Vietnamese Fusion
Vegetarian Cuisine

Chat Mingkwan

Book Publishing Company
Summertown, Tennessee

© 2007 Chat Mingkwan
Background cover photo: Lisa Smith © Fotolia
Cover and interior food photography: © Book Publishing Company

Cover design: Warren Jefferson
Interior design: Gwynelle Dismukes
Food photos: Warren Jefferson
Food styling: Barbara Jefferson

Published in the United States by
Book Publishing Company
P.O. Box 99
Summertown, TN 38483
1-888-260-8458

ISBN 978-1-57067-207-1

15 14 13 12 11 10 09 08 07   9 8 7 6 5 4 3 2 1

Pictured on the front cover:
Fresh Spring Rolls, p. 68
Noodle Soup (Pho), p.76

Pictured on the back cover:
Mango and Coconut Tartlets, p. 142

Printed in Canada

Library of Congress Cataloging-in-Publication Data

Chat Mingkwan.
  Vietnamese fusion : vegetarian cuisine / by Chat Mingkwan.
    p. cm.
  Includes bibliographical references and index.
  ISBN 978-1-57067-207-1
1. Vegetarian cookery. 2. Cookery, Vietnamese. I. Title.
TX837.C4524 2007
641.5'636--dc22   2007031797

The Book Publishing Co. is a member of Green Press Initiative. We have elected to
print this title on paper with postconsumer recycled content and processed
chlorine free, which saved the following natural resources:

43 trees
2,023 lbs of solid waste
15,750 gallons of water
3,795 lbs of greenhouse gases
30 million BTUs

BOOK
PUBLISHING
COMPANY

green
press
INITIATIVE

For more information visit: www.greenpressinitiative.org. Savings calculations
thanks to the Environmental Defense Paper Calculator at www.papercalculator.org

Contents

As I stride through my journey, sometimes I am annoyed by standing still, sometimes upset by stepping back. Now, I am striding with my daughter, Pia—and I never mind getting sidetracked. *Càm Ön!*

A portion of the proceeds from this book will be donated to projects that promote the preservation of endangered wildlife. With your help, they'll keep on roaming.

Foreword

My first vegetarian cookbook, *Buddha's Table: Thai Feasting Vegetarian Style*, has been a source of inspiration, as it often receives hearty comments that encourage me to explore other regional cuisines—this time, Vietnamese vegetarian cooking.

For me, Vietnamese is much more than a third language due to my few sporadic years spent in Vietnam. Even though the Vietnamese alphabet is in English (Latin based), their pronunciations with corrected stress and intonation are incomprehensible to me. I tried mostly to learn the right names of dishes, but even then, my pronunciation often goes astray. My Vietnamese friends, colleagues, and students have had their fair share of my annoying, inexplicable squeaks; even my friend Emily, the Vietnamese grocer, no longer keeps eye contact with me when I approach her busy counter. Thankfully, with their kindness, I was able to translate into English as many words and sounds as closely as possible from the original Vietnamese.

My teaching curriculum now includes a Vietnamese vegetarian cooking class in the Asian section. As usual, my students are testers and tasters. Sometimes my attempts have left them tongue-tied, unable to aptly describe an unappealing taste. As a result, the recipes have been repeatedly worked and reworked until they have reached perfection and finally ended up in this book.

I would like to express my sincere gratitude to everyone, including you, the reader, for using the following recipes. Because of your support, I am inspired to take on another vegetarian challenge and turn all cuisines, one at a time, into more beneficial and nutritious eating.

Chào

Chat Mingkwan

Introduction

When I was young, growing up in Thailand, I often heard horrendous news about neighboring Vietnam—casualties from napalm bombs, brutal communist Vietcong, and the miserable conditions endured by the Vietnamese people. My heart went out to them when I heard that young children my age became orphans and homeless when their parents and families were taken away. Not once did I hear about the beauty of Vietnam, the friendliness of the Vietnamese people, and the delicious complexities of their cuisine. During that tough time, the Vietnamese people, and even Miss Saigon, probably had little concern about their nationalism; rather, they were preoccupied with survival—escaping bombs and finding sustainable food. After more than three decades of recuperation since the war ended, Vietnam slowly returned to normalcy and embraced foreign contacts, opening the country to businesses and tourism. I was among the first wave of visitors to witness the comeback of Vietnam and, from my culinary profession and background, their cuisine impressed me the most.

I began my journey at Hanoi, the center of the northern region, going through Hue, the old capital of learning and culture in central Vietnam, and ended up in Ho Chi Minh City, previously known as Saigon, the home of Miss Saigon, in the south. Streets were crowded with mostly bicycles, motorcycles, and a few automobiles that were drowned out by the distinctive sounds of bells and horns. Every rider and driver made noises for the right-of-way as they navigated through the jammed traffic. Pedestrians, including myself, had to consolidate and garner the courage to cross Hanoi streets, where there were very few traffic lights and crossing paths. The chaotic state of traffic had little effect on the genial disposition of the people of Vietnam. After years of war, internal conflicts, and economic hardships, they remained calm, friendly, and gracious to each other and to everyone.

The streets were lined with beautiful and well-preserved buildings from the French colonial era—grand and imperial—especially those in Hanoi that were designed to duplicate Paris on a smaller scale. After business hours, certain streets were transformed into food courts with a variety of hawker food stands. It was dinnertime and a chance to pick and choose a delicious Vietnamese meal. Locals had a variety of choices for dinner, which could be a one-plate dish, such as a bowl of noodle soup called *pho*, a crêpe, a Vietnamese baguette sandwich, or a put-it-together-yourself meal of multiple courses from different food stands. The course meal in a traditional Vietnamese setting, for instance, could start with an appetizer of mousse, followed by hot-and-sour soup, papaya salad, an entrée flavored with lemongrass, and a French-influenced *gâteau* (cake) for dessert. I often washed all these delicious dishes down with a cup of hot, slow-dripped Vietnamese coffee.

Hanoi was a little cold and overcast during the winter months, so the local food was hot and hearty to keep you warm and comfortably full, with such dishes as *pho*. The cold climate of the north limited the cultivation of many spices; as a result, the food was lighter and less spicy than in the central and the southern regions. The northern region shares a border with China, and the Chinese culinary influence of stir-fries is common in this area. Hue, in the central region, was the ancient capital of Vietnam, where once the country's royalty resided. Vietnamese culinary culture was developed here among many royal kitchens. The food is elaborate and highly decorative, using various spices grown along the region's mountainous terrain. A classic Hue meal consists of small portions of many dishes that are meticulously prepared and grossly time-consuming. The southern region's fertile lands and hot and humid climate produce a large variety of vegetables, herbs, spices, fruits, and livestock. Foreign influences, notably French and Indian, landed ashore and introduced white potatoes, asparagus, tarragon, shallots, and curry spices to this region. Seafood is mainly used and is plentifully supplied by the vast areas of the southern shoreline. Most dishes are tasty and fragranced with herbs and spices; they are often served with plenty of fresh vegetables.

The Chinese have had a strong influence in Vietnam, which is evident throughout, particularly on local architecture, including the concept of feng shui, styles of furniture, color themes, and animistic beliefs. The French later inserted their presence during the colonization era, and it continues even now. Both Chinese and French influences are intertwined in everything Vietnamese. One of the most obvious is the cuisine of Vietnam, where the prominent culinary culture of the East meets the West. Some consider Vietnamese cuisine as French cooking in a Chinese kitchen or vice versa. The Chinese concept of yin and yang and stir-frying techniques are used as often as French caramelizing in Vietnamese cooking. Indian influences are also prevalent, as their curries and spices add more depth to South Vietnamese meals. Ingredients and techniques of both cultures are utilized and give rise to a Vietnamese cuisine of unique and endless possibilities in tastes and flavor.

Characteristics of Vietnamese Food

Fresh is the first obvious characteristic of Vietnamese food. An array of fresh ingredients is used in cooking, and additional fresh vegetables and herbs are essential accompaniments to every meal. Most Vietnamese dishes are designed so that fresh vegetables and herbs play an important part in completing the dish. For example, fresh vegetable leaves may be used as wrappers, as their mild flavors will dilute the intense taste or spiciness of a dish. Ideally, the meal is a balancing act among the flavors of the dish and the accompaniments. The dish can also be completed by using a variety of fresh herbs, which adds various flavors to be savored in every bite. Herbs can be eaten individually, or they can all be combined to make each bite multiflavored. Not only does the unique variety of Vietnamese herbs make every bite different, it offers new flavor sensations to the Western palate.

Nutritious is another characteristic of Vietnamese food, whose array of fresh vegetables and herbs supplies important vitamins, minerals, phytochemicals, and fiber, not to mention the medicinal properties of certain herbs, such as mint and ginger. The Chinese concept of yin and yang, the hot and cold property of food ingredients, is also a factor in healthful Vietnamese cooking and eating. In most Vietnamese dishes, the ratio of meat to vegetables averages 1:2, 1:3, or even 1:4, where a small portion of meat in the dish is to be eaten with a larger portion of fresh vegetables and herbs. This same proportion is prevalent in most Asian cuisines, especially Chinese, where a small portion of meat can be stretched for a big meal when cooked with a lot of vegetables. Although Vietnamese cuisine has absorbed much Chinese influence, Vietnamese dishes utilize significantly more fresh vegetables and herbs, and they are often eaten raw. In Western cuisines, meat is the main focus. Therefore a large portion of the dish is comprised mainly of meat and accompanied by a small amount of vegetables and starch. But for the Vietnamese, the reverse is true: fresh vegetables and herbs are served in large portions with small amounts of meat; the main focus is on the nutritious vegetables and herbs. In fact, in Vietnam the accompanying fresh vegetables and herbs are provided at no limit with the dish. They are usually arranged in large amounts, in large containers, and placed in front of diners, who share and choose their favorite fresh accompaniments to go with their food.

The fusion of two worlds is another main characteristic of Vietnamese food, where the major cuisine of Asia meets its European counterpart. This is where the best of both worlds combine as French cuisine from the Chinese kitchen or Chinese cuisine from the French kitchen. Either way, Vietnamese cuisine has got the right fusion. Vietnam is a very close neighbor to China, sharing a border in the north and sharing the South China Sea in the east. Their association has lasted for centuries through trade and cultural exchanges. China, a powerful country in both economic and military might, has asserted much influence throughout Southeast Asia, and more so on their next-door neighbor, Vietnam. Chinese ingredients such as noodles and techniques such as wok stir-frying are common among Vietnamese households. Chinese education, economy, and military traditions were sought and taught in Vietnam, and later the communist ideology was also a part of learning and became a cause of the military conflict. The French came upon the shore of Vietnam for trade and later to secure a place for their military presence and a balance of power among colonizers in Indochina. As with their Chinese predecessor, French education, economy, and military traditions were taught and assimilated into Vietnamese society. French coffee, baguettes, and pâtés have been a part of the Vietnamese diet, and caramelizing sugar is a major method used to season Vietnamese dishes. Indians have also had a prominent role in the development of Vietnamese cuisine. As their trade ships came ashore at the southern seaports, their spices and curries were introduced and became a part of many signature dishes. Notwithstanding both major influences on their cuisine, the Vietnamese assert their own personalities by using unique herbs and spices that are found locally, thereby creating subtle tastes and flavors to call their own. An abundance of ingredients, a profusion of techniques, and an endless way of combining concoctions have given rise to many delicious Vietnamese dishes that bring out a nostalgia of French, Chinese, and Indian cuisine.

Soy Products

Most Vietnamese dishes use fish sauce (*nuoc mam*), primarily because of its saltiness and value as a flavor enhancer. Other exotic ingredients, such as shrimp paste and fermented fish, also add authentic flavors to Vietnamese cuisine. But none of these products are vegetarian. Therefore, various plant-based seasonings are used in this book instead.

Many types and brands of soy products make good alternatives to fish sauce, from light-colored soy sauce for cooking a white sauce to double-dark soy sauce for dark brown glazing. They also range in saltiness from low sodium (lite soy sauce) to those with a high salt content. There even is a sweet soy sauce made with a thick molasses and soy mixture. Instead of using animal products, a stir-fry soy sauce made from mushroom extract and a variety of soy pastes can easily replace the oyster sauce in stir-fry dishes. Black or yellow fermented beans and fermented tofu lend pungent, authentic flavors to a vegetarian dish and can be used in place of shrimp paste and fermented fish. These products are described in detail in the section that follows.

Nowadays, thanks to creative vegetarian chefs and merchants, innovative vegetarian foods with various tastes, textures, and colors occupy supermarket shelves. In addition to traditional products, seasoned tofu is made to simulate the flavor, texture, and appearance of meat products such as chicken, beef, pork, smoked duck, goose liver, and more. Products from the rivers and oceans, such as water plants and sea vegetables (seaweeds), replicate fish and seafood ingredients. Some of these products need a little getting used to, as they are considered acquired tastes. For those who want to understand the very basics of food preparation, making your own tofu can be a fun and fulfilling project. (For a recipe for homemade tofu, see page 20.) You can make tofu from an assortment of beans and create diverse flavors and textures to produce a wide variety of dishes.

SOYBEAN OR SOYA BEAN (GLYCINE MAX)

The Chinese have cultivated soybeans for centuries, dating back to 2838 BC. In China they are considered one of the five sacred grains (*wu lu*). The United States has now become the largest producer of soybeans, supplying about 75 percent of the world's total production. There are more than one thousand varieties, ranging in size from a small pea to a large cherry. The beans come in various colors and combinations of red, yellow, green, brown, and black. They grow in pods that have fine, tawny hairs. Unlike other legumes, the soybean is low in carbohydrates and high in protein. Soybean products are also a good source of iron and contain vitamins B_1 and B_2 and linoleic acid, an essential fatty acid that is one of the omega-6 fatty acids. Soybeans are used to produce *kecap* (Indonesian sweet soy sauce), *miso* (see "soybean paste," page 16), *natto* (Japanese fermented beans), *okara* (the residue from soymilk), soybean oil, soy cheese, soy flour, soy ice cream, soy margarine, soy mayonnaise, soymilk, soy nuts, soy sauce, soy sour cream, soy yogurt, *tamari* (Japanese dark soy sauce), tofu, *yuba* (tofu sheets or skins), and soy pizza. Dried soybeans should be presoaked like any other dried beans before being cooked and used in soups, stews, casseroles, or other dishes. Bean sprouts grown from soybeans can be used in salads or as a cooked vegetable. Green soybeans (also called edamame) are those picked when they are fully grown but not fully mature. They are sold fresh or frozen and come in their pods, which are bright green and covered with fuzz. Steam the pods for twenty minutes and serve them as a snack or appetizer. They can be shelled and eaten just like peanuts.

Soy Products

Bean Sauce and Bean Paste

These soy products are seasonings made from fermented soybeans. They can range from thin to thick and from smooth to chunky. They should be stored in a nonmetallic, tightly sealed container in the refrigerator for up to one year.

Black Bean Sauce is a thin, salty, full-flavored mixture made with mashed fermented black beans and flavored with garlic and sometimes star anise.

Brown Bean Sauce, or Fermented Yellow Bean Sauce, is thick and made with fermented whole yellow soybeans, salt, and water.

Hot Black Bean Sauce has a medium consistency and is a combination of black soybeans, chiles, garlic, sesame oil, and sugar.

Fermented Black Beans, also known as Chinese black beans or salty black beans, are a Chinese specialty consisting of small black soybeans that have been preserved in salt before being packed into cans or plastic bags. They have an extremely pungent, salty flavor and must be soaked in warm water for about thirty minutes before using. Store tightly covered in the refrigerator for up to one year.

Soybean Paste, called miso, is essential in Japanese cooking. It has the consistency of peanut butter and comes in a wide variety of flavors and colors. This fermented soybean paste has three basic categories: barley miso, rice miso, and soybean miso. Each has a different salt content and some have added sugar. Miso can be used in sauces, soups, marinades, main dishes, and salad dressings. Stored in an airtight container in the refrigerator, it should keep several months.

SWEET BEAN PASTE is made with fermented soybeans and sugar. It is quite thick and has a sweet-salty flavor.

SOYMILK

Sua dau nanh is an iron-rich liquid made by pressing ground cooked soybeans. It has more protein than cow's milk. Soymilk is a cholesterol-free, nondairy product that is low in calcium, fat, and sodium. It makes an excellent alternative to cow's milk for vegans. Soymilk has a tendency to curdle when mixed with acidic ingredients, such as lemon juice or wine. It is an important ingredient in making tofu.

SOY SAUCE

Si dau is a dark, salty sauce made from fermented boiled soybeans and roasted wheat or barley. China and Japan produce a number of varieties ranging in color from light to dark and in texture from thin to very thick.

DARK SOY SAUCE is the "regular" soy sauce. It has a rich soy flavor and color. This soy sauce is generally used when a particular type is not specified in the recipe.

DOUBLE-DARK SOY SAUCE is a lot darker than regular soy sauce and is used mostly for glazing and for sauces that need a dark brown color.

FERMENTED BEAN CURDS are tofu curds that have been fermented with salt, water, vinegar, rice wine, and/or spices until they develop an extremely pungent taste and flavor equivalent to shrimp paste or Limburger cheese. They come in a small jar and should be stored tightly sealed in the refrigerator for up to one year.

Soy Products

FERMENTED YELLOW BEANS (*toung*) are whole yellow beans that have been fermented in water and salt. They often come in a bottle and are ready to be used in stir-fries and sauces. Close the lid tightly and store the bottle in the refrigerator for up to one year.

LIGHT SOY SAUCE (*nuoc dau nanh mantrang*) is much thinner and lighter but saltier than regular dark soy sauce. It is also called thin soy sauce, white soy sauce, or cooking soy sauce, as it has less soy flavor and a lighter color that won't turn sauces dark brown. Light soy sauce is the best substitute for fish sauce in a vegetarian Vietnamese dish.

LITE SOY SAUCE is regular soy sauce with less sodium.

SUSHI OR SASHIMI SOY SAUCE is a milder soy sauce with added rice products to sweeten its taste. It is more expensive than regular soy sauce and is often used as a dipping sauce.

SWEET SOY SAUCE (*nuoc dau nanh ngot*) is a thick, sweet, dark sauce made from soy sauce and molasses or palm sugar. It often is used instead of sugar and is valued for is dark color, thick texture, and sweetness.

TAMARI is Japanese dark soy sauce. It is rich, thick, and extremely dark.

TOFU OR BEAN CURD

Dau hu is made from curdled soymilk, resulting in curds that are drained and pressed in a fashion similar to making cheese. Tofu has a bland, slightly nutty flavor that easily takes on the flavor of the food it's cooked with. Tofu comes in regular, low-fat, and nonfat varieties, and in textures ranging from soft to extra-firm.

BAKED TOFU is baked tofu in a sealed package. Baking rids it of most moisture, making the tofu extra dry and firm with an intense flavor. It is often prepared with added spices, such as Chinese five-spice powder. Store it in the refrigerator for up to one week.

FRIED TOFU (*dau hu chim*) is deep-fried tofu in a sealed package. It is semicrunchy on the outside and soft in the inside. It contains small air pockets that readily absorb sauces and flavors. Store it in the refrigerator for up to one week.

PRESSED TOFU (*da hu tuol*) is sold in small squares. It has a "meaty," chewy texture and may have added coloring or flavorings.

SILKEN TOFU (*dau hu non*), named for its silky smooth texture, comes in soft, regular, and firm styles. It is usually packed in water and is sold in a sealed plastic container. It also may be vacuum-packed in plastic without water. Silken tofu is also available in aseptically sealed packages that may be stored unopened at room temperature for up to eight months. Once opened, silken tofu should be stored in water, which should be changed daily. The cake should be kept refrigerated for no longer than one week.

TOFU SHEETS OR TOFU SKINS (*dau hu mong nhi da*) are thin layers of tofu that curdle on the surface of hot soymilk. They are sold three different ways: fresh in water; fresh and folded or rolled in a sealed plastic package; and dried in a big sheet, or packed airtight in a plastic bag. Dried tofu sheets can be kept for up to one year and must be reconstituted before using. Fresh tofu sheets will keep for about one week in the refrigerator. Fresh or reconstituted dried tofu sheets can be cut to desired sizes and used as wrappers or additions to soups and stir-fries.

Homemade Tofu

Dau Hu Lan Tai Nha

Serves 6

1 pound dried soybeans or yellow mung beans

1/2 gallon hot water

Flavorings or spices (such as salt, soy sauce, or Chinese five-spice powder; optional)

1 tablespoon magnesium or calcium sulfate

Either soybeans or yellow mung beans can be processed to make tofu. The soybean (Glycine max), or soya bean, was domesticated in China by the third millennium BC. The soybean has many varieties that differ in seed size and color, including white, green, red, brown, and black. The most common kind is smallish and pale brown and is known in Indian cuisine as white gram. The mung bean, on the other hand, is the seed of the plant Vigna radiata, a native of India. It is known as golden gram or green gram, depending on its color, and is often used as a main ingredient in the Indian dish dal. All varieties of mung beans, after being shelled and split, have a small, pale yellow seed inside. The Chinese regularly use mung beans to grow bean sprouts, which are different from soya or soybean sprouts, and as a source of starch for mung bean vermicelli, or cellophane or glass noodles. Dried soybeans and mung beans are sold already hulled (the pod has been removed) and are available whole or split.

Soybeans or yellow mung beans are soaked in water for three hours before they are processed (blended with water) and the liquid is extracted for "milk." Both firm and soft tofu can be made from soymilk or mung bean milk. To make firm tofu, magnesium sulfate is added to the bean milk; to make soft tofu, calcium sulfate is added. The firmness also depends on how much whey (the liquid that remains after the solids have been coagulated) has been extracted. Without magnesium or calcium sulfate, a thicker milk with more bean pulp is required, along with using not-too-fine cheesecloth to strain the processed blend. The pulp will help solidify the mixture, but it will only make a soft tofu after more water has been squeezed (pressed) out. The tofu will be very crumbly; handle it carefully.

Square or rectangular wooden or plastic frames are used in commercial tofu making to form the tofu. For homemade tofu, large round cookie cutters, empty aluminum cans cut open at both ends, or small square milk cartons cut open at both ends can be used as the frames.

Pick through the beans and rinse them with cold water to rid them of debris or small stones. Soak the beans in hot water to cover for 2–3 hours, or until the beans have swelled and fully absorbed the water.

Combine one-third of the beans with some of the soaking water in a blender, and process until the beans are well puréed. Place a strainer on top of a medium pot, and line the strainer with cheesecloth. Pour the mixture into the cheesecloth, and pull the cloth's edges together. Squeeze as much soymilk out of the mixture as possible and discard the solids. Continue processing the remainder of the soaked beans in a similar fashion.

Put the pot over medium heat and bring the soymilk to a boil. Boil for about 3 minutes, stirring constantly. Add any optional flavorings at this point. Remove from the heat and let cool for 10 minutes, or until lukewarm. Slowly stir in the magnesium or calcium sulfate to help the soymilk curds congeal. Let the tofu sit undisturbed for 5–7 minutes, or until lightly firm.

Place a rack on a baking sheet, and place four 4 x 4 x 2-inch or 3 x 5 x 2-inch frames over the rack. Line the frames with an 8 x 8-inch or 6 x 10-inch piece of fine cheesecloth. Alternatively, place several large cookie cutters or homemade frames made from aluminum cans or milk cartons on the rack and line them with oversized fine cheesecloth. Scoop the tofu into the cheesecloth to overfill the frames, and fold the edges of the cheesecloth to completely wrap the tofu. Place flat, heavy objects (such as a piece of brick in a zipper-lock plastic bag) on top of the tofu for 10–15 minutes, or until it is at your desired firmness, to squeeze out more water and make the tofu firmer. Steam the wrapped tofu on a rack over boiling water for about 5 minutes, or until it is completely heated through. Let cool, and unwrap the tofu for further use. Store the tofu by submerging it in cold water. It will keep refrigerated for up to 5 days (be sure to change the water daily).

Other Ingredients Essential to Vietnamese Cuisine

Vietnamese food is a combination of subtlety from Chinese and French cuisine, personalized by local ingredients with flavors that are unique to Vietnam. Many varieties of Vietnamese herbs and their flavors are difficult to describe, and they are often eaten fresh as accompaniments to various dishes. Vietnamese cooking frequently uses "raw" (unrefined and unprocessed) sugar, such as rock sugar and block sugar, to add sweetness; lime, tamarind, and vinegar contribute sour notes; hot chiles add heat; and fish sauce or soy sauce is used instead of salt. Some of the ingredients are new to Western kitchens, though they are available through Asian markets in the United States. Don't be discouraged to try cooking Vietnamese food because of its unfamiliar ingredients and cooking techniques. In fact, Vietnamese food preparation uses a lot of simple French and Chinese techniques that are recognizable to the Western cook. By getting acquainted with the ingredients and their uses, even novices to this style of cooking can easily prepare any dish on a Vietnamese menu. Only ingredients that are unfamiliar to the Western kitchen are mentioned in this chapter, including where to find them and how to use them.

HERBS AND SPICES

What makes Vietnamese food unique is the special herbs and spices. The ingredients and cooking methods from the Chinese and French have greatly influenced Vietnamese cuisine. Noodles, which originated in China, have been adopted and modified to create many classic Vietnamese soup dishes such as *pho* (page 76). French baguettes, pâté, and *gâteau* (cake) have suitable places in Vietnamese meals, often with a touch of local flair. Surprisingly, from as far away as Central America, chiles have traveled on Spanish and Portuguese fleets to land on fertile Indo-Chinese soil and become part of spicy Vietnamese dishes. These herbs and spices usually grow in tropical climates and find their way to Western countries. Nowadays, fresh Vietnamese herbs and spices can be produced in the United States, especially in the hot climates of Florida and Hawaii, and in California during the summer months. As the popularity of Vietnamese and Southeast Asian cuisine grows, so does the market for these popular herbs and spices. Vietnamese mint and lemongrass have earned commercial shelf space in the big-name grocery stores.

As the weather permits, I cultivate my own herb garden. Some of the herbs do well in the ground and some are very content in pots. Most nurseries now carry exotic herb seeds and starter plants for both cooking and decorative purposes. Most of the herbs are perennial and do very well in the ground during the hot months. The ones in pots can be conveniently moved indoors during severe weather and generally last for two to three years. Though most Vietnamese herbs and spices can be cultivated locally, some must be imported in various forms: fresh, dried, powdered, frozen, and canned in brine. For some herbs and spices, substitutions can easily be made by using items more readily available outside Vietnam. However, to maintain an authentic essence, the herbs and spices with an asterisk (*) cannot be replaced.

BASIL

Many varieties of basil can be cultivated in Vietnam, but only a few varieties can be successfully grown in the United States. It may be hard to find the exact basil to use. You can alternate among them or just use the widely available Thai sweet basil or Italian basil.

LEMON BASIL (*charh rau que*) (*Ocimum basilicum*) has light green leaves with a slight speckle of hairs, green stems, and sometimes white flowers. It has a nippy peppery and lemon flavor that goes well with soups and salads, especially with noodle soups.

THAI SWEET BASIL (*rau que*) (Ocimum *basilicum*) has small, flat green leaves with pointy tips, and its stems and flowers are sometimes reddish purple. It imparts a very intense taste with a strong anise or licorice flavor. It's often used as a flavorful fresh accompaniment and garnish for leafy vegetables. Ordinary sweet basil makes a good substitute. Sweet basil is available year-round.

CHILES

Ot are available in many types, from large to small and hot to sweet. They come in three colors, each indicating a different stage of maturity and spiciness: mild yellow, hottest green, and sweet and hot red. Many varieties of fresh red chiles are preferred in Vietnamese cuisine for their fragrance, heat, and bright red color.

BIRD'S-EYE OR THAI CHILES (*mat chin va ot*) (*Capsicum minimum*) are the smallest chiles, and with Thai chiles, the smallest are the hottest.

They are yellow, red, or green and have an extremely pungent taste. Bird's-eye chiles are used for chili sauces and dips and are added to salad dressing for spicy heat. They are available in most Asian grocery stores under the label "Thai chiles."

SERRANO (*Capsicum annum*) are green chiles with smooth skin and round bodies. As they mature their color changes from bright green to scarlet red then yellow. They are easily found in markets in the United States. Their flavor is as mild as the *ot*, making them a good multipurpose chile.

VIETNAMESE CHILES (*ot*) come in red, yellow, or green and are the size of a forefinger. They look similar to a jalapeño chile but with a pointy tip. They are a lot milder than bird's-eye chiles and are used both fresh and dried. If fresh *ot* are not available, use fresh serrano or jalapeño chiles. For the dried chiles, large dried Mexican chiles, such as guajillo chiles, California chiles, or New Mexico chiles, are good substitutes.

CHINESE FIVE-SPICE POWDER

Huong-liu is a Chinese ground spice mixture, also sold as "five-fragrance powder." It is golden brown in color and consists of star anise, fennel, cloves, cassia (Asian cinnamon), and Sichuan pepper (or ginger and/or cardamom). The flavor of star anise is the strongest in the mixture.

CILANTRO*

Ngo (*Coriandrum sativum*), or Chinese parsley, is indispensable to Vietnamese cooking and is used generously. Each part of the plant, from the roots to the leaves, can be utilized for different purposes. The roots are very pungent and are an important ingredient in marinades and sauces and for flavoring clear soup broth. The stems and leaves are used both for flavoring and as a leafy green garnish. Cilantro has delicate, light green leaves and stems with white or light pink flowers, which are all edible. In most supermarkets in the United States, cilantro is sold without roots, but the stems can be substituted for the roots in cooking.

GALANGAL*

Rieng (Alpinia officinarum), or white ginger, is a perennial rhizome plant similar to ginger but with a larger and more brightly colored root. The root tips are pink and have a strong medicinal taste, so it can't be eaten directly like ginger. Galangal is used as a pungent ingredient in most Vietnamese aromatic and hot-and-sour soups. Galangal is available as the fresh root or in frozen, dried, and powdered forms in most Asian grocery stores. If using dried slices of galangal, soak them in warm water for at least thirty minutes, or until you can bend the pieces. If a substitution is needed, replace fresh galangal with dried galangal, using half the amount called for in the recipe. Regular ginger cannot duplicate the authentic essence of galangal. Only as a last resort should ginger ever be used instead of galangal.

GARLIC CHIVES

He (Allium tuberosum), or Chinese chives, have a stronger aroma than European chives. They have long, flat, slender leaves and long stems topped with white flowers. They are used exclusively for stir-fry dishes and as a garnish over noodle dishes. Green onions are a good substitute.

JASMINE

Nuoc hoa are flowers of the jasmine shrub (*Jasminum* species). Their strong, sweet fragrance is often used in Vietnamese desserts in the same manner as vanilla extract. Jasmine extract in a bottle is available at well-stocked Asian grocery stores. Jasmine water is made by floating a handful of flowers in a bowl of cold water overnight, or by diluting the extract with water. Use rose water or vanilla extract as a substitute.

LA-LOT LEAVES OR PEPPER LEAVES

La-lot (*Piper* species) have shiny, heart-shaped leaves and small nuts that can be chewed like tobacco. The la-lot leaves, or pepper leaves, are from a plant in the pepper family. The leaves are often used as wrappers, and when cooked, mostly grilled, they release a mild anise flavor and camphor aroma into the food. La-lot can be found in well-supplied Vietnamese and Thai markets. Perilla leaves, or Japanese shiso leaves, are faintly similar in flavor and make an exceptional substitute.

LEMONGRASS*

Xa (*Cymbopogon citratus*) resembles a grass with a strong lemon aroma. To use lemongrass, cut off the grassy top and root end. Peel and remove the large, tough outer leaves of the stalk until you reach the light, milky white inner leaves. Chop it very finely for use in salads, grind it into a marinade, or cut it into two-inch portions and bruise it to use in soup broth. Lemongrass can be found fresh in most grocery stores because it has a very long shelf life. Dried and frozen lemongrass are also available in most Asian stores.

PANDAN OR PANDANUS

Nuoc hoa (*Pandanus odoratissimus*), or screw pine leaves, are the long, slender, bladelike, dark green leaves of a tropical plant. They impart a sweet floral fragrance that is popular in Vietnamese desserts. Their intense green color is valued as a natural food coloring. Pound and grind the leaves with a little water, and strain the mixture to get a liquid extract. Bottled pandan extract is available in well-stocked Asian grocery stores. The Vietnamese use pandan instead of vanilla in their cooking. Use rose or vanilla extract as a substitute.

PERILLA LEAVES: See "shiso leaves" and "la-lot leaves."

PRESERVED TURNIP

Tan xai, or Chinese pickled radish, is a salt-cured Chinese turnip or radish. It is a flavor enhancer that is salty and sweet with a crunchy texture. Chop it into small chunks before using. It is available in the dried goods section of all Asian markets.

SAW-LEAF HERB*

Ngo gai (*Eryngium foetidum*) have slender, bright, shiny green leaves with serrated edges. They emit a unique fragrance that is a combination of cilantro and mint. *Ngo gai* are eaten fresh as an accompanying herb to many dishes and are also added as a major herb in salad dishes.

SHISO LEAVES

Japanese shiso leaves (*Perilla frutescens*) have heart-shaped, serrated-edged leaves tinged with purple on their underside. They are related to mint, with a faint aromatic flavor of ginger and cinnamon. Their other names are perilla and beefsteak leaves. They are used in salad and noodle dishes.

STAR ANISE

Hoi huong is a major spice in Chinese cooking and is frequently used in Vietnamese cooking. These eight-pointed, star-shaped seedpods are products of a slender evergreen tree of the magnolia family (*Illicium verum*), native to China, and have a sweet licorice flavor. They can be used whole or ground into a powder and are often added to long-simmering dishes. Star anise is one of the key elements in Chinese five-spice powder.

SUGARCANE

Mia is the fresh, bamboolike stem of the sugarcane plant. Before using, peel off the green or yellow skin and use only the yellowish white meat. It can be cut into small chunks and added to food for a sweet taste and the fresh flavor of sugarcane. Alternatively, cut it into strips to use as skewers for grilling. Peeled and canned sugarcane in brine is available in five- to eight-inch sticks.

TAMARIND*

Me chau (*Tamarindus indica*) is a fruit pod of a very large tamarind tree with fine, fernlike leaves. Fresh green tamarind can be used in sauces or pickled and served as a snack. The ripe brown pulp is extracted for tamarind liquid and is used to impart a sour flavor without the tartness of lime. The tamarind liquid is often used in soups and sauces. At Asian grocery stores, it is available in a pulp block, powdered, or ready-made in a jar. To make tamarind liquid from the pulp, soak a one-inch cube of tamarind in one-half cup of hot water for ten minutes. Work the tamarind with your fingers until it disintegrates and the water turns brown and thickens. Alternatively, boil the pulp with water for five to seven minutes, or until it disintegrates. Strain the mixture through a sieve; it will make about one-third cup of tamarind liquid.

TURMERIC*

Bot nghe (*Curcuma domestica*) is another plant rhizome that is bright yellow, making it good for both coloring and flavoring. Ground turmeric is used mainly in curry powders. Fresh turmeric is hard to find; dried or ground turmeric can be substituted.

VIETNAMESE MINT OR POLYGONUM LEAVES*

Rau ram (*Polygonum odoratum*) have green and purple slender leaves with an herbaceous flavor that is cool, zippy, and spicy. This exotic herb is often added fresh to salads and soups for authentic Vietnamese dishes. An exact substitute is unlikely; regular mint is acceptable.

VEGETABLES AND FRUITS

AGAR-AGAR

Thach-hoa is a gelatin derived from refined seaweed. It is available in two forms: packages of two (ten-inch-long) rectangular sticks (*kanten* in Japanese), or two-to four-ounce packages of fourteen-inch translucent strands that resemble crinkled strips of cellophane. It is widely used in Southeast Asian cooking for molded jellied sweets. To use agar-agar, soak it in warm water for thirty minutes and squeeze the pieces dry. Add to cold water in a pot and simmer until the agar-agar is completely dissolved. As a general rule, one-half stick of *kanten* or two-thirds ounce of agar-agar strands will thicken four cups of liquid.

Ready-to-use dried agar-agar sticks are also available in many sizes and colors. They need to be boiled in water until tender and are used in iced desserts or sweet drinks.

ASIAN GOURD OR BOTTLE GOURD

Loofah (*Lagenaria siceraria*) is a long, slender, green vegetable similar to a green zucchini. Sometimes its skin will be ripped and tough and the gourd will need to be peeled before it is cooked in stir-fry and soup dishes. Mature bottle gourds have a hard dried shell that is water-resistant and can be used as a bottle. They are also called loofahs.

BABY CORN

Bar non (*Zea mays*) is young corn that has been harvested before maturity. It is very sweet and tender and is used in stir-fries or in a fresh vegetable side dish. Fresh baby corn is available in well-stocked Asian produce markets, but cooked and canned baby corn is widely available. There is no comparison in taste between fresh and canned baby corn.

BAMBOO SHOOTS

Mang (*Phyllostachys*, *Bambusa* and *Dendrocalamus* species) are the young sprouts of the bamboo bush. They have a neutral taste with a crunchy texture and absorb flavors well in various dishes. You can buy bamboo shoots fresh, cooked, or canned in Asian supermarkets. To prepare fresh bamboo shoots, trim the tips and remove the tough outer shell. Cut off the tough bottom ends. Boil the shoots with two or three changes of water, boiling each time for three to five minutes, or until they are tender but still crunchy.

CHINESE BROCCOLI

Cai lan (*Brassica oleracea*), *or gai lan*, has dark green leathery leaves that grow on thick stalks. The leaves, stalks, and flowers can be eaten. Peel the tough skin off the stalk before using. Regular broccoli is a good substitute.

CHINESE CELERY

Rau can (*Apium graveolens*) is smaller than Western celery and has a stronger flavor. It is served fresh in salads or cooked in clear broth. In traditional Vietnamese cooking it is used mostly in soup broths and seafood dishes to counteract the fishy flavor.

COCONUT

Dua (*Cocos nucifera*) is the most versatile plant—its leaves and trunk are used in construction, the shell of the fruit is used for fiber and in the garment industry, and its fruit is used for food and in medicines. Coconut sugar, or palm sugar, is extracted from the sap of the coconut flower, and palm wine, or toddy, is further refined by fermentation and distillation.

COCONUT CREAM (*sua dua*) is the rich and creamy liquid from the first pressing of coconut milk.

COCONUT MILK (*nouc dua*) is derived from processing the grated white meat of the ripe brown coconut, not to be confused with the clear coconut water (the liquid inside the fruit). The process involves steeping the freshly grated coconut meat in boiling water and letting it stand for five to ten minutes before pressing it and straining out the thick white liquid. The first pressing usually is set aside for a rich coconut cream. The second and third pressings yield a less creamy coconut milk. In markets in the United States, you now can choose from many forms of ready-processed coconut milk and cream—fresh from a ripe coconut, frozen, powdered, in a milk carton, and canned. After standing on a shelf awhile, the canned coconut separates into a thick top layer of cream and a bottom layer of more watery milk. By opening the can gently and scooping out the thick layer, you can obtain coconut cream. If you shake the can before opening it, you will get coconut milk.

SMOKED COCONUT (*dua nuon*) is a young green coconut that has been smoked. This process intensifies its flavor, giving it a slightly smoky aroma and taste.

YOUNG COCONUT (*dua non*) is popular for its clear, refreshing, flavorful water which is often served with its tender white coconut meat. Young coconuts normally have green skins and moist husks that make them heavier than dry ripe coconut. In most Asian grocery stores, young coconuts are sold already peeled, without their green skins, often in moist white husks or young white shells. Using a large cleaver or large, heavy knife, chop off a small pad of the white shell and collect the clear coconut juice (known as coconut water) inside. Then cut the coconut in half, and use a spoon to scrape out the tender white meat. Young coconut juice and meat are also available frozen in tightly sealed plastic bags.

DAIKON

Cu cai trang (*Raphanus sativus*) is the root of a giant white radish; it has a long, cylindrical shape resembling a white carrot. Daikon has a pleasant, sweet flavor and a crunchy texture. It is often used to make soup broths.

EGGPLANT

Ca nau comes in many varieties—its size ranges from a small marble to a base-ball, its shape may be oval to spherical, and its color extends from white to yellow to green to purple. Four Asian varieties are available in U.S. markets:

INDIAN EGGPLANT (*Solanum torvum*) has an intense purple color and shiny skin and is about the size of a plum. It is quite crunchy and suitable for salads and stir-fries.

LONG EGGPLANT OR JAPANESE EGGPLANT (*ca nau dai*) is a long purple or green fruit with a denser texture than regular round purple eggplant. It often is used in salads, stir-fries, curries, and grilled dishes.

MARBLE EGGPLANT (*ca nau cosoe*) (*Solanum torvum*) grows in clusters. It is bright green and is the size of small marbles.

THAI EGGPLANT (*Solanum melongena*) is the size of a golf ball. It is light green with a crunchy texture. It is used as a vegetable in stir-fries and curries.

Jackfruit

Mit (*Artocarpus heterophyllus*) is a very large fruit with short, spiky, brownish green skin. Its ripe meat is a brilliant yellow or orange and has a unique, sweet flavor. Ripe jackfruit is often used in Vietnamese desserts because of its neutral sweetness that goes with almost anything. Young jackfruit has white or pale green flesh and is popular in salads. In the United States, ripe jackfruit in syrup and young jackfruit in brine are canned and readily available in Asian grocery stores.

Jicama

Cu dau (*Pachyrhizus erosus*) is an underground tuber with crunchy, juicy, ivory colored flesh and a sweet, bland flavor that suits everything from fruit cups to stir-fries. Jicama can be eaten raw or cooked after its thin, matte, sandy brown skin has been peeled. Shredded jicama is very good in Vietnamese salads with lime dressing.

Kabocha

Bi ro (*Cucurbita moschata*) is considered a winter squash in the United States. It has a jade green rind with celadon green streaks. When cooked, its pale orange flesh is tender, smooth, and sweet. Choose kabochas that are heavy for their size. The rind should be dull and firm; avoid any with soft spots. Kabochas are similar to pumpkins or acorn squash, and they are cooked the same way.

Lily Bud or Lily Flower

Hoa hien/kim cham (*Hemerocallis fulva*) is the flower of a daylily that has been dried. It has a unique flavor with a sweet fragrance and elastic texture. Soak lily buds in warm water to soften them before using them in soups, salads, or stir-fries.

LONG BEAN

Dau dua (*Vigna unguiculata* var *sesquipedalis*), also known as yard long bean or snake bean, has slender green or purple pods that grow up to twelve inches in length. They are excellent eaten raw or cooked in stir-fry dishes. Long beans are available in most supermarkets during the spring and summer months. Green beans are a good substitute.

LOTUS

Sen (*Nelumbo nucifera*) is a symbol of purity. Its root is light brown with an odd appearance similar to a chain of stiff frozen sausages. It is sold in the produce section and is used as a vegetable in soups and stir-fries. Lotus seeds (*hat sen*) are used fresh for sweet dishes or dried for use in stews. Lotus stems can be used in stir-fries and sometimes in salads.

LYCHEE

Trai doi (*Litchi chinensis*) fruit originated in China, but it also has been cultivated in the cool climate of Vietnam. Lychee fruit is round, a little bit bigger than a cherry, with red bumpy skin and a sweet flavor that has a pleasant sour hint. In the United States, imported canned lychee is available year-round. Fresh lychee can be found seasonally in well-stocked Asian markets.

MORNING GLORY

Rau moung (*Ipomoea aquatica*), also called water spinach or swamp cabbage, has roughly triangular-shaped leaves and hollow stems. The tender tips are popular for flambés or stir-fries, or they are eaten fresh as a side vegetable. Spinach is the closest substitute.

MUNG BEANS

Dau xanh (*Vigna radiata*) are yellow and green respectively and are often used in Vietnamese crêpes and desserts. The beans are usually sold dried and prepackaged. Soak the beans in cold water for at least thirty minutes before cooking them. Drain and boil the beans in fresh water for five to seven minutes, or until they are tender.

POMELO

Pomelos (*Citrus grandis*) is the giant grapefruit now readily available in almost all Asian markets in early winter. It is sweeter and less bitter than the local grapefruit and may be eaten either as a fruit or as a main ingredient in salad.

PAPAYA

Du du or *papaw* (*Carica papaya*) usually is eaten ripe as fresh fruit, but unripe green papaya is picked when young and firm and is very popular for use in green papaya salad. Choose a papaya that is very hard and firm with a bright green color. Peel and seed the papaya before shredding or cutting it into fine matchsticks. In the United States, green papaya that is imported from Mexico is available in well-stocked Asian grocery stores.

SEA LETTUCE

Rong bien (*Ulva lactua*) is usually sold fresh in bulk in large, open crocks of water. It has been cleaned, trimmed, and processed, most commonly in the shape of a bow tie, knot, or string. It also is sold dried in packages and is usually reconstituted before using. Sea lettuce can be cooked in soups and stir-fries or poached before using in salads.

TARO ROOTS

Khoai mon (*Colocasia esculenta*) are oval-shaped underground tubers of the taro plant. They have brown hairy skins with encircling rings. In the United States there are two types available—large, almost as big as a football, and miniature, the size of a plum. The flesh varies from white to cream and is often speckled with purple. Its taste is similar to a potato but with a distinctive taro flavor. Taro can be used and cooked the same way as a potato or sweet potato.

WATER CHESTNUTS

Cu nang (*Eleocharis dulcis*) add a sweet flavor, white color, and crunchy texture to many dishes, especially desserts. They are the tuber of a plant in the sedge family and are round with black skin. Fresh water chestnuts are available at well-stocked Asian markets. Choose firm, unblemished ones. Peel off the black skin before using. Canned water chestnuts are available in all supermarkets. There is no comparison between fresh and canned water chestnuts.

Rice, Noodles, and Wrappers

Rice

Gao (*Orya sativa*) is the steamed long-grain rice that accompanies the majority of dishes in a Vietnamese meal.

Brown Rice (*gao luc*) is long-grain rice with only its inedible outer husk removed; it is not ground or polished into a smooth, white grain. The nutritious, high-fiber bran coating gives it a light tan color, nutlike flavor, and chewy texture. Brown rice is subject to rancidity, which limits its shelf life to about six months. Brown rice, or unmilled brown rice, now regarded as a health food, was rarely eaten in rice-staple countries, where people valued the whiteness and tenderness of the milled grains. The brown or reddish outer layers (bran) are rich in fiber and B-complex vitamins. Cook brown rice the same as regular white long-grain rice, but add a little more water and increase the cooking time to about forty minutes.

Fragrant Rice or Jasmine Rice (*gao thom*) is extremely popular and available almost everywhere. Before cooking, rinse the rice well with water to cleanse away any dirt or debris. Cook the rice in a pot with a tight-fitting lid, using a ratio of one part rice to two parts cold water. Bring to a boil. Reduce the heat, cover, and simmer for fifteen to twenty minutes, or until the water has been absorbed. Turn off the heat and let the rice stand covered on the still-hot stove for ten to fifteen minutes to finish steaming before serving. When rice is properly cooked, it will be soft, fluffy, and more than double in volume. If the rice turns out too mushy, cook it with a little less water in the next batch. If using a rice cooker, follow the instructions in the manual that came with it.

GLUTINOUS, SWEET, OR STICKY RICE (*nep*) is the long-grain rice that is often used in desserts. After it is cooked it becomes uniquely sticky and soft and can be easily shaped into a ball. Its flavor is mild and sweet. The uncooked grains are whiter, shorter, and rounder than jasmine rice. The best way to prepare glutinous rice is to soak it for three to ten hours in cold water, using a ratio of one part rice to three parts water. Drain the rice and steam it in a steamer over high heat for fifteen to twenty minutes, or until tender.

GLUTINOUS BLACK RICE (*gao den*) is another variety of sweet or sticky rice. It is also called forbidden rice. It has dark purple grains and a unique fragrance. It can be prepared the same way as its white counterpart, but it will take longer to cook, about twenty to thirty minutes. Black rice is often combined with glutinous white rice, using a ratio of one to one before soaking, to give it a desirable tender texture after it is cooked.

RICE PAPER SHEETS

Bahn trang are indispensable to Vietnamese food as wrappers and a sort of starch, and their mild flavor neutralizes rich, spicy food. Dried, tissue-thin rice paper sheets are made from rice flour and water and are commonly and conveniently purchased rather than made at home. A thick batter of rice flour and water is spread thinly over a piece of muslin that is stretched across a round vat filled with boiling water. After the mixture is cooked, a large, flat wooden paddle is slipped under the sheet of wet rice paper and used to transfer it onto a woven bamboo tray. The tray is filled and then propped at an angle facing the sun to allow the sheets to dry. Rice paper sheets are manufactured in many sizes ranging from six to twelve inches in diameter; eight-inch rounds are the most common. Rice paper sheets need no further cooking; rather, they must be softened

Fresh Spring Rolls, p. 68, Dipping Sauces #2 and #3, pp. 51–52, Vietnamese Coleslaw, p. 94

before use. This is can be done by soaking them in a bowl of warm water or brushing them with warm water until they are soft and pliable.

NOODLES

Bun is from the Chinese and was adopted by the Vietnamese; it is used to make a meal or a side dish. There are many varieties of noodles, all differing in size, shape, and ingredients. In well-stocked Asian grocery stores in the United States, you can buy fresh Chinese wide or medium-wide rice noodles as well as a fresh sheet that you can slice into noodles at home. Dried noodles are readily available in all sizes and qualities. Dried noodles should be soaked or boiled in water to soften.

FINE-THREAD RICE NOODLES (*bahn hoi*) are thin, round noodles made from freshly ground rice flour. In the United States, fresh noodles are difficult to find. The closest substitute is wheat-based Japanese somen noodles, which are sold in well-stocked Asian grocery stores. Cook the noodles in boiling water until soft. Drain and rinse them with cold water before portioning them into small wads the size of a bird's nest.

GLASS NOODLES OR CELLOPHANE NOODLES (*mien/bun tau*) are made from mung bean flour. They are most often available dried in vermicelli threads. After being soaked or cooked in water, they turn clear (hence the name).

MEDIUM RICE NOODLES OR RICE STICKS (*banh pho*) are rice noodles that are one-quarter inch wide. They are the most popular size in Vietnamese dishes, especially in the noodle soup pho. They are available fresh and dried.

SMALL RICE NOODLES (*bun nho*) are vermicelli rice noodles.

Bamboo Shoot Dumplings, p. 56, Dipping Sauce #3, p. 52

WIDE RICE NOODLES (*bun hon*) are one-inch-wide rice noodles.

YELLOW OR EGG NOODLES (*mi*) are small yellow noodles made from flour and eggs. Fresh noodles are available in well-stocked Asian grocery stores. Dried yellow noodles are also sold prepackaged in small balls. A vegan version of yellow noodles is available made with an egg substitute. Cook the noodles in boiling water until soft.

TAPIOCA PEARLS

Bot bing-bang are made from tapioca flour and shaped into small, medium, and large round balls. They are also dyed in various colors. They are kneaded with lukewarm water to make a dough, or cooked in boiling water to make pudding. The large pearls are popular in iced coffee (see Vietnamese Iced Coffee, page 146).

WRAPPERS

Vietnamese cooking borrows many Chinese ingredients, especially its wrappers (*banh cuon*), for a number of dishes. Certain types of ready-made wrappers can be cooked very quickly; this helps speed preparation time instead of making them from scratch. Spring roll wrappers, lumpia wrappers, and rice wrappers are made from a flour-based dough and generally come in three sizes: five-inch, nine-inch, and twelve-inch squares. They are available fresh and frozen. The larger size can be cut according to its use. Wonton wrappers, three-and-a-half-inch squares, are made from a flour and egg dough and come in two thicknesses: very thin for deep-frying, and thick for steaming or for making dumplings. Tofu sheets or skins can be used as wrappers. Rice paper sheets are the most popular wrapper in Vietnamese dishes.

Seasonings

Candy Sugar

Keo duong is also labeled "sugar in pieces." This product is a Chinese invention. It is made from sugarcane that has been minimally processed to maintain its original flavor and fragrance, which is raw and sweet in comparison to nonfragrant, highly processed, granulated white sugar. It often comes in a plastic-wrapped stack of one by five-inch blocks; each block is one-quarter inch thick. It has a light brown color that is similar to brown sugar. It's quite brittle and melts easily when heated. Break or chop the sugar into small chunks, and use it to make syrup or add it to food to impart its raw, sweet flavor. Brown sugar is an excellent substitute.

Chili Sauce:

Tuong ot is a prepared Asian seasoning that can be used as a condiment or mixed into a dish.

Black Bean Garlic Sauce (*dau ot dan nauh*) is a sweet, mild, and smoky chili sauce that often is used as a flavor enhancer in salad dressings and soups.

Chinese White Plum Sauce (*tuong dan nuh va chi*) is a mild, sweet-and-sour syrup. It is used as a sauce for delicately flavored dishes such as spring rolls.

Sambal Oelek is ground hot and sour red chiles in a vinegar mixture. It is popular for adding a chile zest to a bowl of soup and various sauces.

SRIRACHA SAUCE is a hot, orange colored, sweet-and-sour sauce that can add a spicy heat to any dish, especially noodle soup.

SWEET CHILI SAUCE (*tuong ngot*) is sweet and sour with evidence of mild red chile chunks. It is a popular sauce for fried or barbecued dishes.

VIETNAMESE GARLIC AND CHILI SAUCE (*tuong ot tuoi*) is a chili sauce that originated in Vietnam. It is used to add heat to many Vietnamese sauces and is also used as a condiment.

HOISIN SAUCE

This Chinese savory sauce is a mainstay on Vietnamese dining tables. Hoisin sauce (*tuong dau nauh*) is a condiment that is added to soups and snacks and is included as part of the sauce and seasoning in many dishes. It consists of fermented soybeans, vinegar, garlic, chiles, and other herbs and spices. Hoisin sauce adds sweet, savory, and a little spicy flavor to any dish.

MAGGI SEASONING SAUCE

This multipurpose seasoning originated in Switzerland but now is popular throughout Southeast Asia. Maggi Seasoning Sauce (*Nuoc Tuong Magi*) serves as a secret flavor enhancer in most marinade recipes. A few drops can improve flavor dramatically. A similar product sold under the brand name Golden Mountain Sauce is also available.

PALM OR COCONUT SUGAR

Dua duong thiot not is made from the sap of the flower clusters of coconut or palm trees. It has a distinctive flavor and fragrance and a pale, light brown color. In the United States, palm sugar is sold as a paste in glass bottles or as crystal-

tic wrap in most well-stocked Asian grocery stores. Chop or grate it into small chunks, or heat it in a microwave for one to two minutes until melted, to measure it before using. Store it the same way as ordinary sugar.

ROCK SUGAR OR CRYSTAL SUGAR

This sugar also has Chinese origins. Rock sugar (*doung phen*) is similar in shape to small rocks and is light brown or clear in color. Its fragrance depends on the plant it comes from, which can be either sugarcane and/or sugar beet. It's easily melted when heated. Break it into small pieces with a kitchen mallet or the back of a knife, and use it to make syrup or add it to food for sweetness with flavor.

SOY SAUCES See "soy products," page 17.

STIR-FRY SAUCE OR VEGETARIAN OYSTER SAUCE

Nuoc cham xao is similar to oyster sauce but is made from plant-based ingredients, such as mushrooms with sweetened soy sauce, and is used mostly in vegetable stir-fry dishes. It comes in many varieties: mushroom stir-fry sauce, vegetarian stir-fry sauce, and vegetarian marinade sauce. It must be refrigerated after opening and will keep about six months.

VEGETABLE BASE OR BOUILLON POWDER

This product is a flavor enhancer made by reducing vegetable stock into a paste or powder. It adds sodium and an intense vegetable flavor. It is used sparingly to improve the taste of a dish without using MSG.

Special Equipment

CLAY POT OR CHINESE CLAY POT

This simple and inexpensive cooking utensil has its origin in China and is used throughout Asia. It is a cooking and serving tool in one, as food can be cooked and served directly from the clay pot. It is handmade with a natural clay color and is partially glazed around the inside. It usually comes with one large handle or two small handles and a tight-fitting lid. There are many types with different qualities, but most are intended for short-term use. Some of the clay pots are secured with wire to ensure that even if a pot happens to crack during cooking, the food will remain intact and be completely cooked during this last use of the pot. The clay pot with a flat bottom is to be used on top of a stove and can go in an oven for the purpose of keeping food warm or reheating it. The fine clay of the pot lightly filters a smoky flavor into the food. When cooking on the stove with an open flame, start with low heat first to warm the pot, then raise the heat to the desired temperature. Starting with high heat all at once will crack the pot. Clay pots are available in many sizes at Chinese and Asian grocery stores in any Chinatown. A regular metal pot with a tight-fitting lid is a good substitute.

MORTAR AND PESTLE

There are two types of mortars and pestles, each serving a particular purpose: a stone mortar and a clay or wooden mortar. The stone mortar (bowl) and pestle (club) are made of solid stone and are hand carved from a selected piece of the stone by artisans. The mortar is very heavy and sturdy and has a stubby shape; its mouth is wide, and it has a very thick rim. It's perfect for the heavy pounding needed for a fine grind. If this type of mortar and pestle is not available, the next best thing to use, for more convenience and for saving time, is a food processor or blender.

A clay or wooden mortar is easy to make by hand. The mortar is made of clay or carved wood, and its pestle is carved out of wood. It is a lot less expensive than the stone one, but it has a shorter life and is disposable. It is shaped like a tall cylinder, with a wide mouth and a narrow base. It is light, unstable, and not suitable for heavy grinding. Its main function is to serve as a mixing or tossing bowl, with little grinding. The famous Vietnamese Papaya Salad recipe (see page 90) uses this kind of mortar for mixing and tossing the ingredients. If this type of mortar and pestle is not available, a metal bowl and a blunt rolling pin can be utilized for the same purpose.

SHREDDER

Many types of shredders are essential in any kitchen, especially in a vegetarian kitchen where the cook may need to shred different kinds of vegetable into various shapes and sizes. There are hand shredders, box graters, box slicers, mandolins, and other shredding devices with blades that can be exchanged to create specific shapes and sizes—thin to thick slices, julienne, and matchsticks. A shredder helps reduce preparation time when fruits and vegetables need to be cut thinly and uniformly.

Special Equipment

STEAMER

Many types of Chinese steamers (*chun*) are typical in Vietnamese cooking. A multilayer steamer made of metal or bamboo (a type of steamer used for dim sum) in various sizes is an essential cooking tool in the Vietnamese kitchen. A wok with a tight-fitting lid can also be used as a steamer by adding crisscross bars to hold a plate of food over boiling water.

WOK

The Vietnamese people borrowed the wok (*chao*) and stir-fry cooking techniques from the Chinese. This thin metal bowl with a handle serves many purposes: stir-frying, deep-frying, steaming, boiling, smoking, and more. It traditionally is made of rolled steel, which provides excellent heat control, but it also can be made of sheet iron, anodized aluminum, and stainless steel. It comes in various sizes—from small, with one long handle for tossing the food, to large, with two handles to manage a large volume of food. The advantage of wok cooking and stir-frying lies in the speed, which consequently minimizes the loss of vitamins, colors, flavors, and textures in fresh food. A flat-bottom wok has been introduced for use on an electric or flat gas range in the Western kitchen. Good maintenance is required to season the wok after each use so it will not rust. Clean and dry the wok thoroughly; then heat it and rub it with a little vegetable oil.

Sauces

Many types of sauces accompany Vietnamese dishes, including ready-made condiments of various kinds. The most popular and often served is *nuoc cham* (see pages 51 and 52), which comes in many versions and can be used as a sauce or salad dressing. Sauces can be light and delicate or rich, creamy, and nutty, depending on the ingredients used. They can be prepared by using heat to intensify flavors for a rich and complex sauce, or by just combining fresh ingredients for a light and refreshing sauce. They also can be made hot and spicy with the addition of chopped fresh chiles and/or ready-made chili sauce. Small saucers are essential and should be handily available with a Vietnamese meal for many types of sauces. They can be used for a dark sauce, light sauce, chili sauce, soy sauce, sriracha sauce, hoisin sauce, lime or lemon juice, and/or vinegar.

Because of the French influence, many versions of caramel syrup have become indispensable in Vietnamese cooking. It might be a straightforward caramel syrup made with melted white sugar, or one that has an added Asian flair with flavored sugars from sugarcane, beets, or coconuts, or a sour version with added lemon or lime juice, or perhaps a local version with added fish sauce or, in our case, soy sauce. The degree of caramelizing also varies depending on the cook's preference. The sugar can be cooked a little longer for a touch of smoky flavor and to get a deep dark color, a faint bitterness, and a less sweet caramel taste. Or it can be lightly cooked for a light brown color with an intense sweetness. Caramel syrup can be prepared in a big batch in advance and stored in the refrigerator, making it very handy for cooking the next several meals.

Caramel Syrup

Nuoc Mau

Makes ¾ cup

1 cup sugar, candy sugar, or brown sugar
¼ cup cool water
¼ cup hot water
2 tablespoons freshly squeezed lime or lemon juice

Combine the sugar and cool water in a saucepan and bring to a boil. Do not stir. Reduce the heat to medium, and simmer for 10–12 minutes. When the syrup turns dark brown and the bubbles become sluggish, slowly add the ¼ cup hot water. Watch out for the splash! Raise the heat to high, and continue cooking for another 3–5 minutes. Stir in the lime juice, and remove from the heat.

Caramel Soy Syrup

Nuoc Mau-Sí Dau

Makes ¾ cup

As it cooks, this recipe will give off a very pungent odor. Be prepared and use a well ventilated area.

½ cup candy sugar, finely chopped, or brown sugar
⅓ cup soy sauce or light soy sauce
3 tablespoons water

Combine all the ingredients in a saucepan, and place over medium heat. Cook for 10–15 minutes, or until the mixture is reduced to a thick syrup that coats the back of a spoon. Watch closely so the mixture doesn't boil over, and take care that it doesn't burn.

Dipping Sauce #1 (cooked)
Nuoc Cham

Makes I cup

Combine the vinegar, candy sugar, water, soy sauce, garlic, chiles, and salt in a saucepan, and place over medium heat. Bring to a boil and simmer for 4–5 minutes, or until the mixture turns into a light syrup. Let cool. Transfer to a serving bowl and sprinkle with the chopped peanuts and shredded carrots.

1/4 cup rice or distilled vinegar

1/4 cup candy sugar, finely chopped, or brown sugar

2 tablespoons water

2 tablespoons light soy sauce

2 tablespoons minced garlic

2 teaspoons minced red chiles (optional)

1/4 teaspoon salt, or more to taste

1/4 cup chopped roasted peanuts, for garnish

1/4 cup finely shredded carrots (matchsticks), for garnish

Dipping Sauce #2 (uncooked)
Nuoc Cham

Makes I cup

Combine all the ingredients in a bowl, and stir to mix well.

1/3 cup sugar

1/3 cup rice or distilled vinegar

1/4 cup water

1/4 cup chopped roasted peanuts

3 tablespoons light soy sauce

2 tablespoons finely minced garlic

1 tablespoon freshly squeezed lime or lemon juice

1 tablespoon bottled chili sauce (*sambal oelek*) or hot chili paste

Sauces

Dipping Sauce #3 (fresh juice)
Nuoc Cham

Makes I cup

Combine all the ingredients in a bowl, and stir to mix well.

2 tablespoons freshly squeezed lime or lemon juice, or more to taste

2 tablespoons light soy sauce, or more to taste

2 tablespoons sugar

2 tablespoons water

2 tablespoons finely chopped garlic

2 tablespoons finely shredded carrots (matchsticks)

I tablespoon minced red chiles, more or less to taste

Dressing
Nuoc Cham

Makes I cup

Combine all the ingredients in a bowl, and stir to mix well.

5 tablespoons light soy sauce

$1/4$ cup freshly squeezed lime or lemon juice

3 tablespoons sugar

2 tablespoons water

2 tablespoons finely shredded carrots (matchsticks)

I tablespoon minced garlic

I tablespoon minced red chiles, more or less to taste

Hoisin Peanut Sauce

Nuoc Leo

Heat a small saucepan over medium heat and pour in the oil. Add the garlic and fry for 1–2 minutes, or until light brown and fragrant.

Stir in the vegetable stock, hoisin sauce, soy sauce, sugar, and chili sauce. Simmer, stirring occasionally, for 2–3 minutes, or until the mixture is thick and syrupy.

Remove from the heat and stir in the peanuts. Dilute with additional vegetable stock or water, if the sauce is too thick. Let cool and serve.

1 teaspoon vegetable oil

2 tablespoons minced garlic

1/2 cup vegetable stock or water

1/3 cup hoisin sauce

1 tablespoon light soy sauce

1 tablespoon sugar

1 teaspoon chili sauce (*sambal oelek*) or hot chili paste, more or less to taste

1/4 cup minced roasted peanuts

Peanut Sauce

Sot Dau Phong

Place the roasted peanuts and sesame seeds in a mortar with pestle or a food processor, and process until finely ground. Transfer to a saucepan, and add the remaining ingredients.

Place over medium heat, and stir to mix well. Bring to a boil and simmer, stirring constantly, for 5–7 minutes, or until the mixture is thick and syrupy. Take care that the mixture doesn't burn on the bottom of the saucepan. Dilute with additional water or stock if the sauce is too thick. Transfer to a serving bowl, and serve as a thick sauce.

Makes 1 cup

$1/2$ cup roasted peanuts

2 tablespoons roasted white and/or black sesame seeds

$1/2$ cup vegetable stock or water

$1/3$ cup sugar

1 tablespoon vegetable oil

2 teaspoons chili sauce (*sambal oelek*) or hot chili paste (optional)

1 teaspoon salt

Snacks and Appetizers

Following the examples of the Chinese multidish banquet and the French course meal, the Vietnamese stage their dishes and put them in order for a pleasant eating experience. There is a traditional Vietnamese seven-course meal where all dishes are comprised of beef, each one prepared in a different way. In several-course meals, all dishes cannot be served as the main dish, so more than half of them are light in volume and served as snacks or appetizers. Many Vietnamese dishes are considered light eating, and they can be enjoyed between meals or as a small course of the meal. Most snacks and appetizers have been developed from Hue cuisine, the classical Vietnamese food. The city of Hue is in central Vietnam and used to be the ancient capital city where royal families resided. A Hue meal was elaborate, decorative, and painstakingly prepared. Hue recipes have been modified to be more practical to mainstream Vietnamese and have resulted in many varieties of Vietnamese snacks and appetizers.

Bamboo Shoot Dumplings

Baan Tai Miew

Serves 6

This see-through, half-moon-shaped dumpling is an excellent appetizer, borrowing Chinese ingredients and techniques, but adding Vietnamese style with plenty of local herbs. Cornstarch makes the dough light and clear, and the arrowroot or all-purpose flour makes it more elastic. The dough should have a smooth texture that is easy to work with and should not break apart when kneaded into a thin sheet. Adding extra flour or liquid can help improve its consistency. (See photo, facing page 41.)

DOUGH, GARNISH, AND WRAPPERS

2 cups cornstarch

1/2 cup arrowroot starch or all-purpose flour

1 cup boiling hot water, or more as needed

1/4 cup vegetable oil

1/2 cup thinly sliced shallots

1 large banana leaf, or 2–3 flat lettuce or cabbage leaves, or 1 piece parchment paper

FILLING

2 tablespoons vegetable oil

1 1/2 cups matchstick-sliced fresh or canned bamboo shoots

1 cup chopped firm tofu

1/2 cup thinly sliced green onions, white and green parts

1 tablespoon light soy sauce

1 tablespoon stir-fry sauce or vegetarian oyster sauce

1 tablespoon sugar

1 teaspoon vegetable base or bouillon powder

1/4 teaspoon ground black pepper

To make the dough, sift the cornstarch and arrowroot starch into a bowl. Make a well in the center of the starch mixture, and pour in the hot water. Gently mix with a spoon until well combined. When the mixture is cool enough to handle comfortably, knead it for 3–5 minutes to make a smooth dough. Cover the dough with a kitchen towel, and let stand for 20 minutes.

Heat a pan over medium heat and pour in the oil. Add the shallots and fry for 3–5 minutes, or until light brown and crispy. Do not let them become dark brown or burn, as they will be bitter. Remove the shallots from the oil and drain on absorbent paper. Set aside for garnish. Reserve the oil.

To make the filling, heat a pan or skillet over medium heat and pour in the oil. Stir in the bamboo shoots and tofu and cook for 2–3 minutes, or until heated through.

Add the green onions, soy sauce, stir-fry sauce, sugar, vegetable base, and pepper. Stir to mix well. Cook until heated through, about 2 minutes. Remove from the heat and let cool.

Divide the dough and roll it into 15–20 balls, each about 1 inch in diameter. Knead and press each ball into a thin, round wrapper, about 2 inches in diameter.

HERB ACCOMPANIMENTS AND SAUCE

1 head lettuce
1 bunch sweet basil
1 bunch Vietnamese mint (*rau ram*) or mint
1 bunch cilantro
1 bunch saw-leaf herb or dill
1 cup Dipping Sauce #1 (page 51), #2 (page 51), or #3 (page 52)

Fill each wrapper with a heaping tablespoon of the filling, and fold the wrapper into a half circle. Fill and press the edge to seal completely. Repeat the process until all the dough has been made into dumplings.

Arrange the banana or lettuce leaves on a steaming tray, and brush them thoroughly with some of the reserved oil. Arrange the dumplings on top of the leaves, making sure they are not touching each other. Brush the dumplings with more of the oil, and steam over boiling water for 10 minutes, or until cooked through and translucent. Transfer to a serving platter, and top with the fried shallots.

Clean and separate the lettuce for accompaniments into individual leaves to use as wrappers. Clean the herbs, trim the tough stems, and separate into small pieces.

To eat, fill a piece of lettuce leaf with a dumpling and top with the herbs. Wrap all the contents with the lettuce leaf, dip in the dipping sauce, and eat by hand.

Snacks and Appetizers

Braised Mushrooms with Soy

Nam Xao Nuoc Tuong

Serves 6

This simple mushroom side dish creates a flavorful contrast to all fresh salads. Soy sauce and mushrooms provide salty, earthy tastes that pair well with the salad's refreshing flavors. Fresh straw mushrooms are very popular in Vietnam and are best suited for this recipe. They are difficult to find in the United States; canned straw mushrooms in brine are available, but their bland flavor and mushy texture diminish the delicious result. Small, fresh button mushrooms can be used; they may also be combined with fresh straw mushrooms for variety.

1 1/2 pounds fresh straw or button mushrooms, or a combination of both

2 tablespoons vegetable oil

3 tablespoons chopped garlic

3 tablespoons soy sauce

2 tablespoons sugar

1/2 teaspoon cracked black pepper, plus more for garnish

1/2 cup vegetable stock or water

Salt

3 tablespoons chopped cilantro leaves, for garnish

Clean the mushrooms, and trim and discard the tough stems. If using more than one variety of mushroom, cut them into equal sizes so they cook uniformly.

Heat a pan over medium heat and pour in the oil. Add the garlic and cook for 2–3 minutes, or until light brown and fragrant. Add the mushrooms, and stir briskly to combine well.

Stir in the soy sauce, sugar, pepper, and vegetable stock. Cook and simmer for 3–5 minutes, or until the mushrooms are tender. Season with salt to taste.

Transfer to a bowl and garnish with the cilantro and additional cracked pepper.

Fried Tofu with Lemongrass

Dau Hu Chien Xa

When you have little time, a vegetarian restaurant seems so far away, and the dollars in your pocket are running out, this recipe will make for a quick meal. Ready-fried tofu is available in Asian markets. All you need to do is heat the tofu by refrying or baking it to get back its crunchiness. Instead of fresh lemongrass, use its powdered form, which can be stored in your pantry. Everything is thrown into a pan, seasoned, and heated through. In no time, you will have a delicious, nutritious, and affordable meal.

1 pound firm tofu, completely drained of water

1 cup vegetable oil

1/3 cup finely minced lemongrass, tender midsection only, or 1 tablespoon powdered lemongrass

2 tablespoons minced garlic

1 teaspoon minced red chiles, more or less to taste

1 tablespoon soy sauce, or more to taste

1 tablespoon sugar, or more to taste

1 teaspoon Chinese five-spice powder

1/4 teaspoon ground black pepper

Slice the tofu into 1 x 2-inch pieces, 1/2 inch thick. Pat dry with paper towels.

Heat the oil in a saucepan and fry the tofu for 5–7 minutes, or until light brown and crispy, turning it once. Remove from the oil, and drain on absorbent paper.

Pour the oil out of the pan, leaving just enough to coat the pan's surface. Stir in the lemongrass, garlic, and chiles, and cook for 2–3 minutes, or until light brown.

Return the tofu to the pan, and stir to mix well. Add the soy sauce, sugar, five-spice powder, and pepper. Stir to combine well, and cook for 2–3 minutes, or until heated through. Transfer to a serving platter and serve as a snack.

Snacks and Appetizers

Crispy Spring Rolls
Cha Gio

Vietnamese crispy spring rolls can be a hearty meal and are very filling compared to the Chinese version. Instead of eating spring rolls on their own, the Vietnamese tear them apart and stuff them in lettuce leaves along with fresh herbs. All the contents are wrapped with the lettuce, dipped into a sauce, and eaten by hand.

FILLING

10 dried Chinese black mushrooms, or 6 fresh shiitake mushrooms

1/2 cup dried wood ear mushrooms, or 1 cup fresh wood ear mushrooms

2 ounces dried glass noodles, bean threads, or cellophane noodles

2 cups matchstick-sliced firm tofu

1 cup matchstick-sliced jicama or lotus roots

1 cup matchstick-sliced carrots

1/2 cup chopped yellow onions

2 tablespoons light soy sauce

2 tablespoons minced garlic

2 tablespoons sugar

1 teaspoon ground black pepper

1/2 teaspoon salt

If using dried mushrooms to make the filling, soak them in warm water for 15–20 minutes, or until they are soft and fully expanded. Drain and squeeze out the excess water. Remove the tough stems from the black mushrooms, and slice the caps into long, thin strips. Remove and discard the tough knots from the underside of the wood ear mushrooms, and slice them into long, thin strips. If using fresh mushrooms, slice only the tender parts into long, thin strips.

Soak the glass noodles in hot water for 15–20 minutes, or until soft and pliable. Drain and cut into 1½-inch-long strands.

Combine the mushrooms, noodles, and all the remaining ingredients in a mixing bowl and set aside.

If using rice papers to assemble and serve the spring rolls, lay 2 or 3 sheets on a flat, clean surface. Using a pastry brush, brush the rice sheets with hot water, and let stand for 30–60 seconds, or until they are soft and pliable. If using the frozen wrappers, thaw and separate.

Place about 1½ tablespoons of filling across the bottom of each wrapper to form a 3 x 1-inch log. Fold the bottom edge of the wrapper over the log, and then roll tightly. Halfway into the wrapper, fold both side ends toward the center. Continue rolling tightly. Apply water lightly at the open edge, and then seal completely. Repeat the process to make more spring rolls until all of the filling has been used.

Heat the oil in a wok or deep saucepan to 375 degrees F; the oil should have a depth of at least 2 inches. Add the spring rolls so they fit loosely. Fry the rolls, turning them occasionally, for 3–5 minutes, or until golden brown on all sides. Remove from the oil and drain on absorbent paper.

Cut the spring rolls diagonally in half, or leave them whole and arrange on a platter.

Serve with the lettuce leaves, herbs, and dipping sauce on the side.

To eat, tear a spring roll into small pieces and place on a lettuce leaf. Top with small pieces of the herbs and wrap up the leaf. Dip into the sauce and eat by hand.

WRAPPERS AND ACCOMPANIMENTS

1 package (12 ounces) Vietnamese rice paper sheets (8 inches in diameter) or frozen lumpia wrappers

3 cups vegetable or peanut oil, for deep-frying

1 head lettuce, cleaned and separated into leaves

1 bunch mint

1 bunch sweet basil

1 bunch cilantro

1 cup Dipping Sauce #1 (page 51) or # 2 (page 51)

Snacks and Appetizers

Crispy Tofu with Herb Sauce and Papaya Salad

Tong Gar Yarn

Every country in Southeast Asia has its own dish of crispy fried food that pairs well with a local papaya salad. Thai people have chicken and som tum, Laotians have beef and tum som, and the Vietnamese have fish and goi du du. We vegetarians have crispy tofu and papaya salad. Green papaya's crunchy texture and mild flavor is perfect with the cold and crisp lime dressing. If green papaya is not available, green beans, cucumbers, carrots, or jicama can be used instead.

TOFU

1 pound firm tofu or fried spongy tofu

3 cups vegetable or peanut oil, for deep-frying

HERB SAUCE

$^1/_2$ cup light soy sauce

$^1/_2$ cup tamarind liquid

$^1/_4$ cup palm sugar or brown sugar

$^1/_3$ cup very thinly sliced lemongrass, tender midsection only (2–3 stalks)

$^1/_3$ cup very finely diced young ginger, cut into $^1/_8$-inch cubes

$^1/_3$ cup very finely diced red onion, cut into $^1/_8$-inch cubes

$^1/_4$ cup finely sliced saw-leaf herb, Vietnamese mint (*rau ram*), or sweet basil

1 tablespoon minced red chiles, more or less to taste

To prepare the firm tofu, if using, drain it completely of water, and cut it into $^1/_2$ x 1$^1/_2$-inch strips, $^1/_2$ inch thick. Pat dry. If the tofu is prefried, omit the oil and heat the tofu in an oven at 350 degrees F for 7–10 minutes, or until crispy.

To fry the tofu, heat the oil to 375 degrees F in a deep pan over medium heat; the oil should have a depth of at least 2 inches. Gently lower the tofu into the hot oil to fit loosely in the pan, and fry it, turning occasionally, for 5–7 minutes, or until golden brown and crispy on all sides. Remove from the oil and drain on absorbent paper.

To make the herb sauce, combine the soy sauce, tamarind liquid, and palm sugar in a saucepan over medium heat. Bring to a boil, and cook and stir for 2–3 minutes, or until the sugar is completely dissolved. Remove from the heat and let cool. Just before serving, add the remaining ingredients and stir to mix well.

To prepare the accompaniments and serve the tofu, clean and separate the lettuce into individual leaves. Clean the herbs, trim the tough stems, and separate into small pieces.

To eat, fill a lettuce leaf with the Crispy Tofu and top with the fresh herbs. Roll up the leaf and dip it into the herb sauce.

Serve with Papaya Salad.

ACCOMPANIMENTS
1 head lettuce or cabbage
1 bunch sweet basil
1 bunch Vietnamese mint (*rau ram*) or mint
1 bunch cilantro
1 bunch saw-leaf herb or dill
1 recipe Papaya Salad (page 90)

Deep-Fried Crêpes
Chao Thoom Yuan

Instead of pan-fried crêpes, which are lightly crispy around the edges, this recipe uses the deep-fry technique that gives all-over crunchiness. Leftover homemade Crêpes (page 98) or ready-made spring roll and lumpia wrappers can be used. The same filling from Tofu Purée on Sugarcane Sticks (page 72) is normally used. This allows you to make good use of surplus ingredients from each of these dishes.

2 cups chopped firm silken tofu, completely drained of water

I cup chopped water chestnuts

I cup chopped yellow onions

2 tablespoons chopped green onions, green part only

I tablespoon soy sauce

I tablespoon sugar

I tablespoon vegetable base or bouillon powder

I teaspoon ground black pepper

2 tablespoons cornstarch

3 tablespoons boiling hot water, or more as needed

$1/4$ pound spring roll or lumpia wrappers (6- or 8-inch squares), thawed completely

3 cups vegetable or peanut oil, for deep-frying

Combine the tofu, water chestnuts, onions, green onions, soy sauce, sugar, vegetable base, and pepper in a bowl. Mix vigorously with your hands for 2–3 minutes, or until the texture is lightly stiff.

Place the cornstarch in a small bowl, and gradually pour in the boiling hot water, stirring continuously. Mix well to make a thin paste; this will be used to seal the wrappers. Add a little more hot water if the paste is too thick.

Gently separate the wrappers, and cut each one in quarters.

Spread the tofu mixture thinly on each wrapper, leaving an empty narrow rim around the edges. Apply the cornstarch paste along the rim, and top with another wrapper. Press around the edges to seal completely. Repeat the process to make more crêpes.

Heat the oil to 365 degrees F in a deep pan over medium heat. The oil should have a depth of at least 2 inches. Gently drop the crêpes into the pan to fit loosely. Fry, turning once, for 2–3 minutes, or until golden brown on both sides. Remove from the oil and drain on absorbent paper.

Clean and separate the lettuce into individual leaves. Clean the herbs, trim the tough stems, and separate into small pieces.

To eat, fill a lettuce leaf with a fried crêpe and top it with the fresh herbs. Roll up the leaf and dip it into the sauce.

Herb Accompaniments

1 head lettuce

1 bunch sweet basil

1 bunch Vietnamese mint (*rau ram*) or mint

1 bunch cilantro

1 bunch saw-leaf herb or dill

1 cup Dipping Sauce #1 (page 51), #2 (page 51), #3 (page 52), Peanut Sauce (page 54), or Hoisin Peanut Sauce (page 53)

Deep-Fried Rice Spring Rolls

Saow Ja Yío

This is another crunchy, deep-fried spring roll, with steamed rice inside instead of the usual rice on the side. Cold, dry, left-over rice has the perfect texture to absorb all the liquid seasonings and flavors. Wet rice sometimes turns out too mushy after being fried. Again, an entourage of accompaniments brightens up this unusual spring roll dish.

1 cup chopped baby corn or corn kernels

1 cup thinly sliced wood ear mushrooms or mushrooms of your choice

1 cup matchstick-sliced carrots

2 tablespoons light soy sauce

2 tablespoons sugar

1 tablespoon stir-fry sauce or vegetarian oyster sauce

1 tablespoon vegetable base or bouillon powder

1 teaspoon ground black pepper

2 cups cold steamed rice

2 tablespoons cornstarch

3 tablespoons boiling hot water, or more as needed

20 sheets dried Vietnamese rice paper (8 inches in diameter) or spring roll wrappers

3 cups vegetable or peanut oil, for deep-frying

Combine the baby corn, mushrooms, carrots, soy sauce, sugar, stir-fry sauce, vegetable base, and pepper in a medium bowl. Stir to mix well. Gently fold in the cold rice and combine thoroughly.

Place the cornstarch in a small bowl, and gradually pour in the boiling hot water, stirring continuously. Mix well to make a thin paste; this will be used to seal the wrappers. Add a little more hot water if the paste is too thick.

If using rice paper, lay 2 or 3 sheets on a flat, clean surface. Using a pastry brush, brush the rice paper sheets with hot water, and let stand for 30–60 seconds, or until they are soft and pliable. If using the frozen wrappers, thaw and separate.

Spoon about 2 tablespoons of the vegetable mixture across the bottom of each wrapper to form a 1 x 3-inch log. Fold the bottom edge of the wrapper over the log, and then roll tightly. Halfway into the wrapper, fold both side ends toward the center. Continue rolling tightly. Apply the cornstarch paste lightly at the open edge, and then seal completely. Repeat the process to make more spring rolls and use up the filling.

Heat the oil to 375 degrees F in a deep pan over medium heat. The oil should have a depth of at least 2 inches. Gently drop the spring rolls into the pan to fit loosely. Fry for 3–5 minutes, turning occasionally, until golden brown and crispy. Remove from the pan and drain on absorbent paper. Cut the spring rolls into 1-inch bite-size pieces.

Clean and separate the lettuce into individual leaves. Clean the herbs, trim the tough stems, and separate into small pieces.

To eat, fill a lettuce leaf with the spring roll pieces and top with the herbs. Wrap the leaf around the filling, dip in the dipping sauce, and eat by hand.

ACCOMPANIMENTS
1 head lettuce
1 bunch sweet basil
1 bunch Vietnamese mint (*rau ram*) or mint
1 bunch cilantro
1 bunch saw-leaf herb or dill
1 cup Dipping Sauce #2 (page 51)

Snacks and Appetizers

Fresh Spring Rolls

Banh Cuon

Serves 6

When mentioning Vietnamese food, fresh spring rolls often come to mind. An array of fresh ingredients is prepared in advance and ready for the simple technique of filling and wrapping. The tricky part is handling the rice paper, which is somewhat temperamental. In its dry form, it is hard and brittle, and after being wet and made pliable, it must be used right away. If it is too wet for too long, it will fall apart; if it isn't wet enough, it becomes stiff and won't cooperate as a pliable wrapper. After being left out or refrigerated for too long, it will become dry and tough. It also does not help that there are so many brands in the marketplace, and they all behave differently when wet. Some take longer to soften than others, so the timing will need to be adjusted according to the brand; some brands take less than a minute. Wet or soak the rice paper long enough to just make it pliable for wrapping; moisture in the filling will further soften it to perfection. (See photo, facing page 40.)

2 ounces dried glass noodles, bean threads, or cellophane noodles

1/2 pound fried or firm tofu

1 small head lettuce, cleaned and sliced into narrow strips

1/2 cup matchstick-sliced carrots

1/2 cup matchstick-sliced jicama or Asian pear

1/2 cup matchstick-sliced cucumbers (seeds removed)

1/2 cup thinly sliced (chiffonade) mint leaves

1/2 cup thinly sliced (chiffonade) sweet basil leaves

18 sheets dried Vietnamese rice paper (8–10 inches in diameter)

Salt

18 sprigs cilantro or dill, long stems and leaves attached, for garnish

1/2 cup long matchstick-sliced red bell peppers, for garnish

Bring 3 cups of water with a little salt to a boil in a pot. Add the noodles and cook for 3–5 minutes, or until they are soft and pliable. Drain and rinse with cold water. Cut the noodles into 3-inch strands, and set them aside to drain.

Slice the tofu into thin strips, 2–3 inches long. Slice and shred all of the vegetables and herbs uniformly, and set them aside separately.

To roll, fill a large bowl halfway with warm to hot water and soak the rice paper sheets, one at a time, for about 1 minute, or until soft and pliable. Alternatively, arrange 2 or 3 sheets of rice paper on a flat surface, and use a pastry brush to generously brush the sheets with hot water. Let them rest for 1 minute or longer, until they are soft and pliable.

Remove the rice paper sheets from the bowl (or the flat surface) and arrange them on a damp towel. Fill each sheet at the lower third with a little lettuce, noodles, and strips of the shredded vegetables, herbs, and tofu. Sprinkle with salt to taste. Fold the edge over and roll the rice paper tightly to wrap all the ingredients; halfway into the wrapper, fold in both side ends to form a log. Place a sprig of cilantro and a strip of bell pepper along the log with their tips extending over one end of the log. Continue to roll and completely seal. Repeat the process to finish all the ingredients.

1 cup Dipping Sauce #1, (page 51), #2 (page 51), or #3 (page 52), Hoisin Peanut Sauce (page 53), or Peanut Sauce (page 54)
1 bottle hoisin sauce, for condiment
1 bottle sriracha sauce, for condiment

To eat, cut the rolls in half or serve them whole with the dipping sauce and hoisin sauce on the side. Dip a fresh spring roll in the sauce and/or top the roll with dab of hoisin and sriracha sauce before eating.

Snacks and Appetizers

Fried Sweet Rice

Saoy Yang

Rice is staple in Asia, and its different flavors and textures help keep the meal interesting. This dish, which uses sweet sticky rice instead of plain steamed rice, is an accompaniment to many Vietnamese dishes in the same way a basket of bread accompanies a Western meal. Sweet sticky rice has a unique flavor and sticky texture that holds together well, making it easy to eat by hand.

2 cups sweet or sticky long-grain rice

$^1/_2$ cup coconut cream

2 tablespoons sugar, or more to taste

$^1/_2$ teaspoon salt, or more to taste

I cup panko breadcrumbs, or more as needed (see note)

3 cups vegetable or peanut oil, for deep-frying

Note

• Panko breadcrumbs are used in Asian cooking for coating fried foods. They are coarser than standard breadcrumbs and create a delicious, crunchy crust. Panko breadcrumbs are available in Asian markets.

Soak the sweet rice in cold water for 2–10 hours. Rinse and drain. Transfer the rice to a steamer, and steam over boiling water in a pot with a tight-fitting lid for 15–20 minutes. Turn the rice over from top to bottom, and continue steaming for 10 more minutes, or until tender. (If using a rice cooker, follow the instructions in the manual that came with it.)

Combine the coconut cream, sugar, and salt in a bowl. Stir until the sugar is dissolved. Add the hot cooked rice to the bowl, and fold it in until thoroughly combined. Let cool.

Form the rice into small balls, each 1 inch in diameter. Press the balls lightly to flatten them into a round dough. Roll the dough in a plate of breadcrumbs until evenly coated; shake off the excess crumbs.

Heat the oil to 375 degrees F in a deep pan; the oil should have a depth of at least 2 inches. Gently drop the dough into the pan to fit loosely. Fry, turning occasionally, until light brown on all sides. Remove and drain on absorbent paper. Serve the Fried Sweet Rice as an accompaniment to main dishes.

Sweet Rice and Beans

Saoy

In addition to plain steamed rice, a variety of beans—a source of protein—is added to make this side dish more interesting in taste, texture, and nutritional value. This dish should be a favorite addition to your vegetarian repertoire because it is very easy to make. Different varieties of rice and beans can be used, giving you endless alternatives. Each ingredient can be cooked separately and put together at the end, along with any type of seasonings, herbs, and spices that strike your mood and make your day.

2 cups sweet long-grain rice, brown rice, black rice, wild rice, or Arborio rice

1/4 cup dried mung beans

1/4 cup dried red beans

1/4 cup dried black beans

2 tablespoons sugar, more or less to taste

1 teaspoon salt, more or less to taste

Herbs and spices of your choice, to taste

Soak the rice, mung beans, red beans, and black beans separately in cold water for 3–10 hours. Refresh the water at least once.

Using fresh water, boil each kind of bean separately for 7–10 minutes, or until just tender. Do not overcook them, as they will fall apart and turn mushy. Drain and rinse with cold water. Drain the rice and rinse with cold water.

Combine the rice and beans in a bowl and mix well. Transfer the mixture to a steamer, and steam over boiling water in a pot with a tight-fitting lid for 15–20 minutes, or until the rice is tender (the amount of time needed will depend on the type of rice used). Turn the mixture over from top to bottom and continue steaming for 5–10 minutes longer, or until all the ingredients are fully cooked.

Transfer to a bowl and mix in the sugar, salt, and herbs and spices of your choice to taste. Serve the Sweet Rice and Beans as an accompaniment to main dishes.

Tofu Purée on Sugarcane Sticks
Chao Thoom

Serves 6

The original recipe of this item is one of the Vietnamese signature dishes, uniquely using sugarcane as skewers to hold food for barbecuing. The fragrant sweet flavor of sugarcane also rubs off on the food, and when combined with a touch of smoky barbecue charcoal or wood-burning aroma, it can make this dish quite attractive and unusual. Sugarcane sticks are chewed to extract the sweet aftertaste. Fresh sugarcane can be found at your local farmers market or well-stocked Asian grocery stores. Prepared sugarcane sticks in brine or syrup are also available.

4 pieces sugarcane, each 6 inches long

1 pound firm silken tofu, completely drained of water

3 tablespoons chopped garlic

3 tablespoons chopped shallots

3 tablespoons sugar

2 tablespoons cornstarch, or more as needed

2 tablespoons light soy sauce

1 tablespoon vegetable base powder, or 1 bouillon cube diluted with a small amount of hot water

1 teaspoon baking powder

1 teaspoon ground black pepper

¼ cup vegetable oil, for brushing

Peel each piece of sugarcane and spilt in half lengthwise, and then split each half in half again. There should be a total of 16 sugarcane sticks.

Break the tofu into large chunks. Place the chunks in a strainer to drain the water completely, squeezing the tofu lightly, if necessary.

Combine the garlic and shallots in a food processor, and process until finely minced. Add the tofu, sugar, cornstarch, soy sauce, vegetable base, baking powder, and pepper. Pulse the mixture until well blended. Do not overprocess into a paste. The mixture should hold together very well and be able to form a dough.

Start a charcoal grill, wood-burning grill, or searing pan in advance so it reaches medium heat, or preheat the oven to 350 degrees F.

With damp hands, mold about 2 tablespoons of the tofu purée around a sugarcane stick, leaving about ½ inch at both ends of the stick exposed. Place the molded tofu stick in a well-oiled tray, and brush or rub it all over with vegetable oil. Repeat the process with each of the sugarcane sticks until you have used up all of the mixture.

Grill or sear the tofu purée over medium heat for 3–5 minutes, turning occasionally, until it has grill or sear marks all over. Alternatively, bake in the oven for 15–25 minutes, turning once, until golden brown. Transfer to a serving platter.

Fill a large bowl halfway with warm to hot water, and soak the rice paper sheets, one at a time, for about 1 minute, or until soft and pliable. Alternatively, arrange 2 or 3 sheets of rice paper on a flat surface, and use a pastry brush to generously brush the sheets with hot water. Let them rest for 1 minute or longer until they are soft and pliable.

ACCOMPANIMENTS

12 sheets dried Vietnamese rice paper (8 inches in diameter)

1 head lettuce, cleaned and separated into leaves

$\frac{1}{2}$ cup cilantro leaves

$\frac{1}{2}$ cup mint leaves

$\frac{1}{2}$ cup sweet basil leaves

$\frac{1}{2}$ cup saw-leaf herb or Vietnamese mint (*rau ram*)

1 cup thinly sliced English cucumbers, cut into half circles

1 cup Dipping Sauce #1 (page 51), #2 (page 51), or #3 (page 52)

Remove from the water or flat surface, and place them on a serving platter. Stack several rice paper sheets with damp paper towels or lettuce leaves in between so they won't stick to each other.

To eat, place a sheet of rice paper on a serving plate and top with small pieces of lettuce. Sprinkle with a few cilantro, mint, basil, and saw-leaf herb leaves, and cucumber. Strip the tofu purée off the stick into small chunks, and place it in the middle of the vegetables. Roll and wrap all of the contents, dip into the dipping sauce, and eat by hand. Chew on the sugarcane stick to extract its sweetness. Do not swallow the cane.

Snacks and Appetizers

Soups and Salads

Some people classify the Vietnamese as "wet eaters" because they transform all sorts of ingredients into bowls of soup. The most popular Vietnamese noodle soup, *pho*, has several traditional varieties, depending mostly on the meat used and the broth flavor. It can also be served with different types and sizes of noodles: vermicelli rice or glass noodles, medium-size rice or potato noodles, large rice or wheat noodles, or various sizes of egg noodles. For vegetarian cooking, we narrow it down to just vegetable broth, but we can still have a wide variety of choices by using all different types of noodles and an expansive array of tofu and vegetables.

After closely examining Vietnamese food, I hardly find any dishes that are not salad or do not included salad. The majority of dishes come with accompaniments of fresh vegetables and herbs in large amounts, which makes it hard to see a fine line of classification. For example, Fresh Spring Rolls (page 68) come with a fresh vegetable filling and are served with more fresh vegetables and herbs, just as noodle soup (*pho*) is served with fresh accompaniments. I can only make a distinction of the salad from other dishes by looking at the use of dressing, which is generally the famous Vietnamese *nuoc cham* (see pages 51 and 52). With *nuoc cham* dressing, fresh lime or lemon juice is often used, and it is tossed in with other salad ingredients instead of being served on the side as a dipping sauce.

Noodle Soup
Pho

From sunrise to sunset, Vietnamese noodle soup (pho) satisfies hunger at breakfast, lunch, and dinner. Vietnamese start their day with a bowl of noodle soup, or take a lunch break with noodle soup, or end their day with a bowl of noodles; and some even enjoy it for each meal, all in the same day. A variety of pho is offered in many neighborhood noodle shops, which receive overwhelming support from local residents. Pho is more popular and convenient to eat as a one-plate meal at the shops, from where many varieties can be chosen. Because of its many steps of preparation and many different varieties of ingredients, making pho in large amounts to serve many people is worth the effort. For our vegetarian version, homemade is more practical and less time-consuming when making a vegetable broth. A good tasty broth is an essential component that constitutes more than 50 percent of a delicious bowl of pho. (See photo, facing page 81.)

BROTH

12 cups water

1 yellow onion, chopped

1 leek, cleaned and chopped

1 carrot, chopped

1 celery stalk, chopped

1 daikon radish or other vegetable of your choice, chopped

5 whole shallots

8 pieces thinly sliced ginger, each piece 2 x 2 inches

2 cups sliced mushrooms of your choice, cut into bite-size pieces

1 1/2 cups julienne firm tofu

2 ounces (about 1/4 cup) rock sugar or sugar, or more to taste

2 tablespoons light soy sauce, or more to taste

1 tablespoon vegetable base or bouillon powder

1 teaspoon salt, or more to taste

To prepare the broth, combine the water, onion, leek, carrot, celery, and daikon in a large stockpot. Bring the mixture to a boil, and reduce the heat to medium. Skim any foam or impurities off the broth's surface.

Place the whole shallots on a medium grill or over a gas burner. Roast, turning occasionally, until lightly charred and blackened on all sides. Add the shallots and ginger to the broth.

Continue cooking the broth at a gentle boil for 30–45 minutes, or until it is reduced to three-quarters of its original volume. Strain through a fine sieve into a clean pot and discard the solids.

Place the broth over medium heat and add the mushrooms, tofu, sugar, soy sauce, vegetable base, and salt. Cook for 4–5 minutes, or until the mushrooms are tender. Adjust the seasonings if needed.

Reheat the broth over high heat before serving with the noodles.

To prepare the noodles and serve the soup, heat a pan over medium heat and pour in the oil. Add the shallots and fry, stirring frequently, until light brown and crispy. Do not overcook until they are dark brown or burned, as they will be bitter. Remove from the oil, and drain on absorbent paper. Set aside.

If using dried noodles, soak them in cold water for 30 minutes and drain. To cook the noodles (fresh or dried), bring a large pot of water to a boil. Add the noodles and cook for 2–3 minutes, or until tender. Drain well.

continued next page

NOODLES AND ACCOMPANIMENTS

2 tablespoons vegetable oil

$1/4$ cup thinly sliced shallots

1 pound fresh, medium rice noodles, or $1/2$ pound dried noodles

1 cup thinly sliced yellow onions

2 tablespoons thinly sliced green onions, white and green parts

$1/2$ pound bean sprouts

1 lime, cut into 6 wedges

2 red jalapeño chiles, thinly sliced

6 sprigs sweet basil

6 sprigs cilantro

6 sprigs mint

6 sprigs saw-leaf herb or Vietnamese mint (*rau ram*)

1 bottle hoisin sauce, for condiment

1 bottle sriracha sauce, for condiment

Soups and Salads

Arrange the bean sprouts, lime wedges, chiles, basil, cilantro, mint, and saw-leaf herb on a platter, and place them in the middle of a dining table to serve as a side dish with the soup.

To serve, portion the cooked noodles equally into 6 large serving bowls. Top with the sliced onions, green onions, and fried shallots. Ladle the hot broth, mushrooms, and tofu over the noodles.

Each diner, at any time, selects the vegetable accompaniments and adds them on top of the soup, eating the soup with chopsticks and a spoon.

Hoisin and sriracha sauce can also be added as condiments for more flavor and heat.

Vegetable Stock
Nuoc Leo Rau Cai

Stock or broth in any kind of soup is the key to a delicious flavor. A good, flavorful stock contributes a great deal to the success of the dish. There are many ways to produce a good stock from various types of fresh vegetables. This simple recipe consistently gives excellent results. Make it in large batches and freeze it so you always have some on hand.

12 cups water
1 onion, chopped
1 leek, cleaned and chopped
1 carrot, chopped
1 celery stalk, chopped
1 daikon radish or other vegetable of your choice, chopped
1/2 cup chopped cilantro roots and stems
2 tablespoons chopped garlic (optional)
1 teaspoon coarsely ground black pepper
1 teaspoon salt (optional)

Combine all the ingredients in a large pot and bring to a boil. Reduce the heat to medium-low and simmer for 30–45 minutes, or until all the vegetables begin to disintegrate. Pour the mixture through a fine sieve and discard the solids.

Noodle Soup with Lemongrass

Bun Hue

Serves 6

In addition to pho, the subtly flavored soup, Vietnamese enjoy this dish, which uses lemongrass to create an aromatic, herbal noodle soup. Its origin is in Hue, the capital of the old Vietnamese empire in central Vietnam. Hue had been the capital city for more than 150 years and was also the center of classical Vietnamese cooking, where Vietnamese culinary culture was developed in the confinement of royal kitchens.

To make the broth, heat a pan over medium heat and pour in the oil. Add the shallots and fry for 1–2 minutes, or until light brown and fragrant. Stir in the remaining ingredients, and bring to a boil. Simmer for 10–15 minutes. Remove and discard the lemongrass. Adjust the seasonings, if needed. Reheat the broth over high heat before serving with the noodles.

Cook the noodles in a pot of boiling water until tender, 3–4 minutes for fresh noodles, or 5–7 minutes for dried noodles. Drain in a colander, and portion the noodles into serving bowls. Top with the tomatoes, cucumbers, and lettuce.

To serve, reheat the broth to a boil. Stir in the mushrooms and tofu and cook for 1–2 minutes, or until the mushrooms are tender. Ladle the hot broth, mushrooms, and tofu into the bowls, and garnish with the cilantro and green onions. Serve hot.

BROTH

2 tablespoons vegetable oil

1/4 cup thinly sliced shallots

8 cups vegetable stock

3 lemongrass stalks, cut into several 2-inch-long pieces and bruised to lightly split

2 tablespoons light soy sauce, or more to taste

2 tablespoons tomato paste

1 teaspoon salt, or more to taste

1 teaspoon chili sauce (sambal oelek) or sriracha sauce (optional)

1/4 teaspoon ground black pepper

NOODLES AND VEGETABLES

1 pound fresh, medium rice noodles, or 1/2 pound dried noodles

2 tomatoes, seeded and cut into 1/2-inch cubes

1 1/2 cups thinly sliced English cucumbers, cut into half circles

3 romaine lettuce leaves, sliced into thin strips, or 1 cup baby spinach leaves

1/2 pound mushrooms of your choice, cleaned and cut into bite-size pieces

1 pound firm tofu, cut into bite-size pieces

3 tablespoon chopped cilantro leaves, for garnish

3 tablespoons finely sliced green onions, white and green parts, for garnish

Stir-Fried Fresh Mango and Cashew Nuts, p. 113

Hot-and-Sour Soup with Pineapple and Tamarind

Canh Chua Thom

Both pineapple and tamarind have distinctive sweet-and-sour flavors. Pineapple also lends a refreshing touch of tropical taste to any dish. Tamarind has begun to gain wide popularity in Western kitchens due to its unique sweet-and-sour flavor and amber color. It can be used in place of lime, lemon, or vinegar in salads, soups, and sauces. Tamarind in U.S. markets comes in two forms: as a liquid in plastic jars, and as a semidry pulp in plastic wrap. The liquid tamarind comes in very handy in cooking, but it has a limited shelf life and requires refrigeration after opening. With the semidry form, the tamarind needs to be diluted with hot water; then its liquid is extracted. It lasts about a year without refrigeration.

2 tablespoons vegetable oil

1/2 cup thinly sliced yellow onions

3 lemongrass stalks, cut into several 2-inch-long sticks and bruised to lightly split

5 pieces thinly sliced galangal or ginger, each piece 2 x 2 inches

2 tablespoons minced garlic

2 cups white mushrooms, cleaned and cut into bite-size pieces

1 1/2 cups fresh pineapple, peeled and cut into 1/2-inch cubes

1 cup thinly sliced fresh or canned bamboo shoots

5 cups vegetable stock

1/3 cup tamarind liquid, or more to taste

2 tablespoons light soy sauce, or more to taste

1 tablespoon sugar, or more to taste

1 teaspoon salt

1 cup bean sprouts

1/4 cup thinly sliced green onions, white and green parts

1/4 cup mint leaves

2 tablespoons freshly squeezed lime or lemon juice, or more to taste

1/4 cup cilantro leaves

2 red chiles, thinly sliced

Heat a pot over medium heat and pour in the oil. Add the onions, lemongrass, galangal, and garlic, and fry for about 2 minutes, or until the onions are soft. Stir in the mushrooms, pineapple, and bamboo shoots. Cook for 2–3 minutes longer.

Raise the heat to high and add the stock. Bring the mixture to a boil, and stir in the tamarind liquid, soy sauce, sugar, and salt. Cook for 3–4 minutes. Remove from the heat.

Add the bean sprouts, green onions, mint leaves, and lime juice. Gently stir to mix well. Taste and adjust the seasonings, if needed. Ladle into serving bowls, and garnish with the cilantro and chiles. Serve hot with steamed rice, Fried Sweet Rice (page 70), or Sweet Rice and Beans (page 71).

Noodle Soup (Pho), p. 76

Glass Noodle Soup

Gna Maen

Glass noodles are made from beans, and after being cooked they turn clear, hence the name. Glass noodles come in many different sizes and are also called bean threads or cellophane noodles. They have a unique texture, which is a little firmer and more elastic than other noodles. An excellent alternative to the starch and carbohydrate found in rice and wheat noodles, glass noodles provide plenty of protein from beans.

4 ounces dried glass noodles, bean threads, or cellophane noodles

10 dried Chinese black mushroom caps

1/2 cup dried lily buds

10 cups vegetable stock

2 yellow onions, peeled and cut into eighths

2 tablespoons Maggi Seasoning Sauce or flavorful soy sauce

1 tablespoon whole black peppercorns

1 pound firm tofu, cut into 1/2-inch cubes

1/4 cup chopped green onions, white and green parts

1/4 cup chopped cilantro leaves

Soak the noodles in warm water for 10–15 minutes, or until soft and pliable. Cut into 6-inch strands. Soak the mushrooms and lily buds in warm water for 7–10 minutes, or until soft. Drain and squeeze out the excess water. Set aside.

Pour the vegetable stock into a pot and bring to a boil. Add the onions, Maggi Seasoning Sauce, and peppercorns. Reduce the heat to medium, and simmer for 10–15 minutes, or until the onions are tender.

Bring the stock to a boil again, and add the mushrooms and lily buds. Cook until soft, about 3 minutes. Add the noodles and cook until tender, about 2 minutes longer.

To serve, portion the tofu into serving bowls. Ladle the noodles, mushrooms, lily buds, and hot broth into the bowls, and garnish with the green onions and cilantro.

Serve hot with steamed rice, Fried Sweet Rice (page 70), or Sweet Rice and Beans (page 71).

Pumpkin with Coconut Milk

Canh Bi Ro Ham Dua

Serves 4

Older Vietnamese, especially Buddhist monks, comprise the majority of people in Vietnam who become vegetarian to help reduce the workload on their frail digestive systems and to practice compassion toward all living creatures by not eating them. This is a traditional dish for vegetarian Buddhist monks in temples throughout Vietnam. Made with a variety of root vegetables, it is hearty and filling. Coconut milk provides a rich, creamy broth that can be served as a soup. The vegetables in this recipe can be interchanged; use one or all in the same dish to create variety.

1/2 cup dried wood ear mushrooms, or 1 cup fresh wood ear mushrooms

1/2 cup raw peanuts

1 cup peeled and diced kabocha squash or pumpkin, cut into 1/2-inch cubes

1 cup peeled and diced sweet potatoes, cut into 1/2-inch cubes

1 cup peeled and diced taro roots, cut into 1/2-inch cubes

1 cup peeled and thinly sliced lotus roots or baby corn, cut into 1/2-inch pieces

2 1/3 cups coconut milk (one 19-ounce can)

1 cup thinly sliced Asian gourd (*loofah*) or green zucchini

2 tablespoons light soy sauce

1 tablespoon sugar

1 tablespoon vegetable base or bouillon powder

Salt

3 tablespoons cilantro leaves, for garnish

3 tablespoons sliced Vietnamese mint (*rau ram*), for garnish

Soak the dried wood ear mushrooms and raw peanuts in warm water separately for 20 minutes. Drain the mushrooms, trim and discard the tough roots, and slice the mushrooms thinly. Drain the peanuts, clean off any debris, and remove the skins.

Combine the peanuts, kabocha squash, sweet potatoes, taro roots, lotus roots, and coconut milk in a pot and bring to a boil. Reduce the heat and simmer for 4–5 minutes, or until the vegetables are almost tender.

Stir in the mushrooms, Asian gourd, soy sauce, sugar, and vegetable base. Season with salt to taste. Bring the mixture to a boil again and remove from the heat.

Ladle into bowls, and garnish with the cilantro and Vietnamese mint.

Stuffed Cabbage Soup
Canh Bap Cai Cuon Thit

Serves 4

This is an elaborate clear broth soup, and by itself, it can be a meal. It requires a few steps of preparation, including wrapping and tying ingredients into small packages. The end result shows the cook's careful execution that is appreciated by all.

I head napa or white cabbage

20 stems garlic chives or Chinese celery, or I leek

3 tablespoons vegetable oil

¼ cup thinly sliced shallots

I cup chopped shiitake mushrooms or other mushrooms of your choice

I cup chopped firm silken tofu, completely drained of water

¼ cup chopped Chinese celery or celery

I tablespoon light soy sauce

I tablespoon Maggi Seasoning Sauce or flavorful soy sauce

I tablespoon sugar

Separate the cabbage into individual leaves (about 20 leaves) to use as wrappers. Trim off the tough center ridges. Wash and set aside to drain. Trim and cut the garlic chives (or celery stems or leek) into long, narrow strips for use as string ties.

Bring 5 cups of water to a boil in a saucepan. Add the cabbage leaves and strips of garlic chives (or Chinese celery or leek) and poach them until they are soft and pliable, about 2 minutes. Drain and rinse with cold water. Pat dry.

To make the stuffing, heat a pan over medium heat and pour in the oil. Add the shallots and cook for 2 minutes, or until light brown and fragrant. Stir in the mushrooms and cook for 2 minutes. Stir in the tofu, chopped celery, soy sauce, Maggi Seasoning Sauce, and sugar. Cook for 3 minutes, or until heated through. Remove from the heat.

Spread the cabbage leaves, and place about 2 tablespoons of the stuffing on each leaf. Fold in the edges and shape into square packages. Tie and secure the packages with the garlic chive strips.

Place the vegetable stock in a medium saucepan, and bring to a boil over medium heat. Drain the lily buds and add them to the stock. Add the wrapped tofu packages and simmer for 3 minutes, or until they are heated through. Season with salt and adjust the other seasonings to taste.

Ladle into individual bowls, and garnish with the chopped cilantro before serving.

5 cups vegetable stock
$^{1}/_{4}$ cup dried lily buds, soaked in warm water
Salt
3 tablespoons chopped cilantro leaves, for garnish

Hot-and-Sour Soup

Chua Nam Hunong

Serves 6

This recipe starts off as a simple, aromatic broth that can be served as is, but by adding chiles and lime juice, the dish becomes a hot-and-sour soup. As with other Southeast Asian cuisines, such as Burmese, Cambodian, Laotian, and Thai, lemongrass and galangal are often used in aromatic soups. The application of these herbs goes beyond cooking, as they are widely used in folk remedies. Both lemongrass and galangal have medicinal properties as antibacterials and tonics to aid indigestion.

2 tablespoons vegetable oil

1/4 cup thinly sliced shallots

5 cups vegetable stock

3 lemongrass stalks, cut into several 2-inch-long pieces and bruised to slightly split

5 pieces thinly sliced galangal or ginger, each piece 2 x 2 inches

1/2 pound fresh mushrooms of your choice, cut into bite-size pieces

1/2 pound cherry tomatoes, cut in half

2 tablespoons light soy sauce

2 tablespoons sugar

1/2 teaspoon salt

2 tablespoons freshly squeezed lime or lemon juice, or more to taste

3–4 red chiles, finely chopped or bruised to lightly split, more or less to taste

2 green onions, white and green parts, cut into 1 1/2-inch-long pieces, for garnish

1/4 cup chopped cilantro leaves, for garnish

Heat a medium pot over medium heat and pour in the oil. Add the shallots and fry for 3–5 minutes, or until light brown and crispy. Do not let them become dark brown or burn, as they will be bitter. Remove the shallots from the oil, and drain on absorbent paper. Set aside for garnish.

Add the stock, lemongrass, and galangal to the pot and bring to a boil. Simmer for 5–6 minutes, or until the stock is infused with lemongrass flavor. Add the mushrooms, tomatoes, soy sauce, sugar, and salt. Cook for 3–4 minutes, or until the mushrooms are tender.

Remove from the heat and add the lime juice and chiles. Adjust the seasonings if needed. Ladle into serving bowls and garnish with the green onions, cilantro, and fried shallots. Serve hot with steamed rice, Fried Sweet Rice (page 70), or Sweet Rice and Beans (page 71).

Sour Bean Sprouts

Dua Gia

Sour bean sprouts are an excellent accompaniment to rich dishes with caramelized syrup; they help tone down the sweet caramel and balance the flavors on your taste buds. Bean sprouts are the most popular vegetable in Chinese and Vietnamese cuisine, as they are inexpensive, nutritious, and available year-round. They can be grown indoors in any season with artificial light, freeing up land for other produce. Their mild, neutral flavors absorb seasonings and sauces very well. Traditionally with this recipe, the heads and string tails of the bean sprouts are meticulously and monotonously picked and discarded, leaving only the white stems, showing the great effort and attentiveness of the cook. But for our purposes and for better nutrition, the heads should be left intact for consumption.

2 cups water, or more as needed

1/3 cup rice vinegar or white vinegar

1/3 cup sugar

1 tablespoon salt, or more to taste

1 small carrot

1/2 pound bean sprouts

3 green onions, white and green parts, cut into 1 1/2-inch-long pieces

1/4 cup matchstick-sliced red jalapeño chiles

3 sprigs cilantro, leaves only

Freshly squeezed lime or lemon juice

Combine the water, vinegar, sugar, and salt in a pot, and place over high heat. Bring to a boil and cook for 1–2 minutes. Remove from the heat and let cool.

With a vegetable peeler, peel the carrot and discard the skin. Continue peeling the flesh lengthwise into long, thin ribbons. Cut the ribbons into 3-inch lengths.

Transfer the carrot ribbons to a bowl and add the bean sprouts, green onions, chiles, and cilantro. Add the vinegar mixture to the bowl, and marinate for at least 1 hour at room temperature. The liquid should completely cover the vegetables.

Before serving, drain and add lime juice to taste (this will add a refreshing flavor). Serve at room temperature with any dish that has a caramelized sauce, such as stews and those cooked in clay pots.

Jackfruit Salad
Goi Mit Tron

Serves 4

Ripe jackfruit is popular as a fresh fruit in Vietnam. Its yellow-orange flesh represents gold and prosperity, bringing good fortune to those who come in contact with it. Unripe, young jackfruit is also popular and mainly used in stir-fries and salads. The ripe jackfruit has an intense fragrance, sweet flavor, and soft, smooth texture, whereas the young fruit has a mild, nutty flavor and crunchy texture. Fresh jackfruit is hard to find in the United States; canned products are available for both ripe and young jackfruit. For this recipe, if jackfruit is not available, use cabbage or jicama as an alternative.

1 1/2 cups thinly sliced young, unripe jackfruit or cabbage (3/4–1 pound)

Salt

2 tablespoons vegetable oil

2 tablespoons minced garlic

1 cup julienne fried or firm tofu

1 tablespoon light soy sauce

1 tablespoon sugar

1 1/2 teaspoons vegetable base or bouillon powder

2 tablespoons chopped Vietnamese mint (*rau ram*), plus additional leaves for garnish

2 tablespoons roasted sesame seeds, plus more for garnish

1/4 teaspoon ground black pepper

1 bag (4–6 ounces) rice crackers or chips of your choice

If using canned jackfruit, boil it in water for 2 minutes to freshen the flavor. Lightly squeeze out the excess water and slice it thinly. If using fresh young jackfruit, cook it in boiling water with a little salt for 4–5 minutes, or until tender. Drain and slice thinly.

Heat a saucepan over medium heat and pour in the oil. Add the garlic and cook for 1–2 minutes, or until light brown and fragrant. Stir in the jackfruit, tofu, soy sauce, sugar, and vegetable base. Cook and stir to combine well, about 2 minutes. Remove from the heat and stir in the Vietnamese mint and sesame seeds.

Transfer to a serving plate and sprinkle with the black pepper. Garnish with more sesame seeds and mint leaves.

Serve the salad with rice crackers, Fried Sweet Rice (page 70), or Sweet Rice and Beans (page 71) on the side. Use the crackers to scoop the salad up to your mouth, and enjoy both at the same time.

Pomelo or Grapefruit Salad

Goi Buoi

Pomelo is a giant grapefruit that is available in U.S. markets in late spring, but in Vietnam, it is available year-round. There are two varieties: white-meat and pink-meat pomelo. Both varieties are truly sweet, a lot sweeter and meatier than ordinary grapefruits. They are often eaten as citrus fruits or juice. The pink pomelo is suitable for this salad because its sweet-and-sour flavor goes well with the citrus dressing. The pomelo has a thick, spongy skin with white inner membranes that tightly wrap its juicy segments. The skin and membranes need to be removed; the segments are then gently broken into small pockets of pulp and juice. When tossing the salad, tender care must be taken to not break the pockets, or the end result will be a watery salad.

1 pomelo or giant grapefruit
2 tablespoons vegetable oil
1/4 cup thinly sliced shallots
1 cup diced firm tofu, cut into 1/4-inch cubes
1/2 cup matchstick-sliced carrots
1/2 cup thinly sliced English cucumbers, cut into half circles
2 tablespoons chopped mint
1/2 cup Dressing (page 52)
3 tablespoons chopped roasted peanuts, for garnish
2 tablespoons chopped cilantro leaves, for garnish

Peel the pomelo and break up its flesh into small segments. Set aside in the refrigerator to chill.

Heat a pan over medium heat and pour in the oil. Add the shallots and fry for 3–4 minutes, or until light brown and crispy. Do not let them become dark brown or burn, as they will be bitter. Remove the shallots from the oil, and drain on absorbent paper. Set aside for garnish.

Add the tofu to the pan, stir to mix well with the shallot-flavored oil, and heat through. Set aside.

To serve, gently combine the pomelo, tofu, carrots, cucumbers, and mint in a mixing bowl. Add the dressing, a little at a time, and toss gently. Taste and add more dressing, if needed. Transfer to a serving platter and garnish with the peanuts, cilantro, and fried shallots.

Serve the salad with steamed rice, Fried Sweet Rice (page 70), or Sweet Rice and Beans (page 71).

Papaya Salad
Goi Du Du

An abundance of inexpensive and nutritious ingredients makes papaya salad one of the most popular local dishes in every Southeast Asian country. In this part of the world, the papaya grows unattended; its seeds are spread by birds, and its plants are easily established on a small patch of soil. The papaya is hardy and grows fast, profusely producing fruits. Papaya fruits are picked when they are young, green, and firm for the papaya salad; otherwise, they will be left to mature and ripen to be consumed as fresh fruits. Peel off the green skin completely and discard it; rinse the peeled fruit with cold water, and shred only the white meat into matchsticks before using it in the salad. If green papaya is not available, cucumbers, carrots, green beans, and/or jicama are good substitutes. Vietnamese and Southeast Asian women's secret for weight control is eating a lot of papaya salad and perhaps not much of anything else.

Serves 6

1 firm, green papaya (about 1 pound)

2 tablespoons chopped garlic

1 tablespoon chopped Thai chiles, more or less to taste

1/2 cup shredded carrots (matchsticks)

1/2 cup cherry tomatoes, cut in half

2 tablespoons light soy sauce, or more to taste

2 tablespoons sugar or brown sugar, or more to taste

2 tablespoons freshly squeezed lime or lemon juice, or more to taste

1/4 cup chopped roasted peanuts, for garnish

Peel the papaya, making sure the green skin is completely removed; use only the white flesh. Rinse with cold water, cut it in half lengthwise, and discard the seeds. With a hand shredder or box grater, shred the papaya into long matchsticks, making about 2 cups.

In a mortar with pestle (or a metal bowl with a rolling pin), gently grind and pound the garlic and Thai chiles until well combined. Add the papaya, carrots, tomatoes, soy sauce, sugar, and lime juice. Gently pound with the pestle and stir with a long spoon to mix well. Adjust the taste with more soy sauce, sugar, and lime juice.

Transfer to a serving platter, and garnish with the chopped peanuts.

Clean and separate the lettuce into individual leaves. Clean the herbs, trim the tough stems, and separate into small pieces.

Serve the salad with the lettuce and herbs on the side, as accompaniments, along with Fried Sweet Rice (page 70) or Sweet Rice and Beans (page 71).

ACCOMPANIMENTS
1 head lettuce or cabbage
1 bunch sweet basil
1 bunch mint
1 bunch cilantro
1 bunch dill

Green Mango and Apple Salad

Goi Xoai Va Boun

Serves 6

Green mango has a unique sour flavor and crunchy white flesh. It is the fruit of the mango tree that is harvested while still young and firm. Most mangoes sold in markets are ripe; although some are green and firm before they have fully ripened, they are intended to be eaten as ripe fruits. The ripe mangoes are not suitable for green mango salad because of their mushy flesh. The green mango's sour flavor also pairs well with sweet-and-sour Granny Smith apples. Their combination of flavors and textures complement each other and result in a well-balanced dish. Acid from the mango also helps keep the flesh of the apple white. If green mango is not available, use only the apple. Leave its preparation until the last minute, just before mixing with the lime dressing, which will also help the apple stay white.

$1/4$ cup vegetable oil
$1/4$ cup thinly sliced shallots
1 cup julienne firm tofu
$1/2$ teaspoon salt
$1/4$ teaspoon ground black pepper

Heat a pan over medium heat and pour in the oil. Add the shallots and fry for 3–5 minutes, or until they are light brown and crispy. Do not let them become dark brown or burn, as they will be bitter. Remove the shallots from the oil, and drain on absorbent paper. Set aside for garnish. Reserve the oil.

Transfer the reserved oil to a bowl and stir in the tofu, salt, and pepper. Marinate the tofu for 30 minutes. Start a charcoal grill or grill pan in advance so it reaches medium heat. Prepare all the fruits and vegetables.

When the grill is ready, place the tofu over the hottest part of the fire, or heat the grill pan until smoking. Grill the tofu for 2–3 minutes, turning occasionally, until it is brown with grill marks. Remove from the heat and set aside.

Just before serving, combine the mango, apple, carrots, mint, basil, chiles, and dressing, a little at a time. Taste and add more dressing, if needed. Transfer the salad to a bed of lettuce and top with the grilled tofu. Garnish with the fried shallots and cilantro.

Serve with steamed rice, Fried Sweet Rice (page 70), or Sweet Rice and Beans (page 71).

1 small green mango, peeled and sliced into matchsticks (about 1 cup)

1 small Granny Smith apple, sliced into matchsticks (about 1 cup)

1 cup matchstick-sliced carrots

3 tablespoons chopped Vietnamese mint (*rau ram*) or mint

3 tablespoons chopped sweet basil leaves

1 tablespoon chopped red chiles, more or less to taste

1 cup Dressing (page 52)

1 head lettuce, cleaned and cut into bite-size pieces

3 tablespoons chopped cilantro leaves, for garnish

Soups and Salads

Vietnamese Coleslaw

Goi Bay Cai

This is a very nutritious coleslaw. To make it even more healthful with no oil at all, use fresh firm tofu instead of fried tofu. It is an easy and quick dish to put together. As its English name suggests, it often serves as a side dish to a main course, either to balance rich and heavy flavors or to help cleanse the palate and rejuvenate taste buds for the next bite. (See photo, facing page 40.)

DRESSING

¼ cup freshly squeezed lime or lemon juice

2 tablespoon light soy sauce

2 tablespoons sugar

1 tablespoon minced garlic

1 tablespoon minced fresh red chiles (jalapeño, serrano, or hot Thai chiles)

Salt

SALAD

1 pound fried or firm tofu

2 cups matchstick-sliced green cabbage

2 cups matchstick-sliced red cabbage

½ cup matchstick-sliced carrots

½ cup finely sliced (chiffonade) mint

2 tablespoons finely sliced (chiffonade) Vietnamese mint (*rau ram*)

2 tablespoons finely chopped cilantro

2 tablespoons chopped roasted peanuts

1 bag (4–6 ounces) vegetable chips of your choice

To make the dressing, combine all the ingredients in a bowl, adding salt to taste, and stir until the sugar is fully dissolved.

To make the salad, slice the tofu into long, thin, julienne strips. Heat the fried tofu by refrying it in hot oil; alternatively, bake it in a 300–350 degree F oven for 10–12 minutes. If using the firm tofu, use it as it or fry it in hot oil until light brown and crunchy on the outside. Remove it from the oil, and drain on absorbent paper.

Just before serving, gently toss the tofu, green and red cabbage, carrots, mint, Vietnamese mint, and cilantro in a large bowl. Add two-thirds of the dressing, and toss to combine well. Taste the coleslaw and add more dressing, if needed.

Transfer to a serving plate, sprinkle with the peanuts, and garnish with vegetable chips.

Main Dishes

A banquet in Vietnam is an awesome sight to witness, with its bright colors, lively sounds, and delicious flavors. Greater prosperity is equated with more elaborate food made of pricey ingredients.

Many Vietnamese dishes can be served as either an appetizer, snack, or a main dish, depending on the portion size, timing, and occasion. Vietnamese crêpes can be a snack when served in small sizes in between meals, or they can be served as a main dish in a large portion with all accompaniments during the meal. Heavy dishes with rich and intense flavors that often require side dishes of starch, such as rice or noodles, and large amounts of accompaniments are considered main dishes in this chapter. Each can be a large, one-plate meal or part of a several-course meal. As for vegetarians, different cooking techniques and varieties of ingredients can easily make an ensemble for a multicourse meal. Alternatively, by concentrating on a one-plate meal, the result can be an extravagant dish with an entourage of accompaniments.

Clay Pot Glass Noodles
Mien Kho To

Since olden times, Vietnamese have been using handmade clay cooking utensils, such as pots and pans, on clay wood-burning stoves. Cooking with clay on a wood-burning fire infuses the food with a pleasant touch of smoky flavor, much like using mesquite in North American cooking. Recently, some of the clay utensils have been replaced with more durable metal and steel, but clay pots still remain from the Old World for cooking certain dishes with a touch of authenticity. If a Vietnamese clay pot is not available, a flat-bottomed Chinese clay pot or a regular saucepan can be used; these are suitable for the flat-top cooking ranges found in Western kitchens. Both kinds of clay pots are available in many sizes at Asian grocery stores or in any Chinatown.

MARINATED TOFU

1 pound firm tofu, cut into $1/4$-inch cubes

2 green onions (green and white parts), sliced in half lengthwise and cut into $1 1/2$-inch-long pieces

2 tablespoons minced garlic

2 tablespoons minced ginger

2 tablespoons minced cilantro stems and leaves

2 tablespoons vegetable oil

1 tablespoon stir-fry sauce or vegetarian oyster sauce

1 tablespoon Maggi Seasoning Sauce or flavorful soy sauce

$1/2$ teaspoon ground black pepper

$1/2$ teaspoon salt

5 ounces dried glass noodles, bean threads, or cellophane noodles

4 dried Chinese black mushroom caps or fresh shiitake mushroom caps

$1/2$ pound fresh asparagus or snow peas

To make the marinaded tofu, combine all the ingredients in a bowl, and set aside to marinate for 15–20 minutes.

To prepare the glass noodles, soak them in warm water for 15–20 minutes, or until pliable. Drain and cut into 6-inch strands.

If using dried mushrooms, soak them in warm water until soft, about 10 minutes. Drain and squeeze out the excess water. If the mushrooms are large, cut them in half.

Remove and discard the tough stems of the asparagus, and cut the asparagus lengthwise into quarters. Cut them on the diagonal into $1 1/2$-inch strips. If using snow peas, trim and use them whole.

To make the sauce, combine the vegetable stock, Caramel Soy Syrup, and sesame oil in a bowl.

To cook, heat a large clay pot or saucepan over medium heat. Add the vegetable oil and swirl to coat the pot evenly. Stir in the tofu and marinade mixture, and cook for 1–2 minutes, or until the garlic is light brown and fragrant.

Stir in the noodles, asparagus, lotus roots, and mushrooms, and gently toss to mix well. Stir in the sauce, increase the heat to high, and bring the mixture to a boil. Cover the pot with a lid, and reduce the heat to medium. Boil gently for 8–10 minutes, or until the liquid has been absorbed, stirring once or twice.

Remove from the heat and garnish with the cilantro, basil, and mint. Serve immediately, while still hot, with steamed rice, Fried Sweet Rice (page 70), or Sweet Rice and Beans (page 71).

SAUCE

2 cups vegetable stock

$^1/_2$ cup Caramel Soy Syrup (page 50)

1 teaspoon sesame oil

SEASONINGS AND HERBS

2 tablespoons vegetable oil

$^1/_2$ cup thinly sliced lotus roots or water chestnuts

3 sprigs cilantro, leaves only

3 sprigs sweet basil, leaves only

3 sprigs Vietnamese mint (*rau ram*) or dill, leaves only

Main Dishes

Crêpes
Banh Xeo

This recipe is the most obvious example of the French influence over Vietnamese cooking; it is combined with a touch of Chinese and local Vietnamese flavor. Without any subtraction, this dish adds a medley of ingredients—a set for batter, a set for filling, a set for accompaniments, and another set for the dipping sauce. Though there are many sets of ingredients, only simple steps and cooking techniques are required. At the end, your effort pays off with a delicious meal that brings people together as they help each other assemble the dish.

This recipe can be prepared two different ways: you can either make a large batch of filling ahead of time and fill each crêpe one at a time, or you can make the filling and crêpes one order at a time. Vietnamese crêpes can be served as a one-plate meal or, if you reduce their size, the crêpes can be a light meal or snack.

BATTER

1 cup rice flour
$^1/_4$ cup cornstarch
1 tablespoon sugar
1 tablespoon ground turmeric
1 teaspoon salt
$^3/_4$ cup coconut milk
$^3/_4$ cup water, or more as needed
2 tablespoons vegetable oil
$^1/_4$ cup thinly sliced green onions, white and green parts

To make the batter, combine the rice flour, cornstarch, sugar, turmeric, and salt in a bowl. Gently whisk in the coconut milk, water, and oil to make a thin batter. Stir in the green onions and set aside.

To make the filling, drain the mung beans and transfer them to a pot. Add fresh water to cover the beans by 1 inch, and bring to a boil. Reduce the heat and simmer uncovered for 10–15 minutes, or until the beans are tender enough to be mashed between your fingers. Do not over-cook the beans. Drain, if any water is left, and set aside.

Heat a pan over medium heat and pour in the oil. Add the shallots and garlic and cook for 2–3 minutes, or until light brown and fragrant. Stir in the tofu and mushrooms. Cook for 2–3 minutes, or until the mushrooms are tender. Add the cooked mung beans, soy sauce, sugar, vegetable base, and pepper. Stir to mix well, and cook for about 1 minute longer. The mixture should be fairly dry. Remove from the heat and stir in the bean sprouts.

To make a crêpe, heat a 9-inch nonstick skillet or flat-bottom wok over medium-high heat. Brush with vegetable oil to lightly coat the pan's surface. Stir the batter and ladle ½ cup into the pan; immediately tilt the pan to spread a thin film of batter to cover the pan's surface. Cook the crêpe for 1–2 minutes, or until the surface is dry.

Spread about one-sixth of the filling over one-half of the crêpe, and sprinkle with additional fresh bean sprouts (for added crispiness, dribble some oil along the sides of the pan and cook the crêpe a bit longer). Fold the other half of the crêpe over to cover the filling.

FILLING

½ cup dried yellow mung beans, soaked in 2 cups of water for at least 30 minutes

2 tablespoons vegetable oil, plus more as needed for frying the crêpes

3 tablespoons thinly sliced shallots

2 tablespoons minced garlic

2 cups julienne firm tofu

2 cups thinly sliced mushrooms of your choice

1 tablespoon light soy sauce

1 tablespoon sugar

1 tablespoon vegetable base or bouillon powder

½ teaspoon ground black pepper

2 cups bean sprouts, plus more for garnish

continued on next page

Main Dishes

To remove the crêpe from the pan, invert a serving plate and cover the top of the pan. Place your hand over the plate and turn over the pan to flip the crêpe onto the plate. Repeat the process for all 6 crêpes.

Arrange the accompaniments on a serving platter and pour the dipping sauce into a bowl.

To eat, each diner tears off a small portion of the crêpe, places it into a lettuce leaf, and tops it with the fresh herbs and vegetables. The leaf is then rolled up and dipped into the sauce before it is eaten by hand.

To make a small batch of crêpes, one order at a time, heat a 9-inch nonstick skillet or flat-bottom wok over medium heat. Add a little oil and stir in just one-sixth of all the filling ingredients, following the previous instructions for cooking a large batch, but do not remove the pan from the heat. When the filling is ready, sprinkle about ½ cup of the batter all over the filling. Cook until the surface of the crêpe is dry. Top with additional fresh bean sprouts and fold the crêpe in half.

ACCOMPANIMENTS

1 head lettuce, washed and separated into individual leaves

1 cup julienne carrots

1 cup mint leaves

1 cup cilantro leaves

1 cup sweet basil leaves

1 cup saw-leaf herb and/or Vietnamese mint (*rau ram*)

1 cup thinly sliced English cucumbers, cut into half circles

1 cup Dipping Sauce #1 (page 51) or #2 (page 51)

Grilled Five-Spice Portobello Mushrooms

Nam Rom Heo Noung Vi

The original recipe for this dish is quite popular, showcasing juicy pieces of pork chops. Our vegetarian version is as impressive, and all kinds of mushrooms can be used. Portobellos are large enough to substitute for the pork chops and are easy to handle whole. Make sure the marinade get into the gills of each mushroom to maximize flavor absorption.

6 large portobello mushrooms

1/2 teaspoon whole black peppercorns

2 whole star anise

1/3 cup finely minced lemongrass, tender midsection only (2–3 stalks)

2 tablespoons chopped garlic

2 tablespoons chopped shallots

2 tablespoons light soy sauce

2 tablespoons Maggi Seasoning Sauce or flavorful soy sauce

2 tablespoons sugar

1 teaspoon Chinese five-spice powder

1 teaspoon sesame oil

2 tablespoons vegetable oil, plus more for grilling

1 cup Dressing (page 52) or Dipping Sauce #3 (page 52)

Clean and trim the mushrooms. Discard the stems and reserve only the caps. Set aside.

Roast the peppercorns and star anise in a dry pan over medium heat for 3–5 minutes, or until fragrant. Grind them into a powder using a mortar with pestle or a food processor. Add the lemongrass, garlic, shallots, soy sauce, Maggi Seasoning Sauce, sugar, Chinese five-spice powder, and sesame oil. Process into a paste. Rub the paste all over the mushrooms and sprinkle with the oil. Cover tightly with plastic wrap, and marinate for 2–10 hours in the refrigerator.

Start a charcoal grill in advance so it reaches medium heat. Grill the mushrooms for 5–7 minutes, turning them once, until they are nicely charred on both sides. Serve the mushrooms with Dressing or Dipping Sauce #3 and steamed jasmine rice, Fried Sweet Rice (page 70), or Sweet Rice and Beans (page 71).

Main Dishes

Imperial Rice (Vietnamese Fried Rice)

Com Hoang Bao

Fried rice is a common dish in cuisines that have rice as a staple. The Vietnamese have their own signature fried rice dish called imperial rice, and it is traditionally served wrapped in a lotus leaf. The thick tissues of the lotus leaf keep the rice warm for a considerably long time and impart a sweet fragrance that is quite unique to this dish. The lotus represents purity in Vietnamese culture, so wrapping the rice with a lotus leaf has a significant impact on the Vietnamese psyche. Dried lotus leaves can be found at well-stocked Asian grocery stores; if you cannot find them, banana or grape leaves can be used instead, or simply serve the rice on a plate.

½ cup dried lotus seeds, soaked in warm water for 30 minutes, or ½ cup chopped fresh lotus seeds or water chestnuts

4 dried Chinese black mushroom caps, soaked in warm water for 15 minutes

2 tablespoons vegetable oil

½ cup chopped shallots

½ pound firm tofu, cut into ¼-inch cubes

½ cup corn kernels

2 tablespoons light soy sauce

1 tablespoon sugar

1½ teaspoons vegetable base or bouillon powder

½ teaspoon ground black pepper

2 cups steamed rice, crumbled

Salt

Drain the lotus seeds, and boil them in plenty of fresh water for 5–7 minutes, or until they are tender enough to be mashed between your fingers. Do not overcook them until they disintegrate. Drain and lightly chop. (If you are using fresh lotus seeds or water chestnuts, just lightly chop them.) Drain the mushrooms, squeeze out the excess water, and slice them into thin strips.

Heat a wok or saucepan over medium heat and pour in the oil. Add the shallots and cook for 3–4 minutes, or until light brown and fragrant. Add the lotus seeds, mushrooms, tofu, corn, soy sauce, sugar, vegetable base, and pepper. Stir to mix well, and cook for 2–3 minutes.

Add the steamed rice, and stir to combine thoroughly. Season with salt to taste. Cook for 2–3 minutes, or until the rice has absorbed all the flavors and is heated through.

Transfer to a lotus or banana leaf, and top with the green onions. Fold the leaf to wrap the rice in a neat package, turn the package over, and tuck all the edges underneath. Transfer to a serving plate. The whole rice package can be reheated in an oven or microwave.

To serve, cut an X across the package and fold the leaf to make a large opening on top of the package. Spoon the rice onto individual dinner plates.

1 lotus or banana leaf
$1/4$ cup sliced green onions, white and green parts

Main Dishes

Grilled Eggplants and Mushrooms with Lime Sauce

Ca Tim Tai Jun

Serves 6

As an entrée or salad, this dish is a very nutritious choice. Eggplant and mushrooms absorb marinades very well. Grilling them on wood or charcoal over an open flame lends a smoky flavor and provides attractive grill marks. The fresh lime sauce adds a tart and refreshing jolt to a summer barbecue.

2 large Asian eggplants

2 large portobello mushroom caps

$^1/_4$ cup finely minced lemongrass, tender midsection only (1–2 stalks)

3 tablespoons minced garlic

2 tablespoons minced ginger

2 tablespoons minced green onions, white and green parts

2 tablespoons vegetable oil

$^1/_2$ teaspoon salt

$^1/_2$ teaspoon ground black pepper

3 tablespoons freshly squeezed lime juice

3 tablespoons light soy sauce

1 tablespoon sugar, or more to taste

1 tablespoon minced red chiles, more or less to taste

Slice the eggplants diagonally into thin slices, about $^1/_8$ inch thick. Slice the mushroom caps into thin slices, about $^1/_4$ inch thick.

Combine the eggplant, mushrooms, lemongrass, garlic, ginger, and green onions in a bowl, and sprinkle with the oil, salt, and pepper. Fold the mixture gently to combine well, taking care not to break the mushrooms. Marinate for at least 15 minutes.

Start a charcoal grill or grill pan in advance so it reaches medium heat. Grill the eggplant and mushrooms for 5–6 minutes, or until cooked with grill marks on both sides. Transfer to a serving platter, and arrange the eggplant and mushrooms alternately, over-lapping each other.

Combine the lime juice, soy sauce, sugar, chiles, and the remaining marinade, if there is any, in a bowl. Stir until well combined and the sugar is dissolved. Pour the lime mixture all over the eggplant and mushrooms.

Arrange all the vegetable accompaniments on a platter.

To eat, fill a lettuce leaf with some of the eggplant and mushrooms, and top with the accompaniments. Wrap and eat by hand.

Serve with steamed jasmine rice, Fried Sweet Rice (page 70), or Sweet Rice and Beans (page 71).

VEGETABLE ACCOMPANIMENTS

I head lettuce or cabbage, washed and separated into individual leaves

I5 sprigs cilantro, tough stems removed

I bunch mint, leaves only

I bunch sweet basil, leaves only

I bunch saw-leaf herb or Vietnamese mint (*rau ram*)

Main Dishes

Grilled Minced Mushrooms in La-Lot Leaves

Nam Hunong La-Lot

The la-lot plant, which is also called pepper leaf, has shiny, heart-shaped leaves and small nuts that are chewed like tobacco. The leaves can be used as wrappers, and when they are grilled, they release an aniselike flavor and camphor aroma. La-lot leaves might be very difficult to find in the United States; perilla or Japanese shiso leaves are similar in shape and makes an excellent substitute.

To make the mushroom mixture, combine all the ingredients in a bowl and mix thoroughly. Alternatively, combine all the ingredients in a food processor, and pulse several times until well mixed. Do not process into a smooth paste. Cover the bowl and marinate for 6–12 hours in the refrigerator, or for at least 1 hour at room temperature. After marinating, the mixture should hold together like a dough. Add more water or cornstarch, if needed.

Have ready 20 bamboo skewers, 5 inches long, soaked in cold water. Start a charcoal grill, broiler, or grill pan in advance so it reaches medium heat.

Mold 1 1/2 tablespoons of the mushroom mixture into a log about 1 1/2 inches long, making about 30 logs. On a flat work surface, place a la-lot leaf, shiny side down, orienting its stem closest to you. Place a log of the mushroom mixture on the leaf at the stem end, and roll the leaf to wrap the log

Serves 6 (makes 30 pieces)

MUSHROOM MIXTURE

1/2 pound shiitake mushrooms (caps only), minced

1 cup (about 6 ounces) firm silken tofu, drained completely of water

1/4 cup finely minced lemongrass, tender midsection only (1–2 stalks)

3 tablespoons finely minced shallots

2 tablespoons finely minced garlic

3 tablespoons sugar

2 tablespoons light soy sauce

2 tablespoons Chinese five-spice powder

2 tablespoons cornstarch, or more as needed

1 tablespoon vegetable base or bouillon powder

1 teaspoon salt

1/2 teaspoon ground black pepper

1/2 teaspoon ground turmeric

tightly, leaving both ends of the log exposed. Repeat the process for all of the logs.

Arrange 3 wrapped logs horizontally, closely side by side, and skewer or thread 2 bamboo sticks, about one-half inch apart, through the logs. Brush the logs lightly with oil on all sides. Repeat the process for all the logs.

To cook, place the skewered logs on the grill or under the broiler for 2–3 minutes on each side, turning once, until they are light brown all over and cooked through. Remove from the heat.

Arrange the lettuce and herbs on a serving platter and pour the dipping sauce into a bowl.

To eat, pull a grilled mushroom and la-lot leaf off the skewers. Place on a lettuce leaf and top with fresh herbs. Roll up the lettuce, dip in the sauce, and eat by hand.

Grilled Minced Mushrooms can also be served with side dishes of steamed rice, Fried Sweet Rice (page 70), or Sweet Rice and Beans (page 71).

WRAPPERS

30 pieces large la-lot leaves, rinsed with cold water and patted dry

1/4 cup vegetable oil

HERB ACCOMPANIMENTS AND SAUCE

1 head lettuce, washed and separated into individual leaves

1 bunch cilantro, leaves only

1 bunch mint, leaves only

1 bunch sweet basil, leaves only

1 bunch saw-leaf herb and/or Vietnamese mint (*rau ram*)

1 cup Dipping Sauce #1 (page 51), #2 (page 51), or #3 (page 52)

Lemongrass Dry Noodles

Bun Dau Hu-Xa

Vietnamese are considered "wet eaters" and are famous for their wet noodles—all kinds of pho with different meat ingredients. Once in a while, they also enjoy a dry noodle dish that serves as a salad or a main dish. All the ingredients are tossed together at the last minute before serving. Alternatively, the ingredients can be arranged in layers and served with a sauce or dressing on the side so diners can spoon their portion onto a plate and toss in just enough sauce to make it their own dish.

MARINATED TOFU

1 pound firm tofu

1/3 cup finely minced lemongrass, tender midsection only (2–3 stalks)

3 tablespoons minced garlic

2 tablespoons sugar

2 tablespoons light soy sauce

2 tablespoons vegetable oil, plus more for brushing

1 tablespoon Maggi Seasoning Sauce or flavorful soy sauce

1 teaspoon ground black pepper

To make the marinated tofu, slice the tofu thinly into 2 x 3-inch strips, ½ inch thick. Combine all the marinade ingredients in a mixing bowl, add the tofu, and marinate for 2–3 hours in the refrigerator or at least 1 hour at room temperature.

Start a charcoal grill, broiler, or grill pan in advance so it reaches medium heat. Just before serving, cook the tofu for 1–2 minutes on each side, or until it is light brown with grill marks.

To prepare the noodles and finish the dish, bring a medium pot of water to a boil, and cook the noodles for 2–3 minutes, or until soft and pliable. Drain and rinse with cold water until completely cool. Cut the noodles into 6-inch strands, and set aside.

Gently toss and combine the lettuce, bean sprouts, cucumbers, carrots, and herbs in a mixing bowl.

To serve, transfer the vegetable mixture to a serving platter. Top with the cold noodles and grilled tofu. Sprinkle the peanuts all over the noodle dish.

Each diner spoons the mixture onto a dinner plate and sprinkles it with the dressing or dipping sauce. Using chopsticks, each diner tosses together all the ingredients to eat.

Noodles, Vegetables, and Herbs

2 ounces dried vermicelli rice noodles

I head lettuce, thinly sliced into matchsticks

2 cups bean sprouts

I cup thinly sliced English cucumbers, cut into half circles

I cup matchstick-sliced carrots

$1/2$ cup thinly sliced (chiffonade) sweet basil leaves

$1/2$ cup thinly sliced (chiffonade) mint leaves

$1/2$ cup thinly slice saw-leaf herb and/or Vietnamese mint (*rau ram*)

$1/4$ cup chopped roasted peanuts

I cup Dressing (page 52) or Dipping Sauce #3 (page 52)

Main Dishes

Lemongrass Spongy Tofu

Xa Ot

Fried tofu is readily available at Asian grocery stores. It comes in many types, varying in shape, size, and texture. This recipe requires the spongy type that is a light brown color and comes in one-inch cubes. Its spongy, porous texture is ideal for this dish to absorb the marinade and sauce at a maximum level.

MARINATED TOFU

2 tablespoons vegetable oil
2 tablespoons minced garlic
1 tablespoon soy sauce
1 tablespoon sugar
2 teaspoons cornstarch
1 teaspoon ground black pepper
1 pound fried spongy tofu, cut into 1-inch cubes

To make the marinated tofu, combine the oil, garlic, soy sauce, sugar, cornstarch, and pepper in a bowl. Add the tofu, toss gently, and marinate for at least 30 minutes.

To prepare the vegetables and finish the dish, heat a wok or frying pan over high heat, add the oil, and cook the lemongrass, shallots, and garlic for 2–3 minutes, or until light brown and fragrant.

Add the marinated tofu, bell peppers, carrots, and chiles. Stir-fry for 1–2 minutes to mix well. Add the syrup and lime juice. Stir-fry for 2 minutes longer, or until the vegetables are fully cooked. The sauce should have the consistency of a gravy. Add a small amount of water if the mixture is too dry.

Transfer the mixture to a serving platter and sprinkle with the pepper and cilantro. Serve with steamed rice, Fried Sweet Rice (page 70), or Sweet Rice and Beans (page 71).

VEGETABLES AND SEASONINGS

3 tablespoons vegetable oil

$3/4$ cup thinly sliced lemongrass, tender midsection only (3–4 stalks)

$1/3$ cup thinly sliced shallots

3 tablespoons chopped garlic

I cup julienne red bell peppers

I cup julienne carrots

2 tablespoons chopped fresh chiles, more or less to taste

$2/3$ cup Caramel Soy Syrup (page 50), more or less to taste

2 tablespoons freshly squeezed lime or lemon juice

I teaspoon ground black pepper, for garnish

$1/2$ cup cilantro leaves, for garnish

Morning Glory with Bean Sauce

Rau Muong Xao Tuong

Serves 4

Morning glory, or water spinach, is used so often in many Vietnamese dishes that it may be considered the Vietnamese national vegetable. It is an aquatic plant that thrives almost anywhere there is plenty of water. It's abundant, inexpensive, and easy to handle. It can be eaten fresh as a side vegetable to a main dish, or cooked as a vegetable in soups or stir-fries. This recipe is a stir-fry that requires intense heat in cooking; it should take just a little time in a wok. The smaller the batch, the faster it will cook.

1 pound morning glory or spinach

3 tablespoons vegetable oil

2 tablespoon chopped garlic

3 green onions (green and white parts), sliced in half lengthwise and cut into 2-inch-long pieces

2 whole red chiles, bruised to lightly split (optional)

2 tablespoons fermented yellow bean sauce (see "soy products," page 16)

1 tablespoon light soy sauce

1 teaspoon sugar

1/4 teaspoon ground black pepper

Trim and discard the tough stems off the morning glory. Soak in cold water, clean, and rinse thoroughly. Cut both the stems and leaves into 2-inch-long strips.

Heat the oil in a wok over high heat until smoking. Add the garlic, green onions, and red chiles, stirring briskly. Add the morning glory, yellow bean sauce, soy sauce, and sugar. Stir and fold the mixture top to bottom so all of the vegetables contact the heat source at the bottom of the wok. Cook and stir for 2–3 minutes to mix well.

Transfer to a serving platter and sprinkle with the pepper. Serve hot with steamed rice, Fried Sweet Rice (page 70), or Sweet Rice and Beans (page 71)

Stir-fried Fresh Mango and Cashew Nuts

Xao Hot Dieu

Serves 6

Cashew nuts are a cash crop in the southern region of Vietnam. A single cashew nut, which dangles underneath its fruit, is the seed; it develops in this unusual manner outside the fruit. Cashew nuts are a superb ingredient in many dishes and are valued for their unique flavor and texture. They are considered a luxury and are always included in a gift-wrapped basket, which shows that the benefactor is skilled in the art of giving. (See photo, facing page 80.)

3 tablespoons vegetable oil

2 tablespoons minced garlic

1 tablespoon chopped red chiles, more or less to taste

1 cup diced firm tofu, cut into $1/2$-inch cubes

1 cup snow peas, trimmed

1 cup julienne red or yellow bell peppers

2 tablespoons stir-fry sauce or vegetarian oyster sauce

2 tablespoons sugar, or more to taste

1 tablespoon light soy sauce, or more to taste

1 tablespoon vegetable base or bouillon powder

1 tablespoon rice vinegar

1 cup peeled and diced firm, ripe mango, cut into $1/2$-inch cubes

1 cup seeded and diced tomatoes, cut into $1/2$-inch cubes

1 cup roasted cashew nuts

$1/2$ teaspoon ground black pepper

2 green onions (green and white parts), sliced in half lengthwise and cut into $1\,1/2$-inch-long pieces, for garnish

3 sprigs fresh cilantro, leaves only, for garnish

Freshly squeezed lime or lemon juice

Heat a wok over high heat and pour in the oil. Add the garlic and chiles and cook for 1–2 minutes, or until light brown and fragrant. Stir in the tofu, snow peas, and bell peppers. Stir-fry for 2–3 minutes, or until the vegetables are almost tender.

Add the stir-fry sauce, sugar, soy sauce, vegetable base, and rice vinegar. Stir to mix well, and cook until all the vegetables are tender, about 1–2 minutes longer. Remove from the heat.

Just before serving, toss in the mango, tomatoes, and cashew nuts. Transfer to a serving plate, sprinkle with the pepper, and garnish with the green onions and cilantro. Sprinkle with lime juice to taste, and serve with steamed rice.

Mushrooms with Garlic Sauce

Nam Luc Lac

Serves 6

The original recipe is bo luc lac, or the famous shaking beef. Marinated beef is seared in a sizzling hot pan and shaken instead of stirred to evenly cook it. The beef is served warm over a fresh salad with French dressing. It is one course of the famous Vietnamese seven-course meal bo bay mon, beef prepared in seven ways. We substitute beef with mushrooms that are firm and large enough to be cut into cubes. The mushrooms of your choice should be cut so their flesh will have more contact with the marinade, to better absorb it. A bed of watercress salad remains the same from the original recipe, with a modified French dressing.

MARINATED MUSHROOMS

1 pound portobello mushrooms or firm-flesh mushrooms of your choice

1/4 cup vegetable oil

1/4 cup minced garlic

2 tablespoons light soy sauce

2 tablespoons sugar

1 tablespoon Maggi Seasoning Sauce or flavorful soy sauce

1/4 teaspoon salt

To make the marinated mushrooms, slice into 1-inch cubes. Combine the mushrooms with 2 tablespoons of the oil and 2 tablespoons of the minced garlic in a mixing bowl. Add the soy sauce, sugar, Maggi Seasoning Sauce, and salt. Gently toss to mix well. Marinate the mushrooms at room temperature for at least 30 minutes, or in the refrigerator for 2 hours. Prepare the vegetable accompaniments (on facing page) before cooking the mushrooms.

To cook the mushrooms, heat a wok or frying pan over high heat. Add the remaining 2 tablespoons oil to the wok and swirl to coat its surface. When the oil is hot to lightly smoking, add the remaining garlic and stir-fry for 1 minute, or until light brown and fragrant.

Add the mushrooms in a single layer over the wok's surface, and leave undisturbed for 2–3 minutes, or until seared brown. Flip the mushrooms over with a shake of the pan, or use a spatula to turn the mushrooms. Sear the other side for 2 minutes longer.

To make the vegetable accompaniments, 10 minutes before serving, toss together the red onion and vinegar in a mixing bowl. Set aside for at least 5 minutes. Add the soy sauce, oil, sugar, and pepper to the bowl and mix well.

Just before serving, add the watercress and basil leaves to the bowl, and toss with the onion and soy sauce mixture. Season with salt to taste. Transfer the watercress mixture to a serving platter, and top with the mushrooms.

Serve with steamed rice, Fried Sweet Rice (page 70), or Sweet Rice and Beans (page 71).

VEGETABLE ACCOMPANIMENTS

1 medium red onion, thinly sliced into half rings (about 1 $^1/_2$ cups)

2 teaspoons rice vinegar

2 teaspoons soy sauce

2 teaspoons vegetable oil

1 teaspoon sugar

$^1/_2$ teaspoon ground black pepper

1 bunch watercress, washed, tough stems removed

$^1/_4$ cup thinly sliced sweet basil leaves

Salt

Main Dishes

Mushrooms in Vinegar Fondue

Nam Rom Nhung Dam

This is one of the most popular Vietnamese dishes that brings people together, gathering around a tabletop cooking device and having a nice conversation over a self-assembled meal. This dish also brings many culinary cultures and techniques together, both from Singaporean and Chinese hot pot (steamboat) and Swiss and French fondue. All the ingredients are prepared in advance and arranged around the heat source for the actual cooking and final assembly which is done at the table.

VINEGAR FONDUE (BROTH)

3 cups young coconut juice (from fresh green coconuts or frozen coconut juice)

2 tablespoons vegetable oil

2 tablespoons minced garlic

3 lemongrass stalks, cut into several 2-inch-long sticks and bruised to lightly split

1 3/4 cups distilled white vinegar or rice vinegar

2 tablespoons sugar

1 tablespoon vegetable base or bouillon powder

2 teaspoons salt, or more to taste

1/2 teaspoon ground pepper, or more to taste

If using young coconuts to prepare the vinegar fondue, use a cleaver or a heavy knife to swiftly chop off a small pad of the coconut shell. Collect the juice in a bowl. Cut the coconuts in half, and use a spoon to scoop out the tender white meat; reserve it separately from the juice. Discard the coconut skin and shells. If using frozen coconut juice, thaw it and separate the meat from the juice if they come together.

Heat a medium pot over medium heat and pour in the oil. Stir in the garlic and lemongrass. Cook for 1–2 minutes, or until light brown and fragrant. Add the coconut juice, vinegar, sugar, vegetable base, salt, and pepper. Bring the mixture to a boil, lower the heat, and simmer for 10 minutes. Transfer to a fondue pot or a clay pot. Place on a tabletop burner at the dining table. Place the plate of coconut meat around the heat source as a part of the accompaniments.

To prepare the vegetables, clean the mushrooms and gently slice them as thinly as possible using a serrated knife. Cut the onion in half and slice it thinly. Slice the napa cabbage into thin strips.

Arrange all the vegetables and herbs on serving plates surrounding the vinegar broth and heat source. Set a large, shallow bowl of warm water next to the rice paper sheets. Portion the dipping sauce into individual saucers and place next to individual dinner plates and chopsticks.

To cook and self-serve the fondue, heat the vinegar broth to a gentle boil. Soak a rice paper sheet in the bowl of warm water for about 1 minute, or until it is soft and pliable. Remove it from the water, and set it on a dinner plate. With the chopsticks, pick up a small amount of the bean sprouts, carrot, cucumber, and different herbs, and mound them in the middle of the rice paper. Pick up a few slices of mushroom, onion, and cabbage, and submerge them in the hot vinegar broth. Poach them lightly for less than 1 minute, and place them on top of the fresh vegetables and herbs. Sprinkle with the bottled sriracha sauce or pepper for a spicy flavor. (Alternatively, all the vegetables can be eaten fresh or cooked, as preferred.)

Roll and wrap the rice paper into a log, dip it into the sauce, and eat by hand.

VEGETABLES, HERBS, AND ACCOMPANIMENTS

1 pound assorted mushrooms of your choice

1 large white onion

3–4 tender napa cabbage leaves, or 2 cups baby spinach leaves

½ pound bean sprouts

1 carrot, sliced into matchsticks

1 English cucumber, cut in half lengthwise and thinly sliced crosswise

1 cup Vietnamese mint (*rau ram*)

1 cup cilantro leaves

1 cup sweet basil leaves

1 cup saw-leaf herb or mint leaves

1 lime or lemon, cut into small wedges

18 dried Vietnamese rice paper sheets (8–10 inches in diameter)

1 cup Dipping Sauce #3 (page 52) or Dressing (page 52)

1 bottle sriracha sauce or chili sauce, *sambal oelek*, or ground black pepper

Main Dishes

Rice Cupcakes with Savory Filling

Ban Baew

Serves 6

This is an elaborate dish with many steps and lists of ingredients. But they are simple and easy steps to follow, and all can be done in advance and later put together just before serving. Steamed sweet rice cakes are crowned with a tasty topping and then become the filling to fresh vegetable leaves and herbs. Their combination provides a well-balanced meal with a delicious taste and good nutritional value.

CUPCAKE BATTER

2 cups rice flour

2 tablespoons cornstarch

1 tablespoon sugar

1 teaspoon salt

3 cups water

TOPPINGS

1/4 cup yellow mung beans, soaked in 1 cup water for at least 30 minutes

1/4 cup vegetable oil

1/3 cup thinly sliced shallots

2 tablespoons chopped onions or shallots

1 cup chopped mushrooms of your choice

1/2 cup chopped water chestnuts

1 tablespoon soy sauce

1 tablespoon stir-fry sauce or vegetarian oyster sauce

1 tablespoon sugar

1/2 teaspoon ground black pepper

To make the cupcakes, have ready 18 small ceramic or glass saucers, 2 inches in diameter, and 1 large steamer set.

Combine the flour, cornstarch, sugar, and salt in a bowl. Slowly pour in the water and mix thoroughly.

Fill the steamer pot with water, and bring it to a rolling boil. Arrange the saucers in the streamer tray, and heat the saucers first until fully hot, about 3 minutes. Pour the batter into the saucers, filling them almost to the rims. Steam for 7–8 minutes, or until the batter is cooked and firm. Remove from the heat and let cool.

Run a thin blade around the saucers to loosen the cakes. Remove the cakes from the saucers and transfer them to a plate. Set aside.

To prepare the toppings, start by draining the beans and boil them in a pot with plenty of fresh water for 10–15 minutes, or until tender enough to be mashed between your fingers. Drain and grind the beans into a paste in a mortar with pestle or a food processor. Set aside.

Heat a pan over medium heat and pour in the oil. Add the shallots and fry for 4–5 minutes, or until light brown and crispy. Do not let them become dark brown or burn, as they will be bitter. Remove the shallots from the oil, and drain on absorbent paper. Set aside for garnish.

In the same pan, add the onions and cook for 3–4 minutes, or until light brown. Stir in the mushrooms, water chestnuts, and mung bean paste. Cook for 2–3 minutes, or until the mushrooms are tender. Add the soy sauce, stir-fry sauce, sugar, and pepper. Stir to mix well, and remove from the heat.

Clean and arrange all the vegetables and herbs for accompaniments on a serving platter and pour the sauce into a bowl.

Accompaniments

1 head lettuce, washed and separated into individual leaves

1 cup thinly sliced green onions, white and green parts

1 cup sweet basil leaves

1 cup saw-leaf herb and/or Vietnamese mint (*rau ram*) or mint

1 cup cilantro leaves

1 cup Dipping Sauce #1 (page 51) or #2 (page 51)

2 tablespoons matchstick-sliced red jalapeño chiles, for garnish

2 tablespoons thinly sliced green onions, white and green parts, for garnish

To serve, heat the cupcakes and topping to lukewarm. They can be heated in a microwave. Arrange the cakes on a serving platter, and spoon the topping on top of the cakes. Sprinkle with the fried shallots, sliced red chiles, and green onions. Serve the cakes with the vegetable and herb accompaniments and dipping sauce.

To eat, each diner fills a piece of lettuce with a cupcake and tops it with herb accompaniments. The filling is then wrapped with the lettuce, dipped into the sauce, and eaten by hand.

Main Dishes

Rice Porridge

Jaow

Vietnam is the third largest rice exporter in the world, behind Thailand and the United States. Rice is a staple for the Vietnamese and is transformed into many products for their cuisine—rice flour, rice papers, rice noodles, rice crackers, and so forth. Other than steaming, which is the usual method, rice can also be simmered with plenty of water to make a thick porridge, which is similar to pudding in consistency. Rice porridge is a popular breakfast dish, as it is gentle on the stomach. It's also a choice dish after a bout of heavy drinking and is often served during illness, as it's easy to digest.

6 cups vegetable stock

3 cups water

3 yellow onions, peeled and cut in half

1 teaspoon salt

1 teaspoon light soy sauce, or more to taste

1/2 pound white mushrooms of your choice, cut into 1/4-inch cubes

1 cup diced firm tofu, cut into 1/4-inch cubes

1 1/2 cups uncooked jasmine or fragrant rice, or 3 cups steamed rice

Bring the vegetable stock and water to a boil in a pot. Add the onions, salt, and soy sauce. Bring to a boil again, reduce the heat to medium, and simmer for 15–20 minutes. Skim the top of the stock and discard any foam and impurities. Strain the stock through a fine sieve into a clean pot. Discard the solids.

Bring the stock to a boil again and add the mushrooms and tofu. Simmer for 3–5 minutes, or until the mushrooms are tender. Remove the mushrooms and tofu from the stock and set aside.

Bring the stock to a boil again, and stir in the rice. Reduce the heat to medium-low and simmer, stirring occasionally, until the rice disintegrates into a thin, white, gluey paste, 20–30 minutes for uncooked rice, or 15–20 minutes for steamed rice. Be careful not to burn the rice on the bottom of the pot. Add more water as needed. Keep the porridge warm before serving.

Clay Pot Vegetables, p. 132

To serve, ladle the porridge into serving bowls, and top with the mushrooms and tofu. Sprinkle with the pepper, chopped cilantro, and green onions.

Place additional soy sauce and the bottle of red chili sauce on the table so diners can season their porridge to taste.

$\frac{1}{2}$ teaspoon ground white pepper

$\frac{1}{4}$ cup chopped cilantro leaves

$\frac{1}{4}$ cup chopped green onions, white and green parts

1 bottle red chili sauce (*sambal oelek*), as a condiment

Mango and Coconut Tartlets, p. 142

Main Dishes

Simple Stir-Fry

Rau Xao

Wok and stir-fry cooking techniques were handed down from the Chinese. The wok has become an important tool and stir-frying an essential method in all Asian cooking. Vietnamese cuisine also uses wok and stir-fry cooking to maintain the essence of its characteristic freshness. Wok and stir-fry techniques require intense heat to cook foods quickly and preserve their original textures, tastes, colors, and nutrition. A nontraditional wok with a flat bottom was developed to better suit the flat-top ranges that are prevalent in Western kitchens.

1/2 pound firm tofu, cut into 1/2-inch cubes

2 tablespoons stir-fry sauce or vegetarian oyster sauce

1 tablespoon Maggi Seasoning Sauce or flavorful soy sauce

1 tablespoon sugar

1 teaspoon ground black pepper

2 tablespoons vegetable oil, or more as needed

1 cup diced potatoes, cut into 1/2-inch cubes

1 cup diced sweet potatoes, cut into 1/2-inch cubes

1 yellow onion, cut into 1/2-inch slices

Combine the tofu, stir-fry sauce, Maggi Seasoning Sauce, sugar, and pepper in a bowl. Marinate for 1 hour in the refrigerator.

Heat a wok or skillet over medium heat and pour in the oil. Add the diced potatoes and sweet potatoes. Cook and stir for 3–4 minutes, or until light brown and cooked through. Remove from the wok and set aside.

Add a little more oil to the wok, if needed, and raise the heat to high. Stir in the sliced onion and cook for 1–2 minutes, or until light brown. Add the marinated tofu and reserved potatoes. Stir to mix well, and cook for 1–2 minutes, or until the tofu and potatoes are heated through. Transfer to a serving platter and serve with the vegetable accompaniments (at right).

Clean and separate the lettuce into individual leaves. Clean the herbs, trim and discard the tough stems, and separate into small pieces.

To eat, fill a lettuce leaf with the tofu mixture, and top with the fresh herbs. Wrap the leaf and eat by hand.

ACCOMPANIMENTS

1 head lettuce or cabbage
1 bunch sweet basil
1 bunch saw-leaf herb and/or Vietnamese mint (*rau ram*) or mint
1 bunch cilantro
1 bunch dill

Main Dishes

Steamed Tofu with Lily Buds

Dua Hu Hap

Steaming is a nutritious and burn-proof cooking technique, resulting in always-moist ingredients, except when the boiling water in a steamer pot runs out, ruining the food and destroying the pot. Check the water often when steaming. Lily buds are the flowers of daylilies that have been dried. They have an aromatic flowery fragrance and elastic texture. They should be soaked in warm water to soften them before use.

1 pound firm silken tofu or firm tofu

2 tablespoons chopped garlic

2 tablespoons finely shredded ginger (matchsticks)

2 tablespoons soy sauce

1 tablespoon sugar

1 tablespoon stir-fry sauce or vegetarian oyster sauce

$^1/_2$ teaspoon salt

$^1/_2$ teaspoon ground black pepper

5 fresh shiitake mushrooms or dried Chinese black mushrooms

1 cup fresh wood ear mushrooms, or $^1/_2$ cup dried wood ear mushrooms

$^1/_2$ cup dried lily buds (about 30 buds)

1 ounce dried glass noodles, bean threads, or cellophane noodles

1 cup peeled and thinly sliced lotus roots (optional)

2 green onions (green and white parts), sliced in half lengthwise and cut into 1 $^1/_2$-inch-long pieces

1 large tomato, thinly cut into 8 wedges

Drain the water from the tofu completely. Leave the tofu in large pieces, at least 3 x 5 inches. If the tofu is too thick, cut it lengthwise to get a 1-inch thickness. Transfer the tofu to a deep plate, and add the garlic, ginger, soy sauce, sugar, stir-fry sauce, salt, and pepper. Gently turn the tofu to coat it completely with the seasonings. Let marinate at room temperature while you prepare the remaining ingredients.

If using dried mushrooms, soak them in warm water for 15–20 minutes, or until soft and pliable. Soak the lily buds and glass noodles in warm water for 25–30 minutes, or until soft and pliable. Drain and squeeze out the excess water.

Remove and discard the stems of the mushrooms, and slice the mushroom caps into thin strips. Pick out and discard the hard tips of the lily buds, if attached. Cut the noodles into 6-inch strands. In a bowl, combine the mushrooms, lotus roots, lily buds, noodles, green onions, and tomato.

Have ready a heat-resistant plate or a shallow bowl that is big enough to hold all the ingredients, and deep enough to hold the liquid from steaming, that will fit properly in your steamer. Spread one-third of the mushroom mixture on the plate. Lay the tofu on top of the mushroom mixture, and sprinkle it with the marinade. Scatter the remaining mushroom mixture over the tofu.

Bring the water in your steamer to a rolling boil. Place the plate of tofu on the steamer rack, cover with the lid, and steam for 15–20 minutes, or until all the ingredients are cooked through.

Serve the tofu while still hot, by itself or with steamed rice, Fried Sweet Rice (page 70), or Sweet Rice and Beans (page 71)

Main Dishes

Stuffed Grilled or Steamed Eggplants

Ca Tim Nuong

Serves 6

This dish is common in the southern region of Vietnam and eastern Cambodia, where they share borders. Eggplants are grilled or steamed whole, and their skins are peeled off easily. They are later made into pockets and stuffed with a spicy and tasty filling. It is easy to make this dish in advance and conveniently reheat it just before serving.

6 whole, long Asian eggplants

3 tablespoons vegetable oil, or more as needed

¼ cup thinly sliced shallots, for garnish

2 tablespoons minced garlic

2 cups finely chopped firm tofu

3 tablespoons light soy sauce

2 tablespoons sugar

1 tablespoon vegetable base or bouillon powder

1 tablespoon red chili sauce (*sambal oelek*), more or less to taste

Steam, grill, or bake the whole eggplants, stems attached, for 10–15 minutes, or until tender and their skins wrinkle and turn brownish. Remove from the heat and let cool. Peel and discard the skins. Cut a long, lengthwise slit in the middle of each eggplant to create a deep pocket; do not cut all the way through. Set aside and keep warm for stuffing.

Heat a saucepan over medium heat and pour in the oil. Add the sliced shallots and fry for 2–3 minutes, or until light brown and crispy. Do not let them become dark brown or burn, as they will be bitter. Remove the shallots from the oil, and drain on absorbent paper. Set aside for garnish.

Add the minced garlic to the pan and cook for 1–2 minutes, or until fragrant. Add the tofu, soy sauce, sugar, vegetable base, and red chili sauce. Stir to mix well, and cook for 2–3 minutes. If the mixture seems too dry, add a little water. Adjust the flavor by adding more soy sauce and sugar to taste. Remove from the heat.

To serve, heat the eggplants in a microwave for 1–2 minutes, and then stuff them with the tofu mixture, mounding it high. Garnish with the bell peppers, cilantro, green onions, and fried shallots.

Serve the eggplant by itself or with steamed rice, Fried Sweet Rice (page 70), or Sweet Rice and Beans (page 71).

½ cup diced bell peppers (red, yellow, or orange), cut into ⅛-inch cubes, for garnish

3 tablespoons chopped cilantro leaves, for garnish

3 tablespoons chopped green onions, green and white parts, for garnish

Main Dishes

Tofu Stew with Coconut Juice

Dua Hu Heo Kho Nuos Dua

Young, green coconut is a popular fresh fruit. Its fresh juice can easily quench your thirst, and its fresh, tender white meat can satisfy as a snack. Its fragrant, sweet juice is often used as a base or broth in many kinds of Vietnamese stews. Many Asian grocery stores carry fresh whole young coconuts in their produce section; frozen coconut juice and meat are sold in plastic packages in the frozen foods section.

1 whole young coconut, or 2 cups frozen coconut juice and meat

2 tablespoons vegetable oil

1/2 cup finely minced lemongrass, tender midsection only (2–3 stalks)

3 tablespoons chopped shallots

2 tablespoons chopped garlic

1 pound fried spongy tofu, cut into 1/2-inch cubes

1 1/2 cups peeled and diced water chestnuts or jicama, cut into 1/2-inch cubes (about 1/2 pound)

1 1/2 cups peeled and thinly sliced lotus roots (about 1/2 pound)

1/2 cup Caramel Soy Syrup (page 50)

1/3 cup light soy sauce, or more to taste

1 teaspoon Chinese five-spice powder, or more to taste

1 teaspoon ground black pepper

If using young coconuts, use a cleaver or a heavy knife to swiftly chop off a small pad of the coconut shell. Collect the juice in a bowl. Cut the coconut in half, and use a spoon to gently scoop out the tender white meat and add it to the coconut juice. Discard the skin and shells.

Heat a saucepan over medium heat and pour in the oil. Add the lemongrass, shallots, and garlic, and cook for 1–2 minutes, or until light brown and fragrant.

Add the tofu, water chestnuts, lotus roots, syrup, soy sauce, five-spice powder, and pepper. Cook, stirring occasionally, for 2–3 minutes.

Add the coconut meat, coconut juice, and vegetable stock. Bring the mixture to a boil, and skim off any foam or impurities that float to the surface. Reduce the heat to medium-low and simmer for 20–30 minutes, or until everything is tender.

Transfer to a shallow bowl and garnish with the cilantro. Serve hot with steamed rice, Fried Sweet Rice (page 70), or Sweet Rice and Beans (page 71).

1 cup vegetable stock
3 sprigs cilantro, leaves only

Vegetables with Spice Paste

Buen Rau

Farther south, in the warmer climate of Ho Chi Minh City, previously known as Saigon, the capital city of Vietnam, tropical produce appears in many local dishes. Fresh coconut milk makes soup broths creamier, and various spices turn up the heat in Vietnamese dishes. Besides the Chinese and French influences, ingredients from other cuisines landed ashore at Saigon's seaport, and Indian curry powder has had a significant impact on Vietnamese food.

To make the spice paste, combine all the ingredients in a mortar with pestle or a food processor, and process into a smooth paste.

To make the vegetables, combine ⅓ cup of the coconut milk with the spice paste in a pot over medium heat. Cook and stir for 3–5 minutes, or until the paste is fragrant.

Add the remaining 2 cups coconut milk and the potatoes, squash, water chestnuts, taro roots, onion, sugar, soy sauce, and vegetable base. Stir to mix well. Reduce the heat to medium-low and simmer for 10–15 minutes, or until the vegetables are cooked and tender.

SPICE PASTE

10 red Thai chiles, or 5 red jalapeño chiles

3 tablespoons chopped shallots

2 tablespoons chopped garlic

2 tablespoons chopped cilantro roots or stems

2 tablespoons chopped ginger

2 tablespoons curry powder

15 whole black peppercorns

½ teaspoon salt

VEGETABLES

2⅓ cups coconut milk (one 19-ounce can)

1 cup diced potatoes or sweet potatoes, cut into ½-inch cubes

1 cup diced kabocha squash or pumpkin, cut into ½-inch cubes

1 cup diced water chestnuts, cut into ½-inch cubes

1 cup diced taro roots or carrots, cut into ½-inch cubes

1 yellow onion, cut into thick wedges

2 tablespoons palm sugar or brown sugar

2 tablespoons light soy sauce

1 tablespoon vegetable base or bouillon powder

Season with salt to taste, and adjust the other seasonings, if needed. Stir in the cherry tomatoes, and cook for 2 minutes longer.

Remove from the heat and serve with steamed rice, Fried Sweet Rice (page 70), or Sweet Rice and Beans (page 71).

Salt

15 cherry tomatoes

Main Dishes

Clay Pot Vegetables
Cai Kho To

This dish has a deep, intense, sweet flavor dominated by caramel syrup. It should be served with steamed rice to help dilute the intense flavor. Any vegetables of your choice can be used as long as their cooking times and prepared sizes are taken into consideration. All vegetables should be cut into a uniform size so they will cook evenly at the same time; otherwise, those that take longer to cook should have more time on the heat. For example, carrots should be cooked a lot longer than bean sprouts. The longer the vegetables simmer in the syrup, the more intense their flavor and the thicker the sauce will be. (See photo, facing page 120.)

2 cups (1 pound) diced firm or fried tofu, cut into ½-inch cubes

2 tablespoons minced garlic

2 tablespoons minced ginger

1 tablespoon rice vinegar

1 teaspoon ground black pepper

3 tablespoons vegetable oil

2 cups thinly sliced shiitake mushroom caps

2 cups green beans or snow peas, cut into 1½-inch-long strips

2 cups julienne carrots

6 whole red Thai chiles, bruised to lightly split, more or less to taste

½–¾ cup Caramel Soy Syrup (page 50)

½ cup julienne red bell peppers, for garnish

2 tablespoons chopped cilantro leaves, for garnish

4 sprigs sweet basil, leaves only, for accompaniment

4 sprigs mint, leaves only, for accompaniment

4 sprigs saw-leaf herb or Vietnamese mint (*rau ram*), for accompaniment

Combine the tofu, garlic, ginger, vinegar, pepper, and 1 tablespoon of the vegetable oil in a mixing bowl. Marinate for at least 30 minutes.

Heat the remaining 2 tablespoons oil in a medium-size clay pot or saucepan over medium heat. Stir in the marinated tofu, and cook for 2–3 minutes, or until the garlic is light brown and fragrant. Add the mushrooms, green beans, carrots, and chiles. Mix well. The mixture should be mounded high in the pot.

Add the Caramel Soy Syrup and stir to combine well. Close the lid, and continue cooking on medium-low heat for 5–7 minutes, or until the vegetables are tender and the liquid is reduced to a thick sauce.

Remove from the heat and sprinkle with the red bell peppers and chopped cilantro. Serve with the herb accompaniments and steamed jasmine rice, Fried Sweet Rice (page 70), or Sweet Rice and Beans (page 71).

Sweets and Beverages

Other than what is found in French sweets and desserts, which have many varieties and are exhausting to describe, Vietnamese use local ingredients such as fruits, plant fragrances, and coconut products to make desserts that are uniquely their own. Local fruits, in addition to being served fresh, are incorporated into sweets, such as banana and jackfruit pudding. Coconut milk and cream are used instead of cow's milk and cream for their rich and creamy flavors. Fragrances from local plants, such as pandan and jasmine, perfume and add a tropical touch to Vietnamese desserts. Only simple cooking techniques are required for making Vietnamese sweets, in contrast to French desserts, which involve kneading, creaming, and frosting. Most Vietnamese desserts require few or no animal products, which is a vegetarian godsend to complete our meals.

Banana and Tapioca Pudding
Che Chuoi Chung

Serves 6

Most Vietnamese puddings use tapioca pearls for their gelatin-like texture and neutral flavor that easily absorbs other tastes and fragrances. Tapioca pearls are made from tapioca flour and come in three different sizes—small, medium, and large. Some are dyed with various colors, most often red, yellow, green, and black. They are usually cooked in water until they become translucent and soft. When cooking tapioca pearls, pay close attention, stirring occasionally, so they do not stick to the bottom of the pot and burn.

6 large regular bananas, or 10 small exotic bananas (dwarf, Burro, or Mysore bananas; see note)

1 $1/2$ teaspoons salt

4 cups water

$3/4$ cup small tapioca pearls

1 $3/4$ cups coconut cream (one 14-ounce can)

$2/3$ cup sugar, or more to taste

$1/2$ teaspoon pandan, jasmine, or vanilla extract

2 tablespoons roasted black and white sesame seeds, for garnish

Note
• Select bananas that are not fully ripe and that still have greenish skins. Ripe bananas will disintegrate when cooked.

Peel the bananas. Slice them in half lengthwise, and then cut them crosswise into 1$1/2$-inch-long pieces. In a mixing bowl, combine the bananas, $1/2$ teaspoon of the salt, and enough cold water to just cover the bananas. Set aside.

Pour the 4 cups water into a pot or saucepan, and bring to a boil over medium heat. Add the tapioca pearls and cook, stirring occasionally, for 7–10 minutes, or until the pearls are almost clear with tiny white dots in the center.

Drain the bananas and add them to the tapioca pearls. Stir in the coconut cream, sugar, pandan extract, and the remaining 1 teaspoon salt. Continue cooking for 5–7 minutes, or until the bananas are tender.

Remove the pot from the heat. Ladle the pudding into individual bowls, and garnish with the sesame seeds. Serve warm or at room temperature.

Banana Cake
Bahn Chuoi Nuong

Ripe bananas that can't be used up fast enough and old bread that might get stale are put together and given new life in this delicious cake. The remaining ingredients are already in your pantry, making this cake convenient and easy to prepare. It can be served warm or cold with your favorite ice cream.

1 1/2 pounds ripe bananas, regular or exotic
   bananas or a mix

1 1/2 cups sugar

1 3/4 cups coconut milk (one 14-ounce can)

2 tablespoons brandy (optional)

1/4 teaspoon salt

1 teaspoon vanilla extract

1/4 teaspoon ground cinnamon

8 slices sandwich bread (white or whole wheat),
   crusts removed

Peel and slice the bananas as thinly as possible, taking care that the pieces do not break apart. Sprinkle half of the sugar (3/4 cup) over the sliced bananas.

Combine the remaining sugar, coconut milk, brandy, and salt in a pot, and place it over medium heat. Cook and stir for 2–3 minutes, or until the sugar is dissolved. Remove from the heat, and stir in the vanilla extract and cinnamon.

Soak the bread in the coconut milk mixture for 4–5 minutes. Make sure that the bread fully absorbs the mixture. Preheat the oven to 350 degrees F.

Thoroughly oil 1 large, nonstick baking pan (8 x 8 inches or 6 x 8 inches) or 2 (6-inch) round pans. Arrange a layer of the bananas on the bottom of the pan, and cover them with a layer of bread. Continue the process for as many layers as possible, and finish with a layer of the bananas on the top. If any of the coconut milk mixture is left over, do not add it to the baking pan, as it will make the cake too mushy.

Bake for 45–60 minutes, or until a toothpick inserted in the center of the cake comes out clean. Remove from the oven and let rest for at least 12 hours (in the refrigerator or at room temperature) before cutting.

Slice the cake into wedges. Lightly heat in an oven or microwave to serve warm, or serve the cake at room temperature. Serve with vanilla ice cream.

Sweets and Beverages

Cold Tapioca Pudding with Cantaloupe

Hat Chun Chau

Any type of sweet and fragrant melon can be used, but Vietnamese prefer cantaloupe, and many varieties are available, some with pale green flesh and intense fragrances. This dish is often served chilled during the hot summer months when sweet ripe melons are at their peak. Plain white small tapioca pearls are often used for the end result, as they provide a beautiful color contrast—clear tapioca, white coconut cream, and golden cantaloupe.

Serves 6

1 large, ripe cantaloupe
3 cups water
1/2 cup small tapioca pearls
2 cups sugar
1 cup coconut cream
1 teaspoon salt

Cut the cantaloupe in half and discard the seeds. Using a melon baller, scoop out round cantaloupe balls and place them in the refrigerator to chill.

Pour 2 1/2 cups of the water into a pot or saucepan, and bring to a boil over medium heat. Add the tapioca pearls and cook, stirring occasionally, for 7–10 minutes, or until the pearls are almost clear with only tiny white dots in the center. Stir in 1/2 cup of the sugar. Remove from the heat and place in the refrigerator to chill.

Combine the remaining 1 1/2 cups sugar with the remaining 1/2 cup water in a small pot, and place over medium heat. Cook for 7–10 minutes, or until the mixture turns into a thin syrup. Remove from the heat and let cool.

Combine the coconut cream and salt in a small bowl, and stir to mix well. Set aside.

To serve, portion the chilled tapioca pudding into serving bowls. Top with the syrup and melon balls. Sprinkle with the coconut cream mixture and serve chilled.

Mung Bean Pudding

Kae Toaw Sung

Mung beans are a great source of protein, and their seeds are used for growing bean sprouts. Dried mung beans are sold in two colors: green (known as green gram) and yellow (known as yellow or golden gram). They are sold whole with the skin on, whole peeled, or peeled and split. Mung beans are often used to make homemade tofu, savory fillings, or sweet puddings. They should be picked over, cleaned, and rinsed with cold water to rid them of dirt or small stones that might chip a tooth. To reduce their cooking time, mung beans are soaked in cold water for at least thirty minutes before cooking.

1 cup peeled and split yellow mung beans, soaked in water for 30 minutes

3 cups water

1 ½ cups sugar

2 tablespoons cornstarch

3 tablespoons cold water

1 cup coconut cream

1 teaspoon salt

Drain the mung beans and transfer them to a pot. Add fresh water to cover the beans by 1 inch, and bring to a boil. Reduce the heat and simmer uncovered for 10–15 minutes, or until the beans are tender enough to be mashed between your fingers. Do not overcook the beans. Drain, if any water is left, and set aside.

Combine the 3 cups water with the sugar in a pot, and place over medium heat. Simmer for 5–7 minutes, or until the sugar turns into a thin syrup. Stir in the cooked mung beans.

Combine the cornstarch with the 3 tablespoons cold water in a small bowl, and stir to mix thoroughly. Add the cornstarch mixture to the pot. Cook and stir for 3–5 minutes, or until the cornstarch turns clear and the mixture thickens. Remove from the heat.

Combine the coconut cream and salt in a bowl. Set aside.

To serve, portion the mung bean pudding into serving bowls, and sprinkle with the coconut cream. Serve warm or cold.

Sweets and Beverages

Hue Spouse Cakes
Bahn Phu The

This sweet tradition carries a message to all married couples to stick together through thick and thin, just like a thin batter turns into a thick cake. At least we shall hope that the marriage lasts longer than the time it takes to make this cake! This recipe's origin is from city of Hue, the center of classical Vietnamese cuisine. Traditionally, the cake begins by painstakingly transforming pandan leaves into fragrant containers, the size of a tiny jewelry case. Pandan, or pandanus, is a tropical plant with long, slender green leaves. The leaves impart a sweet floral fragrance, which is the essence of so many Vietnamese desserts. Two boxes are tied together with a string of coconut leaf into an inseparable pair called "husband and wife." Preparing the ingredients for the batter and filling are time-consuming when done from scratch, such as shredding coconut meat into fine strips. The boxes are then filled with layers of batter and filling before being steamed. This wonderful dessert has more than just a delicious taste; it also shows great care, skill, and patience. This recipe has been modified to shorten its procedures to fit today's busy lifestyles; hopefully it is not an indicator of the state of today's marriages!

Serves 6/Makes 30 pieces

BATTER
1 pound tapioca flour
1 1/3 cups sugar
1/2 cup sweetened dried coconut flakes

FILLING
2/3 cup (5 ounces) yellow mung beans, soaked in water for at least 30 minutes
2/3 cup corn syrup or maple syrup
1 tablespoon vegetable oil
1 tablespoon orange blossom extract or orange extract

To make the batter, combine all the ingredients in a pot, and place over low heat. Cook for 10–12 minutes, or until the mixture is thick and pastelike.

To make the filling, drain the mung beans and transfer them to a pot. Add fresh water to cover the beans by 1 inch, and bring to a boil. Reduce the heat and simmer uncovered for 10–15 minutes, or until the beans are tender enough to be mashed between your fingers. Do not overcook the beans. Drain, if any water is left.

Transfer the mung beans to a food processor and add the corn syrup, vegetable oil, and orange blossom extract. Process into a paste that has the consistency of peanut butter. If the mixture is too runny, heat it in a pot over low heat, stirring occasionally, until it thickens.

Line 30 muffin cups with paper liners. Have ready a steamer set large enough to hold the muffin pans. To cook, scoop 1 heaping tablespoon of the batter into a muffin cup, and top it with 1 tablespoon of the filling. Scoop another heaping tablespoon of the batter over the filling. Repeat this process with the remaining muffin cups until all the batter and filling are used.

Transfer the muffin pans to the streamer tray. Steam over high heat until the batter is translucent, about 20 minutes. Remove the cakes from the muffin pans. Serve warm or at room temperature.

Steamed Rice Cakes in Banana Leaves

Banh Goi

The banana means much more to Vietnamese daily life than just a fresh fruit. Its leaves can be used for a makeshift thatched roof, biodegradable wrappers and containers, and when dried, rolling papers for smoking tobacco. This recipe utilizes both the fruits and leaves, forming the dessert into neat little packages. Banana leaves can be found in the freezer section of Asian grocery stores. Parchment paper is a good substitute.

Serves 6 (makes 8–12 pieces)

MUNG BEAN OR BANANA FILLING

½ cup (4 ounces) yellow mung beans, soaked in water for at least 30 minutes

3 tablespoons sugar

1 tablespoon vanilla extract

½ teaspoon salt

2 ripe bananas, peeled and sliced into 1 x 4-inch pieces, ¼ inch thick

WRAPPERS

1 package banana leaves, thawed

2 tablespoons vegetable oil

RICE CAKE BATTER

1 ¾ cups rice flour

⅔ cup sugar

2 cups water

1 teaspoon pandan, jasmine, or vanilla extract

If making the mung bean filling, drain the mung beans and transfer them to a pot. Add fresh water to cover the beans by 1 inch, and bring to a boil. Reduce the heat and simmer uncovered for 10–15 minutes, or until the beans are tender enough to be mashed between your fingers. Do not overcook the beans. Drain, if any water is left.

Combine the beans with the sugar, vanilla, and salt in a bowl and let cool.

Is using bananas for the filling, prepare the banana slices and set aside.

For the wrappers, cut the banana leaves into 16 pieces, each piece 8 inches square. Lightly roast the leaves over an open flame, or blanch them in boiling water to make them pliable. Stack 2 pieces of banana leaf together with the grain running in opposite directions to make a set of wrappers. Set aside.

To make the batter, combine the rice flour, sugar, water, and pandan extract in a pot, and place over low heat. Cook, stirring constantly, for

5–7 minutes, or until the mixture thickens and has the consistency of paste.

To wrap, brush a wrapper with some of the oil, and place about 2 tablespoons of the batter in the middle of the wrapper. Top with 2 tablespoons of the mung bean mixture for a bean cake filling, or a piece of banana for a banana cake filling. Cover the filling completely with more batter. Wrap all the contents into a tight package (square or rectangular), and tuck in all the edges securely. Repeat the process to use up all the batter and filling. Transfer the packages to the steam tray of a steamer set, and steam over high heat for 10–15 minutes.

To make the sauce, combine the coconut cream, sugar, cornstarch, and salt in a pot, and place over low heat. Stir to mix well. Cook and stir for 4–5 minutes, or until the mixture thickens slightly. Remove from the heat.

To serve, unwrap the packages and arrange the rice cakes on a serving platter. Top with a generous amount of sauce, and sprinkle with the roasted sesame seeds. Serve warm.

SAUCE
1 3/4 cups coconut cream or milk (one 14-ounce can)
1/4 cup sugar
1 tablespoon cornstarch
1/2 teaspoon salt
3 tablespoons roasted black and white sesame seeds, for garnish

Mango and Coconut Tartlets

Bahn Nuong Dua

French technique cannot be ignored when making small pies or tartlets. To make them more authentic and vegan, coconut milk has been used instead of butter or cream. For the filling, the coconut products must be of high quality with a very rich and creamy taste. Sweet tropical fruits or seasonal local fruits can be used as a fresh topping or with a combination of toppings. In Vietnam, many varieties of mangoes are available, and with new hybrids, they are available all year round. Mangoes are best eaten fresh, and they go well with coconut tartlets. Any type of pie dough can be used, including convenient, ready-made piecrusts, graham cracker crusts, puff pastry sheets, or phyllo dough. (See photo, facing page 121.)

DOUGH

2 cups all-purpose flour, or more as needed

1/2 cup sugar

2 tablespoons cornstarch

1/2 cup vegetable shortening

1/4 cup coconut milk, or more as needed

FILLING

1 3/4 cups coconut cream (one 14-ounce can)

1/2 cup sugar, or more to taste

1/4 cup cornstarch

1 teaspoon fragrant extract (pandan, jasmine, vanilla, rose, etc.)

1/4 cup sweetened dried coconut flakes

2 ripe mangoes

1/2 cup mango or apricot jam

To make the dough, combine all the dough ingredients, mix well, and knead until smooth.

Roll the dough into a flat sheet, less than 1/8 inch thick. Cut the dough to fit 10–15 small, well-oiled tartlet pans or a 10-inch pie pan. Preheat the oven to 350 degrees F.

To make the filling, combine the coconut cream, sugar, cornstarch, and extract in a pot, and place over medium heat. Bring the mixture to a very gentle boil. Remove from the heat and let cool to lukewarm. Fold in the coconut flakes.

Pour the filling evenly into the tartlet pans or pie pan, about three-quarters full. Do not fill to the rim. Bake for 15–20 minutes, or until a knife inserted into the center of the filling comes out clean. Remove from the oven and let cool. Refrigerate to chill.

Peel and cut each mango in half around the seed. Slice each half into thin pieces. Place the mango or apricot jam in a small pot, and melt it over low heat.

Arrange the mango slices on top of the cold tartlets or pie, and brush the surface with a coating of the melted jam. Return to the refrigerator to cool, and then repeat the brushing process with a second and third coat to get a shiny seal all over.

Serve cold, with whipped cream or ice cream, if desired.

Pineapple Tartlets
Bahn Nuong Nhan Thom

Serves 6

Fresh fruits are abundant in the southern plateau of Vietnam, where the city of Dalat, a few miles north of Ho Chi Minh City, is the center of Vietnamese produce. Plantations of fresh fruits are established, growing all varieties, including Western fruits such as strawberries, oranges, peaches, and plums. Pineapple does well in the tropical climate of the south, and Vietnamese pineapple is exceptionally sweet and popular in desserts such as jam, cookies, candies, and pies. Any ready-made dough, such as piecrusts, graham cracker crusts, puff pastry, or phyllo dough can be used in this recipe.

DOUGH

2 cups all-purpose flour, or more as needed

2 tablespoons cornstarch

1/2 cup sugar

1/2 cup vegetable shortening

1/4 cup coconut milk, or more as needed

FILLING

1 pineapple, peeled, cored, and chopped, or 2 cups chopped canned pineapple, drained

1/2 cup sugar, or more to taste

1 teaspoon vanilla extract

To make the dough, combine all the dough ingredients, mix well, and knead until smooth.

Roll the dough into a flat sheet, less than 1/8 inch thick. Cut the dough to fit 10–15 small, well-oiled tartlet pans or a 10-inch pie pan. Preheat the oven to 350 degrees F.

To make the filling and prepare the tartlets, combine all the filling ingredients in a pot, and place over medium heat. Cook and stir for 8–10 minutes, or until the mixture thickens. Fill the pie crust or tartlet crusts, and bake for 20–30 minutes, or until golden brown. Serve warm or at room temperature, with whipped cream or ice cream, if desired.

Four-Precious-Stones Coconut Drink

Suong Sa Hot Luu

Serves 6

Four colors of different ingredients represent four types of precious stones—diamond, ruby, jade, and gold. They mean that good fortune is bestowed upon you, so why would anyone refuse this delicious, hearty drink and good fortune! All the ingredients, such as agar-agar sticks and colored tapioca pearls, are available ready-made and are sold dried, in plastic packages, at Asian grocery stores. They simply need to be cooked and served in the drink. For more good fortune, you can make up your own drink with more ingredients and more colors, including fresh seasonal fruits.

¼ cup yellow mung beans, soaked in water for at least 30 minutes

¼ cup dried agar-agar sticks

¼ cup red and white tapioca pearls

¼ cup green rice flour balls or dumplings

2 cups coconut milk or rich soymilk

1 cup honey or corn syrup, or more to taste

3 cups finely crushed ice

6 sprigs mint

Drain the mung beans and transfer them to a pot. Add fresh water to cover the beans by 1 inch, and bring to a boil. Reduce the heat and simmer uncovered for 10–15 minutes, or until the beans are tender enough to be mashed between your fingers. Do not overcook the beans. Drain, if any water is left, and set aside.

Fill 3 pots with about 3 cup of water, bring to a boil, and cook the agar-agar sticks, tapioca pearls, and rice balls or dumplings separately until tender. They will take about 5–15 minutes to cook, depending on their size and the brand. Taste a little of each item to make sure it is tender. Drain and rinse with cold water.

Combine the coconut milk and honey in a bowl, and place in the refrigerator to chill.

To serve, scoop the mung beans, agar-agar sticks, tapioca pearls, and rice balls or dumplings into tall glasses in distinctive layers. Top with the crushed ice, and pour the coconut milk syrup over all. Garnish with the mint, and serve with long spoons.

Vietnamese Iced Coffee
Ca Phe Da

Serves 6

The most popular Vietnamese coffee is a cup of slow-dripped coffee that is run through a device called a "direct flow filter," a Vietnamese invention. This filter employs a concept similar to the French press coffee filter, but it is made of metal in the shape of a small cup with tiny holes at the bottom. It is small enough to rest on top of a coffee cup. Medium-ground French roast coffee is packed between metal filters, and enough hot water to fill a cup is poured over the coffee. Slow brewing using gravity allows the water to pass through the coffee, collecting the flavors and dripping into the coffee cup, which traditionally is about one-third filled with sweetened condensed milk. After every drop of the coffee has been collected, the contents are stirred well, and it is drunk either warm or poured over a glass of ice for a creamy iced coffee. Occasionally, large tapioca pearls of all colors are added to the iced coffee for something a bit more solid to chew on during a chat over coffee or for a little snack to settle the stomach. Since the direct flow filter makes only one cup of coffee at a time, the following recipe has been modified to make a big batch of coffee enough for six or more people.

$^1/_2$ pound large black or white tapioca pearls

$^1/_2$ cup sugar, more or less to taste

$^3/_4$–1 cup medium-ground coffee (French roast, Colombian, etc.)

$^1/_2$ cup honey or syrup of your choice

4 cups crushed ice

2 cups sweetened soymilk

Bring 4 cups of water to a boil in a pot, add the tapioca pearls, and simmer for 10–15 minutes, or until tender and fully expanded. Drain and place the cooked tapioca pearls in a bowl. Add 2 tablespoons of the sugar and mix well. Set aside.

Bring 5 cups of water to a boil in a pot, and add the ground coffee. Turn off the heat and let stand for 7–10 minutes. Strain the mixture through a fine sieve and discard the solids. (Finely ground coffee can be brewed in a coffee maker or in a filter to get about 4 cups of very rich, strong coffee.)

Add the remaining sugar and honey to the coffee. Stir to mix well, and set aside to cool in the refrigerator.

To serve, scoop about 2 tablespoons of the tapioca pearls into each tall glass. Fill the glass with crushed ice. Pour the coffee mixture almost to the rim of the glasses and top with some of the soymilk. Alternatively, the coffee mixture, crushed ice, and soymilk can be blended in an electric blender and poured on top of the tapioca pearls.

Serve with large straws or, if you prefer, small spoons.

Sweets and Beverages

References

Aiemsabuy, Oopchaeal. *Tofu Aroi, Delicious Tofu.* Bangkok: Sangdad Books, 1997.

Culinaria Konemann. *Southeast Asian Specialties.* Cologne: Konemann, 1998.

Davidson, Alan. *The Penguin Companion to Food.* New York: Penguin Group, 2002.

Gruenwald, Joerg. *PDR for Herbal Medicines.* Montvale, New Jersey: Medical Economic Company Inc., 1998.

Herbst, Sharon Tyler. *The New Food Lover's Companion.* New York: Barron's Educational Series, Inc., 2001.

Hlengmaharnaka, Vanida. *Arharn Vietnam.* Bangkok: Sangdad Books, 2000.

Holzen, Heinz von. *The Food of Asia.* Singapore: Periplus Editions (HK) Ltd., 1999.

Jue Joyce. *Savoring Southeast Asia.* San Francisco: A Weldon Owen Production, 2000.

Jue, Joyce. *Asian Appetizers.* Emeryville, California: Harlow & Ratner, 1991.

Kongpun, Sisamon. *The Best of Vegetable Dishes.* Bangkok: Sangdad Books, 2000.

Mahidol University. *The Miracle of Veggies 108.* Bangkok: Kopfai Publishing, 1997.

McNair, James. *James McNair Cooks Southeast Asian*. San Francisco: Chronicle Books, 1996.

Megal, Christophe. *Asian Tapas*. Hong Kong: Periplus Editions, 2005.

Mingkwan, Chat. *Buddha's Table: Thai Feasting Vegetarian Style*. Summertown, Tennessee: Book Publishing Company, 2004.

Mingkwan, Chat. *The Best of Regional Thai Cuisine*. New York: Hippocrene Books, 2002.

Owen, Sri. *Classic Asian*. London: DK Publishing Inc., 1998.

Poladitmontri, Panurat. *Thailand: The Beautiful Cookbook*. San Francisco: Collins Publishers, 1992.

Thonanong, Thongyao. *Royal Court Recipes*. Bangkok: Sangdad Books, 1998.

Trieu, Thi Choi. *The Food of Vietnam*. Singapore: Periplus Editions (HK) Ltd., 1998.

Walden, Hilary. *The Encyclopedia of Creative Cuisine*. London: Quarto Publishing Limited, 1986.

Mail Order Sources

Vietnamese food has become very popular in recent years. Ingredients for making Vietnamese food at home can be found in local Asian markets. You can also conveniently shop on the Internet. Just type "Vietnamese ingredients" into a search engine, and you'll find many Web sites related to Vietnamese food and online retailers who sell ingredients. Here are a few good places to start:

To find Vietnamese markets near you:

www.vietworldkitchen.com

For online retailers:

www.importfood.com

www.orientalpantry.com

www.templeofthai.com

www.diamondorganics.com

Index

ABOUT THE AUTHOR

As the youngest boy in an urban family in Bangkok, Chat Mingkwan was often left behind to help his aunt prepare the family dinner while his older brothers and sisters ran off to play. At first he despised the task of cooking, but he later learned to enjoy the knowledge and skills he gained, including discovering the sweet revenge of spiking and overspicing his brothers' and sisters' meals. Chat often intentionally prepared their meals with almost unbearable spiciness and got away with it. The food was so spicy but still so delicious that Chat's siblings were unsure whether to punish or praise him. Eventually, cooking became his passion. He gradually fine-tuned his skills and continued cooking, although praise was his only reward and encouragement.

Chat came to the United States to pursue higher education in a design field, while cooking and training part-time in a French restaurant as a hobby. This was his first big step in the culinary profession. With a degree from California State University, Chat worked for several years in the hospitality design business, specializing in kitchen and restaurant design. Later, he followed his culinary passion by apprenticing in provincial French cuisine at La Cagouille in Rayon, France. Returning to the United States, he offered his French cooking always with a twist of Asian and perfected his Asian cooking with a hint of French techniques to fit the Western kitchen. Chat traveled extensively throughout Southeast Asia and realized a wealth of culinary knowledge among these countries and their unique cuisines. He again became an apprentice, this time of Vietnamese cuisine, and easily mastered the skill with his Thai cooking background. Chat put his skills to the test for several years in the culinary metropolis of San Francisco at a restaurant that specialized in Southeast Asian grilled food before realizing his call for sharing the knowledge. He's now doing what he likes most: cooking, teaching, traveling, writing, and making sure that people who come in contact with him have a full stomach and a good time.

Chat's overall philosophy is similar to his cooking simplicity. Untie the knot, either the one in your stomach or the unclear one in the recipe. Make it simple, straight, and true to yourself. Let's walk this path together.

Visit Chat at www.unusualtouch.com.
There is something for everyone.

BOOK PUBLISHING COMPANY

since 1974—books that educate, inspire, and empower

To find your favorite vegetarian and soyfood products online, visit:
www.healthy-eating.com

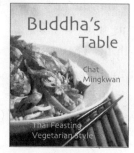

Buddha's Table
Chat Mingkwan
978-1-57067-161-6
$14.95

Indian Vegetarian Cooking at
Your House
Sunetra Humbad,
Amy Schafer Boger, MD
978-1-57067-004-6 $12.95

Japanese Cooking:
Contemporary & Traditional
Miyoko Nishimoto Schinner
978-1-57067-072-5
$12.95

Authentic Chinese Cuisine for
the Contemporary Kitchen
Bryanna Clark Grogan
978-1-57067-101-2
$12.95

Flavors of Korea
Young Sook Ramsay
Deborah Coutrip-Davis
978-1-57067-053-4
$12.95

Flavors of India
Shanta Sacharoff
978-1-57067-023-7
$12.95

Purchase these health titles and cookbooks from your local bookstore or
natural food store, or you can buy them directly from:

Book Publishing Company • P.O. Box 99 • Summertown, TN 38483
1-800-695-2241

Please include $3.95 per book for shipping and handling.

As the gond⬛⬛⬛⬛⬛⬛⬛⬛⬛⬛⬛⬛e
darkened wate⬛⬛⬛⬛⬛⬛⬛⬛⬛⬛⬛

"I'm very gla⬛⬛⬛⬛⬛⬛⬛⬛⬛

I suppose so—⬛⬛⬛⬛⬛⬛⬛⬛ered, suddenly cautious, afraid to let this man know how quickly he had come to matter so much.

"Just 'I suppose'?" He laughed. "I know American women have a reputation for coolness. But my dear, you are half Italian. Can't you do a little better than that? I want very much to kiss you right now, but I must have some encouragement."

She looked into his eyes, and she had no words at all. He bent his head and took her lips gently, teasingly, as if they were a delicacy made for nibbling. The touch of his mouth filled Alicia with an almost unbearable sweetness. It had been such a long time since a man had held her in his arms . . .

───────※───────

SOMETHING OLD, SOMETHING NEW
by Lillian Africano

SOMETHING OLD, SOMETHING NEW

LILLIAN AFRICANO

A JOVE BOOK

The author is grateful for permission to quote from the following:

"A Deep-Sworn Vow" by William Butler Yeats. Reprinted with permission of Macmillan Publishing Co., Inc., from *Collected Poems* by William Butler Yeats. © 1919 by Macmillan Publishing Co., Inc., renewed 1947 by Bertha Georgie Yeats. Also reprinted with permission of A.P. Watt Ltd., London, England.

SOMETHING OLD, SOMETHING NEW

A Jove Book / published by arrangement with
the author

PRINTING HISTORY
Jove edition / February 1983

ISBN: 0-515-05865-3

Jove books are published by Jove Publications, Inc.,
200 Madison Avenue, New York, N. Y. 10016. The words
"A JOVE BOOK" and the "J" with sunburst are trademarks
belonging to Jove Publications, Inc.

PRINTED IN THE UNITED STATES OF AMERICA

ACKNOWLEDGMENTS

Special thanks to my editor, Beverly Lewis, for her excellent editorial direction; to my agent, Elaine Markson, for her expert guidance; to my children, Arthur, Nina, and David, for their invaluable support and loving presence.

A friend is in prosperitie a pleasure,
a solace in adversitie, in grief a comfort,
in joy a merry companion, at al times
an other I.

John Lyly: EUPHUES

PROLOGUE

As the heavy brass doors of the walnut-paneled elevator opened, Jenny Ashland took a deep breath, stepped in, and pressed the button marked PH. The elevator climbed quickly and smoothly to the top. Nice piece of symbolism, Jenny mused—climbing to the top alone—except she hadn't been alone, not really. There had been her darling baby, Rebecca, now all grown up—and now there was Scotty.

But Lord, it had been a bumpy ride, up and down and sideways—and now she was here: Penthouse A was hers. She had made it hers, and she felt triumphant—and a little afraid.

She fitted the key into the lock. It was one of those new high-security mechanisms, not at all like the simple lock she and Sally had been permitted to open with their very own keys after they had become teenagers. So many years—so many memories ago.

The door swung open to reveal dazzlingly white walls washed with sunlight. And there it was—the feeling she had always loved best about this apartment—the feeling of being outdoors. The parquet floors had been buffed and waxed to a mellow patina. Jenny winced as she thought of the movers who would be coming today, bumping and dragging heavy pieces of furniture against the unmarred surface. Ah well, she thought, the floors had survived other moving days. The nicks and scars made them more interesting, gave them character. Like people. Sometimes—if they were lucky.

She walked through the spacious gallery, past the double living room, straight to the terrace. She threw open the leaded glass doors and flooded her senses with the panorama she had always loved—a bird's-eye view of Greenwich Village. Town house roofs, church spires, lush hidden gardens, the arch at Washington Square, and in the distance—a newcomer—the twin towers of the World Trade Center. No matter that she had grown up in New York, Jenny had never taken the city's charm for granted, never looked at its beauties with jaded eyes.

Now, more than ever, she felt the intoxication of the city below. Now it was part of her view from the top. It had cost a small fortune to buy back the view of her childhood, and she had earned it all herself. She, Jenny Richman Ashland, had picked herself up from the rubble of her own failed choices, left behind the regrets and recriminations of all her "might-have-beens." And here she was at thirty-seven, with all her own teeth, her sense of self stronger than it had ever been, making yet another beginning.

And yet—and yet. Her eyes flickered, almost involuntarily, to the dining room, where the morning light was refracted into a thousand sunbursts in the mirrored columns that had been installed a few years ago. Jenny's throat constricted with pain, her shoulders shuddered, as she felt for a brief moment the presence of death. It was there, in the apartment. Jenny had thought the ghosts had all been laid to rest, but now—now she wasn't so sure. The women of Jenny's family had known love and conflict and pain—even death—right here, within the walls of this luxurious aerie.

Now there would be good times, she promised herself. Only good times, she whispered, with the silent urgency of a prayer. She moved into the kitchen, the sprawling old-fashioned kitchen with a butler's pantry that was bigger than many apartment living rooms. Here, too, some concessions had been made to modern living—a sleek Pirelli floor, the finest of professional appliances, a formidable array of highly lacquered and extremely efficient storage cabinets. She opened the refrigerator—she had stocked it with fruits and cheese and drinks for moving day—and took out a bottle of Perrier and some ice cubes. She filled a paper cup, then lifted it to no one in particular. It was her toast to her own new life.

1

As the horse-drawn carriage clip-clopped through the gray slush that carpeted Madison Avenue, the slender dark young man in the passenger seat shivered and pulled the collar of his camel-hair overcoat closer to his neck. This was his fourth winter in New York, but he thought he would never get accustomed to the biting cold, not after the mild winters of his native Egypt.

The driver brought the carriage to a halt in front of a three-story brick town house with an enormous wreath of holly on the door. The young man paid the driver, then bounded up the steps two by two, heading straight for the welcoming beacon of light that issued from the windows of the parlor floor.

He rapped the brass knocker three times, and the door was opened by a rosy-cheeked maid. A loud surge of conversation and the tinkling of glasses told him the holiday party was well under way.

"Good evening, Sofia. I hope I am not too late?"

"Not at all, sir. But Mme. Rubichou said I was to bring you directly in to her."

No sooner had the maid relieved the young man of his coat and opened the leaded glass doors that led to the front parlor than a tall striking woman with sharp features and flaming red hair rushed forward and flung long slender arms around his neck. "Sharif, my darling boy," she said, punctuating her words with hugs and kisses. "I was afraid you might disappoint me."

"Dear Syrie—I could never do that. Something came up just as I was about to leave, but I would have been here even if I had to walk all the way from Riverside Drive."

She flung her hand against her forehead in a gesture of mock horror. "Perish the thought, *chéri*. You would have been chilled to the bone—you might have contracted *la grippe*. And then I would have had to answer to your dearest mother.

1

Alors—let us go inside and you can meet the angel I have been telling you about.''

She took his hand and pulled him into the parlor, through the clusters of guests, past the enormous Christmas tree that stood in the middle of the room, toward a fair young woman with porcelain-perfect skin, clear green eyes, an aristocratic forehead, and hair the color of summer wheat. She stood alone in a far corner of the room, a vision in green velvet, a cup of punch held in her small delicate hands.

"Here she is," Syrie announced proudly, as if she were personally responsible for all this loveliness. "Carlotta, my love, this is the young man I've been telling you about—Sharif Hazzi, the son of my oldest friend, Amina.

"Sharif"—she turned to the young man—"this is Carlotta Barzini, the niece of another very dear friend, Adela Barzini. I am depending on you to amuse my little guest. She has been with us for more than a week, and all she has seen are old people like me."

"*Chère* Syrie," he protested, "you are not at all old—" But before he could finish, she was gone, a flurry of pure energy bustling among the other guests.

He turned to the young woman, and although he was normally a gregarious and articulate man, he found himself silently staring at the perfection of her face.

"I am very pleased to meet you," the vision said, in a lilting, charmingly accented English.

"The pleasure is entirely mine, signorina," Sharif answered, finally finding his voice. "What happy fate has brought you to New York? A visit perhaps?"

"A very long visit. Zia 'Dela—my aunt—she sent me to visit Syrie, so that I might improve my English and see something of the world."

"But your English is quite marvelous."

"You are very kind," she said, lowering her eyes, managing to look provocative and mischievous and shy all at the same time. "I have studied the language—and French, as well—at the convent school. But I have had very little opportunity to speak it. Then Syrie was kind enough to invite me—"

"Forgive me, signorina, if I ask a personal question, but if your aunt sent you to a convent school, how is it that she permits you to come alone, such a long distance, to a city like New York?"

Carlotta smiled, revealing a tiny dimple in her left cheek. "If you knew Zia 'Dela, you wouldn't ask that question. When she makes a decision, she does not worry about whether or not she is contradicting something she said the day before. She is a wonderful and original woman."

"She must be. And I am grateful that she has sent you here. Perhaps I may have the privilege of meeting her one day."

Carlotta blushed, and Sharif watched with delight as the delicate tracings of pink crept up the creamy perfection of her cheeks.

He pressed Carlotta to tell him more about herself. He listened attentively, murmuring sympathetically as she told of being orphaned at five, of being sent to live with her aunt in her ruined "but quite marvelous" palazzo in Venice. She described the regal but very drafty corridors and drawing rooms, the "guests" who came often and paid for their "visits," discreetly wrapping their currency in bouquets of flowers or packages of bonbons because Zia was too proud to admit she accepted rent for her "hospitality."

He laughed as she described the rigorous "interviews" her aunt conducted with prospective guests, during which she required detailed histories of their lineage, their social connections, and, in some cases, their education and their health.

He smiled as she described Zia 'Dela, who was now sixty years old, and who never appeared outside her own bedroom without her full maquillage, gowned and shod and wearing most of her remaining jewels, who rose at dawn and exercised for an hour before she rang for café and melon—the same breakfast she had eaten every day of her life.

"She is magnificent, my zia," she continued, "and she loves me so much, though I think it was sometimes tiring for her to raise a small child. But she was always thinking of ways to make me wise and strong like herself. Because she knew, you see, that I would be alone one day, when she goes to heaven."

Sharif murmured a protest. What a monstrous idea, he thought, that this angelic creature should spend a single moment bereft and alone.

Carlotta saw his expression and reacted. "No, no, it is not something to be sad about. That is why Zia sent me to the nuns. She is not so very religious, but she said they would give the best education for the least money."

Counting on her fingers her recently acquired skills, Carlotta recited: "Now I can sew, I can embroider, I can cook—very well—I can make fine lace, and I can scrub a floor until it shines. Zia 'Dela says there are many ways I can earn a living, if it becomes necessary—especially if my English is very, very good."

"And what else does she say, your very wise aunt?"

She dropped her eyes again, taking on the slightly naughty expression he was beginning to adore. "She also says that if I find a rich husband, who is also very handsome and very kind, why then, I can be a very superior wife. And I can make certain the servants are doing their work properly."

Trying hard not to laugh, Sharif assumed a serious air. "I must congratulate you and your aunt, signorina. You both seem to have prepared for every eventuality."

"But now I must stop talking about myself, signor. That is not very polite. Syrie has told me that you are Egyptian, and that you are a very brilliant student at Columbia, and that you speak many languages."

Sharif smiled. "Syrie is always generous with the people she loves. I am Egyptian—I was born and raised in Cairo—but I'm not at all certain my professors would agree with Syrie's estimate of my brilliance."

"Have you been in this country very long?"

"About three and a half years. I graduate in six months."

"And then?"

"Then I shall go back to Cairo. I have not seen my family for a long time." There was something in his voice, something in the expression on his dark, handsome face that touched her.

"You have been lonely here?" she asked gently.

"Yes," he said, his voice almost a whisper. "At times it was very hard. But Syrie and her husband, Pierre—they have been like a family to me. And now," he added, "I have met you. And so I can only be glad to be in this city—and very grateful to Syrie for inviting me here, to this wonderful party."

Carlotta dimpled again. "But Signor Hazzi, I could not help but overhear the call Syrie made to invite you. It was my impression that you did not wish to come at all."

"Impossible!" he said, searching his memory hastily for a recollection of that conversation. Then he smiled, a little sheepishly. "Ah, yes—well, you must let me explain, signo-

rina. It was not that I did not wish to be here. It was simply
that one of my classmates invited me to spend the holidays
with his family. I had already accepted the invitation. But
when Syrie explained that she wanted me to be here—and to
meet someone very dear to her—why, then, the matter was
settled. And if you, or she, had the impression I was at all
reluctant, then I must humbly beg your pardon. Will you
forgive me?''

"There is nothing to forgive, Signor Hazzi. But I see our
hostess signaling us to take some refreshments. Shall we have
some holiday turkey?''

"If that is what you wish, dear lady. For myself—I have
an entire feast before me, right here.''

Carlotta blushed again. "Really, Signor Hazzi, you are
very extravagant. Why,'' she said, "I might almost believe
you were Italian and not Egyptian at all.''

"Signorina, for you I will be anything at all. This is not
extravagance but truth. From my heart.'' Sharif thumped his
chest with such emphasis that he started to cough.

"Come, come,'' Carlotta said, laughing and patting his
back at the same time. "I think we had better have some
supper before you do yourself an injury.''

Reluctantly Sharif turned his attention to the Rubichous'
holiday table. Mechanically—eager to return to Carlotta's
side—he filled two plates with turkey and ham and smoked
oysters.

After a few perfunctory passes at his own supper, Sharif
watched, enchanted, as Carlotta consumed, with relish, every
morsel on her plate. "Tell me, signorina,'' he said, "tell me
more about your life at the convent. Was it not very rigorous
for you, the regimen of the good sisters?''

"Oh, no,'' she replied. "To others, the convent life might
seem difficult, but to us, it was often quite merry. We had
many *regolamenti*—rules—that is true. But we ourselves were
not sisters, and so it was understood we would break these
rules. Not very often, you understand, because that would
have been disrespectful. But occasionally, it was permitted.''

"And you, Carlotta—may I have the privilege of calling
you by your given name? What kind of student were you?''

She smiled mischievously. "Why Signor Hazzi—Sharif—I
was, of course, a model student, very obedient and—''

"Always?''

"Well—almost always.''

"And the other times?"

"Well, the other times"—she rolled her eyes upward to heaven—"Mother Superior would become very unhappy, and then I would have to do penance—for my own welfare, you understand. So I could be a better person."

"What kind of penance?"

"Ah, well, that would depend. Sometimes it was to remain silent for a very long time. That was very hard for me." She laughed at herself. "Or I would have to say my prayers kneeling on a handful of rice. The usual."

For Sharif, who was born a Copt but whose ideas of religion were more mystical than dogmatic, whose concept of God was that of a beneficent and not very demanding deity, this notion of physical penance was extremely suspect. He frowned, and Carlotta caught his change of expression at once.

"Oh, no," she protested. "You must not think that penance is a bad thing. It is really very good—because then the sin is finished and the slate is washed clean. But," she added, mischievous again, "the penance was not always for the students. Sometimes, when one of the sisters was unkind without reason, then one or two of us would go, very, very quietly, and put the powder that makes one itch in that sister's bed." She started to giggle at the memory, and when Sharif laughed too, she went on, "Or if the sister was really cruel, it would be the laxative in the pitcher of drinking water.

"Of course"—now her voice took on a somber quality—"that would mean punishment for all of us, because no one would confess or tell who did it. But it was worth the trouble, you see, because everything seemed more fair that way."

As she finished her recital of life at the convent, Sharif knew he would marry this woman and no one else. And although he was reluctant to leave her at all, he looked around and saw that most of the other guests had left, that the servants were discreetly clearing away the remains of the meal. His good manners told him it was time to take his leave.

"Signorina," he said, bowing slightly and pressing her fingers to his lips, "it seems I must say good night. I hope to see you again—very soon."

"Good night, Sharif. I have enjoyed this evening very much."

Before he left, Sharif took his hostess aside. "Thank you, dearest Syrie. Thank you for the best evening of my life."

The older woman smiled and patted Sharif's head affectionately, as she had done when he was a small boy. "You liked my lovely Carlotta, little one? Are you sorry you were so naughty when I asked you to come?"

"Syrie," he said passionately, "you were wise, as always. Forgive me." He smiled the little-boy smile that had always engaged her as he kissed her hand. "*Au 'voir*. Say good night to Pierre for me. And Happy Noel to you both."

When he returned to his lodgings on Riverside Drive, the two comfortably furnished rooms he had let from an elderly woman who took in student borders, he could not stop thinking about Carlotta. He thanked whatever Providence had taken him to the Rubichou home, so that he would not have to live another day without knowing there was a perfect woman for him. And it was all Syrie's doing.

Syrie Rubichou and Sharif's mother had known each other since childhood, and they had managed to keep the bond between them alive, through the years and across several continents, with letters and occasional visits. Before Sharif had left Cairo to study at Columbia University, he had promised his mother that he would spend all his holidays with the Rubichous. Like so many Egyptian sons, he was completely devoted to his mother, close to her in a way that transcended the usual mother-son rituals. Their relationship was genuinely intimate, remarkably frank, the bond between them unconditional.

"Promise me," she had said, on the eve of his departure, "promise me that you'll make Syrie's house your second home. It will make our separation easier for me, if I know that you won't be all alone."

"Of course, *Maman*," he had promised. "Anything that will ease your mind. But I won't be all alone for very long." He had smoothed her still jet-black hair and tried to reassure her. "I'm sure that I will meet many interesting people. I will write to you very often and I will tell you everything I am doing."

Sharif had kept his promise. He had turned up on Syrie's doorstep his first week in New York, and she had welcomed him with tears and hugs and kisses, as she exclaimed over his good looks. "When I look at you," she said, "it's almost as if your dear mother was with me. You have exactly the same beautiful face—and the same expression in those wicked eyes.''

And although Sharif first came to Syrie from a sense of duty, he returned over and over again, to dispel the dismal fog of homesickness that soon enveloped him. With Syrie, he could play at "remember when," in conversations that recalled her visits to Cairo or shared holidays when his family had vacationed at her villa in the south of France.

Eventually he had met interesting people at the university, but there had been few real friendships. America might be the melting pot of the world, but the wealthy and privileged who attended the university did not expect to find exotics cluttering their hallowed halls of academe.

True, Sharif's family was wealthy, aristocratic, and very well known in Egypt. But his skin was the color of café au lait, his impeccable English shaded with an accent. Sharif did not push. He had too much pride and too much style to try to force his way into social circles that did not want him. Instead, he had applied himself to his studies. Although he had come to Columbia—a rare choice for Egyptians of his generation—for a gentleman's education, his pride spurred him to do well.

His free hours were spent with the Rubichous, enjoying superb dinners prepared by their temperamental and supremely talented French cook. Syrie was always "receiving," ready to share her parlor and the bounties of her kitchen with anyone who craved a splendid meal, a sympathetic ear, or some hearty conversation, in one language or another. And he enjoyed the quiet relaxation of a game of whist or backgammon with Pierre, whose quiet intelligence had made a success of his shipping business, just as his endless capacity for listening had made a success of his marriage.

In time Sharif had made a few friends. His aloofness, his obvious ease with money, his finely tailored English wardrobe, and his excelence in class had attracted overtures from a few young men who were secure enough not to require the hallmarks of uniformity in others. But his closest friend was still Syrie. And now she had introduced him to the woman he knew he would love forever.

Just as he was drifting off to sleep, he allowed himself to remember, for the first time that evening, the fact that he had been betrothed, at the age of fourteen, to the daughter of his father's best friend. Quickly he pushed the thought away. It had all happened so long ago. It was a complication, but it could be managed. It had to be.

Late Christmas day, Sharif called again on the Rubichous, bearing flowers for Carlotta, a bottle of Napoleon brandy and a box of chocolates for Pierre and Syrie. *"Joyeux Noel,"* he said, kissing Syrie on both cheeks.

"Come in, my darling," she urged, drawing him into the library, where he could hear the sounds of *Aida* from the windup Victrola.

"I hope you are well today," he said politely, as he took a comfortable chair by the fire. All the while his eyes ranged over Syrie's shoulder, searching.

"I am very well, thank you. What is it?" she asked with feigned innocence. "Are you looking for something? Ah, where are my manners! You must be very cold. You want some tea . . . or perhaps a small cognac—"

"No, no—please don't trouble yourself. I am fine, really. But I was wondering . . . your houseguest . . . Signorina Barzini . . . she is not here today?" he asked, with such disappointment in his voice that Syrie laughed out loud.

"Oh, I should be shot for being so cruel," she said. "Carlotta is upstairs, having a small siesta. We have had so many guests, so much excitement, the poor lamb is quite exhausted."

"But she is all right, Syrie, isn't she? She is not ill?"

"She is fine, my darling. And she will undoubtedly join us shortly. I hope you will not mind entertaining me in the meantime?"

"It is always a pleasure to visit with you, Syrie. You are one of those rare people who—"

"Please, little one, no flattery."

"Not flattery at all. I was just thinking last night how very unusual you are—and how much I owe you—how kind you have been to me—how much your friendship has meant to me. And now—now you have made me so happy."

"Tcha! I have done nothing at all. Your visits have been a great pleasure for Pierre and me. You have given me a delicious taste of what it is like to have a grown-up son—a most delightful and charming one. So naturally, since I have under my very roof a young woman who is equally delightful, my common sense dictated that you should be brought together."

"Still, I must tell you—"

"Hush. All this gratitude will make me ill, like too many sweets. Ah—look—just in time to divert your extravagant gallantry. Carlotta, dear child, *comment ça va? Tu as bien dormi*?"

"Very well, thank you, Syrie. Signor Hazzi—what a very pleasant surprise. And so soon . . ."

To his horror, for he had always been comfortable in the company of women, Sharif felt himself redden. "I could not stay away," he blurted. "Not even if I had wanted to."

"Come here, my dear," Syrie said. "Sharif has brought you some lovely flowers. And for me—look at these marvelous chocolates. Come . . . sit down and entertain our guest while I go into the kitchen for a vase. And possibly someone who will make us some tea. If this young man has anything to say that he does not want me to hear, why, then, he'd better do it while I am out of the room, so I can discharge my duties as chaperone with a good conscience."

Again he blushed, and he could not for the life of him articulate any of the speeches he had rehearsed. His eyes were riveted to the lace ruching on her gray watered-silk dress—at precisely the spot where it delicately caressed her neck. He could see the hint of a pulse beating there, and he felt as if he had drunk a great deal of wine.

"You are still on holiday from the university?"

"*Si.*"

"You did not tell me last night what you were studying."

"A little of everything, *chère* Carlotta. Some mathematics, some history, some science, some English literature—so that I will not be an embarrassment to my father. He is a truly learned man."

"I think you are very modest. I think that you must be a formidable scholar and that you will find my poor education very limited."

"Impossible. You would not be so kind in your estimation of my abilities—not if you could see how I have struggled with my English. I can manage to read Byron and Shelley in their native tongue. That is all very well. But when I attempt Molière or your wonderful Dante in English—why, that is a pain to my ears. To express ideas of beauty or love, I feel I must reach for your very rich language—or French—or even Arabic— Ah, now there is a language for love."

Carlotta lowered her eyes and let her lips turn upward. This stirred Sharif as applause would an actor. He rushed on: "I wish I could share with you some of my favorite Egyptian poets. I wish I could show you my Cairo. You would love it. I know you would. It is so cosmopolitan, but gentler, kinder than Paris. And Alexandria in the spring . . . *sur la plage . . . c'est si . . . si . . .*" His eyes turned liquid and dreamy as he conjured up a vision of the two of them walking barefoot in the sand that bordered the Red Sea.

His reverie was interrupted by Syrie's noisy return. "*Alors*— I see that you have amused yourselves in my absence. And now we shall have some lovely Darjeeling tea with some Christmas pastries. I took the liberty of telling cook to set another place for dinner. I assume you will grace our table, Sharif? Yes? Good. In fact, I was just thinking that Sharif must share the remainder of his holiday with us. Pierre is so busy at the office, and we must have someone to accompany us. I have promised to show Carlotta the city. I thought we might begin tomorrow with a drive. One of the horses is lame, so we can try out Pierre's Christmas present to himself, his new Packard automobile. What do you say to that?"

Sharif's eyes lit up. During his years in New York he had become enamored of American automobiles. The prospect of seeing Carlotta again and the pleasure of a new machine seemed doubly delightful. "*Mais oui,* Syrie. I shall be only too happy to accompany you tomorrow—anywhere you choose."

The excursion was a great success. Sharif had marveled at Pierre's auto, a Packard runabout in heliotrope and white, its interior sumptuous with gold-leaf decoration and upholstery of white patent leather.

"*Regardez,*" Syrie said. "Have you ever seen anything so disgustingly ostentatious? I told Pierre it was an automobile for an actress—or a madam. Not suitable for a businessman at all. But you know Pierre—when he gets an idea into his head, there is no use arguing with him. And since he has spent five thousand dollars for this machine, we may as well use it.

"Now, Roger," she instructed the chauffeur, "I want you to be careful. Drive very slowly. The streets are treacherous, and Ma'mselle Barzini is here to see some sights, not to run a race.''

"Yes, Madame,'' the chauffeur replied. "I won't go faster than ten miles an hour.''

"That's what he always says,'' Syrie whispered to Sharif. "And always he accelerates, when he thinks I am not paying attention. Watch him, *chéri*. Be sure to caution him when the needle in the front begins to jump.''

To Carlotta she said, "You are fortunate to have no automobiles in Venice. I have just read an authoritative report by a distinguished American physician. He says the human body is not fitted for high-speed automobiling, and that those who persist in this filthy habit may suffer serious consequences.''

She finished this last pronouncement in such a funereal tone that Sharif could not resist teasing her. "And what are these consequences? Surely you have warned Pierre?''

"I have indeed. Some of these are physical and affect the one who drives the machine.'' She dropped her voice so Roger would not hear. "Others are more subtle. This very doctor says that he has seen instances of nervous prostration and melancholia. Alas, Pierre only laughed, even when I showed him the article.''

Sharif restrained himself from smiling, for in fact it was often difficult to take Syrie's pronouncements seriously. She was a veritable encyclopedia of information, but it was impossible to determine which of her "facts'' were gleaned from reliable sources and which were the result of random gossip.

"Here''—she pointed outside—"is B. Altman and Company, and close by is the Macy store. Roger will take us past Arnold Constable and Brentano's and oh, yes, you must see the Siegel-Cooper emporium on Eighteenth Street. It was built just a few years ago—I'll take you there one day this week. Shopping here,'' she said to Carlotta, "can be quite an adventure. These new department stores are so large. Do you know they can sell in one day what a small shop would take a year to sell? It's true. In just one year, I have read, these stores sold more than two hundred thousand pairs of silk stockings? Imagine!''

Carlotta murmured politely, and Syrie went on. "Here,'' she said, as they passed a construction site on lower Broadway, "here they are building what will be the tallest structure in the world. It belongs to the Woolworth Company, and it will be almost eight hundred feet high.''

Syrie continued her travelogue, pointing out buildings and shops until it was lunchtime. Then she instructed Roger to drive to Pell Street. ''I hope this will be a treat for you, my dear,'' she said to Carlotta, as they sat down at a marble-topped mahogany table in one of the neighborhood's Chinese restaurants.

Carlotta looked around the small establishment with its tile floors, its tin ceilings trimmed with exotic latticework, at the Chinese diners rapidly maneuvering clumps of rice with chopsticks. ''This seems very different from any restaurant I have seen,'' she said, ''but I have not been to many.''

''Well, then,'' Syrie said confidently, ''you will certainly enjoy this.''

They began their meal with bits of sugared ginger, dried nuts, and candied apricots. ''Isn't this marvelous?'' Syrie said. ''So enriching to try different food from different cultures, don't you think?''

''Oh, yes,'' Carlotta agreed, though in fact she found the taste of ginger somewhat overpowering. ''Thank you, Syrie, for bringing me here.''

''I'm so glad you like it.'' Syrie beamed. ''And I'm certain you will enjoy another treat I have for you. Of course, we cannot ask Sharif to come along, but tomorrow I am going to take you to my Turkish bath club.''

''A Turkish bath in New York City?'' Sharif asked.

''Oh, yes,'' Syrie said. ''It's on Seventieth Street, near Lexington Avenue. I find it so refreshing—a brisk swim, then the steam, a massage, perhaps the pedicure. Of course, most of the patrons are quite stout, not like my little angel—or even myself,'' she said, drawing herself up so that anyone might see there was not an ounce of surplus fat on her tall angular body.

''I hope you will both have a pleasant time,'' Sharif said. ''I am only sorry that I will not be able to see you tomorrow.''

''But of course you shall see us, silly boy. You must come for dinner. Perhaps Pierre will take us to Chez Mouqin or to Petitpas. The cuisine is French,'' she explained to Carlotta, ''but the clientele is very literary, very artistic. We have dined there often with Sharif, so now we must introduce these places to you.''

• • •

In the weeks that followed Sharif spent virtually all his free time with the Rubichous and with Carlotta. Syrie's active imagination concocted dozens of excursions that took them to concerts, to the theater, to the opera, and to the city's landmarks that she considered noteworthy.

As the weather grew warmer, she took the young people to Central Park, where Carlotta found a nostalgic reminder of her home—an authentic Venetian gondola which would convey them around the lake for only ten cents.

Although no formal declarations were made, it was understood that Sharif's intentions were serious. The word "marriage" had not been spoken, but it was there, by suggestion and innuendo.

When Syrie and Pierre chaperoned the young couple on a trip to Coney Island, the first attraction they visited, on Surf Avenue and West Tenth Street, was the "Streets of Cairo" —painted bright yellow with blue hieroglyphics, and complete with camels and donkeys and a ragtag array of Arabs and Egyptians. Carlotta seemed quite impressed, but Sharif was appalled. "But this is nothing like Cairo," he said indignantly. "I don't want you to look," he told Carlotta. "You must close your eyes and come away at once. I will show you my Cairo soon enough. Come away from here and choose something else to do."

"Can we try that?" She pointed to the giant Ferris wheel.

"Of course, my dear," Syrie said. "Pierre and I will watch. You two go ahead."

Carlotta's bravado left her when the metal cage in which she and Sharif were sitting suddenly stopped, almost at the top of the enormous wheel. She clutched Sharif's hand and whispered. "*Dio*—I'm afraid. Are we going to fall?"

Sharif put his arm around her shoulder. It was the most intimate gesture that had passed between them. He wanted very much to kiss her, but his sense of propriety restrained him. "Don't be afraid," he said, his heart pounding with excitement. "There—you see, it has started again. You must not be afraid of anything when I'm with you. Ever."

It was late in spring, with his graduation just weeks away, that Sharif put his intentions into words. He spoke first to Syrie. "I think you know that I want to marry Carlotta," he said. "Do you think her aunt will agree?"

"Dear boy! I am so happy. Of course she will agree. She must. I will see to it. I will assure her there is no one else in this world who is better suited to her Carlotta. And your own dear parents—I think they will adore her. I'm quite certain of that as well. This is a wonderful match, made by a very wise cupid, if I do say so myself."

Sharif hesitated a moment, then decided to take Syrie into his confidence. "I wish it were that simple," he said. "But I'm afraid there are some difficulties. You see, it was decided a long time ago that I should marry Najla Abou-Saif, the daughter of my father's good friend. I was fourteen and she was seven at the time—you know how these things are arranged. If I had not met Carlotta, if I had not loved her, I could have done as my father wished. But now . . . now I must go home and explain to my parents what has happened. I know they will be disappointed, but—"

"Oh, my dear," Syrie interrupted, "I'm so very sorry. I've been so stupid. Your parents never told me, but oh, I'm afraid they will blame me for all this."

"Please don't be upset. Carlotta and I—I feel this was fate. My parents will certainly understand. You'll see. Everything will be fine."

"I hope so, *chéri*. I hope so."

"There's just one thing. I don't want you to mention this conversation to Carlotta. I don't want her to worry. I will tell her myself—after the problem is resolved."

"Of course, Sharif. I think that is wise. Perhaps you might want to postpone your proposal until after you have spoken with your parents?"

"No!" He heard the vehemence in his voice and quickly added, "Excuse me, Syrie. I didn't mean to . . . But you see, I don't want to wait. There is nothing in the world that can change my feelings. I want to go to Egypt knowing that I have her love as well. All I will postpone is the sharing of problems."

And so when Sharif spoke with Carlotta, there was no mention of a fiancée in Cairo. He led her into Syrie's garden, though the spring air was still a little cool. "I hope you have read my heart," he said, "so that these words are not really necessary. Will you be my wife?"

She sighed, and Sharif held his breath until she turned on him a smile of radiant happiness. "Oh, yes, Sharif. I want very much to be your wife. I have been hoping you would ask me," she said with a frankness he had seldom found in young women. "I was so afraid you would go back to Cairo and that I would lose you."

"Dearest Carlotta, I must go back to Cairo, but only to settle some family business. But first I shall go to meet your aunt. And when I return, we can make plans for our wedding. Does that suit you, my love?"

"Of course."

$$=\!\!\!\!\succ 2 \succ\!\!\!\!=$$

Sharif sailed from New York on a sunny day in June. Syrie and Pierre and Carlotta accompanied him to the pier, laden with champagne and fruit and flowers. They toasted the future, and then blew teary kisses and threw gaily colored streamers as the great liner pulled away from the dock, beginning its voyage to Genoa.

Two weeks later Sharif boarded a train for Venice. When he arrived at the crumbling palazzo on San Paolo Square, there was not a hint of fatigue in his young and very handsome face. His linen suit had been carefully pressed by the valet at the Albergo Danieli; his toilette was immaculate. His manner was excited and eager as he approached the intricate swirlings of the massive iron gate, then pulled the chain hanging from the large brass bell. After a long wait came the sound of shuffling. The household's single manservant, a gangly old man known simply as Old Gaetano opened the gate, to the accompaniment of such sterterous breathing that Sharif feared for his health.

He was shown into a small salon, given an undistinguished but pleasant sherry, and told to wait for "La Contessa." The room reminded him of a sepia photograph that had faded in the sunlight. The furniture and the rug were very fine and very old. The fabrics and the colors still had a delicate beauty, worn though the fibers were. The walls were flaking, and there was more than one water stain where the rains had seeped through the ancient roof tiles. Yet the overall impression was one of quality and something indefinably aristocratic, something rarer than mere surface beauty.

Sharif had the same impression as Adela Barzini made her entrance—a tall, ramrod-straight old woman with tightly crimped and hennaed hair, dressed in an elaborate old-fashioned gown of mauve silk trimmed with fine pointelle lace. Adela had never been conventionally beautiful, but Sharif, who had a keen appreciation of bone structure and breeding, whether in people or animals, admired the well-defined clean features that had not blurred with age, the clear emerald eyes that were so much like Carlotta's. When she spoke, it was with an almost martial air: "So you're the young man who wants to marry my niece."

Sharif was astonished. "But how did you know?" he asked, forgetting his manners.

Adela laughed, obviously pleased with her advantage. "It seems that both my good friend Syrie and my niece were afraid I might overwhelm you if you arrived unexpectedly. So I have had not one but two cables suggesting I welcome you into the family. Such as it is. And that I employ more delicacy than usual. Does that answer your question?"

"*Si,* Contessa Barzini, *molto grazie.*"

"Well, I must say you are not hard to look at. And you speak passable Italian—for a foreigner."

"You are very kind. And you are exactly as I hoped you would be."

Now it was Adela's turn to be caught off balance. "What an extraordinary thing to say!"

Sensing that he now had some advantage, Sharif flashed his most engaging smile. "I know how much Carlotta loves you, Contessa Barzini, and I wanted very much to see you as she does."

"Very commendable, young man. But I will spare you any further anxiety. No need to charm a difficult old woman. I give you my blessing. You had it before you arrived. Unless you were afflicted with some irredeemable flaw. So—now— tell me about your plans."

"*Grazie . . . mille grazie,* Contessa. I promise you I will take good care of Carlotta."

"I'm sure your intentions are good, and that is all I ask for." She paused a moment, then went on: "Tell me, aren't you a little curious about why I give my niece to you so quickly? She means a great deal to me, you know.''

Sharif looked a little sheepish. ''I haven't really had time to be curious, Contessa. I'm just grateful you will accept me, whatever your reason.''

''I'm going to tell you, so you'll understand what I expect of you. How little and how much. Now pay attention to what I say. I want to see more than a polite expression on your face. I want to see some movement, some understanding in those beautiful eyes of yours.''

''I assure you, Contessa—''

''No more 'Contessa'—you may call me Zia 'Dela, as Carlotta does.''

''*Mille grazie*, Zia 'Dela.'' Sharif leaned over, picked up the old woman's hand, and lightly grazed the fingers with his lips. ''I will try—''

''I'm sure, I'm sure. . . . *Ecco*—now just listen. I don't know how much Carlotta has told you about me, other than myths about my fierce reputation. No—don't interrupt. A display of temperament is my favorite affectation. I would be disappointed to be told I had failed in this. Years ago, I was different. I was not lovely like Carlotta, but I was a handsome and elegant young woman. And there were several suitable men who wished to marry me. Instead, I chose Leonardo—and made my own Romeo and Juliet story.

''Not that our families hated each other. On the contrary, we were all very good friends. But we were not meant to marry. Our families, you see, were too much alike. We had the same needs—specifically, a great deal of money. My family and the Barzinis, we were what you would call faded aristocrats. We had titles—minor ones, but titles nevertheless. Palazzos and land—you see in what condition. But again, not the shacks of the poor. I was one of two children, and Leonardo—the only surviving son in his family. We were the last chance. So to speak. To bring some money into our families. Good solid banking money. Merchant money. To once more add the luster of gold to our titles. But Leonardo and I fell in love. And married each other.''

She paused, and Sharif sensed that some comment was expected. ''And were you happy?''

''Ah, now that is the essence of what I am trying to tell you. My Leonardo was not a strong man. Not physically or temperamentally. I say that, but I loved him nevertheless.

And I don't deny there were problems in the eight years we were married. But those eight years—before he died—I would not exchange them for anything this world, or the other, has to offer. It is the kind of happiness I want for my Carlotta. In all the years I have lived, I have found nothing to equal those moments that a man and a woman share when they love each other.''

"If that is what you wish," Sharif said, with a fervor that made the old woman smile, "then I can tell that she shall have it as long as we live. But tell me—if I may ask—you never thought of marrying again?"

"I did. Once. Leonardo had been dead for many years. The first shock of grief had passed. It was more difficult to sustain myself with his memory. I was quite lonely. A very fine man proposed. Ironically, he was exactly the kind of man my parents had wanted from the start. Very wealthy, and not noticeably bourgeois. I did not love him. But there seemed to be many empty years ahead."

"What happened?"

"My brother died. My sister-in-law soon after. Carlotta came to live with me. I adopted the child and suddenly the years ahead did not seem so empty."

"I understand."

"Do you? I would be surprised if you did. Young people don't really seem to know how imperfect this world of ours is. Their dreams are so large. And so perfect. But from something Syrie said in her message, I suspect you may soon find some imperfect realities yourself."

"If you mean my parents—yes—I anticipate some difficulties. But I feel that once my father realizes that I mean to marry Carlotta no matter what, they will wish us well."

"I hope with all my heart you are right. But I also hope that you are prepared for the possibility that your love may not bend everything that stands in your way."

"With all due respect, Zia 'Dela, nothing will stop this marriage."

"Good. I think you'll find that Carlotta is not as fragile as she looks. She has the qualities needed to be a strong and resourceful partner."

"For which I must thank you."

"Yes. I suppose you must. And that's enough talk." The woman took two small velvet boxes from her pocket. "When I die, whatever I have will belong to Carlotta. For now, I give you these small things which meant very much to Leonardo and to me.'' She opened the first box to reveal a slender circlet of rose gold exquisitely set with pearls and garnets. ''This was the first gift Leonardo ever gave me. And this,'' she said, indicating a small stickpin set with a single perfect diamond, ''this was my wedding gift to him. I hope you will experience some of the love that surrounded these things.''

Sharif's reunion with his parents began with a deluge of hugs and kisses, a torrent of questions, barely half answered before the next wave began. Then came seemingly endless rounds of food and drink: great brass trays laden with small dishes of *mezza,* the Middle Eastern smorgasbord of hors d'oeuvres; whole roasted lambs and chickens; steaming platters of rice; crisp salads adorned with fresh mint. And then the pastries—miniature mountains of sweets made with tissue-thin dough, filled with nuts and creams and drenched in aromatic sugar syrup perfumed with attar of roses.

Sharif felt like visiting royalty. He was almost overwhelmed by his family's outpouring of love and affection. He appreciated, as he had not when he lived in Egypt, the almost surreal beauty of his native country, the tenderness of its people, the absence of abrasiveness in its daily life, and, most of all, the graciousness of his own home. He had lived in pleasant but modest circumstances in New York, and now he realized how much he had missed the airy and broad-balconied white stucco villa that overlooked the Nile. He took notice, for the first time in years, of its furnishings—an exquisite meld of European antiques and Islamic art—and he looked with fresh eyes at the inlaid tables, the priceless rugs and tapestries, the filigree silver lamps and engraved brass vases, the lush well-tended gardens of jasmine and bougainvillea.

But most of all, he realized how much he had missed his father and mother—their company, as well as the emotional infusion he got from their presence. His father seemed not to have aged much in four years. There was a little more silver in the thick wavy black hair, a slight stoop in the shoulders. His mother seemed virtually unchanged, her hair still done in the familiar raven coils at the neck, her porcelain skin—untouched and unblemished by cosmetics—dusted ever so lightly with fine lines, her figure still trim and immaculate in the simple Paris dresses she had made each year by her French seamstress.

After the reminiscences, the anecdotes, when it was time to sit and talk about the future, whenever Najla's name came up, Sharif adroitly changed the subject—a gesture that was not lost on his mother. But of course the confrontation did come. Amina sat quietly and listened, watched as her son tensed himself. When, for what seemed like the hundredth time, Jamil said, "Now, my son, we must make some plans for your marriage, for your future," Sharif interrupted, "Father—listen to me. I've been trying to tell you. Something has changed . . . something important."

"Of course, of course. You are older now—a man."

"Something else, Father. I've met the woman I want to marry."

Jamil's face was filled with confusion. "Woman? Marry? What are you saying? The woman you will marry is—"

"I can't, Father. I'm sorry, but I can't. I don't love Najla. And I do love someone else—very much. It's unthinkable for me to spend my life with Najla."

The impact of what Sharif was saying began to register, and Jamil began to understand that his son, this favored child who had barely given him a moment's worry, really meant what he was saying. His bewilderment gave way to the first flush of anger. "I will tell you what is unthinkable, and I will tell you only once. In my house it is unthinkable that a son would shame his father by making a liar of him, by breaking an honorable contract made years ago."

"Father, I'm sorry to embarrass you. That wasn't my intention. But surely something honorable can be arranged. Perhaps we could say that Najla refused to marry me, for whatever reason her family chooses to give. Then they wouldn't lose face. And I could postpone my marriage for a decent period—"

"Stop!" Jamil shouted, his ruddy face turning crimson, his eyes blazing. "Do you think people are fools? Najla will be disgraced and humiliated. She may not find another husband. And I—your father—I will be called a liar and a man who cannot command the respect of his children."

"But Father . . ."

"There are no 'buts,' Sharif. I want you to think on this: As far as I am concerned, you will marry Najla Abu-Saif and no one else. We will not discuss this . . . this lapse of yours any further. But if you insist on defying me, then you will leave this house. And I will say that my son is dead, that he has been killed in an accident.''

With this last sentence hanging in the air like a cloud of poison, Jamil abruptly left the room. Sharif sat, silent and dazed. He had expected resistance, perhaps even some shouting, but not this. Not a choice between Carlotta and his family. He had been raised with love and affection and infinite patience. The ties that bound him to his family were as soft as velvet, yet as strong as tempered steel. He felt as one with his parents, especially with his mother, and he could not imagine tearing himself out of their lives. It would be like dismembering a living thing.

Yet the price for staying was beyond his ability to pay. If his father had asked him to give up Carlotta, that would be painful enough. But to be forced to marry another woman, to look at her face instead of Carlotta's—to hold her, to pretend to care for her—it would be like spending his life in a prison constructed of his own lies.

His mother's voice broke into his thoughts. "What is she like, this young woman of yours?"

"She is wonderful, Maman. She is very beautiful, and she makes me so happy. If only you could meet her, I know that you would love her, too."

Amina reached over and brushed her son's hair from his forehead, a gesture she had carried over from his childhood. She understood what he was feeling, perhaps better than he would ever know. "Yes," she said, "I am certain I would love anyone who makes you happy."

"What can I do, Mother?" He looked at her with such pleading in his eyes, like a little boy bringing a hurt to be kissed and made better. And she thought her heart would break because she had no remedy for him. None.

"I cannot tell you, dearest child, my love, my precious. Whatever you choose will bring you some bitterness and some regret. You will have to decide which kind you can live with better. I will talk to your father, but I don't believe there is any hope of changing his mind. He, too, feels he has no easy choices."

"I feel there is no choice at all, Maman. Even if I could never see Carlotta again, I could not marry Najla Abou-Saif. I cannot, Mother, I just cannot." Once again he turned his eyes to her, entreating her understanding.

Amina Hazzi gave her son what it was in her power to

give, although she knew it meant that she might not see him again, might not share any part of his life or hold any of his children in her arms. "If you have the courage to live your life in a foreign land, if you have the strength to leave us behind, then—God forgive me for saying this—then, marry the woman who will make you happy. And know that I will always love you and pray for you, no matter what your father says or does."

Sharif hugged his mother and put his head on her shoulder, as he had done so many times in childhood. "Your father will not leave you any money, but I am not a poor woman. I have a great deal of land and property. For now, I will give you whatever I can convert into cash. And you must choose whatever you like from the house in Alexandria. Everything there belongs to me. I will arrange to have it sent to you at once."

"I couldn't, Mother—I couldn't take money from you."

"You can, and you will. As your father's heir, you would have been a rich man one day. I will not have you living like a beggar. It would kill me to think of you in need, without . . ."

Though her voice cracked with the strain of held-back tears, her head was held high, and he knew that she meant what she said, that she was proud to have this power, the opportunity to help her son, even at the cost of defying her husband.

They sat together for a long time, mother and son, long after the blazing midsummer sun dissolved into a pink and violet ball and was swallowed up in the tranquil blue-gray waters of the Nile. It was as if they were memorizing each other, the features of face, the sound of voice, the texture of skin.

The following morning, Sharif went to a hotel, where he stayed until his mother completed the financial transactions that would give him and his bride a comfortable beginning, a generous cushion against need. "I will send you whatever I can, from time to time," she said, on the day she came to say good-bye. "And when Syrie comes to Egypt or when we meet in Europe, she will tell me how you are—and she will bring you news of me." She handed him an inlaid box filled with bracelets, earrings, brooches, and necklaces. "I want you to take these things. Don't look so sad—they aren't my favorite pieces. Pierre will tell you where you can sell them, where you can get the best price. They will mean much more to me if I know they are helping you."

"Thank you, Mother. Thank you from both of us." He took both her hands and kissed them tenderly. They embraced silently, crying soft tears, taking the last possible moments of warmth from each other.

"Just be happy, *mon petit*, just be happy."

It was the last time he would hear her voice.

3

Sharif had left New York a hopeful young man in love. He returned an exile. He loved his native country, as he had loved his family. Now he would never again take a morning stroll along the banks of the Nile, never hear the muezzin's wailing call to prayer, never inhale the pungent aromas of the old *souk* in Khan Khalili.

The words "never again" were like a lament that haunted his brain and brought tears to his eyes. The memory of Egypt was a constant pain, and he vowed that it would be his alone, that he would not burden Carlotta with it.

"Tell me," she said eagerly, the first time they were together again, "tell me everything. Zia 'Dela—was she well? How did she look? I have been so anxious for you to return."

"Your aunt sends you her love. She is well. What a remarkable woman she is! I can understand why you are so unique and lovely. She has given us her blessing and a wedding gift which I will give you now since you have been so patient in my absence." He took the small silk box from his pocket and placed it tenderly in her hand.

"Oh, Sharif—oh, *caro mio*—this is Zia 'Dela's greatest treasure. Oh, I think I am going to cry. Do you know, this was a gift from Leonardo, her husband?"

"I know, my love. She wanted you to have it. Here"—he brought out another box—"this was her gift to me."

"She must have liked you very much to give you Leonardo's stickpin."

"Of course she did. She saw at once how much I loved you. She welcomed me to the family—and gave me permission to call her Zia 'Dela."

"And your family, my dearest—did you find them all well? What did they say when you told them of our marriage?"

In spite of his resolve to hide the truth from his fiancée, Sharif could not prevent the spasm of pain that crossed his face. He tried to keep his voice light, but the effort made the words sound strained and halting. "My mother wishes us well. She, too, has sent you a gift. She hopes that you will wear it on our wedding day."

"What else, Sharif? There is something else. I can see it. You must tell me."

"There is something, my darling. It has nothing whatever to do with you. My father is . . . displeased with me. He had intended me to marry . . . someone else. The arrangements had been made when we were both children. I didn't want to concern you . . . until the matter was resolved."

"But you were not able to . . . resolve it?"

"No."

"But this is impossible! How can we marry if this will estrange you from your family? I know how much they mean to you. I cannot be the cause of this. I cannot. I love you too much."

"Hush, dear Carlotta. It is finished now. What has been said cannot be unsaid. My family understands we are to be married. And that is what we shall do. Now, I don't wish to discuss anything sad. We must make wedding plans. And we shall have to look for a place to live. And," he concluded, "I suppose I must think about finding work."

"A garden wedding," Syrie was saying. "There will still be roses and geraniums and impatiens. We must hurry before the weather gets too cool—but, yes, I think we can arrange a very lovely wedding. Now tell me, what have you done about a place to live?"

"Nothing yet, Syrie," Sharif answered. "I know we must—"

"Yes, you certainly must. Well, leave it to me. Tomorrow I will begin to find some suitable places, and we can all look together. Is there anything else we have not thought of?"

"There is one thing," Sharif said, hesitating. "I hate to

impose on you any more, but I will need to find work. I
thought perhaps Pierre might direct me—''

"Of course he will direct you," Syrie interrupted, speaking, as she often did, for her husband. "He has many friends
in business. For that matter, I'm certain Pierre would be
happy to offer you a position with his firm. Wouldn't you,
dear?''

"Yes, that would be possible. The shipping business is
growing very rapidly in this country, and I would be very
pleased to have Sharif work with me. But I don't know if he
would enjoy the work. It suits me very well because I enjoy
the accumulation of money and the various crises that arise. I
don't mind the long hours—my Syrie seems to amuse herself
quite well in my absence. But for newlyweds, well . . .''

This was one of Pierre's longer speeches, and it was followed by a respectful silence.

"Pierre is right, as usual," Syrie said. "Perhaps something
else . . . you children are both so beautiful, you know and
appreciate beautiful things. And you are not without means.
A commercial venture—perhaps the buying and selling of
antiques and objets d'art. With your wonderful taste, your
elegance—and of course, you speak several languages—I
think you will do very well.''

Sharif and Carlotta looked at each other. In another time or
other circumstances, neither of them would have thought of
trade as a way of sustaining life. Sharif would have managed
his father's properties, seen to the breeding of Arabian horses
in the family stables. He would have been called upon to do
nothing more strenuous than riding with friends at the Cairo
Horse Riding Club or engaging in repartee at the glittering balls
of the Egyptian court. Carlotta might have been courted by
dukes, painted by classic artists, while she played the piano
or worked a fine needlepoint. Now they were both strangers
in a foreign country, far from impoverished, but also far from
the cushioning class structures of their native environments.

Carlotta had not been raised in the affluence that Sharif had
known all his life. She had seen her aunt struggle to live
without selling her pride. Now she watched her young fiancé
as he turned over the idea of buying and selling things. She
guessed that for him the notion was somewhat distasteful.

"*Ecoutez, mes enfants,*" said Syrie, who had also guessed
Sharif's thoughts. "What I am suggesting is not the same as
keeping a shop in Cairo or Rome. I am proposing something

very elegant, very refined—something which you both are well suited for. And if it is not quite upper-upper class, well, let me be blunt. Here in America, there are two kinds of society: the Brahmin blue blood—for these people you will always be far too exotic—and the society of wealth—here is where you will mix well, and here is where a shop will never be held against you, if you earn enough money. Money, *chers petits*, will make you *comme il faut*."

She saw Sharif's expression change, his attitude become more attentive. "The first thing you will need," she continued, "is a good location. That is very important. I think Pierre can help us there. Will you, my dear?"

"Yes, of course, I have friends with properties in the city. And I believe I can also be of assistance in locating living quarters."

"Wonderful," Syrie said. "Something charming, my love—that is important. And a good neighborhood. Not very costly. But—well, never mind, *chéri*, I leave the details to you. Now, we have certainly done enough work for today. And Pierre has promised to take us all to the theater. He tells me the *Ziegfeld Follies* is very amusing this season, but I think my husband simply enjoys looking at young ladies with very long legs and very short costumes."

Within a few days Pierre had assembled a list of locations for the prospective gallery. In his methodical way, he explained the advantages and disadvantages of each as Sharif and Carlotta listened respectfully and Syrie tapped her foot.

Pierre smiled. "I can see that my lovely wife is growing impatient. So I will tell you that the location which I recommend to you is an empty shop of medium size. It adjoins a fine tailoring and dressmaking establishment in the Gramercy Park area. The rent is quite reasonable, and the owner is a friend of mine. I think I can persuade him to make the initial lease even more attractive, with a provision for a higher rent, say, in two years. By then, you will know if everything is going well—"

"Of course things will go well," Syrie interrupted. "Please, Pierre, let us not discourage the children with 'ifs.'"

Pierre smiled again. "Syrie, my love, the best way to ensure that things go well is to anticipate what things might go wrong. I have no wish to discourage Sharif and Carlotta—I only want to give them the benefit of my experience."

"You are right, as usual. Please go on."

"Well, first of all, Gramercy Park is quite a solid neighborhood. It is young by European standards. In fact, less than a hundred years ago, that lovely park and all the houses around the square were nothing but a festering swamp. A very clever gentleman bought the land with an eye to creating a very exclusive, very chic residential neighborhood. Later, a number of artistic people—not bohemians, mind you—settled there, without changing the character of the neighborhood. It is very respectable, very solid—the kind of place I should choose if I were starting a business like yours.

"But the most important advantage of this particular location is the quality of the clientele of the tailor who would be next door to you. These people are all very well off, precisely the sort of customers you will hope to attract. You will quickly capture their attention with an attractive window display."

Syrie jumped up from her chair and ran to plant a very loud kiss on her husband's cheek. "Brilliant! This man is brilliant. Am I not the luckiest woman in the world? Well, then, since you have found the perfect place, we must see it. Can we go now, Pierre?"

"If you wish. I'll have Roger bring the car."

At first glance, the empty shop was not terribly impressive. Carlotta thought it dark and narrow, but she waited for her fiancé to say something. "Well . . ." murmured the fastidious Sharif, who was repelled by the dust and cobwebs.

Determined not to begin on a gloomy note, Syrie took charge. "Look," she exclaimed. "Look at the potential we have here. Of course, we must have the shop cleaned and painted. But look, we don't have too much harsh sunlight—perfect, because we can create a wonderful ambience with electrical lights—some of those lovely pieces by Mr. Louis Tiffany. And see—the dimensions are very intimate, so the gallery will not look like a commercial establishment. We can create the illusion of a gracious drawing room. Here—we can get a carpenter from one of Pierre's warehouses to install a *faux* fireplace . . . a brilliant chandelier in the center . . . and at the far end, perhaps a dining table covered with fine linen. I will lend you my Alençon lace, if you promise not to sell it. Oh, my dears, it will be *merveilleux, n'est ce pas?*"

Carlotta and Sharif nodded in unison as they tried to follow

Syrie's recitation, to keep up with the picture she had been painting.

"Well, then," Sharif said, "if this is where we are to begin, perhaps Pierre will draw up the necessary papers for us."

"Certainly, dear boy. Now we can return home and talk a little further, over some sherry."

"Please, Pierre," Carlotta said. "You and Syrie go on. I think Sharif and I will stay awhile. And then tomorrow we must begin looking for a place to live."

When they were alone, Carlotta took Sharif's hand. "What is it, *caro mio*? I feel that you are not altogether pleased with these plans we are making. If you don't like this place, we can ask Pierre to find another."

He shook his head. "It all seems so . . . so sordid. This place . . . it's so small and dreary. And the idea of a shop . . . No matter what Syrie says, the idea of selling things— like a barefoot merchant in the bazaar—I don't know if I can do it. I just don't know. . . ."

"I understand, *tesoro*," she said. And she did. Carlotta knew that Sharif had not been tested before, not where his pride and self-esteem were concerned. Men of his class were born to be better than those around them. They learned in a thousand spoken and unspoken ways, from the moment they were born, that they were part of a privileged order. Now, because he had met and loved her, he had left behind the amenities of rank and privilege. And although he had expressed only his indignation, Carlotta knew that he was also afraid. "Listen to me, *amore*. I know you think that Syrie is only trying to be kind to us. But she is right, I think. This can be an adventure for us—something we can do together. The shop is very ugly, it's true. But it can be made beautiful. We can do it together. And I can be with you all day. I won't have to kiss you good-bye in the morning and wait for you to return in the evening. We are going to make a great deal of money, and," she finished triumphantly, "we are going to do it together."

He looked at her with something like horror. "You are not telling me that you intend to work at this . . . this shop with me? It will be difficult enough for me, but to bring you here, to allow you to be spoken to by all kinds of people . . . it's unthinkable!"

"It is not unthinkable," she said quietly, but firmly. "I

know that sort of thing is not done in Cairo. But we are in America, *caro*. Customs are different here. Why, they even say that women will soon have the vote. I want to be close to you in whatever you do. You are my family—I have no one else. There is one more thing—one very important thing you must remember," she added, teasing now, trying to lighten the argument she knew she must win.

"What is that?"

"I have no friends here, no one but Syrie, and nothing in particular to do. If you leave me at home all day, I shall eat kilos of marzipan and grow very, very fat." She puffed up her cheeks and held her breath until he laughed. "You must let me do this. Zia 'Dela would agree, I know. She is a very practical woman. At least you must let me try. And then," she said, lowering her eyes, "later, when we have some babies, then I will have something to do at home."

He drew her to him and held her quietly. He knew he would agree, not because her arguments were so convincing, but because it was difficult to refuse her—and because he was afraid, and he sensed that he could draw from her the strength to resist that fear.

"What shall we call it, this enterprise of ours?" he whispered against her ear.

"I shall leave that decision to you, *tesoro*."

"If it were a ship, I would name it after you—the S.S. *Carlotta*. But I could not put your lovely name on a shop."

"Then we must think of something secret, something only the two of us would understand."

"I have it. What about Principessa Gallery, in honor of my own *principessa*? No, actually you are my queen, the queen of my heart, but we don't wish to appear grandiose, do we, my love? Especially in such cramped quarters?"

"No," she laughed. "I think you are right. Principessa will be sufficiently elegant for our gallery. And you'll see, it will be wonderful. Because we will be together."

"Well, what do you think, children?" Syrie asked as they stepped from the elevator of the massive châteaulike building on the west side of Central Park.

"It is so modern," Carlotta said. "The bathrooms are so grand, and that device in the kitchen—what was it called? A dumbwaiter? I think it would be very simple to keep house here."

"And you, Sharif? Does it suit you?"

"If Carlotta likes the apartment, then it will be fine. But there is something . . . I don't know . . . the neighborhood seems a little . . . underdeveloped."

Syrie laughed. "Perhaps you are right. They called this building the Dakota because it was so isolated when it was built. Well, if you are not completely satisfied, I have saved my best until last. Dear Pierre has been so helpful. There is a building that is owned by yet another of his friends. The old gentleman who owned it previously lived in the very apartment we are going to see. And the neighborhood—my dears, it is one of my favorites.

"We are going to Greenwich Village," she told Roger, who had been napping behind the wheel of the auto. "Some years ago, this was the most affluent area in all of New York. It is now very much favored by artists and writers. I think you will find it amusing—a little bohemian, but very comfortable."

As the car passed Fourteenth Street, Syrie said: "Some of your favorite American writers have lived just a few streets away, Sharif—Mr. Mark Twain and Mr. Bret Harte, and that Arab artist, the one who writes poetry—Kahlil Gibran—he lives in a studio on Tenth Street, not far from the building I'm going to show you. I should also point out that this building is only a short distance from the location we have chosen for your gallery."

"Ah, here we are—stop the car, Roger." The three passengers left the car and walked up the steps of a ten-story building with a classical facade on Fifth Avenue. "A distinguished structure, is it not? Pierre tells me it was built by a Mr. Stanford White—a fine architect. There was a *scandale* surrounding his death." She dropped her voice and rolled her eyes in a manner that did not exactly indicate disapproval. "Something about another gentleman's wife. But look here." She pointed to the massive brass doors. "These were brought from Italy, as was the marble of the lobby. Very baronial, don't you think?

"Take us to the top floor," she instructed the liveried elevator operator.

As they left the elevator, Syrie produced the key to Penthouse A and admitted the couple with a flourish. "You will notice," she said, "that there is only one other apartment on this floor, so you would have a great deal of privacy. *Voila!* What do you think?''

Carlotta caught her breath. ''Oh, Syrie,'' she said, ''there is so much light, so many windows.''

''Yes. I'm told the old man was very fond of the outdoors. Come,'' she said, leading them through the enormous living room, with its ornate moldings and dazzling crystal chandeliers, straight to a pair of broad leaded glass doors that led to a vast terrace. ''There you are—a garden in the sky!''

And for once Syrie was not exaggerating. Neglected and overgrown though it was, the terrace garden was still very impressive—obviously tended once by expert hands. On the curlicued brass railings grew English ivy, which seemed to enclose and shelter the evergreens and the apple trees growing from elaborate stone tubs that lined the red tile floor. To one side was a white lattice arbor, where the last roses of summer bloomed, red and gold and pink and white. And off in one far corner was a cupid with bow and arrow, captured in mid-flight, a mischievous smile upon his face—a stonecutter's fantasy that made Sharif and Carlotta smile.

''Now,'' Syrie said, ''I must show you the other rooms.'' And she did, pointing out the graceful proportions of the formal dining room, the floors of costly parquet—each in a different design—the carved marble fireplaces in each of the main rooms, the spacious kitchen with its floor-to-ceiling cupboards, and the equally large adjoining butler's pantry. ''This is very modern, very convenient,'' she said. ''And there are four baths, one for each of the bedrooms. You will not need so many now, but later, perhaps.'' She nudged Sharif, so he would not miss her meaning.

''It's very nice,'' he said.

''It's wonderful,'' Carlotta said. ''But,'' she hesitated, her common sense tempering her pleasure in what seemed to her an idyllic place to begin married life, ''this may be too costly for us.''

''Nonsense,'' Syrie said. ''Leave the details to Pierre.'' She waved airily, confident in her husband's abilities to make everything manageable. ''If you like this apartment, then you shall have it. And now that you have a place to live, let us stop for refreshments.''

Outside, she instructed Roger to take them to Hegeman's Drug Store.

"A drugstore, Syrie?" Sharif asked. "Are we to refresh ourselves with some mysterious potion, then?"

"Oh, *la*, you are always so quick with the questions. Well, if you must know, I am going to introduce Carlotta to my favorite American confection—the ice cream soda."

When they arrived at the drugstore, Syrie led her party directly to the soda fountain—an ornate wonder with an onyx counter topped with a pierced brass pagoda supported by four marble Corinthian columns. "This looks like an oriental seraglio," Sharif said, laughing. "Really, Syrie, where do you find all these places?"

"I find these places," she said indignantly, "because I have a lively curiosity about the city in which I live. And you should, too, if you're going to become authentic New Yorkers. Do you know," she began, "how many of these soda fountains have been built in the past ten years? According to a newspaper story which I read . . ."

— **4** —

The garden wedding ceremony was brief and simple, performed by a young priest from St. Patrick's. Carlotta was beautiful in her white silk organza dress with long sleeves and a high neck, bordered in handmade lace. Her blond hair, which was piled high on her head, was covered by a flowing veil the texture of fine cobwebs, which fell in graceful folds to the hem of her dress.

When she saw her groom, slender and elegant in his gray morning dress, the intensely loving expression on his face as he tried to find her eyes beyond the bridal veil, she whispered a prayer to the Madonna, thanking her for the blessing of a husband she adored.

As the midwife to this match, Syrie watched the couple anxiously, knowing that the day must be a bittersweet one, particularly for Sharif, who had grown up surrounded by a loving family. She had kept the festivities to a minimum, inviting a few friends, people who could contribute to the illusion of a happy atmosphere.

After the couple had been toasted with French champagne, after they had danced together to the romantic music of a string quartet, Syrie told Sharif that her chauffeur would drive them to their new home whenever they were ready. When she saw the expression of relief on his face, she was glad that she had restrained her own preference for large, noisy parties.

As Sharif and Carlotta stepped out of the walnut-paneled elevator and walked the few steps to their new home, they saw, leaning against the door, a clumsily arranged bouquet of chrysanthemums sitting precariously in a glass jar and decorated with ribbons and tissue paper. On it there was a small card, painfully lettered, as if by a small child, spelling out the words "Good Luck And Happiness."

Mystified, since they knew very few people other than the Rubichous, Carlotta picked up the flowers. "For luck," she laughed. "It's a wonderful omen, but who could have brought them?"

"I don't know, my dear, but I gratefully accept the sentiment. Though I don't think I need any more luck than I have right now." He picked up his new bride, feeling a fierce sense of pride in her Botticelli beauty, a rush of gratitude that she had entrusted to him her life and her future.

"Careful, *carissimo*," she cautioned, laughing as he swung her across the threshold, then whirled her around and around. She tightened her arms about his neck, then looked deep into the gray eyes that could sparkle like tourmaline—or smolder like autumn smoke.

"Welcome home, *amore*," he murmured against her neck, as he set her down gently on the antique prayer rug that now covered the floor of the entrance gallery.

"You are my home now," she whispered, taking his hand and leading him through the living room and out to the terrace. The October air was cool and pleasant, the fading sun just slightly frosted with the suggestion of autumn.

They had been man and wife just a few hours, but at this moment they both felt as if they had been together since time immemorial, as if life had just begun for them.

"I wish I had the words to tell you," Sharif said to his new bride.

"I know," she answered. "I know, my love."

"Well, then, you must tell me how you feel, Madame Hazzi. Are you having any second thoughts about making such an undistinguished match? Marrying a poor expatriate Egyptian? After all, such a beauty as you deserves a king, or at least a prince."

Carlotta laughed, a musical sound that always made Sharif think of delicate crystal. "*Che cosa dici?* Why do you say such silly things? We are not at all poor. Just look at this splendid apartment and all the wonderful things we have in it." She waved her hand to take in the exotic mélange of East and West that made up the furnishings of their new home: the savonnerie carpet that had come from her mother-in-law's bedroom, the familiar armoire that had sat forever in Zia Adela's palazzo, all the wondrously crafted bits and pieces of seasoned wood, of polished brass, and faded tapestry that made up their joint heritage. "Was it not wonderful of Pierre to ship all these things for us? And so quickly! Syrie tells me it usually takes months to bring anything from such distances, but, for us, he has made a miracle!"

"Yes, I know. We owe Pierre and Syrie so much. But I am already looking at everything I need. Yet for you, I feel there must be more. Why, I'm not even giving you a proper honeymoon."

Carlotta sighed with mock impatience. "We have already discussed this, my love. I thought we had agreed. It's foolish to waste money on travel right now. We have years and years ahead of us. And there is so much to do now. In *tutti i casi,* we have no need to visit strange new places, *adorato*—we have each other to discover." She looked at him with such intensity that her eyes seemed to take on the color of precious emeralds, just as they had the first moment he had seen her.

"So wise—and so beautiful," he whispered. "No wonder I was bewitched." He pulled her close, feeling himself tremble. This was the first time he had held her like this, knowing she was his, confident that no one could interfere or disapprove. She pulled back slightly, flushed with what he thought was embarrassment, and they both stood still for a moment, self-conscious in their newlywed status.

Sharif realized that for all her womanly airs, her perfectly formed body, Carlotta was still, in some ways, probably a child, a girl who had spent many of her eighteen years in a convent school. He did not want to spoil their first days of marriage with his overeagerness. He tried to establish a new mood, for although Sharif was also young in years, he was remarkably sensitive.

"Come, my dear," he said, "if we're not going to have a proper honeymoon, at least we shall have a fine wedding supper—unless Delmonico's has failed us." He led her into the dining room, where a waiter from the Fifth Avenue restaurant had earlier laid out a light supper on the massive refectory table. It was a simple but elegant meal of cold chicken, garden salad, cheese, and apple tart. Off to the side, in a silver bucket, a bottle of Dom Perignon reclined invitingly, chilled to a delightfully drinkable temperature.

Sharif lit the tall white tapers that stood in their handmade silver holders, adorning the Venetian lace cloth that covered the table. He popped the cork on the bottle and poured the sparkling wine into two crystal glasses. "To you, my wife," he toasted, raising his glass. "*Solo tu . . . così lungo come viverò.*"

Carlotta smiled. She loved to hear Sharif's Italian. He spoke it with such a fluid charm, as he did all the languages in his repertoire. She raised her glass in response. "To you, my husband, *mi sposo.*"

Sharif was not really hungry, not for anything but his bride, but he put on a convincing display of relishing his meal. "Excellent chicken," he said. "Do you remember, my dear, the first meal we shared together? I could hardly do justice to Syrie's holiday table, when all I wanted to do was look at you."

"Really? All I can remember of that night was thinking that you were surely the most handsome man I had ever seen, and that my heart would break if I didn't see you again."

"No! Did you really think that?" He sparkled with pleasure. "And to think I almost didn't come to Syrie's party."

"What a horrible thought." Her delicate heart-shaped face grew somber. "I have often wondered what would have happened if I had come to Syrie's a few months later, after you had gone back to Cairo. I think I would have gone to my grave without marriage."

"I don't believe you, my sweet, not for a moment. But thank you for saying that. And you have reminded me—we must toast Syrie Rubichou, our patron saint and guardian angel."

"Oh, yes, yes she was." Carlotta giggled, remembering girlish conspiracies, romantic intrigues, all lightly cloaked with the prevailing customs of good manners and good taste. "You never knew it, *caro*," she confessed, a smile dimpling her face, "but after you started coming to call, she was always trying to arrange 'accidental' moments when we could be alone."

Sharif laughed, dropping the chicken leg he had been chewing. "Well I'll be damned—*scusami, cara*—but here I believed it was my Eastern cunning and charm that were responsible for those bits of freedom from Syrie's supervision!"

"It doesn't really matter, does it? Really, it has all been a miracle, from the first moment we met until now. Everything except . . ." She stopped and her face grew sad. "If only . . . Oh, if only . . ."

"Hush," he said, getting up from his chair and rushing to take her in his arms. "We are never going to discuss 'if only.' Never. I absolutely forbid it. You said yourself—we have so much, and we will not spoil it by looking back at what we cannot have."

"But it's not for me I feel so sad. I've lost nothing, and I can't help thinking how much this marriage has cost you."

"For the last time, my love, I am going to tell you that for me, the price is—manageable. It wasn't your fault, but after I had seen you, it was simply not possible for me to marry anyone else." He looked down on his bride, her head resting against his chest, her eyes looking up at him with an expression that was part gratitude, part adoration. As he bent to kiss her neck, her ears, he began to pull the pins from the luxuriously thick topknot in which she bound her hair.

"Wait," she said, then took his hand and led him into their bedroom. She sat him down on the eiderdown quilt that covered the feather mattresses of the Venetian canopied bed— the same rose-hued, gold-leafed bed that had sheltered Carlotta's parents and her grandparents before them.

Sharif had planned to be gentle and tender and patient with his convent-school bride. What he had not been prepared for was the little gamine who began directing their wedding night with a mixture of shyness and mischief—and insinuations of a desire that threatened to match his. He watched with surprise and a little apprehension as she loosened her hair till it fell past her shoulders, halfway to her waist, then slowly and deliberately unfastened each of the score of tiny pearl buttons that bound her embroidered silk blouse. Next, she undid her skirt, beginning with the small metal snaps that held the delicately pleated waistband which circled her diminutive waist.

Once undone, the yards of silk organza whispered past her legs, down to the floor. Daintily, she stepped out of the soft heap of fabric. Quite unexpectedly, Sharif felt his eyes fill, as she stood before him, in the best of the hand-stitched chemises she had made in the convent. She took his face in her hands and whispered, "*Marito Mi*, my love," then kissed him full on the lips, lightly at first, her touch as delicate as flower petals, then with passion, her mouth soft and strong at the same time, returning the pressure of his kiss, her lips opening hungrily against his. He picked her up and laid her head on the down pillows while he loosened his tie and undid his collar and studs. As he removed his clothing piece by piece, Carlotta sighed deeply, a sound of complete and utter contentment.

Later, Sharif lay awake, looking at his sleeping wife, thinking what a miracle it was that she belonged to him, this wonder of innocence and full-bodied sexuality, this child who had almost overwhelmed him with her passion.

Like most men of his time, he had expected to marry a virgin. But he had believed this innocence would come at a price. He had expected to treat his wife with restraint, with less enthusiasm than he usually displayed with professional women, in whose beds he had learned about sex.

Instead, Carlotta's ardor had taken his breath away, delighted him. He thought that if they both lived to be a hundred years old, she would never fail to enchant him with the unexpected.

5

The following afternoon, after Sharif had gone to Pierre's office for some financial advice, a gentle tapping brought Carlotta to the door. On the other side, she found a slender, dark woman, about twenty or so, with enormous black eyes set against olive skin and masses of curly black hair, unsuccessfully restrained by hairpins and combs. A happy woman,

Carlotta concluded, in one of her characteristic snap judgments, as she took in the almost palpable effervescence that surrounded Rachel Levine.

"Hello, missus," the visitor introduced herself. "I'm your neighbor from down the hall." She inclined her head in the direction of the only other apartment on their floor. "Mrs. Simon Levine," she explained, with a grave formality that showed how seriously she took her marital status. "I wanted to say 'welcome,' and ask if you needed anything."

"How do you do," said Carlotta, with an awkward formality, because she did not quite know what to say. Then, as she noted her neighbor's heavily accented English, the careful speech, she had a flash of comprehension. "The flowers—you left them?"

"Oh, yes! Did you like them? I wanted to bring maybe a nice chicken, some sponge cake, but Simon—Mr. Levine—he says, 'Rachel, don't be pushy'—Rachel, that's me—he thinks I'm pushy—but that's because he's so quiet. I don't like to go against him, so I said—" Here she took a breath, and Carlotta wondered how anyone could say so many words at once without stopping for air. "So a few flowers, I said—how could that be pushy?"

Not knowing what to say after this Niagara of words and accompanying gestures, Carlotta asked, "Would you like to come in?"

This was clearly what Rachel had hoped for. "Oh yes, yes indeed I would. But just for a while. Simon says you are newlyweds, so I won't stay more than a little minute."

Rachel's "little minute"—the first of many such visits—stretched into two hours. First she exclaimed over every piece of furniture, every bibelot, recognizing in them an elegance she had never seen in the homes of people she knew. Then she somehow moved directly into the story of her life, explaining to Carlotta how she had come from Russia when she was just eight years old, how she had met Simon in the hallway of the East Side tenement where they had both lived for a time, how she had loved him from the start, and how all her prayers had been answered when he had proposed eleven years later.

"He makes a nice living now," she added, with uncharacteristic understatement. Rachel was usually extravagant in her retelling of Simon's incredible success, of the ambition and drive and incredible luck that had taken him from master tailor and pushcart entrepreneur to the ownership of factories producing a better-than-average line of women's ready-to-wear. Perhaps she sensed that Carlotta belonged to a different world from the one into which she had been born, the one from which Simon had worked so desperately hard to escape, thus earning her gratitude as well as her love.

Rachel seemed to feel that Carlotta was what she would describe as "a real lady," one who would not be impressed by her favorite litany of accomplishments, the harrowing tales that told of impossible dreams winning over equally impossible odds. She allowed herself: "Simon has worked very hard to be where he is now," well aware that "where he is now" was a place occupied by Carlotta and her husband with no apparent effort at all.

In return for all this information, Rachel extracted from Carlotta, with a skill and perserverance that would have been the envy of a professional interrogator, the news that she was an orphan, that she and Sharif had also fallen in love "at first sight," that they had been married under less than ideal circumstances, that consequently they had begun their married life more or less alone.

In Carlotta's story, Rachel saw a series of remarkable similarities to her own. Perhaps it was the motif of aloneness. She declared dramatically—this may have been the result of two glasses of sherry—that destiny had brought them together, that clearly they were meant to be lifelong friends.

Somewhat alarmed by Rachel's irrepressible personality, Carlotta cast a rather unsubtle glance at the ormolu clock on the piano.

Instantly, Rachel responded. "Oy, look what I've done," she lamented, clapping her palm to her forehead. "Simon would kill me. He said, 'Rachel, don't be pushy with the newlyweds.' Now look what a long time I stayed."

Before Carlotta could supply a polite disclaimer, Rachel plunged on, "Never mind, darling. I'm leaving. But you come for a real visit, you promise? Me, I'm always home with my bee-yootiful baby, my little Robert—isn't that a nice American name? Only three years old and already he talks like a professor. So you promise you'll come?"

Carlotta, who had been nodding vigorously during this last verbal onslaught, steered Rachel to the door, promising to visit soon. After she heard the heavy door down the hall open and close, she allowed herself a long and heartfelt laugh. Yes, she thought to herself, Rachel Levine was a most interesting neighbor. Kind and generous and sensitive. But whether she would enjoy living so close to such relentless energy, well—that she would have to see.

Although Sharif and Carlotta were almost all alone in the city, the days following their marriage passed quickly, swallowed up by the myriad of practical details accompanying the opening of Principessa. And although Sharif had protested his wife's working, he was secretly glad she had insisted. The days spent with her were less lonely than they might have been without her. And her practicality, for which he constantly blessed Zia 'Dela, kept him from making certain mistakes. He was accustomed to plenty, while she had learned how to shepherd limited resources and to make little seem like much.

Pierre had arranged for the shipping of dozens of massive crates of furniture and bric-a-brac from Sharif's mother and Carlotta's aunt. He had also arranged for Sharif to have direct access to a friend of his, a Parisian banker who involved himself in the discreet disposition of personal valuables for distressed members of European society. At Pierre's suggestion, the banker gave Sharif introductions to a number of middlemen who rendered similar services in London and Rome and Vienna.

Pierre also promised to supply the young couple with a mailing list of his wealthiest and most influential clients.

But it was Syrie who came up with a plan for making certain that Principessa's opening would be adorned with the luster of high society. "*Ecoute,* Carlotta," she said. "There is someone who may be a great help to you. If you agree, I shall invite her to my home, introduce you, and leave you to charm her."

"Of course, Syrie. I am always ready to take your advice. But who is this lady?"

"Her name is Marina Vanderbeck. She is quite elderly, a widow. Her husband did not leave her much except his very distinguished name and the most superb social connections. So this very clever lady makes her way in this world by selling these connections—though, of course, it is never referred to in that way—to those who do not have them. For example, if a young lady of a good bourgeois family wishes to make a debut in society, Mrs. Vanderbeck will arrange it, for a fee. If some elegant names are needed for a second-rate ball or a not-so-chic charity, Mrs. Vanderbeck can also be of service.''

"But this is perfect for us, Syrie. I think the resourceful Mrs. Vanderbeck will be a fine investment for us.''

"Yes, I thought so. But a word of caution, *chérie*. In spite of her limited means, Mrs. Vanderbeck will not work for just anyone. She still has a great deal of pride. And if a wealthy merchant makes the mistake of treating her without the respect she requires, as if she were one of his employees, why, then, that is the last he will see of her. *Tu comprends?*''

"*Mais oui,* Syrie. I think perhaps this Mrs. Vanderbeck is very much like Zia 'Dela. I think we shall understand each other very well.''

"*Bon.* Then I shall arrange a meeting as soon as possible.''

Marina Vanderbeck was genuinely charmed by Carlotta, for she recognized that the beautiful young woman was, unlike so many of her other clients, "one of us," an authentic aristocrat, albeit one produced by a foreign culture. The young woman treated Marina with such courtesy, such genuine appreciation, that a bargain was quickly struck. For a fee that Carlotta considered quite reasonable, Marina would deliver at least a dozen, possibly more, genuine blue bloods to the champagne celebration that would mark Principessa's opening.

Over tea and biscuits, Carlotta offered Marina still another proposition—a discreet bonus each time one of her contacts made a purchase or turned over an unwanted piece of furniture or jewelry for sale. In this way, Carlotta forged a long-term alliance with Marina Vanderbeck, giving the woman a vested interest in Principessa's success.

With this final piece of business out of the way, Carlotta turned her attention to the addressing of invitations, in the fine calligraphy she had been taught by the nuns, on heavy bond paper—invitations to partake of champagne and view the treasures of Principessa Gallery, on January 10, 1912, at 5:00 P.M.

The debut of Principessa was a glittering success. Mrs. Vanderbeck outdid herself. A sizable contingent of the rich and near-rich turned up to consume Sharif's champagne, to nibble delicately at Carlotta's robust pâté, and to express at least a polite interest in the choicest pieces artfully arranged within the gallery's silk-covered walls.

Diligently, Carlotta mingled with the guests, smiling and nodding and straining to overhear bits of conversations. "Rather charming, this little place, don't you think?" "Yes, really, and the owners seem so accommodating—and quite knowledgeable." "Much more personal than the larger places." "Quite—when my fellow left Parke-Bernet, I had the devil of a time finding anyone who would look after me properly." "I quite understand. And some of the pieces here are rather unusual, don't you agree? Not like the ordinary gallery stuff." "Pity some of the best things are sold already—strange they should have gone before the opening."

Unknown to the chattering guests, the "sold" tags that dotted the merchandise were also part of Carlotta's selling strategy. In the years to come, Sharif would joke that he provided the broad back while Carlotta contributed the brain in their business.

Just two days before Principessa's opening, Carlotta had decided something was needed to put the imprimatur of success on the gallery, no matter how its first customers reacted. She returned to the apartment with Sharif and ran through the rooms. "Here," she said, pointing to her favorite armoire, a massive and rare example of classic Venetian cabinetwork. "Take this to the gallery. And this"—indicating a museum-quality tapestry that had been a gift from Sharif's mother. "This—and this—and this." She had made a complete circuit of their apartment, picking out their finest and most treasured possessions. "All these." She turned to Sharif. "We must call the movers and have them take these to the gallery at once."

"But you're not serious?" He was incredulous that she would consider parting with the only tangible relics of their joint heritage. "We can't sell these things!"

"Of course not," she said, laughing. "We're not going to sell any of them. But these are much better than anything we have in the shop. We will display them with very small cards that say 'sold.' That will show that we are already very chic, very prosperous. We will say that several customers requested private viewings and that they purchased those pieces. What do you think, *chéri?*"

"I think you are as devious as you are adorable, and I think I am the luckiest of men, though now I'm certain you have a

Borgia or two tucked away in your family tree. It's a brilliant
idea. We cannot fail.''

Carlotta's idea was indeed a good one, and it seemed, at
least from first reactions, that they would not fail. There were
many among their first guests who recognized that Sharif and
Carlotta offered something special, merchandise that was more
interesting than expensive. They were impressed by the gallery's size, which indicated exclusivity, and by the prospect
of discretion and personal service. If they were disappointed
by the ''sold'' cards that eliminated the gallery's best pieces,
they found the second-best interesting enough.

After the last bit of pâté had disappeared, the last champagne cork had been popped, and the last guest graciously
ushered out, Carlotta and Sharif toasted each other, confident
that they had no reason to fear the future.

Once the shop had been locked, they stepped out into the
cool early night air, and into the shiny Buick that Sharif had
bought the week before. ''I still don't know if I can accustom
myself to these American machines,'' Carlotta complained,
as she arranged the skirt of her beige silk suit over her half of
the front seat. As she secured her hat and veil over her
carefully arranged hair, she looked the picture of American
fashion, but in truth she did not share her husband's passion
for American automobiles. ''And such an extravagance,'' she
teased. ''Here we have so many expenses and you buy a
costly new toy.''

''It wasn't so costly,'' he said. ''In fact, it's one of the
cheapest models available. It didn't even cost a quarter of
what Pierre paid for his.''

She remembered his admiration of Pierre's car and realized
how much he wanted one like it—and how difficult the
practice of even minor economies was for a man like him.
She stroked his cheek and said, ''Well, then, one day you
will buy a car that is even better than Pierre's.''

When they got home Sharif and Carlotta once more found
an offering from Rachel Levine laid at their door. This time it
was a bottle of champagne, beribboned in red, white, and blue,
and accompanied by a childlike drawing of a horseshoe, with
the message: ''Congratulations and Good Luck.''

''Oh look, Sharif, *guarda quisti—que gentile.* Come, *caro,*
let us knock on their door and share a toast with Rachel and
Simon.''

''*Ma perche bella*, it is late—we are so tired. Another

time." In truth, it was not very late, nor was Sharif very tired. But while he appreciated the fact that Carlotta, in spite of her early reservations, had found a devoted friend in Rachel, he always found himself somewhat uncomfortable in the company of Rachel's husband. No matter how hard Sharif tried to make small talk, no matter how many clever anecdotes he offered his neighbor, the atmosphere between them remained as serious and somber as the three-piece suits the man wore every day, regardless of temperature or season.

By his fine nose and broad forehead, his well-barbered beard and carefully brushed hair, not to mention his heavy gold watch and chain, Simon Levine appeared to be a judge, a banker, a scholar—someone refined and distinguished. But when he spoke, the illusion was dispelled. Try as he had for years, he could not completely lose the speech of the unlettered immigrant. The greenhorn he had been kept getting in the way of the gentleman he had hoped to become. As a result, Simon Levine said very little in the company of people he did not know well, of people he hoped to impress. Thus he gained a reputation as a man of few words, a man who measured his speech and wasted no time in idle chatter, a deep man with no sense of humor.

Sharif conceded that the man was probably a good fellow. He was considerate of his wife and doted on his son. But he was so damned quiet. It was unnatural, thought Sharif, whose own home had rung with the sound of jokes and laughter and spirited debate. Though Sharif occasionally thought he could hear a pealing laugh, then a baritone counterpoint, coming from the apartment down the hall, he found it hard to connect this sound with his somber and serious neighbor. Simon's eyes rarely betrayed a sparkle of happiness, unless he was looking at his wife or son. No, he was not the sort that Sharif could be friends with. Sharif did not like to work hard at getting to know someone, and Simon Levine did not inspire in him a desire to make the effort.

Still, Carlotta was fond of Rachel, and if it was necessary for him to suffer occasional discomfort so she might have this friendship, then he would do it. So when Carlotta turned on him the full force of those green eyes, stuck out her lower lip ever so slightly, and said in a small voice, "Please, *caro mio*—just one small drink?" he shrugged his shoulders in a gesture of acquiescence. "Of course, my love, if that is what you want."

When the door to the Levine apartment opened, Rachel gave a cry of delight and threw her arms around Carlotta. "*Mazel tov, mazel tov!* So now you are officially open for business? Come in, come in, and tell me all about the fancy party."

"All right, all right, thank you for the champagne. We'll share it together, and then I'll tell you everything that happened."

Rachel ushered them ceremoniously into what she called her "parlor," a room with lovely proportions that were somehow lost in the jumble of overstuffed pieces that Rachel added each time her husband's wealth increased a notch or two. Great armchairs upholstered in opulent damasks or prickly mohair flanked formidable rococo mahogany end tables, topped with grotesque bits of "art."

Yet although the room itself was mercilessly ugly—Sharif shuddered and Carlotta smiled each time they visited—the parlor was saved from total disaster by Rachel herself. When she was there, with her bubbling laugh and the nervous energy that could scarcely be contained within her short plump body, then the visitor might say, "Aha—now I understand." For Rachel and her surroundings were all of a piece. She dressed with the same enthusiasm and innocence of aesthetic standards with which she decorated her home.

After she seated her guests, Rachel went to her china closet to bring forth her "company glasses"—great goblets of heavy lead crystal which she set ceremoniously in front of her guests. "So come and join us, Simon darling," she called out. "We're going to have a toast with our neighbors." To her guests she said, "Simon has been going over his books tonight. The accountant was here all day, but Simon has to do everything himself—just like a schoolteacher, he goes over everything." She smiled indulgently, implying no criticism of her husband, but rather praising his acuity, his executive abilities.

When Simon came into the room, he nodded formally to his neighbors. "Good evening," he said, then sat down.

"Will you open the champagne, Mr. Hazzi?" Rachel asked.

"Perhaps Mr. Levine would like to do the honors, since he is our host?"

Simon shook his head. "Please, go ahead," he insisted, not so much out of courtesy as from the insecurity he always felt with the little social rituals, like the popping of champagne corks, which he associated with the upper classes.

As the ceremony was completed, the cork duly removed, the glasses clinked, Rachel asked again, "So, *nu*—your opening—how was it?"

"Please, Rachel," Simon remonstrated, "speak English—our guests don't understand Yiddish."

Carlotta laughed. "Oh, Mr. Levine, Rachel and I understand each other perfectly, whether I speak a little Italian or she speaks Yiddish. And I am happy to say that the opening was very nice—but I wish you had come to share it with us."

"Oh, no." Rachel shook her head vigorously. "We are not uptown people, and this is business. We don't fit in with the people you will want for customers."

"But Rachel, we are not uptown people either. We are not even Americans. How could you think we would not want to share a happy moment with our friends? We don't have so many friends, you know."

"Oy, what a baby you are." Rachel shook her head from side to side. "You are better than uptown people. You are real quality. Anyone can see that. And I am proud to be your friend." Rachel's voice faltered with the sincerity of her sentiment.

Carlotta felt her own tears coming, so she changed the subject. "I must also thank you for sending Mary Rose to me. I don't think I could have managed nearly so well without her."

"Wait for a little while with the 'thank yous.' Her sister Cathleen works two years in this house now—and we still don't know who is the boss. Every time I show her something, it's 'yes mum' and 'no mum'—and then in one ear and out the other. And every five minutes, she makes those crosses on herself—like a dybbuk was after her and she needs protection."

"Well, Rachel, I am still grateful to have Mary Rose look after the house while I am at the gallery. And as long as she does not break so much, I will be content. I don't really mind if Mary Rose crosses herself so often. After all the years at the convent, I am quite used to it."

"Oy, stupid—" Rachel clapped her hand on her mouth. "Carlotta darling, I did not mean to insult your religion—I forgot."

"Don't trouble yourself, *chère* Rachel, I am not at all

insulted. I think the pious Mary Rose does not often remember I am Catholic either. I think she really believes it is a terrible mistake that the pope is Italian, and that in truth all good Catholics must come from Ireland. I am afraid that Sharif and I seem to her what she calls 'heathen.' "

Rachel laughed, recalling her own maid's mutterings about "heathens" and her suspicion that these imprecations were directed at her. Even Simon allowed himself a thin smile at this point, though he said nothing.

"Never mind," said Carlotta. "No matter what we are, our children will be Americans one day."

"Oh yes!" Rachel concurred, raising her glass in a toast to the future. Now Simon's face took on an almost beatific expression, as if he had just heard the expression of his most treasured prayer.

Sharif, on the other hand, winced visibly, struck with the painful thought that his children would break the thread of life that had begun so many centuries ago in the warm life-giving cocoon of the Nile valley. Unlike Simon, Sharif had not experienced the ghetto, the pogroms, the hunger and despair that had sent him wandering from his native country. No, Sharif had been cast out, and the pain of that expulsion would stay with him for the rest of his life.

Carlotta saw the change in her husband's face. She reached out and put her hand over his. As if on cue, a cry came from the nursery. Robert Levine began to whimper softly.

Rachel moved reflexively to minister to her son, but Simon held out his hand to stop her. "I will see to the boy."

A moment later Sharif looked at his watch and said to his wife, "I think we must say good night. Tomorrow will be very full for us."

And as the door closed behind them, Simon sat in the nursery—a room which Rachel had decorated to exemplify her idea of the phrase "fit for a prince"—rocking his son in his arms, his stern face transformed by love as he hummed an old Yiddish lullaby.

"I wish you liked Simon as much as I like Rachel," Carlotta said, when they had returned to their own apartment. "Then we could all be such good friends."

"I have tried, *cara*," Sharif protested. "For your sake, I have really tried. But the man is damned difficult."

"I know he is not so very charming, but he is a good man. And he has had a very difficult life."

"He's a rich man now, *tesora*. He has everything—a wife who loves him, a son, and still he always looks as if he's eating sour fruit."

"Listen to me, Sharif. Rachel has told me how Simon began his business—with a single sewing machine and then a small tailoring shop. When they were first married, Rachel never saw him. He wanted so much to give his family a good life, he worked sixteen hours a day, even more."

"But I've seen his store—Levine's—it's a full city block, three stories high. Do you mean this was the result of a single sewing machine?"

"Not exactly. Simon had an uncle who died and left them a small inheritance. He and Rachel opened a dry goods store. They were like us, don't you see? But their shop was for the poor, not the rich. Simon had the idea that he could sell good merchandise in the neighborhood where he lived, at prices his friends and neighbors could afford."

"A good idea, I suppose. The man has a good mind, I've never doubted that."

"It was an excellent idea, and soon Simon's customers came from other places, to buy better things for less money. But Simon was still not satisfied. Rachel told me that she was very frightened when her husband decided to open a store uptown—where there were so many stores for the rich— Altman's and Macy's, for instance. But he insisted that even the rich knew the value of money. And he was right, you see."

"Well, if he is so right, as well as so rich, then why is he not more like his wife? She has such a happy nature—it is always a pleasure to share her company."

"Think a minute, *caro*. You have seen Simon, and you have met many of Pierre's fine friends, men of wealth. They are not the same. This difference—it matters very much to Simon. Rachel does not care. She is happy in what she has. She is not concerned that they do not belong with 'uptown' people. But Simon cares, very much. Do you understand, my love? He is a man with a deep hunger. He still wants to give his family everything, but he does not know how to get it for them."

Sharif took his wife's hand and kissed her tenderly on her

forehead. "All right, my dear. Since I am so blessed, I will try to understand your Mr. Levine. And now we really must get some sleep."

The next day was as busy as Sharif had predicted it would be, and so were the days that followed. Thanks to word of mouth spread by Principessa's first clients—and by the efficient workings of Marina Vanderbeck's grapevine—there was a brisk traffic through the shop. At first most of their customers—many of them an overflow from the popular tailor next door—came to look rather than to buy. But from the beginning neither Carlotta nor Sharif coaxed or cajoled or intimidated customers. They presided over the gallery as if it were an extension of their home, and not a place where they expected to earn a living.

They treated clients as if they were honored guests, and not merely potential sources of revenue. And they listened carefully to both the criticism and the praise from all their "guests." They nodded sympathetically when Mrs. Stoddard lamented that Principessa did not have a single piece of that beautiful glass she had seen at Mrs. Pierce's last night—and immediately made a note to try a small display of the glass. They noted Mrs. Ransom's delight when she scooped up a delicate bit of Dresden and declared that all her friends had been "searching everywhere" for just such a treasure.

Carlotta listened and she learned. She learned, for example, that there were items—fine, beautifully crafted items—that you could not give away at any price, because they were not in fashion. These she packed away carefully in the storeroom, to be brought out again when fashion made them valuable. On the other hand, she learned that during a particularly lively period, she could move an unlimited number of china dogs. And although she and Sharif found these creatures rather ugly, they compromised by keeping the stock in the rear of the shop.

Sharif and Carlotta listened, too, to their clients' decorating problems, to their social insecurities and vulnerabilities. They tried to understand what kind of atmosphere these people wanted to create in their homes. And they offered their help—advice based not on any formal training, but on the good taste that had been bred into them in a lifetime of gracious surroundings. They suggested how a Chinese vase might best be displayed in a formal entrance gallery, how a garden room might best be rearranged to accommodate a new French corner chair, and so on. This "personal decorating" they offered at no charge to regular customers. And soon, because their own personal elegance lent such credibility to their judgments, because their suggestions almost always made a room a little more "special," in time, their opinions came to be as valued as their merchandise was admired.

No matter how many customers were in the shop, Carlotta always took the time to offer coffee or tea or lemonade, served in Limoges cups and Waterford glasses, sometimes with the help of the sturdy Mary Rose, who alternated her housekeeping duties at the Hazzi apartment with chores at Principessa.

And just before the gallery closed at seven o'clock, Sharif always offered a sherry to any customers who lingered. Then he and Carlotta would take the short ride home, later to sit down to one of Mary Rose's half-hearted attempts to reproduce one of Carlotta's continental recipes, or, worse yet, one of Sharif's favorite Egyptian dishes.

Time after time, Carlotta patiently explained, "*Ma chère* Mary Rose, this pasta—these noodles—must be cooked *al dente*. You understand? This means in a way that the teeth will still have some work to do. Not like a pudding—*tu comprends*?"

The stalwart Mary Rose always accepted these instructions in silence, standing ramrod straight, arms folded across her chest, thinking her own thoughts. In the end, she cooked everything according to her own notion of what was "fittin'," muttering into her pots and pans about her employer's attempts to seduce her into the mysteries of "furrin' " cooking.

In desperation, Carlotta sent Mary Rose to a cooking school on Lafayette Place. The girl obediently attended the classes, though she was insulted at the suggestion that her skills were wanting. She resisted the instruction, and ultimately the Hazzis surrendered to her iron will.

6

When Carlotta vomited her breakfast three mornings in a row, when she had to lie down in the storage room because she felt faint, she dared to hope that she might be able to give her husband a child—a gift to ease the pain of what he had forsaken to marry her.

Because her neighbor had already borne a child, she asked Rachel what symptoms she might look for next. Rachel crowed with delight. "Darling girl, of course you are pregnant. Just look at the roses in your cheeks. And your eyes—oh my, just look—a regular madonna. *Mazel tov*, dear friend, *mazel tov*."

"Oh, I hope so, Rachel. I hope you are right. A child would make Sharif so happy. We could be a family, then—not just two people alone."

"And you, too, darling. A baby will make you happy, too. Wait till you see what a child will make you feel, a little baby with skin like silk, and . . . wait, you'll see for yourself."

So Carlotta had waited, not very patiently. And when her first symptoms were followed by a swelling in her breasts and a new roundness in her belly, Carlotta visited Rachel's doctor. He confirmed the fact of her pregnancy and assured her that she could expect a fine, healthy baby in about six months.

On her way home, she planned a celebration, a quiet Sunday dinner, when she would tell her husband he was to become a father. Then, later in the day perhaps, they would share the good news with Syrie and Pierre and Rachel and Simon. But the following morning, just as she was showing her favorite set of Lalique sherbet cups to a customer, she felt suddenly lightheaded. Then the room started to spin, and her knees gave way under her. When she opened her eyes, she saw Sharif's face, contorted with anxiety, as he dabbed her face and forehead with a cool, wet handkerchief.

"*Tesoro?*"

"*Si, bella*—how are you feeling?"

"I am all right now, really I am."

"I think I will call a doctor. This is not the first time you have not been well. I have seen it. *J'ai peur, chérie.* If something were to happen to you . . ."

"Non, non, mon amour, j'ne suis pas malade. Je suis enceinte."

Sharif looked completely startled, as if the possibility had not even occurred to him. "Are you sure? Let me call a doctor to make certain."

"I have seen a doctor. Yesterday. I was going to tell you this weekend, when we had some time to ourselves."

Sharif stared at his wife in wonder, as if he had never seen her before. He had no words to tell her what he felt.

The following months were rich and happy ones for the young couple. Now they would no longer be strangers alone in this new world. Now there would be a child, a living product of their love.

Although Sharif fussed and fretted over Carlotta's health, her well-being, she insisted she felt wonderful. And although he suggested that she rest in the evenings, she would laugh and suggest they go dancing instead at one of the local hotels. As they whirled to the strains of "Dardanella" and "Japanese Sandman," Carlotta declared that she was the happiest woman in all of the United States.

And then, as miraculously as it had begun, so suddenly and abruptly, it was over. Carlotta went into labor at seven o'clock on a Wednesday evening in the eighth month of her pregnancy. An hour later, Dr. Aram Tataryan took charge, with Mary Rose in assistance.

At midnight a son was born, a perfect five-pound boy with the face of a Titian cherub. And only the faint blue tinge of cyanosis told the story—that Carlotta's baby had failed to breathe, that the child who was to be called Jamil, after Sharif's father, was dead.

Mary Rose was consumed with a frenzy of "Hail Marys" and frantic crossings. And even Aram Tataryan was shaken from his usual professional detachment by the sight of the child, whom he described later, in a hushed voice, as "the most beautiful infant I have ever delivered." Sharif was rent with a grief so profoundly physical that he left the room to weep—savage, tearing sobs that left him exhausted, but unrelieved of his pain.

Carlotta lay in the semistupor induced by the morphia given her by the doctor, tossing fitfully and muttering unintelligible sounds. Later, in the quiet time just before dawn, as Sharif sat at her bedside, staring anxiously at his wife's face, she bolted upright. Her eyes flew open and she spoke, as if her words were a continuation of some dream conversation she had been conducting. "Where is my baby? Give him to me."

Sharif rose from his chair to soothe her, to settle her back against the pillows. Her voice rose sharply, to the edge of hysteria. "Where have you taken him? I saw my child. I saw him. Where is he?"

With no strength left to give his wife, Sharif lost control. His face crumpled, and the sobs started to come again, harsh and cruel and without hope. And Carlotta, even in her befuddled condition, understood at once. Her body went rigid, then her face also set, as if it had been cast in plaster.

Her expression did not change, not then, nor in the hours and days that followed. No matter who spoke to her, no matter what was said, she remained exactly the same. She did not cry, nor did she wail bitter tears against the wanton fate—or cruel god—that had stolen the breath of life from her son. She simply put herself beyond the reach of everything, beyond tears or joy or feeling of any kind. She sat, day after day, in her bed, or reclined on her chaise—if someone carried her there.

Every few hours, Rachel Levine knocked softly on her door, bearing small gifts and good things to eat—flowers, a custard as light as an angel's kiss, a pitcher of beef tea, brewed lovingly and long from lightly seasoned bones and choice tidbits of lean beef. Leaving her own little Robert with Mary Rose's sister Cathleen, Rachel treated Carlotta as if she were a child herself, holding the rigid form against her ample bosom, rocking, soothing, cajoling—willing her friend to return from the dark place where she had wandered all alone. But Carlotta would not come back. And Mary Rose's cluckings and crossings grew more frequent, as did her vocal speculations on what would become of the missus.

Sharif had closed the gallery for a few days, leaving on the door a black-bordered sign that read: "Death in the Family." On the Monday following his son's birth and death, Sharif reopened the shop. But he moved among his treasures like a shadow, without knowing what he was doing, without remembering when it was done. He left his home each morning wondering how Carlotta would survive another day, and he returned each evening thinking only of how he might find her.

And when days, then weeks, passed without a change in her condition, a nagging fear took hold of him and penetrated the numbing shell of his grief. It was the fear that his Carlotta had left him forever, leaving behind only a wooden puppet with vacant eyes and no soul, to fill her bed.

He spoke to Dr. Tataryan, who confessed that he had done all he knew how to do. "Your wife has a severe melancholia—not so unusual in a case like this. In fact, I have seen less severe instances in mothers who have given birth to healthy children. Time is usually the best healer."

"But, doctor, when time fails . . . there must be something else."

"I have no medicine to give you, Mr. Hazzi, but perhaps I might recommend—"

"Anything, anything at all—you must tell me something. I cannot just watch my wife remain like a statue without trying to help her."

"Perhaps a change of scene. Being in a place that isn't so familiar might help her to take notice of life again. It could be a first step. . . ."

"What kind of place do you recommend?"

"Any place that would be pleasant for the two of you. Mind you, I'm not saying that any good will come of it—I simply don't know—but perhaps a sea voyage. I have seen the ocean air act as a restorative."

After he had spoken to the doctor, Sharif realized that if he was to take the advice they had just discussed, he would have to close the gallery—and perhaps lose the prospects they had generated in the short time they had been open. The young boy who had been hired to clean and perform odd chores could not be left in charge. There was no one to whom Sharif could entrust his infant business.

He spoke to Marina Vanderbeck, but the grande dame shook her head emphatically. "I'm sorry, Mr. Hazzi. I would very much like to help you and your dear wife, but no one in my family has ever been in trade."

Sharif smiled in spite of himself.

"Don't be impertinent, young man. I know exactly what you're thinking. But what I have done—for our mutual benefit—is not the same as keeping a shop."

"Well, I certainly did not mean to insult you, *chère madame*," Sharif said, "but I find I will need someone as elegant and genteel as yourself if Principessa is not to founder now. My wife may be indisposed for some time, and if I wish to spend time with her, I cannot leave the gallery in the hands of a young boy. It must be someone who can give our clients the kind of attention I want them to associate only with Principessa."

"Yes, I quite understand," Marina Vanderbeck said. "I see that what you have managed to do is to avoid the atmosphere of commerce, even while you create the very ambience in which it can best flourish."

"Precisely, Madame Vanderbeck. If we lose that, then I think we lose the very quality that will make us prosper. But if I cannot find what I need soon, then I may have to choose between the welfare of my business and the future of my marriage."

Mrs. Vanderbeck sighed sympathetically. "I am so sorry, but perhaps . . . if you would care to try an . . . arrangement with someone other than myself, then there is a young man who might serve your purposes."

"Yes?" Sharif waited for details.

"Geoffrey Harwood has proved to be a great disappointment to his family. He has, this past year, been dismissed from the third institution of higher learning which his father had . . . persuaded . . . to accept him. He has, if I may put it delicately, a predilection for the less serious pursuits of life. Geoffrey is a bright lad, extremely likable in his way, but he lacks the desire to apply himself. So his father has told him there will be no more education—and no more allowance— until he spends a year learning perseverance and responsibility, specifically by finding a position and keeping it."

"Please forgive me, Mrs. Vanderbeck. I can certainly see why this young man might be seeking employment. But why do you think I should give him a job?"

"Because," she said, with exaggerated patience, "Geoffrey is neither stupid nor without ability. His parents made a mistake in not requiring him to test himself sooner. Incidentally, I should tell you that Geoffrey is my favorite nephew.

He is frivolous, but he is also scrupulously honest. Further-more, he has fine manners—and an excellent tailor.'' She added these last qualifications as if they constituted an irrefut-able case for Geoffrey's eligibility. But Sharif knew exactly what she meant. In the world where he sought his clients, the attributes of a young man like Geoffrey were more valuable than the virtues of diligence and perseverance.

Marina Vanderbeck turned out to be right. Geoffrey Harwood made a fine appearance. He was almost sinfully handsome, a fact that was not lost on Principessa's female clientele, and, moreover, he was a quick learner. The novelty of earning his daily bread appealed to him, at least for the moment, and he listened carefully to Sharif's instructions as to what he must do when he managed the gallery on his own. To allay his own fears about leaving his business in such inexperienced hands, Sharif had extracted a promise from Pierre that both he and Syrie would regularly visit Principessa to check its books and its inventories for any alarming developments.

And so on a warm September day, Sharif and Carlotta boarded the S.S. *Marianne*, bound for Genoa. The ship be-longed to Pierre's firm, and since the firm was enjoying a breathtaking surge of prosperity, he and Syrie offered the trip as a gift to their young friends.

To see them going up the gangplank, Syrie thought any-one would have imagined they were a golden couple with the world at their feet. But a closer look, a look at Sharif's worried face, at his eyes that kept returning to the blank doll-like creature who was his wife—that look would have told the truth, that these were two people who were lost. Sharif and Carlotta had belonged only to each other, and now these ties had become dangerously loose, casting each of them adrift.

≈ 7 ≈

The S.S. *Marianne* was a freighter, but the limited accommodations it provided for passengers were extremely comfortable and inviting. The crew, mainly Italian and Greek, were friendly, and anxious to please the handsome couple—the dark-haired man who spoke such fine Italian and the sad-eyed lady who rarely spoke at all.

In other circumstances, the ship might have been the perfect place to spend a belated honeymoon. But Sharif was too filled with the worry that had become his constant companion to fully appreciate the beauties of long leisurely days at sea.

Carlotta behaved like a dutiful child, taking Sharif's arm when he led her into the dining room, eating small portions of whatever was put in front of her. This, too, worried Sharif. Although Carlotta's belly was still rounded—a last sad reminder of her pregnancy—the rest of her body was becoming sharp and angular. The cheekbones in her finely structured face had the look of stilettos, threatening to pierce the delicate layer of translucent skin.

When Sharif walked the deck to take the sea air with its healing powers, she allowed him to take her hand and guide her. And when he spoke to her, she answered—when she answered at all—in sentences of few words.

To find a strength he did not feel, to pretend a cheerfulness he had forgotten, he made imaginary bargains with fate. "I will accept the loss of my son," he murmured, to whatever power might be listening. "I will do whatever I must to make Carlotta better. But please, oh please, let her be better."

But hope became harder to hold on to, as the bow of the *Marianne* cut across miles of open sea, and still there was no change. One night, as he began to help Carlotta into bed, the sight of her vacant expression, of her thin body, so pale and white against the pink of her nightgown, roused in him a fresh rush of misery and despair. He pulled his wife's body close to him, holding her tightly, desperately, crooning into her ear. He felt her grow rigid, and when he looked into her eyes, hoping to see something—anything—there, he found that the vacant stare had been replaced by an expression of stark terror.

It was too much for him to bear. He ran from the small stateroom, a man pursued by demons, leaving in his wake the dull moan of anguish that had been torn from his throat.

It was this naked animal sound that penetrated, ever so slightly, the fuzzy blanket of anesthesia that had separated Carlotta from the rest of the world. Ever since the death of her son, she had been overtaken by a dark dread that had always been part of her religion, a darkness she thought had been left behind in Italy along with the sisters, with the whispered questions in darkened convent bedrooms: "Oh, Carlotta, do you think it's true that God sees everything, that he will punish us for every bad thought we have?"

And her own answers, solemn and certain: "Oh, yes, everything bad we do will be punished. And if we're not sorry, we'll be damned to hell, forever and ever."

For Carlotta, the list of damnable offenses was long and rather vague, a compendium of biblical commandments and social missteps. High on her list of imperatives was the solemn invocation to honor one's parents.

She had felt a deep and genuine distress when Sharif had forsaken his parents to marry her. She had had moments of fear and foreboding before their wedding. But she had pushed the uneasiness aside, with the power of her love for the handsome Egyptian with the smoky eyes. But when her child— the sweet angel she had seen for just a moment—was taken from her, Carlotta knew she was being punished. And she was remorseful and afraid—afraid of what else might lie in store for her.

Day after day she lived in numb terror. On the periphery of her consciousness she noticed that people came and went, touching her, leading her through the motions of living. And just now, she had felt his arms around her—and then that awful sound. It pulled her, like a magnet, from her bed. Like an automaton, she got up, walked mechanically to the door that still hung open.

Now she was alone. All alone. Now he was gone, too. Her eyes wandered vaguely around the room—and stopped at the nightstand. She walked to it—and picked up the glass carafe.

When Sharif returned to his stateroom, the first thing he saw was the open door. His misery gave way to the fear that Carlotta had wandered outside, fallen into the sea.

And then he saw her, kneeling on the floor, in a bed of broken glass, her eyes shut, her face waxy, her lips moving in a familiar litany of Hail Marys. He cried out her name, ran to her. He picked up the frail body—and cried out again when he saw her knees, covered with blood and bits of glass.

He laid her on the bed and began to sob as he tried to staunch the flow of blood with a towel, to pick out the razor-sharp splinters that had penetrated her skin.

Her eyes opened. She reached out a slender arm and touched him. "Sharif?" It was the first time she had uttered a sound without being spoken to. He reached for her.

"Carlotta—*carissima*—you must speak to me. You must let me help you. Carlotta—please don't leave me. I can't live without you. Carlotta—look at me." He shook her, as if she were a rag doll, willing her to focus her eyes on him. "Listen, my darling, we must share this loss together, or it will destroy us both. He was my son, too, Carlotta. . . ." His voice cracked and he began to cry again.

She spoke with the voice of a schoolgirl reciting a catechism. "My baby—yes, my baby—God took my baby because I was wicked. And soon"—she took a breath and the words came out, the thought that had lingered, unspeakable, for weeks—"and soon, God will take you, too."

"No!" he shouted, as he began to perceive the nature of the darkness that had covered his wife. "No, no, no." His voice took on authority now, as he understood exactly what it was he was fighting. "Listen to me, Carlotta. It was not God who took our child. It was a weakness. The doctor told me. If he had lived, it would not have been for long. It was better this way, Carlotta. We can have more children. You have done nothing to be punished for. Believe me. Nothing at all."

"Oh, yes, yes I have. I made you sin against your parents. We should never have married. It was wrong. . . ."

"Carlotta—no—it was my father who was wrong. It was his pride that made him do what he did. My mother understands. She blessed our marriage—and so did your aunt. My father will change his mind. You'll see. And then we'll all be happy.'' He reassured her with words he did not believe. But Carlotta was listening.

"Really, *caro*, really?'' She asked, in the same small voice.

"Really, my darling, really and truly. You must come back to me. It is the only thing that matters now. Perhaps life would have been simpler if we had not met. But when I think of growing old, of dying without knowing what it was like to love you—I can't imagine it. And God help me, I couldn't choose it. Look at me,'' he commanded, as he noticed her eyes were starting to drift again. "You and I—we are everything to each other. If I lose you, I will be all alone in a strange country, a strange world. Now I want you to tell me everything you have been thinking. And I will help you to put it behind you.''

They sat together and talked for most of the night. They talked of Sharif's pain at being cut off from his family. They talked, haltingly, of their mutual sorrow, of Carlotta's profound feeling of failure. And again she put into words her fear that she would lose her husband to the same cruel fate that had taken her son. "No,'' her husband said, making her a vow that no human being could make. "No. I promise you that I will not die and leave you. Not ever.'' And somehow they both believed that promise.

Although Dr. Tataryan had suggested that Carlotta not conceive another child for at least six months, she came back from her holiday pregnant and happy. And while both she and Sharif had some fears about her condition, they reassured themselves with the thought that this early pregnancy was a good omen, that it was meant in some way to diminish the loss of their first child.

They came back to find their business thriving. Aided by his aunt's energetic but discreet assistance, Geoffrey Harwood was a great success. "Buy'' was the watchword in New York these days—buy on Wall Street, buy one of the shiny new automobiles and join the nine million Americans who owned them. Buy the fine antiques that had once graced the elegant salons of France and England and Italy, buy the collector's items that had languished in a sultan's harem in Constantinople or a ruined pasha's palace in Alexandria. All of these sat briefly in the tasteful confines of Principessa Gallery—before they found a new home in a Park Avenue maisonette, a Madison Avenue town house, or even, occasionally, in an elegant Harlem bordello.

Woodrow Wilson was in the White House, women were campaigning for the right to vote, and the newspapers were filled with stories of the war in Europe.

Prospects for international trade seemed extraordinarily bright. In spite of many strikes and demands for higher wages, the shipyards were running at full tilt. International Mercantile Marine common stock, which had doubled the year before, was continuing its steady upward climb. Pierre and Syrie Rubichou were growing richer by the month.

In the midst of this surge of growth and prosperity, Alicia Adela Hazzi was born—exactly on the day the doctor had forecast for her debut into the world. It was probably the last time that Alicia would be so predictable—or so cooperative.

At seven pounds, two ounces, Alicia was a black-haired, blue-eyed bundle of raw energy, unabashed in her willfulness and greedy for life. The first time she put her mouth to Carlotta's breast, she sucked it hungrily—then punched with two small fists when the milk did not come quickly enough. Sharif laughed, delighted that he and Carlotta had produced such a robust life-loving child. But beyond the laughter, there was sadness, for Sharif knew—as he would soon have to tell Carlotta—that the doctor had said there would be no more children—no more daughters and, most regretfully, no sons.

Perhaps it was because they both realized how fragile and precious was the life of a child, that from the beginning Sharif and Carlotta adored their vivacious little girl. They spoiled her outrageously, and she, the child born reaching for life with two deliciously plump little hands, became a creature of large and varied appetites.

Her parents were, on the whole, pleased that Alicia was not to live her life as a pallid observer, that she was likely to savor experiences of all kinds. They applauded when she sat up at five months, her cupid's lips pursed in concentration, her cobalt-blue eyes serious and intent in her cherub face framed by glossy black curls. And six months after that, she pulled herself up with the aid of a dining room chair, bottom lip thrust out, and propelled herself on wobbly but determined legs, chubby arms outstretched for the chocolates Sharif held in his hand.

At sixteen months she articulated her first words—"give

me''—a demand she would repeat often and without apology throughout her life. Yet there was something innocent and appealing about Alicia's single-minded insistence on gratification. She never whined or whimpered on the rare occasions when her parents failed to accommodate. When, now and then, she found herself facing a setback, she was frankly puzzled. She approached defeat or disappointment as a problem requiring a solution rather than as a lesson. Why had it happened, she would ask herself, and how could she avoid a similar experience in the future?

Remarkably, Alicia also took physical hurts with an equanimity that was rare in adults, and even more so in a child. When she was eight, Sharif had made her a birthday present of a Shetland pony, simply because she had once ridden in a pony cart and subsequently asked if she could have one of her own.

Alicia took the responsibility for the little animal, which she named Dusty, very seriously, lavishing on it more care and attention than she could give to the people she loved. Three days a week Mary Rose would pick her up at school and take her to the stable at Central Park where the pony was boarded. The child would ride for an hour, trying hard to sit her mount as her father had taught her. Then she would solemnly follow the rituals the groom had shown her, walking the pony to cool him down, washing the animal and brushing him until he fairly crooned with pleasure.

One hot summer day, Dusty, made frantic by a bee sting, threw Alicia, breaking her collarbone. Sharif raged and swore he would have the animal killed. "No, Daddy, no," Alicia begged, even while the doctor was tending her injury. "Dusty wasn't naughty. It wasn't his fault. The bee hurt him. You mustn't punish Dusty. He won't do it again. I promise."

Sharif smiled in spite of his concern for his only child. "All right, Alicia. If that is what you wish, Dusty will have another chance."

At Marina's suggestion—and intervention—Alicia was enrolled in Miss Schuyler's School, a genteel Madison Avenue establishment dedicated to the educational standards deemed appropriate to the daughters of the rich: a generous helping of art and music appreciation, a smattering of languages, and, most important of all, tutoring in the importance of wealth and social status as well as the attendant rules of decorum and deportment.

Somehow Alicia could not achieve either the attitude or the behavior that might have helped her slip smoothly and safely through Miss Schuyler's. As the hierarchy of the school was to learn, Alicia was simply not the sort of child to pass quietly through any social machinery. From the tip of her always slightly tousled head down to her always slightly disreputable shoes (Mary Rose applied brush and polish faithfully every night, but to no avail), from her unruly exterior to her more unruly heart, Alicia was not the raw material of which conformity is made.

In kindergarten she refused to take the preordained morning "nap," explaining to her teacher that she just wasn't tired. When she was sent to the headmistress's office, she offered an explanation that made Miss Schuyler smile. "I don't mean to be such trouble, ma'am, but it seems silly to rest when you're not tired. I mean," she went on with what seemed to her perfect logic, "you don't eat when you're not hungry, now do you?"

Trying hard to control a smile, for in truth she thought Alicia was an enchanting child, Miss Schuyler made her voice even, but not harsh. "What you say makes perfect sense, Alicia, but I am going to tell you something that perhaps you can understand. Sometimes it is necessary, in the interest of more important goals, for us to do things which seem unnecessary—or even silly. You see, there are too many people living in this world for each person to do things as he sees fit. Do you understand, Alicia?"

Alicia had been listening very carefully, for she liked Miss Schuyler very much. "I'm not sure, ma'am." Then she went on in a conciliatory tone that almost caused the woman to burst into laughter. "I can see that I have caused you some trouble, and I didn't mean to do that. If it will make you feel better, I will lie down with the other children." With this, Alicia looked up, like a parent who has solved a problem for a not-very-clever child.

"Well, I certainly thank you for your cooperation," Miss Schuyler answered. "I know that you and I are going to be very good friends. But I hope you will be patient as you try to accustom yourself to the school's rules and regulations."

On that occasion Alicia nodded solemnly and left the room. But not all her brushes with authority were resolved so neatly.

Hers was a generation educated according to the "spare the rod" philosophy; it was a time when teachers held a position of unquestioned authority, a time when juvenile precocity was highly suspect. With the exception of Miss Schuyler herself, the staff at the school did not appreciate either Alicia's attitude or her penetrating questions.

Whenever she was in the class of a teacher who taught by rote, she would unfailingly ask the kind of question such a teacher could not answer. And when she was told to "look it up for yourself so you can learn it properly," she would inevitably throw out yet another challenge.

By the time she reached the second grade, Alicia had a reputation for being a "difficult" child. Her second-grade teacher sent for Sharif and Carlotta, with a euphemistic request for a "conference." When the parents presented themselves at the appointed hour, they were told that their daughter had an unfortunate habit of "talking back." As if on cue, Alicia, who had been sitting toward the back of the room, listening very intently, marched up to the teacher's desk, placed her hands on her hips, thrust out her lower lip, and said, "I do not." The teacher turned to Sharif and Carlotta, raised her eyebrows and her shoulders in a gesture that said, "Do you see what I have to put up with?"

Sharif and Carlotta looked at each other and simultaneously stifled the impulse to smile. They were more than a little amused by Alicia's spirit, but they realized that she would need to learn when and how to curb that spirit—and to hold her tongue. To the teacher, Sharif said, "I understand, Miss Shelby. We'll speak to Alicia about it."

"Why did you say that to Miss Shelby?" Alicia asked Sharif, as she sat with her parents around the dinner table.

"Why did I say what?"

"Why did you say you would speak to me? You sounded like you believed Miss Shelby."

"I did believe Miss Shelby. That is, I believed she meant what she was telling us."

"But I told you—I don't talk back. Not the way she made it sound. She says a lot of dumb things, and she hates it when you tell her. That's not talking back."

"Alicia, listen to me. There are many people in this world who are exactly like Miss Shelby. And there are many situations where you will find yourself knowing more than people who feel they have the right to tell you what to do. There are rules for these situations, and you will have to follow them. If you don't, then you may be punished. Your mother and I don't want that to happen to you, so we are asking you to conform."

"Does that mean you want me to do stupid things, even when I know they're stupid?"

"Well—sometimes."

"Which times?"

Sharif shook his head. "That, Alicia, you will have to find out for yourself. But until you are a little older and better able to decide, I think you had best do as you're told—in school, at least."

"Yes, Papa," she said, with a frown that made her father doubt her acquiescence.

Later that evening, as Carlotta and Sharif lay in bed, drowsy but not sleeping, they felt a small warm body crawl between them. "What is it, Alicia?" Carlotta asked. "Did you have a bad dream?"

"No, Mama, but it's lonely in my room. I want to sleep with you and Papa. Why do I have to sleep alone and the two of you sleep together?"

"Because Papa and I are married, and married people sleep together."

"But why can't I be married with you?"

"Because only two people can be married together. And when their children grow up, they can get married, too."

"But that's such a long time to wait, Mama."

"Hush, little one, it's not so very long. Close your eyes now and stay with us tonight. Make a wish and close your eyes and go to sleep."

"I wish you loved me the way you love Papa."

Carlotta stroked her daughter's hair. "Papa and I both love you very much, Alicia. Sleep now, *bella*, sleep."

After her father's little talk, Alicia managed to behave well enough to avoid major recriminations—but not meekly enough to avert the small skirmishes that became a familiar part of her young life.

Her teachers, with the exception of those who taught social or domestic skills, reported that she was unquestionably blessed with remarkable intelligence. But her performance was uneven, bringing her to the point of failure at least half a dozen times throughout her stay at Miss Schuyler's.

Assignments which were, in her opinion, "stupid" or unnecessary were either not handed in or completed in such an offhand way as to invite a large red F on the top. But when she was presented with what she saw as functional work, she almost always performed well, handing in papers that impressed and sometimes disconcerted her teachers.

Whatever satisfactions and problems Alicia faced at Miss Schuyler's, she usually faced them alone. In spite of her rare beauty, her incandescent core of pure energy, her presence that could fill and dominate a room, Alicia was not popular.

She was usually invited to parties and dances, for the girls who ran those affairs noticed that Alicia had considerable drawing power when it came to young men. But on the whole, her youthful individualism made her more of a loner than a leader. To the other girls her flamboyance seemed suspect, as did her outspokenness, which could be enjoyed vicariously in the classroom but not outside it.

Her parents did not seem to notice the scarcity of friends in Alicia's life, nor did she confide in them. Although her parents often told her how beautiful she was, how much they adored her, there was something in their love for each other that seemed, often in subtle ways, to close her out.

After school she rode her chestnut gelding, Pasha—a gift from her father after she had outgrown Dusty—at least twice a week, or whenever she needed to feel the freedom and power of a thousand pounds of horseflesh carrying her into the wind.

Other days, she would wander to the Levines' apartment to soak up the warmth from Rachel's ever-fragrant kitchen or to play poker with her "best friend," Robert.

On one such day Alicia looked accusingly at her neighbor while she swept her winnings—twenty-two cents—toward her side of the table. "Did you just let me win that hand, Robert Levine?"

"Of course not, Alicia. You're just a better player than I am."

"I am?" She fairly beamed at such a compliment from the boy she saw as an endless source of wisdom.

"Yes, you are. You like to win, so that makes you play well. Anyway, even if you weren't any good, I wouldn't lose on purpose. That would be like lying to you. And I don't do that."

"I know you don't, Robert. That's why you're my best friend. I'd rather play cards with you than do almost anything else."

"Silly little Alicia. I like to play cards with you, too. But you're a girl. You should be doing other things after school."

"Like what?" she demanded.

"Like being with girls your own age."

"I hate them. All the girls in school are so dumb. All they do is giggle and flirt with boys. And they hate me."

"I'm sure that's not true, Alicia." Robert's face grew thoughtful for a moment. "Maybe they're jealous."

"Of me?" Alicia was incredulous, for she had never imagined that she possessed anything that was enviable.

"You're very pretty. Don't you know that?"

"Oh, well—Mama and Papa say that sometimes. But parents are supposed to say things like that."

"But it's true. You are pretty. And that makes people notice you. Just like they do when you're ugly or different, like I am."

"Don't you dare say such a thing, Robert! You're not ugly at all. I think you're very handsome. Almost as handsome as Papa."

"Friends don't lie to each other. Remember that, Alicia. I know that I'm short and skinny and I'm not good at sports. And if that wasn't bad enough, I have braces on my teeth and pimples on my face."

Quick tears filled Alicia's eyes. "I'm not lying, Robert, honest I'm not. I do think you're handsome. Lots of famous men in history were short—like Napoleon. Your braces will come off soon, and then you'll have beautiful teeth. And if you put some stuff on your face, maybe the pimples will go away. Besides, they're not so bad. They give your face character," she concluded, quoting a remark she had overheard somewhere.

Robert laughed and ruffled her hair affectionately. "Dopey. You're impossible. Come on—let's go ask my mother for something to eat. I smell apple strudel."

"You're so lucky, Robert. Your mother is always home, and she's always making wonderful things for you. My mother's never home. It's always dark when she comes back with my father. And then we eat and they tell me it's time to do my homework and go to sleep.''

"My mother likes to stay in the kitchen. Maybe your mother likes to do other things more.''

"But, Robert, that's what I'm telling you. She just likes to be with my father better than she likes being with me. Otherwise she wouldn't leave me with Mary Rose all the time.''

"Did you ever say that to your mother and father?''

"Lots of times. They just pat me on the head like they don't even hear me.''

Robert grew thoughtful again. "I don't know, Alicia. Maybe that's one of the things you're supposed to understand when you're older.''

"Huh,'' she said, indignant now. "Maybe I won't wait that long. Maybe I'll just come over and live with you. It's more fun here, anyway.''

8

There were those who had said the bubble might burst. But few believed that the world could come to a crashing, grinding halt. Yet that day did come, the day that the stock market later called it blackest day—October 29, 1929.

For a fortunate few who had never dallied with the rainbow vendors of Wall Street, who had not succumbed to the gilt-edged lure of "common" or "preferred," the crash of '29 brought marginal hardship rather than disaster and ruin.

Carlotta and Sharif were among the fortunate. Although sales at the gallery fell off sharply, they did not panic. They were the products of older cultures, cultures that viewed human affairs in cycles—cycles that alternated between prosperity and depression. They maintained a guarded optimism that a country as rich and powerful as the United States would soon recover.

For specific advice, Sharif turned, as always to Pierre, who reinforced their feeling that economic depression was a temporary condition. "Listen, my boy,'' he said, "I have lived in this country a great deal longer than you have. I have seen this kind of crisis begin on Wall Street and spread like a plague. Back in 1907, we saw very much the kind of thing that is happening now—bank failures, general panic. Then the day was saved by an American financier, J. P. Morgan. The old man was seventy years old, but he personally lent twenty-seven million dollars to various member firms of the stock exchange. And when that was not enough, he announced that he would underwrite a thirty-million-dollar bond issue which would save the city from bankruptcy. It was a bold stroke, and it worked. The panic soon came to an end.''

''So you think we should just retrench a bit and wait, until we see some signs of recovery?''

''No, not at all. Retrench where you must. Cut your household expenses, certainly. But where your business is concerned, now is the time to expand. What you do now can make you very rich in the future. This is my advice, and I urge you to take it. Buy whatever you can now—prices will never be so low—and wait. If you need money, I will lend you what you need. Unlike some of my American competitors, I have always maintained a very sound liquid position where my capital is concerned. It is part of my European background, I suppose, but it is a practice with which I have prospered.''

So Carlotta and Sharif cut their personal expenses, with Mary Rose's salary and Alicia's school tuition their only remaining luxuries. With Pierre's help, Sharif decided to gamble on future prosperity.

Many of his richer clients rushed to liquidate precious objects for even more precious ready cash. For a few dollars—often pathetically few—Sharif acquired a large inventory of Georgian silver, rare books, near-priceless tapestries, and antique jewelry—an inventory that would one day make him a rich man. For a modest cash payment he took over the lease of the tailoring shop next door. He would use the space as a warehouse, and later, when times were better, he would break through the walls and expand Principessa's selling area.

The Hazzis' apparent solvency at a time when ruin was rampant increased Alicia's isolation at school. The fact that her parents became the receivers of family treasures from her classmates' homes added a strain of resentment to her already limited relationships.

Once again she found a kindred spirit in Robert Levine,

who was suffering from a similar kind of ostracism at the Redfield Academy.

Like the Hazzis, the Levines managed to escape the disaster that befell so many of the recently rich. Throughout the years of Simon's increasing success, they had lived well below their means. To them, luxury had been every small possession they had acquired since their life in a cold-water flat on Delancey Street.

When bad times came, Simon took his losses in that season's stock. Then, like the shrewd street merchant that he was, he converted his merchandise to necessities, all but eliminating luxury items from his stock. He kept his stores open by closing off entire departments, by reluctantly paring his sales staff to the bone. To his son's classmates, this survival only reinforced the myth of the cunning Jew. Robert told himself that he did not care.

To Alicia, he explained, "I don't want to be like the boys at school. I never wanted to be like them—or to go to that stupid place. It was all my father's idea. He's ashamed of being Jewish. He thinks it's something you can get rid of—if you spend enough money and go the the right schools. And then you're supposed to spend the rest of your life pretending you're someone else. I hate it. And I won't do it."

"I hate it, too," Alicia agreed. "I don't want to be like everybody else, either. Those girls at school—all they think about is how they look. And boys." She said this so scornfully that Robert laughed.

"That doesn't sound so terrible. Give yourself another couple of years and you'll like boys, too. Just wait and see."

"Oh, no, Robert. Boys are dumb. Except you. You're the only boy I like. When we finish school, we can get married. And then we'll both be happy."

Robert started to smile, but when he saw the earnest expression on Alicia's face, he tried to match her tone. "Alicia, listen to me. I like you, too. A lot. We're friends. More than that, actually—you're like a sister to me. But when we get older, we'll both be marrying other people."

"But why, Robert? Why?" Alicia was bewildered. She had made up her mind that she would marry Robert, that a life with him would mean the end of her loneliness. It had not occurred to her that he might have other plans.

"Because," he explained, "when I get older, I'm going to

marry a Jewish girl and have a Jewish family. I have to. It's part of who I am.''

Alicia's eyes started to tear. ''But Robert, it's not my fault that I'm not Jewish. It isn't fair.''

He ruffled her hair. ''I know, Alicia. But that's the way it is. I'll always be your friend—you know that.''

Her lip trembled. She bit down, not wanting to let him see her cry. ''If that's the way you feel, then I'm not going to be your friend anymore. You're mean, Robert. You don't really care about me, either—and you're not my friend.''

So Alicia lived her teenage years friendless, but not quite alone. Her beauty and vivacity, her willingness to take a dare, to flirt with the forbidden, made her a natural candidate for the ''fast'' crowd at school.

She learned to smoke, to carry a package of Camels stuffed into the lining of her purse, to blow perfect smoke rings on the terrace of her home. She learned to drink—and was proud of the fact that she could outlast any girl in her crowd.

Though she secretly thought this crowd was no less ''dumb'' than the one which had snubbed her, she had one strong bond with them. They were all renegades who belonged nowhere but with each other.

For them, bonding together was an act of defiance. And for them, there was no standing still. It was as if they were driven—to drink even more, to keep later hours, to push their parents to the limits. It was only a matter of time before someone would suggest a weekend house party—without chaperones.

Alicia was one of the first to agree, though she realized with a small twinge of conscience that this would mean lying to her parents—for the first time.

The lie was quickly forgotten, as she made the drive to the New Jersey shore in a crowded Chevrolet convertible—one of a three-car caravan. As she puffed a cigarette, enjoying the wind that ruffled her hair, she felt bold and daring and quite sophisticated. She let her date, a boy named Ray, put his arm around her. She had picked Ray because he was the best-looking boy in the group, as well as the best dancer. She made no protest when he let his fingers trail along the top of her breast.

When they arrived at the house, which had been closed for eight months, they found it dark and musty. There was a quality of gloom and disuse that did not quite dissipate even when the lights were turned on and the windows opened.

Bottles of whiskey were opened, records were put on the Stromberg-Carlson, couples started pairing up to dance. Alicia accepted one drink, then two more, and when she and Ray began to dance, she allowed him to press her body close, to grind against her to the rhythm of the music.

Someone suggested a walk on the beach, and the couples gradually drifted outside, carrying blankets and bottles of rye and Scotch.

Alicia had never been given any instruction in the morality of sex. She had gathered that it was something you were not supposed to experience until you were married. But she had also gathered that this rule, like most other rules, was made to be broken. She knew that her date would expect to ''do it,'' if that was what everyone else was going to do. She was willing to go along, if that would take her one more step into the adult world—and away from the isolation of childhood.

She sat with Ray on the blanket, drank beer, and listened to the waves break on the beach. He put his head on her lap, his fingers working upward along her bare leg. She watched him take off his shirt, his shoes and socks, and then his trousers. She helped him remove her skirt, her blouse, and her bra. She allowed him to fondle her body—not knowing what was expected of her. The rest was over very quickly. Ray passed out on the blanket, and Alicia walked to the water and threw up.

She returned to the house alone, took a hot shower, and went to sleep in one of the bedrooms. She stayed in the house until it was time to go home on Sunday night.

What had happened to Alicia at the house party seemed to her sordid and rather painful, but it did not end her yearning for the kind of secret closeness shared by her parents. It would have been different with Robert Levine, she told herself. Robert would have made her happy. He would have looked at her in the same way Papa always looked at Mama. He would have touched her in the same knowing way that always made Mama smile.

But Robert was lost to her. His skin had cleared, as she had assured him it would. And the braces had gone, leaving behind straight teeth and a lovely smile, a smile he turned in her direction from time to time when they met in the elevator or the lobby. She never smiled back, and she knew she would not forgive him for not choosing her, for bringing other girls to share the warmth of Rachel's affection, the treasures of her kitchen.

With Robert's rejection, Alicia was left with an aching void in her life, a sense that she had to find someone who would love only her and make her feel whole. No wonder all the girls she knew were so anxious to get married, she thought. Then the restlessness and the searching could end, and they could really get on with their lives.

When Alicia first laid eyes on Charles Richman, she suspected that for her the search might be over. She was a freshman at Barnard, the women's college of Columbia University. Although Marina Vanderbeck had hinted that Alicia might do better with a school that was less "intellectual" and more "social," Alicia liked the idea of obtaining a fine arts degree at her father's alma mater.

It was in a required course in English literature that Alicia first saw Professor Richman. "Isn't he dreamy?" the girl in the next seat whispered, as Charles came into the classroom. "He looks just like Tyrone Power—only blond—don't you think? Or maybe it's George Montgomery. . . ."

Alicia gave the girl a scornful glance. Honestly, she thought, movie-star fantasies in a classroom. No wonder some people thought it was a waste of time to educate women.

Then, in spite of herself, Alicia conducted her own careful inspection of Professor Richman, noting the clear brown eyes, the fine character lines that looked as if they had been etched into his patrician face by sun and wind. His boyish body had an easy grace that reminded her of her father. And his clothes, she observed, were good things, well cut, well tailored—and well worn. Charles Richman, she decided, bought things when they were needed, and not on whim. A sensible man, she decided, constant and dependable.

"Good afternoon, ladies," he said, in a mellifluous, perfectly accented baritone that might have been the instrument of a trained actor. "My name is Charles Richman, and I shall be spending the next fourteen weeks guiding you through the mysteries of English 101. Since this course is a required one, I am aware that I have in you a captive audience. Let me assure you that there is a good reason for this minor abridgment of your freedom of choice. I assume that most of you have mastered—or at least are intimately acquainted with—the fundamentals of English grammar. Experience has proved, however, that most college freshmen do not have the skills necessary for precise, effective written communication. These are the techniques which we shall analyze and use. The course is not an easy one, but I promise you, the time will be well spent. There is no text for the class—I've prepared a suggested reading list, which you can pick up as you leave. The first assignment, due a week from today, is a personal essay. I want you to write briefly—about five hundred words or so—about something or someone important to you. There will be no letter grade for this assignment, so please keep in mind that what I shall be looking for is not your placement of commas and periods, but rather a sense of how well you can make me understand how and why you feel about something close to you. From this I can get an idea of your strengths and your weaknesses, collectively and as individuals. And I can plan future assignments accordingly.

"Now, before I let you all leave, I'll just ask you to pass around this seating chart and to put your name in the appropriate space. And, oh yes, one last point that might particularly interest the English majors among you. At the end of the semester, those of you who seem inclined to go beyond the fundamental work of this course will be invited to join a freshman seminar next semester. This will mean extra work, an extra credit point—and an exemption from English 102. Good afternoon, ladies. If there are any questions about the assignment, I can be found in my office during the hours I've noted on your reading list."

Even before Charles had finished speaking, Alicia had begun to search her mind for an essay theme, something that she could write convincingly on, something that would make him think of her as a good student. Not like the bubbleheads who probably cluttered up his classes, sitting around making calf's-eyes at him. Besides, being a good student was something she knew how to do. Making calf's-eyes was not.

By midweek she had started and discarded half a dozen papers. She had tried to write about her parents, but her words failed to capture the beauty of those two elusive, enchanted people. She thought for a moment of writing about her friendship with Robert Levine—but the memory was still too raw and painful.

She decided finally to write about Pasha. She closed her eyes and thought of the exquisite lines of his body, the graceful movement of his limbs when they cantered through the park, the quick surge of power when she put him into a gallop, the gentle response of his eyes when she stroked his head or fed him bits of carrot or sugar lumps.

Quickly she began to draw word pictures of her splendid animal, of the strong mystical bond she always felt when they were together. She finished her essay by saying: "There is nothing in the world like the affection and loyalty of an animal. It is absolute and unconditional. An animal will never disappoint or abandon you, and only death can take him away from you."

She handed in the paper and waited anxiously for Professor Richman's verdict. And when it came, she felt a quick rush of pleasure, tempered by a small twinge of disappointment. On the top he had written: "You write like an artist, Miss Hazzi. I congratulate you on the lyricism and strength of your prose. Your paper touched me. The single flaw I find in your work is a technical one—a lack of discipline (and even an artist must have discipline) in your style. Perhaps your next project should be a research paper, which would help you organize and structure your material."

As Alicia read and reread Charles's comments, she nearly snorted when she came to the word "discipline." It was a word she had seen before—often—in other classrooms, written by other teachers. Why did they all have such one-track minds, she wondered ruefully. Suddenly she had the feeling that she was being watched. She looked up quickly, just in time to catch Charles staring at her. She smiled, but he looked away at once and resumed his lecture. "Poetry," he was saying, "has become a Cinderella among the language arts. It has fallen on hard times, and that is a pity. Poetry is neither mysterious nor contrived, although it certainly can be mindless in some of its modern manifestations. But when it is well conceived and well executed, poetry can have the power of clarion speech and the beauty of music. Consider, for example, this piece by Yeats:

> Others because you did not keep
> That deep-sworn vow have been friends of mine;
> Yet always when I look death in the face,
> When I clamber to the heights of sleep,
> Or when I grow excited with wine,
> Suddenly I meet your face.

"Now—who can tell me what the poet is saying here?"

As Charles read, his voice seemed to caress her ears; his passion touched her heart, warming her eyes with tears. He is magnificent, she thought. So wise, so knowing. She wondered what it would feel like to be held very tight by Charles Richman, to be pressed against the rough tweed of his jacket, to know the touch of those long tapering fingers, to hear the richness of that voice soften to a loving whisper. She dropped her glance to her notebook, fearful that he would see the questions in her eyes.

All right, she resolved. Professor Richman loved poetry. And he had faulted her for a lack of discipline. She would show him. She would do a paper that would knock him on his ear.

When the class ended, she hesitated a moment at his desk. "Miss Hazzi? Is there something I can do for you?"

"Actually, I was wondering who your favorite poet is."

He looked startled. "John Milton. Why?"

"Well," she said sweetly, "you did suggest that I make my next project a research paper. So I thought I'd choose a poetry subject. But I couldn't think of the right poet."

"I think you'll find John Milton's work rich with possibilities, Miss Hazzi. And I commend you for getting such an early start."

"Discipline, Professor Richman," she said, even more sweetly. And she was almost certain that Charles Richman blushed.

Sharif stood in the doorway of his daughter's room, watching her quietly as she scribbled furiously on the yellow pad in front of her, surrounded by untidy piles of books. He started to say something, then changed his mind and walked back into the living room, where Carlotta sat in front of the fireplace, warming a brandy between her long slender fingers.

"Our daughter seems to have become a serious scholar," he said, smiling.

"Yes, I have noticed. All that energy—it makes me tired sometimes to watch. Our Alicia attacks the schoolwork with the same passion she gives to her riding. Still—" she sighed— "I don't see much joy in it, this passion. I worry sometimes, *tesoro*. She does not seem to have any . . . calm in her life, our Alicia. And there do not seem to be many friends."

"Perhaps she does not feel the need for them," Sharif

suggested. "I cannot believe she would not have friends if she desired them. She is so beautiful—so intelligent—so spirited. Perhaps all she needs is to find a man who will love and cherish her, as I cherish you."

The concern in Carlotta's eyes melted away as she held out her arms to her husband.

In the quiet of her room, with only the strains of a Bach fugue to keep her company, Alicia pored over her growing pile of notes, taking pleasure in the feeling of accomplishment. This paper would certainly mean an invitation to join the freshman seminar. Then Professor Richman would notice her. She would find a way.

She had been studying Charles Richman as she would study a problem in mathematics. He liked good students, she observed, but not those who were dreary—not when he tried so hard to keep the class work from being dull and routine. He forgave errors, but not pretentiousness or long-windedness. He was a generous marker. And he seemed to appreciate originality.

Originality—that was the reason she decided against choosing *Paradise Lost* as a theme. He had probably seen dozens of freshman papers on that poem. Instead she had chosen Milton's *Samson Agonistes*. She liked the Samson myth—the story of a mighty warrior enslaved by a woman's charms.

She reread the Old Testament story several times, then turned to every book on Milton she could find, to books on the Renaissance. As she wrote, she warmed to her subject and thrilled to her own prose as she told the story of "God's faithful champion who stumbled and fell," who was "as noble as any Greek hero, who was infinitely more human." When she finished, she knew she had a project that would make the other students' work pale by comparison. All that remained was Professor Richman's reaction.

Alicia was not disappointed. Her mark was an A+. At the top of her theme Charles had written: "Your paper is exceptionally fine in both content and treatment. You have obviously assimilated your research, and this gives assurance to the organization of your paper and to your own conclusions. I thoroughly enjoyed reading this paper, and I learned much from it."

While Alicia was still glowing from Charles's praise, she heard him say: "Ladies, I'd like to read some passages from one of the papers. I've chosen this example because it is full of information, yet it is not a turgid piece of sterile research. It combines accuracy with truth. It is serious, thoughtful—and thoroughly readable. Miss Hazzi, I wonder if I might have your paper back so that I might share it with the class?"

She handed him the paper wordlessly, then shivered with pleasure as Charles began to read:

> "And there was a certain man of Zorab, of the family of Danites, whose name was Manoah; and his wife was barren, and bare not. And the angel of the Lord appeared to the woman . . ."

Alicia listened, mesmerized, to Charles's voice, giving sound and substance to the words she had written. It was as if a new, intimate connection had been forged between them.

When he finished, he handed back her theme. She dropped her eyes intuitively, without really knowing what a pretty picture her long dark lashes made against the pink and white skin of her cheeks. And when the class was over, he said quietly, "Miss Hazzi, would you stay for a moment?"

She listened demurely as Charles complimented her again on her work. "I rarely see this kind of research in freshman papers," he said. "Actually, even my graduate students sometimes have to be bullied into doing the level of work you have accomplished here. I can see that you're more than capable of handling the assignments in the freshman seminar next term. The choice is yours, of course, but I hope you'll consider the advantages of the smaller class, the stimulation of the specialized work. We'll be covering some of the classics like—"

"Oh, yes, Professor Richman, I'd love to take your seminar. Thank you for asking me." She gathered her books and started to leave.

"Miss Hazzi?" he said quickly, as if he had just come to a sudden decision.

"Yes?"

"Miss Hazzi—this is my last class of the day. I wonder if you would join me for some tea? If your schedule permits, that is."

This was more than Alicia had hoped for, and without a second thought, she decided to cut her next class. "Of course. I'd love to have tea with you."

But once they were seated together at a small table in a

neighborhood coffee shop, Charles seemed to retreat again into his academic stance. "You show a remarkable maturity in your work, Miss Hazzi. I'm certain you'll do well in whatever field you choose, but I wondered if you had considered an English major?"

"No—no, I hadn't. But if you think I should . . ."

"Actually, 'should' has nothing to do with it. There's such verve and passion in your writing—one rarely sees those qualities."

She did not tell him that the "verve" was caused by his presence, that the "passion" was directed at him—that for another instructor she might well have turned in the same indifferent work she did in some of her other classes. Instead she smiled. "Couldn't you call me Alicia? Outside of class at least?"

"I suppose I could," he said, seeming less confident than he did when he was teaching. "That would make another 'first' for the day."

"Another? What else have you done today?"

"I've asked to see you outside of class. Look here, Miss Hazzi—Alicia—this feels damned awkward, with you being my pupil, but actually, I wanted to ask if I could see you some evening. A concert? Or a play perhaps? Do you like musicals?"

"Yes—yes, I do. I don't think it's awkward at all," she said, assured now that he had noticed her. As a woman. "It's not as if you were teaching third grade. I am nineteen, after all."

"Ah, yes—well, that does put a different complexion on things—your advanced age."

"You're making fun of me." She pouted prettily, flirting as if she had been doing it all her life.

"Just a little—and just because I'm nervous."

"Are you telling me that I make you nervous, Professor Richman? I find that hard to believe."

"Call me Charles—please. But only after class, if you don't mind. I wouldn't want my students to slip into anarchy."

"I don't think that would happen. Your students like you very much."

"Really?" He flushed with pleasure and embarrassment. Alicia was surprised at how boyish and ingenuous he looked— as if he really did not know how popular he was, or how many of her classmates would give a month's allowance to be sitting in her place right now. She was oddly touched, because that little show of human vulnerability made Charles Richman seem eminently accessible.

Alone in the serenity of his book-filled study, Charles allowed second thoughts to diminish the pleasure of the time he had spent with Alicia. He knew it wasn't prudent or practical to spend free hours with students. He was aware that the college's history had included a few scandals—whispered gossip, followed by quiet resignations, discreet transfers.

Charles loved his work. It was the very core of his existence. Yet it was a lonely existence. He knew that the faculty wives thought of him as an eligible bachelor. He was always invited to the myriad teas and receptions that made up the college's social life. But he had never met a woman who held his attention, who made him want to linger.

And then she had appeared. A freshman student. A dark-haired beauty with an aura about her—a mysterious, indefinable, seductive quality. Once he had seen her, it had been difficult to keep his eyes from her face. Then she had written her first paper, filled with a sadness, a loneliness that drew him. She seemed like one of those tragic heroines of nineteenth-century novels. Then she had asked him about his favorite poet—and written that extraordinary paper. It was as if she were reaching out to him. It was an invitation he could not ignore.

"I'm going to the theater tonight," Alicia announced to her parents. And just as they began to smile their approval, she added, "With Professor Richman, from school." She watched with pleasure as uncertainty crept into their expressions.

"When did all this come about?" Sharif asked cautiously.

"Don't look so worried, Papa," she said, laughing. "Professor Richman is a gentleman—like you. He is very handsome and very brilliant. Also like you. He thinks your daughter is an extraordinary pupil. Yes, that is what he said. Extraordinary. Oh, Papa, all the girls in my class will be wild with envy. They all think he's wonderful. But it was me he asked to tea. And now we're going to the theater. To see *The Barretts of Wimpole Street* with Katharine Cornell. And then we're to have supper at the Algonquin. Oh, I think this is going to be the best evening."

"Well, if all this makes you happy, we shall certainly make your professor welcome—won't we, my love?"

Carlotta nodded. "Of course. I look forward to meeting your young man. He is a young man, isn't he, Alicia? How old is this Professor Richman?"

Alicia waved her hand airily. "Oh, Mama, I'm sure I don't know. It would have been too gauche to ask. And what does it matter? He thinks I'm very mature. He said so."

Sharif and Carlotta exchanged glances, but said nothing.

They greeted Charles Richman cordially, offering polite conversation and Sharif's best sherry. Alicia watched Charles as he stood with her father, drawing him out about his own university days. She thought there would never be two other men as attractive as these—her father, dark, unusually somber; Charles, fair, aristocratic.

Charles had rehearsed any number of speeches for Alicia's parents, for he was anxious that they not misunderstand his interest in their daughter. "Mr. Hazzi," he began, "I know you must have some reservations about my seeing Alicia. Certainly it is not accepted practice for faculty members to mingle socially with students. But Alicia is an unusual young woman. She is—"

"Quite mature," Sharif finished, with a touch of irony.

"Well, yes, actually," Charles continued, "but if you have any objections, I will certainly respect them. Let me assure you—"

"That is not necessary, Professor Richman. I don't see anything particularly sinister in your interest, nor in the fact of your being Alicia's instructor. I can see that it gives Alicia great pleasure to spend time in your company. For the moment, that is all that concerns me. And," he added with another ironic smile, "in any case, she has assured me that you are a gentleman."

As they sat in the darkened theater, Charles's eyes shifted frequently from the stage to Alicia's profile. Once, without thinking, he put his hand over hers. She turned and smiled at him, radiant and content.

Their comfortable mood prevailed while they shared a late supper at the Algonquin. "I've always loved this place," Charles said. "It seems to live and breathe literary tradition."

"Then I love it, too," Alicia agreed, her eyes sparkling

with pleasure. "Thank you for taking me to the theater. It was beautiful. And so sad."

"I imagine that you go to the theater often, Alicia. Surely this isn't such a rare treat for you?"

"Oh, well, my parents go fairly often. Sometimes they remember to invite me."

Something in her voice made him more gentle. "Your parents seem like exceptional people."

"Yes," she said quietly. "I've always thought so."

"They are a very handsome couple."

She nodded, hesitated a moment, then went on, encouraged by the concern in his face. "To me, they've always seemed perfect. Like a beautiful painting. Perfect and unreachable. You can appreciate it, admire it, but you can't really be a part of it. Do you know what I mean?"

He did not quite understand what she was telling him, but he knew instinctively that it was important. "I'm glad they didn't object to this evening. I want to do this again, Alicia. Often."

"Me, too. They won't object. They probably won't even notice."

"I can't believe that. How could anyone not notice you?"

Her mood shifted, and she teased him. "Really, Professor Richman, is that what you think? It took you long enough to notice me."

"Really, Miss Richman. I can tell you now that it didn't take me long at all. But I told you before—I don't make a practice of dating my students."

"Lucky for me. Half the girls in the class think you're very attractive. And sexy," she added mischievously.

"Really, Alicia."

"Really, Charles."

"Now you've humbled me, Alicia. I had thought it was my teaching ability that held my students' interest."

"Oh, Charles, I'm only teasing you. Everyone thinks you're a wonderful teacher."

"Thank you for that." He looked at his watch. "Perhaps we'd better leave now. I don't want to keep you out too late."

She wanted the evening to go on forever, but she did not argue. When he brought her to her door, she stood waiting, expectantly. He squeezed her shoulder and said, "Good night, Alicia. I'll see you in class."

"Good night, Charles," she whispered.

Before he slept, Charles Richman thought about his own parents. They had been happily married, yet he had never felt excluded from their happiness. His father had been the dean of a small junior college in Vermont; his mother, a woman of no particular beauty. Their marriage had endured until the day James Richman died.

Charles's mother had an enormous talent for living, a gift she had shared generously with her family and with all who knew her. Boredom and ennui were strangers to Sarah Richman. Life had given her a good marriage, a child. In exchange she had given her husband a lifetime of contentment. To Charles she had given boundless affection, an enormous respect for women, and the hope—no, the conviction that marriage was a sublime condition.

In Alicia he thought he saw the same boundless energy that made his mother a perpetual source of nourishment, the same quick intelligence that had delighted her husband. He did not really know much about this pupil of his, yet he felt he knew all about her. She roused in him the need to protect, to soothe and comfort and love. He felt that in cherishing Alicia, he would bring a richness and beauty to his own life.

"Well, Charles, this is certainly something of a predicament you've brought me." Henry Adams, chairman of the English department, puffed vigorously on a cigarette and shook his head. "A freshman, you say?"

"Yes, Henry, a freshman. I had hoped you would advise me. Surely there's a way to keep this from becoming a 'predicament'?"

"Don't know, Charles, my boy. I'm thinking. Last time something like this came up—before your time—it was a fellow from the science department. Left his wife. Married the girl. Left the school, too. Messy, it was. Devilishly messy. Hear he went out west somewhere."

"Look, Henry, I don't have a wife. I'm serious about this girl. I've met her parents, and they don't seem to object. I'll talk to the dean, if you think that's best. I don't see why this can't be honorable and aboveboard."

"P'raps we can see the dean together, Charles. But it

won't be simple. First thing you'd better do is get her out of your class."

"But she's one of my best students!"

"Then she'll do well with someone else. Don't want all those other girls in your class to start whispering. Telling their parents. It's the nature of the little creatures. They'll notice. And they'll talk."

"All right, Henry. I see your point. Is there anything else?"

"Discretion, Charles. It's not my place to tell you this. But you'll have to be like Caesar's wife, you know. Above reproach. You can count on me, Charles. You're a fine teacher, and I don't want to lose you. Be careful and p'raps this will all work out."

"Thank you, Henry. I couldn't ask you for any more."

But when Charles began to explain his position to Alicia, he found her less than sympathetic. "It's outrageous, Charles. What do I care for small minds and petty gossip?"

"Alicia, please—keep your voice down. Your parents will think we're quarreling."

"What does it matter what they think? Oh, Charles, this was such a pleasant evening—why do you have to spoil it for me?"

"It was a lovely evening, and I want many more evenings with you. That's why we have to behave in an intelligent, reasonable way. I'm not talking about petty gossip and small minds. This involves your reputation—and my career."

Her face softened, her tone became less shrill. "I'm sorry, Charles. I wasn't thinking about you. Please don't be angry with me. I just don't want to be in someone else's stupid class. I want to be with you. I don't care if the other girls know about us. I want them to know."

"Alicia."

"All right, Charles. I'll transfer into another class next semester."

When Charles left Alicia he felt optimistic. He did not see her slam the door, then kick it viciously, muttering, "Damn, damn."

As she turned around, she ran into her mother.

"Is something wrong, Alicia?"

"Charles wants me to leave his class. To find another instructor."

"*Ma perchè?*"

"He doesn't want people to talk about us. It's so stupid. Really."

"He sounds like a sensible, thoughtful man, this Professor Richman."

"Sensible, sensible—oh God, how I hate *sensible*," she complained, kicking the nearest chair as she stamped toward her room.

Carlotta smiled. Perhaps this relationship was just what Alicia needed.

Sharif and Carlotta watched fondly as Charles Richman courted their daughter. They agreed that his quiet calm had a leveling influence on Alicia, but more than that, they saw that his affection seemed to nourish a new serenity in her. Alicia's disposition appeared to mellow, yet Carlotta did not quite trust the lowered eyes, the "Yes, Charles" that came to her daughter's lips so readily whenever Charles made one of his quiet pronouncements.

"It seems unnatural," she complained to Sharif. "It's as if she's pretending to be someone else."

"You worry too much," her husband said. "She's happy with Charles. Happiness has a way of changing people. Why shouldn't Alicia change a little for Charles? He's a good, solid chap, very intelligent—his books on English poetry are quite brilliant. And he is devoted to our daughter. Stop fretting, my love. Alicia and Charles will be as happy as we are."

Alicia's newfound calm evaporated on a Sunday morning at brunch, when Charles mentioned casually that his summer plans included an extended visit with his mother in Vermont.

"You don't mean that," Alicia said accusingly. Carlotta held her breath and passed a silver plate to her daughter. "Alicia, darling, have a warm brioche. They are very good this morning."

But Alicia would not be distracted. "How can you think of leaving me, Charles?"

"Alicia," he said gently, embarrassed to have Sharif and Carlotta witness any discord, "I haven't seen my mother since last summer. I always plan to spend time with her during the summer break. She's old, dear, and I don't know how many years we have left together. Surely you can understand?''

"Take me with you, then. I'll understand if you take me with you." She thrust her chin forward, daring him to refuse her.

Charles shook his head and looked to Carlotta for assistance. "Alicia dear, there's nothing I'd like better. I want you to get to know Mother. But I thought we'd wait until we're engaged. I didn't think it would be proper—"

"Proper! What do I care . . . Did you say *engaged*, Charles? What a novel way to propose!" The sullen pout became a smile.

Charles looked again at Carlotta. "Well, naturally, I hadn't planned to say anything so soon. I had planned to talk to your parents—perhaps next year. I thought we could marry after graduation."

"Oh, Charles, let's be engaged now. It will be such fun. Then we wouldn't have to skulk around the campus. And I could go with you to Vermont. We wouldn't have to be separated. Say yes, Charles—please say yes."

"Well—if that's what you want—if your parents have no objection . . ."

Alicia fingered the small diamond that twinkled on her left hand, watching, as if from a distance, while Charles embraced his mother, kissing her warmly on both weathered cheeks. What an ugly woman, she thought, as Charles took her hand and drew her close. "And this is Alicia, Mother. I know you'll be great friends."

Sarah Richman smiled a welcome at Charles's fiancée. "Charles has told me so much about you. Welcome to our home. And please think of this as your home, too."

Alicia smiled politely and looked around at the well-worn furnishings, the rugged bits of antique Americana, the cozy clutter. It all seemed to go with Sarah Richman, but somehow Alicia could not visualize Charles in this setting—in spite of the clusters of photographs that sat on the old player piano, on the rough-hewn oak mantel, on almost every table surface in the living room. A dull place, she decided at once. No wonder Charles had left.

"We have so much to talk about," Sarah was saying. "I'll give you some of my recipes—Charles's favorites. And perhaps I can help you avoid some of the pitfalls of academic life. I had my share of disasters. Oh, yes, I certainly did." She laughed, a loud hearty sound. "But I learned—thirty-five years smoothed out all my rough edges."

Alicia squirmed against the flowered chintz of a sagging love seat. She did not like the sound of "academic life." It sounded like work. Boring work. She did not like her future mother-in-law's assumption that she would pattern her own married life after anyone else's. Especially not homely Sarah Richman's. She yawned. "Oh, my," she said. "The trip seems to have tired me out. Could you please show me where I'm to sleep?"

"Oh, I am sorry," Sarah said. "Of course you're tired. Charles will probably want to take you hiking tomorrow. And I'll have to get to work right after breakfast."

"Work? Charles didn't tell me you worked."

Sarah laughed again. "I'm always doing something or other. This summer I'm working at a day camp. I must say it's a change for me. Keeps me stepping smartly. I've been learning new things every day."

Alicia yawned again.

"Here I am rambling," Sarah apologized, "and you're asleep on your feet. Upstairs," she directed. "First room to the left. Charles will take your things up. Sleep well."

"Thank you," Alicia said—and retreated hastily up the stairs.

The following morning Charles's childhood home looked a little less dismal—even though Alicia nearly gagged on the huge heavy meal that Sarah Richman called breakfast. Alicia had been raised on breakfasts of café au lait and croissants and jam. She watched, fascinated, as Sarah set out steaming platters of ham and sausage and eggs, a heaping basket of biscuits, and a pitcher of cloyingly sweet syrup she proudly described as "Vermont's best." She tried not to look as Charles filled his plate twice and ate with apparent relish. She murmured, "Not hungry," when Sarah complained, "This child eats like a sparrow."

She was relieved when the older woman announced it was time to go to work and left in a last flurry of kitchen activity, promising she would fix pot roast and dumplings for supper.

As Charles began to carry dishes and cups from the table to the sink, Alicia stepped in front of him and slid her arms up his chest and around his neck, murmuring, "Aren't you glad

I came?'' before she pressed her lips against his. Caught by surprise, he forgot the restraint he usually exercised and pulled her close, pressing her body into his. She slipped her hands under his pullover. He shuddered, then gently pushed her away. ''Alicia—we have to stop. Right now.''

''But why?'' she coaxed. ''We're all alone. And we're going to be married.''

''Because that's not the way I want to love you. We'll wait until we're married, and it's my responsibility to see that we do.'' He spoke quietly and firmly, and she knew that he would not change his mind. ''Let's take a nice long walk. I want to show you the pond where I learned to swim.''

Almost in spite of herself, Alicia was impressed with the Vermont landscape—the rolling acres of majestic virgin forests set against granite mountains, the crystal clarity of Charles's favorite pond. She watched with pleasure as he peeled off his shirt and pants, felt the pride of ownership when she saw the lean contours of his body, the rippling muscles as he executed a clean dive into the pond, cutting the water with lazy unhurried strokes.

''Come on in, Alicia,'' he called. ''The water's perfect.''

''In a minute,'' she answered. ''I'm enjoying the sun. And the view.''

For Alicia the day took a downward turn when Sarah Richman returned to the gray clapboard farmhouse and Charles's attention shifted from her to his mother. He insisted on helping Sarah prepare dinner. This left Alicia two choices: to sit in the living room alone, leafing through the piles of *National Geographics* that seemed to be Sarah's favorite reading material—or to sit in the kitchen, listening to mother and son reminisce about Charles's childhood. She wouldn't have minded hearing Charles tell her some of those stories. But to listen to the two of them—well, it was just too tiresome.

She pasted a smile on her face and let her attention wander, taking in the well-worn, well-polished pots, the shelves of preserves—fruits and vegetables—all neatly stacked and carefully labeled. She had heard that New Englanders were frugal. Sarah probably ate the harvest of her garden all winter long.

'' . . . don't you think that's true, Alicia?''

She realized that Sarah had been speaking to her. "I'm sorry," she said. "I was just admiring your preserves."

"I'll give you some when you and Charles go back to the city. I was saying that when a woman marries a college professor, she acquires a very large extended family. She has to treat them with care, because they can have an enormous impact on her husband's career. Why, I remember the first time I gave a dinner party for James's colleagues—I was just a bit of a bride then, and I did everything wrong. James's department chairman was a vegetarian. I'm sure James had told me, but it had gone clean out of my mind. I prepared a New England boiled dinner—so all the poor man could eat was bread and butter and salad. Then I made the mistake of getting into a heated discussion on the subject of vegetarianism —he was quite fanatical about it, I can assure you. But that wasn't all. My seating arrangement was all wrong. James explained to me later that some academic people are very sensitive about that sort of thing. Well, I had a lot of making up to do after that. I baked raisin bread and brownies for the department head for weeks. But I learned. . . ." She smiled fondly.

Alicia smiled back, thinking she had never heard anything so tiresome or depressing in her own life. This was certainly going to be a long visit. A very long visit.

Yet the relationship survived the visit, as well as the rules that Charles had laid down for their courtship. For the most part, Alicia held her tongue and her temper, turning the strength of her formidable will on herself. She did not press Charles for more than the light, tender embraces he offered. Nor did she protest the lengthy engagement.

Carlotta and Sharif approved of Charles's insistence that Alicia finish school. Yet they noted also the growing tally of small victories that Alicia scored with the use of a pretty pout or a seductive "please, Charles."

"I'm afraid," Carlotta said to her husband. "I'm afraid that when they marry, it will be like a man trying to break a wild horse with soft words. Without a miracle, it cannot be done."

"I think you may be right, my love. But she seems quite determined to marry him."

"I know." Carlotta sighed. "I don't like to interfere, but I think I will talk with Charles. Perhaps you can speak with Alicia. She may listen to her papa.''

When Carlotta suggested to Charles that he might be wise to offer a stiffer resistance to Alicia's whims, he smiled indulgently. ''But why, Mrs. Hazzi? I love Alicia, and I want to make her happy. I don't see any reason to create disagreements. I believe that two people who love each other can live in harmony. Do you know,'' he added, ''I can't remember my parents ever raising their voices to each other. Not in all the years they were married.''

Carlotta smiled at her prospective son-in-law, though her uneasiness had grown.

For his part, Sharif had barely begun to speak to Alicia, to point out that there were certain important temperamental differences between her and her intended, when her temper flared. ''Stop it, Papa. Just stop. I won't hear this. Charles is the first person who has really loved me. He doesn't criticize me, and he doesn't think other people are more important. You can't spoil this for me, Papa. If you try, I won't ever forgive you. I'll marry Charles whether you like it or not.''

Sharif knew she meant exactly what she said, and so the subject was permanently closed.

Alicia and Charles were married in June 1936, a week after her graduation. It was a lavish wedding, for Carlotta and Sharif would spare no expense in marrying off their only child—no matter what reservations they had about the match.

Alicia took no particular interest in the celebration attending her marriage. The assembled guests—the Rubichous, the Levines, selected Principessa employees and clients, Charles's colleagues, and, of course, Sarah Richman—were barely noticed by the bride. As she took her vows, radiant in her Lanvin wedding gown, she had eyes only for Charles. Now he belonged to her. And now she would never be lonely again.

Charles had suggested a honeymoon in New England, for he had always loved the countryside in Maine and New Hampshire and Vermont. But Alicia had vetoed this idea and insisted on a trip to Paris.

He was glad to accommodate. A honeymoon, he reckoned, was part of a bride's prerogative. And when he took his bride in his arms on their wedding night, when he saw the trust and adoration in her eyes, he knew he had been right.

Alicia had never told anyone—not even Charles—about her first and only sexual experience. In this one area she was shy and timid and not at all secure. In this one area she put all her trust and confidence in Charles, hoping—no, praying—that he would make it right. She was not disappointed.

In Charles's arms she felt treasured and sheltered and warm. The old fear was forgotten. Love was everything she had hoped it might be. And after they had made love for the first time, Alicia thought she had never felt so happy, so complete in all her life. She knew then that she had been right—that happiness and fulfillment came from finding the right man.

She knew she was lucky to find a man who loved her so much. She reflected fondly on how he had let her have her way on the question of the honeymoon. And then there had been the matter of their first home. Dear Charles had assumed they would live in his little bachelor apartment on Riverside Drive and 112th Street. "You're joking," she had said the first time he had mentioned the idea. Then, seeing the stricken look on his face, she had softened her voice. "It's a charming place for you, Charles, but what on earth would I do up there? It's the end of the earth. It's practically not even in Manhattan. Oh, Charles, it's not safe up there. And my parents have offered to buy us a place of our own. You wouldn't be so selfish as to make me do without, would you?"

Of course, Charles had agreed. Such a dear. When she remembered the conversation, she smiled and went to sleep.

9

The newlyweds began their married life in a lovely wide town house on Seventy-ninth Street, a few steps from Fifth Avenue and Central Park, a short distance from Alicia's favorite museum. Charles was a bit uncomfortable at first at accepting such largesse from his in-laws. But, he reflected, it *would* have been selfish to deprive Alicia of a comfortable home. The neighborhood was unquestionably more elegant than his. And when children came, yes, it would make a difference.

Though Charles made this first adjustment with ease, he was soon called upon to make others. He had expected the same kind of domestic felicity his father had enjoyed, and he was somewhat distressed when the furnishings in the lovely new house grew dusty, when the floors took on a grimy cast and the accumulations of daily litter could no longer be ignored. Charles gently brought these conditions to his young wife's attention. Her reaction was quick and unapologetic.

"But Charles—I don't like to clean and dust and scrub. I've never done it before. Why should I have to do it now? Really, Charles—why should I?"

Charles had no ready answer. Although his salary and the royalties from his books did not add up to a large income, his wife was quite well off, thanks to a trust fund set up by her parents. There was no reason for her to live far beneath her means. So he did not object when a cleaning woman began to appear in the morning and disappear in the afternoon, leaving an infinitely more appealing home in her wake.

He made a similar adjustment in his expectation of home-cooked meals. After a few perfunctory forays in her beautifully remodeled kitchen, Alicia presented her husband with another reasonable argument. "Charles, dear, surely you can see that my cooking isn't worth a damn. And frankly, darling, I really don't have any interest in learning. I'm just not good at these domestic things. I'm bored sitting at home while you're off at the university. I've had a really good idea. Before you say anything, just let me tell you. I want to hire a cook. And I want to go to work—at the gallery. I'm sure my parents can find something useful for me to do there. Then we'll both have something to do during the day. And we'll eat so much better. Isn't that a fine idea?"

Charles wasn't at all sure it was. He wanted his wife to be at home, waiting for him, as his mother had waited for his father. But he was a fair man. If his beautiful wife would rather not perform domestic chores, if she would prefer to spend the day working with her parents, he could see no reason to make her unhappy.

And so a cook was hired, a stout German woman with a

remarkably varied repertoire. "See, Charles," Alicia exulted, after they had sampled a week's worth of fine roasts and salads and soufflés. "Isn't this better than eating my awful cooking? And I've had such a good time at the gallery. Mother said I could start out as a general assistant to everyone—make myself useful wherever I'm needed. The day just flew by. . . ."

Yet, although she had had her way, Alicia was perhaps less pleased than she might have been. It had occurred to her, rather suddenly, that perhaps her victories with Charles were just a little too easy, that when he deferred to her, it was not so much out of love as from weakness. The idea grew, tainting her pleasure in getting her own way. It made her test her husband in unnecessary disagreements. She pushed him, challenging him, daring him to stop her. But he did not. And each time he failed to meet her silent challenge, her love for him was soured by the bitter taste of contempt.

She began spending longer days at Principessa, wondering if he would object, if he would insist that she come home before he did so that she might greet him with a drink, some conversation, a daily ration of affection.

But Charles said nothing. He found himself readjusting to the same kind of empty home he had known as a bachelor, filling the time with research for a new book and wondering why his wife had changed so much.

In one area the marriage remained the same. Neglect her husband as she might in the day, worry him, bewilder him, still at night she turned to him, seeking solace and tenderness in his arms.

Alicia's reaction to the news of her first pregnancy was a curious one. Although she had been casual about contraception, she seemed incredulous, as if she could make no connection between what she and Charles did at night and what was now happening to her body.

From the beginning she was at war with the child growing within her. She was visited by the most racking attacks of morning sickness, not just in the morning, but at regular intervals throughout the day. She felt tired all the time. And when she was not tired, she was sick to her stomach and wishing she were dead.

Carlotta offered sympathy and help with household chores,

although in fact Alicia had done little homemaking even when she was feeling well. Her mother assured Alicia that what she was feeling was normal, that the pain and suffering would seem worthwhile after her baby was born. Alicia was not convinced. "I hate you," she whispered one night to the fetus that seemed to be growing at her expense, taking control of her body and her well-being. "I hate you—do you hear?"

As if the unborn child did hear, Alicia woke up the next morning to find her inner thighs smeared with blood. She reacted with fear and fascination. When Charles came into the bathroom to see why his wife had not come out, he found her hunched over the sink, willing herself to throw up, as if that somehow might make everything all right. "What is it, Alicia?" he asked, face twisted with concern. "What's wrong." For an answer, she showed him the blood.

He picked up her unresisting body and carried her back to bed. Not wanting her to hear the worry that would surely be in his voice, he went into the next room to call Roger Tataryan, the son of the doctor who had delivered Alicia. Once help was summoned, he called his office to cancel his classes for the day. Then he returned to the bedroom to sit on the bed, holding his wife's hand, murmuring reassurances from time to time.

Before he had married Alicia, Charles had assumed that he and his wife would recreate the kind of partnership he had seen growing up in his own home. When he had failed to find the same serenity, the same mutual contentment in his life with Alicia, he grasped at the hope that time might smooth out the jagged edges that kept the two of them from forming a harmonious partnership, might gentle the spirit that kept tugging Alicia outside the periphery of their marriage.

And when time alone had failed to produce this result, Charles had turned to yet another hope—a child. This hope had soared with the news of Alicia's pregnancy, had remained alive in spite of the unmistakable signs that she was less than happy with the condition that would make of her a mother.

Now, as he sat just inches from the body that had rebelled so vigorously against the child they had conceived, he worried quietly. For the child, yes, but also for Alicia. For all her high spirits, her stubborn unwillingness to bend or accommodate, Alicia could be frail and vulnerable. She was like a thoroughbred—unbeatable, uncatchable, yet perhaps easily destroyed.

When Roger Tataryan appeared at the door of their town house, Charles let him in and, in a voice scarcely louder than a whisper, explained Alicia's symptoms. The doctor's examination was brief, and when he took Charles aside, his manner was serious, but not grave. "I know how emotional Alicia can be, Charles, so I want you to put this episode in perspective. Alicia is staining. Not too heavily, but it's a sign you can never ignore."

"Do you think she might lose the baby?"

"That's a possibility, of course. And if it happens, it's usually for the best. It means that the baby—"

"Is there anything we should do for her? Would it be better if she went to the hospital?"

"Not yet. I just want her kept quiet. If the bleeding gets heavy, call me right away. Then call this number for an ambulance."

When Charles returned to resume his watch over his wife, he found her subdued, but not depressed. As he reached to take her hand, she turned ferocious eyes on him. "It's not my fault," she said vehemently.

"Of course not," he soothed her. "Roger said it was just—nature. It doesn't mean anything will go wrong. You'll be fine in a day or two."

Again the blue eyes blazed. "This baby has been nothing but trouble." And then the sedative took hold and she fell into a restless sleep.

By the end of the following day, the staining stopped and there was no pain. Roger seemed satisfied that Alicia's condition had stabilized. "Well, children," he said, smiling, "it looks as if everything will be fine."

"Thank you, Roger, thank you for everything." Charles spoke while Alicia lay silent against white sheets, eyes half open, cheeks slightly flushed.

"Don't thank me. It was all decided somewhere beyond me. But"—he pointed a finger at Alicia—"we don't want to press our luck. I want you to stay in bed for a few days. After that you should take it easy. Don't overdo physically. And avoid any kind of stress or strain. I'm hoping there won't be any more problems, but we'll keep a close eye on you. Come to see me next week. See that she does, Charles."

Alicia spent the requisite number of days in bed. But when she got up to resume her normal routine, she seemed to ignore the "take it easy" admonition with reckless abandon. She went early to the gallery and stayed past closing. On weekends she filled her days with strenuous physical activity. One Saturday morning Charles opened his eyes and saw his wife pulling on her riding boots. He bolted upright. "Alicia!"

"Go back to sleep, Charles. I didn't want to disturb your rest."

"You're not planning to ride today?"

"Of course I am. I'm feeling fine—thank goodness—for the first time in months. I don't see any reason to behave like a cripple. I've been sick and miserable and I'm not throwing any more precious time away."

"The baby, Alicia. Roger said you shouldn't—"

"Oh, the baby. If having a baby means not living like a human being, I'm not even sure I want one." Alicia knew she sounded cruel, but she couldn't stop herself and she couldn't take the words back. Instead of telling Charles that she desperately needed to feel that she belonged to herself again, that she was feeling claustrophobic and trapped, that she had to be outdoors, she simply turned on her heel and left.

As Charles watched the back of her Harris Tweed hacking coat disappear, the thought came to him that if his mother had felt the way Alicia did, he might never have been born.

Although her mother did not seem particularly anxious for her arrival, Alicia's daughter was born—alive, healthy, and extraordinarily beautiful. Alicia went into labor at high noon on a chilly Saturday in the fall. She did not feel pain so much as a rhythmic cramping, which she was determined to ignore as long as possible. Charles assigned himself the job of making periodic calls to Roger—and periodically asking Alicia if she was ready to go to the hospital.

To Charles's queries Alicia answered no, for she had a fear of illness and death that translated into a fear of doctors and hospitals. The sole exception in her mind was Roger. Now she had a superstitious conviction that if she postponed the hospital until the last possible moment, her chances for survival would be improved.

But when she spent the entire day doing inconsequential chores, and when she insisted on lingering over dinner and coffee, Charles lost patience. "For heaven's sake, Alicia, you're acting like a child. I can see from your face that it's time to go. What's the point of staying here, darling? Isn't it better to be at the hospital? You'll be looked after. . . ."

"I'm not ready, Charles. Stop harping on the hospital. I'm just not ready. In fact," she said, her voice taking on a hint of defiance, "I think I'd like to look at the papers before I go. Would you get them for me?" Then, seeing his face harden, she changed her tone. "Please, Charles? Then I'll go—I promise."

He did as she asked, watching anxiously as she paged through one section after another. He made no comment as he timed the spasms he saw reflected in her face. Finally, after she doubled over, holding her abdomen, she looked up at Charles and said quietly, "I'm ready to go now."

As they made the seemingly endless trip to St. Vincent's Hospital, Charles saw a new Alicia, white-faced, teeth clenched—and he realized that his indomitable wife was not only in pain, she was obviously frightened almost beyond endurance.

"Alicia, darling," he said, "it's going to be all right. As soon as we get to the hospital, they'll give you something for the pain. Roger is waiting for you, and I'll be there until the baby is born. There's nothing to worry about. I hope you're not thinking about the problems you had a few months ago. Roger said that everything is normal and routine. . . ." He kept up a running stream of conversation, voice low and soothing, and watched her jaw relax just a little.

When they reached the hospital, Roger took one look at his patient and said dryly, "You haven't left us much time to play around with, my dear." Then to a waiting intern he added, "Let's go."

Alicia reached up from the examining table and took Roger's hand. "I don't want to be a nuisance, Roger, but could I have something for the pain?"

He looked down at her face, which was now covered with sweat. "I'm sorry, Alicia. It's a bit late—I can't do it now. Just hold on a little longer. You're going to deliver in a very little while."

The "very little while" seemed like an eternity to Alicia. She was racked with waves of unrelenting pain that she felt would surely split her body in two. This baby is going to kill me, she thought, as she was wheeled into the delivery room.

Thi̧s is the last day of my life—and the notion filled her with wonder and resentment. Within a few minutes, the ether took away consciousness and all sensation of pain.

The next time Alicia opened her eyes, she was settled in a private room, with Charles sitting at her bedside. "Welcome back," he whispered, and she could see that there were tears in his eyes.

She opened her mouth to speak, but it felt dry and cottony—her tongue, thick and clumsy. "Thirsty," she croaked, and he jumped up to fill the glass on her nightstand. He cradled her head gently in his arm and held the glass to her lips.

"Just a little now," he cautioned. "And drink it slowly." When she was finished, he laid her head back on the pillow. "How are you feeling?" he asked, his concern showing in the anxious tilt of his body, the rumpled suit, the tousled hair that had not been combed since the morning before.

"Hurts," she answered, then fell back to sleep.

He noted that she had not asked about the baby, about whether it was alive and well, about its sex and appearance. He shrugged off this lapse with the reminder that she was too exhausted from her ordeal. So he went off to the hospital nursery to look and marvel at his infant daughter.

Later that evening Alicia was almost herself again. She sat up in bed now, wearing the French lace bed jacket Carlotta had brought, surrounded by the flowers that had cost Charles nearly a half week's salary. She was a queen, receiving guests—her mother, her father and her husband.

"She is so beautiful, your daughter," Sharif said. "And she looks so much like my magnificent Carlotta—it is quite incredible." He was holding her mother closely, protectively, and Alicia thought how curious it was that her ordeal was still another occasion for bringing her parents closer.

"Thank God you are well, *bella*," said Carlotta. "I have been praying for you all day. And yes, your baby is beautiful—but not half as beautiful as you were."

Alicia did not tell her family that she had not yet seen her child, that she had told the nurse she was too tired. Conversation grew strained during the visit because each time the subject of her baby came up, Alicia's interest seemed to drift. It was as if the infant in the nursery had nothing to do with her. Smiling politely, she accepted the good wishes and concern of her family, but there was no joy or sense of involvement in her responses.

When Carlotta and Sharif left, Charles made a new effort. "Have you thought of a name for the baby?" he asked.

She turned vague eyes on him. "Oh—I don't know." She gave him a bright, artificial smile. "Why don't you choose? After all, you're her father."

A bitter response came to Charles's lips. This was one of the few times in their brief—and disillusioning—married life that Alicia had deferred to him, and he realized it was simply because she did not give a damn. Then he bit the harsh words back, not wanting a confrontation of cruelties that could not easily be taken back.

"I was thinking," he said evenly, "that if you didn't mind, I'd like to name her Sarah—after my mother. We could call her Sally. You know," he went on, "she does look very much like Carlotta. She has the most beautiful eyes, and her forehead . . . she looks like a painting by Botticelli. I look at her and I can't believe how lovely she is. Even the nurses agree—and they think that most infants are quite plain.

"You must see her, Alicia. Let me ask the nurse to bring her—just for a few minutes. I know you're tired," he said, giving credibility to her excuses, "but you'll feel better after you've seen her."

Alicia closed her eyes and nodded. Charles spoke to the nurse, who was charmed not only by the Richman baby but by her handsome father, and she agreed to bend regulations "just this once."

When she had placed the blanket-wrapped infant in Alicia's arms, Alicia took a long appraising look. With her critic's eye, she examined the porcelain complexion, the button nose, the china-blue eyes, touching the skin that was as soft as silk. She scrutinized each little finger, extended and counted every toe, ran her fingers over the dimpled knees and the plump little elbows. And when she was finished, she rewrapped the baby carefully and settled back on her pillows, a satisfied smile on her face. As Charles watched this little tableau, he thought it was not the smile of a beatific Madonna but of a Cheshire cat.

◄ 10 ►

It was decided that Sarah Miranda Richman and her mother would come home a week following the baby's birth. Waiting for them would be the baby nurse–nanny hired by Carlotta to do the chores which her daughter would surely view with indifference or distaste. Charles was agreeable to this arrangement, for although his family had been far from wealthy, he did come from a Brahmin tradition that included the baby nurse.

Alicia came home to a spotless house and a bedroom made festive by flowers and fresh fruit and a bottle of champagne chilling in a silver bucket. "Welcome home," Charles said, as he led his wife, laughing and protesting, to their bed.

"I'm not at all tired," she said. "I haven't done anything today except get dressed and come home."

"Humor me then," he coaxed, as he settled her under the handmade down quilt. As soon as she laid her head on the nest of pillows he had made, he took a small box from his pocket. "For the mother of my little princess."

"Charles! A surprise—oh, let me see it." She tore the pink tissue and the Burgundy satin ribbon and opened the old velvet jeweler's box. Inside was a handmade gold locket. "Oh, Charles—it's simply beautiful. Wherever did you find such a wonderful piece?"

"It was my grandmother's. My father gave it to me when she died. He told me to give it to my wife—on a memorable occasion. I can't think of anything more memorable than this."

She accepted the kiss he dropped tenderly on her cheek. "I hope," he said hesitantly, "that this might be the beginning of something new—something better for us, Alicia."

She opened her eyes wide. She knew exactly what he was talking about. But since she felt the core weakness in their marriage was Charles's flawed character, she failed to see how a new baby would change anything. She was saved from

101

having to make an answer by a tap on the bedroom door. It was the nurse, Annie, carrying Sally in her arms.

"I know you must be anxious to get settled with this little angel, so I brought her up to you. I can warm her bottle and let you feed her this first time home."

"No, Annie." Alicia waved both the nurse and her infant daughter away. "I think I'm too tired right now," she said, contradicting the statement she had made moments before. "You take care of it. And in the future, I'll let you know when I want the baby."

On that first day the pattern of the Richman family was more or less established. Annie became no less than Sally's surrogate mother, while Alicia became a kind of resident godmother, paying attention to the child when she felt maternal—that is to say, when it amused her to think that she was the mother of a child.

As soon as she felt fit, she began spending most of her days at Principessa. When Carlotta suggested that this was not such a good idea, she snapped, "Why? You did it when I was a baby. Why was it all right for you and not for me?"

"Because I was with my husband. I was helping him build a business. I was building for our family's future."

"Oh, really? Did it ever occur to you that you were building something else? A cozy little world for the two of you? A world that didn't really need or want a child?"

"Alicia, my love," Carlotta protested, understanding in a flash that her daughter was saying something dangerous—something true—about the ways in which she had failed her child—because she had loved her husband almost too much. "No, Alicia, your father and I, we loved you very much—"

"But you did what suited the two of you at the time. And that, Mama dear, is what I am trying to do. Furthermore, I wish, just once, you would listen, just once give me—"

Carlotta stared at this magnificent dark-haired creature who was her child, and she remembered a night years ago, a night when she believed that her love for her husband had cost her the life of a son. And she wondered if her love for Sharif was now to be measured out in the happiness of their only child. Although Carlotta was not close to her daughter, she knew that Alicia had a need that drove her, that she was searching for some sanctuary she had not yet found. She had not found it in her marriage; she would not, Carlotta suspected, find it in her child, and she would probably not find it in the business she now seemed to want so much. Perhaps, Carlotta thought, as a wave of guilt and pity washed over her, perhaps she might never find it. She put her arms around the stiff, unbending form of her daughter.

"*Cara,* Alicia," she sighed. "Perhaps you are right. Perhaps your father and I have been selfish. I don't know if you can understand this, but when we fell in love and married, it was as if we were completely alone in this world. We had to be everything to each other—lovers, parents, friends—everything. Perhaps we continued to feel that way after it was no longer true. Perhaps we were too close to give you the kind of love you wanted from us.

"But if we disappointed you, don't let that disappointment cloud your life with your husband, with your child. It's up to you, *tesora,* to make something of that. Alicia, my sweet, if your marriage is not what you hoped for, it is within your power to mold and shape it. Charles loves you very much— now, I think, more than ever. Talk with him, help him understand you better. Help yourself to understand him. If you ignore your marriage now, if you avoid the things you don't like, they will not get better, I promise you. And you will never know the power of your own strength, the ways it can make you happy."

Alicia had relaxed visibly in her mother's arms. She leaned slightly into Carlotta's bosom and nestled her head there. For a few moments she was a little girl again, believing in the possibility of happy endings, willing to listen to those who promised them.

Carlotta went on talking. "Your father and I—you may not believe me—but we have worried about you ever since you were a young woman. We felt that you were a rare and special individual, someone who did not fit into a mold. We loved you for being special, for having fire and spirit. But, my darling child, you did not seem to have a purpose or a direction, and we did not know how to give you one, or even if we should try. If we failed you, I am truly, truly sorry. But now you are old enough to take those responsibilities for yourself. You must realize that the kind of fire and spirit you have—these can consume you if you do not direct them." Carlotta had been stroking her daughter's hair as she spoke, and now she brushed her forehead with her lips.

"Oh, Mama," Alicia sobbed, tears coming for the first time since she was a child. "Oh, Mama, I wish . . . I wish

we had always talked like this, just the two of us. I wish . . .
Oh, Mama, I love you.''

Carlotta drew her daughter close. She felt her heart splinter
with remorse for the small omissions that might have meant
so much, for the wasted moments and unseen opportunities
that had made of her daughter an emotional orphan. She
swore silently that she would do everything she could to help
her daughter find serenity. ''I'm sorry,'' she said. ''But at
least we are talking now. And we have many years ahead of
us to make up for what was lost. And then, as your papa
says, *inshallah* . . .''

In the time that Carlotta had been speaking, her words had
taken root in Alicia—the idea that it was somehow within her
power to take hold of her disappointments, to reshape and
restructure her life. She thought perhaps she would spend a
little more time with Charles and the baby, and try to find
there whatever it was that gave other women such satisfaction, that sense of completion that had always eluded her. She
shut her eyes and held her mother close.

Less than a week after their talk, Carlotta announced that
she and Sharif were setting off on an anniversary trip, a
cross-country drive from New York to Los Angeles. Sitting in
the living room of her childhood home, warming herself from
the fire in the marble fireplace, sipping some of her father's
fine cognac, Alicia thought how much in love her parents
looked, even now, after so many years of marriage.

As she listened to them eagerly describe this trip—the first
time they would explore at leisure the country that had been
their home for so many years—what she felt was hunger, and
some envy. In spite of her mother's encouraging words, she
wondered if the bond between her parents was born of some
magical formula conceived and executed by fate, and whether
it could possibly be imitated.

She appraised the atmosphere they had created around
them, the details that had been added to their home over the
years—the profusion of flowers, fresh and dried; the myriad
candles that complemented the elaborate lighting system, designed by Principessa's resident lighting expert; the hundreds
of artifacts they had accumulated. Strange, Alicia thought,
that Carlotta had never been a conventional housewife, and
yet this home had a quality she could not explain, a personality that reflected and complemented the people who shared it.

Sharif's voice broke into her reverie: "Alicia, your mother and I have been talking about how the gallery will be managed in our absence. We want you to work with Geoffrey while we're away. He'll be in charge, of course, but I think this will be a good opportunity for you to acquaint yourself with the administrative part of the business. Geoffrey is the best person to teach you. When we return, the three of us can all sit down and talk again. You'll have a better idea of whether or not this is something you really want to do. And you'll know how much time you really want to spend. . . . Perhaps Charles might join us as well. . . ."

Alicia realized that Carlotta must have discussed their conversation with her father. Of course she would have. And once again she envied the kind of relationship her parents had. But now her father was saying she could have a chance at being a part of what they did together. A real part. She smiled at him and at her mother—the fairy prince and princess of her childhood. "Yes, Daddy," she said, "I'd like that very much." At last they had let her in.

"Voila, my sweet," Sharif said proudly, pointing to the new Mercedes touring car he had bought to carry them across the United States. "This automobile is the finest, most comfortable machine money can buy. I'm sure you will agree. Once we begin our journey, you won't even know that you are in an automobile."

Carlotta laughed. "Every year you visit the automobile shows, every year you study all the new toys. And every year you say you have bought the best of all."

He smiled back. "Ah, but it is such a small vice, *cara mia,* don't you agree? Perhaps I am a little fickle with my machines, but I am always constant with my love."

"Macché—I see how the ladies at the gallery look at you. And very often I see you looking, too. I think you are much naughtier than you admit."

"Never, *bellissima,* never. If I look at other ladies, it is only with the appraiser's eye, because I know I have married the most beautiful of all women."

"Oh *davvec* . . . I don't believe you. Not for one little minute. But I shall pretend I do—since we are going to be all alone in this metal monster for so many weeks."

"Cara! It is not a monster. It is the best car in the entire world. You'll see. This will be a great adventure for us. We

have lived in this country for so many years and we have seen so little of it. Now we have time—and leisure. Aren't you happy, my love?''

"Of course. Still . . . I wish we were not leaving Alicia at this time. There is so much she has felt for so many years, things she never told us. Sharif, I believe our child has never been really happy. And I think she feels it is our fault."

"Impossible!"

"No, I think this is what she feels. She told me that if I had really loved her, I would have stayed home to look after her, as Rachel Levine did with her child."

"But Rachel is a simple woman. Forgive me—I know you like her very much, and I know she is a good person—but what else would Rachel have done? She was happy when she created a kettle of barley soup. She was triumphant when she made her furniture shine. You were not made for tasks like these, my love."

"Nevertheless, it seems our daughter felt deprived."

"Deprived of what? We gave her everything it was in our power to give. I was brought up in the same way. My mother did not work, but she had her own pursuits. I had a wet nurse, a governess, and then a tutor. I did not eat at the same table with my parents until I was twelve—and moderately civilized—but I never doubted that my parents loved me."

Carlotta laughed. "What a revelation—I have always believed you were born civilized. But I understand what you mean. Perhaps it would have been the same for me, if my parents had lived. But this is America. Children perhaps have different ideas here. I don't quite understand, but our daughter believes we have somehow cheated her. As I look back, *tesoro,* I don't know. . . ."

"All right, my dear, we'll do whatever you think best—after our holiday. Now we shall enjoy this . . . this honeymoon of ours. You must let me show off my new toy, as you call it."

She looked at him, thinking how little he had changed since she first saw him, so many years ago, in Syrie's crowded parlor. He had grown a mustache, which made him look even more distinguished. And there was a frosting of gray in his thick black hair, which gave him the look of substance and maturity. But her own reactions to this man were constant; scarcely a day went by that she did not thank the blessed Virgin for sending her such a love.

•   •   •

It was just such thoughts that crowded her mind as they drove steadily toward Chicago. She reached up to stroke his cheek, her head nestled snugly on his shoulder. His face was serious, his concentration focused on the darkened road, the heavy rain that sheeted the windshield in spite of the rhythmic *clickety-clack* of the wipers. They had traveled so many miles, so many years, together. How lovely it would be to sleep in a warm bed together. A half hour or so, Sharif had promised.

It had been a lovely holiday—the two of them, like children, carefree and together. Suddenly she felt Sharif's body go rigid. "*Dieu!*" he cried hoarsely, as he turned the wheel sharply, trying to avoid the headlights that were bearing down upon them. She started to make the sign of the cross.

Within a few seconds the lovely new toy was a twisted, flaming wreckage, and the holiday was over.

Charles sat in the darkened bedroom, listening to his wife sobbing in her sleep. It had been a week since the phone call had come in the middle of the night, the call that had made Alicia an orphan. Charles had answered the telephone. When he had turned to Alicia, her lips were moving soundlessly. Before he could find the words to repeat what the Chicago police had told him, he saw the color leave her cheeks, watched her crumple to the floor.

He had put her to bed, held her as she exhausted herself with tears. When he tried to talk to her the following morning, to discuss funeral arrangements, she had refused to listen. "Please, Charles," she said, her eyes entreating him to spare her. "Please, Charles—you do it. Whatever you think best. Don't ask me."

This morning she had refused to go to the funeral, relenting only when she realized she would be left at home with only Sally for company. She had stood, rigid and still, during the brief service, her face covered with a thick black veil so she would not have to see anyone, not have to return more than a brief nod to those who offered their condolences.

Later she had embraced her husband desperately. "Make love to me, Charles. Please—make love to me now."

He was startled, but he had understood her need to take life and warmth from him. He had held her, stroked her, not with passion, but with all the tenderness of which he was capable.

She had fallen asleep. But now the crying had started again, and he had no more remedies for her grief.

She knew he was there in the room. Even with her eyes closed, she sensed his presence. He was so good, so kind. He was all she had now, she thought, forgetting the little blond baby who slept in the nursery. But Charles could not heal the pain she felt.

They had gone away. Together. They had left her. It was like a book without the final chapters. They had left her—unfinished. Just when there was the chance of a new beginning for them, the chapter that would initiate her into the mystery that had been her parents. She clenched her teeth in silent rage. She could almost imagine that they died happy, because they were together. They had cheated her. Again.

It was a different Alicia that Charles saw at the reading of her parents' will—a calm, composed Alicia who sat in the offices of Partridge & Hubbard, the law firm that had handled the Hazzis' personal and business affairs for twenty years.

The provisions of the will were not particularly surprising. With the exception of a few bequests to friends and trusted employees, everything—including control of Principessa—was left to Alicia.

"Of course, this includes the apartment on Fifth Avenue. . . ." Alicia's head nodded rhythmically, to show she was paying attention to the drone of legal details that issued from the lips of Lawrence Partridge, the senior member of this old and respected law firm. "I know how painful this must be for you, Mrs. Richman . . . so tragic, and so sudden. Should you wish to sell the apartment, I can refer you to someone who will handle all the necessary—"

"No," she said firmly. "I'll be keeping the apartment. But I may ask you to dispose of some other properties. I'll make an appointment to see you after I've had an opportunity to examine my parents' holdings more closely."

Charles marveled at her apparent composure, her cool demeanor—at the contrast between this Alicia and the one who had clung to him after that terrible phone call and whimpered like a lost child. Somehow that scene had remained with him—had made him certain that when the subject of her parents' home came up, Alicia would be only too glad to turn the matter over to someone else, someone who could make the painful memories disappear, quickly and efficiently. He could not imagine what was behind those measured words: "I'll be keeping the apartment." But by now he had come to realize that his wife was not an easy woman to second-guess.

When the legal formalities had been completed, he led her to a small neighborhood bar across the street from Partridge & Hubbard. Although it was only eleven in the morning, he ordered two brandies. "How do you feel, darling?" he asked, covering her hands with his, rubbing them gently to take away the chill.

"I'm fine," she answered, her voice steady, her eyes clear. "Really, Charles, I'm quite all right. I appreciate everything you've done for me. But there's no point in just—wallowing. My parents would be the first to agree with that."

"I'm glad you're better, my dear. But I wish you wouldn't always test yourself against the hardest possible measure. You've been bruised, and I think you should allow yourself some time to heal. It's not an admission of weakness to feel normal human emotion, Alicia. It's healthy and intelligent."

Alicia smiled at her husband, a thin thread of a smile that said: I know you mean well, but you couldn't possibly know what's going on inside me.

Charles did not seem to notice, and so he went on. "What I don't understand, dear—though it is your decision, of course—is why you don't sell the apartment. I don't think you can keep it for investment purposes. The board probably wouldn't let you rent it for more than a year. . . ."

"I don't want to use it as an investment, Charles. I want to live there."

"Live there? In heaven's name, why? We have a perfectly fine house. And what would be the point? I don't want to be cruel, but wouldn't it be healthier to just let it go? I would think the memories would be very painful for you. Darling, have you really thought this through?"

"Yes, Charles, I have. There is no way that I am going to let strangers live in that apartment. I want to move in as soon as possible."

Charles opened his mouth to argue, and then he realized, not without some bitterness, that if Alicia had really made up her mind, it would be futile to argue. "Well . . . if it means that much to you," he offered, as a face-saving device for both of them.

"It does, Charles, it does," she said with an intensity that she herself did not quite understand.

As the Richman family moved into Penthouse A, the apartment took on a new atmosphere. While Sharif and Carlotta were alive, it had been, for them and for those who knew them, an oasis of serenity and charm. Now it took on a temporary quality, as if it were the resting place of people in transit.

This was partly because Alicia was reluctant to give up any of her parents' furnishings. Charles persuaded her to store some of the larger pieces to make room for things from their own home—for Charles's books and Alicia's personal belongings. Perhaps if Alicia had put her designer's eye and artistic instinct to work at home, she might have made a warm and eclectic nest for her family. But Alicia did not have a taste for nest building, and Penthouse A became a composite of two separate households, with two entirely different personalities, neither of which was comfortable with the other.

Alicia decided that she and Charles would occupy her parents' bedroom, which was almost unchanged. But Charles found the room uncomfortable, unsuitable for the long quiet hours of work he did at home. He chose for himself a medium-sized room at the far corner of the apartment, a room with two exposures, highly polished parquet floors, and a charmingly ornate ceiling. Within a few weeks, he made the space his own. Its principal furnishings were an eighteenth-century English desk and a music cabinet of the same vintage, which he used to store term papers, research notes, and the assorted appurtenances of an academic career. On the wall hung a pair of brass rubbings taken from an English country church—of a knight and his lady; a fine Wyeth landscape, rugged but not bleak; a few engravings he had found in a trunk in the Vermont house. On the floor he had laid a colorful Moroccan rug, a souvenir of a trip his father had made many years ago.

Although the room was almost always cluttered, it was a pleasant confusion, and the impression was one of warmth and character. Charles's study was perhaps the most appealing room in the house; it made the same strong statement of personality that Charles made in the classroom.

Not coincidentally, "Charles's room," as it came to be called, adjoined the space that Alicia designated as Sally's nursery. This was a healthy distance from the master bedroom— "Alicia's room." "It's quiet back here," Alicia explained, pointing out that the sunny room had its own bathroom, as well as a small adjoining chamber that would become the nurse's room—serving notice on Charles that a nurse or some other surrogate mother would be a permanent member of the Richman household.

This arrangement made of the Richmans a family of separate individuals living under the same roof, each with his private area, each with his personal isolation.

As Alicia assumed control of Principessa, she fulfilled her father's prophecy. With Geoffrey Harwood's capable direction, she quickly learned the administrative details of the business.

The first decision she made was to move the gallery uptown, to Madison Avenue near Fifty-seventh Street. "I don't think Gramercy Park will do anymore," she explained to Geoffrey. "It's charming, it's idiosyncratic, and there's still some 'old money' in the neighborhood. But if we're going to move with the times, I think we must be located where most of the important spending takes place."

"You're absolutely right," Geoffrey agreed, thinking that it might be interesting after all to work with Sharif and Carlotta's daughter.

And although her own home reflected an indifference to style and detail, the new Principessa would become a testament to Alicia's prolific imagination, her own distinctive tastes. The new gallery was less old-world, more contemporary in flavor. Working closely with Geoffrey, depending on him to interpret for her the whims and vagaries of the born-rich, Alicia installed a softer, subtle lighting system, a starkly simple mode of display, calculated to suggest that each of the gallery's offerings was a museum piece.

The move to the new location coincided with a shift in the national mood. Franklin Roosevelt had launched a new economic era. The wheels of industry had started to turn again, the ranks of the unemployed had thinned, and there was a guarded optimism among those who predicted rises and falls in national fortunes. And although there was a Democrat in the White House, the rich were spending again. They did a fair amount of this spending in the new seductive ambience of Principessa, where the monthly sales tallies climbed steadily upward.

At first Alicia spent long hours at Principessa because, she rationalized, she owed this attention to her parents' memory. But within a short time she was irrevocably wedded to her own success. In the management of Principessa, Alicia found something that had heretofore been missing from her life—an opportunity to test herself, an outlet for her talent and energy, a place where she could enjoy the security of the total control that relationships with people had never given her.

If her parents' death set the course for Alicia's marriage, it also cast the mold for her relationship with her daughter—a relationship that never quite "took." Alicia was pleased with, even rather proud of, the perfect china doll she and Charles had made. She loved Sally in the same way she loved the coromandel screen on the second floor of Principessa or the Hittite necklace displayed in the entrance gallery; they were all things of beauty, pleasing to the eye and soul.

To the child of flesh and blood who needed more than objective approval and admiration, Alicia seemed remote and distant. As if she intuited from the start how little claim she could lay to her mother's attention, Sally was that most treasured commodity—a "good child." She rarely cried. When she was hungry or wet, she whimpered softly. If no one answered her muted appeal within a few minutes, she turned her lovely face into the pillow and cried herself to sleep, with her tiny thumb tucked daintily between her rosebud lips.

"An angel," her nurse Annie would say whenever she looked at her little charge, nestled in the Irish linen bed-clothes her grandmother had bought before she died. "Who could resist this little angel?" she would ask pointedly when-ever she had the opportunity, for she found it vexingly hard to understand the kind of mother who would pat such a lovable child in passing, who would smile absently, but who rarely found the time to hold her close, to give her a bottle, or to kiss her sweet-smelling hair.

But if Sally failed to engage her mother, she captured and held her father's heart. "My little princess," he whispered, the first time he bent over the brass cradle that held his infant daughter. And this was what he called her from infancy through girlhood—and past the wedding day that took her away from him. Her first steps, when she took them, were toward her father, who reassured her with extended arms and soothing words of encouragement. "Come on, sweetheart," he coaxed. "Daddy's here. Daddy will help you." And believing him, Sally came, daintily, placing one foot in front of the other, gurgling with delight when she reached the safety of her father's arms.

For so many of the years to come, Charles Richman would be there for his little princess, arranging his life, his career, so that she would always have the comfort of his presence, would know that her daddy was there to help with whatever troubled her.

— 11 —

Alicia sat on the other side of Roger Tataryan's scarred oak desk, a stunned look on her face. "I don't believe it."

"Believe it. I won't be completely sure until your tests come back, but all those years of experience tell me you're pregnant again."

"No," she said firmly, as if her disbelief could alter what he was telling her. "No, it can't be."

"Alicia, dear—" He smiled, all goodwill and patience. "It can be and it probably is. You told me the last time that you weren't using any contraception, and if that's still the case, you shouldn't be so surprised."

"But I am. I started right after Sally was born."

"All the time?"

"Of course," she snapped. But even as she said the words, she realized how often she reacted with annoyance at the mechanics of birth control and willfully defied nature.

"Well, my dear, I'm sure you know best," he went on, all patience again, "but clearly something went wrong—or right— because with such a beautiful child as Sally, I'm sure you and Charles want more than one?"

"Actually, we haven't discussed it," she half-lied, because although Charles had once voiced his desire for several children, he had not brought up the subject again after Sally was born. "But I don't know if either one of us is ready for another child. After all, Sally isn't even two yet."

"But with the nurse and the housekeeper, and all the other help you have, surely that isn't a serious problem. And," he concluded on a note of hearty medical finality, "whether you're ready or not, this baby is almost certainly on the way."

Charles knew that something was wrong when Alicia came home at four in the afternoon. She asked Annie to "get the baby out of the way," and she ordered an early dinner, "something light," from the housekeeper. Then she went straight into her bedroom, explaining to Charles that she had a "raging headache."

"Is everything all right?" he asked.

"No, actually, it isn't. We'll talk about it at dinner." And she left him to wonder.

When she came to the dinner table, she had refreshed herself somewhat with two aspirins, a snifter of brandy, and a cold compress on her forehead. She announced flatly and without preamble, "I'm pregnant again." Her tone left no doubt about her own feelings on the subject.

"Are you sure?" Charles asked, buying time with the most inane question he could think of.

"Not absolutely. But Roger is fairly certain."

"How do you feel?" It was another safe question, but with this one, Charles knew he had run out of neutral conversational ploys.

"I'm not deathly ill, at least not yet."

Silence from Charles's end of the table. When he had heard similar news more than two years before, he had experienced a rush of pleasure, a surge of hope. Now there was only apprehension. The single positive thought he had was that Sally would have a brother or sister, someone to grow up with, someone who could give her another portion of love.

Alicia's voice cut into this thought. "I don't want it."

Silence again.

"I said I don't want this child."

"I heard you." Charles was shocked, not so much by the sentiment as by her bald-faced expression of it.

Now Alicia lost patience. Charles was being deliberately dense, forcing her to spell it out, refusing to help her. "I want to do something about it."

"Do something?"

"Damn it, Charles, stop acting so dull-witted. I don't intend to have this baby. Do I have to spell it out for you? I don't intend to spend the next nine months wishing I were dead. And I don't intend to take on any more responsibilities. I'm simply not cut out for this sort of thing."

"What you're talking about is illegal—and immoral—and dangerous."

"Oh, Charles, don't be so sanctimonious. It's perfectly safe if it's done by a qualified physician, and I intend to find the best."

"What did Roger say?"

"I haven't discussed this with Roger. I suppose he'd take the same dreary stand that you're taking."

Another brief moment of silence. Then: "You can't do it, Alicia. There has to be a more compelling reason for killing an unborn child than the whim of a woman who doesn't feel like bearing it."

"Why do you always manage to make my wishes sound so—so invalid? Now you're making me sound like a monster. You talk about an unborn child. But that child is living in my body. Don't I have anything to say about that?"

"Well, my darling," he began, with uncharacteristic sarcasm, for his wife's selfishness had provoked him to a cold, calculating anger, "since you don't seem to object to sexual activity—in fact, I would say that you rather like it—I don't see why you act so violated when a pregnancy results."

Alicia flinched, and two bright spots of color appeared on her cheeks. Charles had crossed an invisible line, escalated their quarrel into an area that was forbidden. And so she lashed back with words she did not mean at all. "You know, Charles, you are least charming when you become the quintessential WASP. From what book of Puritan ethics did you find that bit of philosophy? Paying the piper, is it? If you're telling me that you expect me to suffer a dismal pregnancy as the price of marital bliss, I just may decide to forgo that pleasure."

Now it was Charles's turn to flinch, for Alicia had attacked the one facet of their marriage where he was in charge. He heard the threat she had issued, and he countered with one of his own. "I can see that this discussion is deteriorating. I don't see any point in going on with it and saying things we may regret later. But I will say this—in earnest, Alicia, believe me: If you do anything to harm this child, then understand that you are jeopardizing our very marriage.''

Alicia absorbed this information, stifled a moment of utter panic at the thought of losing Charles, then responded with as much dignity as she could muster, determined to have the last word, ''Very well, Charles, I shall certainly take your threat under advisement. But let me tell you, my dear—I think you will live to regret it.'' With that, Alicia left the table and returned to her bedroom. She threw herself on her bed and pounded her pillow in a silent rage. A short time later she fell asleep.

Alicia's counterthreat to Charles did not materialize. In spite of her vehemence about not wanting the baby, she had never made the mental transition from not wanting to actually being ready to destroy it. In a curious way, she was actually relieved when Charles's ultimatum put aside that option. She was also pleased by his show of strength. Unfortunately, she could not find the words to tell him how she felt, and the moment dissipated. Charles never realized how much she wanted him to be exactly as he had been during their quarrel— self-assured, in control, a match for her headstrong, unfocused attacks.

As for Charles, although he no longer had the hope that the mere birth of more babies would create a family, he never regretted the fight he had put up for his second child. He had not been quite the Puritan that Alicia had mocked him for being, but he had felt a strong repugnance to the idea of destroying a child, particularly when they lived in circumstances that should have been ideal for the raising of children.

Jennifer Amanda Richman had no more of a claim on her mother's attention than had Sally, but she did not come into the world apologetic and diffident. She had given her mother an easy pregnancy—none of the morning sickness, the cramping or fatigue that had marked Alicia's first time. But after that, Jenny asserted her right to live, her right to be noticed and nurtured, at every opportunity. When she was wet, she howled. When she was hungry, she screamed.

''A handful,'' Annie remarked on more than one occasion, although her tone of voice made it clear she loved the newcomer, extra work and all.

Curiously, the vinegar in Jenny's disposition intrigued Alicia in a way that Sally's sweetness had not. When her mother attempted to give her equal time—namely, perfunctory embraces and brief rocks of the cradle—Jenny would not be bought off so easily. She would fix her mother with a stare so intense that Alicia would look away, almost unnerved by the infant. And when she would try to put the baby down, Jenny would fill her lungs and shriek. Instead of being annoyed, Alicia would laugh and hold the baby just a little longer than she had intended, captivated by the child's spirit.

Physically, Jenny was a maverick infant, a rather homely one at that, resembling neither her father nor her mother, with her shock of red hair, the wide dark eyes that almost had an Oriental quality. Temperamentally, she seemed very much her mother's daughter, a resemblance that delighted both her parents.

For a time the new baby did improve the Richmans' marriage. Alicia was drawn into her own domestic scene. The result was a frantic burst of activity, including the decoration of the nursery. It seemed that Alicia suddenly fancied the idea of having two daughters, enjoyed the compliments and admiration she gathered when she took them, with their nurse, for a walk. She saw in these children the kind of challenge she relished—the possibility of shaping and molding raw material, of making her two daughters the best in every way.

She engaged another nurse, a young Frenchwoman, with the idea of making her daughters bilingual before they started school. They would also be beautiful, accomplished, and socially correct. Alicia believed these were practicable goals, provided she made wise choices.

As Alicia played at mothering, as she planned what would be Jenny's first Christmas, suddenly the country was plunged into another war. In Charles's classes, the girls talked of nothing but war, of fiancés and boyfriends enlisting. For Alicia, the war brought new customers, spending more money.

"It's amazing, Charles," she said one evening over dinner. "We have more clients than ever. They buy without even looking at price tags. It's extraordinary when you consider that we're in the middle of a war."

"It's not so extraordinary," he said dryly. "Wars have always been profitable for the rich. It's the poor who pay the bills—with husbands and sons who get killed and maimed."

"Oh, Charles," she said, suddenly thoughtful. "I'm so glad that you don't have to go. I don't know what I'd do without you."

"You'd do very well," he said quietly. "You're a very capable woman. I wish I could go. I don't feel fortunate—I feel old and useless."

"Charles!"

"It's true. There doesn't seem to be anything I can contribute, except to sign up for the air-raid warden program. I've written letters—I know I could get leave from the college—but no one seems to need an aging professor of English."

Alicia was appalled and fascinated. She assumed that Charles did things she didn't know about, but this took her by surprise. "Surely you don't mean it—you really would leave us?"

"Don't look so alarmed, Alicia. I told you—no one in the War Department wants me. So here I'll stay."

"Well, I should hope so. You have a family," she said earnestly, not noticing the ironic smile this evoked. "There are plenty of single men who have no responsibilities. Oh, Charles," she said softly, going over to sit on his lap and stroke his hair. "I know you get impatient with me sometimes, but we do need you, Charles. I couldn't think of life without you."

Strangely enough, Charles believed her, but her words gave him no comfort.

If Charles was not to be allowed to contribute to the war effort, he resolved to give more to his daughters. At first he did this out of a pious sense of duty. If Alicia was going to shirk, then, by God, he would take up the slack. And although he loved his daughters, he did not really expect to derive much pleasure from doing his "duty."

He thought often of his own childhood, which had been filled with bounteous family dinners, with joyous snow-glazed Christmases, with scenes that might have been taken from Norman Rockwell paintings. Memories of his father evoked the smell of good pipe tobacco, the feel of rough tweed and mellowed leather, the sense of kindness tempered with authority. His mother . . . thoughts of his mother always made him smile. She was very much against "spoiling" children, but she always managed to arrange something special for Charles's birthday, to give him his heart's desire at least once a year. She was loving patience itself, losing her temper with Charles only when he displayed some meanness of spirit or pettiness of character. In raising him, as in everything else, his parents had worked in tandem, each complementing the other's efforts.

He had imagined he would bring up his own children in a similar environment. He had envisioned evenings in his study, dandling a child on each knee, after the day's work had been done. He had not expected to sit on sickbeds, cutting out paper dolls or coloring pictures of cats and dogs and horses. He had not expected to arbitrate quarrels over who "started it" or to answer the hundreds of questions that sprang from the imaginations of two little girls.

Yet he did all this—and more. In return, his daughters gave him more pleasure and love than he had thought possible. They gave him entrée into a whole new world, the world of little girls, the mysteries of women.

Each, in her own way, gave him something precious and unique. In Sally's growing beauty he found a constant wonder, an affirmation that no matter how flawed his marriage to Alicia might be, it was capable of producing this perfection. In Jenny he found another kind of pleasure. Jenny was both her mother's daughter and her comeuppance—a questioner, a disagreer, the kind of child who could exasperate and delight.

When Annie lectured both girls on the dangers of hot stoves and high places and sharp objects, Sally nodded gravely, perfectly willing to take her nurse's word on the mysteries of the adult world. After hearing the same lectures, Jenny invariably tested the information for herself—keeping both Annie and Charles busy applying Band-Aids and kisses to fingers and knees, and effecting rescues from the tops of furniture.

Although she created problems, Charles admired his younger child. She could dare more, and often get away with it. She could stand up to her mother in a way few adults could. She would demand Alicia's attention. When Alicia attempted to embark on one of her frequent evenings out, Jenny would exact a penance—she could always coax or bully her mother into a few extra hugs, a short bedtime story, or even a brief game.

Between Alicia and Jenny there was a connection, something that happened when those two pairs of eyes locked. "Just like her mother," the servants said. And Charles worried that they might be right. He worried that Jenny would spend her life as her mother had, searching for happiness in the most unlikely ways.

• • •

"Come on, Sally, open your mouth" Jenny coaxed. "I won't hurt you. I promise."

"All right," Sally agreed. "But don't do anything until I tell you."

"Okay." Jenny stuck a finger into her sister's mouth and gently wiggled a loose molar. "It's practically out. If you close your eyes, it will all be over in a minute."

Sally did what she was told, scrunching her eyes shut, opening her mouth wide, and holding her breath.

"Here I go now," Jenny said, grabbing the tooth firmly with a piece of tissue. "There! Here it is Sally. You can open your eyes now." She brandished the tooth triumphantly.

"Oh, yuck, Jenny, take it away—it's so ugly. I don't want to look at it."

"It's just an old tooth, Sally. I'll wrap it up in this tissue, and you can put it under your pillow."

"You do it, Jenny. I don't want to touch it. Oh, Jenny, I'm bleeding—it's getting all over my dress. What should I do, Jenny?"

"Come with me," Jenny instructed, taking the maternal manner she had adopted with her older sister. "Now just put your head over the sink and rinse your mouth out. That's it. Take your dress off, put on your nightgown, and get into bed. I'll bring you some ice cream. Cold stuff is good for bleeding." She went into the kitchen and spooned a generous dollop of vanilla ice cream—Sally's favorite—into a dish. Then she watched protectively as her sister took the first bite.

"Ooh—it feels funny in there. It's a giant hole, Jenny—I'll bet it looks awful."

"No, it doesn't. And nobody can see it anyway. Finish your ice cream and go to sleep. Then the tooth fairy can come and leave you a present."

"I'm not tired, Jenny. Besides, I have to stay up and tell Mommy that I broke her perfume bottle. She's going to be so mad, Jenny. She's going to yell at me, I just know it. I made such a mess. I tried to glue it back together, and then the glue went all over the vanity table." Sally looked utterly miserable and close to tears.

"Don't cry now, Sally, I'll tell Alicia about the perfume bottle. She won't yell at you, I promise. She'd better not or I'll yell right back at her. Do you want me to read to you for a little while?"

"The Three Musketeers?"

"Okay—but just for a little while. I have to do my homework before Daddy gets home."

"That's my favorite. It reminds me of us—you and me and Daddy."

"Yes—and Alicia can be Cardinal Richelieu."

"Jenny—he's so wicked!"

"Well, she is, too—sometimes. But don't tell her. It can be a secret. And don't tell Daddy either. He won't like it."

When Charles came home, Sally was asleep. "I took care of Sally today," Jenny told her father proudly. "I took out her tooth, and I gave her some ice cream, and I did all my homework. Now you can check it for me. And don't forget to put a dollar under Sally's pillow. I promised her the tooth fairy would come."

Charles smiled and patted Jenny's head. "Thank you, dear, I appreciate everything you've done. How did you get to be so grown up so quickly?"

"I just thought of what you'd do, Daddy, if you didn't have to work late today. And Daddy—can I ask you for something? For me?"

"Of course, Jenny, what is it?"

"Well—could you come to my school on Thursday morning? Please, Daddy? I know you have classes, but it's· so important. Remember I told you about the play my class was going to do? Well, it's Thursday, and I want you to see it so much."

Charles's face softened. "I'd be proud to see your play, Jenny. I'm sure I can arrange a makeup class with my students. Perhaps we should tell your mother. . . ."

"Oh, no, Daddy, don't do that."

"Why not, sweetheart? I know she's busy, but maybe she'd come this time."

Jenny looked down at her shoes. "I already told everybody my mother couldn't come. She never does," she added. "I told them she was away on a secret business trip. Oh, Daddy, I'm sorry I lied—I just didn't want to tell the teacher she was too busy again. You won't tell her, will you?"

Charles smiled. "No, I won't tell. But next time—"

"I know, Daddy—next time I'll think of something better."

Later Jenny sat up in her bed, fighting sleep, like a sentry on night watch. She was tired, but she had promised her sister

she would inform Alicia that her Lalique perfume bottle had
been broken—and that her vanity table had been smeared
with Elmer's glue during a futile attempt at repair. When she
heard the door open and close, she got out of bed and went to
meet her mother.

"What is it, Jenny? Why are you out of bed? Are you
sick?"

"No, Alicia," she said. She had picked up the habit of
using her mother's first name when she first learned to talk.
"I have to tell you something."

"And you waited up all this time? Really, I'll have to
speak to Annie."

"No, you can't do that." Jenny planted her hands on her
hips, just as Alicia used to do. "It wasn't Annie's fault. I just
waited in bed. She didn't know I was awake."

"Well, what is it then? I'm tired, Jenny—we had a very
long day at the gallery today."

"We had an accident today."

"What kind of accident? Was someone hurt?"

"No. That perfume bottle you like—the one with the pretty
top—it got broken."

"What were you doing with my perfume bottle, Jenny?
You know I don't like anyone to touch my things."

"It was an accident. And we tried to fix it. But the glue
spilled. On your vanity table. And you'd better not yell at
Sally," she finished in a rush, waiting for her mother's anger.

"Why would I yell at Sally? And why shouldn't I yell if I
want to? Here I come home after a very long day and you tell
me that you girls have made a mess in my bedroom—"

"Well, you can yell at me if you want to. But Sally feels
bad when people are mean to her. Especially you."

Now Alicia was fighting back a smile. "And what about
you, Jenny? Don't you feel bad when I'm mean?"

"I can take it," Jenny answered, quoting a line she had
heard in a John Wayne movie.

"Go to sleep, Jenny," her mother commanded, no longer
trying to hide her amusement. "I'm not going to yell at
anyone. In the future please stay away from my vanity table.
And ask your sister to do the same. Good night, dear."

"Good night . . . Richelieu," Jenny muttered, as she
retreated to her room.

•   •   •

As her daughters grew older, Alicia administered the external details of their lives, just as she administered Principessa. She selected dresses from small boutiques, from Saks and Bergdorf's—cunning imported knits from Italy, embroidered pinafores from Spain, coats from England. For their birthday parties she hired the finest caterers in New York. Piano lessons were given by a former concert artist while teeth were coaxed into perfect straightness with the best orthodontic care money could buy. Alicia had decided that her daughters would be a success, just as her business was. They would belong as she had never belonged.

Yet, emotionally, the "three musketeers" belonged to each other. Charles accepted without comment Alicia's decisions about what the girls would wear and what schools they should attend. The rest he took upon himself—the "family" picnics, the trips to museums and concerts, the little, loving day-to-day attentions.

Charles was the cornerstone of the Richman family, just as Alicia was the cornerstone of Principessa. He was, for his daughters, a never-ending source of love and warmth and security. In turn they gave him adoration and affection, the companionship that Alicia was too preoccupied to give.

They hovered protectively when he worked on his manuscripts, bringing tea and coffee and offers of help. They listened while he read aloud from his work, applauded vigorously—a perfect audience—declaring that their father was the wisest, the most brilliant man alive.

When Charles entertained colleagues or groups of students, Sally and Jenny passed trays of hors d'oeuvres, trying to take the edge from Alicia's frequent absences on these occasions.

If their family life was flawed, Sally Richman provided its note of perfection. Adolescence and puberty only enriched her beauty. The tentative quality disappeared, the anxiety to please softened into a kind of old-world graciousness. There was a vulnerability to her loveliness which made Sally well-nigh irresistible.

For Jenny, growing up was not so smooth a transition. She became a gangly thing, all elbows and knees, emotionally and physically. She felt her shortcomings even more as she watched her sister blossom. When she looked in the mirror, she did not see any sign at all of her grandmother's ethereal fairness or her mother's striking good looks. Yet she had heard the phrase "her mother's daughter" often enough to know there was something of Alicia in her. She concluded it was Alicia's "badness" that others saw in her. Sally had never had it; Sally was so comfortable with people, so at ease, so trusting of the world around her. It was Jenny who would have to beware. That flawed bit of self-awareness made Jenny quieter in her adolescence, more subdued. The lively child seemed to lose her nerve as she banked her own spirit.

Once she decided she would never be a beauty, Jenny determined to be something else. She was particularly proud of her intelligence, her ability to learn quickly. It was her special link to Charles, and she worked hard to sharpen her intellect.

In school, she found solace and stimulation, challenge and reward. Here there were rules, clearly laid out, and if you followed them, if you did what was required, you could count on enough praise and attention to satisfy the hungriest ego. Jenny acquired an ever-growing collection of gold stars and notes from teachers, assuring her that she was exceptional.

And if these pleasures were one-dimensional, well, Jenny tried not to notice. She had made a rule for herself: You can't have everything. It was a rule that helped her control the restlessness and hunger. It helped her to create order out of uncertainty, to avoid risks and foolish chances. Perhaps it would help her avoid the curse of being "her mother's daughter."

12

Of all his bequests to his daughter, Sharif had left her one—a living legacy—who would help her make all the others work. This was Geoffrey Harwood. Over the years he had spent at Principessa, the ne'er-do-well nephew had become an éminence-grise; the smart-aleck playboy had become an avid capitalist.

Geoffrey had lost his lazy insolence, his casual disrespect for commerce. Now he took money-making very seriously indeed, and he dressed and behaved accordingly. He had become very buttoned up—almost dull, his aunt had lamented before she died.

He taught Alicia all she needed to know about running the gallery, about doing the "right" things at the "right" time, about attending the right functions, giving the right donations to the right charities—about the right way to enhance Principessa's already distinguished client list.

Almost inevitably, Geoffrey became Alicia's escort and companion—after Charles declared his disinterest in the constant stream of social functions Alicia wanted to attend. Geoffrey developed a subtle language for teaching Alicia what he knew without making her feel that he was in any way superior, without making her aware that there were gaps in her background. Although Alicia had lived among the rich, had been exposed to the material trappings of wealth, she had never really been assimilated into that world. Geoffrey taught her nuances, subtleties, little signs of arrogance that only the very rich and overbred could afford, taught her how to avoid the worst gaffes of the newly rich, the overeager.

Alicia never deluded herself that she could become integrated into the world she serviced—her social ambitions were for her children. With Geoffrey's help her aim would be possible. He taught her about the right places to vacation, to ski, about schools and coming-out parties, about where to dine and where to worship.

And, quite unexpectedly, he changed her life by introducing her to Gardiner Crowne.

It was at a charity dinner for the Heart Fund. The theme of the ball was "Holiday in Spain." Alicia wore the costume of a Spanish dancer, her dark hair piled high on her head, partly covered by a mantilla. The rich colors of her costume and the slash of red lipstick showed her vivid beauty to stunning effect. When she made her entrance on Geoffrey's arm, she noticed any number of female heads turn ever so slightly, saw an even greater number of male heads turn toward the figure in black lace.

Usually Alicia spent an evening like this making contacts with old customers, offering a warm smile, a flattering bit of personal attention that they would remember. She began by paying court to Elizabeth Simon, an aging dowager who was on her fourth husband and third face-lift, and who had bought more then sixty thousand dollars worth of merchandise from Principessa during the past year. She was trying to look attentive, which was a little difficult due to Elizabeth's unsettling habit of relentlessly repeating herself. While this valued client was going on about a new villa in Porto Ercole—and speculating on what she might buy from Alicia to make this twenty-room "cottage" habitable, Alicia's eyes wandered. They were caught and locked by a slender flamenco dancer who was just walking into the ballroom, alone.

Alicia forced her attention back to Elizabeth. A few minutes later the stranger materialized at Elizabeth's elbow. Geoffrey spoke. "Alicia," he said, "I don't think you've ever met Gardiner Crowne?"

"No," she said, with what she hoped was cool sophistication. "I don't believe I have."

"Well," the stranger said, "that has been my loss, I'm sure." He took Alicia's hand and squeezed it with more than polite pressure.

"Gardiner, you naughty boy," Elizabeth said querulously, annoyed at losing the spotlight for even a moment. "We haven't seen you for ages. You simply must come to tea—and very soon—or I shall be extremely annoyed with you."

"Dear Elizabeth." He bowed from the waist, in a gesture that was courtly and mocking at the same time. "I should be flogged for neglecting you. But I promise I shall do better—yes, I promise." He took the septuagenarian's mottled hand and brought it tenderly to his lips.

And then, just as Elizabeth began to simper, he put his arm quickly around Alicia's waist and plucked her away. "Excuse us," he said, in passing, "but I simply must dance with this lady before another minute goes by."

When they were out on the dance floor, he lowered his eyes to hers and drawled, "Well, aren't you going to thank me for rescuing you?"

"Rescuing me?" Alicia protested, all mock indignation. "From one of my best clients? You must be crazy. She's going to make me pay for this, you know—and it's all your fault."

"So speaks the redoubtable Alicia Richman, doyenne of Principessa Gallery—a woman who is all business."

She felt the blush begin at her scalp, travel at alarming speed along her neck, linger at her groin, and speed down to her toes. She was inordinately pleased that this man knew who she was, and a little alarmed that it mattered at all. "Of course," she said, sounding slightly stuffy. "My business is very important to me."

"I see." Through those two words he managed to insinuate that he did see—a great deal.

She lifted her gaze past the shoulder level of his costume and studied his face. It was a bandit's face, the face of a breaker of hearts. Yet Alicia guessed that he was probably what she called a "blue blood." It was there in the way he carried himself; like Geoffrey, he moved through the world around him as if it belonged to him.

Gardiner's complexion was rather tawny, which perhaps accounted for his exotic, somewhat disreputable quality. His nose was aquiline, his cheekbones sharp—almost Slavic—his hair, dark and wavy, and his eyes—well, these could best be described as "bedroom eyes," seductive, with eyelids permanently at half-mast. Though Geoffrey would later tell Alicia that the drooping lids were related to a medical condition which two operations had failed to correct, as with all other women, this information in no way diminished the impact that those eyes had on Alicia.

"Have you know Geoffrey long?" she asked, trying to get a "fix" on the man, to determine why she had never seen him before.

"We met at school." He refrained from naming his distinguished prep school, correctly suspecting that she knew perfectly well what school Geoffrey had attended. Then, as if he had read her mind and seen exactly what she wanted to know, he explained: "We probably haven't met because I've spent the last ten years in California. Irene—my wife—prefers the climate there."

Alicia reckoned that this last piece of information was given very deliberately. Although she was relatively innocent of the intrigues and machinations of extramarital sex and adultery, she was aware of this one gambit. She thought of it as the "married man's gauntlet"—the throwing out of information relating to a wife and/or children shortly after meeting a woman with whom one might conceivably want to stray. This was nearly foolproof insurance against future recriminations:—"But I told you from the beginning I was married, didn't I?" Alicia usually despised this kind of thing, but this time it made her smile.

Mistaking the reason for her smile, Gardiner became more expansive. "But," he said, "I have always appreciated the rich variety of the Northeast. Especially now.'' He dropped his voice to underscore his point.

She looked up at him quickly. Good heavens, she thought, he thinks I'm flirting. And then she realized she was doing just that—and enjoying it. ''And what brings you here now, if Irene loves California so much?''

He smiled at her, as if he had been waiting for her to ask. ''Actually, it was Irene's doing. She told me I must find honest work. And there doesn't seem to be much I can do in California, so I thought I'd try my luck in New York.''

''And what is it that you plan to do, Mr. Crowne?''

''Gardiner, please.'' He shrugged his beautifully tailored shoulders without missing a beat of the music. ''I really don't know. Let me see.'' He closed his eyes, affecting a pensive mood. ''What am I suited for? I can usually get a good table at a restaurant. And I can tell a good Margaux from a mediocre one. I play a decent game of squash. . . .''

''Why, Mr. Crowne—Gardiner—those are enviable accomplishments. I'm surprised you haven't been besieged with offers.''

''I know, I know.'' He shook his head. ''Most employers are so conventional. They can't see beyond paper credentials and job experience. Well, I don't have much of that, and I'm not ashamed in the slightest. I don't think anyone should work who doesn't have to, and I've not had to. Until now. And it's my own fault. Irene got fed up with some of my— quirks—and she laid down the law. Maybe if she thinks I'm sufficiently reformed, I'll get a reprieve.''

And well you might, Alicia thought, for Gardiner, she suspected, had a guileless quality that probably protected him from the worst consequences of his ''quirks.'' At that moment her businesswoman's brain went into gear. And she had a mad idea, an idea that seemed less mad as she mentally embellished it. She looked at him and laughed out loud.

He laughed too. ''Well, Madame Richman, what is it? Is the joke on me or can you share it?''

''The joke may be on both of us. But if you're interested, I think I can offer you a job.''

13

That meeting at the charity dinner began a relationship that would bring both Gardiner and Alicia financial profit. It would bring Gardiner something entirely new in his experience—the possession of respectable sums of money that he had earned himself. It was a novelty that he enjoyed.

For Alicia's first instincts were right. Although Gardiner seemed like a stereotypical idler, a decorative man with very little inside his head, Alicia thought he might be very useful to her particular business. She remembered her parents' experience with Geoffrey, and she thought that history might repeat itself. Gardiner, with his West Coast connections, might be the perfect linchpin for a project that had been taking shape inside her head for a long time.

Not everyone was so sanguine about Alicia's discovery—or "Madame's protégé," as Geoffrey dubbed Gardiner. Geoffrey's waspishness came from a certain insecurity about his own position. With Gardiner in attendance, Geoffrey was no longer Principessa's single "token socialite." And since no one knew exactly what position Madame had in mind for Gardiner, Geoffrey fretted that Gardiner's prospects might somehow disturb his own.

Nor was Charles Richman very pleased with his wife's new employee. There had been an instant chemical reaction—all bad—between the two men. For all the years that they had been married, Alicia and Charles had been at least free of one problem—jealousy. Whatever differences there had been between them, each had been certain of the other's fidelity. For Charles, that feeling came to an end when he met Gardiner, when Alicia invited the man to their home for dinner. Charles watched him eat the meal that had been set before him, watched him fondle the after-dinner brandy with just the right touch of practiced ease, watched him, in fact, being perfect in every superficial way.

And after Alicia and Charles had said good night to Gardiner, she turned and asked, "What do you think of him?"

Charles snorted. "He has all the substance of a coat hanger."

Alicia smiled. "I know."

That smile made Charles more uneasy than any defense of the man might have.

While the employees of Principessa whispered and giggled about Gardiner and "the boss," Alicia was perfectly aware of their speculations. In fact, she rather enjoyed the gossip, because she knew it was not true.

And while others speculated about what was presumed to be a torrid affair, Alicia enjoyed a relationship which was in some ways curiously like the one she had shared with Robert Levine. With Gardiner she felt a similar easygoing camaraderie, as well as a sharing of the play and the play-acting part of life. There was never any question of approval or disapproval—which marked so many of her days with Charles. Gardiner never expected anyone to do "the right thing."

With his thoroughbred's instinct, Gardiner did not try to make love to Alicia. He guessed—rightly—that sex for her would not be a casual thing. Yet they both enjoyed the flirtation, the admiring glances, the seductive touches; in short, they both enjoyed each other thoroughly, and always with the moral conviction that they had done nothing wrong. And while Gardiner cared nothing about right or wrong outside his own personal code of honor, this did matter to Alicia.

Knowing that she was technically faithful gave Alicia the defenses she needed against Charles's searching glances, his silent air of reproach.

Gardiner began his career at Principessa with genuine curiosity and zest. Like a child embarking on a fresh adventure. He found the surroundings aesthetically pleasing. And with his instinct for manipulation, he was a natural salesman, although he would never have admitted it.

When Alicia tried out her idea on Gardiner, he was full of enthusiasm. "Of course," he said. "It's a natural. California would be a perfect place for Principessa to expand. And that is a place where I could help you. I mean really help. You should do very well there—I'm surprised you haven't thought of it before."

"I have. I've thought about this a number of times over the past couple of years. But I wasn't sure I could make it work—until I met you. My parents were always against expansion for its own sake. They always said that Principessa was built on the personal touch. And when we met—I felt perhaps you could help me do just that.''

"I'm flattered, Alicia, that you waited for me. I'll do my best not to disappoint you."

"Let's not have any talk about disappointment. I expect you to just be yourself, and you've had plenty of practice doing that, haven't you?"

"Indeed I have—far too much, if you listen to my critics."

"None of that either. If we have a great success together, your critics will be humbled."

When Alicia brought up the subject of Principessa West at home, Charles's reaction was fairly explosive. "Damn it, Alicia, this is too much. We barely have any family life as it is, and now you're talking about flying back and forth to California. There's no need for this venture. We have more money than we'll ever need. The girls don't need anything—except a mother—and your new store isn't going to give them that. What's it for, Alicia? Tell me what it's for."

She looked at him with a mixture of condescension and pity. "Really, Charles, you don't build a business just to make money. You simply don't seem to understand. It's a question of keeping up with the times. If you don't expand, you stand still, and then you start to slip because your competitors are moving. One day you're successful, and the next—you're yesterday's news."

"Would that be so terrible, Alicia? As I said before, we could still live very nicely."

She did not have a ready answer for that, and so she started to filibuster. "How can you suggest that I just neglect Principessa, just let it go under, after all the years my parents spent building it up. Do I ever suggest that you leave your precious manuscripts? That you stop—"

"Perhaps I wish you would. Perhaps it would make me feel that you noticed. And perhaps I would be glad to give up time with my 'precious manuscripts' if it meant having a life with you."

The yearning in his voice stabbed her with guilt. She knew she could not give him what he wanted, just as she realized he was a good and decent man who loved her, who deserved to have what he was asking for. She reached out and touched his

hand. "Charles, dear, I understand what you're saying. But I
wish you could understand something about me—so I wouldn't
feel I was failing you. I don't think I can be what you wish
me to be. It doesn't fit me, Charles. Maybe you find this hard
to believe, but you do mean a great deal to me. I know I
don't show it, but that seems to be something else I don't
quite know how to do." As she spoke, she realized that she
was not just placating her husband. She meant what she was
saying, and that knowledge made her inexplicably sad.

Perhaps it was because she did not have Charles's approval, perhaps it was because Geoffrey took a dim view of the
project—ill-timed and overreaching, he said—or perhaps it
was because the girls suddenly seemed more whiny, more
irritable about her comings and goings. Whatever the reason,
Principessa West was not getting off to a good start.

Alicia and Gardiner had found a perfect location—on Wil-
shire Boulevard. The property was available for a price that
Gardiner's attorney had deemed "very sound." And that was
the last thing that went right for a long, long time.

Shortly after construction began, one of the workmen fell
from a scaffold. In the hospital, it was discovered that the
"man" was a boy of fifteen, which meant that Principessa
and its contractor would be liable for massive damages should
the boy suffer any serious disability and should his parents
decide to sue.

Nor was that the only disaster. Alicia had handpicked, with
Gardiner's advice, some of the New York store's choicest
pieces to lend the Los Angeles gallery for its opening. Somehow an entire railroad car carrying these pieces disappeared
somewhere between New York and Chicago. Although this
loss was covered by insurance, the problem of finding and
shipping items of the same caliber seemed insoluble.

Alicia knew that first impressions for openings like
Principessa West were crucial. She had planned a gala event,
lavishly catered, with Lester Lanin's band as well as a modern jazz quartet, procured by the expensive press agent she
had hired. With Gardiner's help, all this preparation would
bring out an army of California's beautiful people. But she
knew something would be missing if Principessa West, on its
first public showing, turned out to be a perfect jewel box
displaying only second-rate gems.

"Really, Alicia," Gardiner consoled her, "we can reschedule the opening. One of us could take a quick swing through western Europe, perhaps Hong Kong—I'm sure we could find enough interesting merchandise to cover what was lost. Maybe the missing things will turn up. After all, even if they were stolen, someone will be fencing them somewhere. I'll ask some friends to look into it."

Alicia laughed in spite of her mood. "You're a constant surprise, Gardiner. Are you telling me that you have friends who would know about stolen merchandise and fences? A 'gentleman' like you?"

He smiled, one of those self-deprecating smiles that she found so charming. "A 'gentleman' like me has more need of all kinds of friends, my dear. Since I've lived with no visible means of support, as they say, I've depended on the goodwill of people in all kinds of places. I'm sorry if that disappoints you, Alicia my dear, but I just have never been able to afford the luxury of moral fastidiousness. But perhaps my wicked ways can help us this time."

"Maybe they can, Gardiner. I hope so." She wondered what Charles would say if he heard this last bit of conversation. He'd probably forbid me to see Gardiner or some pompous thing like that, she thought. And then she would have to ignore him—as usual. Gardiner may have been kept by his wife, but Alicia would bet he wasn't owned by her.

Alicia soon found out about Gardiner and his wife. "What does your wife think," she asked, feigning an air of innocence, "about your finding a job that brings you back to California so often?"

"Come and see for yourself. Come to the house for dinner. I think it would be a good idea—for a number of reasons."

The invitation made her uneasy, yet she saw the logic of it. She and Gardiner were spending a great deal of time together. In New York it might go relatively unnoticed. But here in California, where he was very much married, it might seem strange if she did not at least meet Irene Caswell Crowne. "Yes, all right," she said. "Find out what would be a convenient night for Irene."

"Alicia, dear," he said, with mock reproach, "I may be Irene's house pet, but I can still make dinner invitations on the evening of my choice. Let's say Friday—about eight."

• • •

Alicia found dressing for dinner difficult. She had made a few discreet inquiries from time to time, through Geoffrey and other New Yorkers. "What's Gardiner's wife like?" She had tried to keep her tone light, but the question had invariably brought knowing glances, a hint of a smirk. Sizing up the competition—that's what Geoffrey had imagined she was doing.

But what she really wanted was to try to get along with Irene. It was like wanting your school friends' parents to approve of you. Alicia was aware that her appearance, even unadorned, was fairly eye-catching, so she decided to dress as simply as she could. She discarded a black suit, because even without jewelry, she looked too "New York." She settled instead on a simple brown wool suit. The color had never looked right on her, but she had kept the suit around as "filler." With it, she selected a tailored linen blouse and the locket Charles had given her.

The woman who met Alicia at the door was a surprise. Irene Crowne was tall and a little thick around the middle. The body was athletic, the skin deeply tanned. Her hair was several shades of blond—sun-streaked, Alicia reckoned, rather than man-made. Her dress was a column of white jersey adorned with a long strand of lapis beads.

Alicia felt suddenly dowdy, but she did not mind. She hoped that Irene would feel comfortably superior. She put on what she hoped was a cordial smile. "I'm so glad to be meeting you at last, Mrs. Crowne."

"Well, yes," Irene Crowne drawled, in a husky voice that seemed incongruous with the accents produced by fine boarding schools and expensive tutors. "I should say so. Here Gardiner has been talking for months about Alicia Richman, and I wasn't even sure she existed. I began to wonder where he was hiding you—and why."

The remark unsettled Alicia, and she tried to cover her feelings with a short laugh. "A sin of omission," she quipped and immediately regretted her use of the word "sin." She added: "We've been frightfully busy with all the disasters that seem to be overtaking us here."

"Oh, dear," Irene drawled, raising her eyebrows. "I do hope that's not an omen of some sort. I would so hate to see Gardiner's career nipped in the bud. Poor dear. It's taken him so long to find himself. It would be unfortunate to see him idle again. The dear boy does get into such mischief." Her tone would have been appropriate in describing an adorable but somewhat naughty child.

Alicia's cheeks flushed when she realized that Irene probably felt it was necessary to state her claim as unmistakably as possible.

She made no reply, and Irene continued smoothly, now all graciousness and hospitality, "Oh, dear, where are my manners? Do get comfortable. I think the garden room would be nice this time of day. And let me get you a drink. Do you like sherry?"

"Sherry would be fine, thank you."

"Gardiner should be done in a minute. Honestly"—she rolled clear brown eyes heavenward—"he is so undisciplined. It's fortunate we never had children. . . ."

Alicia bit back a response. She found the woman most unappealing, and she knew she would have to watch herself.

When Gardiner appeared on the wide marble staircase, Alicia relaxed a little and allowed herself to look around at the house he shared with his wife. It was a little like Irene herself—quality without ostentation—a California house made from natural materials. Gardiner had told her that they owned several homes and that this one was Irene's favorite.

Somehow Alicia had expected traditional design, antiques. This place was comfortable, unpretentious, a good marriage of fine materials and clean design. It was a relaxed environment, all white and sand and interesting textures, Mexican hangings, and a lot of glass. Alicia liked the house very much, but she wasn't sure how it fit the picture she was forming of the woman before her.

Gardiner interrupted her survey with a warm greeting. "Alicia—welcome to our home." She was glad he hadn't heard the comments Irene had made a few moments ago. To hear his wife talk, the "our" would have been an exaggeration.

"I see you have a drink," he said, "so let me show you around. Irene can give you the tour of her kennels if you're interested—she breeds dogs. But I think you must see the view. It's nearly dark—and still quite lovely."

He took Alicia's elbow and guided her out to a side patio. As she left the room, she could have sworn that Irene's well-bred face went a shade or two darker.

"I don't think your wife likes me," she whispered.

"I think you're probably right," he whispered back, squeezing her elbow in reassurance. "But I didn't expect her to like you. I just wanted her to see you. To Irene, the known is always much more manageable than the unknown.''

Alicia was startled. This was the first time Gardiner had mentioned that his wife had more than a casual interest in her existence. She didn't know what to say.

"Here," he pointed, pushing open the sliding glass doors to reveal a Pacific paradise. "I like to take my meals here when Irene's busy, which is quite often. It's so peaceful. . . .''

As he spoke, Alicia had a picture of a different Gardiner from the one she knew—a Gardiner who wasn't always ready with a facile quip, a Gardiner who ate his meals alone near a quiet stretch of beach, and who just might be a genuine romantic. We all make our little deals, she thought. At least Gardiner pays his bills—and without a whimper. She thought of just how much she really liked this man, and she was afraid that if she wanted to, Irene might find a way to end their friendship.

When they returned to the garden room, which was redolent with the scent of roses and lilacs, Alicia tried hard to win Irene's favor. She tried to talk about dogs—a subject she knew virtually nothing about. Irene answered her timid questions briefly, without embellishment. She did not want to talk about the gallery because she was afraid Irene might feel left out. She asked some questions about the house, and Irene recited a full description, with just an edge of boredom in that husky, well-bred voice.

Alicia started to sigh, then caught herself—and looked up quickly to see if Irene had noticed. She caught a momentary glance of pure dislike. Later, she told herself it might have been her imagination.

The meal was almost as difficult as the visit. Although Irene's home was lovely, her clothes perfect, she did not set a good table. The food was all of good quality, well prepared, but somehow it lacked soul or passion. Alicia suspected this might be true of the lady herself, and the thought gave her some satisfaction. She tried to concentrate on chewing and swallowing her roast, and washing it down with a not very interesting wine.

As soon as the meal was consumed and a decent interval of labored conversation had passed, Alicia excused herself, pleading an early appointment in the morning. Irene did not press her to stay.

• • •

The following morning, Gardiner appeared at Alicia's hotel suite with a "business as usual" demeanor. He had no intention of saying anything about the comments that Irene had made following her departure.

"So," she had drawled. "So that is the famous Alicia."

Gardiner had not answered, and she went on, "I can't see that there's very much to her."

Again Gardiner had not answered, sensing, quite accurately, that his wife's taunts had nothing to do with genuine conversation.

Seeing that she would get no response from her husband, Irene had cut directly to the point. "Still," she had said, softening her voice to an ominously low level, "I wouldn't want you to spend any more time with her than was absolutely necessary, Gardiner. No, I think that would not be a good idea at all."

He had thought—briefly—of saying something to the effect that since Alicia was his employer, it was not his place to decide the amount of time that was "absolutely necessary." But since he realized very well what his wife was implying, he made no comment.

Gardiner had had many affairs, yet these had been conducted with his wife's tacit consent. She allowed him to assert the masculinity he was rarely permitted to flex at home, but when she sensed that any relationship was becoming too interesting, she made certain it ended.

When Gardiner overindulged his fondness for women—as he had done not so long ago—Irene tightened the purse strings. This last time, Gardiner had completely overstepped his boundaries—he had been indiscreet enough for one of his affairs to surface regularly in the gossip columns. For this, Irene had made him pay—by forcing him to get a job. Now she was more than a little annoyed that the punishment had turned out to be so pleasurable for him.

Gardiner said nothing of this to Alicia. When she remarked again about Irene's apparent dislike of her, he dismissed her anxiety. "There aren't many people—or things—that Irene approves of. And I can assure you that none of them would appeal to you. So please don't give her another minute's thought."

• • •

In the weeks to come, Gardiner would find himself doing all kinds of things he had never attempted before. In the various crises preceding the opening of Principessa West, he took on the roles of comforter, adviser, and all-around pillar of strength—none of which he had ever attempted in his marriage. He enjoyed these roles. They gave him a secret, made him feel slightly less inconsequential at home.

For her part, Alicia was pleasantly surprised at Gardiner's unexpected qualities. She had hired him as window dressing, and he was turning out to be a valued associate. On the surface he had seemed attractive but inconsequential, yet he was able to give her life more dimension, not to mention the fun of a shared interest.

He proved remarkably versatile, and effective, in difficult situations. Although she had hired him for his connections with the wealthy and socially prominent, he had indeed contacted his less savory "friends"—including friends who miraculously "found" the missing train shipment, and soon enough so that the gala opening did not have to be postponed. Still another of his "friends" had managed to avert disaster in the matter of the injured workman. With the help of a sizable check from Alicia, the matter was settled quietly, without a lawsuit or unpleasant publicity—and without compromising Principessa's insurance coverage.

Each time Gardiner reached out his hand and helped her along, Alicia felt her feelings for him grow—feelings of gratitude and closeness and something that might have been sexual attraction. This had never happened during her marriage to Charles, and Alicia felt fascinated—and afraid.

She kept these feelings hidden and under control, until the night before Principessa West's gala opening. One by one, those who had been working in the gallery left until only Alicia and Gardiner remained, checking guest lists, the caterer's preparations, the wine deliveries, the dozens of details that would make the opening a success. They worked well in tandem, one double-checking the odd item, the other remembering the missed detail.

Finally it all seemed to be finished, and neither of them could think of another single thing to do. "Let's have a drink to celebrate before we call it a night," Gardiner suggested. "I've been to my share of openings, and I think this one is going to be the best."

She agreed. They were both fatigued and exhilarated at the

same time, a little reckless—a little intoxicated with the anticipation that hung in the air.

As Gardiner opened one of the bottles of Dom Perignon that had been reserved for the VIP bar, it seemed as if they were in a fairyland—a magical place filled with beautiful crystal, fine china, lacquer and bronze, and semiprecious stones. And they were all alone in it.

They clinked Baccarat glasses and Gardiner offered a toast: "To Madame Richman of Principessa," he said, bowing slightly and reprising the phrase he had used when they first met.

"And to her knight in shining armor," she answered, for that was how Gardiner seemed to her.

Without either of them knowing how it happened, they came together. The kiss lasted only a few moments, but for Alicia it was as if time had been suspended. When they drew apart, there was a look of wonder and disbelief in her eyes.

She found an answering look on Gardiner's face. "Well," he said.

"Yes. I know."

"We'd better talk." He took her by the hand and led her to one of the gray silk couches.

"I'm afraid I don't feel like talking," she said, in a voice that was not very steady.

"No, I don't either." He held her shoulders and looked into her eyes. "What I really want to do is take you in my arms and—"

"But? There is a 'but,' isn't there?"

"You know there is, but if you want me to say it, I will. The 'but' is tomorrow, Alicia. We're friends. I don't want to give that up. I've had women before, but not women friends. I don't think this is something that either of us could do lightly, and burning bridges is not what you and I are prepared to do. Which would only leave us the choice of not seeing each other. And that, Alicia, would cause me a great deal of pain."

Alicia had not cried often in her lifetime, but she felt the tears collecting in her eyes. She agreed with Gardiner, yet she felt she would care for this man as long as she lived. "You're right," she said. "I don't want to give you up. If we leave things as they are, maybe that won't ever have to happen."

Without speaking, they made a final survey of the gallery, put the lights out, and then Gardiner drove Alicia back to her hotel. He kissed her tenderly on the forehead and said good night.

Later, she lay in her bed and wondered if things ever came together, all at once, for anyone. She wondered how it felt to be content, to be free of whatever it was that drove her.

The gallery opening was almost monotonously perfect. Everything and everyone moved according to plan. The turn-out of exquisitely dressed and beautifully coiffed guests was remarkable—a fact that was duly noted by the large number of press representatives who had come. Everything went smoothly, at least until Gardiner and Irene arrived.

Irene extended a hand in greeting to Alicia—while her eyes flicked over her husband's associate. She took in the red Lanvin silk, the mass of black hair pulled back with a diamond clip. This was a different Alicia from the one who had tried to impress Irene with her lack of style. This Alicia looked less like a businesswoman—and more like a threat to Irene's marriage. In spite of her good breeding, Irene could not hold back an expression of dislike mingled with fear. Alicia caught the look—and returned it in kind. She avoided both Gardiner and his wife for the remainder of the evening.

When Alicia returned to New York, she did not notice that Charles was particularly quiet, that his welcome was restrained. She was too absorbed with the new gallery, with the turbulent feelings stirred by her flirtation with adultery.

Nor did she notice that Sally was the only family member who greeted her warmly. "Look, Mother—Daddy's new book came out while you were away. Jenny and I had a lovely party for him. Everyone said it was wonderful. Here, I saved the *Times* review to show you. Look—it says that 'Charles Richman has produced the first original commentary on Keats in decades.' Isn't it wonderful? And look, Mother—the book's dedicated to us. Jenny helped with the notes—I'm not very good at that sort of thing—but Daddy says that we were both 'a constant source of love and support.' Imagine—he said that right on the front page of the book."

"That's nice, darling. Congratulations, Charles," she said absently. "I want to hear all about it. But I'm so exhausted from the trip. Why don't we have a nice talk tomorrow?"

Seeing her father's pained look, Jenny whispered to Sally; "Richeliu strikes again."

Alicia went directly to bed and fell asleep without giving another thought to Charles's book. She did not know that in her absence, one of Charles's more precocious students—a young woman much as she had been—had attempted, unsuccessfully, to seduce him. Nor did she consider the possibility that Charles might have found a certain serenity in her absence, that if she did not offer him more than a half-marriage, she might one day lose him.

⋆ 14 ⋆

Charles had known that one day his girls would discover boys, that it was only a matter of time before they married and left him behind. He wanted this for them, yet he watched with a mixture of pride and regret as they left childhood behind.

Sally grew tall and willowy, developing a figure that was riveting in its perfection. Her blue-gray eyes seemed twice as large when her face lost its childish contours and her cheekbones became more prominent. She was an authentic American beauty.

Jenny changed too. The bright red hair of childhood turned auburn, the figure became full and rounded and very feminine, the face took on a frank, open quality that some found as appealing as beauty.

If Sally was the classic beauty, then Jenny was the universal kid sister. Boys competed for Sally's attention. With Jenny, they wanted to be friends. Both sisters had their share of dates at the progressive but chic coed high school Alicia had chosen for them.

Unlike Alicia, Charles paid close attention to the boys who came to see his daughters. For both his girls, he wanted only the best. Secretly he felt that Jenny might survive, perhaps even thrive on something less than perfection. But Sally—that was another matter. He worried about that fragile beauty. She would need a protector—if not a Galahad, then someone who would understand and treasure her. He found most of her admirers wanting.

So did Jenny, who kept up a running commentary on her sister's beaux. "I think that Bill is a drip," she might say, and perhaps add, "But what do I know? *All* my boyfriends are drips."

Charles always made soothing fatherly disclaimers, but in truth he found little of interest in any of the boys who came to call on either daughter.

The first exception was Elie Lowenstein, a scholarship student at the girls' school, a boy who began life over a delicatessen in the Bronx. The first time Elie sat in the Richman living room, Charles saw the boy's eyes range nervously over the furnishings and the artwork, and watched him biting his lip. Under Charles's gentle interrogation Elie spoke of his father, who had come from Poland and who now ran a delicatessen; of his mother, who had died when he was born. He told Charles that he had wanted to study law as long as he could remember. "I'm going to be a good lawyer," he said, with a quiet determination that was neither prideful nor arrogant. "And then," he added, "I plan to go into politics. I would like to be a judge." In another teenager, this might have been just a "When I grow up . . ." recitation. But from the lips of Elie Lowenstein, the words were entirely convincing. Strange, Charles thought, that this dark intense boy with fire in his eye and hunger in his soul should be courting Sally.

For all her wonderful qualities, she had never been possessed of a strong intellect or a penetrating curiosity. She seemed perfectly content with her life, and she looked forward to marrying and to going on more or less as she had always done. The future she envisioned for herself seemed to encompass neither struggle nor change, while Elie clearly had plenty of both ahead of him.

Jenny might be a more suitable choice, Charles had first thought, for a young man with a quick mind, a nice edge to his wit, and a surfeit of ambition. But as Elie came to the house more and more often, as Charles watched the boy's eyes worship his elder daughter, he understood what it was that Elie sought. For a poor boy with rich dreams, Sally was like a prize, a trophy—perhaps even a good luck piece. When Elie Lowenstein arrived wherever it was he planned to go, a wife like Sally would save him the embarrassment of a mate who belonged to his past. In the end, it was Elie's unadulterated adoration that made Charles think this boy might, after all, be good for his princess.

"What do you think of Elie Lowenstein?" he asked Alicia one night—one of the rare nights they were spending together, sitting in front of the fireplace and sipping second cups of coffee.

"Who?" she asked, her mind obviously elsewhere.

"The boy Sally's out with tonight. They had sherry with us, remember?"

"Oh, yes. He's Jewish." For a moment, memories came to her—memories of herself, loving Robert and hearing: "Oh, no, Alicia. I could never marry you."

"Yes, darling. He is." Charles had never been able to understand why his wife, with her exotic background, seemed so much more sensitive to ethnic and racial variations than he was—in spite of the fact that his ancestors could be traced in a direct line to the *Mayflower*. When he had once mentioned this to his wife, she had answered, "Exactly, Charles. Exactly."

Yet Alicia did not discourage Elie's courtship of Sally. She remembered how her father and mother had tried to point out the obvious incompatibilities between herself and Charles and how this unsolicited advice had only accelerated her rush to the altar. And although Sally was clearly a different breed from her mother, Alicia had become a fatalist on the subject of marriage. So she said nothing at all about the frequency with which Elie came to call.

Charles thought the two children made a curious couple. Sally seemed content in the circle of Elie's admiration—perhaps a little livelier somehow, as if with him as her guide she might venture now and then outside her usual behavior. Elie stopped biting his lip. He also stopped calling Charles "sir" every time he spoke to him.

Yet Elie's confidence was short-lived. Competition loomed sudden—and formidable—in the person of Bradford Jeffers III. It was early on a Sunday morning when Celia Jeffers called Sally. "Could I bring my cousin Brad to your brunch today?"

"Of course. I don't think I've met your cousin, have I?"

"No, he's been away at school. And now he's just starting a new job with his father—they're in banking, you know. Anyway, Brad used to be an awful pest when we were kids, but he's really super now. I thought it might be fun for him to meet some of our crowd. He's been a little out of touch. Do you mind? Tell me if you do. . . ."

"I don't mind at all. It's always nice to have an extra man. Don't give it another thought. I'll see you later."

The first meeting between Sally and Bradford Jeffers III was not exactly love at first sight. But it was noteworthy. As soon as Jenny got her first look at Celia's cousin, she let out a shriek of laughter. "Good Lord," she said. "He's Sally's twin. Look at those eyes. That hair!"

Sally shot her sister a reproachful look. But her eyes did open wide when she got a good look at Brad (who indeed might have been a close relative, if not a twin), took in the tall, slender, beautifully muscled body—by lacrosse and rugby, he later explained—the streaked blond hair, cut short at the neck, full on the top and sides, falling in a soft, seductive wave, almost into his clear, incredibly blue eyes.

Sally blinked once or twice at this man who seemed to be a reflection of all that was attractive in her, and then she smiled, a truly dazzling smile. "Hello," she said. "I'm Sally Richman. And I'm so glad that Celia brought you along."

Brad bowed from the waist, allowing his hair to fall even more seductively into his face. "Miss Sally," he drawled, in the mock-southern style he had picked up during four years at William and Mary, "I am surely pleased to make your acquaintance. You are even prettier than Celia said you were."

Sally flashed yet another high-voltage smile, linked her arm in Brad's, and led him into the living room. "Why thank you, suh," she said, emulating his tone and manner. "Let me show you the hospitality of mah home. Allow me to fetch you a plate of eggs and grits."

"Thank you, ma'am. Ah would be most grateful." And then he looked quite deliberately into Sally's face, until she broke away to get the food she had promised.

As he watched this tableau, Charles Richman was not as impressed as his daughter seemed to be. The young man seemed personable enough. With blood of the bluest variety. Good looks. Too good, really. Perhaps that was it. Although he himself was a handsome man, Charles mistrusted too much physical beauty in a man. It was the vaguest kind of suspicion he felt toward Bradford Jeffers III, certainly not one that could be voiced.

To his credit, the boy had more than a gentleman's education. This past year, he had finished a master's degree at the Harvard School of Business and now he had a job with the family's very old, very solid banking firm. Alicia would no doubt be impressed.

There was one more person who was not altogether pleased at this meeting. Off in a corner, Elie Lowenstein glowered and sulked as he watched Sally, the prize that had seemed within reach, obviously enjoying the attentions of another man. Feeling hurt and ignored, he marched over to the golden couple. "I'm leaving, Sally," he announced.

She looked away from Brad. "But it's so early. Can't you stay awhile?"

He had gambled that she would ask if something was wrong. Then he could say yes and tell her how hurt he was by her attentions to the newcomer. Now there was nothing to do but leave.

Charles watched the rivalry between Elie and Brad with some concern. He would have cast his vote for Elie—although he conceded that the newcomer had some obvious advantages.

For one, Brad could entertain Sally in the fashion she and her friends customarily enjoyed. The best Elie could offer was an occasional movie followed by a modest snack—or perhaps a low-priced seat at a concert or play. With Elie, there were no weekends at beach houses or ski holidays in the mountains. Sally had not seemed to mind Elie's limitations. Yet when Brad offered something else, she accepted eagerly.

"What do you see in him?" Elie asked one day, in a fit of jealousy and frustration.

Sally looked a little surprised at the question. "Brad? I don't know—he's nice."

Elie snorted derisively at this description of Brad Jeffers, but he was afraid to say exactly what he thought.

Yet the threat that Brad posed made Elie move a little more quickly than he might have. He pressed—trying to crowd Brad out, to take so much of Sally's time that there would be little left for anyone else.

This strategy worked for a little while, for Sally did not like to refuse Elie or to hurt his feelings. But when he tried, on Friday evening, to get her to make a commitment two weeks ahead, she refused with some impatience. "For heaven's sake, Elie—I don't know what I'll be wanting to do two weeks from now. I can't decide right now. I might want to spend a little time with someone else, you know. You haven't given me time to breathe.''

He tried to make a joke. ''That's the idea, Sally. I want to overwhelm you with my winning personality.'' Then, more seriously: ''I don't want to see anyone else, Sally. Don't you feel the same way?''

She answered as gently as she could, ''I don't know, Elie. I'm very fond of you. But I do like to see other people sometimes.''

''You mean Brad.''

''Well—yes—Brad, too.''

Elie felt suddenly desperate. He had no argument to offer. He only knew there was a good chance he would lose his golden princess. He took her hands in his, went down on his knees, and bowed his head. ''Please, Sally,'' he whispered. ''Please choose me.'' His shoulders began to heave, and although she could not see his face, Sally knew he was crying.

She stared, fascinated and repelled at the same time. Raw emotion was not a part of her makeup, and she did not quite know how to handle it in others. If Sally had her way, life would always be a series of photographs, with all the flaws erased by flattering makeup and cunning lights—loveliness frozen for posterity through a gauze-covered lens. Although she recognized unpleasantness, unhappiness, she felt they could be avoided—or quickly healed—if only people did what they were supposed to do.

Right now Elie was making her unhappy because he was not behaving as he should. And so she did the only thing she could. She pulled inside herself—and away from him.

Sally was finally lost to Elie during a visit she made to meet Brad's parents. From the first, she thought they were the most elegant couple she had ever seen.

Brad Jeffers II was an older version of his son, slightly heavier, his hair gray instead of blond. His wife was a small, slender woman, her short gray hair slightly rinsed with silver, her clothes simple and well cut. She did not speak much, and when she did, it was in a soft, deferential voice—as if she were testing, gently, to see what her husband's reaction might be.

As Sally sat at their dinner table, enjoying a delicate Dover sole and a lovely Mersault, she thought how handsome and strong Brad's father was—and how proud a woman could be with a husband like him.

— 15 —

"Don't you think Brad is a drip, Daddy? He's just so perfect, it's disgusting."

Charles considered Jenny's question for a moment. "He seems to be Sally's choice, and I think we should respect whatever choice she makes." Then, almost to himself, he added, "I think Sally could make a happy marriage with anyone. Anyone who respects her and appreciates how special she is."

"Daddy—why did you marry Alicia? Did you feel like you'd just die if you didn't have her?"

Charles was startled by Jenny's question, but he had always been frank and open with his daughters, so he tried to answer it. "I'm not sure what I felt at the time, Jenny. I was drawn to your mother. She had fire and spirit. Yet there was something sad about her—something I thought I could reach and change."

Jenny did not want to hurt her father, but she felt that she had to ask another question, the question that had run through her mind so many times. "So what happened, Daddy? Didn't she love you back?"

"Yes—yes, she did love me back. I don't know if I can explain what happened, except to tell you that sometimes love isn't enough. There's something to be said for compatibility, Jenny—two people thinking along similar lines, wanting the same things from life . . . that's important. I didn't realize how important it was, perhaps because my own parents had been so sublimely compatible together. Your mother was . . . different. It was perhaps part of the attraction we had for each other. But in time our differences came between us."

Jenny tried to digest what her father had said. And then she asked the other question that had plagued her for so long. "Do you think I'm like Alicia, Daddy? People say I am, but I don't want to be."

Charles chose his words carefully. "Yes, Jenny, I think

you have some of your mother's qualities. But they are fine qualities—curiosity and independence and spirit. What you must do is become the mistress of your passions—so they don't make you and the people you care about unhappy. You must take the time to think of others. You must choose what you want and direct yourself accordingly. You mustn't be diverted by passing fancies—remember the story I told you when you were a little girl? About the dog with the bone in his mouth? Remember what happened when he saw his reflection in the water? He dropped his bone to reach for the other dog's bone—and then he had nothing. Passion, hunger—they're fine qualities, but you mustn't let them rule you.''

Jenny didn't completely understand what her father meant. But she felt comforted by what he said. She didn't have to be like her mother. The choice was hers.

After the talk with her father, Jenny reviewed the brief list of boys she had dated. She had had her share of crushes on "unsuitable" boys. Perhaps her most dangerous attachment had been to Lenny, a hulking linebacker from a boys' school in Riverdale. When she had brought Lenny to a school dance, her classmates had snickered and made jokes about "the Brain and the Beast."

The memory made Jenny smile. Dating Lenny had been pure excitement—the excitement of forbidden thrills. They had almost nothing in common except a strong physical attraction. When they danced together, it was as if every cell in her body came alive, responding to his every movement and touch. And later—later, when they had parked on a quiet street, they had kissed until she was dizzy with excitement. He nibbled on her ear, his tongue teasing, insinuating—and suddenly she found herself trembling with a spasm of such intensity that Lenny had laughed with delight. She did not go out with him again. That momentary loss of control, the power that it had given Lenny over her, had absolutely terrified her.

Now she knew she had been right. Boys like Lenny were not for her. Now she was ready to make thoughtful, sensible choices, ready for a boy like Jeffrey Ashland. Daddy would approve of Jeffrey, she was certain of it.

High school crushes were a thing of the past. She was a college girl now, a Barnard girl, like her mother—though she had chosen the school to be closer to Daddy. Columbia was a family tradition. She knew her father had been just a little disappointed when Sally had to go to Briarcliff. It was understood that Sally was not up to the rigors of a Columbia education. Still, Charles had been obviously pleased when Jenny had announced her intention to go to Barnard and to "get the best marks ever."

A week ago she had met Jeff at a Columbia freshman mixer. He asked her to dance, and she sensed almost at once that he was the very essence of suitability. He was attractive in a slightly off-center way. His features were a little too irregular to be conventionally handsome, but she thought there was something honest and wholesome in his closely cropped wavy brown hair, his clear brown eyes.

They danced one dance. She liked the way he held her, easily, confidently, without any attempt at instant intimacy. He led well, and although she had never been a good dancer, she followed him easily.

Then they sat down on the sidelines with cups of fruit punch. "I'm in premed," he told her.

"That's wonderful," she said. "I think anyone who studies medicine must be really dedicated. So many years . . . and all those science courses—they've always seemed so mysterious and complicated to me."

"They aren't really, not when you've been exposed to them all your life." He smiled slightly, showing slightly crooked teeth, which seemed to Jenny more appealing, more honest than the products of expensive orthodontia. "I come from a long line of doctors—my grandfather, my uncle, my father. Medicine has never been a mystery to me. But I agree with you about the hard work. I'll have to work my tail off to get into medical school—just because you want something isn't any guarantee you'll get it, especially something like medical school. There are more than a hundred premeds in my class. I bet maybe two dozen of us will make it."

"You'll get in, Jeff—if you want it and you work for it, you'll get in."

He smiled again. "Thanks for the vote of confidence, Jenny. What's your major? Not science, I guess."

"No—not science. I'm a fine arts major," she said, a little apologetically.

"Fine arts—now that's a mystery to me."

"You're kidding."

"No, I'm not. I've been pretty single-minded about medicine ever since I was a kid. I've never really taken the time for much of anything else. I guess you must know a lot about painting and music and such."

"I wouldn't say that. I've just been surrounded by it—the way you were with medicine."

"I think you're being modest. I'll bet you're quite an artist yourself."

"Well," she said modestly, "I did win a couple of prizes in high school. And one of my watercolors did hang in the Museum of Modern Art for a couple of weeks. But that was part of a school exhibition—just kid stuff. I'm not that good. I think I'll concentrate on art history—academic stuff, like my father."

"I'm impressed. No matter what you say. Maybe you can help me fill in some of the gaps in my education. If you have the time, that is."

"Sure," she said, pleased that Jeff wanted to see her again. "Sure, I'd love to."

Jeff insisted on taking her home, though she had insisted she could manage on her own. He walked her to the door and gave her a kiss, a chaste kiss on the mouth, a kiss that smelled of a woodsy shaving lotion, masculine yet so manifestly pure that Jenny suspected she had met the man she would marry.

"I'll call you soon," he promised. "As soon as I can, that is. I have a couple of first quizzes to study for, but as soon as I get on top of things—"

"I understand, Jeff. Whenever you're ready."

Their first real date took place two weeks later, on a Saturday night. Jeff called for her wearing a pair of chino pants, a tattersall check shirt, and a beige cashmere pullover. How wholesome he looks, she thought—just the sort of man who should father your children, who should take you strolling into the sunset. It never occurred to Jenny that at eighteen, she was a little young to be concerned with children and sunset years. But she had seen what happened when people got together without thinking ahead.

"There's a Fellini film playing right here in your neighborhood—on Twelfth Street. We could see that if it's all right with you."

"I love Italian movies, Jeff. Especially Fellini."

They watched the movie in respectful silence and then walked over to the Reggio Café for strong, dark espresso served with paper-thin slices of lemon. "European movies always make me think," Jeff said. "The use of symbolism is so effective—it makes me feel like the director is saying something to me, not just trying to make a piece of junk that makes people laugh and earns a lot of money."

"Oh, yes," Jenny agreed. "European films are really a serious art form—not just a commercial product. I'm so glad the picture wasn't dubbed, aren't you? I don't understand much of Italian, but at least you can try to catch some of the nuances of the original language."

"I'm afraid you're ahead of me there, too. I have to depend on the subtitles. But I agree with you—they're much better than dubbing."

"How is school going for you, Jeff? Did you do all right on those quizzes you told me about?"

He seemed pleased that she remembered. "Yeah, I did all right. But I can't afford to get overconfident. Too many rough spots ahead. How about you?"

"I'm just loving it, Jeff. I thought high school was great, but college is just . . . oh, I don't know—it makes me feel like I'm grown up, like I'm ready to live my own life. The teachers treat you differently. They just tell you what they expect, and then it's up to you to plan your time. If you want to cut a class and go to the library instead, no one watches over you. I like that—the way they assume you're mature enough to decide for yourself."

He smiled at her. "I know what you mean. That's why a lot of kids flunk out freshman year—because they're not mature enough for that kind of freedom. I don't want that to happen to me, and I figure the best way of avoiding it is to be aware of the danger. This is the first time I've been away from home like this. There's too much at stake to treat it like a big vacation."

"You're so wise, Jeff. Where are you from, by the way? You never told me."

"Upstate. Kingston."

"Will you go back there? To practice medicine?"

"No, I don't think so. My father's happy enough there, but I've always wanted to work in a big city—I want to have access to the latest technology and the newest techniques. I don't ever want to lose a patient and know there was a piece of equipment a thousand miles away that might have saved him. I want to be the best, Jenny. The best I can be.'' He flushed a little. ''Maybe you think that sounds conceited. I just meant—''

''I know what you meant, Jeff. I don't think it's conceited at all. I think it's wonderful.''

They sat quietly for a few moments, looking at each other in the dim light of the café. ''You know,'' he said, ''I really hadn't planned on doing much dating for a while. I figured most girls wouldn't understand the kind of hours I'd have to keep, the pressures. . . .''

Jenny waited expectantly, not knowing where this was leading.

''Then I saw you at the mixer. You looked so pretty, and I just wanted to talk to you.''

''Pretty? Me?''

''Sure. I said to myself: That's a great-looking girl. I have to meet her.''

She laughed, delighted that Jeff thought she was pretty. ''So you did.''

''Yeah, so I did. What I'm trying to say is that I want to keep seeing you. But I want to be fair and tell you that my work comes first. For a while, until I get where I want to be. If you can understand that—''

''Of course I understand, Jeff. I admire you for thinking that way. I'd be happy to see you, when you have the time. Maybe we can study together. And I'm a whiz at typing term papers—just try me.''

''You've got a deal, Jenny—I'm going to take you up on that offer. Soon.''

When Jeff brought Jenny home, he gave her a warm hug and two light kisses. Again the smell of pine woods filled her senses, making her feel clean and warm and cozy.

As she got ready for bed, she thought how lucky she was to have found someone like Jeff. They could be compatible together. She was sure of it. She loved the idea that he was going to be a doctor. It made him seem noble and dedicated and wise. She loved, too, the fact that he knew what he wanted, that he wouldn't let anyone or anything divert him. She would help him as she had promised. She had seen what could happen when a woman was selfish and preoccupied with her own interests, when she ignored her husband instead of helping him. It was not a lesson she would soon forget.

Jenny and Jeff soon fell into a comfortable routine. During the school week, they met after class and studied together at the Columbia library. Dinner on those nights was either a pizza on Amsterdam Avenue or "Chinese" in a small restaurant on Broadway. Around nine or ten o'clock he would put her into a taxi for the five-mile trip downtown.

When Jeff's schedule permitted, Saturday was "date night" —which usually meant a movie or an off-Broadway play, and dinner at Monte's or one of the Village's other small inexpensive restaurants.

Unlike Sally and Brad, Jeff and Jenny did not have a "crowd." They studied and had fun with each other. Occasionally Sally teased her sister gently about "settling down like old married people," but Jenny didn't mind. She and Jeff regularly congratulated themselves on their appreciation of life's quiet pleasures, on the fact that they didn't need to look for good times at noisy parties or in smoky overpriced nightclubs.

Physically, their relationship progressed from woodsy kisses to tentative touching. The first time Jeff put his hand on Jenny's breast, they were sitting in a Greenwich Village movie theater, watching a Peter Sellers movie. At first Jenny thought she might have imagined it, but later, when they were parked in Jeff's old Chevy, on a quiet side street off lower Fifth Avenue, the hand returned. She reminded herself that Jeff was "different" from the other boys she had known, that touching him was normal and nice.

When he gave her his class ring and announced that they were officially "going steady," the touching escalated. As they snuggled together in the front seat of his car, he reached under her sweater and unhooked her bra. She yielded to his embrace, a little stiffly at first, but this, too, turned out to be all right.

By the time senior year began, they talked confidently of "we" and "us." Jeff never actually proposed, but an understanding was reached one evening in early fall. He had been invited by one of his professors to a party at The Players, a Gramercy Park actors' club that had been founded in the late nineteenth century by Edwin Booth.

"This is super," Jenny said, as she and Jeff climbed the stairs to the main room, where a Sargent portrait of Booth hung over the fireplace. "I've seen this building so many times from the outside, and I've always wanted to see what the inside looked like." She lingered over the letters and theatrical memorabilia that were displayed in glass cases. Then she and Jeff visited Booth's upstairs bedroom, which had been preserved intact since the actor's death.

"Do you know," she said to Jeff when the party was over, "my grandparents started the family business just a couple of blocks from here?"

"Really? Let's go look."

"Nothing to see now. The old place has been torn down— there's a new apartment building on the spot now."

"Okay, then let's go sit in the park. I want to talk to you."

"Can't."

"Why not?"

"It's a private park. Only the people who live around it have keys."

"Hey—I like that. Let's live here after we're married."

It was the first time he had used the word "married," and Jenny sensed it was his way of testing her response. "Yes," she said, "I think that would be nice."

That night, when Jeff took her home, his caresses became more intimate, as if something had been settled between them. At that point Jenny was more than ready to dispose of her virginity, but something in Jeff's attitude held her back, something in the way he separated girls into "cheap" and "nice" categories. It was too risky, and Jenny had lost her flair for taking risks.

Senior year was filled with small pleasures and rewards. She suspected (although the school was very secretive about class standings) that she would be one of the few who graduated summa cum laude—the highest honor the college accorded.

She had already made Phi Beta Kappa. Jeff had immediately given her a delicate gold bracelet so she could wear the little key around her wrist. And when the chairman of her department summoned her for a meeting, she assumed it was to inform her that her honors paper had been accepted—that she would be receiving a special certificate, stating that she had completed her department's honors program.

"I wonder if you've made any plans for after graduation," the department chairman asked.

"Well—no, Dr. Harcourt. Not really. I had thought about teaching. But I'm just not sure yet."

"Your grades are very fine, Miss Richman. Your work has been consistently excellent, and your honors paper was splendid—as well done as many master's theses I've seen."

"Thank you, Dr. Harcourt."

"If you've thought about teaching, I assume you've also thought about graduate school."

"Well . . ." Actually Jenny had thought about graduate school, not so much as a means to a career, but because she was reluctant to see her school days end. But the idea had been indefinite, linked conditionally—she did not quite know how—to her relationship with Jeff.

"I called you in here," Dr. Harcourt continued, "because I wanted to urge you to apply for the Harding fellowship. It provides for a year's study in Paris, at the Sorbonne. When you return, I could arrange a teaching assistantship for you. You would have ample time to work on your doctorate while you teach one or two classes a week. Does that interest you?"

"I don't know what to say. I'm really honored that you want me. I just hadn't thought about anything like this. . . ."

"Think about it, Miss Richman. Take your time—not too much time, mind you—but think about it, and let me know."

"I will, Dr. Harcourt. Thank you—thank you so much."

Jenny was enormously flattered that Dr. Harcourt had singled her out—of all the department majors—for such an honor. She couldn't wait to tell her father. He would be so proud of her. First she would tell Jeff, share her pleasures with him, as they had come to share so many of their thoughts.

But as she started to tell him of her meeting with Dr. Harcourt, savoring each little detail in the telling, she saw a frown crease his forehead. By the time she had finished her story, Jeff looked serious, almost angry.

"You're not thinking of taking it," he said accusingly.

His reaction was so unexpected, so unsettling, that she became flustered, defensive. "I don't know, Jeff. I haven't even had a chance to think. What's the matter? Why are you looking at me that way? I thought you'd be proud of me."

"I would be proud," he said, in a controlled voice that

chilled her, "if you had said thanks, but no thanks. And what's the matter is that you seem to have forgotten that we were planning to be married."

"Oh, Jeff," she said, in a quick rush of relief. "Of course I haven't forgotten. But we haven't really set a date. You'll be starting medical school next year. You've told me how that's practically a twenty-four-hour job. I didn't think you'd really miss me that much if I took the fellowship. I could come home for holidays. And if I did go to work for Dr. Harcourt, I'm sure I could arrange the hours. We could be married, and—"

He was shaking his head before she could finish. "No good, Jenny, that's just no good. I'm really disappointed. I thought getting married was important to you. I thought you wanted to make a home for us and help me get a good start in my career. I don't want a woman who can only give me part-time attention. I won't live that way. As for a year in Paris—well, I would have thought you'd appreciate the fact that I've treated you with respect. I've never tried to take advantage of you because I want you to be my wife. But there's a limit, Jenny, to what a healthy man can put up with. I can't wait forever. And I don't want to wait a year while you do heaven knows what in Paris. If you leave—if you leave—then I can't promise I'll be here when you get back."

Jenny was stunned. She knew that Jeff had very definite ideas about the proper order of things—she had once heard Charles refer to him as "opinionated" when he didn't realize she was listening—but she hadn't expected such a stern, angry reaction.

"I didn't realize you'd be so upset, Jeff. I never said I would take the fellowship. I just liked the idea. I want the chance to think about it—for a little while, anyway."

Jeff's face relaxed and his voice softened. "Maybe you think I'm being selfish, Jen. But I've never kidded myself about the grind that's ahead of me. I don't want to live a makeshift life while I'm trying to get there. I need someone who understands my goals, who wants to share them. If you want something else, Jen, I'll try to understand. Think about it."

It was the second time that day that someone had told her to "think about it." But there really wasn't much to think about. The fellowship excited her, stirred thoughts of adven-

ture and romance, but the risk of losing Jeff was unthinkable.
Jeff was the first boy she had ever wanted to marry, the first
boy who had wanted to marry her. She remembered the story
of the dog with the bone. Suppose she lost him. Suppose
there was no one else. Ever.

She told Jeff there would be no fellowship, no year in
Paris. She assured him that she would be happy staying
home, helping to lighten the burdens of his professional life.

She could not bear to face Dr. Harcourt and to explain her
reasons for not applying for the fellowship. She wrote him a
brief note, telling him she had certain family commitments
that kept her from accepting his kind and generous offer. She
thanked him for the interest he had taken in her—and firmly
closed the door on what had been a satisfying part of her life.

Jeff decided they would marry shortly after graduation, to
allow time for a nice honeymoon and some relaxation before
he settled into the rigorous routine of medical school. The engagement was celebrated during Christmas holidays at a small
family party.

Sally hugged her as Jenny dressed in a pink brocade dress
and matching flats—the latter in deference to the fact that Jeff
was barely an inch taller than she was. "I'm so happy for
you," Sally said. "Now the two of us are getting married.
Aren't we lucky? Now we can have our own families. Real
families."

"But we have a family."

"You know what I mean. A family the way it's supposed
to be. Not like—"

"Yes, I know what you mean."

"Jenny—I've just had a wonderful idea. Why don't we
have a double wedding? Brad and I talked about getting
married in the spring, but I'm sure he wouldn't mind waiting
till June. Why don't we both have a June wedding?"

"Oh Sally—I love the idea. You don't think a June wedding is too corny?"

"Corny? I think it's romantic and wonderful." The sisters
hugged again, and Jenny went out to greet her guests and
display her ring—a perfect two-carat stone, not ostentatious,
but large enough to be "important." When it had been
admired, along with Jeff's engagement gift of a dainty watch,
Brad stood up, champagne glass in hand. "I'd like to make a

toast now—to Jenny and Jeff. Sally tells me we're all going
to be in-laws on the same day—sometime in June.''

Hugs and kisses followed Brad's words. The photographer
hired for the occasion snapped frantically, trying to capture
the merriment of the moment. Later, when the pictures were
processed, there would be one, taken at almost the exact time
of Brad's announcement. It showed Alicia standing on one
side of the room, an expression of panic on her face, while
Charles Richman stood in an opposite corner, holding a drink
in his hand, his face a study in inconsolable sadness.

—◄ **16** ►—

The third Sunday in June was a beautiful day. It was warm
enough to allow the flimsiest of summer dresses, yet cool
enough so the men in their formal clothes would not be
uncomfortable.

Penthouse A was a visual delight. Orchids and baby's breath
and peonies were massed in lush arrangements. Silver and
crystal sparkled against purest linen. Wood and brass and
pewter were buffed to a warm mellowness. Alicia had emptied all her cupboards, digging out family treasures that had
not been seen in years, and her daughters had squealed with
delight. For once, they had all behaved as mother and daughters
should, sharing the joy and anticipation of the moment.

On this day, all three women looked magnificent. Alicia
wore her black hair coiled in a topknot. Her dress of gray
chiffon would have washed out a less striking woman, but it
made her look regal.

Sally was a latter-day Juliet, all ivory silk and seed pearls,
face framed with blond tendrils. Dozens of guests would
remark that she looked like an angel. Now she put on the
diamond earrings that were a gift from Brad—and thought for
the hundredth time how lucky she was.

Just across the hall, Jenny was folding her "something
blue"—a linen handkerchief that had belonged to Carlotta—
inside her garter. In her princess-line dress of Alençon lace,

with her short auburn hair, her nose dusted with freckles, she looked like the classic girl next door. At this moment she was thinking of a tea she had attended during her last week of college, of a conversation she had overheard between Dr. Harcourt and another professor. "Look at these girls," Dr. Harcourt had said, his voice tinged with sadness and exasperation. "We educate them, we teach them everything we know, and then the best of them go out and get married, and drop out of sight for ten or fifteen years—maybe for good. It all seems a little ridiculous, doesn't it?"

She had gone home from the tea and cried, not because the professor's words were harsh, but because she felt them to be true.

As she arranged her veil around her face, she thought perhaps there might never be an alternative—because she was certainly not going to be one of those lonely, dried-up career women. And she was not going to be like her mother. And so she would promise to love, honor, and obey. She would be a good wife, a conscientious mother. And later—well, later she might find something else.

When Charles escorted the two brides—first Sally, then Jenny—the dozen steps from their bedrooms into the living room, there were audible murmurs, appreciative sighs and comments on their beauty. It was a storybook scene. The terrace doors were thrown open, exposing the trees and shrubs outside, allowing the sun and light to wash over the hothouse flowers inside. The ceremony was traditional, brief, and perfect in every detail.

When it was over, the mother of the brides came in for her share of admiration. Yet for once Alicia did not luxuriate in compliments on how young and lovely she looked to have such beautiful daughters. She was, for the moment, preoccupied with other thoughts. On the one hand, she was relieved that her daughters had grown up so well, that they could "fit" anywhere. This wedding, she was certain, would undoubtedly rate more than a short paragraph on the *Times* society page. Oh, she was aware that the girls were much closer to Charles than they were to her. But she was not an unreasonable woman. Charles had put in the time—and he deserved whatever rewards this brought him.

Yet along with the sense of accomplishment at a job well

done, Alicia felt anxious about her own life. The loss of both girls at once was going to cause some dislocation in her own marriage. After all these years of an established pattern—no matter how imperfect—she was afraid of change. How would Charles fill the giant holes that would be left in the fabric of their marriage? Could they be filled?

Although he felt light-years away from his wife, Charles was thinking similar thoughts. He remembered, briefly, how Alicia had looked on their wedding day. He thought, with some bitterness, that she was probably even more stunning now. Yet when he looked at her, there was no more hope, no more expectation—only a profound sense of disappointment.

The sight of his two daughters, so radiant and so lovely, made his heart swell, his eyes fill. He wanted them to be happy, but he could not hold back the tears. They had been his love, his family, his friends. Now they belonged to two other men. Now there would be just empty hours—hours that had once held their laughter, their voices, their plans and schemes and triumphs. The tears started to fall, and when he looked over at Alicia, watched her laughing with the guests, he thought he almost hated her.

Later, after the four newlyweds had left, after the last guest had said good-bye, after the caterer's helpers had departed, bearing the litter from the wedding feast, Alicia and Charles were left in the quiet of their home, each turning into a separate room, each into a private anxiety.

Alicia creamed her face, lit a cigarette, and put out her light. She sat in an upholstered wing chair and looked out her window at the city lights spread out before her. She was still very beautiful, quite rich, enormously successful. she had just married off two daughters. And although she had every creature comfort she desired, she felt lonely and more than a little afraid.

She stepped into her satin slippers and took the few steps— the few very long steps to Charles's room. He sat in bed, half-glasses perched on his nose, reading one of his eternal dissertations. He looked up when she came into the room, but he said nothing. She slid into the bed beside him. How boyish and attractive he still looks, she thought.

"Charles," she whispered, burrowing her head into his shoulder. "Charles—it's late. Why don't you put that away for now?"

"No, Alicia," he said, his voice calm and deliberate. "I'm not tired, and I would like to finish these pages tonight."

She lay quietly as he went through the pages, making little marks in the margins. Her eyes were closed, but she knew by the sounds he made exactly what he was doing. When at last he put the pages aside, he reached over and turned off the bedside light. She snuggled closer to him. Very deliberately he turned over on his side, with his back to her. "Good night, Alicia," he said.

— 17 —

If the success of a honeymoon was a portent of things to come, then Sally and Brad Jeffers were certain to have life smile upon them. They went from their reception to the St. Regis, where they would spend their wedding night. The following morning they would fly to Europe for a two-month grand tour.

When they reached the hotel, Brad tipped the bellboy and told him to go on ahead. "Just put the bags in the room," he said. "We'll be upstairs later."

"What is it, Brad?" Sally asked.

"I want to carry you over the threshold," he whispered, "and I don't want the help grinning at us."

True to his word, Brad opened the door, then swung his bride up in his arms. "Here we go, Mrs. Jeffers—the first threshold for us." He kissed her tenderly, and Sally knew that this was the best day of her life, that from now on, only wonderful things would happen to her.

Inside, they found a basket of fruit, a vase of flowers, and a bottle of champagne chilling in a bucket—a reminder that their families were thinking of them. They looked at these offerings, then at each other—and then Brad Jeffers took his bride directly to bed.

She had planned to brush her hair, to wear the luxurious peignoir set her mother had bought for her. But when Brad took her in his arms, these seemed like inconsequential de-

tails. She was his wife, and he wanted her—and this knowledge made her very, very happy.

They began to peel away their clothing, self-consciously at
first. Then he opened his arms, took her into them, and said,
"I love you very much, Sally. I'm a very lucky man to have
such a beautiful bride."

Oh no, she thought, I'm the lucky one. She pressed closer
to him.

Somehow they found their way into the bed. Although they
had never gone "all the way," Sally's first experience of
making love was as wonderful and warm as she imagined it
might be. Brad's touch was like the prince's kiss for Sleeping
Beauty—it awakened her body to pleasures she had never
imagined. It was magic, she thought—it happened because he
made it happen. And Sally Richman gave herself completely
to her husband. The giving gave her so much joy that from
that day forward, Sally Richman almost ceased to exist as an
individual. She was Mrs. Bradford Jeffers—completely and
irrevocably a married woman.

Nearby, at the Plaza Hotel, Mr. and Mrs. Jeffrey Ashland
were also settling in for their wedding night. Tomorrow, they
too would begin their honeymoon trip—a two-week holiday
in Bermuda, a gift from Alicia and Charles.

Their wedding night was proceeding according to ritual.
Jeff, resplendent in a pair of silk pajamas, was setting out the
champagne that had been left for them while Jenny lingered
in the bathroom, swishing mouthwash through her teeth and
checking her hair in the mirror. When she was finished, she
looked as lovely as a picture in *Bride* magazine but she felt as
nervous as a cat. And she did not feel much like making love.
Still, she supposed, there was no getting away from it. Tonight was her wedding night.

Besides, Jeff would think she was insane if she even hinted
at her hesitation. She remembered his impatience these past
few months each time they went through their repertoire of
"allowed" caresses, his muttering: "Jesus, Jenny, I don't
know how much longer I can wait."

She had been a little embarrassed. She understood that men
were like that, even nice men like Jeff. But why was it all so
clumsy and hard for women, she had wondered. It seemed
like one of nature's not very funny jokes. Oh, she had been
aroused by Jeff's hands on her body. But that arousal had not

made her want to take the next step. It had only made her afraid.

But here it was. The wedding night. And according to the rules, there was no getting on with the marriage until the wedding night was satisfactorily concluded. So. She squared her shoulders and marched into the bedroom. Jeff promptly handed her a glass of champagne. His attitude was that of a man anxious to get the formalities over with. She swallowed the bubbly liquid quickly, hoping that perhaps it would put her "in the mood."

But when Jeff set down his glass and took her by the shoulders, she felt as excited as if she were going to the dentist. "Don't be shy," he said. "It's all right, now. We're married—we don't have to hold back anymore." And somehow those words frightened her even more.

Jeff addressed himself to the ritual he called "foreplay." This, he had once told her, with some self-satisfaction, was something most men knew nothing about. "It's the reason most couples have lousy sex lives," he said. And then he had informed her they would be among the lucky exceptions. But as he applied himself conscientiously to this chore, Jenny felt detached. As she watched his display of superior foreplay, she thought it had all the romance of a garage mechanic servicing a car. She prayed for this night to be over.

When Jeff had finished his attentions to Jenny's body, he took her, quickly and efficiently. For a fleeting moment, she thought this awful pain must be her punishment for something she had done.

When it was over, Jeff seemed satisfied and pleased. He kissed her good night and suggested they "have another go at it" in the morning. "I don't know if I can," she said apologetically. "I seem to be bleeding a lot."

"Oh, don't worry," he said. "That's to be expected. It'll be all right in a few hours."

She did not believe him.

Jenny knew exactly what kind of wife she should be. She would make a real home out of the cozy rent-controlled apartment they had taken in a red-brick town house on Gramercy Park. The apartment was a genuine find—a four-room floor-through, with a spare room that could serve as Jeff's study.

The place was a little run down, but they had been thrilled with the working fireplace, the view of the back garden—and their own key to the private park. Together, they had scraped years of neglect from the oak floors, restoring them to their original beauty. And together they had peeled plaster from one of the kitchen walls, uncovering some lovely old bricks where Jenny could hang one of her favorite wedding presents, a matched set of copper pots.

They haunted neighborhood antique shops for bargains—a battered old brass teapot, some iron fireplace tools, a braided rug for the living room. And when Jeff began his studies at Columbia Medical School, Jenny started her own homemaking studies in earnest. She bought and studied cookbooks and homemaking magazines. She visited butchers and greengrocers and listened attentively when they instructed her in the mysteries of well-marbled steaks and perfect mangoes.

She tested recipes, eschewing the shortcuts that a less loving wife might use. And when she was satisfied that she could produce a variety of well-prepared meals—so that her husband would never be bored at the dinner table—she moved her sights higher, into the realm of do-it-yourself books that instructed her in sewing, in hanging wallpaper, in laying tile, and in repairing small appliances.

Jeff applauded her efforts and her accomplishments. Early in the marriage, he had spoken to her about living modestly until such time as his career could support a more luxurious standard of living. He suggested that she not touch the substantial account Alicia had established when Jenny was a little girl, that she leave it in reserve for "important things we might need later on."

She agreed willingly, appreciating his strength of character and sound values. And since economy seemed to please her husband, she applied herself to budgeting. She set her table with fine linens, but she laundered and pressed them herself.

She didn't mind the extra work. It all made the day go faster. She found that when she did not set projects for herself in advance, the hours seemed long, in spite of the television game shows and soap operas she watched while she worked.

At the end of each day, she would list her accomplishments in her diary: new dishes she tried, chores she performed for Jeff, a new way of ironing shirts so they had a "professional" look.

One evening, however, when she had finished her list, which included preparing a perfect roast and a heavenly light crème brulée, and typing a term paper for Jeff, her hand continued to write, almost involuntarily: "So what."

She put the pen down, stared at the entry, then closed the diary. And that night, when she and Jeff made love, she left her diaphragm in the bathroom medicine chest.

Nine months later, Rebecca Susanna Ashland was born. Her father was proud, her mother optimistic. Although Rebecca was a colicky baby, a child who demanded almost constant attention, Jenny deferred to Jeff when he said no to bringing in a baby nurse. "I don't want our child being brought up by a stranger, Jen. There's a lot of psychological bonding that goes on in those early months. We don't want our daughter getting attached to a nurse, do we?"

This, like Jeff's objections to professional diaper service and commercial food, made sense. So Jenny devoted herself to Becky, while she tried valiantly not to allow any slippage in her general homemaking. She struggled to keep up with the dusting, the cleaning, the ironing, the cooking. Empty hours became a thing of the past. More than once, her diary entries read: "Tired." or "So tired." Or "I wish I could sleep for a week."

Jenny had never been clothes-conscious, but now she noticed, with some distress, that there were days when she did not properly comb her hair, when she never changed out of blue jeans and a sweat shirt into the kind of dress or hostess gown that Jeff preferred to see in the evening. She knew, as her magazines constantly reminded her, that she was risking losing her husband's affection, his sexual ardor—indeed, risking her very marriage—if she let herself go. Well, she reasoned, nothing worthwhile was easy. Her husband, her child—they would be happy and whole. They would know that they were loved. Even if she killed herself proving it.

— 18 —

If Jenny's domestic scene was occasionally bumpy, with Sally it was all smooth sailing. Of course, Sally's married life was made much easier by a full staff of servants. As the son and heir of old money, Brad saw his wife as a kind of chatelaine, and certainly not as a person who actually performed household chores.

Brad's mother instructed her daughter-in-law in the preferences of Jeffers men. She told her how to open accounts with the tradesmen who serviced their Beekman Place neighborhood, told her which details she should take care of herself and which she could properly delegate to servants. She taught her floral arrangements and seating plans for various types of dinners, sample menus, and preferred wines.

Sally was an apt pupil, a natural innovator who took everything she learned from others and made it in some way her own. More than once Brad congratulated himself on his choice of a wife. Sally seemed to be perfect in every setting— at the dinner table, at his side, and in his arms.

Others agreed with Brad. Almost at once young Mrs. Jeffers began to gain a reputation as a charming hostess. She and Brad were so much in love, so pleased with each other, that their buoyant mood communicated itself to everyone around them. Invitations to their home were eagerly sought, gratefully returned, and the Jefferses' social circle grew wider and wider.

Brad and Sally vowed that their marriage would never grow tired, that they would never take each other for granted. They reinforced this promise with tender notes, lovingly laid beside a dinner plate or under a pillow, with tiny bouquets of flowers bestowed for no reason at all.

Sally knew she couldn't be happier. Whenever Jenny saw her, she was always bursting with good news. "Oh, Jenny," she said once, "aren't you so glad you got married? Isn't it heaven?"

"Sure, Sally. It's just fine."

If Sally noticed that Jenny was not quite as enthusiastic, she made no comment. If life was indeed less than perfect, she did not want to know.

Charles and Alicia were now almost strangers. It was as if, for Charles, the marriage of their daughters had brought their own marriage to an end.

Alicia was hurt and bewildered, for whatever else had gone wrong, she had always been able to turn to her husband for physical warmth and solace. It had never occurred to her that he might one day deprive her of her cushion against loneliness. She tried to make overtures—to come home early from the gallery, to prepare simple dinners herself. But now it was Charles who was preoccupied.

He rarely took meals in the dining room, choosing instead to eat from a tray at his desk while he pored over the notes for yet another book. More than once Alicia tried to penetrate this sanctuary, bringing with her small offerings—a fresh pot of coffee, some bright questions about his work.

Charles suffered her presence politely but without interest. And this detachment chilled her more than his anger ever could. Loneliness came to Alicia, more frightening, more intense than before. She vowed she would not let Charles shut her out. He would relent. He had to. She would simply wait him out. And she would win. She was the stronger one. They both knew that.

"Goddammit, Rebecca—what are you doing!" Jenny screamed.

Frightened by the shrillness of her mother's voice, Rebecca dropped the toothpaste she had been mashing into the rug and started to cry.

Immediately remorseful, Jenny put aside the batch of dough she'd been kneading and gathered her daughter into her arms. "Don't cry, baby," she soothed. "It's all right. Mommy's sorry. It's all right. Don't cry, baby."

God, Jenny thought, this is not one of my better days. Becky had been fussy all night with teething pain. "Keep the baby quiet," Jeff had mumbled. "I've got a big day tomorrow."

So Jenny had moved into the nursery, held Becky in her arms, and rocked for hours, right until sunup, when the baby had finally fallen asleep. After breakfast Becky seemed to feel better, but she kept getting into one mess after another. First there had been the bag of flour left untended for just a few minutes, on the counter next to the high chair. Jenny had bitten her lip when Becky had sent it flying—all over her freshly waxed kitchen floor. Jenny had barely finished that cleanup when Becky had—Oh, what was the use of rehashing the morning's disasters. Becky was just a child. She didn't know that her mother was shaking with tension and fatigue. Jeff would have been horrified if he had seen her temper tantrum. It was not the first time Jenny had lost control, and each time she'd hated herself. She would just have to do better, that's all.

She covered the dough with a thick towel and put it aside in a warm corner of the kitchen. Becky probably just wanted some attention, and she would give it to her. "Come on, little one," she coaxed. "Do you want to play with your blocks? Come on—Mommy will help you." Becky rewarded her with a grin, and she felt a little better.

For the next half hour she sat on the floor, making lopsided block towers and watching Becky knock them down. It was hard for Jenny to do this while dozens of chores demanded her attention, but she forced herself to wait patiently, until Becky's eyelids drooped, signaling that she was ready for a nap.

There, Jenny thought, that wasn't so hard. Daddy was right. You didn't have to let your feelings control you. As she tucked Becky into her crib, watched for a moment that angelic face, relaxed in sleep, a tiny pink thumb stuck into the little cupid's-bow mouth, she reminded herself how lucky she was. She contemplated with some satisfaction the little nursery she had created from Jeff's study—the mural of nursery rhyme characters she had painted on the wall, the embroidered canopy she had made for the crib, the patchwork quilt that covered her child—all of these were testaments to how hard she tried, how well she succeeded.

Energized by the prospect of an hour or so of quiet freedom, Jenny attacked the clutter in her own bedroom, gathering up the scattered litter from Jeff's quick morning shower, the Hänsel-and-Gretel trail of used towels and haberdashery that invariably accompanied her husband's rushed morning departures. Sometimes she resented the unspoken rule that made her have to clean up after everyone else. But not today.

She caught a glimpse of herself in the large dresser mirror and grimaced. A real mess, she decided, taking in the unruly, uncombed hair, the oversize man's shirt covered with reminders of Becky's breakfast and morning messes. Quickly, she stripped and showered and changed into a clean sweater and slacks. She gathered her hair into a topknot and finished her toilette with some lipstick and a little blusher. By the time Jeff came home, Jenny was in a fine humor.

"How are my girls?" he asked.

"Wonderful!" She hugged him warmly, rubbing her cheek against his.

"Hey, what's all this? My lucky day? It smells great in here—and you look wonderful." He pinched her cheek. "I don't know how you do it. What have you got cooking?"

"Everything you like. Veal chops and string beans with almonds—and lemon mousse for dessert."

"Terrific. Wait—hold everything for a couple of minutes. I'm going to run down to the corner and get some roses for my wife."

"Jeff?"

"What, hon?"

"Never mind the roses. You know what I want to do? Let's go out to a movie after dinner. I can put Becky to sleep. I'll call that girl we had a few weeks ago—the super's daughter— Oh, Jeff, say yes?"

"Well," he hesitated, "I was going to work tonight. . . ." He looked at his wife's eager face. "Sure—let's do it. We don't want to get stale, do we? But I'm getting you the flowers anyway. And don't argue with your doctor."

She smiled as he went out the door. Not many women had husbands who smelled like pine woods and who brought them roses for no reason.

They came home laughing like the teenagers they had once been. But as they walked through the front door of their apartment, the baby-sitter rushed to meet them. "There was an important call right after you went out. I didn't know where you went, so I didn't know how to reach you. Mrs. Ashland is supposed to call her mother. Right away."

Jenny dialed the number at once. The telephone was answered by a man, a voice she did not quite recognize. "Hello? This is Jenny Ashland. I had a message to call—"

"Jenny, dear—this is Roger Tataryan. Jenny—it's your father. . . ."

"What is it?" she demanded, her voice rising with panic. "Has he had an accident? Is he going to be all right?"

"He's gone, Jenny. A heart attack. Very quick. I don't think he suffered. He was napping. He just didn't wake up. Your mother found him when she went to wake him for dinner. I hate to tell you like this, Jenny. Do come over now. I'll be here."

Jenny put the phone down with fingers that had turned to stone. She turned a face filled with despair and agony toward her husband, and when she opened her mouth, she could not utter a sound.

Roger Tataryan attended to Charles's death certificate, his kind face drawn as he tried to console the women Charles had left behind. He had expected Sally and Jenny to be grief-stricken. He knew how close they had been to their father, how much more than the usual parent-child love had bonded the three of them.

But Alicia—Roger was not at all prepared for her reaction. He had known Alicia since she was a teenager, since he had taken over his father's practice. He had thought of her as a beautiful, headstrong, and willful woman—appealing in her way—and most definitely the dominant partner in her marriage. He expected her to handle Charles's death with strength and quiet dignity. He was shocked when it seemed she would not be able to handle her bereavement at all.

For Alicia, in the days after Charles's death, it was as if she had suddenly become two people—one of them numb, inert, occupying the body that had once housed a spirited, vivacious woman. The other was a disembodied observer who hovered over the flurry of activity that surrounded her husband's death. It was this second Alicia who watched, almost uninterested, as her daughters made gestures of comfort, as friends and business associates came by to offer their respects. This detached Alicia saw the movements of people's mouths as they chewed the food that had been placed there, took careful notice of the clothes they wore, listened to the rhythms of their speech, although she heard not a single word that was spoken. She did notice, however, that Gardiner—impeccable Gardiner—had a tiny food spot on his Countess

Mara tie. But none of this seemed to have anything to do with her.

In fact, she felt a sense of growing irritation when this company of mourners tried to involve her in conversation or in some form of activity. When they brought food, she waved it away. When they tried to make small talk, she refused to answer. She wished they would all go away and leave her alone.

And yet alone was not what she wanted to be. When everyone left her, the two Alicias came together, and she felt the pain, the anger, and the guilt that now surrounded all thoughts of Charles.

"Why did you go and leave me?" Alicia sobbed into her pillow, pounding it with her fists, enraged at the fate that had robbed her of the husband she had not properly valued while he lived. Memories came back, memories of joking conversations, when she had teased him about what he would do if she died. Alicia had been certain that she would die first, she of the high-strung temperament, the churning gastric juices that kept her popping antacids from morning till night. It was she who had the wildly volatile mood swings, the manic excitability that would—she had been certain—give her a heart attack or, worse yet, a stroke. And it was she who had the chain-smoking habit that would give her cancer, if some other disease did not claim her first.

Yet none of these things had happened. It was Charles, of the quiet gentle disposition, the even temper, the soft voice rarely raised in anger—it was he who was gone. And gone so suddenly that Alicia could not shake the mood of disbelief that had enveloped her ever since that horrible moment when she had allowed herself to admit, just for a moment, that she would never, ever see Charles again, that he would never hold her, never love her, never comfort her or make her feel whole. The thought was so grotesque, so enormous in its implications, that Alicia slammed the door on it, and tried instead to focus her complete attention on what now seemed like insurmountable tasks—things like putting one foot in front of another, washing and dressing, combing her hair or eating a meal, when she had no interest at all in where she was or how she looked or what she put into her stomach.

And when she was alone—as she assured everyone she wished to be—then came the turmoil, and, yes, the guilt. When Charles was alive, Alicia had always been defensive about her treatment of him. When her daughters criticized or disapproved of her neglect, she had nipped their comments in the bud with a curt "That's none of your business." Or: "Your father and I understand each other very well. He knows that I love him no matter what I say."

Yet Alicia knew that her daughters were right. Once she had shaken her head impatiently when she heard criticisms that cut too close—as if she could shake off any unpleasant thoughts before they could cling. Now they clung to her. She knew that Charles had deserved better than what she had given. He had offered love and tenderness and respect and loyalty—and a special kind of healing balm for the malady that so often made Alicia feel raw and ragged. He had soothed the restlessness that had made her run like a hunted animal.

And she. What had she given back? Love? Yes, perhaps, but only after her fashion. Loyalty? Yes. But in the other things, things that mattered to people like Charles, there she had failed him. How much had it cost him not to look elsewhere for what he needed? Now she would never know.

When she thought about Charles, who had been impoverished in so many ways because he had married her, the guilt slashed away at her, peeling away the little genuine composure she had.

— 19 —

At a cozy corner table in one of Sally's favorite restaurants, she and Jenny toyed with glasses of white wine and watched the waiter prepare the house fettuccine, adding mustard and Worcestershire sauce to the butter and cream that simmered in the copper saucepan. The aroma burst into the air as he turned up the portable burner.

Sally inhaled—but distractedly, almost professionally—nodding with approval as she decided the dish would probably meet her very high standards. Sally's talents with food were as sharpened and refined as her other domestic skills.

Though she did very little food preparation herself, she was a sensitive and creative cook; she and Brad had even spent part of their European honeymoon learning the mysteries of cor-. don bleu cooking. She supervised her kitchen in a way that elicited the best possible efforts from her help. "Mrs J. buys the best," her cook Paula loved to boast—within earshot of those cooks who worked for more penurious employers.

When the fettuccine was set before them, Sally pronounced it excellent, but neither sister ate with any great relish. Jenny spoke first. "What are we going to do about her?"

Sally shook her head. "I'm not sure we should do anything. What she's going through seems very natural to me." Actually, Sally felt that her mother's mental state was almost stoic, considering she had lost her husband. When she tried to think of herself facing the same situation, she invariably broke into a cold sweat.

"Oh, please, Sally," Jenny said impatiently, "she's not even trying. She never seemed to need him that much when he was alive. If we're going to be honest—at least with each other—then I'll tell you that I don't understand this sudden attachment of hers."

"I think you're being a little hard on her. I know she wasn't a model wife. But Jen—you can't know how much she loved him. And you can't say how much she should miss him now."

Jenny smiled at the unexpected reproach. "You're such a good person, Sally. And you're right, of course. Grief isn't something you have to earn. I guess I'm reacting the way I am because I just don't understand what's going on. I mean— if any woman alive was independent and self-sufficient, it was our Alicia. Now she acts like she's ready to throw herself on the funeral pyre—it just doesn't make any sense to me. I guess it seems hypocritical. I feel that if she had shown Dad just one tenth the emotion we're seeing now, she might have made him happy."

"Well, I don't agree with you. I mean, I do, about the way she treated Daddy. He would have loved some attention and some affection. But as for understanding her—I never understood her before, but she's just starting to make some sense to me now."

"Maybe she just wasn't as sure of herself as we thought. She always seemed so darn perfect—it never occurred to me to make any allowances."

"Me, too. In fact—" Sally hesitated a bit. "I never really told anyone this, and now I feel a little ashamed when I see what Alicia's going through. . . ."

"Really, Sally, what have you *ever* done to be ashamed of? I mean, when we were kids, I used to hate you sometimes because you were so good."

"So good? How strange it is to hear that." Sally's face took on a look of distress—which passed as quickly as it had appeared. "Today must be our day for family secrets. Actually, I never felt quite good enough. I always envied you. Yes, I did," she insisted, seeing the disbelief on her sister's face. "Oh, I knew I was more beautiful. But I always thought you were much more interesting—a thinker, not just someone to look at."

"Oh, but Sally—" Jenny started to protest, to tell about the many times she had seen one of her sister's admirers staring into those blue eyes with a look of sublime enchantment. She started to say that Sally did have something more than just a lovely face and perfect figure, to explain that she had an incandescence that drew people and held them.

But as she tried to put these feelings into words, she burst out laughing. "Look, dear sister, I feel really silly telling you something that should be so obvious to you. Trust me—you are now, and always have been, very, very special. You have a magic that's all yours, that's pure Sally—and it will be the same when you're very, very old. What I think is so funny is that here we are, all grown up and married—and just finding out things about each other. Anyway, you never did finish telling me what terrible thing you did."

"Oh, yes. Well, I don't remember how old I was—but I had come home from college. It was a lovely summer day, and I think I was going to go sailing with Brad or something. The apartment was so very still and quiet. Not a cozy kind of quiet. It was just—empty. But then I realized it wasn't empty. Daddy was sitting there in that study of his, all alone, with a pile of papers on his desk. He wasn't working—I caught him before he could pretend to be doing something. He was just sitting there, staring—and he looked so lonely it almost broke my heart.

"I sat down and we talked awhile. I asked him where Mother was. 'At the gallery,' he said. 'Where else?' I felt so sad for him. He had given us all so much. A real life. A real family. And he seemed to have so little. So—I don't know what made me say it—but I did. I said, 'Daddy, I wish you had somebody special—just for you.'

"He just looked at me. There were tears in his eyes. He didn't say anything—he just squeezed my hand. I went into my room because he seemed so embarrassed. I've wondered so many times since that day if it might have made a difference."

"What?"

"If he had found somebody—just for him."

Even while her daughters tried to draw up a battle plan to rehabilitate their mother, to ease the rough edges as she took on the role of widow, Alicia was mentally trying on the various shadings of this new status. She decided it did not suit her at all.

Before Charles's death, Alicia's life would have seemed rich and full to anyone who had tracked her movements. Her day began with breakfast—a cup of coffee and two cigarettes. Then she would leave, lean and elegant, in one of her classic suits by Chanel or Dior, to head straight for the office that was nearly as elegant as she was. Amid her French and Italian antiques, she would spend an uninterrupted hour screening the mail that already had been sorted by her secretary.

Next she would check the gallery floors, carefully appraising how well each of her employees was carrying out his designated functions. Then came the time for returning phone calls, answering correspondence, and eventually going to lunch—with a buyer, a European agent, a committee dedicated to one of her several charities. After lunch she would nap—a custom learned from her parents and rarely abandoned, even when she was exceptionally busy. The remainder of the afternoon was devoted to loose ends.

Dinner was prepared and served by one of a succession of cooks, at a relatively early hour; this was a habit they had begun at Charles's insistence, so that the meal might be shared with Sally and Jenny. The custom had continued after the girls left home. Evenings, Alicia rarely spent at home. There was always some function to attend which she justified as good business. Principessa and its director were rarely absent from the society pages or the gossip columns.

To a dispassionate observer, Alicia seemed to have it all. At a time when few women had half so much, Alicia had an intelligent, gentle, and kind husband, two beautiful daughters, an engaging and satisfying career, a social life as giddy and ego-nourishing as any enjoyed by a brand-new debutante.

But when Charles died, it was as if someone had pulled the linchpin from the entire structure of her life. Without him, it was as if she suddenly had nothing at all.

Her daughters seemed like strangers—like someone else's children. The prospect of "social" evenings now seemed as dull and tasteless as Charles had often said they were. And when Gardiner called—Gardiner, who had once made her sparkle like a young girl—he now seemed like a shallow poseur compared with Charles, dear, solid, stuffy Charles.

As she had done so many times in her life, Alicia drew into herself, rejecting offers of solace, of diversion, of help. And then, suddenly and without explanation, she appeared one morning, unannounced, at her office. Her secretary, who had not seen her since Charles's funeral, was shocked at the changes that the past month had wrought. Alicia's face was tense and drawn, the once-fine lines beginning to etch deeply into her skin. Although she had made an obvious effort to groom herself, the image she projected was just a little askew.

"It's good to see you again, Mrs. Richman," Peggy said. "Is there anything I can get for you?"

"Yes—yes, there is. Bring me the account books, the monthly report. Fill me in on what's been happening this month. And bring me any mail that wasn't routine."

For the next three hours Alicia did not leave her office. She pored over accounts receivable, over all the cables and letters of condolence that had come to the gallery from business acquaintances, over all the routine data that she normally left to others. At the end of the day, she found that she was physically fatigued, yet emotionally less exhausted. For all the hours she had sat at her desk she had been able to avoid feeling or thinking about her pain.

She was elated at this discovery, for in it, Alicia thought, she had found the key to her survival. And from it came a new life-style. Each morning, after the coffee and cigarettes which became her constant companions, she went directly to the office, where she remained—but without the usual nap or lunch break—until seven or eight at night. Back at her apartment, she picked at whatever meal her cook had prepared and washed it down with two or three glasses of wine. Then came bed and seven or eight hours of restless sleep.

At first Sally and Jenny were glad to see her taking an

interest in the business again. But the relief gave way to renewed concern as they observed the mechanical nature of her new way of life, as they saw that she was not really taking an interest at all, but merely anesthetizing herself, pushing herself as if she were being pursued by invisible demons.

They intervened, pleading with their mother to slow down, but Alicia did not seem to hear. Until the day, eight months after Charles's death, when she simply collapsed at her desk.

Peggy summoned Roger Tataryan, who in turn summoned Sally and Jenny. After Alicia had been mildly sedated and tucked into her own bed, Roger addressed her daughters: "All right. Now it's time to take charge of your mother's life. Perhaps this incident was a fortunate one—your mother was well on her way to destroying her health. Now we have a chance to intervene. Alicia is simply not to go back to that office, or else the next time I'm called there will be no second chance. Do you understand me?"

The sisters nodded in unison.

"I don't want to frighten you, but you must have noticed that Alicia has lost a substantial amount of weight. She smokes enough cigarettes to kill an elephant, and she has nothing whatever in her life that would qualify as rest or recreation. She may believe she's found an antidote to her grief over Charles, but it's an antidote that will kill her."

"What can we do, Roger?" Sally asked. "You know Alicia never really listens to anyone."

"She'll listen." The doctor's jaw set. "She'll listen because I'm not giving her any choice. One way or another, that woman is going to take a very long vacation. She has a capable staff who can manage perfectly well without her.

"I'm going to recommend that she travel, maybe go out of the country. I want you to help me. One of you stay here—pack her bags if you have to. And don't let up on her till you see her get on a plane."

So Jenny and Sally alternated "mother-sitting," praising the attractions of Juan-les-Pins, of Málaga, of Portofino and Cap D'Antibes. But strangely enough, Alicia did not need a great deal of coaxing. As she slumbered in her bed, lulled into a state of rest by Roger's medications, she began to dream, dreams of childhood, of her parents, of days that now seemed much happier than they actually had been.

With the present so painful, and with the future so frightening, Alicia's thoughts lingered in the past. And slowly, without really formulating a plan in words, she found herself thinking of the places where her family had started, of Egypt and Italy. The idea took hold that it was there she might find something to help her contemplate the start of a new day without anxiety and dread.

So when Roger, allied with Sally and Jenny, told Alicia that she was to leave her office and take an extended holiday, they found her remarkably docile. "Yes," she said, "yes, you're right. It's best that I leave here for a while. I think I shall go to Europe—actually to Italy."

"Italy?" Sally and Jenny echoed.

"Yes." Alicia smiled. "I had a mother, too, remember? Or maybe you don't actually remember. But she was very special to me. And I have been thinking that I would like to go back there, to see where she grew up."

Neither of her daughters had ever suspected Alicia capable of sentimentality. They had indeed forgotten that she had once had a father and a mother; at least, they never conjectured how much she had loved them or how she might have felt when they died.

But both Sally and Jenny were delighted that Alicia had solved her own problem, that she had prescribed for herself and thus relieved them of any responsibility for her welfare.

Alicia's staff assured her that the gallery would prosper in her absence, and Gardiner, who had come to know the workings of her mind so well, added a suggestion. "You know, my dear, you don't have to feel the slightest bit guilty about taking the time off. After all, you'll be in a marvelous position to do some very leisurely buying for us. I know this is supposed to be a holiday for you, but while you're traveling do keep an eye open. Particularly in Italy—I think the new European things will be the next big rage. Do think about it." Gardiner knew he was being slightly less than candid. But he hoped that somewhere during her trip, Alicia would indeed think about what he had said, that the businesswoman in her would surface—and force the grieving widow to take a serious interest in the world around her.

When Alicia left for Italy, it was as if a chapter had ended for Sally and Jenny; they might have been orphans, who now had only each other. But instead of drawing together, each sister pulled more into her own marriage.

For Sally, this would be a busy time. She was pleased and excited at the prospect of taking over her parents' apartment— Alicia had made it clear she would not live there again. Sally liked the idea of leaving Beekman Place for Greenwich Village. The move bespoke a certain chic eccentricity, a quirkiness that their friends would certainly appreciate.

Once a haven for artists and authentic bohemians, the Village had been thoroughly and completely colonized by the affluent. With them came fine restaurants and all the support services required for gracious living. An apartment in the heart of all this, on Fifth Avenue, offered wonderful possibilities for a couple like Sally and Brad.

With her unerring instincts, Sally decided to make of Penthouse A a sublime whimsy, to blend old and new in hybrid perfection. She hired one of the city's popular decorators and made it clear that he was not to impose his standards of elegance, but rather interpret Sally and Brad's tastes.

This did cause some conflicts, but the decorator did not quit. He knew that in the end Penthouse A would be a marvelous advertisement for him. It would be seen, admired, photographed.

The decorator was right. The apartment was a triumph. Lavish use of mirrors, of glass construction blocks, and of highly polished metals proclaimed it a home for contemporary people. Yet it was a comfortable home for family heirlooms, for fine paintings and porcelains and bronzes.

The first party the Jefferses gave there was a smashing success. The guest list included two best-selling authors, a United States senator, an avant-garde painter, several foreign industrialists, and a playboy millionaire with his latest covey of starlets. One of the numerous press people present—a gossip columnist who doted on Sally—wrote: "Last night, this reporter had the good luck to be invited to one of this season's best parties . . . given by Sally Jeffers, the town's youngest and most beautiful hostess. . . . Among those nibbling pâté—Oscar-winning Margo Hunt, who absolutely refused to discuss rumors of a spat with leading man Roscoe Lang. . . . Incidentally, the new Jeffers apartment is a knockout."

Jenny smiled when she read the item in her morning paper. She and Jeff had been invited, but he had declined in favor of dinner with an influential hospital administrator he had been

courting. Such evenings always followed an elaborate choreography of rituals and prescribed behavior. This one had gone
well, and Jenny had been rewarded at the end of it with an
appreciative hug and a warm "Thanks, hon. I hope you
didn't mind missing Sally's party, but this was important to
me. Besides, if I know Sally, she'll be having another 'do'
before you know it."

Jenny hadn't minded. She liked the feeling that came from
knowing she was a help to Jeff. It soothed—at least tem-
porarily—the restlessness, the lurking suspicion that there
was something "more" out there.

She had so much, she reminded herself: a good husband, a
pleasant home, a lovely child—solemn, wide-eyed Becky,
who seemed as wise and knowing as many adults. Jeff had
wanted a son, but his disappointment had been brief. He had
vetoed Jenny's suggestion that they "try again."

"What's the point, Jen?" he had argued. "I never wanted
a big family, and I don't see any reason to change my mind.
I'm happy with Becky. Besides—it wouldn't be fair to you or
Becky. I hardly spend any time with you now as it is, and
that's not going to get any better—not for the next few years,
anyway."

Jenny had agreed. Another child, at a time when she had
just managed to reestablish some order in their household
routine, would not be wise. Jeff liked her to be well turned
out, to entertain regularly all the people who might forward
his medical career. He was ambitious on several fronts, aim-
ing for prestigious hospital affiliations and a visible place in
the medical political hierarchy. He was a man moving up,
according to his own timetable.

Jenny was proud of her husband, grateful that he had made
her a partner in his success. She glowed when he said, "I
couldn't have done any of it without Jen. She kept me going
all those late nights—her coffee was better than Dexedrine.
And no one else could have typed all those notes and term
papers—because no one else could have read my handwriting."

For his sake, she had joined medical auxiliaries, attended
luncheons, gotten involved in the "causes" sponsored by
doctors' wives, volunteered her time for hospital benefits and
fund raisers. And for his sake, she dieted regularly to get rid
of the extra "padding" he teased her about.

Her days were heavy with commitments, and if they gave

her little pleasure in themselves, she reminded herself that a good marriage demanded sacrifice. She was infinitely better off than her mother, who was now wandering around a foreign country, trying to forget that she had destroyed her marriage—and killed her husband.

━━ 20 ━━

Alicia rang the bell, and the heavy oak door was opened by a rosy-faced nun who could not have been more than twenty-one or twenty-two. "Signora?"

"Signora Richman. Is the Mother Superior here?"

"*Si, Signora—prego.*" The young woman led Alicia up a massive staircase to a small frescoed reception room. So this is where she came from, Alicia thought, that lovely creature who was my mother. Yes, it all fit. Beauty and a small suggestion of something magical. It was all here—old and ruined, but all here—the kind of elegance that money can't buy.

"Signora." Alicia looked up to see the Mother Superior, a tall rawboned woman who looked as if she might be more at home on a farm. "Welcome to Venice. Welcome to the Convent of the Sacred Heart." The nun's voice was kind, her manner welcoming, and Alicia was suddenly very glad she had come.

"*Mille grazie,* Mother Superior. Do you speak English?"

"*Poco, poco,* my dear. How can I help you?"

"I don't wish to trouble you, but would it be possible for me to walk through the convent—just once?"

"May I ask why you are making this request?"

"Yes, of course. My mother grew up here, in this house. I've never seen it. She died when I was a young woman, but lately I've been thinking about her a great deal. And somehow it seemed important for me to come here. My husband died recently," she added, not really understanding why she was telling this stranger in the somber habit so much about

herself. "I don't know why, but I feel that if I'm to start
over—alone—then it must all begin here."

The nun nodded. "Life takes us in circles, but sometimes it
takes something important—the *tragedia*—to make us see
this. Of course you may visit your *madre*'s home. Take as
long as you like. I did not know her, but we speak often of
her aunt. She was our great *benefattore*, you know. Our little
school was in such a *condizione*. It was *finire in rovina*. Ours
is a poor order. We had no money, no way to make the
repairs. And then—a miracle! *Grazie a Dio*—the good Signora Barzini, she left us the villa. And then, within the
month, another *benefattore* gave a most generous gift to make
everything in *buono stato*. So—we were saved. Every morning at mass we remember your great-aunt in our prayers."

Alicia was unexpectedly moved by the Mother Superior's
narrative. It made her feel warm and alive and somehow
connected both to the woman and to this place. "Thank
you," she said quietly, and the nun nodded, as if she understood exactly what Alicia was feeling.

Alicia refused the nun's offer of a guide, saying: "If it isn't
an imposition, I would like to walk through alone. I promise
not to get in anyone's way."

"Please, Signora. Be at ease here. Our home is your
home." She chuckled at the small joke.

As she began her pilgrimage, Alicia was unusually con-
scious of each step she took. She listened to the tapping of
her heels on the marble floors, and she thought that had she
believed in God, then this was what a visit to a church would
feel like. She walked past black-garbed nuns gliding silently
through the corridors, and she felt as if she were invisible, as
if somehow she had been taken back secretly through time, to
visit, for a little while, her own history.

She climbed up dozens of marble stairs, holding on to
rococo bannisters, passing ancient icons and candles lit to
honor the Blessed Mother. Up she went, to a corner tower
which now seemed to serve as a storage area. She shimmied
her way past wooden chests and cardboard boxes to a small
iron-railed window overlooking the courtyard. She pressed
against the high sill, resting her chin against it, oblivious to
the dust and the cobwebs. She looked through the grime-
covered glass, and she felt as if she were seeing with the eyes
of a child, those of the young Carlotta.

She knew that her mother must have come here often, must have stared out into the courtyard, as she was doing now, eyes misting over with dreams and fantasies, seeing beyond the rust-cobbled pavement, perhaps into a future peopled with princes so charming and so handsome that her heart would surely overflow with love.

Carlotta had found her prince thousands of miles away from this narrow casement window. And she had loved him with all the richness and passion of her entire being. She—Alicia—had been born of that passion. And then—what? She had met Charles, who had cherished and sheltered her from the aloneness that had dominated her life. But had they loved each other as her parents had? They had created two daughters, who had belonged to Charles more than they had ever belonged to her. And what else?

After Charles's death, Alicia had come to believe that her punishment for her failures was to live a life of loneliness and isolation, in which she would at best be tolerated by her daughters. She knew they blamed her for Charles's unhappiness, for the haphazard and selfish way she had mothered them. Only in Principessa could she see herself as something other than a failure.

Yet here—standing in the very shadows of her mother's memory—she felt something else. It was as if Carlotta herself were reaching across the distance of time and space to give her something, something that would make her life more than a succession of days following one after another in monotonous sameness. This secret, this talisman—Alicia felt it settle upon her. She did not know exactly what it was, there in the fading twilight in the white-washed tower room. But she knew, just as if Carlotta had actually spoken to her, that it had something to do with love.

She turned from the window, suddenly happy, and filled with a warmth she had not known in years. She fairly flew down the stairs, feeling light of heart and very, very young.

"Thank you, Mama," she whispered, as she ran through the courtyard and out the massive iron gate. She would not be back here. But she would never be exactly the same. "Thank you, Mama." She felt her mother's presence so sharply that she thought she would burst with the new feeling of strength that filled her. Her mother had seen her, alone and unloved. Her mother had somehow reached out to Alicia, her only child. Now—after all these years—her mother would love her.

When she went back to the Danieli and stopped at the reception desk to ask if there were any messages, her face was lit with a radiance that had not been there before. Her eyes sent out a sparkle, her body seemed filled with energy.

"Signora Richman has had a good day?" the desk clerk asked with more than routine politeness, noticing for the first time since she had checked in that the Signora was a very handsome woman.

"Oh, yes," she answered, "it has been a very good day. Tell me," she asked impulsively, "can you arrange some sort of excursion for me—for tomorrow morning? Nothing too strenuous . . ."

"What do you enjoy, Signora?" the clerk asked, his voice now slightly seductive as he gave her his full attention.

"Oh—I don't know," she said, feeling coquettish, as she had not felt for years, responding to something in the young man's eyes. "Something for tourists. Not churches or museums—something frivolous."

"Would the Signora care perhaps to visit Murano? You can watch the glass being blown, and then you can buy a souvenir or two."

"Yes—yes, that sounds exactly right. Please make the arrangements."

"With pleasure, Signora. The boat leaves at ten o'clock, directly in front of the hotel. If you wish, I can have the operator ring your room."

"No, that won't be necessary. *Grazie*." She flashed the young man a smile, and he acknowledged her departure with a small bow.

She took the elevator up to her room. She decided that tonight she would dress for dinner and enjoy the delectable view from the rooftop terrace. She would not feel self-conscious about being alone, and she would savor her meal instead of merely consuming it, without ceremony, from a tray in her room.

She had so much to be grateful for. She was alive, in good health, rich enough to enjoy the pleasures of a hotel like this, young enough to anticipate the joys of another tomorrow.

She went into the bathroom, noticing for the first time the beauty of the mosaic tiles that surrounded her. She sprinkled some lavender-scented bubble bath into the tub, then inhaled deeply as the powder and water combined to fill the air with scent. When the tub was nearly full, she undressed and stepped in slowly, enjoying the rich creamy water as it covered her body. She closed her eyes, cupped her hands, and rubbed the bubbles over her skin. Her palms hit bone as they passed over her midsection. Too thin, Alicia, she said to herself. You have allowed yourself to become much too thin. She poked at her thighs and found no soft cushion of flesh between finger and bone. Yes, she was definitely too thin.

Now she inspected herself critically. Actually, she didn't look too bad—the slightness of her figure gave her a waifish quality. Not altogether unattractive. I could be an older Audrey Hepburn, she thought, someone vaguely European—with just a hint of dissipation. Perhaps I'll cut my hair. Yes, she liked the idea of becoming someone different, someone who looked and acted very unlike the woman who had boarded that plane in New York—how many days ago?

She soaked until the water turned cool. Then she dried herself and went to the massive Venetian armoire, flipping through the hangers until she found the dress she wanted. The white jersey, she decided. Just the thing when your body is built like a clothes hanger. I need a tan with this, she thought. She resolved to spend some time at the beach. Perhaps a week on the Lido would give her body a glow.

In the meantime, artifice would have to do. She opened her Louis Vuitton makeup case and found a pancake makeup that simulated the ruddy look of suntan. Carefully she applied the color to her face, then highlighted her cheekbones with a deeper shade, darkened her eyelashes, and smudged her lids with charcoal shadow. For her lips, she chose a glossy shade of burnished copper. And when she pulled back her thick black hair into a smooth twist, the total effect was quite exotic. She resembled a dusky goddess, mysterious, mature—and dangerously beautiful.

When she swept into the terrace restaurant, her entrance was lit by nature, for the lavenders and pinks of the summer sunset were just beginning to play on the waters of the canal, to bathe the rooftops of Venice in an aura of pure romance. She walked purposefully into the restaurant, a rustle of white jersey following the maitre d'.

The restaurant was more than half full, and heads turned as people took long, lingering looks at the beautiful woman who seemed somehow more interesting because she was alone. She asked for, and was given, a table at the rail overlooking the water. As the waiter stood deferentially to the side, she became aware of the stir she had created, and she decided to enjoy it.

She asked for a wine list, and since she knew very little about wine, she scrutinized the prices and, having decided that the costliest vintage might be a bit obvious, ordered the second most expensive item listed. Then she settled back in her chair, much more comfortable than she had imagined she could be. She had rarely been in restaurants alone.

Tonight, however, she did not mind not having someone to talk with. She knew she could stare over the water and look desirable and mysterious. Tonight she felt as if all the people in the restaurant were her companions, and she was certain the meal would be very, very nice.

When the langoustine that she had ordered arrived, she breathed deeply the scent of garlic. She ate with gusto, dipping her bread into the butter sauce, smiling her compliments at the waiter. By the time she ordered dessert and espresso, the staff was enchanted with Alicia. She was, the maitre d' declared, better than a film star. And when she departed, she distributed outrageously large tips, enjoying the delighted flurry of excitement she left in her wake.

Back in her room, she removed all her clothes and stretched out naked on her bed, allowing her after-dinner brandy to course leisurely through her veins. Although it was quite early, she closed her eyes and did not open them again until eight the following morning.

She awoke with the kind of buoyancy she had rarely experienced in recent years. She called room service and ordered rolls and cappuccino. In the bathroom, she cleansed her face of last night's makeup, then splashed it with cold water. She thought she looked less pinched around the mouth and eyes. She put one of her silk wrappers on, enjoying the feel of the feather-light fabric on her skin. Funny, she thought, to be a widow of fifty-seven—and just beginning to take notice of life's more obvious pleasures. Better late than never, she added, smiling to herself, just as she heard the room-service waiter's discreet tap on the door.

She had him serve the rolls and coffee on the small desk

under the window that overlooked the gondolas bobbing on the water. She ate slowly, watching the quickening pace of early-morning Venice—the commuters boarding the ferries, the souvenir vendors setting up their wares in the shadow of the doge's palace.

For her morning excursion, she chose white slacks and a navy middy shirt. A little too ingenue, she thought critically, as she inspected herself in the full-length mirror. But oh, she did feel young today. She took down her long black hair, brushed it thoroughly, then arranged it in a braid that began high on her head and hung down to her shoulders.

She felt attractive, and the looks she received when she walked through the lobby confirmed it. As she passed through the door that was being held open by one of the porters, she heard him say: "*Guarda quisti—que carina.*"

She smiled. To be described as *carina*—cute, adorable— well, it certainly opened up new possibilities at her age. It gave an extra spring to her step as she walked toward the motor launch.

The ride to Murano fairly flew by in the pleasure of the early morning sun, the breezes speeding past her face. The little island was geared up for tourist season. Boat loads were regularly ferried back and forth, from morning till night, in the hope that they would dig deep in their purses and buy with abandon. Dozens of shops displayed glassware of every possible shape and size—from vases to candelabra to fire-places; from overblown cherubs to emaciated saints.

Alicia arrived fully prepared to cooperate. She did not want to be sensible. She would look and bargain and buy. Yes, she would definitely buy—something she couldn't possibly use.

Dutifully she tagged after the guide, who took them to one of the island's many glass factories. She watched as one of the craftsmen took a blob of molten glass and, with a few deft strokes, fashioned it into a whimsical horselike creature. There was a sprinkling of applause from their group, which then filed into the factory showroom. Alicia browsed through the merchandise, which included a few genuinely lovely items among the sea of ordinary pieces. The businesswoman in her took over.

Although Principessa carried a selection of Italian imports, including some unusual glass, Alicia thought she might fol-low Gardiner's advice and do a little looking while she was here. Perhaps she might expand the stock which her Italian agent had shipped, possibly add some items according to her personal taste. She had been thinking of adding moderate-priced boutiques to Principessa galleries—small shops that would showcase the kind of whimsical collectibles that appealed to younger shoppers.

She decided to break away from the tour guide and browse a little on her own. She imagined that the official stops on these tours were not necessarily the most creative places, but rather those establishments whose proprietors had made the best financial arrangements with the tour operators. She asked her guide if she might spend a few hours on her own. He assured her: "*Si, Signora*. You can take a later boat back—from the spot where we docked. Or if you wish a private launch at another time, just call the hotel and they will send one." Alicia smiled and thanked him, sweetening her departure with a generous tip.

For a time she simply wandered along the narrow streets that were bounded on one side by water and on the other by shops and courtyards and pretty pastel stucco houses. She stopped at a small footbridge and took some photographs of a church that looked quite old. She walked on—until she was drawn to the irresistible smell of coffee coming from a small café. Since she was no longer following any particular schedule, she sat down and ordered a cappuccino and an *acqua minerale*. The sun was now fairly high in the sky, but not unpleasantly hot. Alicia turned her face to it, closing her eyes and enjoying the warmth that played gently on her skin.

She literally jumped when a voice—a seductive, husky voice—broke the mood. "*Que bella visione.*" Her eyes flew open and locked into a pair of the most compelling green eyes she had ever seen. They belonged to a face that looked as if it might have been copied from a Roman coin. It was a face dominated by a strong forehead, a long aquiline nose, prominent cheekbones, and a full sensual mouth that seemed unquestionably to have been made for love and laughter.

Alicia had no ready answer for this very attractive and very forward man. And so she merely stared, taking in the lean, well-muscled physique that was displayed, rather than hidden, by clothes that subtly suggested the skill of the tailor. She noted the air of the man—a quality that came close to, but was not quite, arrogance, a seductiveness that was flattering rather than brazen. The twitch at the corner of his mouth suggested a mind that loved to play with small ironies.

Alicia's stare did not seem to unnerve the man in the slightest. He bowed slightly, "Signora, I humbly apologize for my rudeness." He managed to suggest by his manner that he was neither apologetic nor capable of rudeness. "But I could not help myself. When I saw your face, turned to the sun in that way—you were like a goddess—a Cleopatra—a Helen of Troy—I simply could not help myself." He threw up his hands to emphasize his helplessness in the face of Alicia's irresistible charm.

She could not help but laugh at the out-and-out theatricality of the man. "Well, then," she said mockingly, "I must accept full responsibility for your lapse in etiquette."

"Ah, Signora"—he bowed again, the twitch at the corner of his mouth becoming more pronounced now—"you are as gracious as you are beautiful. Will you allow me—please, I beg you not to say no—will you allow me the privilege of sharing a coffee with you? Perhaps I can redeem the good name of Italy's men. . . ."

"Well, we certainly can't leave a tarnish on Italy's manhood. Please—sit down, Signor . . . ?"

"Paolo—please—Paolo Reini." He was in the seat opposite her with one fluid movement. And with another effortless gesture, he summoned the waiter, who scurried off instantly to fetch Paolo's espresso.

"So, beautiful lady, will you tell me your name, or must I invent one for you?"

"Now that might be quite interesting. But I'll save you the trouble. My name is Alicia—Alicia Richman."

"And you are an American—yes?"

"Yes. But my mother was Italian."

"Ah, well then, you still belong to us, to Italy, no matter where you have lived."

"What a charming idea—perpetual citizenship. But I think your government has a more pragmatic view of these matters."

"It is of no importance what governments say—they have no soul whatever. But what is it that brings you here now?"

"Oh . . ." She thought for a minute and decided she wasn't ready to talk about Charles to this dazzling stranger. "I decided it was time to see the country where my mother was born. I had never been here."

"Never? Ah, *Dio*—how could the beautiful daughter of a most certainly beautiful mother never visit Italy?"

"I don't know, actually. I suppose there was never time."

"And Signor Richman—is he traveling with you?"

"Signor Richman . . . died," she said. Then fearing she sounded brusque, she added, "Earlier this year."

"I am so sorry, Signora. Please forgive me for—"

"It's all right. I shall have to get used to talking about it. Other people have had losses, too. Mine is not particularly unique."

"Regretfully, you are right, Signora. I, too, have experienced a loss such as yours—my Carla—but it was a very long time ago. We had been married only a year, so now it is not so painful anymore. The sadness remains, you understand, but it is a distant feeling. But no more talk of sadness now. Tell me what you have been doing in Italy . . . in Murano. Shopping?"

She shrugged and laughed. "What else is there to do in Murano, if you are not having a cappuccino with a handsome Italian with impeccable manners?"

He smiled at the mock-compliment. "But did you not come with a group?"

"Yes, I did. But I thought it might be boring to follow a tour guide from one glass factory to another. So I went off on my own."

Paolo made an elaborate gesture of distress. "My dear Signora Richman, if the glassblowing bores you, then I have been rendered speechless."

Alicia looked puzzled. "You see, Signora," he explained, "I was just about to invite you to my factory—where we blow glass!"

She laughed. "Well, that is quite different from what I was talking about. Of course you must invite me, and of course I would be delighted—really I would."

Paolo flashed her a full smile. After he paid the check, he held out his hand to help her up from the table, and she was shocked to find that she responded to his touch. It was unsettling for Alicia, who had not really had a romantic thought about any man since she had first met Gardiner so long ago. She was middle-aged, but she had all the sexual savoir faire of a not-very-bright teenager. She knew that she looked and dressed like a sophisticated woman, and she did not want this man—this man who looked as if he could ease you into bed before you knew what was happening—to know that she was suddenly shy and perhaps a little frightened.

Paolo's factory was a short stroll from the café, but to

Alicia each step increased her physical awareness of the man beside her. For the most part, it was Paolo who made conversation, mentioning minor points of interest on the way. But the conversation seemed to be an excuse for him to stare at her. As for Alicia, she found she could not stop looking at his mouth.

He took her arm when they came to a small alley. "Here we are," he said, as he led her into a large courtyard and then through a large workroom where half a dozen glassblowers worked, in various stages of undress, in the midday heat.

He walked her around the room and introduced her to each of his employees as if she were an old and valued friend, and not a woman he had picked up an hour ago in a waterside café. To one of the workmen, a young man with an unruly head of red hair, he gave some instructions in Italian. Alicia suspected the conversation had something to do with her, and before she left the workroom to visit the front showroom, the young man presented her with an exquisite little unicorn, blown from a rich blue glass the color of lapis lazuli.

"Thank you—oh, thank you so much. *Grazie*!" To Paolo, she said, "I saw a man make a horse at the place I visited this morning but it was not half as lovely as this."

"For you, dear lady, an ordinary horse would not do. It must be something extraordinary, something magical—*ecco*, a unicorn."

"I see," she said solemnly, and she did see, for within an hour of meeting Paolo she had a sense of being touched by something magical.

In the showroom, he took her through rows upon rows of vases and bowls and bottles and figurines, explaining to her the skills and specialities of his workers. Most of the stock was routine Venetian glass, but there were many witty, clever pieces made, Paolo told her, by his star, the young man who had created her unicorn. Alicia was intrigued by his work, and when she expressed her interest, Paolo took her into a small anteroom. "Roberto is ambitious—and imaginative. He has been asking me to begin a new line—these things." He pointed to a group of pieces crafted of ceramic and leather.

"I haven't seen anything like this," she said. "Have you been making them long?"

"Actually, no one else in Venice makes these. They are Roberto's originals. He has half a dozen other ideas as well. I really can't keep up with him."

As Alicia looked over the young man's handiwork, an idea took shape—the idea of working out some sort of arrangement with Paolo for exclusive United States distribution through her Principessa boutique. But she held back, not wanting to talk business. She did not want to be Alicia Richman, director of Principessa galleries. She just wanted to be Alicia, the mysterious lady in the café. And this womanly Alicia felt it would be a mistake to introduce the subject of money and profits into the chemical equation that was taking place between her and the gorgeous stranger.

Later, when Paolo took her back to the dock, where one of the hotel launches was waiting, he asked, "May I take you to dinner this evening? Someplace very Venetian—impossible to find for any tourist, unless she is accompanied by a citizen of the city."

Her delight made her coy. "And why should you be so generous to me, a total stranger?"

"Because I intend to overwhelm your senses with wine and music and an incredibly romantic atmosphere. And then I intend to seduce you." He delivered this speech with a straight face—except for the twitch at the corner of his mouth.

Alicia took a mischievous delight in his answer, although she was thrown off balance by the possibility that he might be serious. She returned his banter with an ease she did not quite feel. She was thrilled that Paolo wanted to see her again, but she was not at all sure how she might handle anything resembling a seduction.

Back in her hotel room, she peered into the mirror and saw, with dismay, several fine lines she had not noticed before. A nap, she thought—perhaps a nap will soften them.

She tried to sleep, but sleep did not come, and she forced herself to lie quietly with her eyes closed while a rush of romantic fantasies played through her brain.

Eventually she gave up the idea of rest and decided to take a long soak in the bathtub. But now she was no longer so content with the body that had seemed perfectly adequate last night. Now she inspected it through the eyes of a heart-stoppingly sensual man, and she had no patience with any of its flaws.

But she refused to let anything spoil the pleasure of anticipating Paolo's return. If she could not change what she did not like about herself, she would concentrate instead on making what she had as appealing as possible. Patiently she creamed every inch of her body with lotion. Though her toilette had for years been swift, efficient, and, for the most part, routine, she now worked intently.

Her makeup she decided to keep simple—the less she put on her face, the less the lines would show. She applied a bronze blusher to her cheekbones, creamy taupe eye shadow to her lids. For a touch of drama, she outlined her eyes with a charcoal pencil, then thickened her heavy lashes with a brown-black mascara. For her mouth she chose a bronze lipstick coated with a shiny gloss that made it look almost shockingly provocative.

Now she smiled at the reflection in the mirror. Although she felt like an awkward teenager, she thought she might learn quickly. She pulled her hair into the same twist as the night before.

She checked her closet, but she knew already that for tonight she would wear something black, something simply cut and very expensive, something that would show off her creamy white skin. And with it she would wear very sheer stockings and sandals with frivolously high heels.

Precisely at eight o'clock, the reception desk rang to announce the arrival of Signor Paolo Reini. Although her heart—or was it her stomach?—was doing flip-flops, Alicia was determined to appear poised and serene, a woman of the world. She squared her shoulders, fixed a confident smile on her face—and opened the door.

Her breath caught when she saw the man she had left just a few hours before. He had changed his clothes, and now he wore a beige linen suit with a white silk shirt, open at the neck. My God, she thought, he looks like a film star—or a gigolo. I don't care which, she thought, I just don't care.

He caught her by the shoulders and greeted her warmly, European style, with a kiss on each cheek, just as if they had known each other for years. "Alicia," he said, and on his lips her name sounded like a caress. Then he drew her back, admiring her, frankly and openly, from head to toe. "You look beautiful," he said, making the very ordinary phrase sound original and fresh.

"Thank you," she answered. "You look beautiful, too."

He nodded his head gravely in acknowledgment of her compliment, the corner of his mouth tugging against a smile.

"Well, my dear, are you ready?"

And when she said she was, he took her elbow possessively, in a gesture that suddenly seemed as intimate as a kiss, as exciting as anything she had experienced in years. She felt a flush begin at her neck and work its way up past her ears and into her hairline. Oh, God, she thought, don't let me act like a teenager. Although she had just met Paolo this morning, she knew with certainty that this evening was going to matter very, very much.

He guided her to one of the gondolas that waited outside the hotel. She was surprised to find that Venetians actually used this mode of travel so popular with tourists. Paolo began a conversation with the gondolier. He seemed to know the man quite well because the dialogue was spirited and lively. He was apparently giving the man directions. At one point she heard a reference to herself—something a little bawdy and explicit, she guessed. Paolo then said something sharp to the man, who ended with an apologetic gesture. Alicia felt unreasonably pleased at this display of chivalry. It told her that perhaps Paolo felt something of what she did—that a chance meeting at a sidewalk café might just be the beginning of something that mattered.

As the gondola began its journey through the darkened waters of Venice, through the narrow byways that tourists rarely saw, the night seemed quite still, except for the distant sound of a mandolin and the rhythmic slapping of the oar cutting through the water. Strangely enough, neither Paolo nor Alicia felt a need to speak. For the time, they enjoyed the comfortable silence usually shared by people who have known each other well for a long time.

Alicia wondered briefly what Paolo was thinking as he put his arm around her. There was no further intimacy, and she drifted contentedly. For so many years she had lived her life as if she were always running for a train just about to leave. She had failed to enjoy the company of those who should have mattered to her.

She would not make that mistake again. She would taste the food she put into her mouth; she would feel the texture of fabrics against her skin; she would inhale the scents that were carried to her nostrils. Like that almost intoxicating fragrance of Paolo's cologne that overlaid the sharp male scent of him. It made her feel alive.

She turned her face, and Paolo broke the silence. "I'm very glad we met, Alicia. Are you?"

"I suppose so—yes," she answered, suddenly cautious, a little afraid to let this man know how quickly he had come to matter so much. She had always been so much in charge of her own emotions, so much in control.

"Just 'I suppose'?" He laughed. "I know American women have a reputation for coolness. But, my dear, you are half Italian. Can you do a little better than that? I want very much to kiss you right now—but I must have a little encouragement."

She looked into those wonderful eyes, and she had no words at all. He bent his head and took her lips as if they were a delicacy made for nibbling—gently, teasingly, as though he was in no hurry because he knew there would be more later. The touch of his mouth filled Alicia with a feeling of almost unbearable sweetness, mingled with the sad recollection that it had been such a long time since she had held a man in her arms.

Suddenly the boat bumped against something solid. The gondolier announced to Paolo that they had arrived at their destination.

The minuscule restaurant was housed on the ground floor of a private home. It consisted of some half-dozen tables and was operated by a family that constantly fussed and flurried around these tables, fetching food and bearing it away to the kitchen. Paolo had apparently ordered their meal in advance, and one delicious course followed another—a most exquisite *paglia e fieno*, a salad of lightly seasoned fennel, and delicate slices of the tenderest veal.

The food was perhaps the best she had eaten in her life. The entire evening was a bombardment of her senses. As she savored each morsel she put into her mouth, Paolo kept refilling her glass with a white wine that tasted like ambrosia—and touching her fingertips with a delicacy that seemed to send her heart into her throat.

The finale to the meal was an aromatic espresso and some Napoleon brandy. Alicia teased Paolo about the presence of the bottle on the table. "I see that you have allowed a foreign element into this very Italian meal."

"Dear Alicia, I am willing to concede to others what they do better than I."

"You mean there are such things?"

"Indeed. But I think it is only fair not to prejudice you in advance. I think you must find out all about me for yourself."

She felt a rush of pleasure at his words. He was saying they would share more than this very lovely evening. His words conjured up a series of scenes in her mind, scenes of them driving together, talking together, sitting together in front of a fireplace, and—she flushed—scenes of them in bed. Shame on you, she scolded herself. But she could not manage to feel any shame at all. She felt only the pleasant warmth of desire, fueled by the wine and brandy she had drunk. Paolo made a quick visit into the kitchen to settle the bill, and within a few moments they were back in the gondola.

As they relaxed into the cushioned seat, Paolo drew Alicia's head down on his shoulder. She left it there, as if she had found a place to rest after a long journey. During the quiet trip back to the hotel, Alicia wondered if Paolo would make love to her—and if she should let him. She knew that people today did that without thinking twice. Things were different now. But how different? she argued back. She did not want to seem cheap.

Was there such a concept now? she wondered. Aha, she thought, but Paolo wasn't a "now" man. He belonged to her generation. And he was European to boot. If she fell into his arms so quickly, he would certainly think she was cheap. Alicia didn't like this conclusion to her polemic, so she started again.

Look, she said to herself, I have already done all the things I was supposed to do. I married, I was faithful, I had children. I did all those things—perhaps not very well, but I did them. Now who will I hurt if I do something impulsive, something perhaps not wise? Who will I hurt—with the possible exception of myself? The answer was no one. Alicia smiled and was content.

As Paolo helped her out of the gondola, Alicia decided she would let him create the scenario for the evening. He took her arm and walked through the lobby, then to the elevator. When they reached her room, she gave him the key. He opened the door, then closed it quietly behind them.

Before she could think of any light conversation to bridge the small awkwardnesses of the moment, he pulled her to him and kissed her—not the light delicate caress he had given her a few hours before, but a long, hard, searching kiss, a kiss that was probing, demanding. When he released her, she looked into his face. "Paolo," she whispered, "I . . ."

"Hush, *bellissima*." He put his finger on her mouth, tracing its contours lightly. "Hush. We are going to have many, many opportunities to talk in the future. But for now I want very much to make love. Alicia, *amore,* I want you." He buried his face in her neck for a few moments, then he took her hand and drew her to the bed.

The next moments were like nothing she had experienced before. She could not remember such pure, unadulterated physical pleasure, not even from the days when she had first loved Charles. Although it had been a long time since she had loved any man, since she had touched any man but Charles, Paolo helped her quickly lose any awkwardness. He was a generous and skillful lover, and she let him lead her, take her to the edges of exquisite sensations. And then she found she was returning his touch with a complete lack of inhibition, with an eagerness and ferocity that surprised her. "Alicia, *amore,*" he murmured, against her throat, her breasts, and she felt that she was completely lost.

Later—she did not know how much later—Paolo propped himself up on his elbow and looked down at her. "Now that you have been thoroughly and completely compromised, I think I shall have to marry you."

Alicia laughed, delighted with the outrageousness of what he was saying, enchanted with the notion that he wanted her. She felt unreasonably happy, even while her rational mind told her that this was all incredibly silly.

"We don't even know each other," she said, reaching for the obvious.

"We'll have time for that later. It will keep us from getting bored with each other."

Feeling a little as if she had stepped into the looking glass, Alicia sighed contentedly and went to sleep in the shelter of Paolo's arm.

She did not awaken until she felt his body stir. "Where are you going?" she asked, drawling her words out between a yawn and a stretch.

"I shall have to go to the factory this morning, *cara.* I will be back later, and then we can go to Amelie's for dinner."

Alicia was amused at Paolo's peremptory manner. She thought with a twinge that Charles probably wouldn't have dared to take such an attitude with her. What's happening to me? she wondered. But all she said was: "Who's Amelie?"

"*Mia madre, bellissima.* If we are going to be married, she will have to meet you."

Alicia took a quick look at her lover's face to see if he was joking. He seemed to be serious, though the ever-present hint of a smile was there. "I think you must be mad to be talking to me like this, Paolo. And I must be equally mad to listen."

"Not at all, my darling. I am old enough to understand that life is finite and young enough to enjoy what is left. I have been with enough women since my wife died to know what I don't want and to recognize what I do want when I see it. I know that I want you. Why should I waste precious time with ridiculous maneuvers, when I already know where I wish to finish?"

"But what about me? What if I don't have your certainty?"

"Then I will just have to help you find it. In the meantime, let us just plan on visiting my mother. If it will make you feel better, I will tell her that I have decided to marry you but that you have not yet accepted my offer."

"I'm not sure we should do that. What will your mother think?"

"She will think that you are completely mad not to leap at such a magnificent stroke of good fortune. But that is not what she will say to you. Amelie is not a typical Italian mama. She will congratulate you on being a strong and independent woman, and then she will tell you in a thousand subtle ways just why I should be your husband—or at least your lover."

"Will she really? I'm not sure I'm ready to hear all this, from the mama of a man I've just met."

"Of course you are, *tesora*." Paolo made the final adjustments on his clothes, slapped her on the rump, and bent to give her a farewell kiss. "I will come for you at six-thirty. Amelie doesn't like tardiness, so be ready."

Before she could answer this last command, he was gone.

After Paolo had left, Alicia showered and washed her hair, musing at the fate that had taken her and a total stranger and somehow fused a "we" within the space of a single day. She breakfasted slowly, dawdling over her coffee, enjoying the afterglow that bathed her in a lovely feeling of warmth.

It was with a great effort that she roused herself and dressed, simply, in a pair of cotton slacks and a knit shirt. She took the short walk to the Piazza San Marco, where she ordered another coffee and sat down to watch the daily rituals of summertime Venice: the arrival of clusters of tourists eager to explore the clock tower or the church; clouds of pigeons converging for the handouts of grain from photo-snapping visitors; shopkeepers preparing for the long business day ahead.

The morning was cool and gray, an appropriate atmosphere in which to examine just what it was that had happened to her. It all seemed mad and crazy—and what exactly did she know about this man who had announced that he was going to be her husband? He might be neurotic—or dangerous—or a fortune hunter.

She wondered just what it was about her that had captured Paolo's heart—or whatever it was she was supposed to have captured. In her mind's eye, Alicia conceded that she was a handsome woman. But did she look well off? Was she wearing expensive jewels? No, actually, there was little about her to suggest more than a comfortable way of life. And clearly Paolo was not a poor man. His business was not huge, but it seemed to be thriving.

Surely he could not be in the business of picking up random tourists with the idea of some sort of gain? Even on short acquaintance he seemed too elegant, too fastidious for that.

You certainly don't think much of yourself, Alicia Richman, a small voice in her head said. What's wrong with you that you can't imagine a desirable man wanting you for yourself? She tried to answer the rhetorical question. Well, I'm not young. But neither is he, the small voice countered. And where is it written that older men are desirable, but older women are not? It must be written somewhere, she answered, because that's the way it has always been. Nonsense, the small voice came back. This is a new era for women—don't you read the newspapers and magazines? Very well, she conceded, I am at least as attractive as Paolo is, certainly his equal intellectually, and no doubt better off financially. So why am I so suspicious when he says he wants to marry me? This time the answer was clear and true: because I have already failed one man, badly, and I cannot believe that fate will reward me with another chance.

She spent most of the morning strolling rather aimlessly, in a way that was not at all typical of her. She window-shopped a little and then she came back to the piazza. She drank one coffee after another in the Quadri and listened to the over-blown string arrangements of songs she had never liked before. Suddenly she found them ineffably sweet, fraught with meaning and heartbreaking truths. She hummed along as the orchestra played "Summertime," then segued into "As Time Goes By." And when a passing tourist grabbed a woman who was sitting at the table near hers, to whirl her in frantic waltz-time to the "Blue Danube," she joined heartily in the scattered applause.

I think I could be happy with all this, Alicia thought—Venice and summer and love. I think I could be very, very happy. But was it real, or just a vacation fantasy? Could she make Paolo part of her life?

As the time drew nearer to six-thirty, Alicia emptied the contents of her wardrobe still another time. She had changed twice already and she was still not satisfied. Meeting someone's mother, at her age—it was almost obscene. But she did want Paolo's mother to like her.

Paolo had said his mother wasn't typical. Did that mean she was one of those crazy eccentrics whom only a son could love? The thought made Alicia shudder. Even though this entire brief affair had an air of unreality, she could not bear the thought that Paolo's mother might scrutinize her and find her somehow wanting. What might she wear to win a favorable verdict? How should she look?

She rejected a pants suit that did marvelous things for her figure as being "too American." She tossed aside a frilly white silk blouse and a simple black skirt as being too schoolgirlish. Finally, with only minutes to spare, she settled on a pearl-gray silk shirtwaist. If the woman knew anything about fashion, she would realize it was beautifully made. If not, it would just look simple. Around her neck she wore the pearls Papa had given her for her sixteenth birthday, and on her ears the clips Charles had bought their first Christmas together. Enough, she said to herself. She sprayed her wrists and hair with Chanel and waited for Paolo, standing up, not wanting to sit lest she wrinkle her dress.

Promptly at six-thirty, he arrived to collect her. He kissed her warmly on the lips. "You look lovely, my dear," he said, and there was something pleasingly possessive in his voice, as if matters had already been settled between them, as if he felt she already belonged to him.

This time there was no gondola, and Paolo indicated that they would walk. "Did you have a pleasant day, *cara*?" he asked.

"Yes, thank you," she answered, in the same vein, thinking that they sounded like a married couple. "And you?"

"I was thinking of you." He turned those eyes on her. "It has been a long time since I sat in my office, trying to look at numbers and seeing instead a woman's face in my mind. I wanted very much to make love to you. That is what I want to do right now. And I think Amelie will see it."

"Oh, my God, I hope not," Alicia said, blushing at the idea that the redoubtable Amelie had a built-in lust-detector which would most certainly pick up the powerful signals that Alicia's own body had begun sending out since Paolo had first walked into her room.

"Surely you're not worried about this meeting," he teased. "She will adore you. And you, my love—if you are the woman I think you are, then you will find her very *simpatico*." Paolo's air of confidence was a great change for Alicia. And yet it seemed right that he did not consult her, did not ask what her wishes or opinions were, but instead told her what he expected.

They walked quietly, hand in hand, like young lovers, until

they came to a high iron fence beyond which lay a lush and fragrant garden. A small sign hung from the top of the gate: ALBERGO FLORA. "Here we are," Paolo said.

"This hotel? Your mother lives in a hotel?"

"Wait—you shall see." Paolo took her elbow and guided her through the garden, through an open courtyard paved with beautiful mosaic tiles, and finally through a small moorish arch that served as the hotel's entrance. They were greeted by a short, bald man in evening clothes. "*Buona sera*, Dottore Reini."

"*Buona serra*, Giovanni."

"Dottore Reini? Are you a doctor?" Alicia asked.

"Not at all, but I have been to the university, and in Italy that makes you a 'dottore.' Now come with me."

As Alicia followed Paolo past the reception desk, she took note of the small but exquisitely proportioned lobby, which resembled the foyer of a gracious private home. In fact, there was really no particular sign that this was a hotel. Even Giovanni might have been a butler. Paolo took her off to one side, to the door of a suite that backed into the garden. He tapped gently and waited. No one answered. "Are you sure she's expecting us?" Alicia asked.

"*Pazienza, cara*. If Tatiana is coming to open the door, we will have to be patient. She is not quite as nimble as she once was."

"Tatiana? Who's Tatiana?"

"Many years ago she was Amelie's maid. But now I suppose you would call her a sort of companion."

When the door was finally opened, Alicia saw a woman whose age, she imagined, might have been counted in centuries. She was a small, frail woman whose face was almost completely seamed with wrinkles and framed by a fluffy cap of white curls. Her eyes, which once might have been blue, now seemed almost as pale as the fair skin surrounding them. At the sight of Paolo the old face became radiant. "*Buona sera*, Tatiana," he greeted her, with a hug and a squeeze.

The old woman dimpled and blushed like a young girl. "*Buona sera*, Paolo. Come inside."

"Will you tell Amelie we are here?"

"*Si*, Paolo, she is coming."

Alicia looked about her, trying to take in everything at once—the old woman, the apartment crowded with large, heavy European furniture, voluminous memorabilia, including hundreds of photographs, which Alicia couldn't really inspect properly.

Tatiana led them into what seemed to be a formal sitting room. The atmosphere was less stiff than the massive furniture had led Alicia to expect. When they were seated, the old woman inched ever so slowly to a glass-fronted cabinet, extracted three cut-glass goblets, and began to pour some sherry. Before she could begin the slow return trip to the guests, Paolo had walked over to her and taken the glasses. *"Mille grazie,* Tatiana." Once again, she blushed with pleasure.

"Paolo, my son." Three heads turned in the direction of the voice. It was a deep, husky sound, almost a baritone, yet it was sweetened with a suggestion of warm honey.

Paolo covered the distance between himself and his mother in three quick strides. He clasped her in a hug that was born of true affection. She stepped back to look at him, as if she had not seen him in a long time. Then she reached up and touched his face with her palm. He took her hand and kissed it.

How lovely they are, Alicia thought—he, tall, fair, elegant; she, small, dark, and very slender. She must be close to eighty, Alicia reckoned, but she might have passed for sixty. Her hair was almost a gunmetal gray, pulled back in a bun that might have been severe on a woman who did not have such a patrician profile. She wore a white oriental-style robe embroidered in gold and crimson. So much for simplicity, Alicia thought wryly. It was the first time she had been outdone by someone's mother.

Amelie turned now to Alicia. "Paolo, we are being very naughty. Let me welcome your friend. She is very lovely, your American lady. How do you do, my dear. I am Amelie, and I am sure Paolo has told you many wicked stories about me. Welcome to our home."

Alicia reached out to take Amelie's outstretched hand. "I'm very happy to meet you. Actually, no. Paolo has only told me that you are a very special woman. We haven't really had an opportunity to talk at length. After all, we only met yesterday."

"Yesterday? How extraordinary! When Paolo told me about you, I somehow had the impression that you had known each other for some time. Well, well, perhaps this boy has a bit more imagination than I had credited him with. *Bene,* I am delighted. Come," she said, "walk with me a bit in the garden, so we can become friends before dinner. Tatiana will be delighted to have Paolo all to herself.''

The two women walked out into the courtyard, where the table had already been laid for dinner. ''If you have just met Paolo,'' Amelie said, ''then perhaps you have some questions I can answer.''

''Well, actually,'' Alicia laughed, ''I don't even know him well enough to formulate any questions.''

''But he has asked you to marry him?''

''Not quite—he announced that we would.''

Amelie laughed, a deep throaty sound that Alicia liked at once. ''Yes, that sounds like my Paolo. With women, he has always had the confidence.''

Now it was Alicia's turn to laugh. ''I'm sure. I could see that at once.''

''This quality—do you like it? Or no?''

''Which quality?''

''The ease with women. Me—I have always been attracted to men who have a rapport with women. I don't like men who are not attractive to many women.''

''I haven't really thought about that. You see . . . I haven't really been . . . involved with that many men.''

''Pity. Different men give a fullness to life. A variety.''

Alicia did not have an answer to this comment, except to agree silently that Amelie was certainly not anyone's idea of a conventional mother—or mother-in-law, for that matter.

As if she knew what Alicia was thinking, Amelie went on, ''But of Paolo's announcement that you will marry—have you agreed?''

''I haven't disagreed. The whole idea seems unreal—and somehow reasonable at the same time. Do you know what I mean?''

''Yes—yes,'' Amelie answered, the smoky laugh bubbling up to the surface again. ''Paolo and I, we are very much alike, and I think we affect people in the same way. We are very forceful, very direct when we want something. We are northern Italians, you know. We can be very practical, but at the same time we live by our passions. To other people this may seem strange—unless they respond to our sense of destiny. I think Paolo must have felt that very strongly to think of marriage with you. I know he has not felt this way with anyone else, and Carla has been dead for many years now—and there have been many women, obviously.''

"Yes, obviously," Alicia agreed, with a touch of irony that was not lost on Amelie.

"But what about you, Alicia? You must tell me about yourself. Have you been married? You must have been. Are you a passionate woman? For Paolo, this is a vital thing." She went on, asking questions and answering them as she thought they should be answered, until Alicia lost track.

"Wait—you must give me a chance to catch up with you, Amelie. Yes, I was married, for many years. My husband died recently." Amelie made a sound of condolence, and suddenly Alicia felt she must tell this woman the truth, that she must be as candid as she knew how—even if this cost her the approval she wanted. So she plunged on: "I loved Charles— at least, I cared for him—but I think I never made him happy. I was not a good wife."

"Davvero? In what way?"

"I took advantage of him."

"Ah—you were unfaithful then?"

Alicia smiled at the older woman's conclusion. "No. What I did was much worse. I walked all over Charles. I made decisions that should have been his. I robbed him of his masculinity." In quick, clean strokes, she described the business, the part it had played in her life and the life of her family. She painted herself as she now saw herself—black.

"But my dear"—Amelie's voice was unexpectedly gentle— "no woman can do things like that unless a man lets her. Paolo would not have allowed anything such as you described for even a minute."

"Charles couldn't help it. He didn't like conflict. He liked serenity and quiet, and I took advantage of that. I must have, because I so often found myself doing the most awful things."

"Poverina." Alicia was shocked at the sympathy she heard in that word. Everyone—her children, her friends—had cast Alicia in the role of villain. It was a role she had accepted and lived with since Charles's death. Amelie's reaction was almost unnerving.

"You don't understand. Charles was a good husband, a wonderful father—and mother as well. He deserved a wife who would give him respect and consideration. I'm afraid I did not give him much of that. Yes, I was faithful, but I cheated him of so much. . . ."

"If you cheated your husband, my dear, then perhaps it was because you, too, were cheated. You were, I think, a spirited young woman—and you needed a man who could appreciate that spirit, who could take delight in it, and meet it with his own strength. A man like Paolo would know that instinctively. It is not as you imagined—a choice between confrontation or a lifeless peace. I think a man like your late husband—please do not take offense, but I think a man like that robbed you of many pleasures of femininity, and so there was nothing for you to do but to take some of his masculinity. If there is no contrast between a man and woman, a relationship loses its greatest pleasures. He did not make you feel like a woman, so you did not make him feel like a man.''

Alicia tried to consider the implications of what Amelie was saying. She was not yet ready to give up the burden of guilt she carried, but so much of what Paolo's mother was saying seemed true. How many times had she deliberately thrown out a challenge, silently hoping that Charles would meet it? How many times had she craved the stimulation of a will that could match her own? And how many, many times had she felt the frustration of being matched with a personality that did not complement hers? Now here was Amelie saying that she'd had a right to feel as she did, suggesting that Charles was not a victim in the failures of their marriage, but a willing accomplice. If she could only believe that.

Amelie continued talking: ''If this marriage has been the sum total of your experience—you have just told me that you have not known many men—then I think you would never forgive yourself if you did not marry Paolo. I think you owe this experience to yourself. You are a lovely woman, Alicia, an extraordinary woman who should have many lovers. But it is not always so easy to find what you Americans call the correct 'chemistry.' ''

''You seem so sure of what you say. Actually, that is very much like Paolo. Tell me, have you always been right about the men you've known?''

''*Si*—yes, most of the time. No one can always correctly predict the course of a love affair, but the men I have loved—yes, I think I have understood them quite well.'' She smiled and closed her eyes for a moment, as if to remember— and Alicia envied her the ability to conjure up past pleasures so readily.

''Paolo's father—you loved him very much?'' Alicia felt she had to ask the question, though it sounded childish and ingenuous as she posed it.

"Ah—with Paolo's father, I had what you might call the conventional marriage."

Alicia smiled at this description because by now she doubted whether Amelie had ever done anything totally conventional. The older woman caught the look.

"Indeed, yes, it's quite true. I told you—we northern Italians are very practical people. I was a dancer. I had a small talent—and some beauty—and not much else. I saw that I was not going to have a great career, and I could not bear to make a marriage that would make me old in five years—we have so many of those in Italy, you see. I met Paolo's father. He was an industrialist. His family was not so old, not quite so fine as mine. He was older and quite well off—and he was in love with me. Out of all these ingredients we made a match."

"Was it difficult for you?" Alicia tried to remember her own headstrong teenage years, tried to imagine marrying someone for practical reasons, someone her family had perhaps chosen. She could not.

"No," Amelie answered. "It was not difficult. Julio was a perfect husband for me at that time of my life. He loved my beauty, my talent—such as it was—and his love made me feel cherished. From him I learned many skills, many refinements I would not have known. He taught me how to run a fine house, taught me to appreciate food, wine, and all the luxuries that money can buy. We traveled, and he taught me about conversation and laughter. I had been very limited in my life, you see. All I had really known was my dancing. And, of course, he gave me Paolo.

"Perhaps the greatest gift he gave me was that he did not try to make me into the 'lady of the house'— a housewife. You see, I had made a conventional marriage, but I was blessed enough to have married a remarkably unconventional man."

"So you loved him after all."

"I loved Julio, yes. Perhaps it would be truer to say that at first I appreciated him enormously. I respected him, and I came to care deeply about his welfare. In the beginning, I was like a child—actually, I was a child. I took what he had to offer, and I felt as if my presence in his life was all the recompense I owed. Later, the bond between us grew stronger, deeper.

"If you are asking about passion, then I will tell you there was none on my part, though I know that Julio did have very strong feelings.'' She saw the questioning look in Alicia's eyes and went on: "We were very good together nevertheless. For a young girl like myself—a virgin with no experience of any kind—a man like Julio, a skillful and considerate lover—I believe he was quite perfect. Better, I think, than a clumsy man who rouses passion.''

"It sounds as if you had a perfect marriage.''

"My dear Alicia,'' the older woman said, almost pityingly, "there is no such creature as a perfect marriage. There are successful marriages—and the other kind. I was fortunate, and when Julio died, I was grateful in the years to follow for all he had done for me. He had made me into a woman who is comfortable and easy in company. In short, he had made me into a woman who could easily become a perfect mistress.''

Alicia laughed, thinking that Amelie had tossed off a brittle witticism.

"But I'm quite serious,'' Amelie insisted. "That is precisely how I spent the ten years following Julio's death.''

"But why?''

"For many reasons, dear girl, but mainly because I wanted to. And that is another story—too long for an antipasto—and I'm sure my son will be wanting his dinner now. So—let us go back.''

Dinner was simple: paper-thin prosciutto served with melon of a perfect ripeness; light, delicate pasta in a cream sauce that was rich without being heavy; veal lightly flavored with butter and lemon, accompanied by a small green salad. It was a meal that could be prepared and served with relative ease by two elderly women, a tasteful meal, artfully arranged and served in a garden redolent of summertime perfume. Conversation was like the meal—rich and light and overlaid with caring. Suddenly it struck Alicia that the atmosphere at this dinner table was very much like that of her childhood, like the evenings Carlotta and Sharif had spent relaxing at the end of the day. It was painfully different from what she had known in her own home.

No more, she said to herself, with an urgency that bordered on commitment, no more of that. Life is finite, just as Paolo had reminded her. She would squander no more time on things that gave back no warmth, no tenderness, no love. Amelie's voice brought her out of her reverie. "So, Paolo,'' she said, turning to her son, "you told me that your friend was a lovely woman, but you did not tell me she was accomplished as well.''

"Of course," he answered. "It goes without saying, and that is why I did not say it."

Amelie persisted. "But to be at the head of such a large important business—well, you might have mentioned that."

Paolo's eyebrows lifted, and he looked inquiringly at Alicia, who now felt uncomfortable about the fact that she had failed to tell her lover anything about Principessa. "It's my fault, Amelie," she said. "There really hasn't been enough time to talk about—details." Here she blushed, realizing what kind of interpretation might be put on her words.

"But Principessa Galleries," Amelie persisted, "is not exactly a detail."

Now Paolo's glance became accusatory. The incipient smile at the corner of his mouth had disappeared, and Alicia sensed that a storm was building.

When she realized that she had probably catalyzed a lovers' quarrel, Amelie stepped in. "Don't sulk, *caro*," she admonished her son. "It's most unbecoming. Later, when the two of you are alone, you can have a jolly quarrel—and a glorious reconciliation. But for now I absolutely forbid you to look at Alicia in that way. A woman is not obliged to give you the gift of all her secrets at once. Perhaps you must earn them, a little at a time."

"*Si,* Mama, you are wise—as always," Paolo conceded. But his eyes conceded nothing. They told Alicia that she still had something to answer for.

For Alicia the remainder of the evening was filled with extraordinary sensations. The contretemps with Paolo had charged the atmosphere with a tension that was somehow sexual. The hint of the combat to come did not frighten her in the least. Somehow she felt that she had passed her initiation in the little group that sat around the dinner table. She felt that Paolo was as much "hers" as she was "his."

When the meal was over, Tatiana produced a pot of thick, dark espresso from the kitchen and a tray of assorted liqueurs from the glass-fronted cabinet. And as soon as Paolo put down his coffee cup, Amelie issued another of her "suggestions": *"Caro mio,* why don't you take a small walk in the garden before you leave? I would so much like to have Alicia to myself for a few more minutes."

After her son had left the room, Amelie took Alicia's two

hands in hers. *"Bene,"* she said, "I approve. I think Paolo will enjoy you. And I think you will very much appreciate what he can give you. You will both be happy. I will teach you how to be Paolo's mistress, and he will never leave you. Now—go and find him."

She dismissed Alicia, who walked into the garden to find Paolo leaning against a tree, arms folded against his chest in an attitude of waiting. She called out to him softly and he came. *"Andiamo,* Alicia. It's time for us to say good night."

Farewells were made with a round of kisses and warm embraces, given with promises to see one another soon.

As they began the short stroll back to the hotel, Alicia spoke. "You still haven't told me why Amelie lives in a hotel."

"I'm surprised she didn't tell you that story herself. Willy left her the hotel when he died."

"Willy who?"

"She didn't tell you about Willy? Well, Willy was a prince—a minor one, but a prince all the same, a Hapsburg. Perhaps because he was a minor prince, he had developed some very sound business talents. He seemed to have fallen in love with Italy and bought a great deal of property—some vineyards, some hotels, some undeveloped resort property. He and Amelie were lovers after Papa died."

"They never married?"

"Willy was already married. He visited from time to time, but he and Mama spent most of their time in this hotel—in the apartment we just left. When he died, he left the hotel to her. Oh, yes, he left her Tatiana, too."

"What a romantic story."

"Amelie is a romantic person. There has never been anything dull about her."

"Did you mind? About her having a lover, I mean?" Alicia couldn't help wondering what Sally or Jenny might say if she introduced Paolo as her lover.

"Why should I mind? She had made Papa very happy. And when he was gone, I knew she would find another man. She was still very beautiful, very vital. It would have been a terrible waste if she had not."

"Did you like him?"

"Yes I did—very much. Willy was very generous, very clever. He made Mama laugh. I think what I remember most about the time I spent with them was the sound of laughter.

Even late at night, when they thought I was asleep, I remember how merry they seemed to be. And that, dear Alicia, was my first lesson in making love. I learned that it was something very merry, and that it made two people very, very happy."

Alicia flashed back in her own memory to her recollections of Carlotta and Sharif, to the first time she was aware of what married love was. She had learned a different lesson from the one Paolo had just described. She had believed that love was very private, very mysterious, something that excluded everyone else—even the very children born of that love. She sighed.

"*Coraggio, cara* Alicia, there is nothing so heavy that it can't be lightened by love. And now you have me to love you."

"How sure you are of everything. That must be a gift your mother passed on to you."

"One among many, Alicia. But it is the only way to live. You cannot be tentative, uncertain. It makes life a very timid affair—*senza gusto.*"

"I see," she said, though she wasn't quite certain she did.

When they reached her room, she imagined that Paolo would take her in his arms again, that there would be another night like the one they had shared before. But she saw his entire attitude change after he closed the door behind them.

"Now," he said, placing his hands on his hips, "before we say anything else, I want you to explain why you did not tell me important things about yourself. Like the fact that you are apparently a rich woman." Before she could find an answer, he went on, "Did you not trust me, Alicia? Is that it? Were you afraid to tell me? Did you think I would take advantage of you?"

As Paolo fired his questions at her, Alicia again was struck by the unfamiliar rhythms of this kind of relationship. She supposed that she and Paolo were quarreling. But the feeling was very different from those generated during her Pyrrhic battles with Charles. There seemed to be a choreography to this quarrel—which made it seem devoid of any threat of real danger. She remembered Amelie's prediction that they would quarrel and make love, and she realized that this was exactly what would happen—that fighting with Paolo did not mean the loss of love, but rather an extension of it.

She took a deep breath and answered: "Yes, Paolo, that's exactly right. At first there didn't seem to be any real reason to tell you about myself. We had just met. Then—well—there was my own insecurity, more than any doubts about you. You must realize—I don't know you well enough to have doubts."

Now Paolo sighed. "You have disappointed me, Alicia. I thought you felt something of what I felt. I thought you felt that we knew all we needed to know about each other—that the rest could come later."

"Well, yes and no. Please understand, Paolo—I was very drawn to you from the first moment I saw you. But I'm not accustomed to thinking and feeling the way you do—not about people and relationships. This is all very new to me."

Paolo looked as if he were about to relent. But then his voice took on a hard edge. "But you thought I was a man who might make love for money."

"I don't know if I thought that or not. I told you—I just wanted some time before I talked to you about—my business."

"Time! Now you are sounding too much like an American. I don't like that at all—talk about time, time, time. Americans talk about time more than any other people in the world, but they know nothing at all about how to use it well. They save it, they waste it, and in the end they don't know how to enjoy it."

Alicia had no answer, so he went on. "Look," he said, "you and I—we have known each other for two days. In America we might have taken two months to get this far. We would have had to 'date' before it would seem appropriate for me to tell you that I want you for my wife. It's ridiculous, is it not? And yet, an intelligent woman like you, instead of thinking for yourself—instead of knowing that what you feel is right—you vacillate and allow yourself to be troubled by questions. False questions." Now he was holding Alicia by the shoulders, scolding her as one scolds an unruly child.

He went on for a time, his voice rising and falling in a kind of querulous symphony. She listened some more, amused rather than alarmed. And then she became impatient. "All right, Paolo, you have every right to be annoyed. But do you have to construct an entire litany out of one complaint?"

Paolo looked startled, and then he laughed—a laugh of pure delight. "Brava, Alicia, I knew there were many things you had to learn—and that you would learn them quickly."

He pulled her to him. "And it is going to be my pleasure to teach you."

Those were the last sensible words spoken that night as Paolo took Alicia to bed and made love to her until she cried out with pleasure. Just before she fell asleep, she buried her face in his chest. "I love you," she murmured. "I love you so much."

"I know," he whispered. And they both laughed before they drifted off to sleep.

— 22 —

In the days that followed Paolo decided that they would marry before the summer was over, and that they would have two homes, in America and in Italy.

As she came to know Paolo better, Alicia realized that he was strong enough to accept her stewardship of Principessa—and proud enough not to like it. She knew that he would never live in her shadow as Charles had done, nor would he allow her to create a place for him in the business—a place that would make him the target of knowing smirks and patronizing attitudes from Principessa's staff. Paolo could deal with a wife who was richer than he was, a wife who had a life and a career of her own, but he would not tolerate a wife who made him a mere accessory to that life.

"I feel so blessed that I found you," she said to him, speaking more frankly with him than she ever had with Charles. "I feel as if my mother sent you to me—and please don't laugh," she added as she told him about her experience in the convent.

"Why would I laugh? I believe in destiny, and in the kind of intuition you have just described."

"I'm glad. But no matter how you came to me, I feel you are a gift, a second chance. But you will have to tell me what to do so I won't drive you away, so I won't make you miserable as I did Charles."

"I have told you, my darling, that I am not Charles. And

as much as I adore you, I simply would not allow you to do those things. I love you too much to let you cause either of us unhappiness.''

''So what is the answer, Paolo? Shall I give it all up and just be your wife? Perhaps I could help you with your business.''

''First of all, *amore*, being my wife is not something you should think of as 'just'. And second, I don't believe the answer to your question is to contrive something false—to pretend that you are not a rich woman or that you do not run a business. But I do not want you to spend your entire day throwing your energies into something which I do not share.''

The solution they reached was one in which Alicia would turn over the active management of Principessa to Gardiner and Geoffrey, who seemed to be doing very well in her absence. Their new home would be not in New York, but in California, where, together, they would launch the first of Principessa's boutiques—which would feature original works created by Paolo's artisans. It would be a new venture, full of challenge and risk, and they would be doing it together. This would be a genuine merger of Paolo's world and hers.

In the passing days of summer, Alicia spent most of her time with Paolo, at his factory, looking at samples, approving, rejecting—convincing him, when she had to, of what would appeal to American buyers and what would not. Working like this, side by side with a man she loved, was a new experience for Alicia. It was so intoxicating that she wished she never had to leave. She was afraid the formula for happiness that worked so well in Venice might somehow fail in the States. When she voiced this fear to Paolo, he laughed and held her tight. ''Nonsense, *carissima*, nothing will happen to make us less happy than we are today. I promise you.''

Their evenings were often shared with Amelie, who took upon herself the responsibility for instructing her prospective daughter-in-law in the art of conjugal bliss. This she did with a series of tales, some true, some fabricated, from her own life. ''I have no daughters,'' she said, ''so I will pass on to you everything that I have learned. You are one of us, a European, so I think you will understand. You must not be an American wife when you go to America. Paolo is a European man, and he can make you happy as no American can. But you must remember to do the same.''

"I didn't realize there was such a difference."

"*Ma, si,* the problems of your marriage—they could not have happened here. We understand that marriage is a contract, like a business. To carry it out, we must first understand what it is that each partner wants from the other. Americans make a great deal of fuss about love, and expressing true feelings, but none of this necessarily makes for a good marriage."

"But Paolo and I do love each other," Alicia protested.

"Yes, yes." The older woman waved her hand, impatient at the interruption. "That is all to the good. It will give your marriage a special richness. But without the other, love will not have the opportunity to survive. You must take the time to find out what each of you wants—and then you must make up your mind to give what is wanted—at least most of the time. If you are feeling cross or ugly, then you might imagine these to be your true feelings. But I suggest that this is not at all what your husband will want. Nor do you really wish to know if he finds another woman more desirable for a moment or two. These might be his true feelings for that moment, but they would do nothing to enhance your love or your marriage. And so that is not the kind of face you will show to each other."

"Are you saying that married people should lie to each other in order to be happy?"

Amelie sighed. "*Ecco,* my darling, was it not Shakespeare who said that all the world is a stage? *Bene*—if we are all actors, then either we can do our parts beautifully and with grace, or not so beautifully. If you take the role of wife, would you prefer to do it with panache and originality? If so, then that is your true feeling, and the others—the whims of the moment—they should be ignored."

Alicia had never heard theories for marital happiness like Amelie's. Yet they conjured up images that were not at all unappealing. "Tell me the truth, Amelie," she asked. "Were you always able to be the same, with Julio—and with Willy—no matter how you felt?"

"Of course not. In the first place, my role changed. To Julio, I was a child bride, someone to be displayed and cared for. Later, with Willy, I was a woman of the world. Thanks to Julio, I was prepared to be the mistress of a worldly and refined man."

"You make it sound like being in service."

"Not at all, dear child." Amelie shook her head impatiently. "You are deliberately misunderstanding me. I am simply putting into words what people usually do not. In your country, before marriage there is only talk of love, not of what a man and a woman are expected to do. I think this is perhaps why so many of your marriages are not satisfactory—whether they ultimately finish with divorce or not. For me, I prefer to understand exactly what is expected—and also to understand what it is I expect."

Alicia stopped to think just what it might be that she expected from Paolo. "But I feel all I want now is for Paolo to be there, a part of my life."

Amelie laughed. "For now—perhaps. But I think you are too substantial a woman to be satisfied with an attractive body that wears trousers. My Paolo is capable of much more. You must demand the attention and the love. If you do not take all he can give, he will lose the gift for giving. And these things you must give him too. Italian men—they are actors of a very special kind. They are brought up to the sound of applause. The mama and the *nonna* and all the aunts and cousins, they say *bravo, bravissimo,* for every small accomplishment. Perhaps this makes them a little arrogant. But in all the years I have lived, I have found that if you create a Narcissus—do you know this story?—then he will always need the mirror in which to see his beauty. If you hold up the mirror which makes him feel ugly, he will not forgive you. But if you show him only his beauty, then my dear Alicia, he will love you with all his heart."

"My God, it all sounds so calculated."

Amelie shrugged. "You are saying it is less good to plan for the important things in your life? That it is better to just blunder along and let things happen as they will? *Dio!*"

"I'm sorry I'm such a bad pupil, Amelie. It's just that I never thought about things you are saying. Not even when I was a young girl."

Amelie softened. "Of course. You really are still very young in some ways. I think this in itself will give Paolo pleasure. You are clever—and yet you need to be taught so much. This will give him the excuse to strut and preen and teach you. Italian men are also like peacocks, you see." As Amelie went on to describe the plumage and social habits of her countrymen, Alicia found herself shaking with laughter.

"What's going on there?" Paolo demanded, from his place in the garden, where he and Tatiana were playing *cinquilio*.

"Instructions for marriage—I am telling Alicia all she needs to know to make you happy."

"What's so funny about that? And why is she laughing so hard?"

"Dear boy—that is the most important lesson of all!"

The wedding was a small one, held in the chapel where Paolo had been baptized. There were no more than a dozen guests—Tatiana and some friends of Amelie and Paolo. Because Alicia had no family or friends in Italy, Amelie was her witness, while one of Paolo's childhood friends stood up for him. After the ceremony, the small party returned for a champagne breakfast at the Albergo Flora.

So different from the first time, Alicia thought as she looked around her. Her first wedding had been a theatrical presentation of which she was the centerpiece. It was the end of her childhood and the beginning of her greatest confusion.

Now at this simple gathering of well-wishers, there was no tension, no stage fright. It was a very human moment, a step in the road that she and Paolo had pledged to walk together. It formalized a commitment they had already made, locked in each other's arms.

She felt so good, so right, so relaxed—in short, she was a different Alicia. She was eager, and open to the simplest pleasures. Whereas her first honeymoon had been a two-month affair, now she and Paolo had planned nothing more than a quiet dinner in his apartment. They both agreed that they would start married life with nothing so contrived as a ritualized honeymoon, that after they returned to the United States, they might perhaps take an extended trip there.

But even without the "trimmings," Alicia Hazzi Richman Reini felt every inch a bride—radiant and fresh and new.

Sally and Jenny learned of their mother's marriage through twin cables, sent to each of them on the day of her wedding. Later she wrote each daughter a letter, telling a little of how she had met her new husband, how happy she was, and adding the hope that they would not think badly of her for remarrying.

Jenny's first reaction was resentment—and then a reluctant

admiration for her mother. "What do you know," she said to Sally over the phone. "Our Alicia has done it again."

"Don't be mean, Jenny."

"I'm not being mean. Here we send off a grieving widow. Now she's coming back—how many months later?—a new bride with a gorgeous new husband, if you believe her description."

"Well, I'm glad for her."

"You would be. Sweet Sally."

"Aren't you glad she has somebody to look after her?"

Jenny laughed. "Is that what you think? Lord, Sally—I'd like to see the man who can 'look after' Alicia."

"Don't laugh, Jenny. She needs looking after, just like anyone else. She just has a different way of showing it, that's all."

"If you say so."

After she had put down the phone, Jenny quickly lost interest in her mother's marriage. It was her own life that preoccupied her. She reviewed the week ahead. Monday, she had promised to make a costume for Becky's school play. Tuesday, it was her turn to play hostess for her chapter of the women's auxiliary of AMA. Wednesday, she had to take Bruno, their pet Labrador, to the vet, for his annual heartworm examination. Thursday, there was dinner with the chairman of the nominating committee for AMA. That day was starred in her head. Jeff hoped to run for national office next year, and making a good impression on the nominating committee was important. Friday, Becky was having some of her little friends over for a pajama party. Jenny had promised to provide a dinner of lasagna and chewy fudge brownies. Saturday—nothing special, perhaps she and Jeff might go out to dinner and a movie. Sunday—what was Sunday? There was something she was supposed to do. But she couldn't quite remember.

Depressing, she thought. Depressing and dull. Not one really interesting thing to do. All the magazines she read warned against the dangers of becoming dull and boring. A good wife owed it to her husband, if not to herself, to keep up with the times. To keep her mind active and lively.

Jenny started to draw up a list of things she might do. She could take a cooking class with James Beard. Jeff would like that. She could study transcendental meditation at the Y. Jeff would probably laugh at that. She could study auto repair at night, at Stuyvesant High School. Jeff would love that. Or, she could take an art class at the New School. She considered these possibilities—and circled the last.

— 23 —

Jenny's first class with Rinaldo Fine was almost a theatrical experience—which was exactly what the instructor intended. The catalog had described the course as "Anyone Can Sculpt," and it had listed the instructor's credentials.

None of this gave any clue to what Rinaldo—the result of a mating between a Mexican dancer and a Jewish tailor from Brooklyn—was really like. From an artist's point of view, he had an almost perfect face—a broad clean forehead, a long straight nose, high sharp cheekbones, a full mouth which suggested cruelty rather than sensuality and which therefore made him all the more attractive to women. The only imperfection was a thin white scar that began just above the left eyebrow and ran diagonally toward the bridge of the nose. Although the scar was the result of a stickball accident that had happened when Rinaldo was just ten, it somehow suggested street fighting and gang war—an impression which Rinaldo fully exploited.

He was very dark, with a swarthiness that suggested all kinds of delicious dangers to the kind of women he described contemptuously as "wimpy WASPs." To men, Rinaldo's appearance suggested a knife strapped to the leg; a character capable of violence, swift and quiet, in an alleyway down a deserted street.

He had made his reputation as an artist of the left—as an outstanding iconoclast at a time when iconoclasts were everyday fare. He managed this with the help of his extraordinary looks, a fair amount of talent, a remarkable flair for generating publicity, a prodigious sexual appetite (which he tended to satisfy where it would do his career the most good), a surfeit of physical energy—an aura, really, of vitality and success. In short, Rinaldo was a self-fulfilling prophecy.

Yet although the world of midtown galleries was his, Rinaldo liked to keep in touch with the artistic communities of Greenwich Village, of Soho and Noho and Tribeca—the world of loft dwellers, still struggling for recognition and trying to keep as much distance between themselves and starvation as possible.

In the duplex apartments, the town houses and penthouses of Fifth Avenue, of Madison and Park, Rinaldo held his own, at least when he was surrounded by women. But it was in the downtown pockets of art and culture that he had the perfect audiences. To the artists who still labored for a tiny portion of what he had, Rinaldo was an inspiration, to them he could deliver his bits of wisdom on art and life—and dismiss as sour grapes the occasional suggestion that he was like an empty walnut which makes a great deal of noise.

Rinaldo taught the New School course in Greenwich Village because he liked the academic connection. It gave him, he imagined, a certain intellectual cachet, without requiring him to do any hard work or to sacrifice what he thought of as his individuality. The New School was a perfect showcase for his particular assets. It was a place that encouraged the eccentric, even the outrageous. It was one part academe, one large part show business. And Rinaldo's class was a solid hit. The enrollment for his course invariably filled quickly.

He firmly resisted invitations to expand his teaching schedule from one night a week to two or more. Rinaldo liked to keep his nights open for his social life, which, freely translated, meant women. "The most important part of art," he explained, "is living. When you stop living, you dry out." As Rinaldo had consistently demonstrated, he intended never to dry out.

It was all of this—his reputation, his flair for attracting attention—that had brought Jenny to his class. For Jenny, "Anyone Can Sculpt" was another stop in her search for "something," for herself.

The first Wednesday night she was in her seat at seven sharp. There was an air of anticipation in the room which was heightened because Rinaldo was fifteen minutes late. He walked in with a gait that was part swagger, part slink, and it was a tribute to his personal style that he carried this off without looking ridiculous. There was an audible buzz of excitement at his entrance.

Rinaldo played his audience by staring into each of their faces, eyes ranging from one person to another, eyes locking with eyes, then moving on, leaving the feeling that a physical touch had taken place. Finally, when every man and woman in the room was in the palm of his hand, Rinaldo began to talk. "Good evening." The voice was soft and low, curiously elegant and feral at the same time. "I'm Rinaldo Fine." This, of course, was completely unnecessary. Everyone knew who he was, what he was. His picture, along with stories of his work, his parties, his public brawls, his women, had appeared in virtually every newspaper and magazine of note.

"I'm very flattered and grateful for the confidence in me you've shown by coming to my class. I want you all to know that I will try to give you back something of value." He paused for a beat, then shifted gears, the charm suddenly disappearing, to be replaced by a hint of the toughness that they all had come to see. "But," he said, his voice hardening, "if I'm going to give you what you came here for—the chance to be as good as you can—if I'm going to be fair and honest with you, then I'm going to ruffle a few feathers. So, if any of you are very sensitive, if you think you may react badly to the kind of criticism I dish out—and I warn you, I'm very, very tough—then I should give you the chance to leave this class and choose another."

Of course no one ever left after this stock speech. They all knew about Rinaldo Fine—part drill sergeant, part psychotherapist, part lover. They were ready and eager for everything he would dish out.

After his opening speech, Rinaldo took care of mundane details, discussing supplies, reading material, and references in a few short sentences. And then, lest anyone imagine for a minute that this was a conventional art class, he turned his much-photographed face directly to his audience. "And now—I think we should get to know one another. I think we need to know who we are and what we want. Why we're here, and how we see life. Tell me about it—you." He pointed to the most striking woman in the room, a slender blonde, about twenty-five, with gray eyes and an opulent bosom. "Your name, please?"

"Christy Reynolds."

"Now, Christy—do you mind if I call you Christy?"

...n it was clear that Christy did not mind at all, he went on, "Tell us about yourself, why you're here, what you do when you're not here, what you want from this class—and" —he paused—"from me."

"Well," she began, slowly, shyly, "I'm married—to a dentist." For some reason, this piece of information evoked a snicker from one corner of the classroom—but the sound died when Rinaldo shot a look of pure venom in its direction. "I study dance," Christy continued, "and sometimes I work in clubs. I want to study sculpture because I think all art is related. I want to learn more about it—and more about me. I guess that's all I expect."

"That's quite a lot, Christy. Some people spend a lifetime in analysis and don't succeed in learning more about themselves. But—I'll do what I can to point you in the right direction." He gave her one of his best Rinaldo Fine smiles, then added, "Stay a minute or two after class, will you?"

The brief autobiographies continued, although clearly none of those that followed interested Rinaldo as Christy's had. Jenny held her breath each time he scanned the group to choose another speaker. Everyone else seemed to be doing interesting things, and she felt stupid and dull and boring. She did not want to stand up and announce this fact to a roomful of strangers.

Rinaldo did not point to her. After about half the class had spoken, he gave his watch a perfunctory look and said abruptly, "That's all."

As Jenny left the class, she cast a wistful glance at the fortunate Christy, who had captured Rinaldo's interest at once. And when she went to sleep that night, it was twin fantasies of making love and making art that warmed her sleep. In her diary, she had written simply: "Rinaldo Fine."

Although she had memorized his features long before the first class had ended, Rinaldo seemed to take no particular notice of her, at least not until the third session was well under way. As he walked from table to table, between the work areas, he stopped at a point just behind Jenny's shoulder— and she knew he was watching her.

She wondered how the piece looked to him, this lump-like woman she shaped with now-trembling fingers, this figure with arms outstretched in an attitude of supplication. In her mind, Jenny had called it "The Searcher."

Finally he spoke. "Not bad," he said. "It's a little timid—cramped. A piece like this either lives or it doesn't. There's nothing in between. It's an absolute condition—no equivocation. It's yes or no."

She waited for more, but that was all he said. Moments later she realized how lucky she had been when he stopped to examine an abstract linear piece, highly polished, highly refined, the work of a computer programmer. It was a piece that Jenny had admired. But Rinaldo looked as if he had just stepped into a pile of dog droppings. "What the hell do you call this?" He almost spat the words at the offending student, shoving his face so close to him that the young man stepped back.

"I just intended . . . I planned . . . uh." The hapless object of Rinaldo's scorn seemed tongue-tied and embarrassed.

"You intended? You planned?" Rinaldo's voice rose with each word. "No wonder this—this thing—is so gutless. If this is the best you can do, you're better off staying home and jerking off." He picked up the piece and threw it to the floor. No one spoke, no one moved. Eyes were involuntarily, irresistibly drawn to the young computer programmer's white face.

Rinaldo turned on the staring class. "What is this? A class or an exercise in voyeurism?"

Everyone suddenly became very busy. After that incident, there were other, less spectacular displays of Rinaldo's pique. And Jenny found herself torn between a craving for some personal attention and the fear that she might bring down on her head the wrath of his disappointment.

Although she found it hard to concentrate, she tried to make her work as good as it might be. She stared surreptitiously, greedily, at his profile, watched in fascination as he moved among the students, quiet and lithe—and, she thought, incredibly sexy.

At home, she felt as if she were hiding a guilty secret. She started to tell Jeff about the class, about the effect that Rinaldo had on his students. Perhaps she thought she wouldn't feel so guilty if she shared her feelings with her husband.

But Jeff smiled absently and squeezed her shoulder. "He's a pro, hon. A big-shot artist. Some eccentricity goes with that territory. I know it's hard for you to understand."

Jenny had no answer, not because of what Jeff had said, but because of what she heard between the lines. She, Jenny

Ashland—wife, mother—she was a world apart from a "pro," from Rinaldo, from Jeff himself. It was true, but it bothered her that Jeff had articulated this truth.

Whenever she had such feelings, feelings that implied any criticism of Jeff, she felt like an ingrate.

To make up for her error, she brought Jeff several small things that had earned a nod or two from Rinaldo. She waited for his inspection, even his approval. But when he looked, she felt he was not seeing, and she found his effusive praise hollow sounding and insincere. His "Very nice, Jen" reminded her of the kind of compliments she had lavished on Rebecca's nursery school creations. Somehow, Rinaldo's silent nods gave her much more to treasure.

She recorded her treasonous feelings in her diary, but her guilt vanished one Friday evening when one of Jeff's associates, Harvey Grunwald, stopped by for a drink. Harvey lived in Westport, where his wife ran a small boutique called Mimsey's Whimsy. Harvey Grunwald never tired of boasting about Mimsey's exquisite taste, her creative flair, her business acumen.

This time Jeff handed Harvey a Scotch, neat, and immediately dragged him into the bedroom, where he had built special shelves to hold Jenny's work. "Have a look, Harv— see what Jen's been up to these days."

"Well, well—beauty and talent, too. You're a lucky guy, Jeff. I hope you know it."

"I guess we can't let your Mimsey monopolize all the feminine creativity now, can we?"

As they spoke, Jenny wondered if they ever discussed things that really mattered in the fake-hearty tone they were using, a tone reserved apparently for children and idiots—and wives.

That night she wrote: "Harvey Grunwald is a pompous ass. And when Jeff is with him, he seems to suffer from the same affliction." And: "I am a coward."

It may have been an accident of fate—but it probably was not—that Jenny crossed paths with Rinaldo just at the time her desire for Jeff was at its lowest ebb. As she watched Rinaldo week after week, a different kind of desire built in her. She envied Christy, who was married to the dentist, but who left the class each week with Rinaldo's arm wrapped possessively around hers. Rinaldo's affairs with his students were part of his public legend. His liaisons began quickly, without preamble; for him they were almost an exercise of *droit du seigneur*. And just as quickly, they were over.

Invariably these affairs were a source of delicious gossip for his classes. When Rinaldo's interest in the beauteous Christy started to wind down, it was almost as if she was the last to know.

The kiss-off came one Wednesday evening, when he did not issue her his usual invitation to remain. Yet she lingered anyway as the other students filed out of the room. At first he pretended not to notice her. But when she remained there, rooted to the floor near his desk, he rapped out, "I'm busy, Christy," then dropped his eyes to his papers in a gesture of dismissal.

If Christy had ever talked to Rinaldo's previous castoffs, she might have known that any protest at this point would be futile. She might then at least have salvaged her pride with a breezy farewell, a casual "see you" thrown over a shoulder. But Christy stayed where she was, eyes filling with tears— and immediately earned his contempt. Then she made yet another mistake. "But Rinaldo . . . I thought. . . ."

He stared at her, eyes hard as agates and said, "Then you thought wrong. School is out. Now please don't get boring." He got up and walked away, making it clear he would not waste another breath on her.

Jenny had lingered, had watched the exchange with a fascination that was a mixture of revulsion, fear—and something else. She found, to her horror, that the man seemed more dangerously attractive than ever.

That night she wrote in her diary: "What would I give to have Rinaldo Fine? To borrow him?"

She herself supplied the answer. The following week she brought to class a piece she had started sometime before, had worked on during moments of high energy, of frustration or anger. It was a communication from Jenny Ashland to Rinaldo Fine. It was light-years removed from her first work. This figure was also a woman, but there the resemblance ended.

The new work was not a supplicant, not a seeker. This woman was arrogant, powerful, fearless. She stood, feet firmly planted, shoulders squared, in an attitude of calculated insouciance, head thrown back in laughter. It was what Jenny sometimes wished to be. It was, in fact, a female version of Rinaldo Fine.

She worked on the figure with her own head down, not stopping, as she usually did, to steal quick looks at Rinaldo. Soon she sensed his presence, silent, watching. "Yes," he said. "Yes." Then he turned his eyes on her and she was forced to look. "Tell me about it," he said. "After class." He did not wait for an answer.

For a moment she was nearly blind with excitement. She went back to her work, but her fingers felt thick and unresponsive.

And somehow the class was over, and somehow it was she, Jenny Ashland, who waited at Rinaldo's desk. It was her elbow he took, while other eyes followed them, with curiosity and some envy, as they left the room.

After they were out of the building, he said. "What took you so long?"

"Excuse me?"

"I said what took you so long? To surface."

"I didn't know I had," she answered, sounding coy and arch and hating it. She had wanted this man's attention for weeks, and now she didn't even know how to talk to him.

"Of course you did," he said flatly. "Let's not waste time with word games." Without asking, he took her directly to a coffeehouse a few blocks away, a place with small dark mahogany tables and stenciled tin ceilings, a place where the strains of a Verdi opera could be heard over the sound of the espresso machine. He ordered prosciutto and melon and espresso. Jenny said she would have the same thing.

"Now Mrs. Ashland—it is Mrs. Ashland, yes?—tell me something about yourself. Save me a lot of questions."

"I thought we all did that at the beginning." She wondered if he would remember that she had not, in fact, told anyone about herself.

"Not that stuff. Tell me the real things. Are you happy? What do you want from life? And what do you think of me?"

"I guess I should be happy. I really have nothing to complain about. I don't think I want anything right now." She lied and lied—and then she told a half-truth: "I think you're a very unusual teacher."

He groaned and looked disgusted. "Keep that up and I'm walking right out of here. What kind of namby-pamby bullshit answers are those? I don't waste my time talking to people who say things like 'nothing to complain about' and 'nice life.' And please—for God's sake—not 'unusual' when you're talking about me. I'd rather have you say I was a horse's ass.''

Jenny flushed. ''I don't think I could say that. I wouldn't mean it. I'm just not used to thinking and talking the way you do.''

''That's one of the reasons I teach—to break people like you out of their little molds.''

Now it was her turn to look disgusted. ''Oh really? Is that what you think you do?''

He laughed. ''Very good. Cut right through the crap. Now go on. Give me a bio. A real one.''

''All right. I'm a frustrated neurotic housewife. I have a good husband and a beautiful daughter. And I do want something—I don't quite know what. And more to the point, I don't know if I can pay the price.''

''How can you know what the price is if you don't even know what you want?''

''I don't know—well, I thought I did. I've never been sure.''

''Have you always been such a 'fraidycat, Mrs. Ashland?''

''I didn't think so. But maybe I have. Maybe it comes from having a mother who wasn't afraid of anything.''

''Bullshit. Everybody's afraid. Either you don't give in to it, or you do—and you end up with half a life. Making excuses. Only you don't really believe them. And you die feeling like you blew it.''

She said nothing.

''Do you know what I see when I see you?''

''What?''

''A virgin. In every way. Makes me want to whisper obscene things into your ear. And watch you blush.''

As if on cue, Jenny began to redden. She thought she probably had started something she couldn't handle, something grown up and very different from the drunken cocktail-party passes she had fended off at medical conventions. True, it was what she had fantasized, but now she reminded herself that she was not twenty and single—that she was a wife and mother. Better to get away while there was still time.

But then he was standing up. ''Let's go.''

''Where?'' She felt stupid the minute the word left her mouth.

He laughed. "Come on, Mrs. Ashland. We're going to my place."

She knew exactly what she should do. She should excuse herself and leave. He would laugh at her, no doubt, but she would be safe. She would have done the right thing. Instead she said, "Well,—maybe just for a drink."

He appeared not to hear. They walked in silence to a converted loft building on East Tenth Street and took the self-service elevator to the third floor. There Rinaldo Fine lived in Village splendor, in a place that was all space and light and spidery green ferns, ficus trees, and twisted jade— and undulating walls that could be recessed at his whim.

Jenny's eyes searched the loft for Rinaldo's work. It was confined to one corner, where, he told her, he worked each morning between eight and noon, no more and no less, whether he felt productive or not. "Anyone who talks 'creative' bullshit," he added, "is just too goddamn lazy to be an artist—or too stupid to be anything. An artist is a worker, just like a plumber or an electrician. And if he's a worker, he has no right to sit around diddling himself and waiting for some no-such-thing like inspiration to strike."

She listened, properly impressed, as she continued her inspection of Rinaldo's home. It was an uncluttered space, reflecting a life pared down to essentials. What mattered to him was his work, and perhaps the work of a few contemporary artists. As she scanned the white walls, she recognized a Jasper Johns, a Rauschenberg, an Agam.

The furniture was spare—a few oversize couches covered in a rough textured fabric that looked Mexican; a large bed upholstered in raw linen and covered with nutria fur; a sleek, functional kitchen area. All in all, the loft told of a man who traveled light and insisted on his pleasures.

Without asking, he walked to a pair of sliding doors, pulled one aside, and took out a bottle of Courvoisier and two balloons. He poured for both of them, then handed one glass to Jenny. "Here. And sit down. You look like a fly waiting to be swatted."

She laughed nervously, then sat down on one of the couches, sinking into the upholstery so deeply that she wondered how she would get up.

"I suppose you want me to tell you about your work." He did not add, "They all do," but she heard it nevertheless.

"Not if you don't want to."

"You have decent technique. Clean. A little too refined for my taste. But you're always holding back. So what you do is always—tentative. A little mushy."

She knew what he was saying was true, but she was disappointed anyway.

"Your work is better than what a Queens housewife would turn out at the Y. But it's formative. Which would be okay for a teenager. But not for you.

"I noticed you the first day," he went on, and instantly the disappointment gave way to a rush of pleasure. "You had on a raincoat with the collar turned up. A big pair of dark glasses. Your hair was in your face. I said to myself, 'Rinaldo—there's a woman in there somewhere.' "

Jenny laughed again, unreasonably pleased that he had noticed her at all.

"If your appearance was any metaphor for your work, I expected you to turn out cryptic blobs."

Now she wasn't quite so pleased.

"I was wrong. Sometimes I am. But you do have to take off the glasses and coat, you know. Otherwise whatever you have will always be stunted—small. Like a bonsai tree."

Jenny tried to take in what he was saying. She was a little embarrassed that he was taking her so seriously. She felt like a fraud, a dilettante. More precisely, she still didn't know exactly why she was in the class. He had once said, "I don't want anyone here who's wasting my time—who's here to meet people or get occupational therapy or fill up some empty hours. If you want that, go take the class in macramé or movie history. I just want serious people here. You don't have to be candidates for the gallery circuit, but heaven help you if I catch any of you jerking me off."

Somehow she, Jenny Ashland, had slipped by. She had fooled Rinaldo Fine. But now she was here, with him expecting her to do God knows what, to break the rules. And she wanted to. She wanted to belong to that magical sorority of his women.

But if Jeff found out . . . he would not forgive her. She knew that. They had never discussed the subject directly, but he was always so judgmental when it came to the weaknesses of women.

Still—might she risk it? And worry about consequences later? He stood behind her now, touching her shoulders and neck with a lightness so exquisite she thought her heart would stop. She closed her eyes and her feelings said yes.

Then suddenly—how had it happened? He was perhaps a little impatient, a little absentminded, a little clumsy. Whatever. He touched her arm and said, "Okay, Christy—let's get on with it."

And for Jenny the moment was over. She had not minded the thought of being one of his student groupies. But she had expected a moment that belonged to her. This—this anonymous tumble just wasn't worth the risk. "I'm sorry," she said, getting up abruptly and knocking a couch cushion to the floor. "I'm sorry—I have to go now. I . . ."

Rinaldo's face darkened suddenly. "Cut it out, Mrs. Ashland. You're starting to bore me." He did not raise his voice, but he began to flay her, methodically, with his words. "You were right before. You are just a neurotic housewife. Neurotic and retarded. You'll never know what being an artist is all about. Go away, Mrs. Ashland. You just don't interest me anymore."

She fled the loft, and she never returned to the class. She planned to tell Jeff that she had dropped out because she didn't have the time to complete her work properly.

But Jeff never noticed the change in her schedule. Not until several months later did he realize she had added no more pieces to the shelves in their bedroom. He asked, "Class over?"

"Yes," she answered. "It's over."

24

Jenny alternately cursed herself for her failure in Rinaldo's class, and then for her pretensions. "A neurotic housewife," she had said. And Rinaldo had agreed.

Better she should concentrate on being what she was. Jeff's wife. Do a better job of that. There must be hundreds of women who would kill for what she had.

How often had Jeff hinted that she try to emulate some of

Sally's flair and style? Certainly she could try a little harder. What was it someone had said? There are no small jobs—only small people.

And so Jenny launched a new campaign: To Be a Better Wife and Mother. She discovered organic foods. Praise from Jeff led her into the realm of wok cookery. More praise from Jeff. Homemade breads and carrot cake followed. Soon homemade ice cream graced their dinner table. And when company came, Jeff pronounced her canapés without peer.

Her parties also began to earn Jeff's approval—though of course they still could not compare with Sally's galas. Over the next few years Jenny's rough edges seemed to disappear. Temper tantrums ceased. Patience seemed infinite. She helped with homework, picked up suits from the cleaners, gladly entertained all the preteen girls who wandered through her home. In short, she became the kind of model parent she had yearned for.

If there was a flaw in all this perfection, it was that Jenny started having stomach cramps with frightening regularity. And sometimes, when she ceased her rounds of perpetual motion, she felt that emotionally she was on the thin edge of survival.

She tried to find satisfaction in the fact that her home had never looked better, that her kitchen had never before given out such delicious aromas, that her daughter had never received such loving care. But she still felt depressed. At times she felt that she herself had been completely erased.

She mentioned the stomach spasms to Jeff. "Sounds like nerves, hon. But what you have to be nervous about, I'll never know. I can give you some Valium. Or you can call Harvey for a GI workup if that'll make you feel better."

She mentally said no to both options. She didn't feel up to Harvey's patronizing heartiness, and she didn't want to go through her day feeling sedated. If the cramps were just from nerves, perhaps they would go away. And if they weren't, well, she would worry about that later.

In her diary, she now began to list the accumulated wealth of her life—to count her blessings, literally, and to remind herself that she had no right at all to want more.

She began to spend more time watching television and concocting Walter Mitty fantasies in which she tried on the lives of people she saw.

Preoccupied as she was, she hardly noticed the small changes

in her husband. Not the new haircut, or the new clothes, or the
diet. It was the new cologne—a musky, overpowering scent
that caught her attention one morning. "I didn't know you
used cologne," she remarked, after he had spent what she
thought was an unusually long time dressing.

"It's new," he said, without further explanation.

"That's a new shirt, too, isn't it?"

"Yes."

When, later, she added up the sum total of new things in
Jeff's life, it seemed considerable, but not necessarily sinister.

When he added a daily run of five miles to his morning
regimen, she laughingly reported this and the entire "new
Jeff" phenomenon to her sister during one of their regular
weekly visits. Sally didn't laugh or even smile. Instead, she
took Jenny's hand and said, in a voice heavy with concern,
"I don't want to alarm you, Jen—but the same thing happened with Marsha's husband. He even went out and bought
a hairpiece—after he had always made fun of anyone who
wore one."

"And?" Jenny probed for the punch line to this story.

"Well—" Sally sighed. "Poor Marsha found out he was
having a thing with his secretary—who was only twenty-
one—and so naturally . . ."

Jenny burst out laughing, not because the thought of Jeff
and infidelity was so impossible, but because she thought of
her husband's nurse-receptionist, a totally efficient, dedicated
woman who drove Jeff crazy with her personal mannerisms.
So that was out. Besides, Jeff wouldn't cheat, she decided.
He was too busy to clutter up his life with more demands. An
affair might have its pleasures, Jenny guessed with borrowed
worldliness, but simplicity, she reckoned, was not one of
them. "No," she said to Sally, "Jeff isn't having an affair. It
would be too much trouble."

Sally did not seem convinced, but she was far too gentle to
press the argument. She scrutinized her sister, taking in the
fly-away hair that could, she knew, be lovely with a little
attention. And those pores around the nose. Just a good
astringent needed there. Maybe a little peel, she thought, to
get rid of those fine lines around the eyes and mouth. "Jenny,
love," she said, "since Jeff has gone in for this self-
improvement program, what would you think about some
'sauce for the goose'? Let me treat, Jen—I would love to take

you to Arden's for a day to begin with. And then, when you have time, we might—''

"Hold it, Sally. Hold it. I love you for what you're saying. You really are one of the world's dearest people. And I think it's wonderful that you take care of yourself. You're a born beauty—it would be a crime if you didn't. That's your style. I don't really know what my style is. But I think I know what it isn't. I'm not even comfortable in 'fixed' hair and 'fixed' clothes. Thanks anyway. But no.''

Having made the one suggestion that came to mind, Sally now seemed to be at a loss. She loved her little sister, but she couldn't completely understand her. She could never fathom, for example, why Jenny took so little pleasure in things that were so satisfying to her—things like grooming, entertaining, beautifying her home. Sally couldn't help thinking that Jenny and Jeff would both be happier if she did.

The reason for the "new Jeff" was not, as Sally had suggested, another woman. In fact, the changes had been precipitated by a lunch with Jeff's old medical school class-mate, Stan Rossiter.

Jeff and Stan had been friendly rivals in school. Both men had been good students, both popular, both ambitious, but in different ways. There the similarities had ended. In his personal life Stan had been an unabashed playboy, eschewing home and family in favor of a series of apartments, each more opulent than the last. With these had come a corresponding series of women, each younger and less demanding than the last.

It was a tribute to Stan's intelligence and skill that these predilections did not interfere with his steady climb in a profession that was fundamentally conservative. He moved from one prestigious grant to another, involving himself in research projects that earned him considerable space in the medical journals. His good looks and flamboyant style assured Dr. Rossiter a fair amount of coverage in the popular press.

Although they had taken different paths, professionally and personally, the two men kept in touch through occasional phone calls and infrequent lunches. For a long time Jeff felt a kind of benign pity for Stan. To him, the rootless life-style and flashy materialism seemed empty and unenviable.

Now, for the first time, Jeff was not sure. As he listened to

Stan talk about his newest interest, a pilot surgical project in
China, Jeff felt a twinge of something. As Stan described the
work he would be doing, he seemed eager, enthusiastic—and
very young.

Jeff studied the fit and lean body ("I run every day," Stan
had explained. "And for good measure, I work out at my
club twice a week"), the perpetual tan, the expensive suit that
seemed to go with the silver Bentley Stan had arrived in.

Jeff had never wanted any of these things before. He had
been right, he believed, to practice serious medicine, to earn
a good living, to establish a family, to put down roots. Now
he had done it all. What he could expect in the future was
simply more of the same. Now Stan's life—the mobility, the
constant change, the absolute selfishness and freedom of
it—suddenly seemed less inconsequential, more seductive.
He tried to shake off that train of thought with his after-dinner
liqueur.

But when he stood in front of the full-length mirror in the
bedroom, he examined Dr. Jeffrey Ashland—and found him
conventionally handsome, trust-inspiring, perhaps a little dull.
He poked at the thickening waistline, frowned—and turned
away.

The change in her life, when it happened, was not like
anything Jenny had ever imagined. In her wicked and disloyal
(she thought) fantasies, Jenny sometimes pictured a Rebecca
partly grown, not needing so much fussing and wiping, not
requiring so many afternoons given over to PTA and teacher
conferences, or to making cookies or costumes for school
plays. And perhaps no more afternoons spent looking after
the growing ranks of children who did not have mothers at
home, who wore keys around their necks, and who flocked to
Jenny's warm and bustling kitchen.

As for Jeffrey, well, when her fantasies turned to Jeffrey,
she fantasized a Jeffrey who had "passed away"—not died,
because she could not bring herself to wish him dead even in
a daydream. No, what she did was to imagine a life where the
part occupied by Jeffrey simply became a blank slate, to fill
in as she wished. She had never thought seriously about
divorce. Divorce meant failure. It was for people who did not
know about commitments, people who had made the mistake
of choosing the wrong partner. Even when she chafed under

the gentle, invisible grip of Jeffrey's expectations, she never thought of him as the "wrong" partner.

And yet. Even though Jenny recognized the virtues and assets of her husband, she wished that somehow Jeffrey might one day pause in the middle of his climb to some private mountaintop. She wished that he might say, "Fine, Jenny. Now that I have most of what I always wanted, maybe we can shift gears for a while. What do you want to do?"

But she always completed this scenario with another question: Why should he? She could imagine Jeffrey patiently explaining to her: "Let me remind you, Jenny, that I expected a certain type of wife when we married. I see no reason to change those expectations now." For she realized now that Jeffrey had chosen her as an ambitious man often chooses a woman—as a partner; no, as an accomplice, really, in the fulfillment of his goals. She, Jenny Richman, had been young and attractive, the daughter of a socially acceptable family, fairly well off in her own right, intelligent but not ambitious, malleable but not entirely characterless. There was no reason for Jeffrey to accept a different kind of wife now. And he had kept his part of the bargain. He was a faithful husband, as far as she knew. And he had not noticeably changed toward her, as so many other men did toward "useful" wives after they had achieved the desired success. If she were to force the issue now, to suggest that perhaps he might appreciate a wife who was more fulfilled, more interesting in her own right, it might prove to be somewhat risky. If he approved the idea, might he not then choose a woman who already had these qualities, a cut-and-polished jewel like himself, sparkling and scintillating—and finished? Not a woman like herself, a woman who, at best, thought of herself in terms of potential.

No, Jenny had never taken the risk. She took, as she always had, the safer course, the preservation of the status quo, and kept, as she always had, the questions, the confusion, for her private moments.

Now something was happening, and it was not quite like anything she had imagined. Jeffrey had sat her down, not in the garden room, where they sometimes shared a predinner sherry, but in the dining room, with a broad expanse of mahogany table between them, as if they were political or diplomatic opponents, about to negotiate a difficult problem. Jeffrey poured himself a serious drink from the sideboard bar, a double Scotch, straight up. Not a drink for trivial chitchat. More a drink to fortify against bad news, against tragedy. Jenny began to feel cold.

"We need to talk, Jenny, about some important things." She sat silently, not supplying him with a cue. He went on. "I don't know if you've noticed, but I haven't really been completely happy."

My God, she thought, Sally was right. There is another woman. She opened her mouth, as if to speak, but her brain refused to supply any words. And so she sat, more frightened than she had ever been.

Jeffrey went on, impatient now, because he saw that Jenny was going to be of no help at all in the demolition of her life.

"This is no reflection on you, none at all. You've been a wonderful wife and mother." Still no response, as Jenny sat in frozen terror, knowing it was over, yet waiting to hear the final clause in Jeffrey's verdict. Guilty—but by reason of what? Abandoned because of incompetence—undesirability? Or that most grievous of all the sins she carried in her heart—the sin of "wrong attitude"? Had Jeffrey always known of it?

"Of course I've seen that your heart wasn't always in it," he said, a small edge of resentment in his voice. "Heaven knows why."

She turned her eyes on him, and they reminded him of a soon-to-be-slaughtered lamb. He repented. "I'm sorry, Jenny, I shouldn't have said that. You have been very good for me. It's just that I realize I've done the things I dreamed about when we were younger. And I still feel unfulfilled. As if I took a wrong turn somewhere . . ."

Now Jenny sat up at attention. She found a voice from somewhere within her. "What is it, Jeff? I'm not understanding what you're saying."

He shook his head. "There's no reason why you should. You and Rebecca are very dear to me. . . ."

"But?"

"But I have the feeling that my life is getting used up . . . I want to do some different things before it's all over."

"What kind of different things? Are you telling me there's another woman in your life?"

Jeffrey looked startled. "How could you think that, Jenny? There's never been anyone else, not since we were married. No—it's just that Stan has been talking to me about a project he's involved with. He's going to China for a year, and he asked me to go along."

"A year," Jenny echoed, grasping at the thin thread of hope that Jeffrey was talking about some temporary dislocation, something with a beginning and an end.

"This is a fantastic opportunity. It's the kind of thing I might have said was out of the question a few years ago. But then we talked, and I started to get excited again, like I did when we were younger. Suddenly I wanted to be the kind of man who could have said 'yes' without thinking twice."

"But I still don't understand, Jeff. Why is this all so terribly serious? If you want to go to China so badly, there's no reason why you couldn't. We can afford the time off. Maybe Rebecca and I could go with you . . . or maybe we could visit . . ."

He shook his head, realizing he would have to spell it out. "It isn't just this opportunity, Jenny. It's what it represents— the excitement, the chance to feel free. . . ."

"Free," she repeated in a monotone. "You mean free of Rebecca and me." It was not a question.

"Maybe it seems that way, and maybe that's how I have to say it, but it's not what I mean at all. Jenny, please . . . maybe this will sound incredibly banal, but I need to rediscover myself—not as a husband or a father or a doctor. Jenny, I need to do it alone."

She started to laugh and cry, on the thin edge of hysteria. "Oh, Jeffrey, oh dear God, Jeffrey, I thought that you—that one of us, at least, knew who he was. What a joke, Jeffrey, oh what a bad, bad joke. What's it all been about then, all these years, if neither one of us has been whole?"

Jeffrey looked bewildered by this outburst. It piqued his curiosity a little, but he was too wrapped up in getting what he wanted to ask Jenny what she meant. He did not really want to know if she had been unhappy. He did not want to know if her little jabs and innuendos, her transient rumblings, had come from something more serious than the usual female neuroses. If she had been deeply, fundamentally unhappy, he did not want to know. Not now. Not when that knowledge might get in the way of his getting loose. Later, perhaps later there would be time for soothing Jenny. So he said, in what she thought of as his best reassuring doctor-voice: "What it's been all about, Jenny, is that the two of us met when we were very young. We fell in love and we tried to make a good life together. But things change, we change. . . .''

She knew that there was a monstrous lie lurking in there, somewhere in that tissue of apparent truths. Somewhere in that gaggle of ''we's'' he was throwing up to obfuscate her vision, she saw and heard the clear and unmistakable sound of a loud, demanding ''I.''

Her first impulse was to cry, to whimper, to do whatever had to be done to stave off this desertion. But from somewhere within her she found the strength—perhaps it came from the pride of Alicia, the self-assurance of Carlotta—to say, ''I assume then that you want a divorce.''

Jeffrey's head snapped back. He had not expected this. ''Well, actually I hadn't thought it through,'' he lied, not quite as easily as he would have liked. ''Maybe a legal separation might serve us better right now. In time we could work something out, something we can both live with.''

Again Jenny heard the lie. And she was right, for Jeffrey wanted his freedom badly, but not at the cost of the substantial financial security he had built for himself. He had reckoned that if enough time lapsed between this first shock and an actual divorce, Jenny might be less inclined to seek punitive damages. After all, he reasoned, it wasn't as if she would be in need. She could live comfortably whether he was in the picture or not.

''No.'' She threw out the single word, to stop him from talking.

''What do you mean—'no'?'' Now Jeffrey's voice rose as his self-control started to slip. This scenario wasn't going exactly as he had planned. He had expected stunned disbelief, some tears, perhaps some anger—then acquiescence or at least resigned acceptance.

''I mean that if you're planning to leave us, I don't think a separation agreement will cover . . . certain realities. I mean I don't want to talk about this anymore. Just leave me alone, Jeffrey. Leave me alone.'' She got up, hoping to end the discussion.

''But we have to talk, to settle things. If I'm going to China, I have to let Stan know by the end of the week.''

''We'll talk, Jeffrey. But not today. And I wish you would pack some things and leave the apartment. As soon as you can.''

''Leave? Really, Jenny, why do you have to be so melodramatic? Why can't I just move into the guest room? Wouldn't that be better for Rebecca? Then we can prepare her. . . .''

Jenny smiled. "I wondered how long it would take you to mention Rebecca. No, Jeffrey, I don't think having your presence in our guest room is going to make this any easier. You can go to your office or to a hotel or anywhere you choose. We'll talk again tomorrow."

Jeffrey was annoyed at the way she suddenly seemed to have taken control of the situation. But he knew he could not afford the luxury of losing his temper with her. "If that's what you want," he said, "I'll leave this evening."

"Thank you," she answered, and she turned and left the room.

When she heard the door slam later that night, Jenny felt her backbone sag. She thought she must get to her bed. She wrote a brief note for Rebecca, who was having dinner with a friend: "Dear Rebecca, I'm feeling a little under the weather, so I've gone to bed early. Daddy is out of town. Sleep well. Love, Mom."

She threw herself across her bed, still dressed in her slacks and shirt, and fell asleep within minutes. When she opened her eyes again, the clock on the bedside table said four-thirty. Now her metabolism seemed to have done a complete about-face. Whereas before her nap she had felt she could sleep for a week, now she felt irrevocably awake—restless. It was as if she had taken one of those diet pills Jeffrey gave her whenever she wasn't looking as thin as he liked her to be.

Since sleep seemed to be out of the question, she took out her diary and began to write: "Mea culpa, mea culpa." She started to catalog the ways in which she had brought about her own downfall—but where to begin? She, Jenny Richman Ashland, had clearly been found out as a treacherous and disloyal wife. What other reason could there be for Jeff to leave her behind? The little bit of anger she had mustered against him, against his selfish and irresponsible behavior, gave way to waves of self-blame.

If . . . if . . . if. If she had been properly grateful for the fine husband she had, if she had followed Sally's gracious example and made him the center of her life, then perhaps Jeff would have found his life more satisfying. And he might not have dumped her. Yes, dumped, she repeated to herself. For no matter how he (or she) tried to dress the situation up with fine-sounding phrases, there was no disguising that fundamental truth. She had been found deficient and had therefore been relegated to a condition she had always found pitiable—the realm of failed wives. Fired. Put out to pasture. The humiliation of it was almost worse than the pain.

She put down her diary and walked softly into Rebecca's room. How was she going to tell that lovely child that her father was going to disappear, that it might be years before she saw him again? And how was she going to explain that she, her imperfect mother, was probably to blame?

Jenny shook her head, as if to shake the problem away, and walked into her kitchen. She looked at the room with fresh eyes, as if she were seeing someone else's home. It was a cheerful, well-equipped kitchen, with flowered wallpaper of yellow and orange zinnias and marigolds and poppies. The warm colors were picked up by the cabinet fronts of yellow and orange formica and complemented by her generous use of butcher blocks throughout the room. Here and there, she saw a touch of whimsy—the giant ceramic foot she made to hold her daily bunch of fresh flowers, the funny Falstaffian face that housed the rich assortment of spatulas and whisks and wooden spoons, and, over the breakfast counter, her "pop art" painting of a peanut butter and jelly sandwich.

It was really a very nice room. And yet—how often had she felt most trapped here. As if her kitchen were a prison that she had decorated and adorned so that she might somehow not notice—or forget for a while—the narrow confines of her life. Now, as she saw only the gleaming equipment, the warmth and comfort of this room, she wished with all her heart that she could turn the clock back. Five years . . . maybe ten . . . so that she might savor the time she spent here instead of resenting it. Perhaps if she had another chance, she could cook and fuss and plan her household chores with joy, instead of with ambivalence.

Too late, Jenny, she told herself. Too late, old girl. You had your chance and you messed it up. Now Jeffrey was starting a new life. He was adding a new, exciting facet to his already full career. She had no doubt that whenever he decided to add a new partner as well, he would have no trouble finding one. This new woman would be eager, agreeable, adoring—and no doubt young and very attractive.

And what about you? She asked herself that most fearsome question of all, the question that was so universally intimidating that it kept men and women everywhere wedded to relationships that were, if not satisfying, at least comfortingly familiar.

She turned on the light near the hall mirror and examined her face closely, scrutinizing the lines, the spray of gray that had begun to fan through her unruly auburn hair. She looked and was not comforted. One female Caucasian, well over thirty. Not a beauty. A strong chin, a straight nose with just the hint of an upward tilt, a generous mouth with too little experience of laughter. She shook her head, dissatisfied, pronouncing the verdict of undesirability. No man she found interesting would find her appealing.

What else did she have to offer this world? This highly competitive new world in which women were expected—no, required—to be more than ornamental, more than well bred and well mannered and well informed. This new world expected women to *do* something—and to do it well enough so that someone would pay for it with hard currency, and not just well-turned compliments. Bereft of a husband, what could she do to make her place in this kind of world?

With one part of her brain, she tried to make a list of her assets and accomplishments, to consider any skill or experience that might apply to paying work. With the other—that part of her that played the resident critic—she demolished every possibility, mocking herself for daring to imagine that the comfortable life she had lived as Mrs. Jeffrey Ashland might have given her any marketable skills. Hah! she kept saying to herself scornfully as she considered one thing and then another.

Yet the alternative was to coast along, doing nothing but looking after what was left of her family, and living on the family money that could cushion her from the harshest realities for the rest of her life. This possibility seemed more comfortable—yet just as frightening—than thinking about work.

No, Jenny, she told herself. You are much too old to while away any more of your life. Much too old, she repeated to her audience of one. You blamed a lot of your own frustrations on Jeffrey. Yes, you did. Don't deny it. And now you cannot afford any more inertia. Or else . . . or else, she finished the implied threat, you are going to wake up one morning and be old. Rebecca will be gone; she will have a life of her own. And you will be an old woman living on half-truths and unfulfilled promises and poisonous regrets.

All right. She would *do* something, she promised herself. She would just have to pull herself together and make a plan. Now she felt very tired again, and she gratefully sought the hours of sleep that freed her from the need to think.

The following morning she tried to send Rebecca off to school with a good breakfast and a healthy dose of normalcy. She knew she would have to talk to the child soon, but first she wanted to find some sort of answer to the question of "what next?" Something that she could use to anchor the life that she and her daughter would be sharing, alone, for an unknown number of years to come.

Over a second cup of coffee, she tried again to plan a life without Jeffrey. What did she have to start with? A fine arts degree. An appreciation of lovely things. Maybe even some talent to translate this appreciation into something through her hands. So what? her personal critic asked. So do thousands of other people. Why should you hope to make a living that way?

She had no ready answer. And still another question materialized: Why don't you ask Alicia for help? With her mother's connections, she might very well find a job. Wasn't that the way things were done? Assuming one was lucky enough to have connections?

Jenny considered this possibility for a moment, and then she banished it with a firm and resounding "no." She almost added "never," then conceded, with some bitterness, that "never" was getting to be as brief as "forever" these days.

Maybe she should go back to school. Get an advanced degree. Then she could teach. That prospect, while not exactly perfect, cheered her up a bit. At least it was a concrete option. She turned to the business of straightening up the house. Today she found the menial chores restful, soothing in their familiarity. And once again she began to feel a nostalgia for the job she had just lost—the job of full-time wife.

Under other circumstances, Jenny and Rebecca might have comforted each other. They might have fallen into each other's arms, touched each other, promised to be there, one for the other. But all Rebecca could think of as her mother spoke words like "separation" and "we both love you" and "we'll work this out''—all she could think of was that she was losing her father.

He was going away, her mother was saying—this handsome, glamorous man who had always dazzled her with his smiles, who had utterly beguiled her the first time he had held her close. And although it had been Jenny who had nurtured and fed and changed Rebecca, Jenny who had listened—often impatiently—to all her childhood complaints, it was Jeff who seemed now to matter most.

To her daughter, Jenny was a constant, to be taken for granted just as the good meals, the comfortable home, the vacations, and the nice clothes were taken for granted. And for the same reason: because they were always there. But her father, her busy, often preoccupied father—he was the icing on the cake, a rare and wonderful treat.

Now her mother was saying that he was leaving. Suddenly. Without warning. Rebecca had rarely even heard her parents quarrel. Nothing had prepared her for this disaster.

And in the absence of any such hints of trouble, Rebecca decided it must have been her mother's fault. She must not have been a good enough wife. Somehow she had made Daddy want to leave. What Rebecca did remember supported this notion. Like those arguments Mommy and Daddy did have. They had called them ''discussions,'' and they didn't raise their voices, but Daddy would say things about Mommy's ''attitude.'' Sometimes Jenny would laugh, and sometimes she would look serious. It was like school, when teachers told you that you had the wrong attitude. It meant that you were doing something wrong, that you had better shape up—or else. Daddy must have warned Mommy, and now the ''or else'' had happened.

Now Rebecca's safe little cocoon had been broken to pieces. Now she belonged to that group of kids whose parents were divorced. She remembered how once, in a moment of pseudosophistication, she had burst into her parents' bedroom to announce that ''Barbara's parents just split up,'' and then to add, dramatically, ''It seems that nobody's still married anymore.'' Now that it had happened to her, Rebecca found that it made no difference that everyone else's parents were divorced. All that mattered was that she felt really, really bad.

And in their separate pain, Rebecca and Jenny pulled away from each other.

• • •

As she had done in childhood, Jenny reached out to her sister. After Jeffrey took his things from the apartment, she telephoned Sally. "Can I come to see you—right away—please?"

"Of course, Jenny. Is something wrong?"

"Oh, God, yes. Everything's wrong." Jenny's voice cracked.

"Stay where you are. I'll come to you." Faced with an obvious crisis, Sally's organizational skills took over. Within fifteen minutes she was in her sister's kitchen, holding Jenny's hand, listening to her blurt out, in disjointed segments, the story of Jeffrey's departure. "Poor Jenny," she murmured at appropriate intervals. "What an awful thing for you to go through."

And when the recital was over, with Jenny crying softly, Sally held her, cradling her head against her breast and trying to soothe her with crooned "I'm sorry's."

Jenny looked up, eyes unfocused, twin rivulets of tears muddying her face. "Oh, Sally, it feels bad. And I don't know what to do now."

"Don't think about it, sweet. Just don't think about it," Sally said, adopting the tone and attitude appropriate to a death in the family. For as her sister talked, Sally felt that Jenny was in the throes of the worst possible catastrophe— short, perhaps, of a slow, painful death. "Come stay with Brad and me for a week or two. We have plenty of room. Let us look after you. We'll serve your favorite things, and you can just rest and get your strength back."

Jenny nodded, grateful that she could postpone making serious demands on herself, that for a little while she could get away from the familiar surroundings—surroundings which seemed haunted now by the memories of good times. Strange, she thought; now that it was over, her marriage seemed filled with good times, and the bad times seemed of much smaller consequence.

25

When Sally announced to Brad that her sister and her niece would be coming for a brief stay, he was not particularly agreeable. "For pity's sake, Sally, I told you about that important German client who's going to be here for the next two weeks. I told you that I wanted to give a couple of parties for him. I need your full attention, Sally. How can you give me that if your sister is hanging around here moping over her husband? That's really going to put a damper on things. And besides," he added peevishly, "if Jeff walked out on her, she probably brought it on herself."

Secretly, Sally thought that perhaps Brad was right, but loyalty to her sister prevented her from saying so. "Brad," she said reproachfully, "I've rarely imposed any member of my family on you. And I have always tried to be hospitable to anyone you brought here—whatever the circumstances."

This was, she knew, a masterpiece of understatement, for in recent years Brad's parents—those models of WASP family perfection—had somehow toppled from the lofty pedestal they had once occupied in her esteem. Bradford Jeffers, II, her illustrious father-in-law, had become more pompous, more overbearing—and somehow less aristocratic during the years of her marriage. As for Constance Jeffers—her pale, self-effacing mother-in-law—in recent years, Constance's afternoon sherries started at ten in the morning and continued until bedtime. And when Constance became blurred and occasionally weepy, her husband became sarcastic and abusive—all of which made their company more than a little burdensome. Sally was too much of a lady to attack her husband with the peccadilloes of his parents' behavior, but she did think Brad owed her some reciprocity—and now she told him so.

"My family rarely intrudes on us, Brad. I don't think they visit more than a few times a year, if you don't count our parties. And whatever you think of Jenny as a wife, she is my sister, and she is in trouble. I expect you to be gracious and

charming while she's here. And I'll see to it that the German
client is enchanted with Jeffers and Jeffers.''

"Why, Sally, if I didn't know better, I would think you
were blackmailing me.''

Brad's wife flashed blue eyes at him, tempering her small
show of strength with a rush of sweetness. "But darling, how
could you begin to think such a thing? You know I've always
been more than happy to help you with your career. And''
—now she dropped her voice, affecting a seductive throati-
ness—"as for my sister—well, I'll just throw myself on your
mercy.'' She got up and brushed his brow with the merest
whisper of a kiss, enveloping him with the familiar scent of
Bal à Versailles—the perfume she always wore because he
had once told her it was his favorite.

And since his wife had restored him to a role he loved to
play—that of reigning household monarch, dispensing favors
to his subjects—Brad thawed considerably. "All right, Sally.
We'll have your sister. And we'll see her through this mess
she's gotten herself into.''

"Oh, thank you, Brad. You really are wonderful.'' Sally
turned adoring eyes on Brad and squeezed his hand in
appreciation.

"I know, I know. But please. Don't let's make this the
beginning of some sort of tradition. Okay?''

"Of course not, darling. This is a unique emergency. We
just don't have divorces in our family.''

By the time Jenny and Rebecca arrived at the Jefferses'
apartment, each with a small suitcase (which reassured their
host that the visit would be one of manageable proportions),
Brad had been coaxed and cajoled into a most convivial state.

"Jenny, dear,'' he said, moving to greet his sister-in-law.
"And Rebecca,'' he added heartily, clasping the two to his
chest. "Please think of this as your house for as long as you
like. And if there's anything you need, don't hesitate to ask.''

"Thank you, Brad.'' Jenny managed a small smile. "It's
good of you to let us impose.''

"Impose! What nonsense. After all—what's a family for
but to lean on when things aren't going well? I just want you
to know that I'm offering two broad shoulders, whenever
either of you needs one.''

Sally noted that her sister seemed a bit embarrassed by
Brad's effusive welcome. "Come,'' she said, "let me get the

two of you settled in. If you're tired, I'll let Tina bring you dinner on a tray. Or, if you're up to it, we can all have dinner together.''

Jenny nodded and followed Sally into what had once been— many years ago—her own childhood room. Now Sally had made it into a warm and welcoming guest room, a room that had a slightly feminine flavor, with its fluffy white flokati rug, the paisley velvet pillows that adorned the stark-white linen bedspread, the floral still lifes that hung on the white walls. "Why don't you put your things away," Sally suggested. "I'll help Rebecca with her things, and then you and I can have a cup of tea."

"Oh yes, Sally, that would be just right."

Sally led Rebecca to a room that was just across the hall from the one which her mother occupied. This had once been Sally's room, and it had once housed a dazzling collection of dolls, which she had since donated to a local craft museum. The dolls had given way to a photo gallery of Sally's suitors, which now resided in a dark corner of her clothes closet. Now the room, tastefully decorated in thickest beige wool carpeting and furniture of finest hand-rubbed rosewood, was generally intended to house business guests. It offered the warmth of a home environment, as well as several amenities generally found in the newer hotels. The adjoining bath, for example, had been completely redone to include a small sauna and a Jacuzzi tub, set into a lushly carpeted platform.

"Here, Rebecca," Sally said. "I think you'll find plenty of drawer space for your things." She indicated a low rosewood chest. "And if you want Tina to press anything tomorrow, just leave it on your bed in the morning. Would you like to take a little nap before dinner? I can turn down your bed—"

"Aunt Sally, I'm twelve years old. And I haven't taken naps in *years*!"

Sally fought back a smile. "I'm really sorry, Rebecca. But you'll have to be patient with me. I don't have any children, so all I can try to do is remember way, way back to the olden days when your mother and I were young." She saw the hint of a smile on her niece's face. "Good. Now we're past feeling like 'company.' I want you to be comfortable here. Just do anything you like—don't feel you have to ask. You can watch television or maybe you'd like to look through the books—we have some here and quite a lot in Uncle Brad's

library. Your mother and I are going to have some tea. Just
tell Tina if you'd like some, too."

"Don't worry, Aunt Sally. I'll be fine. Really."

"I know you will. See you for dinner then."

Minutes later, Sally was pouring tea from a delicate Japanese pot that had belonged to her grandmother. "I don't know
why," she said, "but something warm is always supposed to
cure whatever ails you."

"I guess it's because warmth makes you think of love and
security and life. Cold seems to conjure up images of death
and loneliness. Maybe being abandoned, too. You know,
Sally, ever since Jeffrey and I had that talk, I keep getting the
feeling that I'll never feel really warm again. And it's not
even winter yet."

"What really happened between the two of you, Jen? You
can tell me to mind my own business. But I want to understand. Did you have some sort of argument?"

"No, Sally, we didn't have an argument."

"Well—what, then? He just said he was leaving? Just like
that?"

"Just like that."

"Do you think it was another woman?" Sally's voice
dropped to a funereal whisper.

Miserable though she felt, Jenny almost laughed. "No,
Sally, it wasn't another woman. Jeffrey simply decided he
wanted a new 'life-style'—I think that's what they call it
these days. And he also decided that Rebecca and I didn't fit
it."

Sally looked perplexed. "But I know Jeffrey loves you and
Rebecca. . . ."

"Yes," Jenny said slowly, "I think he does. In a way. But
he doesn't want to be tied to us anymore."

"Isn't there something you could do that might change his
mind?" Sally persisted, for she couldn't imagine letting a
catastrophe of this magnitude just happen. "Maybe if you
talked to Jeffrey, asked him how you could make him
happier. . . ."

Her words trailed off when Jenny sat bolt upright, as if
someone had jabbed her with a cattle prod. "You're saying
it's my fault that Jeff's gone. Because I haven't been the kind
of wife you've been."

"No, no, Jenny. That's not what I meant." Sally flushed
even as she denied it, because her sister had put into words

what she had more or less been thinking. "I just meant that maybe now—after he's had some time to think it all over—Jeff might be able to see more clearly what he's doing. Maybe if the two of you talked now, you might work something out."

Jenny shook her head vigorously. "You're missing the point completely, Sal. Jeff wasn't doing any threatening or accusing—or negotiating. He just calmly said it was over."

"I see," Sally said gravely, looking and sounding more funereal than ever. For although she heard every day about husbands taking flight or marriages breaking up, she blamed these unhappy statistics on the addled state of society, on the women's movement, on the "new morality"—in short, on a variety of factors that had nothing whatever to do with her life. But now her own sister had been rejected by her husband, had been weighed as a life partner and found wanting. Out loud she said, not really believing her own words, "Well, this is Jeffrey's loss. You still have a great deal to offer. I'm sure you'll find someone else. . . ."

"And I'll live happily ever after?" Sally looked so concerned, so earnest, that Jenny's sense of mischief surfaced. "And one day," she went on, warming to the game, "Jeffrey will come back—a broken man—begging to come home. During his absence, I will—miraculously—have become extremely beautiful and dazzlingly interesting. I will say to him, 'Why, Jeffrey dear—how good of you to look in on us. . . .' "

"Stop that, Jenny. You're making fun of me, and I just want to help you." To Sally, the loss of a husband was not an appropriate subject for humor.

"No, Sally, I'm not making fun of you. It's just my—situation. It's so common, it's almost a cliché. And even though I know that, it still feels new and terrible—because it's never happened to me."

"Well, it is terrible!"

"Not really. Here I am—a perfectly healthy woman, with a perfectly healthy child, and enough money to live comfortably. There are millions of women in this world facing real tragedies. You and I, Sal—we were born among the lucky. My problem is that I never knew what to do with my luck. And if I don't learn now, I'll be just as bad at divorce as I was at marriage."

Sally didn't understand what her sister was talking about, so she murmured something about checking dinner and left the room.

• • •

Although Sally had been a little apprehensive about the chemistry at her dinner table, the meal turned out to be a pleasant one. Brad rose to the occasion with some amusing anecdotes about his foreign clients, and even Jenny laughed. Rebecca allowed herself a smile when Brad persisted in describing one of his visits to a Japanese geisha house, in spite of Sally's admonition that there was a "child" present.

Not wanting to tempt fate by letting the meal drag on, Sally got up as soon as the coffee cups were empty. "I don't know about anyone else, but I am rather tired tonight. Jenny—if you're in the mood—I've put some milk bath in your bathroom. Yours, too, Rebecca, but be careful about turning on the Jacuzzi when you put that stuff in the water or you'll have bubbles right out to the front door."

"That sounds like fun, Aunt Sally. How come we never had good stuff like that at our house, Mommy?"

The question caught Jenny unaware. "I don't know, Rebecca. I guess we just never thought of it. I have an idea," she said, trying to share a positive experience with her daughter. "Why don't we sit down and think of all kinds of good stuff we never did. And maybe you and I can change that. Okay?"

Rebecca shot her mother a dark look, full of the suspicion that she was being bribed to overlook the fact that Jenny had alienated her adored father. She made no answer to her mother's question, merely excusing herself and going to her room.

"I guess I'll take advantage of your bubble bath," Jenny said, to fill the silence. "Then maybe I can get some sleep."

"Just call if you want anything."

"Thank you, Sally. I'm sure we'll be fine."

An hour later, Jenny stretched out full length in the oversize bathtub, feeling some of the tension in her neck and arms disappear into the warmth of the bubbly water. Here, in her childhood home, with Sally close by, Jenny felt just a little less abandoned than she had before. After she finished her soak, she found, in the floor-to-ceiling mirrored cabinet, some pristine white towels of luxurious thickness. She flicked on the heat lamp, taking her time toweling her body. Then she treated herself to a body rub with the scented creamy lotion that Sally had put out for her. As she slipped into the

floor-length challis gown she had brought, she had a brief
sensation of well-being. Although the moment passed quickly, she felt sufficiently fortified and relaxed to try to talk to
her daughter. She walked across the hall and tapped on the
door.

"Yes? Who is it?"

"It's me, Rebecca. Can I come in?"

"Okay." There was no enthusiasm or welcome in her
voice.

Jenny opened the door and began, apologetically. "I just
wanted to say good night . . . and maybe talk awhile."

Rebecca shifted a little in her bed, but she made no gesture
of encouragement. Jenny sat down on the bed, but she did not
touch her daughter. She had the distinct feeling that Rebecca
would pull away from her. "Honey—I know you feel miserable. Maybe worse than I do. But we have to try to . . . to
shelter each other. Otherwise . . . we'll both feel lonely now.
And maybe we won't be able to . . . to get together again if
we get too far apart now."

Jenny knew her daughter was listening; she sensed it in the
set of Rebecca's body. But Rebecca said nothing. Jenny
pressed on. "Becky," she said, using the childhood name
that her daughter had discarded the year before but which her
family still used out of habit, "maybe you need somebody to
blame for all this. Maybe it will make you feel better if
you're angry—because God knows this has nothing to do
with you. Blame me if you want to—but please don't pull
away. I know you love your father—but Becky, nobody made
him do what he did. So please, baby, don't hate me for his
failures, too. I don't think I could live through that. Becky?
Say something. . . ."

Silence. And then, just as Jenny was about to get up and
leave, her daughter spoke. "Oh, Mommy," she said, using
the tone she always used when Jenny wandered too far over
the generation gap, "I don't hate you. I just . . ."

"Thank you, Rebecca. Thank you for that." She patted her
daughter's hand, resisting the impulse to scoop her up and
smother her with hugs and kisses. "Good night, baby."

"Good night, Mommy."

The next day was chill and drizzly, and Sally decided to let
her sister sleep while she sent Becky off to school with a
hearty breakfast. While Jenny slept, Sally mulled over one of

her bachelor lists. Actually, it was not a list at all, but rather a prize collection of unattached men that Sally could assemble at any given party—a collection that was the envy of every other hostess in town.

Brad expected her to entertain that German client, and if she could manage to cheer her sister up with an attractive man or two at the same time, well, so much the better. She knew it was too soon for Jenny to notice anyone else—although you never could tell. Still, Sally's intuition told her the best way of handling Jenny was to treat her as if she had just fallen off a horse.

At that moment, Jenny was stirring from what had been a restful sleep, was being led very pleasantly into wakefulness by the aroma of freshly ground morning coffee. Not for the first time, Jenny noted how successful her sister had been at translating the phrase "gracious living" into every detail of her beautifully run home.

After a quick morning wash, she slipped into a terry cloth robe and joined Sally in her bedroom. "Morning, Sally."

"Well, hi. I thought you'd stay in bed awhile. Let Tina bring you a tray."

Jenny squeezed her sister's shoulders. "I'm not sick, Sally. I don't think a wrecked marriage improves with bed rest. Anyway, I did have a nice long sleep. And thank you for getting Rebecca off to school. I don't want you to let us interfere with your routine."

"Not to worry, dear," Sally said rather mechanically, for her attention had already shifted to the doodles on the yellow pad in front of her.

"What are you doing?"

"Oh—just putting together a small dinner for some of Brad's European clients." This was said with as much casualness as Sally could muster, for she wasn't at all sure how Jenny would feel about a major party.

"Mmm." Jenny wasn't going to say it, but the thought of facing a crowd of people, some of whom might ask about Jeff, created a moment of panic. Never mind, she told herself. She would not have to spoil Sally's plans. She could spend the evening at her own apartment, or she could say she wasn't feeling well and go to bed early. Sally was much too sensitive to push.

As it turned out, Jenny did not have to face Sally's guests at all, at least not on this occasion. Her rescue came from a totally unexpected source—her mother.

From her sun-warmed cocoon in California, rich in the reservoir of her husband's constant attentions, Alicia Reini reached out to her daughter as she never had in her younger days. After telling Paolo that she was "uneasy" about Jenny, she translated that uneasiness, Alicia-fashion, into a phone call to Sally. "I'm worried about your sister," she said, "and the last time I phoned her—yesterday, in fact—she wasn't home."

"She's here, Mother. I didn't like the way she was moping around that house. I didn't think it was good for her—or for Rebecca. The place felt like a funeral parlor. So I brought them here for a while—a change of scene."

"Good girl. When you told me about Jeff, I wanted to do something. But since she didn't call me, I thought I'd better mind my own business. Your sister's lucky to have you close by, Sally. You've always had a generous heart."

Sally flushed, not quite knowing how to respond to one of Alicia's rare compliments. But Alicia was already headed in another direction. "Listen, Sally, I have an idea or two. I think this is a critical time for Jenny, and maybe I can help—without being a nuisance. I'm going to fly to New York. Don't worry—I won't impose on you. But if you can both manage to put up with me for one evening, I want to have a long talk with your sister. And I want to see how she is for myself."

"Of course, Mother. Stay as long as you like."

"No. Just tomorrow. And then I'll go to the Pierre. We can't overwhelm Brad with too much family at once. He might think we're planning to make a habit of it."

26

Alicia's arrival seemed like an omen. Her decisive manner, which had often seemed preemptory when she was younger, was now softened by age. It was, in fact, reassuring in this time of crisis. Her arrival—if so tame a word could be used to describe the burst of raw energy that was Alicia—was like a challenge, a gauntlet hurled in the face of the fate that had ravaged her daughter's life.

Now that I'm here, her body language seemed to say, now I will take charge of making things better. And indeed, when she took Jenny into a bedroom for a long mother-daughter talk, her manner was that of a consulting physician, an expert with the power to diagnose and heal the knottiest of human problems.

"You're feeling really low, aren't you, baby?" She began warming the snifter of brandy she held in her long, tapering, and still very lovely hands.

"I can't seem to help it. I've been trying not to let the gloom leak out all over everyone else, but—"

"Never mind about everyone else. Look—I want you to feel free to tell me to mind my own business, which is essentially what I've spent my life doing. What I'm most concerned about now is that you don't spend too much time languishing. Playing Camille can be habit-forming, and you're much too young to spend your life looking pale and wan and sad. Yes, I know what you're thinking—I'm the original iron butterfly, who fell apart when her husband died. But at least let me share that experience with you. Let me give you what I learned.

"I do know how you're feeling now. When your father died, I knew that somewhere outside myself there were reasons to live—I knew there were children and friends and sunshine and good food and places to see. My mind knew there were reasons why I should go on with my life. But I felt numb and completely isolated from all these things. My feelings kept saying: 'Forget it, life wasn't that wonderful before, and now—now it will never be any good.' "

"Yes, I remember. We all wondered if you would ever be yourself again," Jenny said.

"Well at least you wondered. I was sure I would never be myself. But Jenny—and please don't take this as a sign of disrespect for your father—I found that in the larger scheme of things, men are replaceable—husbands, lovers, whatever. It's rarely a once-in-a-lifetime proposition with a man. Other things, things that have to do with you, yourself—they're not so replaceable. And these are really the things that make a solid base for you, a place where you can anchor your life. I know you won't believe me, but you're going to come out of this much stronger, much wiser and—one day—much happier than you have been.''

"Oh, Alicia.'' A heavy sigh signaled Jenny's irritation at Alicia's uncharacteristic mother-hen posture.

"Just hear me out, and then I promise I'll keep my mouth shut if you don't want to talk. I know this is harder for you in some ways than it was for me. At least for me, it was death that ended my marriage. For all my failures, Charles never walked away, never told me that our life together was something he wanted to put behind him.'' She paused as she saw Jenny wince. "But the point is, you didn't deserve that. I know you didn't. You're more like me than you'd care to admit. You're strong and you're independent in spirit and you're curious and questioning—which doesn't make for the easiest of lives. But you were a much better wife and mother than I ever was. Which only proves that whether a man stays or leaves has more to do with him than with what you do. I don't want to say anything against Jeff, but I can assure you that this is his loss.''

"Oh, Alicia.'' Now Jenny allowed herself a smile. "You sound like a doting parent. And it seems like such a funny role for you.''

"Doesn't it though? You know better than I what kind of mother I was. I don't want to get all maudlin now. And I wouldn't insult your intelligence by trying to buy back moments that are gone—especially not with apologies or cheap regrets. I'm just saying what I'm saying now so that you'll know that people generally do what they want to do—not in any absolute sense, perhaps, but they do make the choices that seem best for them at the time. There's very little genuine sacrifice in this world. If someone gives up something, it's really because he gambles it against another kind of gain. And if that doesn't work out, he feels miserably cheated. When I was a young woman, I was self-centered and immature enough to want all my gains at once. You saw that, but you didn't really understand it, so you chose to live another way. Neither one of us was very happy. You weren't really happy with Jeffrey, were you?''

"I thought we had a good marriage.'' This sounded defensive, even to Jenny's ears.

"I'm not trying to pry, baby. I just want something good to come out of this—for you.''

Jenny tried to laugh, but the sound she made was harsh and

unpleasant. "Really, Alicia, I never would have expected to hear about silver linings from you."

"Stop that," Alicia commanded. "It's not your style to be brittle, and I'm not going to let you get away with it. This is your life, not a cocktail-party conversation."

Jenny made no reply.

"I've suspected for a long time that you weren't happy with yourself as Jeffrey's wife. Now you can accept whatever it is you want to be. You can make yourself over—and take the pleasures and the penalties of your own choices. All right," she added brusquely, "now we begin with this very minute. It doesn't feel good now. So how do we make it better for my Jenny?"

Alicia's tone suddenly made Jenny feel a small bit of warmth, the first she had experienced since Jeffrey had left. She smiled at her mother. "I don't know. In fact, if I was certain there was an answer to that question, I wouldn't be so scared."

"Know it, then. I tell you there is. I agree with Sally that maybe you should get away from home for a while, but I'm not sure this is the place for you."

"Why not? Sally has been just wonderful. . . ."

"I'm sure. It's Sally's nature to be wonderful. But I just wonder, right now, in the state of mind you're in . . . I wonder if you might find the atmosphere of Sally's marriage . . . a little too much."

Jenny looked even more puzzled. "Really, Alicia. You're the one who's 'too much.' You sound like a fortune-teller."

"No, baby. I just know my girls a little better than they've ever given me credit for. Sally's chosen one way to live. It's not a way I would have chosen, and I don't think you could have managed it. For Sally, it seems to have worked. I worry about her, sometimes. . . ." Her voice trailed off, then became stronger. "Right now, it's you I'm most concerned about. You're down and you're vulnerable. I don't want you looking back and obsessing about 'what if I had done this or that.' And I'm afraid Sally's little jewel-box home and marriage might make you do that. And lead you to some very wrong conclusions about yourself."

"What do you mean by that?"

"I mean that right now the healthiest thing for you and Rebecca to do is to feel a little bit angry with Jeffrey. Not hate or bitterness, mind you, but a little healthy anger. No guilt or self-recrimination about what you did or didn't do to keep him happy.''

"You don't understand, Alicia. There were . . . things."

"I'm sure. In every marriage there are 'things.' But I know you made a warm and comfortable home for Jeff. Not *Town and Country* like Sally's—but certainly *House and Garden*. When he married you, Jeff found himself a very pleasant situation. Now he's decided he wants something else. All right. I suppose that is his prerogative. But you have every right to feel—at the very least—annoyed with him. After all, your marriage was a kind of agreement. Now one partner says 'cancel'—just like that. Fine. But instead of beating your breast and wondering how you might have made a cushier nest for the man, you might just throw a good old-fashioned temper tantrum. And take a leaf from Jeff's book for the future.''

"How?"

"Jeff created a whole life for himself while he was married to you, a life that is pretty much intact now, that he can take with him wherever he goes. Oh, I'm sure he'll miss you and Rebecca. But after this China thing, he has a life that is fairly full without you. If you can learn from that, then I don't want you to start this new life of yours thinking the answer is to give more of what you don't want to give. There's no real generosity in that. When you start another relationship, I don't want you to begin by thinking of accommodations.''

"Another relationship? Now you're sounding like Sally."

"No, no, Jenny. I don't mean now. In fact, I think that would be a tragic mistake. What you have to do now—can you stand to hear me lecture anymore? I promise not to do it again until the next family crisis.''

"Oh, Alicia, who can stop you when you really want to do something? Lecture away.''

"Well, I know this is going to sound strange coming from me, but you must remember that this is a crisis time for Rebecca, too. Nobody knows better than I do how quickly children slip away from you when you fail them. No, don't say anything. Just take the time now to help your daughter— before you think about anything else. Then, no matter what else happens, the two of you will be a family.''

"I don't know if that's going to be so easy, Alicia. I think she blames me for what's happened. It hasn't been very comfortable to talk, so I've just let her alone.''

"No! That's absolutely what you must not do. If you leave Rebecca to her own thoughts, she'll form all sorts of conclusions—about you, about marriage, and about life in general. And chances are they'll all be off the mark, because they'll come out of her confusion and pain. You'll have an uphill fight trying to change her mind once it's set. *Now,* Jenny, you have to do it now. I think the two of you have to get away together, spend some time alone, someplace warm and very pleasant—someplace healing."

"That sounds nice, Alicia. But I'm just not sure about Rebecca."

"Leave my granddaughter to me. Your daughter may have you intimidated, but I think she'll listen to me. I'll talk to her tomorrow. Then the two of you can spend a couple of weeks in the sun."

To her surprise, Jenny found that she did not resent her mother's offer to intercede with Rebecca, that she was, in fact, relieved. "Thank you, Alicia. I'd appreciate whatever you can do."

And Alicia, for all her customary poise, found that she was unexpectedly moved by this moment with her younger child. "Well, then," she said briskly, "I'll see to it tomorrow."

Then, almost as an afterthought, Jenny asked, "How have you been, Alicia—you and Paolo?"

Her mother's face relaxed, her features softened, and she looked suddenly younger. "We're fine, Jenny. I've never been happier. . . ." Then she stopped herself. "I'm sorry—that was stupid of me."

"No—tell me—I really want to know. Is it all moonlight and roses all the time?"

Alicia hesitated, not sure if her daughter was being sarcastic or just defensively flippant. "There's enough of that for me—but, no, there's more. We argue—quite often. Paolo's even more stubborn than I am." She laughed. "I'm not an easy person to live with—I'm sure I don't have to remind you of that—but Paolo doesn't seem to mind. He loves me anyway," she said softly, as if she were describing a miracle. "We love each other, and no matter what happens between us, that doesn't seem to change. It's what I wish for you, Jenny."

Jenny never knew exactly what it was that Alicia said to Rebecca, but the resulting change was remarkable. True to her word, Alicia had buttonholed her granddaughter as soon as she came home from school. And when they had finished talking, Rebecca marched into her mother's room and announced, "Okay, I'll try not to give you a hard time."

Jenny looked up from the book she had been reading. Caught unprepared, she started to deny that her daughter had indeed been giving her "a hard time." Then she thought better of it and said simply, "Thank you. I appreciate that."

"And I think it's nice that you want to go away with me, just the two of us. Nana says Acapulco is great this time of year. Do we have to wait till vacation?"

"Hold on, hold on a minute. Where did Acapulco come from? I haven't even started to make arrangements, but if that's what you want. . . ."

Rebecca smiled, the triumphant smile of a conspirator. "Nana says it's all settled. We're staying at her friend's house. She says the beach is heavenly, and we can sail and snorkel, and we can stay as long as we like. Isn't that super? I can get a tan now—hardly anyone in school has a tan."

"Yes, Becky, it's super," Jenny agreed, grateful for the enthusiasm in her daughter's voice.

Later, after they decided to return home and to pack at once for their sudden trip, Jenny asked her mother, "Whatever did you say to Rebecca? She's like a little lamb."

Pleased by her first successful performance as family matriarch, Alicia said, "That's our secret, my granddaughter's and mine. But I will tell you this—you must talk to Rebecca. When you think you're protecting her, you're really closing her off. Make her a partner in this life you're going to start together. She's old enough, and she's much wiser than you think. She can help you in ways you probably haven't imagined. She's one of us, Jenny, but much nicer."

"I never really thought about her in that way, you know. We've talked, but it's always been about details, not about the insides of things."

"Well, start doing it. She loves you, Jenny—that child of yours loves you. I'll tell you quite frankly, I don't think she's always liked you—and you should understand how that can happen—but I think there's time to change. Use it, baby, use the time before it works against you."

"I will, Alicia, I'll try." And suddenly Jenny felt a little better, enough to acknowledge that she might feel good one day. "Thank you for everything you've done. You really have helped—a lot. And Rebecca tells me you've actually arranged our vacation for us. When did this happen?''

"Well," Alicia began, half apologetically, after our talk last night, I called some of my friends who have beach houses. It turned out that one couple—the Hallorans—weren't planning to use their place in Acapulco for the next month or so. I didn't mean to take charge, Jenny. I just know that when you've been shaken up the way you have, it's hard to get going again. I wanted you and Becky to have something nice as quickly and easily as possible.''

"Don't apologize. I appreciate what you've done. Before you came I was feeling numb and depressed and rather lost. Now at least I feel as if I might find a direction again. I'm grateful, Alicia, I really am. You know, it's the first time in a long time that I've felt a sense of family unconnected with Jeff.''

"That makes me happy, Jenny. Thank you.''

Jenny and Jeff sat together, one on either side of the butcher-block counter that doubled as work space and breakfast nook. In the week he had been gone, he had phoned a few times, inquiring about her health, her welfare, and Becky's state of mind. Her responses had been perfunctory. Talking to him was extremely painful, an intrusion into her private grief. Her marriage was dead, yet the sound of his voice was a reminder that he was still very much there.

In the short time they had been separated he had somehow become unfamiliar, the planes of his face unremembered. Like a wounded animal, she had retreated from the source of her pain, and now she had to force herself to concentrate on the words that were coming from his mouth, words that had a strange, distant quality—like a bad connection on a transatlantic call.

"'. . . and I wish you had told me you were going to Sally's. I was frantic with worry when I couldn't reach you or Becky. I thought something had happened to one of you. That's when I called Sally. . . .''

Jenny made no reply.

"I want to be fair with you, Jen. I know you and Becky won't really want for anything, regardless of what I do, but still. . . . Have you given any thought to what you would want me to provide?''

"No," she said. "It doesn't matter." Money had been the last thing on her mind.

"Well, then," he said, relief obvious in his voice and expression, "why don't you look over this agreement my lawyer drew up? I've tried to be reasonable—you know my income won't be very high while I'm involved in this China project, and later, I don't really know . . ."

"I'm sure it will be fine, Jeff. Leave the papers here. I'll have Alicia's lawyer look them over."

"If that's what you want . . . and if you decide to go ahead with the divorce . . ."

"I have, Jeff. I don't see any point in staying married."

"I've told my lawyer to stay in touch with you, to facilitate whatever legal action you decide to take."

"Thank you. That's very thoughtful."

He scanned her face to see if she was being sarcastic. He decided she was not, and moved on to the next subject on his mind. "I'd like to spend a little time with Becky before I leave. Maybe I can make this a little easier on her. On both of you."

"You can talk to her when she comes home from school."

"How is she taking it?"

"How do you think?"

"No need to be bitter, Jen. I didn't mean to hurt her. Or you. I've tried to explain to you—"

"I know, Jeff, I know. It's just one of those things."

He flushed red, but held his tongue. "I can understand your hostility," he said slowly in his doctor-voice. "I suppose it's normal under the circumstances. I can wait for Becky outside, if you like."

"You don't have to do that. I have some errands to run. Wait here. But if you want to spend time with Becky, you'll have to do it soon. We're going away for a vacation next week."

"Next week! But I'm only going to be around for a couple of weeks myself."

"I'm sorry, Jeff. Alicia has arranged for us to get away for a while. We both need to be away from here. From this apartment."

Jeff started to protest, then thought better of it. "Then I'd better make the best of the time we have. I don't want her to forget me."

Jenny smiled, and told him she would be back later, after he had had time to talk to Rebecca.

Later, when she came home, she studied Becky's pinched face, noticed the tight mouth—and wondered what her daughter and her husband had talked about. Gently she asked Rebecca if she wanted to talk, but her only response was to shake her head and retreat to her room. There would be time, Jenny thought, when the two of them were alone. There would be time to talk, to ease the sadness and hurt, time to salvage their family in spite of Jeff's defection.

27

The holiday began as soon as Jenny arranged the matter of Rebecca's absence from school. This was not nearly as difficult as it might have been when Jenny was a girl. The faculty and administrators at the Porter Day School saw themselves as overseers and friends of their pupils. In this capacity, they saw their pupils through divorces, deaths, separation crises, learning disabilities, and the like. When Jenny explained to the headmistress that she and Rebecca's father would be divorcing soon, that Rebecca was having a difficult period of adjustment, and that a short holiday might be in order, she found a sympathetic ear. The headmistress clucked her agreement and arranged for a list of homework assignments to be drawn up for Rebecca—in the event she felt up to any schoolwork while she was away.

Next came the business of packing. Both Rebecca and her mother agreed this would be a time for "casual" living. As they folded jeans and T-shirts, Jenny watched the flush of excitement rise in her daughter's cheeks—and she felt an answering response in herself.

"Listen, love," she said, "I've just had an idea. We have tonight to pack. Why don't the two of us start this vacation in style? Let's splurge and have a facial and manicure. And maybe a new dress—just in case we decide to 'do' Acapulco some evening."

Rebecca looked at her mother. This seemed to be a different mom from the one she had always known—the woman who had nurtured and bathed and fussed over her, the woman who had provided most creature comforts—but little or no fun. Rebecca responded at once to this new note in her mother's behavior, thinking with just the smallest twinge of disloyalty that maybe things wouldn't be so bad at home after all.

The surprises continued, on both sides, as Jenny and her daughter yielded up their chilled winter selves to the healing warmth of the Mexican sun and the sybaritic pleasures of their holiday.

The Halloranses' "cottage," as they called it, was a sprawling two-story villa that seemed to grow naturally out of the rolling hills overlooking Acapulco Bay. Inside, the atmosphere was spare, uncluttered, with white walls and cool marble floors, louvered shutters, a cluster of seashells here and there. Yet throughout the house there was a sense of life, a profusion of it, in the tropical plants, and outside, in the birds, the thousands of humming, chirping creatures that made the air pulsate day and night.

At the heart of this tropical kingdom was the Halloranses' majordomo, a tall, slender Mexican of indeterminate years. "Good afternoon, madame," he greeted Jenny upon her arrival, his formal manner a touch incongruous with the lilting rhythm that marked his speech. "My name is Raoul, and I will be looking after you. I will discuss menus with you each morning, after breakfast. If there is anything special you wish, please do not hesitate to tell me. The laundress comes on Wednesday, and the automobile will be back from the mechanic tomorrow. I stay in the cottage at the end of the road." He indicated a small house at the far end of the property.

Rebecca was dazzled by Raoul's manners, but to Jenny, whose recent experience with "staff" had consisted of thrice-weekly encounters with a taciturn cleaning woman, the prospect of all this attention was a little unsettling.

"Perhaps you might care for a bath and a nap to refresh yourselves," Raoul suggested. "Dinner will be at eight-thirty this evening. If you wish to change the hour, I can serve it whenever you wish in the future."

After Raoul withdrew, Rebecca and Jenny laughed with delight. "I think this is going to be fun," Rebecca said.

"Isn't it, though," Jenny concurred. "But I keep getting the feeling that someone's going to jump out of the woodwork and start shouting, 'Miz Scarlett, Miz Scarlett . . .' "

"Oh, Mommy," Rebecca said, affecting a patronizing air, "you just don't know how to appreciate gracious living."

She sounds like Jeffrey, Jenny thought, but she smiled at her daughter and said, "Well, I'll certainly put my shoulder to the wheel and try to learn. Shall we sample that gorgeous white beach—or do you need a nap?"

Rebecca did not hesitate a moment: "Beach."

Ten minutes and a change of clothing later, mother and daughter were strolling hand in hand, scuffling the sand through their toes. They walked silently for a time, then flopped down on the straw beach mats they had brought.

Jenny hesitated a moment before bringing up a subject that had been taboo since Jeffrey had left. "Your father," she said, "would approve of this place. The beauty of nature in a well-ordered setting, everything lovely and manageable and under control."

Rebecca shot her mother a quizzical look. "Is that why you and Daddy are getting a divorce? Because you have different ideas?"

Not knowing what to say, but not wanting to let the moment go by, Jenny spoke slowly, "Well, maybe that's true right now—on the face of it. But I don't want you to think that a marriage has to break up because people have different ideas or values. I think it happens because there are a lot of complicated things that push people apart, just like there are a lot of things that cause them to get married in the first place. Does that make any sense?"

"Sort of. But it still doesn't tell me about you and Daddy."

"All I'm trying to say is that people change, and sometimes that's a good thing. But sometimes the changes turn two people away from each other. And when that happens, well, it's hard for them to stay married."

"But you didn't change, did you? It was Daddy who wanted to leave, wasn't it?"

Put so baldly, Rebecca's question made Jenny ask it seriously of herself. There was a long pause before she spoke. "I think that what I did was what so many girls did in my day. I think I saw marriage as a destination, a place that people searched for. I didn't see it as a dynamic thing, with possibilities for changing and growing. I just thought about getting there and being a good wife. And I'm afraid I didn't really have any clear ideas about that either. In fact, the only thing I was sure of was that I didn't want to be the kind of wife and mother Alicia was.''

''Really?'' Rebecca's eyes widened. She had always thought of her grandmother as a kind of dowager queen of the family. She knew that Alicia and her daughters sometimes disagreed, but she had never heard such a sweeping criticism of Nana as this.

Jenny smiled at her daughter's expression. ''Really. Your nana was an unusual sort of wife and mother for her day. She didn't believe in spending her life looking after a husband and children. She did what she wanted, and we—your Aunt Sally and I—we felt that Nana failed us all. So we both promised ourselves we would do better.'' She laughed, a short, quick laugh ever so lightly tinged with bitterness. ''Well, so much for the arrogance of youth. At least my parents' marriage didn't break up.''

Rebecca reached out and squeezed her mother's hand. The gesture warmed Jenny, and she went on, ''I know I must have seemed like a dragon sometimes. But I found that being the kind of mother I had wished for wasn't so easy. While I was trying to do all the 'right' things, part of me was hungry for the kind of freedom Alicia had taken for herself.''

''But what was so wrong with that, Mommy? That doesn't sound so impossible.''

''I don't know, Rebecca. I didn't know how to do it. Within the kind of marriage your father and I had, it just didn't seem possible.'' She sighed, remembering the unease she had lived with for so many years. ''I know that didn't make me a very pleasant person. . . .''

''I wish I had known, Mommy. Maybe—''

''Never mind, Becky, now we have a chance to start all over.''

For a time they sat without talking, staring into the ripples the afternoon breeze cut into the water. And when they got up to make the trip back up the hill, Jenny felt calm, almost serene.

She felt even better when she reached the house and stepped under a tepid shower, feeling the water sluice the powdery sand from her body. She toweled herself with a luxurious thickness of terry cloth which had hung from a wicker curli-cue set into the bright native tiles that covered the walls.

Dressed in one of the new caftans she had bought for the trip, she padded, barefoot, into the living room. Becky was already stretched out, eyes closed, across one of the bamboo lounges lining the glass wall overlooking the bay. "You look comfortable," Jenny observed.

"Mmm . . ." the girl murmured contentedly, wiggling her bare toes for emphasis.

"Look at this." Jenny laughed with delight, pointing to the "cocktail hour" apparatus that Raoul had apparently laid out for them while they bathed. There was a silver ice bucket, filled to the top and crowned with ornate tongs, a selection of drinks and glasses, several small bowls holding twists of lemon and lime and olives, along with a bowlful of salted nuts. "Would Madame like a drink?" she said, bowing from the waist in the direction of her daughter's reclining form.

"Madame would like a very dry martini," Rebecca parodied back. "Stirred, not shaken."

Jenny paused, pretending to ponder. "Would Madame settle for a Shirley Temple or a club soda?"

Drinks in hand, they sat together, inhaling deeply the aromas that wafted in from the kitchen, enjoying the view that stretched out beyond the glass expanse of the house's back walls. They looked at the sandy beach dappled in fading sun hues of copper and gold that turned rose gold and finally violet. And they savored the moments of quiet that were filled with something better than conversation.

Dinner that evening was a portent of wonderful things to come. Raoul proceeded to drown their senses with an assortment of local shellfish sautéed in delicate sauces hinting of wine and herbs. Dessert was a key lime pie the likes of which Jenny had never tasted before.

Full and content, skin still warm from the sun, Jenny and Rebecca returned to the living room, which seemed even quieter now that darkness had taken over the hillside, with only the pulsing insect sounds to break the stillness. Jenny walked over to the record racks that bordered the stereo system, and after a casual survey of their contents, picked out albums of several Broadway musicals. Rebecca got up, too, and started to look through the various cabinets and storage systems. Suddenly the house seemed like a kindergarten, filled with toys that were new to both of them.

"Look, Mommy." Rebecca called her mother to inspect the contents of a teakwood cabinet she had opened. Inside, there was a treasure trove of games. Rebecca pulled out a Scrabble set. "Do you want to play, Mommy? Oh, do—let's play tonight!"

It was the kind of request that Jenny—the old Jenny, preoccupied, unfocused, and vaguely harassed—might automatically have said no to. But already Jenny was beginning to curb her automatic responses, to hear instead each question as it was asked. And so they played at a leisurely pace through *My Fair Lady,* then alternately accelerated and slowed down as the tempo of *A Chorus Line* rose and fell.

At one point the two of them started to yawn. Jenny said, "Okay, kid, I'm ready to concede the game if we can go to sleep. I can't keep my eyes open. What time is it anyway?"

They both laughed when they saw it was not quite ten o'clock. "Way past your bedtime, Mommy," Rebecca teased. "You must be getting old."

"Fresh kid—it's the time difference. And maybe I am getting a little old."

They started to walk toward the small foyer that separated the two bedroom wings of the house. Just as they were about to go into their respective rooms, Rebecca asked, "Mommy, can I sleep with you tonight?"

Jenny did not show her surprise at such a question—though it had not been asked for years. She merely said, "Sure, I think that would be cozy." And it was, just the two of them snuggled together in the big rattan bed, pulling up crisp cotton sheets just for the pleasure of feeling the freshly ironed fabric against their bodies.

Although she was too tired and too comfortable to write in her diary, Jenny closed her eyes, a contented smile on her lips, and mentally penned the lines: "This has been a good day. I think Rebecca and I will be fine."

In this serene environment, away from the routine that had once demanded so much and offered so little for Jenny, mother and daughter simply drifted, their days like clean calendar pages, waiting to be filled with whatever came to mind. This reinforced the sense of newness they had about themselves and their relationship. It was a feeling that had seemed frightening when Jeff left, but which now held out a promise of something lovely, something Jenny and Rebecca had not known before.

If they had a routine at all, it began each day by their sleeping luxuriously late, then feasting on one of Raoul's imperial breakfasts—a cornucopia of fruits, hot rolls or muffins, and eggs—cooked in all the hard ways that were usually reserved for Sunday morning—served with paper-thin slices of lightly grilled ham—all beautifully presented on fine china platters, in whimsical baskets of wicker, and always accompanied by fresh, crisp linen.

After giving Raoul their preferences for lunch and dinner, they would run down to the beach for a morning of swimming, snorkeling, or perhaps a little sailing on one of the catamarans that dotted the bay front.

Occasionally, Jenny and Rebecca joined Raoul when he made his marketing forays into the "centro," the old part of town, enjoying vicariously the houseman's determined quest for the best that the vendors of fruits and vegetables and fish and meat had to offer.

But when Raoul offered them the opportunity to go sightseeing or visit the city's night spots, they declined with thanks. They found that they preferred the quiet times, the luxury of solitude, the days of pampered idleness, the evenings spent listening to the extensive music collection, sampling the books from the varied library, playing cards or Monopoly or Scrabble. And, inevitably, the early bedtimes, brought on by the surfeit of sun and sea.

"We're living like hermits. Do you realize that?" Jenny asked one evening, after Raoul had served yet another of his culinary triumphs and retired to his own house.

"I know. It's fun."

"Isn't it, though? I never knew it could be so much fun, being a mother. I feel we've both missed so much because I never knew that."

"Oh, Mommy." Jenny knew this was her daughter's signal for her to cut the "mushy" talk.

"Okay. But anyway, I think we're driving Raoul crazy. The other day he was telling me how all the Halloranses' other guests enjoy doing this or that. I think he's never had anyone who just stayed at home. I think he's worried that we're not having a good time."

"Well, maybe we should do *something*. I guess it would be fun to tell the kids at school. . . ."

"Okay. Tomorrow we'll ask him to run down the list of possibilities, and we'll definitely have an excursion of some kind."

They eventually decided on a day spent on one of the boats available for charter. The houseman made all the arrangements, even to supplying them with a well-worn hamper packed with fried chicken, juicy red tomatoes, crisp cucumbers, and a bottle of white Mexican wine, which the boat's captain stowed away in the galley refrigerator.

The "captain" turned out to be a picture-book English expatriate, a character from a Maugham novel—watery blue eyes squinting out from under sun-bleached hair, skin heavily lined and burnished copper from the sun. He wore a pair of old army shorts and a shirt of khaki.

His "crew" consisted of a teenage Mexican boy who giggled and fluttered like a Victorian maiden whenever the captain addressed any remark or gesture in his direction.

Rebecca shot her mother a silent question with the arch of her eyebrows, and Jenny answered with a smile and a shrug. Soon there was more to occupy their interest than the captain's domestic arrangements as they pulled away from the shore and began their rhythmic circuit of the shoreline and beaches.

When the noonday sun reminded them that they were hungry, the captain pulled the boat into a small natural cove along a secluded stretch of beach on a nearby island. "It's very pretty here, ladies. It's a pleasant place to take a swim or look for shells."

"Thank you, Captain," Jenny answered. "It looks lovely."

The captain and the boy skittered off on their own, laughing and joking. Jenny and Rebecca spread a blanket in the shade and unpacked the lunch Raoul had given them. It seemed like a feast, and they both ate heartily.

"Oh, Mommy," Rebecca exclaimed, waving her arms to take in the beach, the blue waters, the clear sky, and the remnants of lunch. "How come we never did this before?"

Jenny opened her mouth—and realized she had no easy answer. "I don't know, love. I just never thought of this" —she imitated the sweep of her daughter's arms—"as part of mothering. Actually"—she paused, bringing to the surface an idea that had been taking shape—"I suppose that when your Aunt Sally and I were growing up, we always thought of our father as the parent we had fun with."

Rebecca thought for a moment, then a look of comprehension flicked over her face. "Just like at our house," she said triumphantly, as though making an important discovery.

Jenny winced at the truth of what was said. "Yes, love, just like at our house. But we'll try to do better now."

Rebecca changed the subject. "Were you ever sorry that you married Daddy and had me? Did you ever wish you'd done something else? Something more fun?"

This was a question that Jenny had asked herself from time to time, and so she had a ready answer. "No, love, I don't think I can be sorry I married your father. And I've never been sorry I had you. I hope I never made you feel that way. It's just that when I was a girl, getting married seemed necessary. The girl who didn't get married was something of an oddball—and I know I didn't have that kind of originality. Anyway, I feel very lucky now. I have a beautiful daughter— and maybe some other things are possible."

Rebecca considered her mother's words. "You know what your problem was, Mommy?"

"No—what was my problem?" Jenny tried to hide the smile that was forming.

"You didn't know what you wanted to be when you grew up. I think I'm going to make up my mind about that before I get married."

Once again Jenny stifled a smile. "I think you're very wise, Rebecca. Much wiser than I was at your age."

After lunch, they walked together, picking up shells and marveling at the quiet of the beach. And suddenly it came to Jenny that she did not miss Jeff, that she had not missed him for some time, that she did not have the feeling that something vital had been lost and that she had been left something less than whole. In fact, she felt more whole than she had for a long time.

Although the days were unstructured, they passed quickly. When it was time for Rebecca to return to school, Jenny felt she was not quite ready to leave the womblike comfort and security of the Halloran cottage for the practical realities of separation and divorce.

"Sweetheart," she asked her daughter, "would you mind if I stayed here for a little while longer, just to collect myself? Nana's still in New York, and I'm sure she'd love to stay with you. If it's all right with you . . . ?"

"Sure, Mommy. I don't mind. I think it will be fun to have Nana at home."

Yet after the arrangements had been made, after Jenny drove back to the cottage from seeing her daughter off, somehow the villa did not seem as warm and inviting as it had before. She put on her bathing suit and went down to the beach, but after a few minutes on the sand she felt restless. She shook her head. It had been a mistake to stay on without Rebecca. The days of closeness and first-time intimacy she had shared with her daughter now made her feel lonely instead of peaceful. She thought perhaps she would give up her idea of a private vacation after all.

Raoul looked up in surprise when Jenny returned so quickly to the house. "Do you need something, Mrs. Ashland?"

"No—yes, actually. Is there someplace nearby to go shopping—or just walk around? I just don't feel like staying around here, today."

"Yes, indeed, there are many new shops, very close by, near the big hotels. Shall I take you in the car?"

"No—no, I don't want to interrupt your day. Perhaps you can call a taxi for me? I'll be able to find another when I'm ready to come back, won't I?"

"Sure, Mrs. Ashland. No problem. What time do you want dinner tonight?"

"Oh, I don't know. Depends on how much time I spend walking around. Why don't you just leave me a salad. And maybe something for a sandwich."

The hubbub and confusion of the downtown streets were a perfect foil for Jenny's mood. Two cruise ships were in the harbor, and most of their passengers were ranging through the city's shops, searching for bargains in straw and silver and leather. Jenny allowed herself to be carried along by other tourists. It was a pleasant sensation requiring no decision-making process, no serious expenditure of energy.

She went along in this fashion until her eye was caught by an unusual silver necklace in a shop window. She stopped and admired it more closely, then decided to walk into the shop.

She felt the refreshing surge of artificially cooled air and found the light dim after the bright sunlight. As her eyes became accustomed to the change, she saw that the shop was filled with pieces executed in the style she had admired—

modern, yet with a strong hint of the classical lines found in the museum jewelry of Mexico. She paused in front of one showcase, admiring the earrings and bracelets it held.

"They are lovely, are they not, madame?"

She looked up, startled by the velvety baritone and by the accent—which, she determined, was Greek rather than Mexican. Her glance found a pair of soft brown eyes that held hers a moment or two longer than mere commerce might dictate. "Yes," she answered, "yes, this jewelry is very striking— not like the things I've seen in the other shops. Did you make it?" She studied the man's face—the deep tan over what must have once been fair skin, the curly blond hair, the long straight nose, the wide, generous mouth.

"Alas, no. These are made by two local craftsmen. The ideas are mine, but I have not the talent to execute them— only to appreciate them."

"Well, I suppose that is at least an equal talent—to design and to appreciate. I mean, some people can look at beauty and not appreciate it at all."

"You're very kind." Again his glance lingered in apparent appreciation of what he saw. Jenny felt herself start to blush. "Is there anything you'd like to look at?" he asked.

"Actually, I wasn't really planning to buy anything—but perhaps that bracelet." She pointed to a slender bangle studded with irregular geometric shapes of lapis and tiger's-eye and a stone she did not recognize.

"This is one of my favorites. Here, try it on," he coaxed, taking her hand and slipping the piece on. "It's beautiful, madame, just beautiful."

Jenny blushed again, forgetting for the moment that this was a shop and she was just a prospective customer. "How much is it?"

"For you—twenty-five dollars."

"And for someone else?" She couldn't resist the teasing rejoinder.

"Ah, well, that would depend. Especially with a piece I am fond of. It would depend on how much I wished the customer to have it."

"I see," she said gravely, as if she encountered this mercantile philosophy every day. "Well, then, if it seems you wish me to have this bracelet, then I shall take it home as my souvenir of Acapulco."

"Madame has come on one of the cruise ships?" he asked suddenly.

"No, actually I've been here for a while, on holiday. But this is the first time I've been shopping."

"Perhaps you will allow me to show you around a bit— offer you a cold drink?"

This was completely unexpected. Jenny stammered, "But what about the shop?"

The man smiled. "Manuel!" he called, and a younger man materialized from the back of the shop. "Take care of things for a while. I will be going out." Manuel nodded, with just the hint of a smile on his lips.

Jenny noticed, but strangely enough, she did not mind. The idea of taking a walk and sharing a drink with a potential Don Juan had a certain appeal for her at this moment. She felt suddenly reckless.

And when her escort took her elbow and gave it an extra, personal little squeeze as he guided her out the door of his shop, she looked up at him and flashed the kind of smile she had not used since the days of her first flirtations with Jeffrey.

She grew even bolder over the piña coladas as she learned that the man's name was Stavros Augustatos. She felt giddy and lightheaded with the kind of romantic flush she hadn't experienced in years.

Over a second round of drinks Jenny and Stavros exchanged capsule histories—not the kind of information shared by people really trying to know each other. Rather, they took perfunctory sightings, quick readings of each other—to gain the illusion that they knew where they were going, and with whom. They determined that she was separated, he divorced, that she had a daughter, he a son.

By the time Stavros called for the check in the little sidewalk café, Jenny knew that he would want to make love—and that she would say yes.

The rest of the day took on a dreamlike—no, a movielike— quality, with scenes she felt might have been played by Ingrid Bergman and Paul Henried. As they left the café, they walked slowly, first separately, then hand in hand, to Stavros's house, a whitewashed cottage overlooking the water.

"Let me show you my home, Jenny," he said, as he led her through rooms which were lovely in their austere, almost monastic simplicity. The walls were finished in white stucco, the sparse furniture made of dark woods. The austerity was relieved by masses of flowers, fresh and dried, and by Stavros's collection of Greek icons, which looked as if they had come from an old Orthodox church.

An interesting home, Jenny thought, and perhaps an interesting man, but she knew that would be something for some other woman to find out, another day, another time.

They stood for a time on a small balcony, then he folded his arms around her. "You are very beautiful, Jenny," he murmured.

Familiar words. Words that lovers had crooned and whispered and shouted since time immemorial. But for Jenny they evoked an almost primitive pleasure. In her years with Jeffrey, she had come to feel utilitarian rather than decorative. And since his rejection, she had lost whatever sense of desirability she had possessed to begin with.

She put her arms around Stavros's neck and met his lips for a long and very pleasant kiss. When he led her to his bedroom, she followed quite easily, just as if she had been doing this kind of thing all her life. Yet when they came to the large double bed, she stopped, suddenly awkward, realizing that she had never before undressed in front of any man except Jeffrey. He seemed to sense her discomfort, for he walked over to the window shutters and closed them, softening the light in the room to a dusky gray. He kissed her again and slowly began removing her garments, one by one, with the practiced proficiency of a man who had done this many times before. Jenny did not mind his proficiency in the least. She was, in fact, delighted that Stavros was giving her the beginning of an interesting past.

He was a gentle and sensitive lover, and he made Jenny's initiation into what she later laughingly called "sin" very pleasurable. In this, her first affair, Jenny felt giddy and wanton and remarkably guilt-free. She felt like a child with a new toy—she felt like a woman of experience.

By the end of the afternoon, Jenny decided to stay a little longer in Acapulco. Stavros had promised to fill her remaining holiday with laughter and pleasure, and Jenny believed him.

Upon returning to the Halloran cottage, Jenny believed that she had lost some of the innocence which Jeffrey had found appealing so many years ago, but which now seemed like an out-of-date dress that sat awkwardly upon her as she tried to fit into today's world. In truth, she was perhaps still quite naive. Her secret fling served as a kind of exorcism. Now that Jeffrey was no longer the only man she had known, she felt ready to step outside the "we" that had made up her world for so many years. It was a prospect which now filled her with anticipation as well as insecurity.

⟢ 28 ⟢

When she flew back to New York, Sally immediately noticed the change in her sister and mentioned it to Alicia. "I think that vacation you gave Jenny has done wonders for her," she said.

But when Alicia looked carefully at her younger daughter, noting the glow that seemed to frost the tropical tan, the hint of a new sparkle in her eye, the suggestion of a newfound vitality, she remembered the time she had spent in Italy—and the first weeks she had known Paolo. She hoped that her suspicions were correct. To Sally, she said, "Yes—yes, I think you're right. I'm so glad your sister seems to have snapped out of her blue mood."

"Why don't we have a party for her, Mother? Before you go back to California. I can invite some people she hasn't met—you know, to keep her spirits up—before she falls into a slump again. Being single in New York—for a woman her age—well, all I mean is that I don't think she's going to have an easy time of it."

As Alicia looked at her older child, her thoughts were not of Jenny, but of Sally. How fragile and sweet she is, Alicia thought. Out loud she said, "I think that's a good idea—yes, very definitely, Jenny should meet new people, people she didn't share with Jeffrey. The less explaining she has to do these next few months—about 'what went wrong' to people who couldn't care less—the sooner she can begin getting on with her life. But Sally, please be a little subtle about it. Your sister has some pride, so we don't want her to feel like one of New York's hundred neediest cases. Tell her you're having a something-or-other party for a good cause. Or ask some of your literary friends. Surely someone you know must have just published a book . . . that's just the thing—make it a party for a book. Then your sister can meet someone other than those doctors Jeffrey always entertained.''

When Sally did tell her sister about the party—in honor of an artist, as it turned out—Jenny was remarkably enthusiastic, not at all wary or suspicious as she had been just several short weeks before. "That sounds like fun, Sally," she said. "I'm so glad you asked me."

Her enthusiasm for her first night out as a single woman built—right until the morning of the party, when she went to her closet and tried to answer the question, "What shall I wear?"

It occurred to her, as she pulled out hanger after hanger, and then shook her head, that her wardrobe seemed to have a distinctly "married" flavor. It was, she decided, a painfully uninteresting selection of serviceable slacks and skirts in basic colors, some classic shirts and pullovers, several "Easter Sunday"–type suits, and a half-dozen "cocktail" and evening dresses of some undistinguished vintage. Not one dress in her closet was a head-turner. Not one item could wrap her in an aura of glamour or intrigue or mystery. These clothes clearly identified her as someone's wife.

How did I let this happen? she asked herself. I've never been poor—and Jeffrey has earned a decent living for a long time. The answer to that question was obvious. The life she had lived had not really been that interesting to her, and the clothes she wore each day were merely a reflection of that state of mind. Except for the shopping trip she had impulsively gone on with Rebecca before their vacation, she had not bought any really good clothes in ages. Nor had she taken the time or trouble to refurbish or reorganize what she had. Or even to throw anything away, she thought wryly, as she noticed all the outmoded things that sagged limply on tired wire hangers.

While she was surveying the fallout that had spread out to her bed, Rebecca came in. "What are you wearing to Aunt Sally's party, Mommy?"

"Oh, I don't know, love. What do you think?"

Rebecca's eyes flicked quickly over the heap of clothing. "Can I tell you the truth, Mommy?"

"Please."

"I hate all this stuff. It's wimpy. I think you should buy something new."

Jenny laughed. "You're right. This stuff is wimpy. And I will go out and buy a new dress. In fact, next week, I think I'll buy a whole new wardrobe. What do you think of that?"

"I think you deserve it."

Jenny hugged her daughter and fairly flew out the door to make a helter-skelter shopping trip—which began and ended in a small Gramercy Park boutique.

But finding a new party dress was not as easy as Jenny had expected. She put on and rejected a whole series of dresses—and the "looks" they represented. She shook her head when the salesperson brought her padded shoulders and Day-Glo colors and see-through blouses. She shook her head even harder when the glossy young creature insisted that these aberrations were "the latest thing." And when the ninety-eight-pound nymph became aggressive about a confection of vinyl and red satin being "today", Jenny snapped, "So is social disease—but I don't want any of that either."

She was just about to leave the shop when the manager, who was also the principal designer, came in. "Perhaps I can help you?"

Jenny took a deep breath and recited, "I need a dress for a 'Saturday night New York-beautiful-people–type party.'" There. Maybe she could shorten what promised to be an ordeal—the chore of finding an attractive dress that wasn't a costume.

The woman looked at Jenny, took in the auburn hair, the fair skin dusted with freckles, the full figure. She reached into the racks and pulled out only one dress. A wool challis of midnight purple, high in the neck, long in the sleeves—a body covering of skillful cut that promised to caress the figure, to hint at its contours without exposing the flaws. "Oh yes," Jenny exclaimed. And then she held her breath while she tried it on, hoping it would fit.

One look in the mirror convinced her it did. And she did not need any urging from the shop owner to take out her checkbook and make the purchase.

On the way home she planned what she might wear with her new dress. Her grandmother Carlotta's amethysts, she decided—a brilliant teardrop pendant with matching earrings—and the single pair of sexy shoes she owned—flimsy deep-plum suede sandals that she had worn only once.

As she dressed, Jenny realized how nervous she was. Not since high school days had she been so apprehensive about going out alone. For so long she had had the protection of a marriage against the small cruelties of single life. The pleasures, too, she added silently, determined to keep her spirits up and her mood positive.

Jenny squared her shoulders when the uniformed maid let her into the Jefferses' apartment. As always, the place looked glamorous. Tonight it might have been the set of a Sondheim musical—the men trendy and the women chic.

Her eyes scanned the women first. They were dressed in a kaleidoscope of styles ranging from expensive call girl to even more expensive gamine. Jenny decided she looked "right." But she was not at all sure that she could feel as confident and self-assured, as soignée, as Sally's friends appeared to be.

She searched for a familiar face, but the only one she could find was her sister's. Sally was surrounded, as usual, by a cluster of people. Jenny hesitated, torn between the awkwardness of standing alone and the clumsiness of barging in on an already-formed cocktail-party group.

She was saved by the appearance of her brother-in-law. "Jenny, dear—how nice to see you again."

"Brad! Hello."

"Do you know any of this crowd?" he asked, properly solicitous because his wife had instructed him to "be nice to Jenny."

"Well, I'm sure you'll find lots of interesting people to talk to. You look smashing, by the way. Come on. For now, I'll introduce you to a good friend of mine." He led her toward a tall, rangy man with sandy hair and an open prep-school face that was just barely touched by lines. He was dressed in a classic Brooks Brothers ensemble—blue blazer with gray slacks—but he managed somehow to look a little rumpled, perhaps even slightly disreputable. "Jenny," Brad began, "I want you to meet Charley Redfield. Charley and I went to Exeter together, and he's began drinking my liquor ever since." He turned to his friend. "Charley, this is my lovely sister-in-law, so I want you to entertain her with some of your better stories."

"I'm enchanted to meet you, Brad's sister-in-law." Charley bowed from the waist. But when Jenny tried to meet his eyes, she thought: He's not at all enchanted. He obviously prefers to stand here drinking alone. And now he's going to force himself to be polite. And sure enough, Charley opened with a standard conversational gambit: "What do you do, Jenny?"

She realized that this was a question she would have to start dealing with. She could not say what she had said for so long—"I stay home and take care of my family." So she improvised: "Actually, I'm looking for a job now."

"Well, you're welcome to mine," he said with that lazy drawl perfected by the rich.

"What kind of job do you have?"

"Investments."

"But I don't know anything about investments."

"Who does, lovely lady," Charley said, with an attempt at levity that made Jenny notice that his eyes were totally unfocused and that he was terribly, terribly drunk. She felt silly standing there, talking to a man in that condition. She found the courage to say, "Will you excuse me, please? I see an old friend over there."

Once again her eyes scanned the room, searching for a direction. She noticed a solitary man dressed in jeans and a sweater, staring intently at a painting. She thought he might be the artist being honored this evening. She walked slowly in his direction, stopping to pluck a miniature quiche from a passing waiter's tray.

She paused in front of the painting and mustered up enough courage to try a conversational ploy of her own. "Do you know the artist?" she asked.

"Sure. Enough to see that he does nothing but garbage." He turned to face her, and she saw that he was serious.

"My goodness. Isn't that a little extreme?"

"No, it isn't extreme. It's exactly what I think."

Torn between politeness and frankness, Jenny decided to say what she thought. "But I think he has a good sense of color. And composition."

"Oh, you do, do you? What are you, some kind of critic or something?"

"No. But I did major in fine arts in school." Jenny was sorry the minute she said it, realizing how breathlessly ingenue and unsophisticated she sounded.

She reddened as the man laughed. She turned to run away, but he put out his hand to hold her. "No, wait—don't go. I

have to find out who you are first. So I can tell old George
that he has at least one fan. Besides the hostess, I mean.''

"So you do know the artist," she accused.

"I should. Old George is my brother."

"Oh." Jenny searched her mind for somewhere to go.
"But you don't think much of his work."

The man snorted. "Putting it that way is an act of charity." Then suddenly he seemed to take notice of Jenny. He
stared at her appraisingly, as if she, too, were hung on the
wall for his inspection. "Are you alone?" he asked abruptly.

"Yes."

"Do you want to split this scene and go somewhere?"

Jenny wasn't particularly attracted to the man, but he seemed
all right. And who was she to be so particular? She had
gathered from Sally's broad hints that she wasn't exactly in a
seller's market with what she had to offer. She supposed she
should be delighted that an attractive man had asked her for a
date. "Yes, I'd like that," she answered, pretending a poise
she didn't really feel.

His next words destroyed her brief illusion. "Listen," he
said, "I don't really believe in a lot of phony romance
garbage. And I don't believe in wasting my time with women
who need to play childish games. Are you any good in bed?"

Jenny's cheeks flamed, as if someone had put a torch to her
face. Her fragile composure failed, and she turned and ran,
straight for Sally's bedroom. She closed the door behind her
and fell onto the bed, wishing she could just disappear,
hoping she could somehow avoid the embarrassment of having to go back out there to leave. How stupid and naive she
had been. Whatever had made her think it was all going to be
so easy? A man she hadn't particularly liked had all but
yawned in her face. And another had checked her out as if
she had been a side of beef. Not even prime beef at that.

Forget it, Jenny Ashland, she told herself sternly. Just
forget it. You had some good years with Jeff. And that is all
you get. Then she remembered her Acapulco interlude. No,
you don't, she admonished herself. That didn't count. Stavros
was nice to you because you were just passing through. This
is the real world. You were passable enough as Jeffrey's
wife. But as a grass widow, you just don't cut it.

She squeezed a few woeful tears from her eyes. And then
suddenly the mental picture of herself sitting there, like a high

school wallflower, crying over a lousy party—suddenly the image seemed totally absurd. She started to laugh.

Just then the door opened. "Well, I'm glad you found something funny at this party. When I saw you run in here, you seemed rather upset."

Jenny looked up to see, standing in the doorway, a rather stately woman of about fifty-five, wearing an obviously expensive dress of gray wool adorned with a diamond bracelet and a pair of matching ear studs of truly impressive proportions. Her steel-gray hair was short, precisely cut, and she wore a pair of oversize white-gold glasses. Seeing the question in Jenny's eyes, the woman said, "I'm Charlotte Lipscomb. I'm an old friend of Sally and Brad's. She told me about you. In fact, she suggested I try to cheer you up."

"Cheer me up?"

"Yes. But don't get mad at your big sister. She may be a bit archaic, but she loves you and she means well. I think Sally still sees divorce as a condition somewhere between chicken pox and terminal cancer. In fact, I suspect I'm the only divorcée in her crowd who didn't take to drinking, psychoanalysis, nymphomania, or compulsive shopping. And I think I'm the only divorcée she knows who likes being single."

"I'm very glad to meet you," Jenny said, realizing she meant those words. The woman standing in the doorway fairly radiated energy and goodwill. "But I'm embarrassed. You probably know more about me than I want anyone to know, and—"

"Stop. Before you go on, let me tell you what I know. Sally told me that you were her sister and that you're having a rough time because you and your husband have separated."

"She must have told you that my husband left me."

"Yes. She did say that."

"Anything more?"

"You mean there's more?"

"No, not really. Anyway—I am glad to meet you. It's nice of you to care about a stranger."

"I'm just indulging a hobby of mine. Someone gave me a hand when my marriage began to fall apart, and it made all the difference in my life. I try to pay back when I see the opportunity."

Jenny wasn't sure how she felt about being someone's good cause. Yet the woman obviously meant well, which was a lot more than you could say about some of the characters who hung around Sally.

"It makes a difference," Charlotte went on, "to talk to someone who has had some of the experiences you're having— someone who came out of a divorce feeling good. Maybe even lucky. And certainly not betrayed or injured."

"How did you manage that? Didn't you have a lot of bad feelings toward your husband?"

"In the beginning. I thought I would die when we split up. But in the end I saw my divorce as a second chance to do things I had never done before."

"A second chance . . ." Jenny mused. She remembered that Alicia had used almost the same words when she came back from Italy with Paolo. And that she herself had started to feel that way about her relationship with Rebecca. "When did it stop? The bad feelings, I mean. What made the difference?"

"A lot of things. I can't reduce it all to a formula for you this minute. It begins with a sense of humor. About yourself. And about your predicament. And judging from the laugh I heard when I came in, you've already taken step one."

By now Jenny was paying careful attention. God knows I can use a guru, she thought. "So what's step two?" she asked.

"Step two is leaving this party before you start thinking there's something wrong with you. Come on. I'll give you a lift home. One of my mad luxuries is to keep a car in the city. I can't stand looking for cabs at night."

Jenny gratefully accepted the chance to leave the party. On the way home, she told Charlotte about her conversation with the painter's brother and about the few moments she'd spent with Charley Redfield.

Charlotte slapped her thigh so hard that Jenny thought she might crash the Alfa-Romeo—"my little Italian sweetheart," Charlotte had called it. "You poor kid. No wonder you ran. Believe me, it wasn't you who bored Charley. He hasn't had a sober evening in the last five years. And when he meets an attractive woman, his brain is too fried for him to notice."

"Well, the other one wasn't drunk. I didn't even get his name, but there didn't seem to be anything wrong with him. If he's a typical New York man, then I don't think there's much out there for me."

"Okay. I'll be brutally frank with you. Yes, he is typical in a way. If you live your life looking for 'Mr. Right,' you'll probably run into a lot of men like him. The trick is to let Mr. Right come looking for you. Then you miss out on all the creeps.''

Jenny laughed. "How did you get so smart, Charlotte?"

"I live right, kid. And I'm going to teach you all my secrets. By the way—how are you fixed for money and a place to live? I know Sally's comfortable, and I know your family has some money, but what about you?"

"I have a nice apartment. I don't really know if I want to stay there. Jeff and I spent a lot of years together in that place—I think it might be hard to stop thinking about him if I don't move. And I don't really have money problems. But I do need a job. I mean *I* need it—a career, actually."

"What can you do? What have you done?"

"Not much of anything. Oh, look, here's my building— you're passing it. Do you want to come up for a drink?"

"Not tonight. Look, Jenny, I have a very early appointment tomorrow with a client—I sell real estate, you know. But why don't we have lunch one day next week? I promise I'll have a ready prescription for everything that ails you. Okay? Here's my card. Call my secretary on Monday, and she'll set it up."

After she had deposited Jenny at the entrance to her building, Charlotte drove away with all the sound and fury the little car could muster. Jenny was dazzled. A woman on her own, no longer young, with an apparently thriving career, a flashy sports car, a secretary, and her own business card. And she was nice as well. Jenny had never known a woman like that close up; she had never counted her own mother, for in Jenny's mind Alicia had dropped out of the human race when she was a child, and Jenny was just beginning to count her in it again.

Jenny considered the party a major success. She had not conquered any hearts, but she had made a friend. It had been, on the whole, a good evening.

— ✦ 29 ✦ —

The promised lunch took place ten days later. Charlotte took Jenny to the 21 Club, and Jenny "oohed" and "aahed," not afraid to be the country bumpkin with this curiously motherly woman.

"I can't believe a New York kid like you is still impressed with '21,'" Charlotte said. "I guess your husband didn't take you to places like this?"

"Not very often."

"Well, don't worry—you haven't missed much. And don't be too impressed. I bring all my good clients here. I'll bet that I pay the salary of at least one waiter. Of course, in my tax bracket the government picks up a nice piece of the tab. I think it's relatively cheaper for me to eat here now than it was to have a burger in a luncheonette when I was a kid. So, enjoy your lunch."

And Jenny did. After the two women had worked their way through excellent steaks and a crisp salad and were well into their coffee, Charlotte asked, "Okay, now it's time to get down to business. Now tell me—what kind of work have you done?"

"I already told you. It wasn't false modesty—I have a degree in fine arts, but I've never done much with it."

"No career experience."

"No."

"I'm curious, Jenny—and you just tell me if I'm out of line, but I'll ask anyway. How come you never worked for your mother? It seems like the perfect place for a bright young woman with a fine arts degree."

"I don't really know, Charlotte. I thought about it, but something kept me away—stubbornness, pride, I don't know. After Jeff left, I thought about it again, but it seemed like a step backward. I went straight from my parents' house to my husband's house. Now if I go to work for Principessa, it would be like going home."

"So? Is that so bad? When I got divorced I would have given my gold crowns to have rich parents to run to."

"You're saying that I'm ungrateful. I don't mean to be. I know I'm lucky to have that. But I just want to make a life for myself. To do something on my own."

"Okay. I thought that might be what you were after. So I'm prepared to offer you a job."

"A job? Doing what?"

"Doing what I do. Selling real estate."

"But I don't know anything about real estate."

"Neither did I when I started. Listen, hon, selling real estate is a natural for divorced ladies and widows. That's why so many of us are in it. You can make your own hours—to a point, anyways. If and when you get really ambitious, you'll stop watching the clock. If you're smart, and if you understand people—and I think that might be you—you can make a lot of money. And you can be doing people a real service at the same time."

"Honestly, Charlotte. You try to sound like such a toughie. But after a little while you come off like a social worker."

"You know why that is? I'll tell you. I am tough, kid. But I'm smart, too. I realized what some people never figure out—that I can make a damn good living without ever pulling a fast one on any of my clients, and without ever pressuring anyone into buying the wrong property. I figure if I don't make a sale one time, I'll get it the next time around. You'd be surprised at the word-of-mouth I get. And my return business—fantastic. One of the highest in New York, I'd bet."

"I'm impressed."

"You should be. Now the reason I want to give you a job is this: If you believe the way I do, then I'll be doing my customers a favor, too. Because right now I have too many customers and not enough help. And I have to send a lot of my overflow to other brokers, who aren't as terrific and honest as I am. Are you interested?"

"Yes—yes, I am." Jenny found Charlotte's enthusiasm infectious. And although real estate was somewhat removed from fine arts, it was an opportunity to stand on her own and to learn something new. People were not going to line up to offer her career opportunities, and she was grateful that Charlotte had come along.

"Any questions?"

"No. Well—yes. How do I start and what do I do?"

"Good questions. But you should have asked about money, about opportunities. I know you're not worried about your next meal, but in any business you should never act as if money doesn't matter. And especially not with a client. A lot of them already think that women are stupid—or soft—about money. So don't add to that impression. You don't have to behave like a barracuda. Just show that you're aware."

"Okay. What about money?"

"What you'll get is a commission on everything you sell—three percent to start, because I'll have to be spoon-feeding you. Then six percent later, when you begin to know what you're doing. But for your apprenticeship, I'll put you on rentals. Less pressure than with purchases—and mistakes are cheaper."

"Is there anything else I should know—for now?"

"About a million things. But for now I want you to sign up for this real estate course." She thrust a brochure at Jenny. "They'll teach you things I don't have the patience for. Things you'll need to get your broker's license. Everything else you'll learn on the job."

Looking across the table at Charlotte, Jenny felt a rush of gratitude. The feeling she had—of being cared for, unselfishly directed—it was one she had once associated with her father and recently—fleetingly, with her mother. She smiled at Charlotte, who now reminded her of an older Eve Arden—with perhaps a dash of Joan Crawford. "Thank you, Charlotte. For everything."

"*Nada*, kid. *Se nada*. You help somebody else out someday and we'll be square. Now—come into the office early tomorrow. You have the address? Good. You have to make it early, before it gets busy, so I can start you off before the phones begin to ring."

Jenny didn't know what she should have expected when she reported for work at eight the next morning. But it certainly was not the unprepossessing barnlike place that served as Charlotte's office. Charlotte caught Jenny's look of surprise and grinned. "Not terribly chichi, is it, kid?"

"Well . . ."

"It's a dump. I like it that way. My less affluent customers feel comfortable here, and the rich ones—they're the tightest with a buck—they think they've found a bargain. Keeps everyone happy. Including my so-and-so landlord who charges me a goddamn fortune for this roach hotel. One of these days I'll buy the building out from under him, the bastard.'' Charlotte took Jenny's arm and showed her around the firm of Lipscomb and Bernstein. ''Bernstein's dead,'' she explained, ''five years ago. But the two names make the company sound bigger.

''Here,'' she said, pointing Jenny toward a corner file cabinet. ''This is the rental file. Go through it. Check out about half a dozen—the descriptions on file—then go see the apartments. That way you'll be able to get a feel for real estate language, see what the descriptions mean. And then you'll learn how to write them yourself when new listings come in.

''What you're going to learn, in time, is that this is like being a marriage broker. Your job is to find the right place for the right person. If you're good, you'll develop an intuition about who belongs where. You'll get to know the buildings—the family buildings, the conservative buildings, the places where singles live, the 'good' addresses, and the ones that are so-so.''

Charlotte's phone started to ring. ''Okay, kid. Get started. The boy from the corner will bring coffee and Danish any minute. Warm your tummy—and then get going.''

Jenny was delighted, dumpy office and all. At last she had her first real job. Even if it was a little low on the ladder of success, it was hers.

Later that night she was still optimistic, although the first flush of euphoria had gone—along with the inches of shoe leather she had walked off, checking Lipscomb and Bernstein's listings.

Her mind had reeled when she examined, in person, just what a ''charming studio, slp alc, wbf, secure bldg'' looked like up close. She had thanked divine Providence for her own spacious place as she went from building to building, seeing for herself what the housing market was like in this city where she had lived—comfortably and graciously—for all her life.

When she returned home to the apartment she had shared with Jeff for so many years, she was greeted by the unexpected aroma of tomato sauce. ''What's going on?'' she asked, as she walked into the kitchen and found Rebecca peering intently into a saucepan.

"Oh, Mommy! It was supposed to be a surprise. I thought you might be tired, so I'm making dinner for you. Look—the salad is all finished. I bought the ravioli from Raffetto's. And I'm making the sauce myself. I called Aunt Sally and got the recipe from her cook."

For about the fifth time that day, Jenny felt almost unbearably lucky, felt an outpouring of love for this child of hers. This closeness was like nothing she had experienced when she and Jeff were together. Maybe, she thought, the same fate that had taken Jeff had also taken away the stereotypical daughter, the one who had sulked about doing chores—and had replaced her with a friend.

Considering Rebecca's inexperience in the kitchen, the meal was remarkably good. Dessert came out of Jenny's pocket: It was a handful of champagne truffles she had bought, on the run, from Teuscher's during her daylong trek through the city. As mother and daughter marveled at the meal, Jenny said, "Thank you, Becky. I can't tell you how much I appreciate what you did."

"It's okay, Mom. I figured if you're going to be working, I should try to help you out."

"Oh, you do, Becky," she whispered, not trusting her voice. "You help me so much."

Not every day in Jenny's infant career was as manageable as the first. Although she found the real estate course relatively easy—she had, after all, always done well in school— the paperwork, the veritable mountain of documents she was expected to know and understand, proved to be very discouraging. But not nearly as discouraging as some of her clients.

There were the couples who insulted her listings, not to mention her intelligence and integrity, when they insisted that Manhattan must be filled with apartments a thousand times better than what she was showing them, then demanded to know how much she wanted "under the table" before she showed them "the good stuff."

The sad clients were even worse—the nice people who were simply priced out of anything decent. Like the old woman who desperately wanted to find "a little place—anything will do" near her daughter. The only problem was that her daughter lived on one of the poshest blocks on Park Avenue, where even a storage room rented for more than the old woman could afford. That dilemma turned out well, as far as

Jenny was concerned, even though the firm, and she, got no commission at all. She had remembered that one of their clients, a finicky elderly bachelor who occupied an entire town house off Madison Avenue, had been complaining about how seedy his place got during his frequent absences from New York. It was the high point of Jenny's week when she persuaded this client to turn over a small downstairs room to the old woman in return for a small fee and house-sitting services.

Then there were the newlyweds—another of Jenny's success stories. They had told her they had been trying to get married for months, but had been unable to find an affordable apartment. Jenny located a sublet for them that was almost a steal, with the chance to renew when the lease was up. "Call it my wedding present," she had said, declining the small commission—and still feeling that she was already something of a success.

She was learning, as Charlotte had predicted she would, to read people, to listen to what they said, to hear what they didn't say, to size them up in a hundred subtle ways. It gave her enormous satisfaction when she was right, and some moments of anxiety when she wasn't—like the time she took a call from a well-known Broadway actor, a man renowned for his portrayals of swashbuckling heroes and lovable villains. This gentleman required, he informed Jenny in an elegant accent that suggested British public schools, "something tasteful, between Park and Madison, not too far uptown. A sublet, nicely furnished. A fireplace would be lovely, dear, though not absolutely necessary. But a terrace, oh yes, a terrace is a must."

When she asked the price range, the voice said airily, "Oh, whatever the going price is, my dear. Rehearsals start soon for a new play, so there isn't much time—you understand."

Jenny was thrilled, for although she had on several occasions rubbed elbows with the rich and beautiful who populated Sally's world, she still felt very much like a fan in the presence of creative people. Her world—Jeffrey's world—had been focused on the eastern medical establishment. And any distinguished people she had met were "secondhand"—they belonged to Jeff, and she doubted very much that any of them had ever noticed her.

Rodney Stevens—he would be all hers. Her first celebrity. She could hardly wait to tell Becky. Her daughter had already pronounced Jenny's business cards "neat." She had a similar reaction to the special phone with several buttons that she'd installed at home to handle client calls. And she had been properly impressed by Jenny's expense account—a very small one, but an expense account nonetheless. And now she had a celebrity story—her own, not borrowed from Jeff or Sally.

She made an appointment to meet Rodney Stevens in the lobby of one of her favorite uptown buildings, a mansion-turned-cooperative just off Madison Avenue, a short distance from Central Park. She wanted to show Stevens a six-room sublet furnished entirely in gallery-quality antiques, a pied-à-terre fit for royalty—with a matching price tag.

If that wasn't to his taste, she had, on her list, a spacious aerie facing the East River, an apartment sparsely furnished in clean, modern furniture. And she had yet another possibility—on the "wrong" side of the park, but with a knockout view and a terrace that would hold a dinner party for a hundred, and at a very reasonable price.

She was feeling rather pleased with herself as she walked past the liveried doorman and into the baroque lobby where Rodney Stevens sat, doing the *New York Times* crossword puzzle. He must have been early, Jenny thought. Unheard of in New York. She hoped he was not annoyed at the wait. She worried for just a moment—and then the actor rose immediately when he saw her. He bowed from the waist and took her hand in a sweeping gesture worthy of a ducal court. Jenny's composure threatened to melt in a blush that started at her scalp and worked its way, in a single movement, right down to her toes.

"Mr. Stevens—I'm sorry if I kept you waiting."

"Nonsense, dear lady. You are," he said, looking at his watch for punctuation, "precisely on time. A lovely trait, particularly in this city. But then," he added, dropping the baritone voice to the dulcet caress that had thrilled thousands of theatergoers, "you are a very lovely lady."

By now Jenny was flattered beyond words. "Thank you" was all she could manage. Then, remembering why she was there: "Shall we look at the apartment?"

"By all means, dear lady. Lead me and I shall follow."

Apartment 10B was unoccupied. Its owner had made his annual pilgrimage to the sun. As soon as she unlocked the door and saw the look of approval on Rodney Stevens's face, she knew she had made the right choice. It was a case of love at first sight. The actor silently appreciated the Chippendale chairs in the dining room, fondled the French armoire in the gallery, and almost swooned when he saw the English clock in the living room. "My dear," he said, "this apartment tells me that you are a woman of exceptional taste and refinement—as well as a great beauty."

This time Jenny laughed. "Mr. Stevens—"

"Rodney, please."

"Rodney, then. You can hardly attribute anything in this apartment to me. I didn't buy or furnish it. I merely have the responsibility for finding a tenant."

"Let's not quibble about details. I know a lady when I see one. There are so few, you know." This time the famous Stevens voice dispensed the compliment in a breathy whisper—at fairly close range. Jenny's pleasure at being flattered gave way to a sense of uncertainty. Back to business, she directed herself.

"The price is two thousand dollars a month," she said, "with a rather large security deposit. You understand, with all these pieces around . . ."

"Quite . . . quite. I'll sign whatever needs signing. Now that I've seen this place, I wouldn't think of living anywhere else while I'm in New York. And of course, you must come to my opening—since you have taken so much responsibility for my well-being."

"Thank you," she said again, knowing how inane she sounded.

"No thanks are necessary," he crooned, taking her hand and pressing her fingertips to his lips. "It is I who should be grateful for your assistance, for meeting you . . ."

Afterward, Jenny wasn't quite sure how it all happened. But somehow, within twenty minutes of crossing the threshold of apartment 10B, she was running around an Empire sofa, saying things like, "Please, Mr. Stevens, this is silly. . . ."

While he, on the other side, was chuckling. "Of course it's silly, my dear. But if you want to play a bit, it's perfectly all right with me."

"No, Mr. Stevens, I'm not playing. We shouldn't be doing this."

"Should . . . shouldn't . . . what do those words have to do with anything? I am a man who appreciates beauty and refinement. And here it is, in all its manifestations. Look, my dear, if you have any doubts, let me assure you that I am a lover of exquisite sensitivity. Acting, you see, is very much like making love, and you must know that I am a brilliant actor. Come, come, let's not waste a potentially delightful afternoon.''

"Mr. Stevens," Jenny had said, with as much hauteur as she could muster, "I am sure you make love with the same finesse you are displaying at this very moment. But I simply can't take advantage of your very kind offer. I am leaving. This minute. I suggest you do not get in my way. If you decide to rent the apartment, you can call the office and I will have the papers sent to you. Good-bye, sir. It has been a pleasure to meet you."

She had gotten out of the apartment and onto the street without further incident. She hailed the first cab she saw. Halfway downtown, she started to laugh. What the hell, she thought, this would make a funnier story than she could have told after a simple meeting with the distinguished Rodney Stevens. Maybe Becky would even think it was "neat."

When she described her encounter to Charlotte, the older woman guffawed. "Welcome to the club, kid. It isn't the first time, and it won't be the last. I must say, I'm impressed with the high-class masher you started with. I think your career is on its way."

"But Charlotte, I think I just lost a client. I think he might go somewhere else for an apartment."

Charlotte shrugged. "If he goes, he goes. I'm not going to lose any sleep over it, and neither should you. It's only a rental—an expensive one, but a rental. Now if you had lost a buyer for a million-dollar property, I might have told you to massage Mr. Stevens's ego—and whatever else needed massaging."

"Charlotte! You're kidding! Aren't you? I mean—you don't do that sort of thing, do you?"

"Not unless I want to, kid. Not unless I want to. That's pretty much how I make all my choices. Figure out how you want to make yours—and stick to it."

Rodney Stevens apparently did take his business elsewhere, since Jenny did not hear from him again. She tried to think of how she might have handled herself better, how she might avoid similar problems in the future. When she saw a course in assertiveness being offered at a midtown Y, she showed the brochure to Charlotte. "What do you think?" she asked.

"I think you've had plenty of schooling, plenty of courses already, kid. What you need is a couple of courses in life. All this will do"—she threw the brochure back at Jenny—"is teach you to say no. I can do that in two seconds. Just wrap your mouth around two little letters—and spit them out. See—no—no—no. But if you're going to be any good at it, you just have to get out there and practice. Nobody can teach you that."

She realized that Charlotte was right, that if she wanted to be one of those people who said and did what they wanted, she would have to make decisions for herself and try to point herself in the right direction.

Determined to avoid embarrassing incidents on the job, she tried to anticipate what kind of situations might come up, to plan how she might handle them smoothly. But in spite of Charlotte's predictions, Rodney Stevens's pass was the last serious one she received on the job.

Slowly she acquired the poise and confidence that kept her from blushing or turning tongue-tied at inopportune moments. And she found that these skills mattered to her as much as the checks she regularly took to the bank.

Her commissions were modest at first, but she was as proud of these checks, of the deposit slips she filled out, as if they were a fortune.

When Jenny passed her broker's examination, Charlotte took her to Le Cygne for a champagne lunch. During the meal, she brought from her purse a small package wrapped in Cartier's distinctive paper with intertwined "C's." "For you, kid. A graduation present. You've been doing great, and you're going to do better."

Not for the first time, Jenny thought how much like "family" Charlotte had become. She opened the package and found a lovely vermeil pen.

"Thank you, Charlotte. I'm going to treasure this."

"Sure you will. In five years you'll have half a dozen expensive pens. But this one will write up your first sale. I'm putting you into sales now, in case you didn't guess. Same principles, more details—which you're supposed to have learned. And more money."

"Thank you again, Charlotte. Look, I don't want to get mushy because I know that embarrasses you. But I wonder if you know how much this job has meant to me."

"Stop right there. I should be thanking you for doing a great job. Incidentally—has anyone told you that you're looking great since you've become a full-fledged career woman?"

"Yes. My daughter. She says I'm much 'neater' than I was when I stayed home and took care of my family. Funny—I thought she'd resent my job, but she doesn't."

"Why should she resent it? You're entitled to have a life, aren't you?"

"Maybe. But I remember how much I resented my mother going off to her office every day. And I had my father at home. Rebecca doesn't."

"But Jenny, how can you compare? You're talking details— about who was where at what time. That doesn't tell anything about what was happening. I'll bet you a hundred bucks it wasn't your mother's career you resented so much as her attitude—whatever that was."

Jenny's fork froze in midair. What Charlotte had said was so simple and so obvious, but she had never seen it. She realized how many of her important choices had been based on that misunderstanding. She had believed, so passionately, that her mother's career had been the villain in their home. And so she had forced herself to be a stay-at-home, just so she wouldn't repeat Alicia's mistakes. Instead, she had gone ahead and committed a whole series of new mistakes. Now she realized that even if Alicia had been bound hand and foot and confined to her kitchen, she might not have been capable of giving her daughters any more than she had given—at least not at that time of her life. The discovery made her want to laugh and cry at the same time. "Oh, Charlotte," she said, "you're wonderful. You're really wonderful! Thank you. Thank you for being my friend, thank you for the job—and thank you for what you just said!"

Charlotte's confidence in Jenny was justified. In her first months as a broker Jenny did remarkably well. Young couples, married and unmarried, were comfortable with her, appreciative of the way she treated them. No matter how limited the budget or how difficult the client, Jenny always remembered Charlotte's advice never to treat a customer like a one-night stand. Her word-of-mouth recommendations were excellent—and her income grew.

As her career prospered, her sense of self began to develop. And as she began to have a clear mental picture of who she was, she rediscovered her physical self—a self she had put to sleep while she had tried to keep a tight rein on her feelings.

Although she had never gotten too heavy during her marriage—Jeff wouldn't allow it—she found her figure as dull and uninteresting as her life had once seemed. She joined a neighborhood health club, and several nights a week she worked for two hours, without mercy, ignoring aches and pains and charley horses, determined to find muscle tone behind the flab. And when she was finished with the calisthenics and machines, she turned herself over to one of the club's masseuses, to be stroked and kneaded and pummeled with a special herbal oil until every square inch of her tingled.

She experimented with perfumes and bath oils, changing them often to suit her mood. She learned to pamper herself, to indulge her senses, with good food, with soft sensual fabrics. She bought silk sheets for her bed, and a fur throw to cover it.

And finally she stopped fighting with her unruly auburn hair, stopped trying to torture it into ladylike submission. "Cut it," she instructed the stylist at Sassoon's. "Not too short—leave it shoulder length—but let it wave. Leave it a little wild—so I can just wash it and let it dry." The result had been astonishing. I could almost be beautiful, she thought, as she looked in the mirror at the shiny copper-colored hair that tumbled seductively around her face.

Buoyed by this experiment, she added more clothes to her wardrobe—funky offbeat clothes that were light-years away from the matronly things she had once worn or the businesslike outfits she'd adopted for work. I can afford it, she thought with delight, each time she purchased a dress or sweater or a pair of shoes that didn't really "go" with anything.

Because of her new success, she was solicited for membership by various business associations. And she was listed in the *Who's Who of American Women*. This she suspected was due to Charlotte's intervention, but she was pleased nevertheless.

When she was honored by the local Women in Business chapter, Sally said to Brad, "Why don't we have a party for Jenny? Now that she's over that business with Jeff—and she's doing so well—wouldn't it be nice if she could meet someone?"

Brad laughed indulgently. "Really, Sally, you're still thinking of your sister as 'poor Jenny.' I know you are—don't deny it. She's looking better than she has in years. She has money of her own, and she seems reasonably happy. She must have a man or two somewhere. But you still think of her as a charity case.''

''Brad! That's not true—well, not completely true. I just don't think she can be so happy living alone. Becky will be grown up before she knows it. I just want her to be as happy as I am.''

''Dear Sally. Have your party. I'm sure Jenny will appreciate the gesture.''

How different it feels, Jenny thought, as she looked around her sister's apartment. She remembered how intimidated she had once been by Sally's crowd. Now, close up, they seemed like ordinary people. Richer. Better dressed. Thinner. But just people, nevertheless.

She took a glass of white wine from the bartender and headed straight for Charlotte, who was engaging one of the waiters in conversation. The young man moved away as Jenny approached.

''Really, Charlotte,'' she teased, ''he's just a child.''

''I know, I know,'' Charlotte sighed. ''But honestly—he's the most interesting man in the room.''

''Look, there's Sally—doesn't she look gorgeous?'' And indeed Sally was magnificent in a lavishly embroidered caftan of a fabric that looked like molten gold, her blond hair plaited in a stunning French braid. ''Who else is here?''

''Tonight your sister has called out the artsy-craftsy crowd. Couple of producers, some actors, a bunch of media people. What do you say we sneak out and get a pizza in Little Italy?''

''I can't do that. This party's supposed to be for me, remember? Besides, it's fun to look at these people. I'll bet there's not a woman who wears more than a size eight in this whole room.''

''True. Which makes me want that pizza even more.''

''Who's that brunette over there?''

''Where?''

''Over there. With Brad. The one with the gorgeous body.''

Charlotte gave Jenny a strange look. ''You don't know who she is?''

''No. Should I?''

"That's Lila Carstairs." She waited, apparently expecting some glimmer of recognition.

"So?" Jenny was puzzled.

"So nothing. She works in radio."

"Is that all? Then why did you think I knew her?"

"Don't mind me, kid. I just thought you might have heard of her somewhere. That's all. Forget it. Look—here comes that cute waiter again. Play your cards right and I'll introduce you."

—— 30 ——

Had Brad tried to remember just when it was that Lila Carstairs became his mistress, he would have had a hard time naming a day, a week, or even a month. One day she was just part of the network of people who passed through his home— guests, friends, useful strangers—and then one day he found himself a regular visitor to her bed.

And had he tried to explain how such a thing had happened, he would have been equally at a loss. It wasn't that Sally was any less serviceable or suitable a wife. It was simply that in Brad's world, adultery had more or less always been a male prerogative. It was a little like fudging one's tax return. People only murmured their disapproval—pro forma— if the IRS caught you and hauled you off to court. And all things considered, adultery was not as socially unacceptable as cheating at bridge or serving bad whiskey.

Still it had not really occurred to Brad to exercise this option until he and Sally learned they would not have children. That he would be the last of the Jefferses. And, more specifically, that it was Sally's "fault." The news was a serious disappointment to Brad, partly because, he told himself, every man wants a son, and partly because he knew his father would be gravely disappointed in him for choosing a wife who was not completely "sound."

Sally was stricken for more personal reasons. Of course she was sensitive to the reactions of her husband and her in-laws, but, for herself, this failure was a serious one. Since she saw herself only as a wife and homemaker, the failure to breed was a grave one.

She mourned for a time, received comfort and consolation from the women in her circle. "But darling," she heard more than once, "look on the bright side. You'll keep that gorgeous figure—no ugly stretch marks—and you'll never be tied down. Anyway, children can be quite awful—especially when they grow up. Really, Sally, count your blessings."

And Sally had tried. She buried her disappointment and her sense of failure in redecorating Penthouse A. The results were little short of spectacular, as half of the city's "style" reporters testified in print.

For his part, Brad buried his feeling of being cheated behind a facade of good manners. And he drifted in the direction that would take him into an affair with Lila Carstairs. It was not that he wanted to punish Sally. On the contrary, he found himself profoundly moved by her tears and self-blame. But if he was willing to go through life deprived of something important, it seemed eminently reasonable that Sally sacrifice her claim to his total fidelity.

Lila Carstairs was an attractive, frankly sensual brunette—on the wrong side of thirty, Brad reckoned, but definitely a woman to catch and hold the eye. As the hostess of a syndicated radio talk show, she had a modest celebrity status. As a self-supporting independent woman, she had a certain glamour and a little eccentricity. Sally referred to her often as "poor Lila," in acknowledgment of her husbandless status. Yet Lila, who had virtually no female friends, was very much a man's woman. She knew instinctively just what to say and do to engage a man's attention. And whenever she visited the Jefferses' home, she was always surrounded by a cluster of male admirers. As for Brad, he had merely admired Lila from afar. Until the night of the Fifth Avenue clambake.

This was one of Sally's annual affairs, a party that took place every Labor Day on the terrace of Penthouse A. A nationally renowned caterer was engaged to serve steamer clams, lobsters, chicken, and corn on the cob to about a hundred of New York's prettiest people. The clambake motif was a cunning conceit, enhanced by the caterer's artful use of gingham checks, and wild flowers and seashells.

It had been five years since Sally had first picked up the

phone to call a dozen of her "dearest friends" to ask, whimsically, "Listen darling—what do you think of this idea? Spending Labor Day in the city. It could be such fun, don't you think? A clambake—on our terrace. Wear beach things if you like."

Sally's friends had agreed that the notion was indeed charming. The event had been duly noted in *Women's Wear Daily* and in *Town and Country*. And the guest list had expanded each year until the party almost had the cachet of the city's major black-tie affairs.

Lila was one of the regulars at the party, and Sally had more than once commented how nice it was that poor Lila could come, since she had no family of her own to spend holidays with. Yet this particular holiday Brad caught a glimpse of Lila in the middle of a tableau on the southwest corner of his terrace. It reminded him of the barbecue scene from *Gone with the Wind*. Only this time it was Lila who was surrounded by gentlemen, plying her with drinks and plates of food. He watched, caught for the moment by his vision of this woman licking the melted butter from an ear of corn, laughing as the runoff threatened to reach her neck. With her eyes sparkling, her hair blowing in the breeze, she did not seem like a "poor Lila" at all, Brad thought. And he wished that he was one of the gentlemen basking in the glow of her attention.

He did nothing about this wish. Not then. No one—not even his closest friends—knew that Brad Jeffers was remarkably innocent sexually. As a teenager at prep school, he had accompanied several of his classmates to a local "house." Fortified by a tumblerful of Scotch, he had managed to perform the deed—barely. And having accomplished the loss of his virginity, he avoided intimacy with women until he was a junior in college. Then he had a fairly staid affair with a young woman he half-expected to marry. She left him for another man, and there had been no one else until Sally.

Although he had been an extraordinarily handsome young man, Brad had never been highly sexed. He liked women, but on the whole he found the company of men more interesting. In some ways he was classically narcissistic, but Sally had found him to be a perfect man. And for many years this was all the approval and admiration he needed.

Now something stirred, something new and untried, and it had to do with Lila. That evening he found himself listening with more than the polite interest of a casual friend to the husky voice, and the generous laugh that came so easily and so often.

At some point she noticed that he was paying more than perfunctory attention to her. She returned the compliment. When he brought her a drink, she held his hand a moment longer than was necessary. She looked into his eyes with an intensity that almost embarrassed him. And when she spoke to him—a few innocent sentences—he began to hear in her voice an entire orchestra of nuance and shading, and he knew without being told that it was all directed at him.

And still nothing specific had happened, not until the spring following the Labor Day gala. Now it was time for Sally's Memorial Day "picnic"—a celebration of the beginning of summer, at least for all those who would be opening their houses in the Hamptons, in Newport, in Deal.

This time Lila found Brad early in the afternoon and managed rarely to be far from his line of vision. "Everyone seems to be going away," she said to him, voice low and suggestive.

"Yes," he said with mock rue, "everyone except the poor summer bachelors who have to struggle between air-conditioned cars and air-conditioned offices."

"Poor men," she sighed, teasing. "And poor me. I still have to do my show five days a week, summer or no summer."

He thought he might have heard an invitation there, but he wasn't sure. "And what will you be doing for fun?"

"Oh, I don't know," she said, lifting her eyes to his so suddenly that he almost moved away. "Just hope that something interesting turns up now and again." Then, as if the idea had just occurred to her: "Perhaps a dear old friend—like you, Brad—might take me to dinner, just to relieve the awful monotony."

"Why, of course, Lila. I'd be delighted," he answered, with a hearty ease he did not really feel. What he did feel was that he had taken a step in a direction that might alter his life.

Brad's affair with Lila began the very first time he had invited her to dinner, after Sally had moved into their beach house in Southampton for the summer. In his mind there had been a certain awkwardness about the choice of a restaurant. Although they had both pretended that this was an innocent dinner between old friends, he thought he would certainly feel guilty if they ran into people they knew. "Where would you like to go?" he asked, leaving the decision in Lila's hands.

"Oh, I don't know," she said. "Why don't we go somewhere different? Off the beaten track."

He knew then that she understood his hesitation, and he was relieved. He suggested a small restaurant in suburban New Jersey, a place that had a decent kitchen and served a local clientele. She agreed, and he could almost hear the smile in her voice.

As he had done that long-ago evening in prep school, Brad fortified himself with Scotch, a great deal of it. He was entirely too nervous to enjoy the meal. Moreover, he had the feeling that Lila was laughing at him, teasing, taking charge. It was quite different from the time he shared with Sally, when there was no doubt whatever about who was in charge. He found that he enjoyed the change. As a man whose entire life had run on schedule, he liked this sense of anticipation, the possibility of surprise.

In the end it was Lila who seduced Brad, with a thoroughness and expertise that left him dazed and shaken, and certain that his life might never be the same.

And in the end he felt no guilt whatever—only a sense of gratitude that it happened. In Lila's extremely sensual hands, he discovered in himself a new capability for pleasure. He left her apartment thoroughly sated, knowing he would be back.

When he put his head on his own pillow, facing the spot where Sally usually slept, he still felt no guilt. Of course he would be discreet, for he still had not the slightest doubt that he would be spending the rest of his life as Sally's husband. But outside the limits imposed by this reality, he knew he would see Lila again—and again.

Just a few miles uptown, Lila Carstairs creamed her face and went to bed. As she snuggled into the hand-embroidered sheets lightly scented with Joy, she thought that perhaps—just perhaps—she might like to have Bradford Jeffers III for more than just an occasional loan.

Although Brad had categorized his affair with Lila as "a physical thing," he found in time that keeping a mistress was not as simple as he had imagined, and that the physical thing was not as small a part of his life as it had been before.

With Sally, there had always been a tenderness, a genuine affection, a respect. But after they had been married a few years, he found he had to remind himself to make love to his wife.

In Lila's presence, he was almost always in a state of arousal. He felt like a satyr, and believed that she somehow held the key to this miracle. With Lila, it was as if all his senses were heightened. Everything was more exciting—the food they shared, the wine they drank, the music they listened to.

Where as Sally's lovemaking was thoughtful, tender, and somehow chaste, Lila was unabashedly curious about the workings of her lover's body—and equally explicit about the mechanics of her own. For Brad, she became a kind of sensual tour guide, exploring, explaining, teaching, showing—until he came to believe that if he had the opportunity to make love to her a thousand times, he would never be bored or indifferent.

Yet, although he might not admit it, there was more than physical hunger that held him. There was also the contrast of Lila's personality with that of his wife. From Lila there emanated so much vitality, so much energy, that Sally sometimes seemed pale by comparison. Lila teased, she joked, she bullied. She often fought with Brad, not because she disagreed, but because she said it "got the juices flowing"—and because making love was so much better afterwards.

She had a strength of character that drew and fascinated him, a kind of femininity that was different from what he had known. And he was constantly intrigued by the multiplicity of her talents. While Sally had sometimes awed him with her meticulous stewardship of their home, Lila had a sloppier, but multidimensional approach to life. She kept a charming, somewhat untidy apartment with no apparent effort; she managed a job that demanded a certain flexibility and quickness of mind; she earned an impressive salary, and she made ingenious investments. She knew how to live well without making it a full-time occupation.

Brad gladly spent two or three nights a week in her company, and he was surprised at how quickly the summer flew by. But as Labor Day drew near, he asked her a question that had been on his mind. "How will you feel about coming to the house when Sally gets back?"

"How should I feel?" She looked up from the slices of zucchini she had been eating, one by one, with her fingers.

"I don't know. I thought perhaps you might feel awkward."

"I never feel awkward, Brad. We're all consenting adults. I understand the ground rules very well. But I will not play the 'Back Street' routine. I won't slink and skulk around Sally just because I've been sleeping with her husband. I understand discretion—if you insist on it—but if you think I'm going to alter my life or my behavior in any other way, then you can say good-bye to me right now. I mean it, Brad. I won't be made to feel guilty or second-rate. I'm single and free to do as I please. It's you who are committing adultery. And if you want to feel guilty or uneasy, go right ahead."

Brad backed away at once. "No, Lila. I wasn't even suggesting that you 'slink,' as you put it. I was just concerned about how you might feel," he lied. "As far as I'm concerned, you're always welcome in our—my—home."

Yet when the annual clambake came around again, it was Brad who felt awkward when Lila came breezing into his living room—calm, self-assured, and apparently very much in control. He shrunk inwardly a little when she caught sight of him and came right over, purposeful and smiling. He felt himself pale when she called out, "Darling Brad—what a lovely day for a party," then tucked her arm possessively in his and dragged him over to the bar. He cast a furtive look in Sally's direction, but she seemed quite serene. She acknowledged his look with a wave and a small smile. Dear Sally, he thought with gratitude. She is such a lady—and I'm so lucky to have her.

He looked around again. He thought he caught a knowing smile from one of his friends. Had he been careless after all? He knew that many of his friends had other women, but right now he felt clumsy and sweaty, and he wondered for a moment whether the affair was worth the trouble.

Then Lila touched his arm. "Your drink, darling." He looked at her, took in the rich, dark hair piled high on her head. Her makeup was not heavy, but it was dramatic, particularly around the eyes. She wore a simple black dress which accented the lush contours of her body, the creamy whiteness of her skin (she was the only woman in the room who did not have an expensive tan). His eyes moved to his wife, then back to his mistress. Sally looked like a duchess. But Lila looked wanton and exciting—a Delilah—and he wanted her very much, then and there. He would go on with it, he thought, a little while longer. There would be time to end it later if things got sticky.

He forced himself to keep calm, though at one point, when he thought Lila was being particularly outrageous, he snapped at her, "For heaven's sake, Lila, can't you tone it down a little? I'm not asking you to be furtive—but do you have to flaunt— things?"

She opened her eyes wide, all injured innocence. "But Brad, dear, you know I love to flirt. Wouldn't it look strange if I ignored you? After all, you're the most attractive man here."

He had no answer for her. But he breathed an audible sigh of relief when she called out her final good-byes.

Later that evening his relief dissipated completely when the maid summoned him to the phone. "Miss Carstairs for you, Mr. Jeffers."

"Lila!" He snapped into the phone. "What do you think you're doing?"

"Why, Brad—how mean you are! I just called because I forgot to tell you something this afternoon. And since this is Labor Day, I thought it needed saying. I wanted you to know that I have no intention of going underground until next Memorial Day. I'm not like the lawn furniture and the outdoor grill. If you want to say good-bye right now— then, fine, we can do that. But if we're still going to be friends, then you should know that I expect a fair amount of your attention. And I expect that attention not to be tied in any way to Sally's geographical whereabouts. I hope you do understand. I won't keep you any longer— so good-bye, Brad dear." And when he heard the click in his ear, Brad felt that somehow he had crossed another line.

"Who was that, dear?" Sally called from the living room, where she was supervising the caterer's helpers removing their paraphernalia.

Since the maid had taken the call, he didn't dare lie. "It was Lila, darling. She asked me to look for an earring she might have dropped on the terrace."

There was a slight pause. "That's strange. I didn't think she was wearing any earrings today."

After the two of them had gone to bed that evening, Brad played back that phrase in his mind. Was it the warning of a wife who suspected that all was not as it should be? Or was it the ingenuous remark of an innocent? He decided on the second possibility—because it was the easiest way to get some sleep.

After Lila's Labor Day ultimatum, Brad established a new schedule that would, he hoped, enable him to spend time with her without arousing Sally's suspicions. He began to visit the Athletic Club regularly, where he would do a few laps in the pool, play a little squash—and then rush off to Lila's, where he would finish the evening, first in her shower, later in her bed.

He was vague about this new regimen, leaving Sally to assume that it had to do with his health ("Can't spend all my time at my desk, darling. Roger warned me that was the surest way to a heart attack") and his business ("Don't like to do too many of those business dinners at home—it's just too boring for you").

Sally had no reason to think otherwise. Brad certainly looked fitter and leaner than he had in years. But for him, it was a little tiring. He knew that if he wanted to keep Lila, he could not afford to let her feel neglected.

He noticed that she could sound petulant, discontented, about the very ground rules she had accepted from the start. He had promised himself that he would give her up if she overstepped certain boundaries, but now he found that he just kept moving the boundaries—like the gambler who says he will try his luck "just one more time." And because he was aware of this slippage, he began to dread the moments when she would stick out her lower lip and pout—a mannerism he had once found sexually exciting.

"Bradford, dear," she might say, voice all soft and trembling, "I'm just feeling so unhappy today. I missed you so much. And I'm so sad that we can only see each other a little bit." Here Brad would feel anxious and a little guilty, because in truth he knew he could not possibly survive a full-time diet of Lila's version of "A Thousand and One Nights."

"And," she would go on, "we hardly go anyplace. I'm a media personality, you know, and I'm just not spending enough time being seen in the right places—or any places, for that matter." Brad would try to pacify her with a piece of jewelry, some flowers, or perhaps a large bottle of perfume.

Sometimes, when he consistently refused to share a holiday

with her, she would go off alone, returning to hint about the male companionship she had found without him. He would pretend to be jealous, because he thought her vanity demanded it. But in fact he was never jealous where Lila was concerned, though he would have exploded with rage had anyone tried to approach Sally. Lila was his bad woman, and part of her allure had to do with her desirability to other men. Occasionally he would ask her about the other men in her life, and when she realized he was more curious than jealous, she became annoyed. He always retreated when Lila turned negative, for he was afraid of the day she would face him with more than just a flurry of pique.

It had happened on her thirty-ninth birthday. He had sent thirty-nine roses, and he brought with him a bottle of Dom Perignon and a pair of small but perfect diamond stud earrings. He found Lila looking unusually beautiful. She wore a simple white sheath, adorned with a single strand of antique silver beads. Her face was pink and flushed, her eyes glittering. He thought that perhaps she had been drinking.

"Happy birthday, Lila." He gathered her to him for a ritual kiss, but she seemed unyielding. "What is it? What's wrong?"

"Oh, Bradford dear," she began, in a voice different from the one she used when trying to coax him into taking chances, "a day like this—it just makes me realize how little we really share. It makes me think that perhaps I'm wasting too much of my life on this relationship."

"But Lila, my dear . . ."

"No. Just listen. While I was waiting for you, I realized that if something had come up, something with Sally, you would have stood me up. After all, it's happened before. Mind you, I'm not nagging. But I did realize today that I've been letting my life be dictated by a third person. And I did tell you I wouldn't do that."

"I have tried not to let you feel that way. . . ."

"I know you have, Brad, darling. It's just one of those facts of life, and I've just realized it's time perhaps to acknowledge . . ."

Brad could not let her go on. Although he had often thought that life might resume a refreshing simplicity without Lila, he could not think of giving her up. Not yet. "Lila, listen—please listen—I want you to stop and think a minute. Think of something that would convince you that what you're saying isn't true. Something that would make you know that what we share is important to me, too.''

She closed her eyes and assumed a position of deep thought. Then she opened them and looked directly at Brad. ''A holiday with you. A real one. Someplace nice. Someplace a man takes a woman he loves—not a woman he wants to hide.''

Now it was his turn to be silent. What she was asking could be very dangerous, but it was clear there would be no negotiating this point.

She reached out and patted his hand ''It's all right, Brad. Forget it. You asked me a question and I gave you an answer. I think I've proved to you that I was right.''

''No, Lila, no you haven't. You just caught me off balance. You're perfectly right. Perhaps I've carried discretion too far. There's no reason why we can't have a bit of time together. A long weekend—perhaps the Bahamas. How would you feel about that?''

She smiled now. ''That sounds simply marvelous.''

''Good. That's settled then. And what about this evening? Where would you like to go?''

''Tonight I don't want to go anywhere at all. I want to open this marvelous champagne. And I'm going to serve you some divine pâté, which I made myself. Then we are going to nibble on some Cornish hens stuffed with wild rice. And then we are going to bed.''

They toasted Lila's birthday and their coming holiday with flute glasses the texture of butterfly wings. Brad hoped that everything would turn out all right.

—◄ 31 ►—

''Happy anniversary, darling.'' Brad kissed his wife tenderly on both cheeks.

''Happy anniversary to you, Brad. And thank you.''

''But you haven't even opened my present yet.''

''The 'thank you' is for making me happy.''

"Well, Mrs. Jeffers, the pleasure has been all mine. Now open your gift."

"You open yours, too. We'll do it together."

Sally's gift was a necklace of small diamonds—fifteen in all, one for each year of marriage—set into a chain of fine platinum. "Thank you again. It's beautiful—and so extravagant."

"You deserve the best, Sally—you are the best. And thank you for this," he said, holding up the malachite lighter from Cartier's. "I hope I don't lose it."

"You'd better not. Put it in your pocket before our guests arrive. And don't you dare take it out and leave it somewhere."

"I promise I'll be careful. In fact, I'll tie it to my wrist. Is that good enough?"

"Silly." She smiled and kissed him, then turned to greet the first of their guests.

Like all of Sally's parties, this one was a success. There had been a few worrisome moments. In the general flurry of preparation, one of the caterer's helpers had broken a favorite vase of Sally's. She supposed the caterer had insurance, but she was afraid if she reported the damage, the waiter might lose his job.

Then the trio of musicians she had hired—well, they turned out to be a little less proficient than she had been led to believe.

She looked around anxiously—and relaxed when it seemed the guests were having a good time anyway. The champagne was evaporating at a brisk rate, and Sally wondered if she might have underestimated the capacity of her guests.

Shortly before midnight Brad raised his glass and called for quiet. "Listen, everybody. Before this day is over I want to offer a toast to Sally."

"To Sally." Glasses were raised.

"Thank you all," Sally said. "Now if you'll excuse me—I want to go into the kitchen to make sure we haven't run out of champagne."

As she worked her way through the crowd, she brushed against a man from Brad's bank—a man she usually avoided because he had an unpleasant habit of becoming familiar when drunk. She tried to edge past him quickly, but she was not quick enough. He reached out and grabbed her arm. "Sally, dear," he began, and her heart sank because she could see that he had consumed a great deal of alcohol. "You haven't let me wish you a happy anniversary."

"Thank you, John, but I really have to go. . . ."

"That's not very friendly, Sally. You have time for an anniversary kiss—everybody gets to kiss the bride, you know." Before she could pull away, the man had tightened his grip on both her arms, pulling her closer, until she could smell the alcohol on his breath. She tried to avert her head, but he was too quick for her. Then his mouth was on hers, wet and insistent, his tongue pushing past her clenched teeth. She felt as if she had stopped breathing, as if she would faint if she did not get away. Panic robbed her of her poise, and in one desperate movement she shoved hard, sending him sprawling onto the floor.

The man's wife was now at his side, apologetic, embarrassed, whispering a suggestion that they leave at once.

"No," he shouted, his face red with drink and humiliation. "No, dammit. Who does she think she is, getting so self-righteous over a little anniversary kiss? Where does she get off being so holy? Everybody knows about her—and them. . . ." He staggered to his feet, pointing a finger at Brad and the dark-haired woman who was at that moment holding his arm.

Conversations died as almost all the eyes in the room traveled from Sally's face to those of Brad and his mistress.

As soon as the words had been spoken, Sally felt the beginning of a nervous laugh, which then caught in her throat as she realized that for a few heart-stopping, life-shattering moments all conversation and laughter had suddenly stopped. The man's words hung in the air like a noxious gas. And in those few moments Sally was poisoned by more truth than she could endure, more than she had allowed to penetrate her consciousness throughout all the years of her marriage. She realized suddenly that she, quite possibly, was the only person in the room who had not known of her husband's affair.

Somehow—she never really noticed how—the party ground to an agonizing end. The guests made hasty, almost furtive good-byes and withdrew, covered with shame and pity for Sally, who had—everyone agreed—never done any harm to anyone. Bits of clichés floated through the air to replace the conversations that had died. Sooner or later it had to come out. . . . Isn't the wife always the last to know? . . . Perhaps it's better this way. . . .

Sally heard nothing. It was as if the contents of her head had been spilled out, leaving only masses of cotton wool in their place. She could not think, could not focus or make contact either with her surroundings or with the people attached to the voices that seemed to be buzzing around her.

She could not have known it, but Brad was looking at her with alarm, for she resembled a life-size doll being handled rather clumsily by a drunken puppeteer. Torn between the fear that she might make a scene if he approached her and a genuine concern for her welfare, Brad yielded to his less selfish impulse. He went to her, put his arm around her shoulder, and guided her gently toward their bedroom. "Come, Sally dear," he said softly. "Come with me."

Had he known his wife better, he would have realized that she was beyond scenes, beyond recriminations of any kind. With one devastating blow to her very soul, Sally had been stripped of the possibility of anger, of rage, of hate—of emotions that might have been her salvation.

She allowed herself to be led, although she was not really able to connect with the man who was saying soothing words in a voice that once had been lovingly familiar, but which now seemed to come from another time and place. She allowed herself to be put into the featherbed she had ordered from Paris.

But now there was no comfort here, in this serene and beautiful womanmade oasis—here where she had spent so many hours arranging and rearranging the life that had, until a few short heartbeats ago, seemed so perfect.

She took the pill that Brad handed her. She vaguely heard him murmur, "Get some sleep, Sally dear, and we'll talk tomorrow. Everything will be all right." She swallowed the tablet, but what was left of her thought process rapped back a silent answer: Nothing will ever be all right again.

Yet somehow the drug did its work, and it was twelve hours later when Sally reopened her eyes. For a few brief merciful seconds, she did not remember the night before. Then she saw the note propped up on the bedside table, supported by the Art Deco clock—a whimsical piece wrought of blue mirrored glass that she had discovered in a small antique shop on Bleecker Street.

She read the words penciled in Brad's precise script: "Dar-

ling, I knew you were feeling pretty awful, and I didn't want
to wake you. I'll be home from the office early, and we can
talk then. For now I'll say I'm so very, very sorry. I would
not have hurt you for the world. I will do anything you ask to
make it up to you.''

Sally read the note twice, but it failed to touch her. What
she wanted was to have her world back—not the real world,
but the world she had fashioned herself, a universe concocted
of Saarinen tables and Eames chairs, of fabrics from Laura
Ashley and wallpaper from Scalamandre, of crystal from
Baccarat and silver from Tiffany. That was the world she
wanted back—the fairy tale, as it had appeared so often on
the pages of *Women's Wear Daily*. She wanted back the
couple that she and Brad appeared to be, and not the couple
that last night's incident had forced her to see—a man and a
woman joined in a stick-figure marriage.

The phone rang, as it would, sporadically, during that
fog-benumbed day, but Sally told her maid she would be
taking no calls at all. She felt she could never talk to anyone
again, never hold her head up or walk into a crowded room
again. She was certain everyone must be laughing at her.
Poor silly Sally, with her head buried in the sand while her
husband and her friend were making a fool of her. She should
have known. Any woman who was not a fool would have
known.

And after the first flurry of laughter and gossip died down,
what then? Looks of pity, condescending smirks—she knew
she could never bear it. But the alternative—what choice did
she have? She could divorce Brad and go out with as much
style and flair as she could muster. But where would she go?
In her world, which required a wealth of inner resources
merely for survival, she would be left a beggar. Somewhere,
sometime, Sally had taken everything she possessed and made
a single investment—in Brad, in her marriage, in her home.
And in so doing, she as an individual had ceased to exist.

Now there was nothing left. When she tried to think of the
future, she felt tired, used. Finished.

Later that evening Brad tried to expiate his sense of guilt,
for he had just begun to see how deeply wounded Sally was.
He launched into the speech he had spent half the day preparing. But the carefully chosen words found no response. Those
words had been calculated to reach someone like himself—a
person to whom marriage was a pleasant and comfortable

foundation on which to build a life—not a person to whom it meant life itself. In Sally's place, Brad would have been hurt, humiliated, embarrassed, but certainly not beyond repair. He admitted to himself that he would probably have required a divorce, but on the other hand, he reasoned that Sally, being a woman, might not need to ransom her pride so dearly.

And so he talked, in stock phrases: "I wouldn't blame you if you wanted a divorce, Sally dear, and if you do, I certainly wouldn't stand in your way. But I hope you can take a minute to reconsider." These phrases he endowed with the utmost sincerity, for he did not, after all, want to be in a position in which Lila would find him to be husband material. After Sally's exquisite housewifery, Lila would just not be—suitable. As a mistress, Lila had been thoroughly engaging. But as a wife—no, Lila was not Sally. And, quite frankly, he did not think Lila could even begin to fill Sally's impeccably made shoes.

He paused, to indicate an air of sensitivity, to convey to Sally that he understood what she must be thinking and feeling. He did not know that she was quite numb and that his best efforts were being wasted on his audience of one. She nodded, since Brad seemed to be waiting for her to do something.

So he went on: "If you can find any reason to forgive me, Sally. If"—again he paused, to play what he thought was his trump card—"if you feel we've had a good life together, except for this . . . this lapse of mine—and it is all mine," he hastened to add. "If you can forgive me, then I can promise you that nothing like this will ever happen again." This declaration was heartfelt, at least for the moment.

"I know I've embarrassed you, Sally," he continued, "and I would give anything if I could buy back what I've done and spare you what you're feeling. But look here"—he flashed a boyish smile, trying to make her a coconspirator in a game of you-and-me-against-the-world—"I'm willing to be as publicly chastened as you want me to be. I'll go to my club for a while. I'll tell everyone you've thrown me out—and that I've begged you to take me back. I'll hire a skywriter . . . I'll take an ad in Times Square . . . right up in lights. I'll say: 'Bradford Jeffers is a fool—and he begs Sally for a second chance.' "

He finished his speech and focused the full force of his considerable charm in her direction. For a brief moment the meaning of what her husband was saying did get through to Sally. And although she was not a woman given to bitterness or bile, an ironic smile played on her lips. She realized that Brad was proposing to mend the monstrous lie that had been their marriage with yet another lie.

She saw that he was again expecting some sort of response. And she saw that nothing he said had made any difference in the way she felt. It was no longer in his power to change anything or repair the damage he had done. He had destroyed her inner sense of self, and all he could offer now was a choice of face-saving devices that seemed rather shabby.

Still, she thought she had better say something or he would go on with this dreary business. "I don't know what I want to do, Brad. I need some time to think. Maybe it would be a good idea if you did go to your club. That will give me some quiet time alone. I'll call you as soon as I can."

Brad was completely startled, but he made a quick recovery. He had been counting on the comfort of continuity to save the day. He felt that the longer they were together after the initial shock of Sunday night's fiasco, the less likely Sally would be to break that thread. He had also counted on his wife's tendency to defer to him. He had thought she might even excuse him, for had she not defended the double standard, not once but dozens of times? Had she not, when the gossip turned to this man or that man who was having an affair, had she not automatically assigned blame to the wife? The wife who had not kept up her appearance, her mind, the quality of her home?

Not that he wanted her to blame herself for his affair, Brad told himself. But dammit, a marriage to the same person did get boring for a man. A man worked hard—he needed a bit of diversion now and then. Dammit, Sally should understand that.

By the time he got up to leave the apartment, Brad was actually starting to feel a little peeved at Sally's attitude. Here he'd tried to be a gentleman, offering her all sorts of reparations, and she was behaving as if nothing at all would do. He didn't like this attitude, not a bit. But on the surface, he maintained the good manners that were the product of his breeding.

"Of course, Sally, try to get some rest. Please take care of yourself. Just know that I love you very much. . . ." Here he reached out to stroke her cheek, not daring to attempt a kiss.

But her face eluded him, coldly and deliberately—and this small gesture, too, struck a warning note. It made him push a bit harder than common sense would dictate. "Maybe one day you'll be able to smile about all this," he said.

She did not answer, and as he rode downstairs in the elevator he thought that he didn't like the idea of Mrs. Bradford Jeffers—the very beautiful and rich Mrs. Jeffers—being on her own in Penthouse A for any length of time. He knew very well that news of her new status would quickly make the rounds of La Grenouille and Le Cirque and Le Cygne, that Suzy might drop a word in one of her columns and then everyone would know. There would be any number of men who would be delighted to make a try for such a delicious prize as Sally Jeffers. He didn't like that idea at all, anymore than he liked the idea that Sally, who had always behaved as if she had made a lucky match with him, might begin to suspect that it was perhaps he who had been the lucky one, that she was still a very desirable woman.

He resolved to send her flowers at once, with a nice note—loving, tender, concerned, but not pushy. Then maybe tomorrow he'd pick up a little something from Cartier's—no, that was bad; errant husbands always ended up at Cartier. Something from Van Cleef, instead, with another tender note. He'd keep it up on a daily basis—meaningful gifts accompanied by meaningful notes. She wouldn't be able to resist for long. Sally was far too much a lady to hold a grudge. By the time he hailed a cab and gave the address of the Metropolitan Club, Brad was feeling much, much better.

32

For three days she sampled life alone, as plain Sally Jeffers, without the cushioning security she had known as Mrs. Bradford Jeffers III. Each morning she got up as usual and drew a lukewarm lightly scented bath. But she bathed herself mechanically, instead of luxuriating, as she had in the time when she could contemplate everything around her with satisfaction.

Mechanically she ran the pumice stone over her heels, her elbows. Taking advantage of the steam from the tub, she covered her face with an almond-honey mask, then gently removed it with a washcloth. Next, a brisk scrub with a loofah across her belly, down her inner thighs—a ritual intended to ward off the creeping invader known as cellulite, but now an empty gesture since she hoped for nothing at all.

She got up from the tub and dried off in her terry cloth burnoose. It was one of a matched pair that she and Brad had bought in Aleppo, during one of their annual vacation-shopping junkets. She walked to her wall-long closet, to survey the neatly hung works of Calvin Klein and Ralph Lauren, of Gianni Versace and Cacharel, of Ted Lapidus and St. Laurent. Superstars all, waiting for her approval, for her unerring touch—the whimsical accessory, the bold accent with jewelry, the Sally Jeffers magic that always made her Halstons, her Norells so much more interesting than those which adorned the bodies of other, less creative women.

Now, even in her distracted frame of mind, she picked up, then discarded a Nippon shift, because she had noticed, while bathing, the premenstrual puffiness around her middle—a flaw that would cause the dress to hang less than perfectly. She chose instead a softly flared French skirt and a full Italian silk blouse.

Then she turned her attention to the problem of filling the day. There would be no parties to give, no business dinners to arrange, no theater openings to attend, no lunches at Lutece or festive evenings at Regine's. And so she found herself with large empty hours stretched out ahead of her—a long frightening void before she could turn to the familiar rituals of bedtime: the shoes returned to the shoe trees, the clothes carefully inspected, and then turned over to the maid, either for a repressing or a trip to the cleaner's; the cleansing cream, carefully applied and scrupulously removed; the tender dabbing at areas around the eyes with the gentlest of Laszlo's ointments; the night cream lavished into the throat and the rest of the face; and finally—the harsh nightly inspection. Was it time for the "full lift"—the inevitable follow-up to the eye tuck she had had done when she was only thirty, when she had noticed that the little pouches were lingering beyond early morning?

Brad had never known. Nor would he have known about anything else she had done to her body. She had never left traces of her serious cosmetic efforts around, never allowed him to see evidence of her menstrual cycle.

Sally had believed it was her job to present Brad with a wife who was as lovely and well turned out as money and science and cosmetology could make her. She acknowledged that it was her responsibility to move from youth to middle age and beyond with as little offense to her husband's aesthetic sense as was humanly possible. She reasoned that since he had married an exceptionally beautiful and fresh young woman, she owed him the courtesy of providing an exceptionally handsome older woman to share the final years of that marriage.

She thought for a moment of spending the day at Elizabeth Arden. She was certain that if she called, they would find the time and space for her. Or perhaps a few hours at Kounovsky's—some brisk exercise, a sauna, and then a massage. But there, as at all the temples dedicated to the preservation and improvement of the female body, she would risk running into someone from her circle. None of them were her friends, not really—they were just women similarly devoted to extracting, by whatever means they could, a few extra moments of beauty before the inevitable came. No—Arden's and Kounovsky were out.

Sally considered whiling away an hour or two at a gallery or museum. Then she rejected that possibility, too. She had never developed a capacity for solitary pleasures. She had thought that this was the last resort of poor, less fortunate women.

Shopping perhaps, she thought. The new crop of furs would have arrived at Bendel's. Or maybe she could have a fitting at Madame Daunou's—to replace those brown suede boots that had finally shown signs of wear. Yet when she considered the prospect, she found that she was suddenly too tired, although it was only eleven in the morning, to give shopping the serious attention it warranted. For Sally was the rare woman who never bought on impulse, who never shopped to cheer herself, who rarely made a mistake. She pitied those women who accumulated closets full of expensive disasters. No, shopping was out.

A movie? No. To sit in the dark alone was quite out of the question.

So Sally went nowhere and did nothing. Instead, she curled up in one of the oversize lounge chairs on the terrace, closed her eyes, and let the sun try to warm her chilled body. Although she was trying not to think, her mind began to range into the past. She remembered a day when she had come home from school with spots on her face and a temperature, afraid that Alicia would scold her for playing with a classmate who had the measles—and for allowing his germs to infiltrate the Richman family. By the time Alicia had returned from the gallery, Sally had worked herself into a state of near-hysteria.

"But Sally, you haven't done anything wrong," Alicia had tried to tell the sobbing child, bewildered though she was by the sobs that shook her daughter's body.

Her father had looked from mother to child and shaken his head. Then he had sent Alicia out of the room. He had fluffed up Sally's pillows and arranged her covers just the way he knew she liked them. "Now, princess," he said soothingly, "I know it seems to you that Mommy is always right and perfect, and that she expects you to be right and perfect, too. But that isn't true. Mommy makes mistakes sometimes—and sometimes she gets sick, too. It's just that she handles these things in ways that other people don't always understand. And I think you should know that her way isn't always the best way. It's human to be weak and imperfect sometimes. And when you're feeling awful—the way you are right now— then I think the best thing you can do is to give in to it. Don't fight it, Sally—just let it happen."

She had fallen asleep to the gentle sound of his voice. And when she woke up the following morning, she was already feeling a little better. How wise, she had thought, how wise Daddy was to know so much.

Now she closed her eyes and repeated his words. Give in to the pain. Let it happen. All day she remained on the terrace, shifting her position from time to time, taking bits of nourishment from the trays Tina brought out periodically. She waited for the bad feelings to wash over her, through her— and then to leave her alone. But nothing happened.

When night came, she was still there, feeling achy and cramped. Of course. She had been silly to imagine that the formula of childhood would still work for her. Nobody could help her now.

The next two days were a repetition of this one. Though she did not consciously realize it, Sally was fighting for her life. Without knowing it, she was trying to reanchor herself in the world around her. But Sally had never developed the constitution of a fighter. Unlike Jenny, who had rebelled and challenged, who had been beaten and come back to fight again, Sally had never tested herself in combat. She lacked the muscle and sinew and nerve to fight. She lacked the animal instincts of the survivor.

Sally was a hothouse woman, a woman nourished by a rarefied, artificial atmosphere who was beaten down by the harsher elements of real life. She struggled against herself, but she did not really know how to put up a fight. And like the gentle creature that she was, Sally surrendered.

Brad carried out his plan to recapture his wife, to reestablish his position and his rights with her. The flowers came regularly, as did the carefully chosen gifts and the sincere notes—all of which were certain to melt Sally's emotional reserve.

But her reactions puzzled him. They were all so unlike the Sally he had known for so many years. She thanked him politely, even graciously, for his offerings, assured him that she had received and carefully read his notes. But he had the irritating feeling that she was somehow not . . . not really there.

He found it hard to make sense of that attitude when he considered how hurt and upset she had seemed to be at the news of his infidelity. One would think, he reasoned, that if he mattered that much to her, then his peace offerings should elicit some livelier response.

He could not begin to imagine that Sally was quite beyond his ability to reach her. Having briefly sampled the prospect of a life alone, Sally decided there was no place she wanted to be, no one she wanted to be with, nothing she wanted to do. With that decision came another—that she no longer wanted to exist.

Once she had reached this juncture, she felt a certain calm, even a peace. She moved as efficiently and smoothly as she ever had in planning one of her better dinners for twelve.

Sally's death would be her final social event. But she could not leave any of it to chance. That would go against the grain. She could not die in one of those lurid tabloid scenarios, leaving tedious details for her survivors. How strange that word seemed—survivors. Yes, the word was altogether appropriate.

What would they do, she asked herself, when she was . . . deceased? Not one of those excessive funerals, she hoped. Might Brad feel he could somehow expiate his "lapse" with a final burst of public grief? She shuddered at the thought that he would probably invite everyone they knew to share with him a last paroxysm of excessive sentimentality.

No, she could not let that happen. If Sally's life had not been exactly what she had thought, then at least her final moments would have some integrity.

She sat down at her antique secretary, took out the creamy vellum Tiffany paper, the vermeil pen from Cartier. In her distinctive, graceful penmanship, she wrote the word "Mother" on one envelope. Inside, a brief message: "Dear Mother, I'm so sorry to hurt you in this way. I love you. Sally."

To her sister, she wrote: "Dear Jenny, Have I ever told you how proud I am of you? I love you. Sally."

For Brad, there was no personal message. She felt that good manners did not require one. Instead, she left a list of instructions. "Dear Brad, No conventional service, please. Just a luncheon at the apartment. If you call the caterer, he will see to everything. No eulogy or anything embarrassingly sentimental. If Jenny wishes to say a few words, that might be nice. Keep the guest list to the names I've listed, please. I don't really have many friends, but I've chosen a few people who might wish to spend an hour or two remembering me. I'd like to be cremated, the ashes to be placed in our family vault. I don't think Mother will mind. Under the present circumstances, I'm sure you'll understand if I don't choose to spend eternity surrounded by the Jeffers." The note was signed simply, "Sally."

She left the three envelopes on her nightstand. She asked the maid to change the sheets on her bed, then told her she could have the day off when she was finished. From the neat symmetrical shelves in her linen closet she chose the violet flowers from Porthault.

From her lingerie drawer she selected a lavender silk nightgown—an antique shift she had found in SoHo, embroidered in fine ecru silk thread.

Still quite calm, she brushed her hair, considered applying makeup, then decided against it, settling instead for a dusting of blusher on the cheekbones and a soft rose gloss on the lips.

In the kitchen, she poured a large bottle of chilled soda into a cut-glass decanter, then placed it on a tray, along with a matching water goblet and the full bottle of pills—pills that Brad always kept handy for coping with jet lag and other lapses in normal sleep patterns.

She carried these back into the bedroom. As an afterthought, she went to the stereo system and twirled the dial on the FM radio until she found the sound of chamber music. She slipped between the sheets, arranging the bedclothes carefully around her. Methodically, she worked her way through the contents of the semi-opaque brown pharmacist's bottle.

She lay her head on the pillow, folded her hands over the covers, and listened to the strains of Dvorak's New World Symphony. She willed herself not to think at all, to hold back the images that threatened, at this final moment, to break through the cotton wool. Soon came the feeling of heaviness through her limbs. But in her head, there was a sense of illumination and peace, and finally—an echo of her father's voice: "Let it happen, princess, let it happen." And her murmured answer: "Oh yes, Daddy, oh yes."

The only contingency Sally could not provide for was the discovery of her body. When Tina came in the following morning, she started to make Mrs. Jeffers's morning coffee as usual. Then she cracked open the door to the master bedroom a few inches, calling out softly, "Mrs. Jeffers? Mrs. Jeffers—are you awake?"

When there was no answer, Tina shook her head and murmured, "Poor Mrs. Jeffers." She was aware that things were not right with the Jefferses. She had even heard that there was another woman somewhere. This had only doubled and redoubled her sympathy for her employer. She was such a nice person, a real lady. But that was the way men were—never appreciated when they had quality at home.

She closed the door and decided to let Mrs. Jeffers get her rest. Poor woman had looked terrible lately. She did not come back to the bedroom until one o'clock. She thought she might coax Mrs. Jeffers into taking a cup of that special consommé she had made the day before. And maybe one of those mushroom omelettes she always enjoyed.

She opened the door a bit. "Mrs. Jeffers," she tried once again. Still there was no response. Now the woman began to feel a stirring of anxiety. Maybe Mrs. Jeffers was sick. She walked to the bed and called out again, then reached out tentatively to touch Sally's hand.

The flesh was waxy and cold, and Tina ran from the room, her shoulders shaking, her stomach heaving.

Later, in the telling, this experience would become a dramatic high point in Tina's life. With each repetition she would embellish the range of her terror, the depth of her sorrow, and most of all—the purity and loveliness of the woman who had taken her life.

⟞ 33 ⟝

When Tina's hysterical phone call came, Jenny fled her home like a madwoman, flung herself into a taxi, and mechanically gave the driver the address on lower Fifth Avenue. During the very brief ride she tried to play back the phone call, tried to find something in the fragmented conversation that might somehow make it all a ghastly mistake.

Maybe when she arrived, she would find that Sally was not dead, that she had suffered some kind of seizure, something that had made her unconscious, even comatose, but not dead. Please God—not dead. Not sweet Sally, who had never harmed another human being. Dear God, she was only forty years old. It wasn't fair.

When she reached the front lobby, passed the familiar face of Sam the doorman, and buzzed for the elevator, she felt a tightness in her throat, a dryness in her mouth. And when she pressed the bell under the brass plate that said "Jeffers," the door opened almost instantly, as if Tina had been waiting on the other side.

She walked into the living room and found Roger Tataryan sitting silent and gray-faced, taking small sips from a cup of tea. "Oh, Roger—" Jenny burst into tears at the sight of the familiar old face. She flung herself at him, demanding to be comforted, as she had done so often when she was younger.

"Ah, Jenny." He sighed heavily, stroking her hair. "Ah, Jenny, I'm so sorry."

"What happened, Roger? What happened to her?"

"Sleeping pills," he answered softly. "By the time Tina

found her, she had been gone a long time. There was nothing anyone could do.''

"But where was Brad? And why, Roger? Why?"

Roger hesitated a moment. "Brad wasn't here, Jenny. He's been staying at his club. I don't like to repeat gossip, but I suppose you'll find out from someone. Tina told me that there was some . . . trouble . . . something about another woman, I believe. Brad moved out the following morning. That's all I know. She left you a note. I'm sure it's all right for you to see it, but you'd better be ready to show it to the police. They should be here soon. I've called Brad, too," he added hesitantly.

As he watched Jenny's lips tighten, Roger knew that the maid had been right. Sally had probably taken her life because her marriage had been failing. Roger did not believe much in modern psychiatry—he felt that common sense gave better answers than did Freudian dogma. But he had seen Sally's development from child to teenager to lovely young woman. And he was not surprised that this delicate beauty had chosen to die rather than face a life littered with broken dreams.

He could see the anger Jenny felt toward her brother-in-law. But Roger felt a twinge of pity for Brad Jeffers. Whatever he had done, he would now have to carry forever the guilt for his own frailties—and for the awful knowledge that something he had done had exposed a tragic weakness in someone else's soul, had driven the woman he had promised to love from despondency to despair and finally to a small brown bottle and oblivion.

Jenny's voice broke into his thoughts. "Can I see her now, Roger?"

He hesitated. Jenny was considerably stronger than Sally had been. But still, the body might shock her. Rigor mortis had begun to set in; the once fresh peach-bloom complexion had taken on a waxy cast, the delicate pink lips had turned cyanotic. Still, the woman had a right to a final farewell. "If you like," he answered. "Shall I come with you, Jenny dear?"

"No—thank you, Roger. I just want a few minutes alone with her."

"Very well. The note she wrote for you—it's just as she left it, on her night table. Call me if you need me."

Jenny nodded and walked purposefully into her sister's

bedroom. She covered the room in a few long strides, then forced herself to touch the form that had been her sister.

There—she had done it. She looked at the body that had already begun its journey back to dust and willed herself to superimpose the vision of another Sally onto the bed—a Sally smiling and radiant, impeccably turned out in one of her perfect costumes, a Sally standing beautiful and majestic in her own living room.

She closed her eyes, wishing to believe that if she somehow concentrated every fiber of her being, she might make Sally know how much she had loved her. "Oh, Sally," she whispered, "I'm so very, very sorry." It was a statement that covered everything, from the ways she might have failed as a sister to the way that Sally had been left so naked and vulnerable at the end.

She read the brief gentle note, and then she cried, grateful for the release the tears brought. She left the note with Roger, after extracting from him the promise that he would make certain she got it back from the police. Then she hurried to leave, not trusting herself to face her sister's husband.

Although it had been Sally's wish to have her final farewell at home, Jenny had wondered if she could make herself go back to Penthouse A so soon. Now she returned to the apartment, her arm linked with Alicia's. Paolo hovered protectively behind the two women, not wanting to intrude in their private grief, yet anxious to do whatever he could to help. Jenny suddenly felt the pressure of her mother's fingers. "I know this is going to be hard for you, Jenny. But try to remember what kind of person Sally was. Think of how she would have wanted us to behave today. We must think of that whenever we're tempted to . . . to get emotional."

Jenny looked at her mother, and as had happened so many times before, she was filled with both admiration and resentment for the strength and equanimity with which her mother faced life—and usually wrestled it to the mat. Jenny had always felt the loss of a child would destroy her, but Alicia seemed to be holding up quite well. Nothing at all like the collapse when Jenny's father died. This will pass, for her, Jenny thought. She's happy with Paolo—anyone can see that. She has him and soon she'll forget Sally.

If only, she thought, if only Sally could have inherited

some of the formidable strength she had carried in those genes. She must have been truly Daddy's girl, gentle and special—and frail.

That leaves only me, Jenny thought, smiling ruefully at the notion that she—her mother's harshest critic—was the one who "took after" Alicia. Well, it had to be one of us, she mused, for it was unthinkable that a woman as vivid and dynamic as Alicia would not have an heir, so to speak.

She cast a quick glance at the profile next to hers. It was still quite elegant, clean in its lines and commanding in its effect, from the top of the broad forehead down to the sharply defined chin. In an unconscious gesture of imitation, Jenny squared her own shoulders and lifted her head, ready for whatever lay ahead.

Now she and Alicia were being shown into the living room. Jenny's eyes scanned the gathering of mourners, looking for familiar faces. She saw her brother-in-law, deep in conversation with the fashion editor of a magazine that had done dozens of articles which had included Sally's image—Sally's face or Sally's apartment or Sally's favorite designers. She looked away quickly, but Brad had seen them. He left the woman and started toward them.

As he advanced toward his mother-in-law and sister-in-law, Brad Jeffers, graduate of all the right schools, successful banker, socially distinguished heir apparent to one of the city's most respectable fortunes, this same Brad Jeffers now looked like a man about to face the guillotine.

He paused a few feet from the two women, started to extend his hand, then thought better of it. He nodded solemnly. "Alicia, Sally." He had given some thought to facing his wife's closest relations, and he had racked his brain for something to say. But everything he considered seemed either banal or utterly tasteless. He found he couldn't even employ the standard murmur "I'm sorry." Of course he was sorry, as he damn well should be. But to these two women, who had lost a daughter and a sister, "sorry" from the man who had driven her over the edge would sound almost insulting. He hoped that Alicia might say something that would set the tone for the day.

Jenny noted Brad's discomfort with some small satisfaction. She decided to prolong it. She threw a curt "Brad" in his direction, then fell silent again.

Alicia moved into the breach. "Bradford, I think this day

will be hard for all of us, so perhaps it would be best if we all put our personal feelings aside and concentrate on getting through these next few hours.''

Brad fairly trembled with gratitude. ''Thank you, Alicia. You're very kind—and gracious.'' His mother-in-law's apparent calm made him go on, to seek a shred of absolution. ''I know I don't deserve . . .'' he began.

Jenny let out a sound that was meant to be a snort of derision and ended up as a strangled sob. ''No,'' she choked out, ''what you deserve is what every murderer deserves. You killed Sally, Brad. We know it, you know it—and everyone in this room probably suspects it.''

''That's enough,'' Alicia snapped, cutting off her daughter's tirade. ''We're here for Sally, and she would be absolutely horrified at this kind of display.''

The blood had drained from Brad's face, and he looked as if he might faint. Alicia took charge. ''Bradford, get hold of yourself. Jenny may have been tactless, but you might as well face the fact that people are going to be saying, or thinking, some unpleasant things. I daresay it won't last long.''

''Yes, you're right, of course,'' Brad murmured. Then his good manners took over automatically. ''Come inside, won't you?'' He led the women toward an empty space on the greige velvet banquettes that lined the far corner of the living room.

Alicia and Jenny sat down, and one of the caterer's white-jacketed helpers materialized, proffering a tray. ''Some wine— or perhaps you'd like something from the bar?''

They each accepted a white wine. Another tray-bearing waiter approached with stuffed mushrooms, miniature quiches, and bacon-wrapped shrimp. Jenny shook her head and clutched at Alicia's arm. ''Oh, Alicia,'' she whispered, as if they were sitting in a church, ''I wish we could have had a regular service somewhere. Then we wouldn't have to deal with all this.''

Alicia turned blue eyes flecked with pain on her surviving child. ''But this is what Sally wanted,'' she said reproachfully. And together they sat quietly while a light lunch was set out. Paolo fetched plates for both of them, but neither of them ate, clinging together as if they were allies in a room full of enemies.

At one point Jenny looked around, trying to determine what possible place the assembled guests might have had in

Sally's life. She recognized a couple of women with whom her sister had lunched on a fairly regular basis. There were several perennial bachelors of dubious sexuality, men on whom Sally had lavished thanks for their dependability and willingness to flesh out any female-heavy guest list, their readiness to bring gossip, repartee, and sartorial splendor to any gathering.

In addition to the fashion editor, a woman Sally had described as "kind," and who was thus automatically added to her circle of near-friends, there were two other members of the press. One was a lesbian gossip columnist who had adored Sally, in print, and who had missed no opportunity to rave about the splendors of Mrs. Jeffers's wardrobe or the perfection of her parties. The other was Vanessa Neville, the dowager empress of the city's fashion press, a woman who had been for two decades the reigning power of New York's press parties, the mistress of a governor, and the senior editor of the acknowledged star among the city's fashion magazines. When Sally had been a young bride, she had met—and impressed—Vanessa. Thereafter, Vanessa had made the younger woman a protégée.

Jenny saw—and almost did not recognize—Elie Lowenstein; it had been so many years since he had courted Sally, in this very apartment. He had married someone else, not the princess of his dreams, but an aggressive young lawyer like himself. Together they had created two bright children and two high-powered careers.

Elie had no real regrets, but every so often he allowed himself the harmless luxury of a brief fantasy, in which he danced until dawn holding a lovely young woman with silver blond hair and blue eyes, a young woman with a sweet full mouth and a soft yielding body. When he had read of Sally's death, he had allowed himself the question of what his life might have been like if she had chosen him. And whether she might be alive today if she had.

They milled around for an hour or so, this collection of professionally decorative people, those who made fashion and those who wrote and talked about it. They seemed uncertain on this occasion about what would be proper behavior at this intimate well-catered lunch. It was so much like other lunches Sally had arranged—except that Sally wasn't here.

Jenny stiffened as she saw Brad working his way across the

room in a shambling, almost crablike gait. His features seemed as blurred as his legs seemed unsteady. Jenny's lip curled. Suddenly her sister's husband, who had at times seemed distinguished, suave, charming—as handsome and desirable as the proverbial forbidden fruit—now seemed not only an immoral monster, but a disgusting one. Poor Sally, she thought, not for the first time that day.

Brad stopped in front of Alicia, as if he might seek some support from her, but he addressed his words to his sister-in-law. "Jenny, I don't want to put you on the spot, but Sally—in her note—she thought that if there were any words to be said, that you should be the one. . . ." He trailed off, waiting for her response.

I couldn't, was Jenny's first thought, as she contemplated saying something personal about Sally in front of this crowd, which had once seemed so glittery and attractive. They, like Sally's husband, seemed infinitely diminished by her death. It would be like talking about a pearl before swine. Yet the alternative—letting Sally leave this life, this apartment, this city without some mention of the fact that she had been there—this struck Jenny as the worst of two alternatives. "Yes," she said to Brad. "Yes, I'll say something."

She waited for her brother-in-law to hush the buzz of conversation. Then she got up and stood in the middle of the room in which she and Sally had played as children, in which she had seen her sister hold court among crowds of people she now felt were utterly worthless. "Sally Richman Jeffers," she began, with an emphasis on the maiden name, "was my sister, and I loved her very much. She was a good and kind person. . . ."

When Jenny finished the few words she had chosen spontaneously for her eulogy, she once more sat down next to her mother. Between clenched teeth she said, "Do you think we can get out of here now?"

"In about ten minutes, darling," Alicia answered. "Do try to be gracious as we leave. There's no need for any of these people to know our business."

"Yes, Alicia," Jenny said, in an imitation of her childhood "let's-humor-Mother" voice. As she waited the prescribed number of minutes, she looked around the room for what she was certain would be the last time. She knew she would never, ever come back here. She was even more certain, as her eyes flicked contemptuously over her brother-in-law, who was now definitely in a condition he usually described as "three sheets to the wind," that she would never knowingly set foot in any room where he might be present.

Two weeks later she received a note from Brad, informing her that Sally had bequeathed all her jewelry to her. These were "family jewels" they had giggled about when they were little, pieces Sally had inherited from Carlotta, as well as a number of things she had been given by her mother.

It was a fine collection, not a large one, but it was truly impressive in the perfection of its craftsmanship and the beauty of its stones. Among the loveliest items were a diamond-shaped lavaliere, given to Carlotta on her tenth wedding anniversary, a confection made of sapphires, with a fiery teardrop diamond at the tip. Then there was the flawless square-cut emerald given to Sharif by his mother, and the Deco diamond watch that Alicia had received on her sixteenth birthday. This bequest, added to what Jenny already had, would make her the owner of a fine jewelry collection.

After Brad explained the disposition of Sally's jewelry, he added another paragraph to his note: "It will take some time for the will to go through probate and for Sally's things to actually come to you, but I've asked our attorney to expedite this matter. If there is anything else of Sally's that you would like to have, just call him and I'll arrange for him to give it to you. I'm planning to give up the apartment and take a smaller place here in town. Since it belonged to your parents before Sally and I moved in, I feel that it should belong to you now. If you would like to take it over, let me know, and I will arrange for my attorney to make the transfer. Otherwise, I shall simply put the place on the market." The note was signed "Brad."

Well, she thought when she finished reading it, at least he has the good sense to know that we don't want anything to do with him, that there's no point in pretending we have anything left to say to each other. She considered making no answer at all, but then she reflected that he might only try to contact her again.

Instead, she took out one of the half pages she used for her office billing, omitted a salutation, and wrote on it the word "No." That should stop him, she thought. And she was quite right.

Although New York could be the smallest of small towns,

Jenny never saw her brother-in-law again. Occasionally, she heard a bit of gossip from "friends" who couldn't resist dropping the news that Brad was looking pretty seedy and that his taste in women had certainly declined. Or that Bradford had never looked better—and wasn't that a smashing young thing on his arm the other night. After a while neither one sort of news or the other had any great effect on Jenny—for neither would soften the loss of Sally.

Jenny's terse note had not surprised Brad, but he had hoped that her response might be different. He did agree with those who blamed him for Sally's death. Maybe it wasn't like first-degree murder, but he had been guilty of a kind of manslaughter—negligent manslaughter. He had been careless with Sally's peace of mind. And if he did not realize how hard she would have taken that fateful drunken outburst, well, he was guilty there, too. After all those years, he should have known his own wife.

Even his own usually taciturn father had been accusatory: "Dammit, Brad—she was a sensitive woman. Couldn't you have been more discreet?" Then, sensing that Brad himself was frayed rather thin, he had added, "Well, never mind, the important thing now is to keep your head. I'm sorry about Sally, but there's nothing to be done for her now. I don't want to see you go to pieces."

He had tried to keep his head—and had done so, just barely. But he felt like a monster at the very idea of profiting in any way from Sally's death. He decided to ask Alicia how he should dispose of Sally's clothes and furs, the pieces of furniture that had been passed down through the family—the apartment that Jenny had just turned down.

When he called his mother-in-law, he found her response civil and calm. "Have Tina box and label all the clothes. I'll arrange for the people from the Lighthouse to pick them up—Sally always donated something to their annual fund raising sale. I'll have one of the gallery trucks pick up the furniture. We can store it in one of our warehouses. Perhaps Rebecca will one day want some of the pieces. As for the apartment, you might as well dispose of it, Bradford. Paolo and I don't often come in from the Coast, and when we do, we usually stay at the Pierre.

"If you feel awkward about taking the money," she added, anticipating precisely what Brad's feelings were, "then perhaps you'd like to put it in trust for Rebecca. Your attorney could arrange it so Jenny would believe it was a bequest from Sally.''

"Thank you, Alicia. Yes, that feels right. I think that will be exactly right.'' He paused, grateful that Alicia was speaking to him as if he were a human being and not a monster. Reluctant to break the connection, he ventured, "Alicia, you must know how sorry I am. If there were any way I could have—''

"Don't, Bradford. I know you didn't set out deliberately to hurt Sally. She was her father's child. I think she was meant to live in a much kinder world than the one we inhabit. That was not your fault. For the things that were your fault I think you will do your own penance. I won't add to it.''

Several months later Sally's will passed through probate and the custodianship of her worldly goods was Brad's. Penthouse A was discreetly listed for sale with the venerable real estate firm of Hollister, Allison and Leeds, a firm that specialized in the management of fine apartment buildings and, more recently, in the resale of apartments in the city's better cooperatives. Brad's instructions to the broker were that the apartment should not be advertised, and that it should only be shown to "nice people.'' The price he left entirely to the broker's discretion.

"The apartment's been sold,'' Alicia told Jenny in an early-morning phone call.

"What apartment?''

"Sally's apartment. Brad called me last night.''

"Oh,'' was all Jenny said, for in truth she did not know how she felt.

"I just thought you'd like to know. It has been a kind of family tradition, that place.''

"Yes, I suppose it has—like being unhappily married.''

"Jenny!''

"Sorry. I'm not really feeling sorry for myself—just a little unsettled this morning.''

"Well, I should hope not. Because if you are, you might at least do so with some accuracy. My mother and father were very much in love with each other, until the day they died. And your father and I—no matter what you thought—we meant a great deal to each other. If there were mutual . . .

disappointments, nevertheless we cared. And we were each an emotional anchor for the other—which, by the way, should not be confused, even by your ironic mind, with a millstone.''

I wish we had been able to talk like this when we were younger, Jenny thought. Perhaps my life and Sally's might then have taken some different turns. To her mother, she said, "Yes, of course, you're right. I suppose it's this last generation of our family that's made a mess of things. Me with Jeffrey and Sally with Brad.''

"I think I still must argue the point with you, Jenny. There was nothing wrong with Bradford. He was a perfectly suitable husband. It's what Sally made of her marriage that was wrong. A relationship between two human beings is by nature imperfect. It simply cannot be idealized until it becomes a kind of shrine. It was Sally's weakness that did that. And I don't think we can condemn Bradford for it.''

"And what about me, Alicia? Did I choose a 'perfectly suitable husband' too?''

"I think in your less bitter moments you know that Jeffrey was not a bad person either. Perhaps more than a little egocentric, somewhat opinionated, a bit pompous at times— not major sins, Jenny. Not at all major.''

"So you think the failure of my marriage was my fault, then?''

"I didn't say it was anyone's fault. And maybe you shouldn't either. Maybe you can say that the marriage worked for a time, and then it simply stopped working, because its time ran out.''

"That's a very contemporary way of looking at things.''

"Well, it might be true. I've thought about this a great deal since Paolo and I were married. He was a perfect man for the season of my life that began after your father died. But in truth, I don't think we would necessarily have been so good for each other when we were younger, though of course I'd never say that to him. With you and Jeffrey, he may have been the perfect man for my Jenny when she was a young girl of twenty.''

"Why? Do you think I was vicariously ambitious? That I needed the promising medical student—that cliché?''

"Something like that. I think you had made up your mind to be a different kind of mother and wife from the one I had been. And you'll forgive me if I sound a little Freudian, but I think you chose the kind of man who would make it impossible for you to change your mind. In a marriage with Jeffrey there was room for only one ego, one career.''

"That's very neat, Mother.''

"No, Jenny, I don't think it was neat for you at all. You weren't like Sally. You weren't cut out to be Jeffrey's alter ego—the keeper of his house, the mother of his child.''

"I wasn't very good at it, was I?''

"Actually, considering the fact that you were a captive of your own choices, you were quite good. I'm sure I've told you this, but you must remember—if you're going to have another relationship with a man—that Jeffrey did not leave you because you failed him in any way. Believe me, if you hadn't been an eminently satisfactory wife, he would have been gone within a year, two at the most. No, my dear Jenny, Jeffrey departed because there was something else he wanted. And being Jeffrey, he thought he should have it.''

"Now you're making him sound unpleasant.''

"Not at all. Just human, as I said before. But—and I hope you don't get angry with me for saying this—I think in time you'll see his leaving as a gift. Now you're really free to choose—in a way you couldn't when you were younger, and certainly not when you were with your husband. You can be a whole person, Jenny, on your own terms. And you can still have love. It's possible. I can see that you're more at ease with yourself than I've ever known you to be. Now, I believe that if a man like Jeffrey came along, he would be totally and completely wrong for you.''

"How did you get so smart, Mother? You weren't always that way, were you?''

"Certainly not. In my own way, I was probably something like Jeffrey when I got married. I think I saw all of you— your father, you, Sally—as fragments of my life, with no unique needs of your own.''

Jenny chuckled, because she was enjoying this moment— and because they were able to talk about something that once had been a source of great pain.

"Something funny?'' Alicia asked.

"Something like that Mark Twain joke—about how wise your parents seem when they get older.''

"Not always. But thank you for saying that, Jenny. I know that Rebecca has always thought you were wise and clever and wonderful. I envy you that. But I know you earned it—in a way I never did.''

Jenny started to make the polite disclaimer, then stopped. "You know, maybe I have. Maybe that is the one wonderful thing I have left from my marriage."

"At least that. And the knowledge—think of it, Jenny, think of it—the pleasure of knowing yourself, and the strength of which you're capable—the strength to stand alone."

— 34 —

"How does it feel to be a success, Jenny?" Charlotte asked at one of the lunches that had become a regular custom for them.

"I don't know that I feel like a success, Charlotte. It's nice to be in charge of my life. But sometimes I miss Jeff—or at least I miss something."

"I know what you mean, kid, and I'm going to give you another of my pearls of wisdom. I don't know anyone who doesn't feel that something's missing at least part of the time. And it usually has nothing to do with getting back something from the past. I don't think you really want Jeff anymore, and he probably wouldn't get along with this new you at all.

"There's more out there, Jen. As long as you're alive, there's always the possibility of more. And wanting it—wanting and looking—that's what gives life extra zest. As long as you can still appreciate what you do have."

"I believe you, Charlotte. At least I can't find any fault with what you're saying. But I just feel as though I probably won't find another man. I mean, let's be realistic—look at all those pretty young things out there, looking for men, and not finding them."

Charlotte shook her head vigorously. "Wrong, kid, wrong. You have a lot to offer that all those pretty young things are missing—trust me. It's true."

"You're telling me that a woman with some miles on her can still attract a man—maybe even what they used to call 'a good catch.' Okay. Then can I ask you a personal question? Tell me if I'm out of line. . . ."

Charlotte's eyes twinkled mischievously. "You want to know about my 'twinkies'? You're wondering why a wonderful, substantial woman like me—a 'good catch,' were I only a man—why I spend my leisure time with sweet young boys with not much upstairs? I'll tell you the simple truth—at this stage of my life, 'twinkies' suit me best. And after all the years I spent being conventional, I figure I'm entitled to a little eccentricity in my old age. Maybe even a little depravity. Are you shocked?"

"No, of course not. I've just never heard anybody—I mean, anybody I know—talk like that."

"Oh, Jenny, Jenny, what a sweet, sheltered, and naive life you've had. And right here in New York City. It's incredible in this day and age."

Jenny stuck out her chin defensively. "That simply isn't true. You're just judging by appearances. Maybe I look like an ordinary housewife to you, but I'll have you know I've had much more experience than you could imagine."

"Really!" Charlotte fought to keep a straight face. "I never would have guessed."

"It's true," Jenny went on, not realizing she was being teased. "I had an affair—with a Greek—right after Jeff and I separated."

"I am impressed. Do go on."

"Well, that was all—besides Jeff—but it was a real affair, so there."

"Well, never mind, kid, that certainly qualifies you as a woman of experience."

"Oh, Charlotte, you're laughing at me!"

"Not at all, Jen darling, not at all. I just wish you knew how dear and precious you are. Now I want you to go out there and get some more 'experience.' "

But more "experience" did not come easily. First Jenny accepted a blind date with a doctor, arranged by the well-meaning mother of one of Rebecca's friends. Jenny thought wryly that her marriage to Jeff had apparently put her into some charmed circle which fitted her to be a companion to doctors.

She found her blind date, who had been described as "a brilliant man," to be as boring and pedantic as anyone she had ever met at a medical convention. Within minutes of arriving at her home, he had antagonized Rebecca by treating her as if she were two years old. Once, when he turned around, Rebecca signaled her mother with a frantic thumbs-down gesture that caused Jenny to burst out laughing. Laszlo Stern, M.D., turned and looked suspiciously at Jenny, the expression on his face suggesting that he might have made a mistake in bestowing his brilliance on this unworthy pair.

The remainder of the evening was no improvement. Although Jenny had expected this obviously well-off man to take her to dinner, he apparently had no intention of taking her anywhere. He had, however, brought with him a bottle of fine wine, which he decanted in an elaborate ritual, lecturing Jenny on the intricacies of treating good wine properly. He emphasized the word "good" a number of times, as if he suspected she was a Philistine who had heretofore known nothing finer than Ripple.

By the time the wine had breathed, the sediment settled, Jenny was starving, her stomach churning at the thought of sampling the wine without food to accompany it. She reached surreptitiously for a Rolaid. Finally she asked, "Would you like me to fix a bite to eat?"

"Why, yes," he said, his tone clearly indicating that she was remiss in not having provided some refreshments.

She foraged around in her refrigerator and found that anything substantial was either frozen solid or in the process of turning green. She inspected her cupboards, then marched out to face Dr. Stern. "We have canned soup and peanut butter," she announced, watching the look of pain that crossed his face. "The soup, I think," he said.

To the accompaniment of Rebecca's barely suppressed giggles, Jenny served her date a bowl of lentil soup while she ravenously devoured a peanut butter sandwich.

As they ate, Dr. Stern recited his curriculum vitae for Jenny. She was suitably impressed by his credentials and then volunteered the fact that she was in real estate. "Oh, really," he said, leaving little doubt as to what he thought of her work.

Feeling somehow responsible for filling the hours that loomed ahead, Jenny dredged her mind for memories of "doctor talk," trying to introduce subjects that would interest her date. Apparently this was the right thing to do, for the man brightened considerably and then told her she could call him Laszlo.

With some considerable effort, she kept up the good work

until, by the end of the evening, her jaw ached with boredom
and fatigue. When he finally looked at his watch and announced he had an early day tomorrow, Jenny's spirits leapt.
She escorted him to the door and held out her hand—to
forestall any possibility of intimacy. Enough was enough.

When he had gone, she mixed herself a stiff drink and went
into her daughter's room to say good night.

"Did you have a wonderful time, Mom?" Rebecca giggled
into her pillow.

"Wonderful. The next person who tells me to go out more
is going to get boiled in oil."

But two weeks later, Jenny was surprised to get a call from
Laszlo Stern. She was certain she had failed his preliminary
interview. When Rebecca answered the telephone, she covered the receiver and stage-whispered, "It's that *doctor*!"

Jenny shook her head frantically and waved her arms. She
panicked about having to choose between yet another dreary
evening and saying "no" to a man asking her out.

Rebecca frowned as she tried to decipher her mother's
frantic semaphores. Finally she caught the word "no." She
removed her hand from the receiver and said, with a poise
that awed her mother, "I'm terribly sorry I kept you waiting,
Dr. Stern, but Mother is unable to come to the phone right
now. In fact, she is leaving for an extended business trip. I
will have her get in touch with you when she is free. Thank
you so much for calling."

She hung up and made a mock bow in her mother's direction.

Jenny laughed with delight. "Oh, thank you, Becky, thank
you. I know I shouldn't have panicked—but I wasn't expecting that man to call again."

"Really, Mother, I'll forgive you this time. But you'll
have to pull yourself together. Don't you know these are
modern times? Men and women are supposed to be equal.
What did you think he was going to do? Bite you? Through
the phone?"

"I know, Becky, I know. It's just that some of us are
better at being equal than others. Your grandmother, for
example. It has nothing to do with modern times. I'll just
have to practice till I get it right. And you'll help me, okay?"

Becky smiled benevolently, pleased at this momentary re-
versal of their roles. "Anytime, Mum, any time."

•   •   •

Jenny tried again. It was spring, and she was far from ready to turn to Charlotte's prescription of bland young men who would stroke the ego, massage the soul, and tune up the body. She was more than receptive when she went to a Real Estate Board press conference at "21" and met Hal Houghton, who covered the real estate beat for the city's most prestigious paper. Hal did not look like Jenny's notion of a newspaperman. From the top of his expensive haircut to the tip of his Gucci loafers he was something of a dandy.

That particular day, Jenny had taken her clothes more seriously than usual. She was wearing a well-tailored beige wool suit, a blouse of cream crepe de chine, a pair of suede pumps. She carried a briefcase of softest leather, exquisitely fashioned and stitched by hand.

Hal approached her at one of the small open bars. Within a few minutes he had verbally skewered the principal speakers and had her laughing heartily at the bitchy wit that seemed effortless. She hesitated for only a second when he asked for her card, and the following afternoon, when he called to invite her to dinner, she accepted at once.

When he arrived at her apartment, she had dressed with care and had a bottle of Montrachet chilling. "Come in," she invited, determined to make this a glamorous New York evening. At that moment, Bruno, the Labrador, lumbered over and jumped up to plant several wet kisses on the guest.

"Get it off," Hal shrieked. "I'm allergic to dogs—get it off!"

Jenny looped her fingers into Bruno's collar and dragged the disappointed dog into her bedroom. "And don't you dare do anything on my rug." She put her face close to his and hissed her disapproval. In reply, he stuck out his tongue and licked her face.

"I'm sorry," she said to Hal.

"You didn't tell me you had a dog," he accused.

"You didn't ask me," she said lightly, not wanting the evening to get off on the wrong foot. "Here—sit down and I'll get you a glass of wine."

"I don't think I should sit on the couch," he said. "It's probably covered with dog hairs. I'll just stand. Maybe we should skip the wine and leave."

"Well, all right," Jenny said, her vision of a sophisticated evening in jeopardy.

Just then Rebecca came into the living room. "Hi, Mom,"

she said. "Hello," she added in Hal's direction. Jenny made a brief introduction.

"You didn't tell me you had a daughter," Hal accused again, after Rebecca left the room.

"But you didn't ask me," she protested, feeling in the wrong and wondering if she should do the sporting thing and let the man leave—alone—right now. Noticing that he was still searching the room anxiously for dog hairs, she said brightly, "Well, shall we go?"

"I've made a reservation at La Goulue," he announced as they rode downstairs in her elevator.

"That sounds lovely."

At the restaurant, Jenny let Hal order, which he did very well. She remarked appreciatively on the food and the wine, and she tried to ask intelligent questions about his work. But she had the feeling she was being measured on some scale—and was not receiving a very good rating. Oh well, she thought, if he could see me in my favorite clothes—she pictured her comfortable gray sweat suit—he'd probably wrinkle his nose and start sneezing.

Although she knew she wasn't making a great impression, Jenny had a good time anyway. Hal was clever and amusing, a master of gossip and small talk. He thanked her for an "interesting" evening. And he did not call again.

Although the men in her life were few and fleeting, Jenny felt more at peace, more fulfilled than she had in years. She and Rebecca continued to grow closer and shared frequent holidays, and she had some wonderful evenings with Charlotte at dinner and at the theater. Her circle of acquaintances grew, so that she seldom had to be alone unless she chose to be.

As for her work, she had found, in this accidental career, a sense of herself she had never known before. Under Charlotte's tutelage, she had grown and prospered, and the figures on her commission checks had increased accordingly. Charlotte had been talking retirement for some time, had mentioned opening a small boutique in a warm climate ("Maybe Acapulco or the Caribbean—something to keep me a little busy so I don't turn into a beachcomber"). Jenny knew that Charlotte was grooming her to take her place. And she marveled at least once a day at the luck that had brought Charlotte and her together. As for Charlotte, she always insisted it had not been luck, but fate.

It was either fate or Charlotte's perspicacity that had brought her heavily into the coop market at a time when coops seemed to have no future at all. In the sixties and early seventies she had never oversold the idea of the cooperative—she had merely directed her customers into sound buildings, where she could assure them, honestly, "If you ever want to sell, I think you'll be able to recover your investment. And I think you'll find the atmosphere much more pleasant than in a rental building."

She had worried, along with her customers, when New York seemed to be on the brink of financial disaster. She held her breath when talk of default filled the airwaves and newspapers, when businesses seemed to be fleeing New York in record numbers, when property owners appeared more than happy to sell.

The coop market fairly ground to a halt. And when some of her worried customers called, she urged them to hold on. "New York isn't going under—trust me. It's just a bad time. Don't sell now. Wait until the market turns around."

For those who insisted on getting out, she tried her best to find buyers. It was a slow and difficult process. Some sellers waited six months to a year for a buyer. Occasionally, when a valued customer wanted out and no buyer could be found, she bought the property herself, with the stipulation that the building's board would let her rent for a year or two.

Then suddenly, dramatically, there was a renaissance in the city. New York was saved. Suddenly the Broadway theater, which had been slowly sinking under the weight of mounting costs and crime and Times Square filth, surged forward with more new productions than there were theaters. Suddenly it was a time for glamour again. New York became attractive not only to the foreigners who had always appreciated the city, but also to suburbanites, people who had raised their families where the grass was greener and mortgage rates lower, people who now wanted to spend the "second season" of their lives having fun.

And almost without warning, Charlotte and Jenny had found themselves with more customers than they could handle, so many that they had to hire several new assistants. The price of apartments that hadn't moved at all the year before now doubled—then tripled—then edged steadily into what an incredulous Charlotte described as "the stratosphere."

One day, in the middle of what she called "this craziness," she invited Jenny to lunch—and announced her retirement. "Don't try to change my mind," she said, over Jenny's protests. "I've been thinking about this a long time—you know that. And now all this craziness has made me rich—my idea of rich, anyway. From here on in, I'd simply be working for the IRS—or I'd have to spend all my time looking for tax shelters. I just want to get away, and I want to turn it all over to you. This business has been good to me. Now it will be good to you. Knowing that will make me happy. And you can come visit me in my villa in Acapulco or St. Thomas. I'm going to make a career of fun now, kid. I'm going to get tan and fat and very lazy."

"That doesn't sound like you, Charlotte."

"Why not? You think I was born wearing a fedora hat and horn-rimmed glasses? You don't see me in a bikini—a pair of shorts?"

Jenny giggled. "Actually, I can see you in almost anything. I just meant I couldn't see you giving up New York—or slowing down."

"Change is what makes life interesting. It's what keeps you young, kid. Did you ever see yourself as a genuine businessperson when you were rattling pots and pans for your doctor-hubby?"

"No, I guess not. I did fantasize a lot, but nothing specific."

"So here we both are. I rest my case."

Jenny considered the implications of what Charlotte was offering. It would mean more money—a lot more money—and everything that came with it. And she would miss Charlotte very much. But the possibility of saying "no" did not seriously occur to her for even a moment.

— 35 —

As a bona fide expert in a growing field, Jenny found that she was gradually acquiring not only money and security, but something of a reputation. This brought her invitations to speak and to teach at lectures and seminars on the subject of purchasing a cooperative apartment. These offers she always accepted, since the exposure invariably brought her new clients and enhanced her reputation as a competent, trustworthy professional.

From there it was only a matter of time before she put together her own three-part seminar on coops, a course which, as fate would have it, she would teach at the New School.

The first time she leafed through the catalog that contained her listing, she turned impulsively to the section on art. Yes, he was still there—Rinaldo Fine—still teaching the same course. How long ago that all seemed. And how different she had been, the Jenny who had been so easily dazzled. She wondered if Rinaldo was still singling out "special" students for extracurricular instruction. She didn't care enough to find out.

And when she stood in front of her own class for the first time, everything that had happened to the old Jenny seemed light-years past. Just as the class was about to start, she detected an audible hum among the students. She glanced up, and there, not two feet from her desk, was Scott Manero, the tall, lean, and extremely sexy anchorman on one of the local news programs, looking every bit as attractive as he did on the small screen.

"Ms. Ashland?" he asked, in that same husky baritone that thrilled so many female viewers when he recited the nightly quota of gloom, doom, and human interest items that made up the six o'clock news.

"Yes, Mr. Manero? What can I do for you?"

"Well," he said, "I had planned to sit in on this seminar with the rest of the group. I'm putting together a report on the

341

changing real estate market in the city, and I wanted to see what level of information was being offered to the coop buyer today. Since you seem to be one of the experts in that field . . ." He threw out the compliment with the same boyish ingenuousness that was his on-camera trademark.

Jenny was flattered in spite of herself. "I thought this kind of research was done by assistants," she said. "I'm surprised that you're here in person."

He laughed. "Very perceptive, Ms. Ashland. I don't usually do this kind of thing. But we're trying out a new concept. It's called 'Knowing Your City,' and it calls for me to do a lot of location work. The first segment deals with finding a place to live. So here I am. I hope you don't mind."

"I don't mind at all. Perhaps it would have been better if you had given me some advance notice—as you can see, you seem to have a lot of fans in this room—but never mind. I'm sure it will all work out. Please—make yourself comfortable." She watched him choose a seat in a back corner, saw half the people in the class turn to watch him while the other half tried to look cool and nonchalant.

When everyone had settled down, she tapped lightly on her desk. "Ladies and gentlemen, this is a seminar on the mechanics and strategies of buying a cooperative apartment, as well as on the tax and investment advantages in making such a purchase. I'm sure you've all noticed that we have a distinguished guest with us this evening. Mr. Manero's presence seems to be a vote of confidence—which I hope will be justified—on the level of information you'll be getting here." There was a smattering of polite laughter. For a moment Jenny felt like a child playing grown-up, and she marveled at all the people sitting there, actually paying money to hear her. But as she started to lecture, she felt herself go into what she thought of as "automatic pilot." It was her defense against stage fright. As soon as she started talking about what she knew, the words seemed to come as if they had a life of their own. All she had to do was push the "start" button. While her mouth formed the words, her eyes watched Scott Manero busily taking notes, just as she used to in school. And once again she felt a moment of pleasure in herself.

When she had finished her basic speech, she asked for questions. A dozen hands shot up at once. She answered each query as crisply, as concisely as possible, and with as much solid information as she could offer. She was sorry that Scott

Manero seemed to have no questions. And she was even sorrier when the clock on the wall indicated that the class had come to an end. She thanked the group for their attendance. And she added, "I'll see you at the next session—and I hope that when you're ready to buy, you'll come to see me."

Although this invitation was always greeted with laughter, she was certain that a decent proportion of this group would indeed take her up on it.

"Ms. Ashland." This time it was a statement, not a question. Jenny looked up from the papers she was ostensibly shuffling, although she had in fact been aware of every step that Scott Manero had taken, from the moment he got up from his seat.

"Yes, Mr. Manero. I hope your time was well spent." My God, she thought, I sound so—so in control.

"Oh, yes, Ms. Ashland. I was really impressed. I think you give as much information as it's possible to give in one sitting." He grinned. "You've saved me or my researchers a lot of digging. I thank you. There's just one thing, though. . . ."

"Yes?" Her eyebrows went up.

"Well, I did have a number of technical questions—for the program, that is—and I didn't think it was fair to take class time with them. Actually, your talk gave me the idea of expanding my series a little. I wonder if I could pick your brain—if we could meet once or twice. I'll give you a spot on the show—how's that?" He grinned again.

"Well, Mr. Manero, that certainly sounds like a fair trade. I'll be glad to give you whatever material you need." She took out her leather appointment book. "When would you like to meet?"

"Well . . . if you're not doing anything now, maybe we can have some coffee or a drink. I'll explain exactly what I'm doing."

"Fine."

It was her perverse sense of history that made Jenny take Scotty to the Peacock, where she had spent that strange evening with Rinaldo Fine. Now she was the teacher. She smiled to herself, remembering again the shy, searching woman she had been.

They both ordered cappuccino, and Scott Manero spent a few minutes explaining his real estate series to Jenny. Then somehow they began talking about his divorce and hers, about the fact that he had no children, that she had a daughter. Later, they both agreed there certainly seemed to be a shortage of worthwhile members of the opposite sex. He explained that all the women he met were either clinging vines or extremely fickle. She nodded sagely, as if she understood perfectly. And he nodded in turn, while she explained that all the men she met were either sex maniacs or boring or, worse yet, both.

By the time they had finished their third coffee—and after she had said, "I really must go now, I have a breakfast appointment"—they agreed that their meeting had been a stroke of good fortune.

"When can I see you again?" he asked. Once again she took out her appointment book. "No," he said. "I mean to go out—as on a date. I'll call you from the office tomorrow to talk business. But I want to see you for dinner, maybe some music later?"

"Yes," she said, without even the moment's hesitation she'd always felt was proper.

"Thursday night?"

"Yes." This without even a token look at her book. "That will be fine."

He walked her to Sixth Avenue to look for a cab, and as they were crossing the street, he put his arm lightly around her waist. His touch made her shiver, and she hoped he hadn't noticed. When a taxi pulled up, he opened the door for her and said, "Good night, Ms. Ashland," with more than a hint of laughter in his voice. He leaned over and kissed her, and she felt as if someone had sent an electric current through her.

Later, she could not recall the cab ride home or opening the door to her apartment, but eventually she found herself sitting on her bed, trying to hold on to the warm glow that enveloped her.

"Mommy?" Rebecca's voice, fuzzy with sleep, came from the next room.

"Yes, darling. Go to sleep. I'll talk to you tomorrow."

" 'Night, Mommy."

" 'Night, baby."

Jenny found herself waiting for Thursday night as a child waits for Christmas. When he telephoned at six that evening and began his conversation with "Look, Jenny, I hate to do this. . . ." she felt a sharp pang of disappointment. Oh no, she thought. He's changed his mind.

"I'm stuck here," he went on. "Late meeting. So I thought I'd ask if you could meet me at Mr. Chow's. I've made a reservation for eight o'clock. I'm awfully sorry to do this. . . ."

She laughed with relief. "Don't be sorry—I really don't mind at all. I've been in a restaurant on my own before."

"Thanks, Jenny. Thanks for understanding."

Who wouldn't? she thought, smiling with anticipation as she hung up the phone.

In fact, she waited only fifteen minutes before Scott arrived, flushed, a little breathless, and obviously glad to see her. Without thinking, they leaned together for a New York air-kiss. He sat down and took her hand. "It's nice to see you again."

"Nice for me, too," she agreed.

They ordered drinks, and, a short time later, some dinner, but neither paid much attention to the contents of glasses and plates. There was an eagerness, an intensity about their conversation, as they rushed to spill out past memories, to empty themselves of past failures and disappointments, as if this would somehow bring them closer.

He told her about his work, about how he had started in a small Philadelphia station, how he had been "discovered," and how he had been brought to New York to become a "semi-star."

She protested his modesty. And then she told him about her humble beginnings in real estate, about the help Charlotte had given her, and how she owed so much to her mentor.

Scott expressed his admiration for her, for Charlotte—and for all women who "do things." And something in that compliment made her want to leave out all those Jeffrey years, years when she had rumbled with vague discontents and conjured unfocused fantasies about "doing things."

And suddenly she felt she had stumbled upon an important truth—that when you started a relationship with someone new, you could be someone new, someone you wanted to be. My God, she thought, maybe that's why self-made men leave their wives so often—to get away from the companion who had known them "when."

She liked Scott thinking of her as active, self-assured,

capable. She didn't want him to know the scattered neurotic who, as Rebecca had said, didn't know what she wanted to be when she grew up.

She listened, very carefully, as Scott told her more about his failed marriage. "She wanted the whole American dream," he explained. "The house in the suburbs, the kind of life that went with it. I never realized it wasn't at all what I wanted until we had been married awhile. Then I started to feel I was cheating Mary, keeping her from finding someone who could give her what she needed. It wasn't so much, after all. It just wasn't for me."

"I'm sorry," she said.

"Me, too. Funny—even after I knew it was all wrong, I still didn't want to think about a divorce. It was Mary who finally pushed it."

"Really?" Jenny found it hard to imagine a woman asking Scott for a divorce.

"Really. You see, after we both realized we wanted different things in life—big things—we started to fight over the smaller things, the details."

"Like what?" Jenny was genuinely curious.

"Like how each of us thought married people should act with each other. That was another thing that was strange. We had lived together for six months before we got married, and we never seemed to notice that we had different needs, and expectations. I thought marriage should be two people, each having his own life and then building something that they could share. I couldn't understand living in another person's pocket or being with that other person all the time. I couldn't see sharing all our friends and all our free time. To me that was boring. After we got married, Mary saw this as a rejection. She felt I was making less of our marriage, less of her, too. She didn't want a life of her own. She wanted mine."

Jenny smiled. "You know—I think Mary might have been happy with Jeffrey. It's too bad that people don't find partners who are more compatible."

"Sometimes they do, Jenny, and even then they have problems. I think it's hard for men and women to stay together these days. Much harder than it used to be."

"Sad."

"Fact of life."

"Well, I don't think I like it. Everything starts to feel so—so temporary."

"Everything is. Empires fall, countries disappear, whole populations die. Next to that, what's one marriage more or less?"

"Oh well, if you're going to take *that* point of view. But that isn't really what I meant. I was thinking how fresh and wonderful something can seem at the beginning, and then how it changes. Sometimes it's so subtle you don't even know it's happening, but then you wake up one morning and you can't even remember what it was like to adore the man who is sharing your pillow."

"Hey, Jenny—this conversation is getting depressing. A lot of things are, but we don't have to talk about them, do we?"

"You're right. We don't."

"Besides—it takes away from the fun of knowing you."

By the time Scott called for the check, Jenny felt as if they had spent hours and hours together. It had been a long time since she had had such an acute sense of here-and-now, since she had savored each passing moment. She was sorry the evening was coming to an end.

During the taxi ride to her apartment, Scott put his arm around her, but that was all.

"Would you like to come in for a brandy?"

"Yes. Yes I would."

The first thing she did was to check her sleeping daughter—and then she put on some music, the kind Rebecca described as "supermarket stuff." She splashed some Courvoisier into two balloon glasses, then joined Scott on the sofa.

The mood was soft, gentle, as comfortable as if they had known each other for a long time. When he kissed her, she responded eagerly. But when he whispered, "Let's make love," she pulled back. His words were not completely unexpected, yet she wasn't ready for them. She was enormously drawn to this man, yet she was hesitant. Making love with Scott would not be like her Acapulco fling. It would mean an emotional entanglement and the risk of pain. She could not put her confusion into words, so she said, "Rebecca's sleeping inside. I can't—I mean I don't do that. . . ."

He put his forefinger to her lips. "Hush. I understand. Do you want to come back to my place?"

"Oh, Scott—it's so late," she said, realizing how childish her excuse sounded.

He sighed. "Okay. Another time." He gathered her to him for another long kiss, and when it was over, she sighed too. "Scott . . ."

"It's okay, Jenny. You're not ready. I understand."

And she was sure he did understand. They saw each other several times—to share a Broadway play, some jazz at the Cookery, a movie. Each time, they kissed with growing intensity. He said nothing—until one evening, walking home from dinner, when he said with studied casualness, "How about coming up to my place for dinner tomorrow night. Since this relationship seems to be getting serious, I'd like to show off my skills in the kitchen."

"Is it—getting serious?"

"Sure—isn't it?"

"I don't know, Scott." She wanted him to spell it out, to assure her that she was safe before she exposed herself in any way. "What do you call a serious relationship?"

"I think a serious relationship begins when two people like each other enough to see each other on a regular basis."

She was pleased at the "regular basis" part of his statement. But she was disappointed he hadn't said something more daring. She wasn't sure what she wanted from Scott Manero. But she wanted him to want her—in every possible way. And then she wanted to be able to choose. Not much, my girl, she rebuked herself. But she smiled to herself because she thought there just might be a chance, just a chance.

What to wear? she asked herself, as she surveyed her closet on the eve of Scott's dinner. She laid out the new underwear she had bought. It was delicate cotton batiste, hand embroidered and very expensive.

She assumed she would be taking her clothes off, and she realized she'd had very little experience in doing this outside the forgiving shelter of her marriage. Something easy, she thought, finally deciding on a silk blouse and black wool pants that were slim, but not too tapered. She started to reach for her soft Italian boots, then chose "no"—and selected a pair of pumps instead. Lord, she thought, I'm nervous.

She went into the bathroom to take her shower. When she opened the medicine cabinet, her eyes were drawn to her diaphragm. What in heaven's name was she going to do with that? Use it now and hope that "it" would happen within six hours? Or tuck it into her bag and dash into Scott's bathroom? No, she would use it now—and hope the timing would be right.

She continued to worry throughout the taxi ride to Scott's apartment. She knew these were modern times, she was aware that she had supposedly lived through the sexual revolution, she understood that everyone was sleeping with everyone else, in combinations she had never heard of when she was growing up. Yet she still had some very old-fashioned, very provincial anxieties. What was she doing, she asked herself, going to a man's apartment, dressed and diaphragmed and ready for bed?

Stop it, she commanded herself. You're a mature and liberated woman. As the doorman buzzed Scott's apartment to announce her arrival, she wondered how many women had made this trip before her. She realized she had not asked how long it had been since Scott's divorce. Did it make a difference?

Yes, she decided, just as the elevator doors opened, it did. She didn't want a rebound relationship. If Scott really liked her, she wanted him to like her after he'd shopped around.

Her heart did a quick somersault when she rang his bell. The door opened at once, as if he had been waiting and didn't mind letting her know. "Well hello."

"Hi, Scotty."

"Come in. I'll give you a drink—and then the grand tour."

"You have a nice place," she said, as she took in the oversize living room, the sweep of windows overlooking Central Park, the fireplace with the marble mantel. Scott lived in what Jenny would call a minimalist apartment. The immediate impression was of whiteness and space and touches of natural colors. Most of the furniture was built-in, constructed of birch and covered with unbleached Haitian cotton. On one wall she noticed a framed fragment of tapestry (French, he explained), on another the room's only vivid colors—a quartet of Chagall lithographs.

"The bedroom," he said lightly, as he pointed her into another airy uncluttered room. Her eyes moved from a platform bed covered with a beige down quilt to an exercise bicycle. She wasn't sure she liked that. Was he vain? A fitness nut? A body freak? Would he recoil from a woman whose body was less than perfect?

Next he showed her into a small library-office. "Here's

where I work,'' he said. She admired the well-read, well-used books that filled the floor-to-ceiling bookshelves, the collection of typewriters—''one for every mood,'' he explained. She pointed to the large telescope that stood, poised for use, at one of the windows.

''Peeping Tom?''

''Yes, actually. I like to look at the city from here. At people, too. Gives a different perspective.''

I don't really know much about this strange man, she thought. Maybe he *is* a strange man. But then she was diverted by the beauty of his kitchen, with its sleek white cabinets and black Pirelli floors. ''You have a cappuccino machine,'' she noted, pleased with this discovery.

''Oh yes. I have lots of kitchen toys. I told you—I'm quite a cook. But I'm not going to do it tonight. I know I promised, but I got stuck at work again. There wasn't time to shop and get started before you came. Do you mind if we go out? There's a nice Japanese place close by.''

''I don't mind at all,'' she said, conjuring up a fantasy of a life shared with a man who cooked—and shopped, too.

The Japanese restaurant was a small neighborhood place, unpretentious but pleasant. The tempura was light, the sake warming, and by the time they finished their meal, Jenny felt relaxed. They walked slowly, arm in arm, toward Scott's apartment. Before they reached his building, he stopped, in the middle of the block, and kissed her. She had always frowned on people who did that, but now it seemed like the perfect thing to do.

When they opened the door to his apartment, she felt awkward again. It would have been better if they'd stayed there all evening, she thought. Now it all felt so calculated.

''A brandy?'' he asked.

''Please.'' He handed her a glass, and then, before she could bring it to her lips, he kissed her again. He took her hand and led her to a sofa. Without speaking, they reached for each other, touching, stroking. But when he started to open the buttons on her blouse, she stiffened a little. ''What's wrong?'' he whispered.

''I feel so . . . so shy,'' she whispered back, feeling more than a little ridiculous.

He got up, walked to a closet, pulled out a terry cloth robe and tossed it over to her. She was grateful that he had not commented on her hesitancy, which seemed to her awkwardly girlish and not at all appropriate to a woman who had been married, divorced, and was the mother of a teenage child. She fumbled with the robe, trying to use it as a kind of screen while she removed pieces of clothing.

At this point, Scott started to laugh. "I can understand a little modesty, Jenny, really I can. But you're not supposed to put the robe on over your clothes. Honestly, that's not the way it goes."

She flushed and tried to buy back some of her lost sophistication by deliberately undoing buttons, unzipping her zipper, pretending he wasn't there. She wrapped the robe around herself, passion somewhat dissipated but determined to get on with it.

She walked into Scott's arms, and together they went into the bedroom. As they leaned against the pillows of the king-size bed, she wished for a state of intoxication, a full-blown, overwhelming passion that would take her right out of herself and straight into tomorrow.

When they kissed, she felt the beginnings of a pleasant warmth moving through her veins. But where was it, she wondered, where was the will-less abandon that drove lovers to fall upon each other, not noticing zippers and buttons—or bumpy knees or imperfect thighs? It had been easy with Stavros, but before she could begin to wonder why, she realized she knew very well. It was because this was not a pleasant interlude. This was part of Something That Mattered.

Scott pulled her closer, his touch more demanding, more urgent. And she began to feel an urgency, too—but of a different kind. She sat up abruptly. "Excuse me," she said, her face flushed with embarrassment. "I have to go to the john." She bolted from the bed, rearranging the robe as she went.

When she returned a few minutes later, Scott was sitting up in bed, smoking a cigarette. He reached out and took her hand. "Okay, Jenny, you win. That's as far as we go tonight."

She went crimson again. "I didn't mean to . . . Scott, I didn't want to be that way."

"I believe you. But I guess I figured out that your heart— or some other vital part of you—wasn't in it. And when it's like that, I can't."

"You can't?"

"No—I can't. Is that so strange?" He sounded defensive.

"I don't know, Scotty. I just never had an experience like this before."

"Well thanks. I hoped this evening would be memorable, but this wasn't quite what I had in mind."

"No, it is. Memorable, I mean. I was never with anyone who noticed whether or not my heart was in it. So thank you. And I'm sorry about—the other. If it bothers you."

He ruffled her hair. "Funny lady. Of course it bothers me. I wanted you. I wanted to make love. It's part of getting closer and showing you how I feel. I care about you and I want everything to be right. That makes . . . things . . . harder."

She looked at him, eyes wide. "Nobody ever talked to me like this before. I always thought men were different—a lot different. I feel like you've told me an important secret. It makes me feel closer to you—knowing that you worry about the same things that I do."

"Well all right, then. So the evening hasn't been a total disaster."

"Oh, no, Scotty, this evening has been special—dopey, maybe, but special."

"Okay, maybe tomorrow I'll believe you. So now let's get to sleep. I forgot to ask—can you stay the night?"

"Yes. I was planning to—if you asked me. Becky's spending the night with a friend. And I don't have to get to work until ten tomorrow."

"Good night, then, sweet lady. Pleasant dreams."

"Good night, sweet Scott. I don't need pleasant dreams. This is nice enough."

Jenny woke up first after a fitful night. Sleeping in a strange bed was certainly not easy, she thought. And it had been a long time since she had shared a bed with a man. After Jeff had left, her bed had seemed achingly empty, even frightening. Now it felt luxurious and peaceful—and hers. If she pleased, she could spread out her body, her books, her snacks. She could read, leave the light on, drop crumbs wherever she chose. She wondered at times how she had ever managed to give up sovereignty in such an important place.

She looked at the man lying next to her, ran her fingers over the dark mosaic of his beard, and told herself there was nothing to be afraid of. She snuggled closer, pressed her nose against his arm and inhaled a mixture of cigarette smoke and soap and sweat. She ran her tongue along his skin, tasting him. Nice. And so different from what she had felt with Jeff.

She was still shy, still a little inhibited, but she was physically drawn to Scott in a way she had not known before. She remembered a fragment of a conversation she'd had with Alicia, who had said, "Someday it may even seem as if Jeff gave you a great gift when he left you. . . ."

Scott stirred and reached for her—a little too automatically, she thought with a twinge, and then silenced the doubt at once. A man like Scott would have had lots of women. *I can handle it,* she told herself. *I'm a big girl. I can handle it,* she repeated, as she surrendered to the fluttering sensations that were radiating from her right ear as Scott nibbled on it. Her arms went around his neck, and she pressed closer, feeling him harden as his hands ranged along her body, gently, insistently. She let herself drift with the feeling of warmth that encompassed her, then gasped with shock as her body seemed to take on an electrifying life of its own.

Later, when they were both still again, Jenny felt a delicious languor settle upon her. She searched for the words to tell Scott how she felt. "Nice," he murmured, before he fell asleep again. That single word, so neutral and noncommittal, stabbed her with disappointment.

An hour later, showered and warmed by two cups of excellent coffee, Jenny was in a taxi, on her way downtown. She closed her eyes and leaned back in her seat, remembering how Charlotte had once assured her that "first times are always ghastly, dear. If you can get past that, you might have something." This certainly hadn't been ghastly, she thought— but she was awfully glad they had got past it.

— 36 —

The first glow of intimacy carried Jenny through that day and the next. Then she began to wonder why he hadn't called—and when he would. She remembered, with the beginning of unease, that he had kissed her ever so lightly as she was leaving his apartment. What was it he had said? Not "I'll see you Thursday or Friday or any particular day," but rather "I'll talk to you soon."

"Soon." Two days had elapsed since they had made love for the first time. It had been an occasion for her. But maybe it was just business as usual for Scott.

Worse yet, maybe she hadn't been very good.

Then she had a thought. A brief lift of hope. Perhaps something had happened. Perhaps he was out of the city. Detained. Anything but indifferent.

Impulsively she went to the phone and dialed his direct line. The familiar baritone voice answered. She hung up the phone quickly, like a thief. An obscene phone caller. Worse. An insecure woman.

She felt humiliated. Then a little angry. The anger made her feel better, so she fed it. Who did Scott Manero think he was? How dare he come on as if he were really interested— and then ignore her? He wasn't a stupid man or a cruel one. Careless, that's what he was. Spoiled, probably, by too many women. Too bad for her.

Suddenly her own phone rang. Somehow she knew, even as she answered, that it would be Scott.

"Jenny," he said, and she had the awful feeling that he knew she had phoned him and hung up, "I've thought about calling you so many times—but it's just been so crazy around here."

Play it cool, she cautioned herself. You know this isn't going to be so easy. "Scott," she said with a confidence she did not feel, "I understand perfectly. I've been busy, too." She hoped the word busy would conjure up images of legions of suitors wining and dining and courting her.

"Would you like to go out to dinner tonight?" he asked.

And she found to her horror that she had said yes—without a single moment's hesitation, without even the pretense of consulting that "busy" schedule of hers.

He was charming at dinner, and for several hours she almost forgot how hurt she had been. She basked in the warmth of his attention, in the sparkle of his eyes. For the first time in her life, Jenny was measuring her own happiness by the expression on someone else's face. It was intoxicating—and frightening.

She wanted so much to tell him how she felt, to ask him all

the questions that would help her understand him. But her instinct—and the bits of personal history that Scott had shared with her—told her you couldn't do that with a man like Scott. He'd think she was one of those clinging women he'd complained about.

No, she thought, she would have to play by his rules if she wanted to keep him. And she did. She felt a warm flush pink her ears as she imagined how, in a little while, he would hold her, how they would touch. . . .

Then she heard him say, as he signaled the waiter for the check, "Do you mind if we make it an early night, Jen? Tomorrow we're shooting a segment in the Fulton Fish Market—and I have to be up at four." He added, with a grin that would have melted any woman's heart, "I promise to make it up to you soon. We can dance until dawn. Or whatever. Sometime when I don't have to get up so early. You don't mind, do you?"

"Of course I don't mind," she said sweetly, thinking: Of course I mind, you idiot. "Why don't I just grab a cab right now," she offered, "and you can get home."

"Are you sure? I'll take you if you'd like me to. . . ."

"No. I'll be fine."

All the way home she kept hearing the echo of the word "soon" in Scott's offer of a raincheck. But now I know what that means, she reasoned. Now it won't be so bad, she promised herself, as she anticipated several days—or longer— of benign neglect.

"Are you going to marry Scotty?" The question came without preamble as Jenny and her daughter shared a Sunday breakfast of scrambled eggs and homemade biscuits.

"I don't know, baby. I really don't know," Jenny answered honestly. Becky looked dissatisfied. "Why do you ask?"

"Well," Becky began, her face serious, "you go out with him a lot. You never did that before. So I figured that you thought he was special."

"You're right, love. He is special." Jenny's voice took on a tenderness that her daughter had not heard before.

"So?" Rebecca demanded. "Are you going to marry him?" Jenny hesitated, so Rebecca plunged on, "Doesn't he want to? Is that it? You like him and he doesn't like you so much?"

"No, that's not it."

"Well, what then? Is he married?"

"No, sweetheart, he's not married. Let me try to make you understand. Scotty and I both have one important thing in common. We both married nice people, and we both had our marriages fall apart anyway."

"So you *are* sorry you married Daddy. You said you weren't. . . ."

"I'm not, truly I'm not. I can't be sorry about a marriage that gave me you. Anyway, I would have been really unhappy if I hadn't gotten married, and your father was a lovely man. . . ."

"Oh, sure," Rebecca said, with a bitterness that shocked her mother. "First he says he'll love you forever—and then he takes off for some stupid medical project."

"Rebecca—precious—listen to me. When people get married, they mean to stay together. But they can't see into the future. I suppose if they felt that staying together was the most important thing in the world, they would do it. But a lot of people don't feel that way. They think it's more important to get the most from their own lives."

"Do you feel that way?"

"I'm not sure, sweetheart. Look—I think you've been hurt a lot, so you've jumped from me to your father, looking for someone to blame. It's over, Becky, it's over now. And to tell the truth, now I'm not sorry anymore. I like our life, Becky. And I wish you did, too."

Now Becky looked surprised. "I do, Mommy. It's much more fun than it used to be. But a lot of things don't make sense."

Jenny laughed. "Welcome to the club. Now you know how being a grown-up feels. But before you think I'm dodging your question about Scotty, I'll try to explain. I care about him. I think I'm in love with him. I think he feels the same way. He's the first man I've imagined sharing my life with."

"Then why don't you live together, Mommy, and see how it goes?"

Jenny laughed again. "Thank you for that very modern advice. But I haven't been invited."

"But do you want to? You could always ask him."

"Oh, Becky, I couldn't do that! These things are . . .

complicated. Sometimes, if you say the wrong thing—or even the right thing, at the wrong time—you ruin everything. You have to wait, to see how the other person feels.''

"That sounds dumb, Mommy.''

Jenny was startled. "It does? Why?''

"It sounds like you're afraid to make mistakes. You're always telling me not to be afraid. How could you like somebody so much and be so chicken around them?''

Jenny started to protest. And then she stopped to consider what her daughter had said. For all her talk about growth and change, was she still a "chicken" when it came to love? "Maybe you're right, Becky. I'll think about it. I hadn't realized you liked Scott so much.''

"It isn't that, Mommy. I like him all right. It's you. You look so pretty and happy when he's around. I just want you to have that.''

Jenny felt the tears come to her eyes. "I love you, baby, a lot. Did I tell you that lately?''

"Sure, Mommy—lots of times. I love you, too.''

It was true, Jenny reflected. Everything Becky had said was true. Knowing Scott had changed her. She felt younger, more vital, charged with nervous energy. She was just surprised that her daughter had noticed.

She had struck up a new relationship with her mirror, depending on it to help her be the best she could be. She had always thought of Sally as "the beautiful Richman," but now she gave herself the same careful attention she gave a piece of pottery.

She had decided she could be "interesting" and even, on some occasions, striking. She bought pots of eye shadow in colors like aubergine and mauve, blushers in shades of copper and coffee, lipsticks in Chinese coral and burnt sienna. For the first time in her life she colored her hair with Egyptian henna, bringing out lights and shadings she had never seen before.

She had spiced up her businesswoman's wardrobe with dresses of burgundy and purple and forest green, with coats of fuzzy mohair and a flowing velvet cape, with butter-soft boots and outrageously impractical sandals.

All of it felt wonderful.

All of it except the fears and the questions. The feeling that the day didn't seem complete if Scott wasn't a part of it. The sense of longing. The feeling that some vital part of her was always with Scott. The fear that if she said what was on her mind, he would turn away.

Dumb. Just as Becky said. She had played it safe during the years with Jeff. She had run the entire course of her marriage taking no chances—not risking his disapproval, not allowing the development of any real intimacy between them. Now the well-ordered life she had built for herself was out of control—and still she was walking on eggs. Chicken, Becky had said.

That was no way to have a real love affair. Charlotte had once told her that the only way to change was to do it. She would have to tell him somehow that for the first time in her life she felt an all-encompassing need for another human being, that this need wasn't satisfied with brief scattered encounters that left her wondering when she would see him again. And if she had questions—like why he had made love to her once, and then seemed in no hurry to repeat the experience—then she would have to ask.

She would be subtle—not demanding—but she would learn to speak her mind.

But when Scott called her, the sound of his voice triggered all her adolescent responses—the sweaty palms, the irregular heartbeat, the high anxiety. And when he suggested they go dancing, she forgot subtlety and blurted out, "I don't want to go dancing. I want to make love."

She felt she would die of mortification when all she heard was a heart-chilling silence. "Say something," she pleaded.

"I don't know what to say, Jen. You've caught me by surprise."

"If you don't say something, I'm going to hang up and drown myself."

He laughed, a little insincerely, she thought. "Well, I certainly don't want you to do that. Look—maybe we should talk."

"Oh—oh—I don't think I like the sound of that. What are we going to talk about? Is it going to make me feel terrible?"

"I hope not. Come up to my place. We'll have some deli and we'll talk. Okay?"

"Okay."

She was sure she had made a mistake. Now he would tell her that she had made too much of this relationship. He would tell her something that had a "but" in it. He would say something like: "You're okay, Jen, but there are ladies I like better." Or: "I like you, Jenny—really I do—but you're not very good in bed, so maybe we shouldn't do that anymore."

When she arrived at Scott's apartment, she found that he had set the table, lit two candles, and put a Segovia record on the stereo. He held out his arms to her. She accepted the kiss he dropped on her cheek, took a breath, and said, "Okay, Mr. Manero—let's talk."

"Not now, Jen. Let's have a bite to eat. I'm starved. I haven't had anything since breakfast."

"Are you kidding? If I tried to eat now—feeling the way I do—I'd probably throw up."

"Okay, then, if you don't want to eat, come with me."

"Where?"

"Hush," he said, taking her hand. "If you want to talk, first you have to listen. So listen up, Jenny Ashland, listen hard." His voice was low and soothing, and he kept on talking as he led her out of the living room and sat her on his bed. Distracted by the touch of his hand on her arm, she was only vaguely aware of his words. Now he was taking her shoes off. "Are you listening, Jen?" he asked, gently rubbing her feet. "Can you hear what my fingers are saying to your toes? No? Well, then," he said, sliding his hands higher, traveling the length of her legs. "See now—that's clearer, isn't it?" He continued talking, not breaking the physical contact while he undressed her and shed his own clothes.

She felt his breath as he murmured, "Sweet Jen," against her neck, and it made her think of summer breezes and old velvet. He twined his fingers in her hair, drawing her face close to his, kissing her forehead, her nose, her lips, lightly, without passion. He stroked her body gently, as if to exorcise the fears that had brought her to his bed. His touch was as delicate as a woman's, soothing and soft, and she felt almost hypnotically relaxed, her body floating with contentment.

"You see," he was saying, his voice suddenly lower, huskier, "it's all right now, isn't it?"

"Mmm," she agreed, forgetting that it had ever been anything but "all right" between them.

He pulled her against him, held her so tightly that she could scarcely catch her breath. Once again his fingers, no longer gentle, were in her hair, arching her body to meet his. Her skin suddenly seemed to be on fire. She dug her nails into his back as she closed her eyes and felt herself rising and falling on waves of exquisite pleasure, hearing from a distance the sound of her voice moaning his name.

She sank back against a pillow, spent and dazed and trying to focus her eyes on the man who lay next to her, propped up on one elbow, grinning.

"So," he said, touching her nose with one finger. "Were you listening carefully, Ms. Ashland?"

"Mmm. Trying to listen."

"And what message did you get?"

"That you're awfully good at this. Too good, maybe?"

"Wrong, wise guy, but thanks—I think. What I was telling you is that it's okay to ask for what you want. That maybe we're past the formalities and maybe we can relax a little. That maybe we can afford to make a mistake here and there without thinking the whole thing's going to go up in smoke."

"You said all that? I think maybe I missed something. Do you suppose you could repeat the good parts?"

He laughed and threw his pillow over her face. "No way, lady, not on an empty stomach. First we eat."

They made a quiet picnic of pastrami sandwiches on rye bread, with "lots of mustard," at Jenny's request, and half-sour pickles, at Scott's insistence.

"Feeling better?" he teased. "Any danger of your throwing up?"

"I'm fine," she said. "Better than fine, maybe."

"Good. Now, since you seem to have cooled off on talking, let me do some. I get the feeling that you're a little bit insecure about . . . the physical part of our relationship. That you think there's something wrong because we didn't come back here the last time we saw each other. Wait—let me finish. I want to tell you something about me first. When I married Mary, I hadn't really been around that much. I had the usual experiences guys my age had, but what I knew about women could fit on one page. A small page. Then later—when things started to break for me—suddenly there were women all over the place. I felt like I had missed out on something. After the divorce, I guess I went a little wild. A lot of faces and a lot of beds.

"I'm not bragging, Jen—that's just the way it was. Then one day I realized I was getting older, and I was still doing the same things, over and over. Spending a nonstop weekend in bed just wasn't a big thrill anymore. Sometimes it was awful. There weren't that many people I wanted to talk to when I got up in the morning. Do you understand what I'm saying, Jen? When I met you, I liked you. I asked you to go to bed with me because that's what I do when I like a woman. You weren't ready—and that was okay, too. When we did, it was good.

"And if it's not on my mind all the time, it's not because I don't think you're wonderful and desirable. You are. I just don't feel I need to run through the same tired paces, where something begins and ends and I don't even have a sense of what it's been about. Do you understand what I'm saying?"

Jenny started to laugh. "Oh, Lord—whatever I thought you'd say, this isn't it. This has to be one of life's bad jokes. You're telling me you're bored with sex—just when I've found out it can be great. You showed me that—and now you're telling me it's not a big deal for you."

He shook his head. "You're twisting what I said. Don't be so defensive with me, Jen. I won't hurt you. All we've found out is that we're in different places when it comes to sex. It's not a tragedy. There are other ways to connect. Like we're doing right now. Okay?"

"Okay."

"Good. Do you want to split another sandwich?"

The listing came to the office in routine fashion, and Jenny almost missed it. These days, her relationship with Scott preoccupied her constantly. Things had been better since their "talk"—she had felt closer to him for a while—but he was still too elusive for comfort.

Fortunately business was excellent. A large stack of new listings on her desk reassured her that while her personal life was a little erratic, the business was sound.

Almost absently, she flipped through the file cards that noted the new listings. Suddenly the words on one leapt up at her. They told her that Penthouse A was up for sale. The pain of remembrance stabbed her. And then there was more—a quick wash of sentiment, and a little curiosity. Jenny decided to handle the listing herself.

"Take messages for a couple of hours, Francine," she instructed her secretary. "I'm going out to look at a listing—the penthouse on lower Fifth. Call the sellers and tell them I'd like to come right over."

There was a new doorman, she noticed, as she gave the man her name and waited for him to ring the apartment. Nostalgia took hold for a moment, to be replaced by panic when she actually found herself with the familiar antique door knocker in her hand. She had not been back since the day of Sally's funeral.

When the door opened, Jenny held her breath and stepped inside. "Good morning," she said, looking around slowly, cautiously, as if she expected to be ambushed by a rush of painful memories.

"Good morning, Mrs. Ashland," Marcia Gillespie answered. "I was a little surprised when your secretary called. Someone else from your office already made an inspection of the place, when we called to list it."

"I have a personal reason for being here, Mrs. Gillespie. My family lived here for a long time, and I realized I wanted very much to see the place again. I hope you don't mind. . . ."

"Oh—so you must be related to the woman who—oh, I'm so sorry, I didn't mean to—"

"She was my sister," Jenny said quietly, amazed that she could say it so calmly, without invoking that feeling of terror and despair that often accompanied thoughts of Sally.

"I really am sorry, Mrs. Ashland. That was very clumsy of me. But you see, I've been so curious about her for a long time. Because of the apartment."

Jenny said nothing. She looked around her, searching for familiar landmarks. It was a little like seeing a relative after a long separation—experiencing the new and the familiar at the same time.

". . . and I loved the apartment when we first moved here. There was something a little 'down' about it, but at first I thought that was just because it was someone else's home. With someone else's things. I thought that when my own decorator worked on it—I thought it would change."

"But that didn't happen?"

"No. In fact it got worse. As you can see, the decorator did a wonderful job." Jenny followed the sweep of Marcia

Gillespie's hand, but "wonderful" was not the adjective that came to mind. She thought the woman's decorator had mongrelized the apartment, had taken its classic features and suburbanized them. Jenny was a little indignant at this abuse, but she did not comment.

"Anyway," Marcia continued, "this place just never felt like a home. It was always like a rainy Monday morning in here. Do you know what I mean?"

"Yes," Jenny answered slowly. "Yes, I do know what you mean." She was not particularly superstitious, but she believed what Marcia Gillespie was saying. She believed that there was an aura that hung over homes and apartments long after their owners had departed. She had been in places that fairly radiated cheer while others gave off intimations of misery and despair. Here Jenny felt something else—a plaintive quality. For all the expensive furnishings and decorator touches, Penthouse A seemed forlorn and abandoned—and perhaps something else that Jenny could not quite define.

"I want to ask you something," Marcia said. "I don't want to be cruel—but your sister—did it happen in the large front bedroom?"

"Yes."

Marcia sighed. "I thought so." For a moment it seemed that was all she would say, but then she continued. "After a while . . . we just couldn't sleep there anymore . . . we moved into one of the guest bedrooms. Then one day I told Daddy I wasn't happy here. He insisted we put the place up for sale. So we called your office."

"I understand," Jenny said. And she did.

"There's just one thing that worries me. I know we can get a good price for the apartment—much more than we paid. But I feel a little guilty, passing it on without saying anything. After all—when we got the place, the broker did tell us what happened here."

Jenny's opinion of Marcia Gillespie went up immediately. "That's very conscientious of you, Mrs. Gillespie. But maybe something can be worked out. . . ." An idea had begun to take shape, and Jenny let it develop while she continued her inspection of the apartment. She forced herself to go into the master bedroom—Sally's room. And strangely enough, she did not feel panic or horror, just an intensification of the plaintive sadness she experienced from the moment she had walked in.

Next she made a perfunctory survey of the other rooms, then she squared her shoulders, took a deep breath, and put her idea into words: "Mrs. Gillespie, have you listed the apartment with any other brokers?"

"No. I told the person who took the listing that we would give your firm a three-months' exclusive. Daddy said that would be more than enough in today's market."

"Yes—I'm sure he's right. Look, Mrs. Gillespie, I'm going to be completely honest with you. I want to buy the place. For myself. I'm not going to haggle or try to get it for less through a third party. I'll give you the asking price, less what the standard broker's commission would be. Then you won't have to feel guilty about selling the apartment to anyone else. Deal?"

Marcia looked confused. "Well . . . I'm sure my husband would be pleased. But I really don't understand why you would want to . . . I mean . . . I would think this place would make you feel awful. Unless"—she hesitated, a shadow of suspicion crossing her face—"unless the price is really too low, and you think you can resell for more. . . ."

Jenny gave the woman points for shrewdness. "I can assure you that the price is a fair one—and that I have no intention of reselling in the near future. I can give you that in writing if you like. Actually, Mrs. Gillespie, I want the apartment for very personal reasons. I know this may seem strange to you, but after being here and talking to you, I felt I had to bring this place back into our family."

Marcia looked a little sheepish. "I'm sorry. I didn't mean to imply that you would do anything—shady. It just seemed a bit odd. Well—this certainly does seem to tie everything up nicely. I'll call my husband and have him contact you about the details."

Jenny had an urge to walk through the apartment again, to spend some time in it, to listen to the memories of her own past. But she didn't want an audience, especially not this young woman who, for all her intuitions, could not understand the pull of this place, where the women of her family had known great joy as well as piercing sorrow. She would wait—until she left behind her the place she had shared with Jeffrey. Now she would leave him behind. Finish the circle. And move on.

— 37 —

Becky was delighted when she heard what her mother had done. She had always loved to hear family stories, about Carlotta and Sharif, about Nana and her grandfather, about Jenny herself. And she was enchanted with the idea of living in the big rambling apartment where her mother had grown up.

Furthermore, she was impressed that her mother could afford the place.

"Wow," Becky said. "Are we rich now? Does this mean I can have my own stereo?"

Jenny was startled by both questions. "I didn't know you wanted a stereo, Becky. Why didn't you ask me before?"

"Well, it's not something I really need. And I didn't want to—you know—make you feel bad in case we couldn't afford it."

"I think we can manage a stereo without getting into trouble."

"Oh thank you, Mommy—and can I put it in your old room? Can I have that room when we move?"

"Yes, love, you can have any room you choose. And by the way—we're not exactly rich, but your old lady is earning a very nice living."

"You're not such an old lady. Ask Scotty and see what he says."

And she did. Later, in the cool quiet of her bedroom, she closed the door and dialed the direct number that was now permanently etched in her mind. When she heard the familiar voice, she said, "Hello, Mr. Famous Anchorman."

"Hello, Ms. Successful Real Estate Person."

"Before we talk—Becky says I'm to ask if you think I'm an old lady."

"Hmmm." He paused, in mock deliberation. "I get the feeling this is a trick question. Do you mean old lady, as in aged female? Or are you talking about female chattel—as in 'my old lady'?''

She caught the tenderness in the last phrase. "Not fair to answer a question with a question. Unless you're a shrink or a rabbi. Have you been holding out on me?"

"Of course, I've been holding out. And so have you—"

She interrupted, not wanting to head into a serious conversation on the telephone. "Before I forget what I called for—I have some news. Guess what I did today? In the space of a single hour?"

"You sold Manhattan back to the Indians."

"Silly. What I did was to buy the apartment I grew up in. Remember the building? I showed it to you once when we were walking."

"I remember. How did that happen?"

"The people who bought it after Sally died—they put it back on the market. They seem to feel it's haunted."

"And do you?"

"Yes. Sort of."

"And that's why you bought it."

"What a smart man you are. Yes, that's why I bought it. What do you think?"

"I think I love you."

Her heart started to pound. It was the first time he had said the words. She realized he was waiting for her to say something. "Thank you, Scotty. I think I love you, too. I have to go now—I want to call Alicia and tell her my news."

But when she hung up and called her mother, the reaction she got was unexpected: "What on earth made you want to live there?"

Jenny realized that "there" was where her father had died, "there" was the setting for Alicia's disappointments in marriage as well as her successes in business. "Just an instinct, Mother. I feel like it's part of me—more than the place I lived in with Jeff."

Alicia was quiet for a moment. "Perhaps you're right, Jenny. God knows you've managed to do things I never did."

"Oh, Alicia, don't try to be so fair-minded," Jenny teased. "If you think I'm making a king-sized mistake, just say so. No—I take that back—don't say anything at all. How is Paolo?"

"He's fine, Jenny. We're going to Milan next week, to

look at some contemporary designers—and then''—her voice took on a schoolgirlish quality—''we're going to spend a week in Venice. . . .''

''You sound happy, Alicia.''

''I am, Jenny. I feel I don't deserve it, but I am—so happy. I wish that you . . . well, you know what I wish for you.''

''I know. Don't worry about me. I'm fine. In fact, I'm better than fine. One of these days I'll tell you about it.'' Jenny was not quite ready to discuss Scotty with Alicia. They had come a long way since she had thought of Alicia as the enemy, but she still felt more comfortable discussing personal things with Charlotte—or even Becky. She hung up with a promise to ''keep in touch.'' And she started to plan. . . .

The closing on Penthouse A was one of the fastest Jenny had ever arranged. Once the place had been vacated, she worked out a kind of superstitious ritual for taking it over. First she hired a contractor to remove all the decorator touches added by the Gillespies and to put a coat of white paint on the walls. She would not launch one of those comprehensive designer blitzes on the place. Instead, she and Becky and the apartment would all live together for a while until she had a sense of what would fit.

She had thought about Scotty—and fantasized where he might fit in this new life of hers. She had casually suggested to him that he stop by and ''take a look.''

He had been full of enthusiasm about her new home. ''It's magnificent, Jen. The place is a palace—those ceilings, those moldings—you hardly see details and space like that anymore.''

She had been pleased that he liked it, happy that he approved.

And now the movers had left. They had done a remarkably good job. Nothing broken, nothing marred. Her furniture looked at home here—better, really, than it had in the Gramercy Park place. Tonight Becky was staying with a friend— and Scotty was coming over to take her out to dinner.

Her pleasure in her new surroundings doubled when he arrived with a bottle of chilled champagne and a set of exquisite flute glasses from Tiffany's. ''My housewarming present,'' he explained, ''for our private housewarming.'' They drank together and once again he told her how much he liked her new home. ''The space is just magnificent,'' he said. ''You could move an army in here and not feel crowded.''

"Crowding is usually a state of mind," she said.

Scott looked solemn, as if she had aimed that remark directly at him. "That doesn't make it any less real, Jen."

She couldn't resist the opening. "So if it's a state of mind and it's real—does that mean it has to be a terminal condition?"

"I don't know, Jen. Look, could we table this and tackle the question of what we do for dinner?"

Jenny was prepared. "I made a reservation at A Bientôt du Soir. It's one of my favorites. Does that sound good?"

"I've never been. It will be brand-new for me—like everything is with you."

Jenny felt a little better. Scott's words didn't sound like the sort of thing he told every woman he knew. Maybe he would go a little further after some good wine and French atmosphere.

Yolande, the petite French proprietress, winked at Jenny when she and Scott came into the restaurant, arm in arm. Jenny often used the place to entertain clients, but she had never been there with a special man. "Good evening, Mrs. Ashland," Yolande said with a Gallic formality that was clearly put on for the occasion. She seated them ceremoniously, and then she discreetly disappeared until Scott looked as if he was ready to order.

"Tonight," she said, "we have some very special pâté with pistachio nuts. The stuffed mushrooms are good also . . . the special entrées are chicken breast with Calvados sauce and swordfish with the chef's special sauce."

Scott looked at Jenny. "What would you recommend?"

"I always have the escargots to begin. And anything with sauce is usually good."

"Okay—then why don't we both start with escargots, and later—maybe the chicken and the fish. We could share if you'd like?"

"Let's." Jenny was delighted. She loved to taste, and Jeff had always been annoyed when she wanted to sample what was on his plate.

"I like this place, Jen. I'm glad you suggested it."

"I come here a lot with clients. But you're the first date I've brought here. In case you hadn't noticed—Yolande is delighted to see you."

"Is that what I'm supposed to be, Jenny—a date?"

She knew that he was teasing, but she took the opening. "I

think you know you're a lot more than that. I don't have a name for it, but you do know, don't you . . .?"

"What I know," he said, "is that you and I are good together. We have good times. We have a nice way of connecting. It's comfortable for me. I want to take care of what we have . . . not spoil it. It's like being married, but without the problems."

Jenny's eyes opened wide with surprise. Was this the same relationship that had been like an emotional roller coaster for her? Was he crazy? Or was she? She didn't think it was better than being married. Better than her marriage maybe, but what did that prove? She had a sinking feeling that his idea of "spoiling" the relationship involved exactly what she most craved from him. Commitment. She shook her head.

"What's the matter?" he asked. "Don't you agree?"

"I'm not sure," she said tentatively, afraid again that the truth would drive him away. "I've never felt this way before. But I don't feel 'connected' to you—except by my own feelings."

"Exactly," he said triumphantly, as if she had just proved his point. "And that's all that matters. It's what was missing in my marriage. We had papers that said we were married, but we weren't really connected. And there didn't seem to be any space to move around in . . . it was awful."

Jenny looked at his face, so earnest and serious—the face that thousands of viewers loved to love. And suddenly she felt sorry for his ex-wife, the woman who had loved him without being loved in return. The insecurity started to creep over her, threatening to ruin her pleasure in his company. Stop it, she told herself. He cares for you. That's why he's telling you these things. "Let's not talk about failed marriages," she said. "How is work?"

"Great!" He appeared relieved by the change of subject. "We've just started a new series on illegal aliens in the city. It's really fascinating—a little hectic, too, because I'm supposed to be breaking in a new researcher . . . the producer's niece. She's fresh out of school, so she keeps stepping on her own shoelaces . . . poor kid," he said, with a note in his voice that sent little pinpricks of jealousy through Jenny. She was relieved when he went on to describe the new project.

At Yolande's urging, they ordered chocolate mousse and apple tart for dessert. When the strong *café filtre* arrived,

Scott reached across the table and took Jenny's hand. The gesture warmed her at once. "This is nice," she said, looking straight into his eyes.

"I told you . . . .it's always nice when we're together," he said, not knowing that she had done a couple of emotional somersaults in the course of one dinner.

I wonder, she thought, if he would still say it was nice if he knew how much I wanted some of his "space."

As if he were reading her mind, he said, "After my divorce, I didn't think I would let another woman get close to me. I just didn't want to go through that whole messy business of getting disentangled again."

Well, of course, you idiot, she wanted to say. Any woman worth having is going to want something in return. Instead she nodded sympathetically, feeling like a traitor to her sex.

"Then I met you," he was saying, "and I hope you won't mind if I say something corny—but you really have been like an answer to a prayer."

And so were you, she thought. But we all know you have to be careful of answered prayers.

"With you," he went on, "I saw it was possible to love a woman without making all the same mistakes."

"But don't you think that's a mistake, too? Thinking you can save yourself from unhappiness by doing the opposite of what you did before? People are different. . . ."

"Maybe," he said without much conviction. "But I know what works for me. And this is it." He squeezed her hand for emphasis. "Do you think I could stay at your place tonight?" he asked softly. "We could christen the new apartment."

"I don't think so," she said, just as softly, unwilling to share her own bed with a man who surrounded himself with space. "Becky will be back early. But," she volunteered shyly, "I'll come to your place if you want me to."

He laughed. "Best offer I've had all day."

They made the cab ride uptown in a comfortable silence. When they reached his apartment, she remembered briefly how she had behaved the first time she had been there and smiled at the memory.

This time, when he reached for her, she went to him, eager for the magic of physical closeness that would shut out the rest of the world. Right now Scott was all hers, and no one else existed. Not Jeff or Mary. Or even the research assistant.

All too soon the magic was over, and it was time to get up from the rumpled bed. "Stay," he said sleepily from the warm cocoon of covers and pillows.

"I can't," she whispered. "I have to be home for Becky."

Silently she put on her clothes and leaned over to kiss him. "Don't get up," she said. "I'll be okay."

In the quiet of her new home, she undressed again and climbed into bed. It felt strange to be in this familiar, yet unfamiliar room. Away from the warmth of Scott's body, her bed seemed larger, less luxurious than it had before.

She wished Becky were home, so that she might wake her up, invite her to crawl under the covers with her. But it wasn't really Becky she wanted to travel with through the lonely hours of night.

"I want," she whispered into her pillow, "oh God, I want him so much." The loneliness that came after making love was almost unbearable here in the stillness of her solitary bed. Did Scott feel it, too? "Stay," he had said. But had he meant it? She fell asleep praying that he might feel as she did, that he would call the very next day and tell her how much he missed her.

But Scott did not call, and although the pattern was by now a familiar one, Jenny thought she simply could not bear it. It was ridiculous, she told herself, that only he could define the boundaries of their affair, that only he could take the initiative, that her only choice was to react to what he did.

It took five days—five lonely days without a whisper from Scott—for Jenny to make up her mind. This won't do, she said. Purposefully, she dialed his apartment. When there was no answer, she was almost relieved. Then came the question: Where was he at ten o'clock on a Thursday evening? And with whom?

She felt she had to know. She continued to call, every half hour, until finally, shortly after midnight, he answered.

"Jenny—what a surprise." He did sound surprised, and not altogether pleased.

"I was thinking of you," she said truthfully. "I hope this isn't too late."

"No—not at all. I just got in," he said, telling her what she already knew.

Now she had to give a reason for her call. "There's a new play at the Public Theater," she improvised, "and I thought you might like to go with me. Saturday night?"

"Umm. Sounds good, Jen—but I'll have to get back to you. Okay?"

"Well . . . okay. 'Night, Scott."

" 'Night, Jen. Talk to you soon."

When she hung up, she felt worse than she had before. Scott had not exactly welcomed her call. Or her invitation. Was someone with him? she wondered.

That possibility stayed with her throughout the night, disrupting her sleep, leaving her to face the morning with puffy eyes and a splitting headache.

She could not possibly go into the office feeling like this. She took two aspirins, drank several cups of coffee. She would use the day to finish straightening out the closets and drawers, not admitting to herself that she needed to wait for Scott's call.

She worked mechanically in the apartment, which now seemed enormous—too big for just her and Becky. It needed to be shared, she thought, and she silently cursed Scott for diminishing her pleasure in the comfortable world she had made for herself.

So this was what love was all about, she thought wryly. All the poems and songs about how the world seemed brighter and better—well, she'd had that for a while. But now . . . these other feelings . . . they reminded her of the TV soap operas she used to watch, in which life moved in slow motion.

To hell with that, she decided abruptly. Though she had sworn last night that she'd rather cut off her finger than dial Scott's number again, she reached for the phone.

She tried the direct line at the station. But it was a female voice that answered. "Mr. Manero's out of town," the voice informed her. "On location upstate."

"Do you know when he's expected back?"

"No, I don't. Next week sometime, but I don't know what day. Would you like to leave a message?"

"No. Thank you."

When she hung up, Jenny was shaking with pain and anger. That's it, she thought. The man had left town without returning her call, without saying good-bye.

"Now you've done it, Mr. Manero, now you've really gone and done it," she muttered, grabbing the offending telephone and hurling it to the floor, feeling anger, hot and pure, coursing through her. The anger energized her, and because there was no other outlet for it, Jenny tore through the apartment like the demon housewives in detergent commercials.

She pushed chairs, pulled tables, arranged furniture, then rearranged it. And when she tired of redecorating, she took up an armful of cleaning supplies and moved methodically, from room to room, scrubbing and dusting and polishing.

When Becky came home from school, she found her mother on her hands and knees, scrubbing furiously at a discolored tile in one of the guest bathrooms. "What's going on, Mommy? A visit from the White Tornado?"

"Hi, baby," Jenny answered, without looking up from the floor. "What's going on is that I'm trying to get this place in shape. I haven't been paying enough attention to things that matter. And that," she said, doubling her tempo for emphasis, "is a lapse I am trying to remedy."

"Scrubbing floors is something that matters? You always hated housework. Mommy, are you all right?"

"I'm fine. Perfectly. And when I finish this floor, I am going to make us a magnificent dinner. With chocolate soufflé for dessert. What do you think of that?"

"I think it's swell. But I still don't understand all this cleaning. The apartment looks great, but it was already clean. Emily scrubbed this floor yesterday. I saw her."

"Emily does her best for us, and I appreciate that. But sometimes it's good to do things for yourself."

Becky shook her head. "You are acting very funny, Mom. But if you want to make that chocolate soufflé, I won't say anything else."

"Good. I'm almost finished here. Give me a hand putting all this junk away, and I'll tell you what I have planned for the weekend."

"The weekend? I was going to hang out with some of the kids on Saturday."

"Hang out if you want to, but maybe you'll change your mind when you hear—"

"What? What are we going to do?"

"What we are going to do, kiddo, is indulge ourselves in

every possible way known to man. Tomorrow morning we are going out for breakfast—maybe One Fifth Avenue, if you like—and we are going to order everything on the menu. . . ."

"Bloody Marys, too?"

"Bloody Marys and champagne and anything we feel like having."

"Okay, Mom—you've got a deal."

"Wait a minute—don't be so easy. After we have breakfast, we are going Christmas shopping. . . ."

"Christmas shopping! Mommy—it's not even Halloween."

"So what? Anybody can go Christmas shopping in December. Anyway, what I have in mind is something a little different. You and I are going to pick out some great big toys for ourselves. Anything we want. Tell me quick—if you could go into a store right now and have anything you wanted, what would you choose?"

"A video recorder! Could I really have one?"

"Absolutely. What else?"

"Oh, Mommy, I can't even think. . . ."

"Well, think. After dinner, I want you to make up a Christmas list. And tomorrow, we are going to wear out my credit cards."

"What about you, Mommy? What are you going to buy for yourself?"

"Oh, I don't know. We'll think of something as we go. You help me. What do you think I should have? A new fur coat maybe? No? You don't like that idea?"

"If you really want it . . . I just don't like clothes that are made . . . you know . . . by killing animals. But if you . . ."

"No, you're absolutely right. Well, then—what about a new car? Something cute we can drive to the beach in the summer? A convertible, maybe? How does that sound?"

"Mommy, are you all right? Really?"

"Sure, kiddo—I just need a little Christmas right now. No sense waiting around for it, is there? And after we finish shopping, we'll go out for dinner. And then we'll pick out a show. Or maybe a hockey game. Are the Rangers at the Garden this weekend? And Sunday morning, we can—"

"Did you have a fight with Scott, Mommy?"

"Why on earth are you asking me that?"

"Because you're talking about all this fun stuff, and you

look like you're going to cry. Did you? Is that why you're acting so weird?''

''Just my luck—a shrink in the family, and a smart one, to boot. No, I didn't have a fight with Scott. I would if I could get my hands on him, but the great man is out of town. Never around when you want him. But I'm really going to take your advice this time, Becky. When he gets back, no more pussy-footing around. Straight talk, that's what we're going to have. And if my life's going to blow up in my face again, at least I'll have a hand in it this time. And now, let's change the subject. Until Scott gets back, I don't want to talk about him—or even think about him. Will you help me do that, Becky?''

''Sure, Mom.''

Yet when Scott surfaced again, telling her, ''I just got in a few minutes ago—you were the first person I wanted to call,'' she nearly melted with relief. But she recovered quickly. No, you don't, she said to herself. Not again.

''I'm not sure I'm speaking to you, Scott.''

''Why?'' His surprise was genuine. ''What's the matter?''

''I remember inviting you to the theater, and I remember you saying you'd get back to me. And that's the last I heard from me. I called your office and they said you'd left town. Without a word to me.''

''Oh, Jen—I'm so sorry. I've been so busy, it just went clear out of my mind. You're not going to hold one mistake against me, are you? Let me make it up to you. We'll go see that show you mentioned—this week—tomorrow. I'll get the tickets—okay?''

''It isn't okay—and it isn't just the play. It's . . . an attitude. I feel you're . . . careless with me.''

''Careless! I don't see how you can say such a thing. I thought we'd established how I felt about you. I didn't think it needed saying every five minutes.''

''Scotty—you're not hearing me. I don't expect you to do anything every five minutes. When we're together, I think I do know how you feel. But when we're not, then I don't know anything. You always talk about the way we seem to connect, but the relationship we have . . . it doesn't seem to have any connective tissue. I never know when I'll see you again. You seem to be able to put me on hold until you feel like making contact. And it doesn't seem to matter how I feel about it.''

"Of course it matters. All right, let's assume there is a little truth in what you say. But I still thought we had a nice thing going. . . ."

"Not for me," she said quietly. "I want it—but no . . . not for me."

"Hold on, Jen. We shouldn't be having this talk on the telephone. I'm coming over. Right now. Okay?"

"Okay." She sighed, pleased that she mattered, but not at all certain how their talk would turn out. One thing she did know. She was going to be open with Scott. No more pretending that everything was fine just because that was what Scott needed to believe. If their relationship was going to survive, it would be on a brand-new basis. I'm too old for games, she thought. I don't have time to wait around and hope.

She ran her fingers through her hair, too distracted to fuss with her appearance. Then, remembering that she was not alone in the apartment, she called out, "Becky—could you come here a minute?"

Her daughter appeared in the doorway of her bedroom, a telephone receiver dangling from her ear, the sounds of rock music issuing from the stereo. "What is it, Mom? I'm on the phone."

"Just listen for a second. Scott's coming over in a few minutes. Could you please give us some privacy? We're going to talk for a while."

Becky covered the receiver with her hand. "Sure, Mom. I have lots of stuff to do in my room. Are you going to make up?"

"I'm not really sure, baby. That's what we have to talk about. I'll tell you all about it later, okay?"

"Sure thing. I hope everything works out."

"Me, too."

Jenny opened a bottle of the Montrachet that Scott liked, poured herself a glass, and downed it quickly. For luck. And nerve.

When the doorman informed her that Scott had arrived, her heart thumped uncooperatively.

Scott's expression, when she opened the door, was serious. For a moment she thought she might be a fool for precipitating a confrontation, for risking a relationship with a man she adored, a man who seemed—at least right now—to feel she was important.

"I came right over," he said. "I'm a little crumpled from the trip. . . . What is it, Jenny? What's wrong? Tell me what I've done to make you feel like this."

She took a deep breath. "Let me just tell you why I feel that way—and maybe you'll understand. I love you, Scott—that's given me some beautiful, happy moments that I'll never forget. But there were some unhappy times, too. I wanted to talk to you about them, but I had the feeling I'd be telling you things you didn't want to hear."

"What things, Jenny?"

"Let me finish. When we started seeing each other, I had no idea where it would go or what I would want. By the time I did know—that I wanted you in my life, very much—I felt we were always dodging the fallout from your marriage. I felt as if I had to avoid doing or saying anything that would make you feel I was like your wife. And every time you talked about 'space' and how great things were between us, I just couldn't admit that I didn't think it was so great. That I didn't like seeing you and loving you—and then not hearing from you for days. I didn't like thinking that you could enjoy being with me—and then put me aside. And I didn't like the idea"—she took another breath—"I didn't like the idea that maybe you were seeing other women too." She stopped and looked at him. "Now it's your turn."

"I don't know what to say, Jen. I never imagined you felt like this."

"That isn't your fault. I never told you. But falling in love with you took me by surprise. It's new for me. And so I don't know how to be in love part-time."

"It sounds to me like you're talking marriage and a common grave," he said, forcing a smile.

"It sounds to me like you think that's a fate worse than death."

"Not for everybody, Jen. I just don't see what technicalities have to do with anything."

"I'm not talking technicalities, Scott. I'm talking about commitment. The kind that two people want to make when they know they've found something special together. If they really feel it, then they know there isn't anything better out there. It seems to me that two people in love should want to start joining their lives, instead of working so hard to keep them separate."

"I can't find anything wrong with what you're saying. I'm just not sure it's for me. I thought you were different, Jen. I know a lot of women feel that way. I just didn't know you did." He looked so solemn, so disappointed that Jenny thought her heart would break.

"I'm not so different. I've been burned, too," she said. "My marriage took me over. But I don't think the answer to one failure is a lifetime of hanging loose and drifting."

He sighed. "I don't know what to say to you, Jen. I love you, but I just don't know if I can give you what you want. I'm not comfortable checking in with another human being all the time, being accountable to one person. I don't know if I can make a relationship with a woman into the center of my life. There's too much else I want to do."

"You mean other women?"

"I mean anything I feel like doing. I like the freedom to decide."

"I see."

"Don't look like that, Jen. I just told you I loved you. Doesn't that mean anything?"

"I guess it means we have different ideas about love."

"Are you saying we can't see each other if I don't feel the same way you do? If I can't give you this . . . this commitment you're talking about?"

"I'm saying it doesn't work for me this way. I can't force you to feel the way I do. I just know it can't work if you don't want me the way I want you."

"Then I guess that's it."

She saw the tightening of his jaw, heard the edge in his voice. She had lost him. She felt the built-up tension and anxiety leave her, felt the energy drain from her body until she thought she would faint. She was barely aware of the curt "good night" and the closing of the door that accompanied Scott's departure.

She sat motionless, suspended in the moment. She felt as if she were made of glass, as if a single abrupt movement might break her, sending a thousand hurts splintering through her heart. "Oh, Scotty," she whispered to the door that had closed behind him, "oh, Scotty, you promised you wouldn't hurt me. You promised."

When Becky found her a few minutes later, she was sitting, perfectly still, in the same place where Scott had left her.

"Mommy?"

There was no answer, so Becky went to her, touched her shoulder. "Mommy?"

Jenny turned pain-glazed eyes on her daughter. "Yes, baby?"

"What's wrong? Did you and Scotty have a fight?"

She shook her head. "Worse," she whispered.

Becky cradled her mother in her arms. "Never mind, Mommy. He's just being dumb. He'll be sorry. You'll see."

Jenny's lips curved reflexively in the shape of a smile. Oh, she thought, if only . . . and then she stopped herself. There wasn't going to be any "if only" this time. She was going to get through this. And there weren't going to be any regrets.

— ✕ **38** ✕ —

Jenny couldn't regret her affair with Scott, not even with the hurting that followed his departure. He had made her feel, had brought excitement and exhilaration to her life, and even the pain of losing him had a fullness, a richness that she could almost savor. It was different from the time when Jeff had left. She knew she had the inner resources to survive—perhaps to love again—even if it meant giving someone else the power to wound her.

Becky was a comfort and, curiously, so was Alicia, who called one night when Jenny was feeling particularly low.

"Are you all right?" Alicia asked, thinking she heard something disturbing in her daughter's voice.

"I'm not sick, if that's what you mean."

"And Rebecca—is she all right?"

"Becky's fine."

"But there is something."

"Yes, Alicia," Jenny said, dropping the last of her usual reserve where her mother was concerned. "There is something."

"A man."

"Yes, Alicia."

"Jenny, dear, I'm not trying to pry—really I'm not. I just want to be 'family.' There's just the two of us now—and Rebecca—and . . . oh, Jenny, it would be such a shame if we didn't even have each other."

"I know, Alicia. There was a man. But it's over now."

"What happened? Can you tell me?"

"There isn't much to tell. I loved him more than he loved me. I wanted, and he wanted less. And when I told him, he went away."

"Then you were right to tell him," Alicia said softly. "Love isn't so easy, no matter how old you are or how long you've lived. But it doesn't have a chance if there isn't a balance—a basic understanding—to begin with."

"That's what I keep telling myself. But 'right' is cold comfort right now."

"I know, baby, I know. Is there something—anything—I can do? Would you like me to come to New York for a couple of days? Or maybe you'd like to come here for a while?"

"Thanks for asking But no—you don't have to baby-sit this time, Alicia. I'll be fine. Really."

"I know you will. I don't doubt that for a minute. It's just . . . I've done so little for you, and my life is so good now . . . I feel a little guilty."

"Don't. I'm glad you're happy—it makes me believe in possibilities."

"Thank you for saying that. And Jenny—I don't know if this is the time to bring it up, but the reason I called was business, actually. If you don't want to talk now, I'll call you another time, whenever you're ready."

"No—it's all right. What is it?"

"Well, Paolo and I have been talking about opening up a Principessa II in New York, on the order of the place we have in Los Angeles—a place that will cater to younger people with a little less to spend. We're going to need a first-rate location. I thought if you had the time, you might handle that for us." -

Jenny laughed. "Honestly, Alicia—there are half a dozen firms in the city who specialize in the kind of commercial space you're talking about."

"I know, baby, but the commission on this is going to be a

big one. I wanted you to have it. Call it a Christmas present—
from old Richelieu.''

"Mother! You knew? Oh God, I'm so embarrassed . . . I
don't know what to say. . . .''

Alicia laughed. "Don't be. That was all a long time ago.
Whatever you meant when you gave me that name, I'm sure I
deserved it. Now think about my proposition. And Jenny, if
you need anything—anything at all—I'm just a phone call
away.''

"I know. 'Bye, Mother.''

When the letter from Jeff arrived, she stared at it for a long
time, studying the airmail envelope, the stamp, the familiar
scrawl in the corner, as if these would give her a clue to why
he was writing to her after all this time. His one year in China
had been extended, by invitation, into a special advisory
position with a Chinese medical school. He had come back to
the United States twice, to visit Becky. Each time Jenny had
arranged to be away. She knew that Becky got letters from
time to time, but she never asked what was in them. Occasionally, her daughter would cautiously volunteer a bit of
information, alert to any signs of distress on her mother's
face.

Finally she opened the envelope and started to read. The
letter was fairly long, filled with a description of the work he
was doing. Her eyes skipped ahead to the final paragraphs:

The work has been exciting and satisfying. I've been
teaching and learning at the same time. I think the
reason I have stayed here so long is that one day I
realized that I no longer had a home to go back to. I'm
not saying this in an attempt to win your sympathy. I
know I don't deserve that. But if it will give you any
satisfaction now, I can tell you that I have had many
regrets.

I know that I left you with a heavy load to carry. You
have managed well, with Becky and with everything
else you've done. Our daughter is proud of you, and I
hope you won't be offended if I say I am, too. I'll be
coming to the States after the first of the year. I'd like
to see Becky, and if you'll let me, I'd like to see you,
too. Maybe we can find some reasons to be friends again.

When she finished the letter, there were tears in her eyes. Time had softened her memories of Jeff. She felt strong enough to see him again, to talk with him—even to be glad that he was happy in his work. Becky would like that.

When Becky came home from school, she handed her the letter. "It's from your father. He's coming here after the holidays. He wants to see you—both of us, actually."

"Oh, Mommy, that's great!" Then she added hastily, "If it's okay with you."

"It's fine, Becky. I'm not mad at him anymore. I guess I haven't been for a long time. It might be nice to see him again. Listen—why don't we go out tonight? Are you in the mood for 'dress-up' or jeans?"

"Medium. Can we have Chinese?"

"Sure. Shun Lee Palace?"

"Yum. Let's go."

Jenny leaned back in her chair and pushed her plate away. "Stop me before I eat another mouthful, baby. I feel like I've gained ten pounds since I walked into this place."

"Oh, Mommy—don't be silly. Besides, food is very soothing when you're depressed."

"Tell that to my skirt—this zipper is ready to explode from all this soothing. I think it's time for me to go back to the health club and get into shape again. Want to come? Not that you need it. . . ." She looked at Becky, but her daughter was not listening. Jenny turned her head to see what Becky was staring at.

There, a few tables away, was Scott, laughing at something his companion, a very young, very attractive blonde, was saying. The meal she had just enjoyed turned to dust in her mouth.

"Do you want to leave now, Mommy? I don't mind."

"Yes, okay, baby, let's leave."

She paid the check, and as she got up to leave, she thought that Scott looked in her direction. Seeing her, if he did see her, didn't seem to bother him, for as she left the restaurant, she saw him smiling at the blonde.

"Hey, lady—want to buy a Christmas tree? Cheap?"

"What?" The telephone call came a week after Jenny had

spotted Scott in the restaurant, and she recognized his voice at once, but couldn't think of anything to say.

"I'm offering you a genuine country Christmas tree—for free—if you come with me to cut it down. Say yes, Jenny. Please?"

"I don't understand." And she didn't.

"I'm going up to my house in Warwick on Saturday. I'll be driving back Sunday night. I want you to come with me."

She still didn't understand. In all the time they had been seeing each other, he had never invited her to spend the weekend at his country place. She had felt it was one of the "off-limits" areas in his life. She had dozens of questions, but she kept her voice steady and said simply, "What time do you want me to be ready?"

"Is nine too early?"

"Nine is good."

"See you."

Jenny turned to face the questioning look in Becky's eyes. "That was Scott."

"Oh? What does *he* want?"

"He asked me to go cut a Christmas tree with him. Upstate. For the weekend." Jenny released each bit of information separately, waiting for her daughter's reaction.

"We already have a Christmas tree."

"Actually, I thought it might be nice to have another one—for outside, on the terrace. We could trim it with those little lights, and—"

"Wait a minute, Mommy. Before we start talking about Christmas trees, do you really need all this aggravation again? You know what I mean."

"Yes, I think I do. Becky, I know this might seem stupid to you, but I—"

"You don't have to say anything to me, Mommy. He wants to make up. And if you want to go, it's okay with me. Really. Just tell that guy he'd better behave himself. Or else."

As Jenny ran down the steps of the building and saw Scott waiting for her, she realized that she had never before seen his car—a blue Maserati. This was clearly going to be a day of firsts. Good ones, she hoped, crossing her fingers.

"Hi," she said, as if they had never said such a painful good-bye.

"Hi. You look different," he said, pointing to her down vest, her flannel-lined jeans and heavy alpine boots.

"I'm wearing my tree-cutting-in-the-country clothes. So are you, I see."

"Yeah, I guess I am."

She slid into the car and wondered if he was thinking what she was thinking—that they had never before gone for a car ride together, never spent a weekend together, never shared any part of a Christmas together. That the list of things they had never shared was, in fact, enormous.

They drove for a time in a silence that was not quite awkward, yet not really comfortable. As they crossed the George Washington Bridge and headed toward the Palisades Parkway, she said, "I didn't expect to see you again."

"I know. Look—before you get the wrong idea, this isn't unconditional surrender."

"I didn't think it was."

"I missed you, Jenny. I thought maybe if you felt the same way, we could sort of . . . reopen negotiations."

She laughed. "You sound as if you're talking about a garbage strike."

"Yeah—well, some days it's felt like that."

He said nothing more, and she didn't press. It had probably cost him a lot to call her, she thought. Strangely enough, she felt calm, less anxious in his presence. After the pain, the acceptance of losing him, she was more aware of what he must be feeling, less needy of reassurance from him.

Scott's house was a surprise. She had expected something very contemporary and slick—nothing like the old two-story stone house set deep on acres of rolling woods, at the very end of a country road.

More surprises waited inside—the utility room that was filled with thriving plants, the country kitchen done in blue tiles and rough pine, the cozy living room with its floor-to-ceiling stone fireplace, flanked by an extensive collection of Indian artifacts.

"How do you like it?" he asked.

"It's lovely—but it doesn't seem like you."

"Sure it does—when you get to know me better."

"Do you let anyone do that?"

"That's one of the things we're going to find out. But first we'd better turn the furnace up and get a fire started or we'll both freeze to death."

"Want some help?"

"I'll do the fire—you can get us something hot to drink. One of the local ladies comes in once a week to clean and fill the fridge. I think you'll find everything if you just look around."

Jenny opened and closed cupboards and drawers, looking for china and silverware and fixings for tea. She was impressed with the order of the house. It was warmer, homier than Scott's apartment, but it was still basically uncluttered. Like Scott, she thought, making a face. Well, maybe she could change that.

She found a box of Chinese tea—no tea bags, she noticed—a pot, some cups and saucers. She put the things on a tray and carried them into the living room. He was already stretched out on a braided rug in front of a promising fire.

"C'mon, Jen. Over here." He moved a little to make room for her, and she stretched out next to him, feeling the warmth from the fire.

"So here we are," he said. "Again."

"Yes."

"Do you think we can get it right this time?"

She smiled at him. "That would be nice. I've missed you so much."

"Yeah—well, it's been pretty bad for me, too. I didn't want to leave you, Jen. I just panicked. You pressed all the wrong buttons, and I ran. So here's my best offer— I'll try to give you what you want. I hope that's good enough."

She looked at his face, flushed with the heat from the flames, serious and intent. This is a perfect moment, she thought. Hearing "I'll try" from Scott meant more to her than a sworn declaration would from anyone else. "I'll try, too," she said. "I'll try not to want so much. Maybe we *can* get it right this time."

He brushed her cheeks with his fingers, then kissed her lightly. "I hope so, Jenny. I do love you. Just remind me of that when I start to get nervous."

"I will. Count on it."

He settled back on the rug, eyes closed, a contented smile on his face.

Yes, she thought, that's just how I feel, too.

They drove back to the city in a mood of giddy self-congratulation. "That wasn't so bad," Scott said. "Two days without another living soul around and we didn't get on each other's nerves. Not once."

"No," she said, laughing. "Not once."

"And we got this spectacular tree. I can't wait to put it up for you. It's going to look great in that big living room."

"Scott—I have to tell you something. Promise not to get mad at me?"

"What is it? Did you run around like crazy with other guys after we broke up? Are you going to confess?"

"Me! You're the one who ran around—I was too busy feeling rotten. But you didn't seem to gather any cobwebs."

"Shows what you know, lady—you're the only one I ever brought up to my secret hideaway."

"Am I really?"

"You are—and you may be the last. You almost killed me in the woods. You're dangerous, did you know that?"

She giggled, remembering how she had tripped and fallen against Scott as they hiked in search of a tree, how they had rolled down the hill until they had been stopped by a massive boulder. Then when they had found a tree that Jenny liked, she had insisted on cutting it down herself—sending the ax flying past Scott's shoulder with her first stroke.

"I hope you appreciate everything I went through to get you a tree," he said, "a tree that is even now probably destroying the paint job on my car."

"No it isn't. I wrapped the blanket very carefully around it. But that's what I wanted to tell you about—the tree."

"Well, what about it? If you've changed your mind about letting me trim it, I won't let you get away with that."

"No, that's not it. You can trim it with Becky and me. But you see . . . actually, we already have a tree in the living room. When you called, I thought it would be nice to have one outside, on the terrace. I didn't tell you because I didn't want you to think—"

"That you didn't really need a tree.. You faker!" He laughed. "But the joke's on you—do you know how many ploys I thought of before I came up with that one? I could have just said, 'Okay, Jenny, I want to see you again.' But—you know."

"Yes—I know."

Becky opened the door for them as soon as she heard the sound of her mother's key in the lock. "So," she said, "what did Santa's helpers bring home?"

"What are you feeding this kid?" Scott teased. "She's starting to sound just like you."

"Watch it, Mr. Manero," Becky teased back, "I'm keeping an eye on you. One false move, and it's coal in your stocking this year."

"Ouch," he said. "No fair—two against one. I'd better get to work before I get into any trouble. Where do you want this magnificent tree?"

"Take it outside," Jenny said. "Maybe we can have a little snack and warm up before we start trimming."

"I baked some Christmas cookies this morning," Becky volunteered.

"Could you manage something a little stronger than that?" Scott asked. "If I'm going out in that cold again—ten stories up—I'll need a little liquid fire in my veins."

"You want some hot punch?"

"Sounds good, kid. Make it strong."

Becky disappeared into the kitchen and returned ten minutes later with a silver tray heaped high with Christmas cookies and a cut-glass bowl filled with steaming punch. "Come and get it," she invited. "My Charles Dickens special. Human antifreeze." She ladled out three generous cups. Scott raised his cup in a toast.

"Here's to us," he said. "I guess we'll be seeing a lot of each other." He looked first at Jenny, then at Rebecca.

"I figured that out for myself," Becky said, laughing. "Now tell me something I don't know."

"Is she like this all the time?" Scott asked Jenny. "Why do I get the feeling I'm taking on double trouble?"

"You are," Jenny said. "But it's not too late to back off. It's only after Christmas Eve, when you share champagne and chocolate fudge with us—that's one of our secret holiday traditions—that you officially become one of the gang."

"I can hardly wait. I love champagne and fudge—and gangs. Did I ever tell you about my early days as a juvenile delinquent in south Philadelphia?"

"No, and I want to hear all about your misspent youth. But I think we'd better get on with our tree before the temperature goes any lower."

The three of them bundled up against the cold. Outside, on the penthouse terrace, they worked quickly, companionably, to set the tree in a metal holder, then to string the tiny candle-shaped lights evenly along its branches. Occasionally, they paused to warm freezing fingers with puffs of frosty breath.

"Do you know," Scott said, "this is the first tree I've trimmed in years—and the first ever I've done under arctic conditions. Maybe I should have brought a camera crew along to do a little human interest story: 'Newsman freezes to death just inches away from warmth and shelter.' Do you think that would be bad for my image?"

"Terrible," Jenny said, taking his hands in hers, warming them gently.

"Oh, yuck," Becky said. "If you're going to start that stuff, I'm going to bed. But I'll be a sport and give you some atmosphere."

"What kind of atmosphere?" Jenny asked.

"You'll see." A few minutes later, they heard the sound of Christmas carols coming through the glass doors and saw the shimmer of multicolored lights from the living room tree.

"She's too much," Jenny said fondly.

"She's a good kid," he agreed. "I think I could get to like her almost as much as I like you."

When the lights were finished, Jenny said, "Do you want to do the honors and turn them on?"

"Well, sure—and they'd better work." He flicked the switch, and the tree was illuminated with hundreds of tiny white lights. "Hey, that's pretty good."

"It's beautiful, Scotty—it's just beautiful. We can go inside now, if you like."

"In a minute. Come over here." He pulled her over to the terrace railing. "I need a last kiss for the road—to hold me until Christmas Eve.'' He cupped her face in his hands and kissed her forehead, her nose, her lips. ''I'm going to leave you in a while,'' he said, ''and I'm not going to see you for a couple of days. I don't want you to worry, and I don't want you to think I've disappeared. I have a lot of Christmas shopping to do—for two special ladies.''

''Oh, Scott, I don't think I need another Christmas present— not a single thing.''

''Yeah—I know what you mean. And Jenny—when I come back—on Christmas Eve—I want to stay over. I want to spend the whole day with you and Becky. Might as well get some practice,'' he added a little self-consciously.

Jenny's heart was so full that she was almost afraid to speak. She snuggled closer to him, and they both looked down on the Village scene below, on the tiny figures hurrying along, intent on their holiday chores, on the huge Christmas tree that blazed bright in the center of the Washington Square arch. ''You know,'' she whispered, ''right now I feel as if all this belongs to us.''

''It does,'' he answered. ''Right now it does.''

She looked into his eyes, saw in them the same love and need that another man and woman had shared, there, in that very place, so many years before. And she felt that she was finally home.

Bestselling Books for Today's Reader